THE EVER-PRESENT ORIGIN

JEAN GEBSER

THE EVER-PRESENT ORIGIN

Authorized Translation by
Noel Barstad with Algis Mickunas

PART ONE:

Foundations of the Aperspectival World

A Contribution to the History of the Awakening of Consciousness

PART TWO:

Manifestations of the Aperspectival World

An Attempt at the Concretion of the Spiritual

Ohio University Press   Athens

Ohio University Press, Athens, Ohio 45701

Library of Congress Cataloging in Publication Data

Gebser, Jean.
    The ever-present origin.

       Translation of: Ursprung and Gegenwart.
       Includes bibliographical references and indexes.
       Contents: Foundations of the aperspectival world :
a contribution to the history of the awakening of consciousness—Manifestations of
the aperspectival world : an attempt at the concretion of the spiritual.
       1. Civilization—History. 2. Civilization—Philosophy. 3. Intellectual
life—History. 4. Civilization, Occidental. I. Title.
CB83.G413   1984   901   83-2475
ISBN 0-8214-0219-6
ISBN 0-8214-0769-4 pbk.

Ohio University Press books are printed on acid-free paper ∞
12 11 10 09 08 07   12 11 10 9

Ursprung und Gegenwart © 1949 and 1953
by Deutsche Verlags-Anstalt GmbH, Stuttgart
English translation © 1985 by Noel Barstad
Printed in the United States of America
All rights reserved.

Contents

PART ONE: FOUNDATIONS OF THE APERSPECTIVAL WORLD
A CONTRIBUTION TO THE HISTORY OF THE AWAKENING OF CONSCIOUSNESS

PART TWO: MANIFESTATIONS OF THE APERSPECTIVAL WORLD
AN ATTEMPT AT THE CONCRETION OF THE SPIRITUAL

Translator's Preface

As early as 1951, even before publication of the second part of Jean Gebser's *Ursprung und Gegenwart*, the Bollingen Foundation contemplated the feasibility of an English-language version and requested an estimation of the book by Erich Kahler (Princeton), the distinguished philosopher of history and author of studies of the evolution of human history and consciousness (*Man the Measure*, 1943; *The Tower and the Abyss*, 1957). In his eight-page review Professor Kahler encouraged publication, calling the book "a very important, indeed in some respects pioneering piece of work," "vastly, solidly, and subtly documented by a wealth of anthropological, mythological, linguistic, artistic, philosophical, and scientific material which is shown in its multifold and striking interrelationship." He also noted that Gebser's study "treads new paths, opens new vistas" and is "brilliantly written, (introducing) many valuable new terms and distinctions (and showing) that scholarly precision and faithfulness to given data are compatible with a broad, imaginative, and spiritual outlook."

Despite this warmly appreciative and incisive estimation, the Bollingen Foundation apparently did not pursue the project further, for Gebser's correspondence with his German publisher mentions a New York option under another name (letter of May 21, 1953) which also was not acted upon. The following year a part of Chapter three was printed in the periodical *Tomorrow: Quarterly Review of Psychical Research* (Summer, 1954 issue, vol. 2, no. 4, pages 44-58) in the author's own English rendering (reprinted here in its entirety pp. 46-60 and p. 106 note 43 below), and later negotiations were taken up by the author with the London firm of George Allen & Unwin, but owing to the death of one of the partners, no agreement was signed.

Because of the continuing interest in Gebser's work by readers and contributors of the journal *Main Currents in Modern Thought*, its editor, Mrs. Emily Sellon, sought to obtain foundation support for a complete translation (also from the Bollingen Foundation), and solicited from the author in 1971 a chapter to be included in the periodical. Unfortunately Jean Gebser's declining health made it impossible for him to prepare a translation himself and the extracts printed in the November-

December issue of 1972 (*Main Currents*, vol. 29, no. 2, pp. 80-88) were translated by Kurt F. Leidecker. Dr. Leidecker subsequently asked Algis Mickunas to collaborate on a translation of the entire work, a project which did not materialize. Jean Gebser died on May 14, 1973.

In 1975 Professor Mickunas invited the undersigned to collaborate on a translation and arranged a contract with the Ohio University Press. A preliminary version of the entire text was prepared jointly during the next three years. After discussions with the author's widow, Dr. Jo Gebser, in April of 1977 the undersigned undertook a complete retranslation and revision of the text and is responsible for the English version in its present form.

The translation is based on the text of the 1973 edition of the German original which the author had revised for publication shortly before his death. Several corrections from Gebser's own papers were supplied following the death of Dr. Jo Gebser in June of 1977 by Dr. Rudolf Hämmerli, Jean Gebser's literary executor and co-editor of the collected edition of Gebser's works (*Jean Gebser Gesamtausgabe*, Schaffhausen: Novalis Verlag, 1975-1981, eight volumes and index). References in the present work to the author's other publications now collected in this edition were prepared for both publications jointly by Dr. Hämmerli and the undersigned.

For the English translation a new index was compiled primarily on the basis of the author's own indexes to the first edition (1949/1953) and the translator's notes (later editions of the original contained abridged indexes by others). The extensive cross-referencing in the index of subjects is intended, as in the original, to draw attention to terms and ideas which are used in the text more or less interchangeably.

The wording of the English title is that of the author himself (letter of August 20, 1971 to Emily Sellon). Included on pp. 277-278 below is the text of an introduction to the second part written by Jean Gebser in 1953 for the house publication *Die Ausfahrt* of the Deutsche Verlags-Anstalt, publisher of the original. A remark on editorial changes in the annotations can be found on p. xxxii.

In conclusion I would like to express appreciation to the many persons who have contributed to the realization of an English version, particularly to Mrs. Emily Sellon and the staff and contributors of *Main Currents*; to the late Dr. Jo Gebser (Bern), the author's widow, who supported the project from its inception and decisively aided its completion; to Mr. Georg Feuerstein (Durham, England), who at the request of the author's widow read and annotated several chapters of the preliminary manuscript and gave much-needed encouragement during later stages of publication; to Dr. Rudolf and Mrs. Christiane Hämmerli (Bern) for providing books and information as well as access to Jean Gebser's archive and library in addition to the contributions noted earlier; to Mrs. Märit Schütt and Ms. Petra Bachstein of the Deutsche Verlags-Anstalt (Stuttgart) for contractual arrangements and extensions, as well as for making available letters of the author and other archival materials relating to the original publication; to Professor Jean Keckeis (Neuchâtel) for permission to include my translation of his "*In memoriam Jean Gebser*" as the introduction to this edition; to Mrs. Alice L. Kahler (Princeton) for placing at my disposal Erich Kahler's review and for providing other materials and information including a copy of a letter by Jean Gebser to Austrian novelist Hermann Broch from the correspondence mentioned in the text (p. 496 below); and to the staff of the Ohio University Press for their interest and co-operation at all stages of preparing and publishing the manuscript.

The text of this fifth printing of the paperback edition, as in the 1986, 1989, 1991, and 1994 editions, has been emended to achieve a more accurate and felicitous wording of several passages and to eliminate some of the remaining typographical errors. I remain indebted to Elizabeth Behnke (Felton, CA), Georg Feuerstein (Lower Lake, CA), and Helen Gawthrop (Ohio University Press) in particular for their many invaluable suggestions toward improving the text.

March 1997   Noel Barstad

In memoriam Jean Gebser
by Jean Keckeis

While completing his studies in Berlin during his mid-twenties—a time of precarious circumstances, as the inflation had abolished the family reserves—Jean Gebser wrote a poem entitled "Many Things are About to be Born," which begins: "We always lose our way / when overtaken by thinking . . . ," a thought which surely reflects a premonition of his later intellectual and spiritual journey.

Born in Posen in 1905, Gebser received his schooling in Königsberg and later in the renowned preparatory school in Rossleben on the Unstrut. He has left us a fine account of how he learned there to "swim free"; ever since a jump from the diving board "into uncertainty," he was in possession of something that he did not fully realize until decades after. "It was then," he wrote later, "that I lost my fear in the face of uncertainty. A sense of confidence began to mature within me which later determined my entire bearing and attitude toward life, a confidence in the sources of our strength of being, a confidence in their immediate accessibility. This is an inner security that is fully effective only when we are able to do whatever we do not for our own sake. . . ."

Following his first-hand experience of the Brown Shirts in Munich in 1931, Gebser left Germany of his own free will and went, penniless, to Spain. There the difficult decision to forego his mother tongue was rewarded by the "enriching knowledge of the Latin way of thinking, acting, and living." He became sufficiently familiar with Spanish culture to hold for a time a position in the Republican Ministry of Culture and even to write poetry in the language of his friend Federico García Lorca (*Poesias de la Tarde*, 1936). Twelve hours before his Madrid apartment was bombed in the Autumn of 1936 he again set out on the path of uncertainty.

By this time he had already formed the conception of his *magnum opus*, *The Ever-Present Origin*, a conception which matured during three years of privation in Paris during his association with the circle around Picasso and Malraux. The necessary repose for completion of the work Gebser found in Switzerland, where he arrived near the end of August, 1939, two hours before the frontier was closed. He became a Swiss citizen in 1951. Unfortunately, Gebser was unable to assume the duties associated with his chair for the Study of Comparative Civilizations at the University of Salzburg; a progressively worsening case of asthma forced him to remain ever closer to his home in Berne and to avoid exertion. The flights of spirit of which he was then still capable are perhaps better known outside Switzerland; and unlike the Swiss, with their predilection for specialized knowledge as such, Gebser went on to transform a prodigious and multifaceted knowledge, gleaned with rare sensitivity from ancient to avant-garde sources, into *Bildung*, wisdom and *sophrosyne*. A glance at the *Festschrift* to commemorate his sixtieth birthday, *Transparent World (Transparente Welt*, Berne: Huber, 1965) provides evidence of the universal emanation of his creativity, which is further attested to by his extensive list of publications.

Jean Gebser did not live to see the completion of a project close to his heart (he died on May 4, 1973 in Berne): the publication of his *Ever-Present Origin* in an inexpensive paperbound edition (Munich: Deutscher Taschenbuchverlag, 1973, three volumes). This edition was to make the work more accessible to students and other young people who have shown their concern with a new consciousness and a new orientation toward the world.

The path which led Gebser to his new and universal perception of the world is, briefly, as follows. In the wake of materialism and social change, man had been described in the early years of our century as the "dead end" of nature. Freud had redefined culture as illness—a result of drive sublimation; Klages had called the spirit (and he was surely speaking of the hypertrophied intellect) the "adversary of the soul," propounding a return to a life like that of the Pelasgi, the aboriginal inhabitants of Greece; and Spengler had declared the "Demise of the West" during the years following World War I. The consequences of such pessimism continued to proliferate long after its foundations had been superseded.

It was with these foundations—the natural sciences—that Gebser began. As early as Planck it was known that matter was not at all what materialists had believed it to be, and since 1943 Gebser has repeatedly emphasized that the so-called crisis of Western culture was in fact an essential restructuration. (It was in 1943 that his *Transformation of the Occident* was first published [Zürich/New York: Oprecht; also Dutch, French, Italian, and Swedish editions], an estimation of the results of research in the natural sciences during the first half of the century.) Gebser has noted two results that are of particular significance: first, the abandonment of materialistic determinism, of a one-sided mechanistic-causal mode of thought; and second, a manifest "urgency of attempts to discover a universal way of observing things, and to overcome the inner division of contemporary man who, as a result of his one-sided, rational orientation, thinks only in dualisms." Against this background of recent discoveries and conclusions in the natural sciences Gebser discerned the outlines of a potential human universality. He also sensed the necessity to go beyond the confines of this first treatise so as to include the humanities (such as political economics and sociology) as well as the arts in a discussion along similar lines. This was the point of departure for *The Ever-Present Origin*.

Here a word might be in order about Gebser's "method." No later than during his sojourn in Spain he must have acquired the "Mediterranean way of thought" (as Ortega y Gasset might have called it) for which existence—the external, the concrete—is more important than the inward, the abstract, the mere awareness of being. What Gebser presents in *The Ever-Present Origin* was incubated, not in the study, but in the warmth of living contact with representatives of all disciplines. His examination of the present restructuration of reality and of the establishment of a new consciousness structure led him to discover earlier restructurations in man-kind's consciousness development. Accordingly, the first part of the book (first pub-lished in 1949), based on research and insights of ethnology, psychology, and philol-ogy, uncovers the "Foundations of the Aperspectival World" in which we now find ourselves (although there is an unwillingness in certain quarters to accept this as a fact). We have evidence that human consciousness has undergone three previous mutations: from the archaic or primordial basic structure the magic, the mythical, and the mental (or rational) structures have emerged. The term "consciousness structures" is to be understood as nothing other than the visibly emerging percep-tion of reality throughout the various ages and civilizations.

This does not imply, however, that the later consciousness structures obliter-ate the earlier—we retain in ourselves irrevocable magic and mythical elements, origin and the present—; nor is it to suggest that a given later consciousness structure is of greater "value" than the earlier, although man has demonstrated at all times the understandable weakness of overestimating and exclusively utilizing the most re-cent potentialities that manifest themselves in him. This is perhaps most clearly ex-emplified by the hubris still evident in many quarters that overemphasizes the *ratio* and attempts to subordinate all else to man's calculating reason and will.

During the interim between the publication of the first and second parts of *The Ever-Present Origin*—the second is an exploration of the "Manifestations of the Aperspectival World"—an important symposium was held at which prominent re-presentatives of the various arts and sciences themselves presented the evidence of the contemporary restructuration which Gebser has demonstrated. Eighteen spe-cialists presented two cycles of lectures at the Academy of Commerce in St. Gallen, Switzerland (1950–51), on the subject of the "New Perception of the World" which were later published in the two volumes of *Die neue Weltschau* (Stuttgart: Deutsche Verlags-Anstalt, 1952–53). A surprising unanimity of basic conception emerged from these lectures: an openness toward questions dealing with transcendence; a scepti-cism about a self-satisfied rationalism; and a courageous humility *vis-à-vis* insights into man's limitations of knowledge and perception—all of these being duly noted in the press accounts. It is such interpretation and sustenance of the life-affirming energies of our epoch that form the substance of the second part of *The Ever-Present Origin*.

The birth-pangs of the aperspectival, integral perception of the world began in the first decade of our century. The major and unique theme of our juncture, according to Gebser, is the irruption of time into our consciousness. It is a matter of our recognizing time as a quality and an intensity rather than as an analytical system of measurable relationships, its perverted and materialized form in the perspectival age. In the new modality of perceiving the world, time appears to be its fundamental constituent; time, being immeasurable and not amenable to rational thought, emerges ever more clearly as a liberation from previous time-forms. It becomes time-freedom. "Just as the conquest of space was accompanied by a disclosure or 'opening up' as it were of surface, of the unperspectival world, so too is today's emergent perception of time accompanied by an opening of space." Today, as the arational-integral begins to supplant the mental-rational, the exhaustion of values at the completion of each consciousness structure becomes evident in the exhaustion and quantification of thought, of our mental capacity, as exemplified by the robot-like thinking of our machines. Nevertheless, the "aperspectival" does not imply the exclusion of the perspectival, rather that its claim of exclusivity must be abandoned in favor of something more encompassing. Gebser has evinced the salient aspects of this new consciousness structure from numerous phenomena in the humanities, the natural and social sciences, and the arts.

In one of his most recent books, The Invisible Origin (Der unsichtbare Ursprung, Olten: Walter, 1970), Gebser has again made evident something hardly describable: "evolution as the realization of a pre-established pattern." Time and again, physicists, philosophers, psychologists, futurologists, artists, and poets have tried to express in words their intuitions of this ever-present origin. In the spring of 1960, the New Helvetic Society (Berne), with the cooperation of Studio Berne, presented a series of broadcasts with the general title: "Paths to a New Reality" (later published as Wege zur neuen Wirklichkeit, Berne: Hallwag, 1960). Besides Gebser, the participants included the physicist Houtermans, the biologist Portmann, the historian Herbert Lüthy, and historian of law Hans Marti. Toward the close of the series, Gebser came to speak specifically about ideologies as typical outgrowths of a purpose-oriented, perspectivistic era, and demonstrated how these ideologies linger about in the world as lost causes, outdone only by the search for new or "counter" ideologies. Particularly anachronistic are the effects of Christian sects posturing like ideologies.

The following year Gebser published another group of essays which had evolved from lectures of his own entitled "Standing the Test, or Verifications of the New Consciousness" (In der Bewährung, Berne: Francke, 1962). His next book, "Asia Smiles Differently" (Asien lächelt anders, Frankfurt and Berlin: Ullstein, 1968), based on his extensive travels in India, China, and Japan, shows yet another notable aspect of his integral "world perception." The book first appeared in paperback in 1962 under the title "Asian Primer" and was intended as a brief vade mecum for Westerners to aid in their understanding of the Asian mentality. (The augmented editon of 1968 followed yet another of Gebser's visits to India.) Both versions of the book document the considerable differences between Western and Eastern ways of thinking. The Asian, for instance, does not experience opposites as dualities or antinomies, as we do in the West, but as complementarities. And in Asia one can still encounter manifestations of what we in the Western world frequently reject as pre- or irrational malfunctions: the magic experience and mythical feeling of the world.

Gebser's later work further explored and elaborated significant aspects of The Ever-Present Origin. He defined polarity, for example, as "the living constellation of mutual complementation, correspondences, and interdependence," which he articulated to counter the deadening effects of dualisms. How many misunderstandings come about because we turn interdependencies into antagonisms! He also addressed the subject of "Primordial Anxiety and Primordial Trust," the subject of his last lecture in October, 1972 at a physicians' congress in Bad Boll (Württemberg). It is a reply from the profundity of wisdom to the three questions: Where do I come from? Who am I? and Where am I going? These and other essays are now collected in the eight volume edition of his works currently in publication in Switzerland (Schaffhausen: Novalis, 1975-1981).

From a poetic fragment written just three weeks before his death are the verses:

Entirely clear and serene
is the heaven within
and farther, in many ways,
the ascent to origin.

Were they a poetic anticipation of an experience of which he spoke in his last lecture: "Death, too, is birth"? Around 500 B. C., at the time of mutation from the mythical to the rational consciousness structure, Heraclitus had expressed it in the words: "The path of ascent and descent is one and the same."

(1973)

List of Illustrations

Preface

"Our virtues lie in the interpretation of the time." (Shakespeare, *Coriolanus*, IV, 7)

"What is now proved was once only imagined." (Blake, *Proverbs of Hell*)

Origin is ever-present. It is not a beginning, since all beginning is linked with time. And the present is not just the "now," today, the moment or a unit of time. It is ever-originating, an achievement of full integration and continuous renewal. Anyone able to "concretize," i.e., to realize and effect the reality of origin and the present in their entirety, supersedes "beginning" and "end" and the mere here and now.

The crisis we are experiencing today is not just a European crisis, nor a crisis of morals, economics, ideologies, politics or religion. It is not only prevalent in Europe and America but in Russia and the Far East as well. It is a crisis of the world and mankind such as has occurred previously only during pivotal junctures—junctures of decisive finality for life on earth and for the humanity subjected to them. The crisis of our times and our world is in a process—at the moment autonomously—of complete transformation, and appears headed toward an event which, in our view, can only be described as a "global catastrophe." This event, understood in any but anthropocentric terms, will necessarily come about as a new constellation of planetary extent.

We must soberly face the fact that only a few decades separate us from that event. This span of time is determined by an increase in technological feasibility inversely proportional to man's sense of responsibility—that is, unless a new factor were to emerge which would effectively overcome this menacing correlation.

It is the task of the present work to point out and give an account of this new factor, this new possibility. For if we are not successful—if we should not or cannot successfully survive this crisis by our own insight and assure the continuity of our earth and mankind in the short or the long run by a transformation (or a mutation)—then the crisis will outlive us.

Stated differently, if we do not overcome the crisis it will overcome us; and only someone who has overcome himself is truly able to overcome. Either we will be disintegrated and dispersed, or we must resolve and effect integrality. In other words, either time is fulfilled in us—and that would mean the end and death for our present earth and (its) mankind—or we succeed in fulfilling time: and this means integrality and the present, the realization and the reality of origin and presence. And it means, consequently, a transformed continuity where mankind and not man, the spiritual and not the spirit, origin and not the beginning, the present and not time, the whole and not the part become awareness and reality. It is the whole that is present in origin and originative in the present.

The remarks above are a prefatory fore-word to our exposition. The book is addressed to each and every one, particularly to those who live knowledge, and not just to those who create it. Our exposition is neither a monologue nor a postulate but a discussion—an intent the author has striven to convey by using the stylistic device of "we" and by including others in the discussion via extensive quotations.

The conception of this work dates from 1932. Any conception, however, is a personal view whose evidential character is valid only for the individual. During the seventeen years since the basic conception was formed, the author has encountered statements here and there in the literature of the numerous subjects treated herein that in part resemble, relate or correspond to aspects of his basic understanding. The quotations and references to such sources are intended to lend a generally valid evidential character to the personal validity of the original conception. In this the author hopes to fulfil the ethical imperative of presenting an expository dialogue instead of a postulatory monologue and thereby convey the probable objective correctness of the basic idea rather than merely a subjective opinion of its correctness.

For this opportunity of being able to express my appreciation, I gratefully acknowledge the aid of my friends and all who have contributed to the success of this venture. My special thanks to Mrs. Gertrud and Mr. Walter R. Diethelm (Zürich-Zollikon), and particularly to Dr. Franz Meyer (Zürich); without their assistance and trust, I would have been unable to carry out the difficult and extended task amidst my economically precarious circumstances.

My gratitude also to the following for permission to reproduce several rare illustrations: The British Museum, London; Messrs. Kegan Paul, Trench, Trubner & Co., London; Hybernia Verlag, Basel; Galerie Rosenberg, Paris; Galerie Gasser, Zürich; and the *Kunsthalle*, Berne.

Burgdorf (Canton Berne); Whitsuntide 1949   Jean Gebser

From the Preface
to the Second Edition

The present work has been out of print for four years, as other pressing obligations have frequently interrupted the author's preparation of this new edition. . . . The text has been revised only where necessary for reasons of style, and where excision of repetitive material and minor rearrangement seemed advisable. Apart from this, the original version has been altered only by the addition of supplementary material and by a substantial increase in the number of illustrations. The additions to the text are written in such a way as to be immediately recognizable, and many have been incorporated into the notes so as not to unduly encumber the text.

The additions have been necessary in the light of many ominous as well as encouraging events since publication of the first edition. The ominous aspects are conceivably outweighed and counterbalanced by insights and achievements which, by virtue of their spiritual potency, cannot remain without effect.

Among these achievements, the writings of Sri Aurobindo and Pierre Teilhard de Chardin are pre-eminent. . . . Both develop in their own way the conception of a newly emergent consciousness which Sri Aurobindo has designated as the "supramental." We defined it in turn as the "aperspectival (arational-integral)" consciousness to which we first referred in *Rilke and Spain* (*Rilke und Spanien*, Zürich/New York: Oprecht, 1940) and later in our *Transformation of the Occident* (1943). It remains the principal concern of the present work to elucidate the possibility as well as the emergence of this new consciousness, and to describe its uniqueness. This same concern is also evident in the author's later works *Standing the Test, or Verifications of the New Consciousness* (2nd ed., 1969) and *Asian Primer* (1962).

The reader will have to judge for himself in what respects our discussion parallels or diverges from those of the authors mentioned, the dissimilarities being occasioned by the differing points of departure. Although both authors have a human-universal orientation, Sri Aurobindo—integrating Western thought—proceeds from a reformed Hindu, Teilhard de Chardin from a Catholic position, whereas the present work is written from a general and Occidental standpoint. But this does not preclude the one exposition from not merely supporting and complementing, but also corroborating the others.

Our exposition has been further corroborated by many scientific disciplines and by the arts. The results of research, the discoveries, insights and creations of numerous creative individuals testify to an attitude closely akin to our own. Not all of these could be considered in our discussion, and we have mentioned only those that seemed to us most significant. The references to these complementary sources may be considered a not insignificant enhancement of this revised version.

There remains the pleasant task of thanking those whose aid has contributed to the success of this edition. I am particularly grateful to the Werner Reimers Foundation for Anthropogenetic Research and its director Prof. Dr. Helmut de Terra (Frankfurt/M.), whose support enabled me to devote myself for a time exclusively to final revisions for this edition. I am equally grateful to Dr. Heinz Temming (Glückstadt) for his extensive assistance in correcting the proofs and compiling the indexes. In conclusion, my thanks to *Editions Gallimard* (Paris) and *Editions de Vischer* (Rhode-St.-Genèse) for permission to reproduce several illustrations.

Berne, February 1966   Jean Gebser

From the Preface to the Paperbound Edition

The present work was written primarily for my generation, or so I thought; but the interest shown by the younger generation has become increasingly evident. The principal subject of the book, proceeding from man's altered relationship to time, is the new consciousness, and to this those of the younger generation are keenly attuned. I am particularly pleased that this edition will make the book more accessible to them. . . .

I would like to thank my wife and my friend Dr. Rolf Renker (Düren) for their invaluable assistance in the preparation of this paperbound edition.

Wabern/Berne, February 1973   Jean Gebser

PART ONE:

Foundations of the Aperspectival World

A Contribution to the History of the Awakening of Consciousness

Editorial Note Regarding the Annotations

Besides references to sources and the relevant secondary literature, the extensive notes following each chapter contain important supplementary information (commentaries and digressions to extend and clarify the questions under discussion). Reference to this supplementary information is made throughout the text by italicized, raised numbers in order to distinguish them from the mere source references.

[In the notes themselves, an asterisk following the number indicates a change or emendation for the English edition. These changes are in almost all instances the substitution of quotations and their accompanying source references for passages originally in English, or for quotations familiar from existing English translations. In one or two instances a clarifying remark has been added.

References to the author's own works have been brought up to date by including in each instance volume and page numbers of the complete edition of his works in the original (Jean Gebser, *Gesamtausgabe*, Schaffhausen, Switzerland, 1975-1981, eight volumes and index).

The author has placed particular emphasis on cross-referencing the notes and source references. Accordingly, his arrangement, although departing from current scholarly practice, has been retained in this English edition. The notes, however, have been placed at the end of each chapter, rather than in a separate volume, as is the case with the second through fifth editions of the original.—Translators note.]

1

Fundamental
Considerations

Anyone today who considers the emergence of a new era of mankind as a certainty and expresses the conviction that our rescue from collapse and chaos could come about by virtue of a new attitude and a new formation of man's consciousness, will surely elicit less credence than those who have heralded the decline of the West. Contemporaries of totalitarianism, World War II, and the atom bomb seem more likely to abandon even their very last stand than to realize the possibility of a transition, a new constellation or a transformation, or even to evince any readiness to take a leap into tomorrow, although the harbingers of tomorrow, the evidence of transformation, and other signs of the new and imminent cannot have gone entirely unnoticed. Such a reaction, the reaction of a mentality headed for a fall, is only too typical of man in transition.

The present book is, in fact, the account of the nascence of a new world and a new consciousness. It is based not on ideas or speculations but on insights into mankind's mutations from its primordial beginnings up to the present—on perhaps novel insights into the forms of consciousness manifest in the various epochs of mankind: insights into the powers behind their realization as manifest between origin and the present, and active in origin and the present. And as the origin before all time is the entirety of the very beginning, so too is the present the entirety of everything temporal and time-bound, including the effectual reality of all time phases: yesterday, today, tomorrow, and even the pre-temporal and timeless.

The structuration we have discovered seems to us to reveal the bases of consciousness, thereby enabling us to make a contribution to the understanding of man's emergent consciousness. It is based on the recognition that in the course of mankind's history—and not only Western man's—clearly discernable worlds stand out whose development or unfolding took place in mutations of consciousness. This, then, presents the task of a cultural-historical analysis of the various structures of consciousness as they have proceeded from the various mutations.

For this analysis we shall employ a method of demonstrating the respective consciousness structures of the various "epochs" on the basis of their representative evidence and their unique forms of visual as well as linguistic expression. This approach, which is not limited to the currently dominant mentality, attempts to present in visible, tangible, and audible form the respective consciousness structures from within their specific modalities and unique constitutions by means appropriate to their natures.

By returning to the very sources of human development as we observe all of the structures of consciousness, and moving from there toward our present day and our contemporary situation and consciousness, we can not only discover the past and the present moment of our existence but also gain a view into the future which reveals the traits of a new reality amidst the decline of our age.

It is our belief that the essential traits of a new age and a new reality are discernible in nearly all forms of contemporary expression, whether in the creations of modern art, or in the recent findings of the natural sciences, or in the results of the humanities and sciences of the mind. Moreover we are in a position to define this new reality in such a way as to emphasize one of its most significant elements. Our definition is a natural corollary of the recognition that man's coming to awareness is inseparably bound to his consciousness of space and time.

Scarcely five hundred years ago, during the Renaissance, an unmistakable reorganization of our consciousness occurred: the *discovery of perspective* which opened up the three-dimensionality of space.[1] This discovery is so closely linked with the entire intellectual attitude of the modern epoch that we have felt obliged to call this age the age of perspectivity and characterize the age immediately preceding it as the "unperspectival" age. These definitions, by recognizing a fundamental characteristic of these eras, lead to the further appropriate definition of the age of the dawning new consciousness as the "aperspectival" age, a definition supported not only by the results of modern physics, but also by developments in the visual arts and literature, where the incorporation of time as a fourth dimension into previously spatial conceptions has formed the initial basis for manifesting the "new."

"Aperspectival" is not to be thought of as merely the opposite or negation of "perspectival"; the antithesis of "perspectival" is "unperspectival." The distinction in meaning suggested by the three terms unperspectival, perspectival, and aperspectival is analogous to that of the terms illogical, logical, and alogical or immoral, moral, and amoral.[2] We have employed here the designation "aperspectival" to clearly emphasize the need of overcoming the mere antithesis of affirmation and negation. The so-called primal words (*Urworte*), for example, evidence two antithetic connotations: Latin *altus* meant "high" as well as "low"; *sacer* meant "sacred" as well as "cursed." Such primal words as these formed an undifferentiated psychically-stressed unity whose bivalent nature was definitely familiar to the early Egyptians and Greeks.[3] This is no longer the case with our present sense of language; consequently, we have required a term that transcends equally the ambivalence of the primal connotations and the dualism of antonyms or conceptual opposites.

Hence we have used the Greek prefix "a-" in conjunction with our Latin-derived word "perspectival" in the sense of an *alpha privativum* and not as an *alpha negativum*, since the prefix has a liberating character (*privativum*, derived from Latin *privare*, i.e., "to liberate"). The designation "aperspectival," in consequence, expresses a process of liberation from the exclusive validity of perspectival and unperspectival, as well as pre-perspectival limitations. Our designation, then, does not attempt to unite the inherently coexistent unperspectival and perspectival structures, nor does it attempt to reconcile or synthesize structures which, in their deficient modes, have become irreconcilable. If "aperspectival" were to represent only a synthesis it would imply no more than "perspectival-rational" and would be limited and only momentarily valid, inasmuch as every union is threatened by further separation. Our concern is with integrality and ultimately with the whole; the word "aperspectival" conveys our attempt to deal with wholeness. It is a definition which differentiates a perception of reality that is neither perspectivally restricted to only one sector nor merely unperspectivally evocative of a vague sense of reality.

Finally, we would emphasize the general validity of the term "aperspectival"; it is definitely not intended to be understood as an extension of concepts used in art history and should not be so construed. When we introduced the concept in 1936/1939, it was within the context of scientific as well as artistic traditions.[4] The perspectival structure as fully realized by Leonardo da Vinci is of fundamental importance not only to our scientific-technological but also artistic understanding of the world. Without perspective neither technical drafting nor three-dimensional painting would have been possible. Leonardo—scientist, engineer, and artist in one—was the first to fully develop drafting techniques and perspectival painting. In this same sense, that is from a scientific as well as artistic standpoint, the term "aperspectival" is valid, and the basis for this significance must not be overlooked, for it legitimizes the validity and applicability of the term to the sciences, the humanities, and the arts.

It is our intent to furnish evidence that the aperspectival world, whose nascence we are witnessing, can liberate us from the superannuated legacy of both the unperspectival and the perspectival worlds. In very general terms we might say that the unperspectival world preceded the world of mind- and ego-bound perspective discovered and anticipated in late antiquity and first apparent in Leonardo's application of it. Viewed in this manner the unperspectival world is collective, the perspectival individualistic. That is, the unperspectival world is related to the anonymous "one" or the tribal "we," the perspectival to the "I" or Ego; the one world is grounded in Being, the other, beginning with the Renaissance, in Having; the former is predominantly irrational, the later rational.

Today, at least in Western civilization, both modes survive only as deteriorated and consequently dubious variants. This is evident from the sociological and anthropological questions currently discussed in the Occidental forum; only questions that are unresolved are discussed with the vehemence characteristic of these discussions. The current situation manifests on the one hand an egocentric individualism exaggerated to extremes and desirous of possessing everything, while on the other it manifests an equally extreme collectivism that promises the total fulfillment of man's being. In the latter instance we find the utter abnegation of the individual valued merely as an object in the human aggregate; in the former a hyper-valuation of the individual who, despite his limitations, is permitted everything. This deficient, that is destructive, antithesis divides the world into two warring camps, not just politically and ideologically, but in all areas of human endeavor.

Since these two ideologies are now pressing toward their limits we can assume that neither can prevail in the long run. When any movement tends to the extremes it leads away from the center or nucleus toward eventual destruction at the outer limits where the connections to the life-giving center finally are severed. It would seem that today the connections are already broken, for it is increasingly evident that the individual is being driven into isolation while the collective degenerates into mere aggregation. These two conditions, isolation and aggregation, are in fact clear indications that individualism and collectivism have now become deficient.

When we have grasped this it is at once apparent that we can extricate ourselves from our dangerous situation only by ordering our relationships to ourselves, to our "I" or Ego, and not just our relationships with others, to the "Thou," that is to God, the world, our fellow man and neighbor. That seems possible only if we are willing to assimilate the entirety of our human existence into our awareness. This means that all of our structures of awareness that form and support our present consciousness structure will have to be integrated into a new and more intensive form, which would in fact unlock a new reality. To that end we must constantly relive and re-experience in a decisive sense the full depth of our past. The adage that anyone who denies and condemns his past also abnegates his future is valid for the individual as well as for mankind. Our plea for an appropriate ordering and conscious realization of our relationships to the "I" as well as the "Thou" chiefly concerns the ordering and conscious recognition of our origin, and of all factors leading to the present. It is only in terms of man in his entirety that we shall achieve the necessary detachment from the present situation, i.e., from both our unperspectival ties to the group or collective, and our perspectival attachment to the separated, individual Ego. When we become aware of the exhausted residua of past or passing forms of our understanding of reality we will recognize more clearly the signs of the inevitable "new." We will also sense that there are new sources which can be tapped: the sources of the aperspectival world that can liberate us from the two exhausted and deficient forms which have become almost completely invalid and are certainly no longer all-inclusive or decisive.

It is our task in this book to work out this aperspectival basis. Our discussion will rely more on the evidence presented in the history of thought than on the findings of the natural sciences as is the case with the author's *Transformation of the Occident*. Among the disciplines of historical thought the investigation of language will form the predominant source of our insight since it is the pre-eminent means of reciprocal communication between man and the world.

It is not sufficient for us to merely furnish a postulate; rather, it will be necessary to show the latent possibilities in us and in our present, possibilities that are about to become acute, that is, effectual and consequently real. In the following discussion we shall therefore proceed from two basic considerations:

1. A mere interpretation of our times is inadequate. We must furnish concrete evidence of phenomena that are clearly revealed as being new and that transform not only our countenance, but the very countenance of time.
2. The condition of today's world cannot be transformed by technocratic rationality, since both technocracy and rationality are apparently nearing their apex; nor can it be transcended by preaching or admonishing a return to ethics and morality, or in fact, by any form of return to the past.

We have only one option: in examining the manifestations of our age, we must penetrate them with sufficient breadth and depth that we do not come under their demonic and destructive spell. We must not focus our view merely on these phenomena, but rather on the humus of the decaying world beneath, where the seedlings of the future are growing, immeasurable in their potential and vigor. Since our insight into the energies pressing toward development aids their unfolding, the seedlings and inceptive beginnings must be made visible and comprehensible.

It will be our task to demonstrate that the first stirrings of the new can be found in all areas of human expression, and that they inherently share a common character. This demonstration can succeed only if we have certain knowledge about the manifestations of both our past and our present. Consequently, the task of the present work will be to work out the foundations of the past and the present which are also the basis of the new consciousness and the new reality arising therefrom. It will be the task of the second part to define the new emergent consciousness structure to the extent that its inceptions are already visible.

We shall therefore begin with the evidence and not with idealistic constructions; in the face of present-day weapons of annihilation, such constructions have less chance of survival than ever before. But as we shall see, weapons and nuclear fission are not the only realities to be dealt with; *spiritual reality in its intensified form is also becoming effectual and real.* This new spiritual reality is without question our only security that the threat of material destruction can be averted. Its realization alone seems able to guarantee man's continuing existence in the face of the powers of technology, rationality, and chaotic emotion. If our consciousness, that is, the individual person's awareness, vigilance, and clarity of vision, cannot master the new reality and make possible its realization, then the prophets of doom will have been correct. Other alternatives are an illusion; consequently, great demands are placed on us, and each one of us have been given a grave responsibility, not merely to survey but to actually traverse the path opening before us.

There are surely enough historical instances of the catastrophic downfall of entire peoples and cultures. Such declines were triggered by the collision of deficient and exhausted attitudes that were insufficient for continuance with those more recent, more intense and, in some respects, superior. One such occurrence vividly exemplifies the decisive nature of such crises: the collision of the magical, mythical, and unperspectival culture of the Central American Aztecs with the rational-technological, perspectival attitude of the sixteenth-century Spanish conquistadors. A description of this event can be found in the Aztec chronicle of Frey Bernardino de Sahagun, written eight years after Cortez' conquest of Mexico on the basis of Aztec accounts. The following excerpt forms the beginning of the thirteenth chapter of the chronicle which describes the conquest of Mexico City:

> The thirteenth chapter, wherein is recounted
> how the Mexican king Montezuma
> sends other sorcerers
> who were to cast a spell on the Spanish
> and what happened to them on the way.
> And the second group of messengers—
> the soothsayers, the magicians, and the high priests—
> likewise went to receive the Spanish.
> But it was to no avail;
> they could not bewitch the people,
> they could not reach their intent with the Spanish;
> they simply failed to arrive.[5]

There is hardly another text extant that describes so succinctly and so memorably the collapse of an entire world and a hitherto valid and effectual human attitude. The magic-mythical world of the Mexicans could not prevail against the Spaniards; it collapsed the moment it encountered the rational-technological mentality. The materialistic orientation of present-day Europeans will tend to attribute this collapse to the Spaniards' technological superiority, but in actual fact it was the vigor of the Spanish consciousness *vis-à-vis* the weakness of the Mexican that was decisive. It is the basic distinction between the ego-less man, bound to the group and a collective mentality, and the individual securely conscious of his individuality. Authentic spell-casting, a fundamental element of the collective consciousness for the Mexicans, is effective only for the members attuned to the group consciousness. It simply by-passes those who are not bound to, or sympathetic toward, the group. The Spaniards' superiority, which compelled the Mexicans to surrender almost without a struggle, resulted primarily from their consciousness of individuality, not from their superior weaponry. Had it been possible for the Mexicans to step out of their egoless attitude, the Spanish victory would have been less certain and assuredly more difficult.[6]

What is of interest to us within the present context is not the historical predicament occasioned by the collision of peoples of differing might, but rather the supersession of the magic group-consciousness and its most potent weapon, spell-casting, by rational, ego-consciousness. Today this rational consciousness, with nuclear fission its strongest weapon, is confronted by a similar catastrophic situation of failure; consequently, it too can be vanquished by a new consciousness structure. We are convinced that there are powers arising from within ourselves that are already at work overcoming the deficiency and dubious nature of our rational ego-consciousness via the new aperspectival awareness whose manifestations are surging forth everywhere. The aperspective consciousness structure is a consciousness of the whole, an integral consciousness encompassing all time and embracing both man's distant past and his approaching future as a living present. The new spiritual attitude can take root only through an insightful process of intensive awareness. This attitude must emerge from its present concealment and latency and become effective, and thereby prepare the transparency of the world and man in which spirituality can manifest itself.

The first part of the present work, which is devoted to the foundations of the aperspectival world, is intended to furnish convincing evidence for this new spiritual attitude. This evidence rests on two guiding principles whose validity will gradually become clear:

1) *Latency—what is concealed—is the demonstrable presence of the future.* It includes everything that is not yet manifest, as well as everything which has again returned to latency. Since we are dealing here primarily with phenomena of consciousness and integration, we will also have to investigate questions of history, the soul and the psyche, time, space, and the forms of thought.

   Since the second part of this work is devoted to manifestations of the new consciousness, the first part must clarify questions relating to the manifestations of previous and present consciousness structures. We shall attempt to demonstrate the incipient concretion of time and the spiritual dimension which are preconditions of the aperspectival world. We shall also attempt to furnish evidence of the increasing efficacy of that spiritual reality (which is neither a mere psychic state nor an intellectual-rational form of representation). This will bring out the validity of our second guiding principle:

2) *Transparency (diaphaneity) is the form of manifestation (epiphany) of the spiritual.*

Our concern is to render transparent everything latent "behind" and "before" the world—to render transparent our own origin, our entire human past, as well as the present, which already contains the future. We are shaped and determined not only by today and yesterday, but by tomorrow as well. The author is not interested in outlining discrete segments, steps or levels of man, but in disclosing the transparency of man as a whole and the interplay of the various consciousness structures which constitute him. This transparency or diaphaneity of our existence is particularly evident during transitional periods, and it is from the experiences of man in transition, experiences which man has had with the concealed and latent aspects of his dawning future as he became aware of them, that will clarify our own experiencing of the present.

It is perhaps unnecessary to reiterate that we cannot employ the methods derived from and dependent on our present consciousness structure to investigate different structures of consciousness, but will have to adapt our method to the specific structure under investigation. Yet if we relinquish a unitary methodology we do not necessarily regress to an unmethodological or irrational attitude, or to a kind of conjuration or mystical contemplation. Contemporary methods employ predominantly dualistic procedures that do not extend beyond simple subject-object relationships; they limit our understanding to what is commensurate with the present Western mentality. Even where the measurements of contemporary methodologies are based primarily on quantitative criteria, they are all vitiated by the problem of the antithesis between "measure" and mass (as we will discuss later in detail). Our "method" is not just a "measured" assessment, but above and beyond this an attempt at "diaphany" or rendering transparent. With its aid, whatever lies "behind" (past) and "ahead of" (future) the currently dominant mentality becomes accessible to the new subject-object relationship. Although this new relationship is no longer dualistic, it does not threaten man with a loss of identity, or with his being equated with an object. Although this new method is still in its infancy, we are nevertheless compelled to make use of it.[7]

In summary, it should be said that our description does not deal with a new image of the world, nor with a new *Weltanschauung*, nor with a new conception of the world. A new image would be no more than the creation of a myth, since all imagery has a predominantly mythical nature. A new *Weltanschauung* would be nothing else than a new mysticism and irrationality, as mythical characteristics are inherent in all contemplation to the extent that it is merely visionary; and a new conception of the world would be nothing else than yet another standard rationalistic construction of the present, for conceptualization has an essentially rational and abstract nature.

Our concern is with a new reality—a reality functioning and effectual integrally, in which intensity and action, the effective and the effect co-exist; one where origin, by virtue of "presentation," blossoms forth anew; and one in which the present is all-encompassing and entire. Integral reality is the world's transparency, a perceiving of the world as truth: a mutual perceiving and imparting of truth of the world and of man and of all that transluces both.

1   See Jean Gebser, *Abendländische Wandlung* (Zürich: Oprecht, 1943, ²1945, ³1950); Ullstein Edition no. 107: ⁴1955, ⁵1960, ⁶1963, ⁷1965; *Gesamtausgabe* (Schaffhausen: Novalis, 1975), I, Chapter 3.—The first references to perspective as a means of disclosing space can be found in our publication *Rilke und Spanien* (Zürich: Oprecht, 1940), written in 1936/39; (also in vol. I of the *Gesamtausgabe*). (The raised numbers preceding the year of publication indicate throughout the present work the edition of the work cited.)

2   Regarding this distinction see Jean Gebser, *Der grammatische Spiegel* (Zürich: Oprecht, 1944), p. 36; ²1963, p. 44f.; *Gesamtausgabe*, I, p. 169. First reference to the scope and application of the term "aperspectival" can be found in the author's *Rilke und Spanien* (note 1), pp. 38-45; *Gesamtausgabe*, I, pp. 40-44, as well as in his *Abendländische Wandlung* (note 1), p. 173; ²1945, p. 200; Ullstein ed. No. 107, p. 150; and *Gesamtausgabe*, I, p. 301.

3   We are referring here to Sigmund Freud's paper "Über den Gegensinn der Urworte," *Jahrbuch für psychoanalytische und psychopathologische Forschungen* 2 (1910), and S. Freud, *Gesammelte Werke chronologisch geordnet* (London: Imago, 1943), VIII, 214-21, which deals with K. Abel's *Gegensinn der Urworte* (1884). See also Karl Terebessy, *Zum Problem der Ambivalenz in der Sprachentwicklung* (Trnava: Urbánek, 1944), p. 5

4   Jean Gebser, *Rilke und Spanien* (note 1), pp. 38-52; *Gesamtausgabe*, I, pp. 40-50.

5   Eduard Seler, editor and translator, *Einige Kapitel aus dem Geschichtswerk des Fray Bernardino de Sahagun* (from the Aztec) (Frankfurt/ M.: Strecker & Schröder, 1927, p. 482. Although this book is long out of print, a considerably abridged edition was published recently including the thirteenth chapter from which we have quoted: *Das Herz auf dem Opferstein*: *Aztekentexte*, postscript by Jahnheinz Jahn (Köln: Kiepenheuer & Witsch, 1962).

6   The victory of the Swiss confederates over the fully equipped Austrian army under the command of Duke Leopold at Morgarten in 1315 can be considered with equal justification as a victory of the new—individual—consciousness over the tradition-bound and clan-grouped Austrian battle-formations: a victory by a smaller number of individuals over the greater numerical strength of the mass. This new individual consciousness was first manifest in Switzerland. The obvious strategic exploitation of the topography by the Confederates was of only secondary importance. Similarly, the Greek victory over the Persians under Xerxes' command could be traced to an analogous context. The strength of the individual Greek consciousness was far superior to the deficient magic consciousness of the despotic Xerxes, who for example had ordered the Hellespont flogged (!) as punishment for its turbulence, which had hindered the crossing of his army to Greece. See Jean Gebser, *In der Bewährung* (Bern and München: Francke, 1962), p. 104; *Gesamtausgabe*, V/I, p. 252f.

7   In this regard see also Jean Gebser, *In der Bewährung* (note 6), p. 119ff.; *Gesamtausgabe*, V/I, p. 267f. The notion of a "world without opposite" loses its apparent negativity whenever antithetical human relationships are transformed into "being with others" or "humanly reciprocal."

2

The Three
European Worlds

1. *The Unperspectival World*

The transformation of European sensitivity to, and comprehension of, the world is nowhere more clearly discernible than in painting and architecture. Only our insight into this transformation can lead to a proper understanding of the nature and meaning of new styles and forms of expression.

Restricting ourselves here primarily to the art of the Christian era, we can distinguish two major self-contained epochs among the many artistic styles, followed today by an incipient third. The first encompasses the era up to the Renaissance, the other, now coming to a close, extends up to the present. The decisive and distinguishing characteristic of these epochs is the respective absence or presence of perspective; consequently we shall designate the first era as the "unperspectival," the second as the "perspectival," and the currently emerging epoch as the "aperspectival."[1]

As we shall see, these designations are valid not only with respect to art history, but also to aesthetics, cultural history, and the history of the psyche and the mind. The achievement of perspective indicates man's discovery and consequent coming to awareness of space, whereas the unrealized perspective indicates that space is dormant in man and that he is not yet awakened to it. Moreover, the unperspectival world suggests a state in which man lacks self-identity: he belongs to a unit, such as a tribe or communal group, where the emphasis is not yet on the person but on the impersonal, not on the "I" but on the communal group, the qualitative mode of the collective. The illuminated manuscripts and gilt ground of early Romanesque painting depict the unperspectival world that retained the prevailing constitutive elements of Mediterranean antiquity. Not until the Gothic, the forerunner of the Renaissance was there a shift in emphasis. Before that space is not yet our depth-space, but rather a cavern (and vault), or simply an in-between space; in both instances it is undifferentiated space. This situation bespeaks for us a hardly conceivable enclosure in the world, an intimate bond between outer and inner suggestive of a correspondence—only faintly discernible—between soul and nature. This condition was gradually destroyed by the expansion and growing strength of Christianity, whose teaching of detachment from nature transforms this destruction into an act of liberation.

Man's lack of spatial awareness is attended by a lack of ego-consciousness, since in order to objectify and qualify space, a self-conscious "I" is required that is able to stand opposite or confront space, as well as to depict or represent it by projecting it out of his soul or psyche. In this light, Worringer's statements regarding the lack of all space consciousness in Egyptian art are perfectly valid: "Only in the rudimentary form of prehistorical space and cave magic does space have a role in Egyptian architecture. . . . The Egyptians were neutral and indifferent toward space. . . . They were not even potentially aware of spatiality. Their experience was not trans-spatial but pre-spatial; . . . their culture of oasis cultivation was spaceless. . . . Their culture knew only spatial limitations and enclosures in architecture but no inwardness or interiority as such. Just as their engraved reliefs lacked shadow depth, so too was their architecture devoid of special depth. The third dimension, that is the actual dimension of life's tension and polarity, was experienced not as a quality but as a mere quantity. How then was space, the moment of depth-seeking extent, to enter their awareness as an independent quality apart from all corporality? . . . The Egyptians lacked utterly any spatial consciousness."[2]

Despite, or indeed because of, Euclidean geometry, there is no evidence of an awareness of qualitative and objectified space in early antiquity or in the epoch preceding the Renaissance. This has been indirectly confirmed by von Kaschnitz-Weinberg, who has documented two opposing yet complementary structural elements of ancient art as it emerged from the Megalithic (stone) age.[3] The first, Dolmen architecture, entered the Mediterranean region primarily from Northern and Western Europe and was especially influential on Greek architecture. It is phallic in nature and survives in the column architecture in Greece, as in the Parthenon. Space is visible here simply as diastyle or the intercolumnar space, whose structure is determined by the vertical posts and the horizontal lintels and corresponds to Euclidean cubic space.[4]

The second structural element in von Kaschnitz-Weinberg's view is the uterine character of Grotto architecture that entered the Mediterranean area from the Orient (mainly from Iran) and survives in Roman dome architecture, as in the Pantheon or the Baths. Here space is merely a vault, a Grotto-space corresponding to the powerful cosmological conception of the Oriental matriarchal religions for which the world itself is nothing but a vast cavern.[5] It is of interest that Plato, in his famous allegory, was the first to describe man in the process of leaving the cave.

We are then perhaps justified in speaking of the "space" of antiquity as undifferentiated space, as a simple inherence within the security of the maternal womb, expressing an absence of any confrontation with actual, exterior space. The predominance of the two constitutive polar elements, the paternal phallic column and the maternal uterine cave—the forces to which unperspectival man was subject—reflects his inextricable relationship to his parental world and, consequently, his complete dependence on it which excluded any awareness of an ego in our modern sense. He remains sheltered and enclosed in the world of the "we" where outer objective space is still non-existent.

The two polar elements which made up the spaceless foundation of the ancient world were first united and creatively amalgamated in Christian ecclesiastical architecture. (The symbolic content of these elements does not, as we will see p. 66 below, emphasize the sexual, but rather the psychical and mythical aspects.) Their amalgamation subsequently gives rise to the Son of Man; the duality of the column and tower, the vault and dome of Christian church architecture made feasible for the first time the trinity represented by the son-as-man, the man who will create his own space.

Understood in this light, it is not surprising that around the time of Christ the world of late antiquity shows distinct signs of incipient change. The boldness and incisive nature of this change is evident when we examine the Renaissance era that begins around 1250 A.D. and incorporates stylistic elements that first appear around the time of Christ. We refer, of course, to the first intimations of a perspectival conception of space found in the murals of Pompeii.[6] Besides their first suggestions of landscape painting, the murals are the first examples of what has come to be known as the "still life," i.e., the objectification of nature already expressed in the Roman garden designs of the same period and heralded by the pastoral scenes of late Bucolic poetry such as Virgil's *Ecloges*. It was principally by incorporating these novel elements of ancient culture and realizing their implications that the Renaissance was able to create the three-dimensional perspectival world from a two-dimensional and unperspectival culture.

2. The Perspectival World

Although already shaped in the Mediterranean world of late antiquity, the perspectival world began to find expression about 1250 A.D. in Christian Europe. In contrast to the impersonal, pre-human, hieratic, and standardized sense of the human body—in our sense virtually non-existent—held by the Egyptians, the Greek sensitivity to the body had already evidenced a certain individuation of man. But only toward the close of the Middle Ages did man gradually become aware of his body as a support for his ego. And, having gained this awareness, he is henceforth not just a human being reflected in an idealized bust or miniature of an emperor, a philosopher, or a poet,[7] but a specific individual such as those who gaze at us from a portrait by Jan van Eyck.[8]

The conception of man as subject is based on a conception of the world and the environment as an object. It is in the paintings of Giotto that we see first expressed, however tentatively, the objectified, external world. Early Sienese art, particularly miniature painting, reveals a yet spaceless, self-contained, and depthless world significant for its symbolic content and not for what we would today call its realism. These "pictures" of an unperspectival era are, as it were, painted at night when objects are without shadow and depth. Here darkness has swallowed space to the extent that only the immaterial, psychic component could be expressed. But in the work of Giotto, the latent space hitherto dormant in the night of collective man's unconscious is visualized; the first renderings of space begin to appear in painting, signaling an incipient perspectivity. A new psychic awareness of space, objectified or externalized from the psyche out into the world, begins—a consciousness of space whose element of depth becomes visible in perspective.

This psychic inner-space breaks forth at the very moment that the Troubadours are writing the first lyric "I"-poems, the first personal poetry that suddenly opens an abyss between man, as poet, and the world or nature (1250 A.D.). Concurrently at the University of Paris, Thomas Aquinas, following the thought of his teacher Albertus Magnus, asserts the validity of Aristotle, thereby initiating the rational displacement of the predominantly psychic-bound Platonic world. And this occurred in the wake of Petrus Hispanus (Petrus Lucitanus), the later Pope John XXI (d. 1277),[9] who had authored the first comprehensive European textbook on psychology (De anima), introducing via Islam and Spain the Aristotelian theory of the soul.[10] Shortly thereafter, Duns Scotus (d. 1308) freed theology from the hieratic rigors of scholasticism by teaching the primacy of volition and emotion. And the blindness of antiquity to time inherent in its unperspectival, psychically-stressed world (which amounted to a virtual timelessness) gave way to the visualization of, and openness to time with a quantifiable, spatial character. This was exemplified by the erection of the first public clock in the courtyard of Westminister Palace in 1283, an event anticipated by Pope Sabinus, who in 604 ordered the ringing of bells to announce the passing of the hours.

We shall examine the question of time in detail later in our discussion; here we wish to point out that there is a forgotten but essential interconnection between time and the psyche. The closed horizons of antiquity's celestial cave-like vault express a soul not yet awakened to spatial time-consciousness and temporal quantification. The "heaven of the heart" mentioned by Origen[11] was likewise a self-contained inner heaven first exteriorized into the heavenly landscapes of the frescoes by the brothers Ambrogio and Pietro Lorenzetti in the church of St. Francesco in Assisi (ca. 1327–28).[12] One should note that these early renderings of landscape and sky, which include a realistic rather than symbolic astral-mythical moon, are not merely accidental pictures with nocturnal themes. In contrast to the earlier vaulted sky, the heaven of these frescoes is no longer an enclosure; it is now rendered from the vantage point of the artist and expresses the incipient perspectivity of a confrontation with space, rather than an unperspectival immersion or inherence in it. Man is henceforth not just in the world but begins to possess it; no longer possessed by heaven, he becomes a conscious possessor—if not of the heavens, at least of the earth. This shift is, of course, a gain as well as a loss.

There is a document extant that unforgettably mirrors this gain and loss, this surrender and beginning; in a few sentences it depicts the struggle of a man caught between two worlds. We refer to the remarkable letter of the thirty-two year old Petrarch to Francesco Dionigi di Borgo San Sepolcro in 1336 (the first letter of his Familiari, vol. 4),[13] in which he describes his ascent of Mount Ventoux. For his time, his description is an epochal event and signifies no less than the discovery of landscape: the first dawning of an awareness of space that resulted in a fundamental alteration of European man's attitude in and toward the world.

Mount Ventoux is located to the northeast of Avignon, where the Rhône separates the French Alps from the Cevennes and the principal mountain range of Central France. The mountain is distinguished by clear and serene contours; viewed from Avignon to the south, its ridge slowly and seamlessly ascends against the clear Provençal sky, its southwestern slope sweeping broadly with soft restraint toward the valley. After a downhill sweep of nearly two kilometers, it comes to rest against the sycamore slopes of the Carpentras, which shelter the almond trees from the northern winds.

Although then unaware of its full significance, the present writer saw the mountain years ago and sensed its attraction. Certainly this attraction must have been sensed by others as well; it is no accident that Petrarch's discovery of landscape occurred precisely in this region of France. Here, the Gnostic tradition had encouraged investigation of the world and placed greater emphasis on knowledge than on belief; here, the tradition of the Troubadours, the Cathari, and the Albigensi remained alive. This is not to say that the affinity makes Petrarch a Gnostic, but merely points to the Gnostic climate of this part of *douce France*[14], which is mentioned in the opening lines of France's first major poetic work, the *Chanson de Roland* (verse 16): "Li empereres Carles de France dulce."[15]

Petrarch's letter is in the nature of a confession; it is addressed to the Augustinian professor of theology who had taught him to treasure and emulate Augustine's *Confessions*. Now, a person makes a confession or an admission only if he believes he has transgressed against something; and it is this vision of space, as extended before him from the mountain top, this vision of space as a reality, and its overwhelming impression, together with his shock and dismay, his bewilderment at his perception and acceptance of the panorama, that are reflected in his letter. It marks him as the first European to step out of the transcendental gilt ground of the Siena masters, the first to emerge from a space dormant in time and soul, into "real" space where he discovers landscape.

When Petrarch's glance spatially isolated a part of "nature" from the whole, the all-encompassing attachment to sky and earth and the unquestioned, closed unperspectival ties are severed. The isolated part becomes a piece of land *created* by his perception. It may well be that with this event a part of the spiritual, divine formative principle of heaven and earth (and nature in its all-encompassing sense) was conveyed to man. If this is indeed so, then from that day of Petrarch's discovery onward man's responsibility was increased. Yet regarded from our vantage point, it is doubtful whether man has been adequate to this responsibility. Be that as it may, the consequences of Petrarch's discovery remain unaltered; we are still able to sense his uneasiness about his discovery, and the grave responsibility arising from it as documented in his letter.

"Yesterday I climbed the highest mountain of our region," he begins the letter, "motivated solely by the wish to experience its renowned height. For many years this has been in my soul and, as you well know, I have roamed this region since my childhood. The mountain, visible from far and wide, was nearly always present before me; my desire gradually increased until it became so intense that I resolved to yield to it, especially after having read Livy's Roman history the day before. There I came upon his description of the ascent of Philip, King of Macedonia, on Mount Haemus in Thessalia, from whose summit two seas, the Adriatic as well as the Pontus Euxinus, are said to be visible."

The significance of Philip's ascent cannot be compared to Petrarch's because Livy's emphasis is on the sea, while the land—not yet a landscape—is not mentioned at all. The reference to the sea can be understood as an indication that in antiquity man's experience of the soul was symbolized by the sea, and not by space (as we shall see further on in our discussion). The famous ascents undertaken by such Romans as Hadrian, Strabo, and Lucilius were primarily for administrative and practical, not for aesthetic purposes. As an administrative reformer, Hadrian had climbed Mount Aetna in order to survey the territory under his jurisdiction, while the fugitive Lucilius, the friend of Seneca, had been motivated by purely practical reasons.

Let us return to Petrarch's letter. Having mentioned the passage in Livy, he describes his wearisome trek as well as an encounter: "In the ravines we [Petrarch and his brother Gerardo] met an old shepherd who, in a torrent of words, tried to dissuade us from the ascent, saying he had never heard of anyone risking such a venture." Undaunted by the old man's lamentations, they pressed forward: "While still climbing, I urged myself forward by the thought that what I experienced today will surely benefit myself as well as *many others* who desire the blessed life. . . . "16

Once Petrarch reaches the summit, however, his narrative becomes unsettled; the shifts of tense indicate his intense agitation even at the mere recollection of his experience at the summit. "Shaken by the unaccustomed wind and the wide, freely shifting vistas, I was immediately awe-struck. I look: the clouds lay beneath my feet. . . . I look toward Italy, whither turned my soul even more than my gaze, and sigh at the sight of the Italian sky which appeared more to my spirit than to my eyes, and I was overcome by an inexpressible longing to return home. . . . Suddenly a new thought seized me, *transporting me from space into time* [*a locis traduxit ad tempora*].17 I said to myself: it has been ten years since you left Bologna. . . . " In the lines that follow, recollecting a decade of suffering, and preoccupied by the overpowering desire for his homeland that befell him during the unaccustomed sojourn on the summit, he reveals that his thoughts have turned inward. Still marked by his encounter with what was then a *new reality*, yet shaken by its effect, he flees "from space into time," out of the first experience with space back to the gold-ground of the Siena masters.

Having confessed his anguish and unburdened his soul, he describes further his perception of space: "Then I turn westward; in vain my eye searches for the ridge of the Pyrenees, boundary between France and Spain. . . . To my right I see the mountains of Lyon, to the left the Mediterranean surf washes against Marseille before it breaks on Aigues-Mortes. Though the distance was considerable, we could see clearly; the Rhône itself lay beneath our gaze." Once again he turns away and yields to something indicative of his poetic sensibility. Helpless in the face of the expanse before him and groping for some kind of moral support, he opens a copy of Augustine's *Confessions* where he chances upon a phrase. It stems from that realm of the soul to which he had turned his gaze after his initial encounter with landscape. "God and my companion are witnesses," he writes, " that my glance fell upon the passage: 'And men went forth to behold the high mountains and the mighty surge of the sea, and the broad stretches of the rivers and the inexhaustible ocean, and the paths of the stars, and so doing, lose themselves in wonderment [*et relinquunt se ipsos*].' "

Once more, he is terrified, only this time less by his encounter with space than by the encounter with his soul of which he is reminded by the chance discovery of Augustine's words. "I admit I was overcome with wonderment," he continues; "I begged my brother who also desired to read the passage not to disturb me, and closed the book. I was irritated for having turned my thoughts to mundane matters at such a moment, for even the Pagan philosophers should have long since taught me that there is nothing more wondrous than the soul [*nihil praeter animum esse mirabile*], and that compared to its greatness nothing is great."

Pausing for a new paragraph, he continues with these surprising words: "My gaze, fully satisfied by contemplating the mountain [i.e., only after a conscious and exhaustive survey of the panorama], my eyes turned inward [*in me ipsum interiores oculos reflexi*]; and then we fell silent. . . . " Although obscured by psychological reservations and the memory of his physical exertion, the concluding lines of his letter suggest an ultimate affirmation of his ascent and the attendant experience: "So much perspiration and effort just to bring the body a little closer to heaven; the soul, when approaching God, must be similarly terrified."18

The struggle initiated by his internalization of space into his soul—or, if you will, the externalization of space out of his soul—continued in Petrarch from that day on Mount Ventoux until the end of his life. The old world where only the soul is wonderful and worthy of contemplation, as expressed succinctly in Augustine's words "Time resides in the soul,"[19] now begins to collapse. There is a gradual but increasingly evident shift from time to space until the soul wastes away in the materialism of the nineteenth century, a loss obvious to most people today that only the most recent generations have begun to counter in new ways.

The transition mirrored in Petrarch's letter of six hundred years ago was primarily an unprecedented extension of man's image of the world. The event that Petrarch describes in almost prophetic terms as "certainly of benefit to himself and many others" inaugurates a new realistic, individualistic, and rational understanding of nature. The freer treatment of space and landscape is already manifest in the work of Ambrogio Lorenzetti and Giotto; [20] but although Giotto's landscape with its hill motifs, for example, is still a predominantly symbolic representation of Umbrian nature, his treatment represents a decided shift away from the unperspectival world. This shift is continued by his apprentices, Fra Angelico and Masolino, and later by Paolo Uccello and the brothers Limbourg (in the Très riches heures du Duc de Berry),[21] who elaborate perspective painting with ever greater detail. What Giotto merely anticipated, namely the establishment of a clear contour of man, is first achieved by Masaccio. It is a characteristic also expressed in Andrea Pisano's reliefs, particularly in his "Astronomer's relief" on the campanile in Florence, and notably evident in the works of Donatello.[22] We must also remember Lorenzo Ghiberti, whose early bronze relief, the "Sacrifice of Isaac" (1401-02), is a remarkably authentic rendering of free, open, and unenclosed space.[23] To the extent that a relief is able to convey spatiality, this relief depicts a space where neither the transcendental gold illumination nor its complement, the darkness of the all-encompassing cavern, are present, but rather one where man is able to breath freely.

All of these manifestations arose as genuine artistic expressions and direct, that is, unreflected utterances of the change in man's attitude toward the world. Not until the third decade of the fifteenth century did European man begin to reflect and theorize, that is, consciously come to terms with the possibilities and expressive forms of the new style.

The intent of our somewhat detailed outline of the history of perspective is to indicate the length of time and the intensity of effort that man required to fully express internal predispositions in externalized forms. An equally detailed description of such specific factors will be required further on in our discussion if we are to apply criteria to the inquiry of our own times that will permit a valid or, at the very least, a considered judgement.

In the third decade of the fifteenth century, Cennino Cennini wrote his celebrated Trattata della pittura, the first theoretical treatise on art.[24] The various investigations that had preceded his work, notably those by the friars of Mount Athos, Heraclius and Theophilus, had been mere formularies.[25] But Cennini, proceeding from a defense of Giotto's style, offers advice on techniques, suggestions for differentiating man from space,[26] and instructions on rendering mountains and space by the use of gradations and shadings of color, thereby anticipating in principle the "aerial and color perspectivity" of Leonardo da Vinci.

About the same time, the brothers van Eyck began to bring increasing clarity and force to the perspective technique of their painting, while a plethora of attempts at perspective by various other masters points up the need for spatialization on the one hand, and the difficulty of rendering it on the other. Numerous works by these frequently overlooked minor masters bear witness to the unprecedented inner struggle that occurred in artists of that generation of the fifteenth century during their attempts to master space. Their struggle is apparent from the perplexed and chaotic ventures into a perspectival technique which are replete with reversed, truncated, or partial perspective and other unsuccessful experiments.[27] Such examples by the minor masters offer a trenchant example of the decisive process manifest by an increased spatial awareness: the artist's inner compulsion to render space—which is only incompletely grasped and only gradually emerges out of his soul toward awareness and clear objectivation—and his tenacity in the face of this problem because, however dimly, he has already perceived space.

This overwhelming new discovery and encounter, this elemental irruption of the third dimension and transformation of Euclidean plane surfaces, is so disorienting that it at first brought about an inflation and inundation by space. This is clearly evident in the numerous experimental representations of perspective. We will have occasion to note a parallel confusion and disorder in the painting of the period after 1800 when we consider the new dimension of emergent consciousness in our own day. But whereas the preoccupation of the Early Renaissance was with the concretion of space, our epoch is concerned with the concretion of *time*. And our fundamental point of departure, the attempt to concretize time and thus realize and become conscious of the fourth dimension, furnishes a means whereby we may gain *an all-encompassing perception and knowledge of our epoch.*

The early years of the Renaissance, which one might even characterize as being dramatic, are the source of further writings in the wake of Cennini's treatise. Of equally epochal importance are the three volumes of Leon Battista Alberti's *Della pittura* of 1436, which, besides a theory of proportions and anatomy based on Vitruvius, contain a first systematic attempt at a theory of perspectival construction (the chapter "Della prospettiva").[28] Earlier, Brunelleschi had achieved a perspectival construction in his dome for the cathedral of Florence, and Manetti justifiably calls him the "founder of perspectival drawing."[29] But it was Alberti who first formulated an epistemological description of the new manner of depiction, stated, still in very general terms, in the words: "Accordingly, the painting is a slice through the visual pyramid corresponding to a particular space or interval with its center and specific hues rendered on a given surface by lines and colors."[30] What Vitruvius in his *Architettura* still designated as "scenografia" has become for Alberti a "prospettiva", a clearly depicted visual pyramid.[31]

Some dozen years later, the three *Commentarii* of Lorenzo Ghiberti also treat of this same perspective;[32] but despite his attempt to remain within the tradition, his treatises describe in a novel way not only perspective but also anàtomy and a theory of drawing (*teorica del disegno*). It is significant that he corrects his principal model, Vitruvius, by inserting a chapter on "perspective" where Vitruvius would have included a chapter on the "knowledge of rules," and consequently intentionally elevates perspectivity to a basic axiom of his time.[33]

There is yet another major artist of that age who continues the discussion of this subject in advance of the definitive statements of Leonardo. Toward the end of his life, Piero della Francesca furnishes a penetrating theory of perspective compared to which Alberti's seems amateurish and empirical.[34] In his three books *De Perspectiva Pingendi* based on Euclid,[35] which were written in collaboration with Luca Pacioli, he defines for the first time *costruzione pittorica* as perspective. He had himself been successful in the practical application of perspective during the time of

Foquet, i.e., the latter half of the fifteenth century,[36] though after the brothers van Eyck[37] (to mention only the outstanding figures). This had facilitated the ultimate achievement of perspectivity, the "aerial perspective" of Leonardo's *Last Supper*.

Before returning to Leonardo, we must mention two facts which demonstrate better than any description the extent of fascination with the problem of perspective during the later part of the fifteenth century when perspective becomes virtually normative (as in Ghiberti's modification of Vitruvius). In his *Divina Proporzione*, Luca Pacioli—the learned mathematician, translator of Euclid, co-worker with Piero della Francesca, and friend of Leonardo—celebrated perspective as the eighth art; and when Antonio del Pollaiuolo built a memorial to perspective on one of his papal tombs in St. Peter's some ten years later (in the 1490s), he boldly added perspective as the eighth free art to the other seven.[38]

At the risk of exasperating many readers, we would venture to point out that this supersession of the number seven, the *heptaos*, can be interpreted as an indication of the symbolic conquest of the cavernous and vaulted heaven of unperspectivity. With the arrival of the eighth "art," which can also be considered an eighth muse, the world of the ancient seven-planet heaven collapses; the "n-", the negation retained in the night-sky [*Nacht*] of the unperspectival cavern gives way to the clarity and diurnal brightness of the eight (*acht*), which lacks the negating "n". The heptagonal cosmos of the ancients and its mystery religions are left behind, and man steps forth to integrate and concretize space.

It is, of course, considered disreputable today to trace or uncover subtle linguistic relationships that exist, for example, between the terms "eight" (*acht*) and "night" (*Nacht*). Even though language points to such relationships and interconnections, present-day man carefully avoids them, so as to keep them from bothering his conscience. Yet despite this, the things speak for themselves regardless of our attempts to denature them, and their roots remain as long as the word remains that holds them under its spell. It will be necessary, for instance, to discuss in Part Two the significance of the pivotal and ancient word "muse," whose multifarious background of meanings vividly suggests a possible aperspectivity.[39] Here we would only point to the illumination of the nocturnal-unperspectival world which takes place when perspective is enthroned as the eighth art. The old, seven-fold, simple planetary cavern space is suddenly flooded by the light of human consciousness and is rendered visible, as it were, from outside.

This deepening of space by illumination is achieved by perspective, the eighth art. In the Western languages, the n-less "eight," an unconscious expression of wakefulness and illumination, stands in opposition to the n-possessing and consequently negatively-stressed "night." There are numerous examples: German *acht-Nacht*; French *huit-nuit*; English *eight-night*; Italian *otto-notte*; Spanish *ocho-noche*; Latin *octo-nox (noctu)*; Greek *ochto-nux (nukto)*.[40] By unveiling these connections we are not giving in to mere speculation; we are only noting the plainly uttered testimony of the words themselves. Nor are we inventing associations that may follow in the wake of linguistic investigation; on the contrary, only if we were to pursue such associations or amplifications as employed by modern scientific psychology, notably analytical psychology, could we be accused of irrational or non-mental thought. It would be extremely dangerous, in fact, to yield to the chain reaction of associative and amplified thought-processes that propagate capriciously in the psyche and lead to the psychic inflation from which few psychoanalysts are immune.[41]

While plumbing the hidden depths of the word roots, we will have to be constantly mindful of connections forgotten by contemporary man. Any attempt to probe this region is likely to unleash a negative reaction in present-day man, since such insights into the shadowy depth are unsettling; they remind him too much of the dark depths which he does not yet dare to acknowledge in himself. Yet it is perfectly permissible today, and to some degree indispensable, to think symbolically while describing symbolic processes. If we insist on such symbolic thinking, however, one precept must be observed: as far as possible we must possess an insight into the particular symbol; that is, we must be certain and aware of the symbolism involved. If we are not, we lose our self-assurance and become victims of the symbol, captive to an unknown power that controls us according to its will. We would expressly warn here of such psychic violation by the symbol, as well as of the psychic bondage that results from an inadequate awareness and knowledge of symbolic thinking.

Let us, however, return to the question of perspectivity. We have noted that perspective is the pre-eminent expression of the emergent consciousness of fifteenth-century European man, the palpable expression of his objectivation of spatial awareness. Besides illuminating space, perspective brings it to man's awareness and lends man his own visibility of himself. We have also noted that in the paintings of Giotto and Masaccio this evident perception of man comes to light for the first time. Yet this very same perspective whose study and gradual acquisition were a major preoccupation for Renaissance man not only extends his image of the world by achieving spatialization but also narrows his vision—a consequence that still afflicts us today.

Perspectival vision and thought confine us within spatial limitations. Elsewhere we have alluded to the antithesis inherent in perspective:[42] it locates and determines the observer as well as the observed. The positive result is a concretion of man and space; the negative result is the restriction of man to a limited segment where he perceives only one sector of reality. Like Petrarch, who separated landscape from land, man separates from the whole only that part which his view or thinking can encompass, and forgets those sectors that lie adjacent, beyond, or even behind. One result is the anthropocentrism that has displaced what we might call the theocentrism previously held. Man, himself a part of the world, endows his sector of awareness with primacy; but he is, of course, only able to perceive a partial view. The sector is given prominence over the circle; the part outweighs the whole. As the whole cannot be approached from a perspectival attitude to the world, we merely superimpose the character of wholeness onto the sector, the result being the familiar "totality."

It is no accident that the ambivalence inherent in the (Latin) primal word *totus* is evident in the word "totality." Although in more recent times the word *totus* has meant "all" or "whole," it would earlier have meant "nothing." In any event, the audial similarity between *totus* and [German] *tot*, "dead," is readily apparent.[43] But let us forget the totality with its nefarious character; it is not the whole. And although the whole can no longer even be approached from the perspectival position, the whole, as we shall see further on, is again being approached in novel ways from the aperspectival attitude.

Perspectivation, let us remember, also includes a reduction; and this reductive nature is evident, for instance, in perspectival man's predominantly visual or sight orientation in contrast to unperspectival man's audial or hearing orientation. The basis of the perspectival world view is the visual pyramid; the two lines extend from the eyes and meet at the object viewed. The image formed by the isolated sector includes the subject, the object, and the space in between. Piero della Francesca clearly expresses this in his remark: "The first is the eye that sees; the second, the object seen; the third, the distance between the one and the other."[44] On this Panofsky comments: "It [perspective] furnished a place for the human form to unfold in a life-like manner and move mimically [which is equivalent to the discovery of space]; but it also enabled light to spread and diffuse in space [the illumination of space is the emergence of spatial awareness] and permitted considerable freedom in the treatment of the human body. Perspective provides a distance between man and objects." Such detachment is always a sign of an emergent objectifying consciousness and of the liberation of previously innate potentialities that are subsequently rediscovered and realized in the outer world.

This example again suggests to what extent perspective is the most tangible expression of an entire epoch. The basic concern of perspective, which it achieves, is to "look through" space and thereby to perceive and grasp space rationally. The very word "perspective" conveys this intent, as Dürer suggests: "Besides, *perspectiva* is a Latin term meaning 'seeing through.' " It is a "seeing through" of space and thus a coming to awareness of space. It is irrelevant here whether we accept Dürer's interpretation and translate *perspicere* (from which *perspectiva* derives) in his sense as "seeing through," or render it, with Panofsky, as "seeing clearly."[45] Both interpretations point to the same thing.[46] The emergent awareness of distantiating space presupposes a clear vision; and this heightening of awareness is accompanied by an increase of personal or ego-consciousness.

This brings us back to our thesis about the antithetical nature of perspective; it locates the observer as well as the observed. Panofsky too underscores this dualistic, antithetical character: "The history of perspective [may be] considered equally as a triumph of the sense of reality with its detachment and objectivation, and as a triumph of human striving for power with its negation of distances, just as it can be seen as a process of establishing and systematization of the external world and an expansion of the ego sphere."[47] Let us for now postpone a discussion of his critical term "power expansion," although he has here noted an essential aspect of perspectival man, and turn back to Leonardo da Vinci on whom Dürer (as Heinrich Wölfflin points out) indirectly based his understanding.[48]

With Leonardo the perspectival means and techniques attain their perfection. His *Trattato della Pittura*[49] (a collection of his writings assembled by others after his death based on a mid-sixteenth-century compilation known as the *Codex Vaticanus Urbinas* 1270) is the first truly scientific and not merely theoretical description of all possible types of perspective. It is the first detailed discussion of light as the visible reality of our eyes and not, as was previously believed, as a symbol of the divine spirit. This emergent illumination dispels any remaining obscurities surrounding perspective, and reveals Leonardo as the courageous discoverer of aerial and color, as opposed to linear, perspective. Whereas linear perspective created the perspectival illusion on a plane surface by the projections of technical drafting, aerial and color perspective achieve their comprehension and rendering of space by techniques of gradation of color and hue, by the use of shadow, and by the chromatic treatment of the horizon.

Above and beyond this Leonardo's establishment of the laws of perspective is significant in that it made *technical drafting* feasible and thereby initiated the technological age.[50] This concluded a process which had required centuries before it entered human consciousness and effected a fundamental transformation of man's world. (In the following chapter we will observe that the roots of this process in fact date back some two millenia.) It is only after Leonardo that the unperspectival world finally passes out of its dream-like state, and the perspectival world definitely enters awareness. Having attempted to show the initial thrust toward awareness of space documented in Petrarch's letter, and to account for the process of painful withdrawal from traditional perceptions, we would here like to indicate the nature of Leonardo's decisive development, for it was he who fully realized Petrarch's discovery.

Among the thousands of Leonardo's notes and diary entries, there are several which, if we compare those of presumably earlier with those of presumably later origin, can document the course of his emergent spatial awareness and thus his extrication from the world he inherited. Of these, we shall select two, one earlier and one later. The first (from Manuscript A of the *Institut de France*) contains one of Leonardo's earliest general definitions of perspective: "Perspective is a proof or test, confirmed by our experience, that all things project their images toward the eye in pyramidal lines." In addition to the fact that we again meet up with Alberti's important idea of the pyramid, now given its valid restatement by Leonardo, the remark expresses the very essence of Leonardo's rather dramatic situation: it expresses his Platonic, even pre-Platonic animistic attitude that "all things project their images toward the eye," which the eye does not perceive, but rather suffers or endures.[51] This creates an unusual and even disquieting tension between the two parts of the sentence, since the purely Aristotelian notion of the first part not only speaks of proof but indeed proceeds from the "experience" of early science. This struggle in Leonardo himself between the scientist demonstrating things and the artist enduring them reflects the transitional situation between the unperspectival and the perspectival worlds.

A note on perspective of presumably later date is illustrative of Leonardo's complete dissociation from the dominant unperspectival structure of ancient and early medieval consciousness.[52] In Manuscript G of the *Institut de France* he writes: "In its measurements perspective employs two counterposed pyramids. The one has its vertex in the eye [he often calls the vertex 'the point'] and its base on the horizon. The second has its base resting against the eye and its vertex at the horizon. The first pyramid is the more general perspective since it encompasses all dimensions of an object facing the eye . . . while the second refers to a specific position . . . and this second perspective results from the first."[53]

These remarks express the change from a *participation inconsciente*[54] to what we may call a *relation consciente*, or conscious relationship. Leonardo was able to place the vanishing point in space (on the horizon) in opposition to the passive or "enduring" point of the eye, the receptor of the stream of object impressions, and thus realized the close interrelationship between the two. As he himself notes, "the second pyramid [realized externally] results from the first." The emphasis has shifted to the eye of the subject—the eye which has realized space and thus established an equilibrium between the ego world (of the eye) and the external world (the horizon).

This statement of Leonardo's is also a conceptual realization or actualization of perspective—a realization that has determined the Western image of the world ever since. Perspective has determined and corresponded to this view to such a degree that even a mere generation after Leonardo (around 1530), Agrippa of Nettesheim was able to include a brief chapter entitled "De Optica vel Perspectiva" in his late work *De Incertitudine et Vanitate Scientiarum et Artium.*[55] There we find the reveal-ing statement: "It [the art of perspective] shows how deformity can be avoided in painting." And in Pietro Aretino's *Dialogo della Pittura*, written about the same time in honor of Titian, there is a verse frequently repeated: "Che spesso occhio ben san fa veder torto," which alludes to the no longer current tendency toward a kind of prejudicial kind of seeing that, as the verse notes, "frequently allows even healthy eyes to see falsely."[56]

Aretino's reproach, as well as Agrippa's more pointed remark, both of which characterize the unperspectival world and its mode of expression as "deformity" and "false vision," demonstrate clearly that space had already entered consciousness and become accepted at the outset of the sixteenth century. Having achieved and se-cured the awareness of space, man in the sixteenth century is overcome by a kind of intoxication with it. This perspectival intoxication with space is clearly evident, for example, in Altdorfer's interiors and in the many depictions of church interiors by the Netherlandic masters that have an almost jubilant expression. It is this jubilation that silences the voice of those who still attempted to preserve the old attitude to-ward the world. The silencing of objections was facilitated to a considerable degree by the fact that Petrarch's experience of landscape and space, as well as Leonardo's application and theory of perspective, had become common property and were evident in the increasing prevalence of landscape painting throughout Europe. We shall only mention a few of the great European masters who repeatedly took up the question of the perception and depiction of space in landscape: Altdorfer, van Goyen; Poussin, Claude Lorrain; Ruysdael, Magnasco; Watteau, Constable, Corot, Caspar David Friedrich; Millet, Courbert; Manet, Monet, Renoir, and finally, van Gogh and Rousseau.

Space is the insistent concern of this era. In underscoring this assertion, we have relied only on the testimony of its most vivid manifestation, the discovery of perspective. We did, however, mention in passing that at the very moment when Leonardo discovers space and solves the problem of perspective, thereby creating the possibility for spatial objectification in painting,[57] other events occur which par-allel his discovery. Copernicus, for example, shatters the limits of the geocentric sky and discovers heliocentric space; Columbus goes beyond the encompassing Oce-anos and discovers earth's space: Vesalius, the first major anatomist, bursts the con-fines of Galen's ancient doctrines of the human body and discovers the body's space; Harvey destroys the precepts of Hippocrates' humoral medicine and reveals the circulatory system. And there is Kepler, who by demonstrating the elliptical orbit of the planets, overthrows antiquity's unperspectival world-image of circular and flat surfaces (a view still held by Copernicus) that dated back to Ptolemy's concep-tion of the circular movement of the planets.

It is this same shape—the ellipse—which Michelangelo introduces into archi-tecture via his dome of St. Peter's, which is elliptical and not round or suggestive of the cavern or vault. Here, too, we find a heightened sense of spatiality at the expense of antiquity's feeling of oceanic space. Galileo penetrates even deeper into space by perfecting the telescope, discovered only shortly before in Holland, and employing it for astronomical studies—preparations for man's ultimate conquest of air and sub-oceanic space that came later and realized the designs already conceived and drawn up in advance by Leonardo.

This intense desire evident at the turn of the sixteenth century to conquer space, and to break through the flat ancient cavern wall, is exemplified not only by the transition from sacred fresco painting to that on canvas, but even by the most minute and mundane endeavors. It was around this time that lace was first introduced; and here we see that even the fabric could no longer serve merely as a surface, but had to be broken open, as it were, to reveal the visibility of the background or substratum.[58] Nor is it accidental that in those years of the discovery of space via perspective, the incursions into the various spatial worlds mentioned above brought on with finality a transformation of the world into a spatial, that is, a sectored world. The previous unity breaks apart; not only is the world segmented and fragmented, but the age of colonialism and the other divisions begins: schisms and splits in the church, conquests and power politics, unbounded technology, and all types of emancipations.

The over-emphasis on space and spatiality that increases with every century since 1500 is at once the greatness as well as the weakness of perspectival man. His over-emphasis on the "objectively" external, a consequence of an excessively visual orientation, leads not only to rationalization and haptification but to an unavoidable hypertrophy of the "I," which is in confrontation with the external world.[59] This exaggeration of the "I" amounts to what we may call an ego-hypertrophy: the "I" must be increasingly emphasized, indeed over-emphasized in order for it to be adequate to the ever-expanding discovery of space. At the same time, the increasing materialization and haptification of space which confronts the ego occasions a corresponding rigidification of the ego itself. The expansion of space brings on the gradual expansion and consequent disintegration of the "I" on the one hand, preparing favorable circumstances for collectivism.[60] On the other hand, the haptification of space rigidifies and encapsulates the "I," with the resultant possibility of isolation evident in egocentrism.[61]

As to the perspectival attitude, it is thus possible to maintain that the domination of space which results from an extreme perspectivization upsets and unbalances the "I." In addition, the one-sided emphasis on space, which has its extreme expression in materialism and naturalism, gives rise to an ever-greater unconscious feeling of guilt about time, the neglected component of our manifest world.

As we approach the decline of the perspectival age, it is our anxiety about time that stands out as the dominant characteristic alongside our ever more absurd obsession with space. It manifests itself in various ways, such as in our addiction to time. Everyone is out to "gain time," although the time gained is usually the wrong kind: time that is transformed into a visible multiplication of spatially fragmented "activity," or time that one has "to kill." Our time anxiety shows up in our haptification of time (already heralded by Pope Sabinus' hourly bell-ringing) and is expressed in our attempt to arrest time and hold onto it through its materialization. Many are convinced that "time is money," although again this is almost invariably falsified time, a time that can be turned into money, but not time valid in its own right. A further expression of man's current helplessness in the face of time is his compulsion to "fill" time; he regards it as something empty and spatial like a bucket or container, devoid of any qualitative character. But time is in itself fulfilled and not something that has to be "filled up" or "filled out."

Finally, our contemporary anxiety about time is manifest in our flight from it: in our haste and rush, and by our constant reiteration, "I have no time." It is only too evident that we have space but no time; time has us because we are not yet aware of its entire reality. Contemporary man looks for time, albeit mostly in the wrong place, despite, or indeed because of his lack of time: and this is precisely his tragedy, that he spatializes time and seeks to locate it "somewhere." This spatial attachment—in its extreme form a spatial fixation—prevents him from finding an escape from spatial captivity. But simple exits and paths are mere phantoms here, for time is not an avenue. Although man's horizons expanded, his world became increasingly narrow as his vision was sectorized by the blinders of the perspectival world view. The gradual movement toward clearer vision was accompanied by a proportionate narrowing of his visual sector. The deeper and farther we extend our view into space, the narrower is the sector of our visual pyramid.

As it developed over the centuries, this state of affairs gave rise to the most destructive of the stigmas of our age: the universal intolerance that prevails today, and the fanaticism to which it leads. A person who is anxious, or who is fleeing from something, or who is lost either with respect to his own ego or with respect to the world—it holds equally true in both instances—is a person who will always be intolerant, as he feels threatened in his vital interests. He "sees" only a vanishing point lost in the misty distance (the vanishing point of linear perspective of which Leonardo once wrote); and he feels obliged to defend his point fanatically, lest he lose his world entirely.

The European of today, either as an individual or as a member of the collective, can perceive only his own sector. This is true of all spheres, the religious as well as the political, the social as well as the scientific. The rise of Protestantism fragmented religion; the ascendancy of national states divided the Christian Occident into separate individual states; the rise of political parties divided the people (or the former Christian community) into political interest groups. In the sciences, this process of segmentation led to the contemporary state of narrow specialization and the "great achievements" of the man with tunnel vision. And there is no "going back"; the ties to the past, the *re-ligio*, are almost non-existent, having been severed, as it were, by the cutting edge of the visual pyramid. As for a simple onward progression and continuity (which has almost taken on the character of a flight), they lead only to further sectors of particularization and, ultimately, to atomization. After that, what remains, like what was left in the crater of Hiroshima, is only an amorphous dust; and it is probable that at least one part of humanity will follow this path, at least in "spirit," i.e., psychologically.

In summary, then, the following picture emerges: there is on the one hand anxiety about time and one's powerlessness against it, and on the other, a "delight" resulting from the conquest of space and the attendant expansion of power; there is also the isolation of the individual or group or cultural sphere as well as the collectivization of the same individuals in interest groups. This tension between anxiety and delight, isolation and collectivization is the ultimate result of an epoch which has outlived itself. Nevertheless, this epoch could serve as a guarantee that we reach a new "target," if we could utilize it much as the arrow uses an over-taut bow string. Yet like the arrow, our epoch must detach itself from the extremes that make possible the tension behind its flight toward the target. Like the arrow on the string, our epoch must find the point where the target is already latently present: the equilibrium between anxiety and delight, isolation and collectivization. Only then can it liberate itself from deficient unperspectivity and perspectivity, and achieve what we shall call, also because of its liberating character, the *aperspectival world.*

3. The Aperspectival World

The full outlines of the aperspectival world can emerge only gradually. It is our hope that it will take on shape and contour as we have occasion to treat its "past" prefigurations and contexts; an object becomes clearly visible and distinct, after all, only when placed against a background or substratum which furnishes sufficent contrast to prevent its being misconstrued. Although that requirement may not yet be fulfilled at this stage of our discussion, it would seem to us necessary here to outline the basic nature of aperspectivity in order to indicate how it came to be expressed. Whether this "indication" is understood as a thesis or merely as a point of departure, it will be convincing only when we contrast the recent forms of expression in painting, as in the other arts, with the background which remains to be described in the course of the present work.

Let us then select and examine from the many new forms of expression a particularly vivid example from the pictorial arts as a first step toward clarifying our intention. During recent decades, both Picasso and Braque have painted several works that have been judged, it would seem, from a standpoint which fails to do them justice. As long as we consider a drawing like the one by Picasso reproduced here (fig. 1) in purely aesthetic terms, its multiplicity of line, even where the individual lines appear "beautiful" in themselves, will seem confusing rather than beautiful. And, as we have been taught to believe, beauty is a traditional category for evaluating a work of art. Yet such pictures or drawings as this demand more of the viewer than aesthetic contemplation based on criteria of beauty; and the relationship of the two is palpably evident, in German at least, from the previously overlooked root kinship of the words schön (beautiful) and schauen (to view, contemplate).[62]

Both words have a predominantly psychological connotation; contemplation is the mode of mystic perception, while the beautiful is only one—the more luminous—manifestation of the psyche. At least to the Western mind, both concepts exclude the possibility of a concretion of integrality (though not of unity). They are only partial activations or incomplete forms of the harmony that is itself merely one segment of wholeness. Mere contemplation or aesthetic satisfaction are psychically confined and restricted, at best approaching, but never fully realizing, integrality.[63]

Yet it is precisely integrality or wholeness which are expressed in Picasso's drawing, because for the first time, time itself has been incorporated into the representation. When we look at this drawing, we take in at one glance the whole man, perceiving not just one possible aspect, but simultaneously the front, the side, and the back. In sum, all of the various aspects are present at once. To state it in very general terms, we are spared both the need to walk around the human figure in time, in order to obtain a sequential view of the various aspects, and the need to synthesize or sum up these partial aspects which can only be realized through our conceptualization. Previously, such "sheafing" of the various sectors of vision into a whole was possible only by the synthesizing recollection of successively viewed aspects, and consequently such "wholeness" had only an abstract quality.

In this drawing, however, space and body have become transparent. In this sense the drawing is neither unperspectival, i.e., a two-dimensional rendering of a surface in which the body is imprisoned, nor is it perspectival, i.e., a three-dimensional visual sector cut out of reality that surrounds the figure with breathing space. The drawing is "aperspectival" in our sense of the term; time is no longer spatialized but integrated and concretized as a fourth dimension. By this means it renders the whole visible to insight, a whole which becomes visible only because the previously missing component, time, is expressed in an intensified and valid form as the present. It is no longer the moment, or the "twinkling of the eye"—time viewed

Figure 1: Pablo Picasso, Drawing (1926) (size of the original: 31 × 46.7 cm)

through the organ of sight as spatialized time—but the *pure present, the quintessence of time* that radiates from this drawing.

Every body, to the extent that it is conceived spatially, is nothing but solidified, crystallized, substantivated, and materialized time that requires the formation and solidification of space in order to unfold. Space represents a field of tension; and because of its latent energy, it is an agent of the critical or acute energy of time. Thus both energetic principles, the latency of space as well as the acuteness of time, are mutually dependent. When we formulate this thought in advance of our discussion, it is to emphasize the basic import that we accord to the present, for both space and time exist for the perceptual capacities of our body only in the present via presentiation. The *presentiation* or making present evident in Picasso's drawing was possible only after he was able to actualize, that is, bring to consciousness, all of the temporal structures of the past latent in himself (and in each of us) during the course of his preceding thirty years of painting in a variety of earlier styles.

This process was unique and original with Picasso. By drawing on his primitive, magic inheritance (his Negroid period),[64] his mythical heritage (his Hellenistic-archaistic period), and his classicistic, rationally-accentuated formalist phase (his Ingres period), Picasso was able to achieve the concretion of time (or as we would like to designate this new style which he and his contemporaries introduced in painting, "temporic concretion"). Such temporic concretion is not just a basic characteristic of this particular drawing, but is in fact generally valid: Only where time emerges as pure present and is no longer divided into its three phases of past, present and future, is it concrete. To the extent that Picasso from the outset reached out beyond the present, incorporating the future into the present of his work, he was able to "presentiate" or make present the past. Picasso brought to the awareness of the present everything once relegated to the dormancy of forgetfulness, as well as everything still latent as something yet to come; and this temporal wholeness realized in spatiality and rendered visible and transparent in a depiction of a human form, is the unique achievement of this temporic artist.

We shall in consequence designate as "temporic" artists those painters of the two major artistic generations since 1880 (i.e., following the classicistic, romantic, and naturalistic movements) who were engaged—doubtless unintentionally—in concretizing time. From this point of view, all of the attempts by the various "movements"—expressionism, cubism, surrealism, and even tachism—show as their common trait this struggle to concretize and realize time. Understandably, such experimentation resulted in numerous faulty solutions; but as we noted earlier, such faults were equally unavoidable during the search for perspective and spatial realization.

The unavoidable attempt to presentiate the past, for instance, was accompanied by a certain chaos; yet this very chaos is always evident wherever a once-valid world begins to undergo a transformation. In this instance many contemporary artists, including a majority of the surrealists and later the tachists, were inundated by an inflation of time; a seemingly endless quantity of exhausted residua was dredged up and revived from the past, engulfing those artists unable to master this reawakened heritage. This has its parallel in the inflation of unconscious residua which have become conscious in the wake of efforts begun by Freud. Instead of the wholeness these artists had hoped for, they inherited a world of bits and pieces; instead of attaining the spiritual supremacy they had desired, they became decidedly psychistic. By "psychistic" we mean contemporary Western man's inability to escape from the confines of the psyche.[65] Even among Picasso's works we find those which mirror such psychic chaos and psychistic inflation. Had he created only pictures in this chaotic manner, we could not definitively number him among the greatest temporic artists; there are, however, many other works by Picasso, notably from the 1930s, that bring his temporic endeavors toward a solution. We shall consider here only two types of pictures: some specific portraits as well as a landscape painting. (The extent to which Picasso's still life paintings exemplify the concretion of time, and also to what extent temporic art is anticipated in impressionism and even in earlier art, as in the work of Delacroix, will be examined later in greater detail.)

Among the portraits to which we refer are several executed since 1918 in which Picasso shows the figure simultaneously "full face" and "profile," in utter disregard of aesthetic conventions (fig.2).[66] What at first glance appears to be distorted or dislocated, as for example the eyes, is actually a complementary overlapping of temporal factors and spatial sectors, audaciously rendered simultaneously

Figure 2: Pablo Picasso, *Le Chapeau de paille*
(*The Straw Hat*)   (1938)

and conspatially on the pictorial surface. In this manner, the figure achieves its concrete character of wholeness and presence, nourished not by the psychistic demand
for beauty but by the concretion of time.

In the drawing on page 25 (fig. 1), as well as in the portraits, the unimaginable
and the truly unrepresentable become evident; its structures rendered transparent,
time becomes visible in its proper and most unique medium, the human body (or
the head).

This type of temporic portrait does not represent merely a willful or fortuitous
playfulness of Picasso's style, but rather reflects his specific need to express and
shape the uncontainable emergence of concrete time. This is evident from his early
incomplete solutions, as well as from similar portraits by Braque done independently during the same period. Two of Picasso's paintings, *Harlequin with a Guitar* of
1918 and 1924,[67] as well as his two major works of 1925, *La cage d'oiseau*, and *Nature
morte à la tête de plâtre*, further manifest his search for concrete time. Picasso himself underscored the importance of these two works by selecting them to appear
among the reproductions of nineteen works printed in Sabartés' collection of 1935.[68]
In addition we refer the reader to two portraits of 1927, *Buste de femme en Rouge*
and *Femme,* as well as to the *Femme au bonnet rouge* of 1932.[69]

With reference to Braque,[70] who by 1939 was at work on his Greek heritage,[71]
we can discern distinct early indications of a temporic treatment in his portraits such
as the *Woman's Head* of 1930 and *Sao* of 1931. There is evidence of his preoccupation
and increasing mastery of this temporic treatment after 1936 (as in fig. 3, p. 28).[72]

The works cited here embody the full creative force of the two most powerful
painters of our era, and even our brief discussion should suggest the extent to which
the concretion of time, and the attempts to formulate it, dominate contemporary
forms of expression. The emergent transparency of time characteristic of the portraits can also be observed in the landscape painting of Picasso mentioned above.
Since there is, so far as we know, only a single and virtually inaccessible reproduction
of this work, we shall venture a description.

I visited Picasso after his return from Britanny to Paris in the autumn of 1938 at

Figure 3: Georges Braque, *Femme au chevalet (Woman before an Easel)* (1936).

his studio, located at that time in the Latin Quarter, where he had done his *Guernica*, the work that almost abolished spatiality. As I recall, he showed me on this occasion the new oils he had completed during the summer of that year. I was especially attracted to one small picture representing a landscape of village roofs as seen from a window; the painting was nearly devoid of depth and any central point of illumination. The entire picture showed nothing but layers of almost flat, multifariously colored roofs suggesting at first glance a mere aggregation of rectangular planes. I felt attracted to it at first, or so I thought, by its abundance of color, until the true reason for my interest finally emerged: its lack of any spatial localization of time. Instead of presenting a temporal moment, the picture renders an enduring, indeed *eternal present*. The shadows that appear among the gradations of hue were not the result of the specific spatial-temporal position of the sun, as in the landscapes of Watteau or Poussin, where one can ascertain the specific park, the particular year, month, indeed the specific day, the very hour, and, from the outline of the shadows, the very second, the exact temporal moment in space.

In Picasso's roof the dislocation and layered arrangement of the shadows mirror the natural movement of time; he has rendered the landscape by audaciously incorporating all of the changes of illumination (visible in the shifts of shadow and shading), the temporal motions brought on by the altered positions of the sun during the time when he was painting. This capturing of the present as it affects nature could not have been bolder, precisely because of its simplicity. What is here visible in this unique painting is not the spatializing temporal moment. It is the present emerging in its transparent entirety—the present corresponding in its indispensable accidentals to our notion of eternity; for neither can be conceptualized or imagined. In Picasso's paintings both the present and the eternity are rendered transparent and thus ever-present, evident, and concrete.

Aperspectivity, through which it is possible to grasp and express the newly emerging consciousness structure, cannot be perceived in all its consequences—be they positive or negative—unless certain still valid concepts, attitudes, and forms of thought are more closely scrutinized and clarified. Otherwise we commit the error of expressing the "new" with old and inadequate means of statement. We will, for example, have to furnish evidence that the concretion of time is not only occurring in the previously cited examples from painting, but in the natural sciences and in literature, poetry,[73] music, sculpture, and various other areas. And this we can do only after we have worked out the new forms and modes necessary for an understanding of aperspectivity.

The very amalgamation of time and the psyche noted earlier, with its unanticipated chaotic effect as manifested by surrealism and later by tachism, clearly demonstrate that we can show the arational nature of the aperspectival world only if we take particular precautions to prevent aperspectivity from being understood as a mere regression to irrationality (or to an unperspectival world), or as a further progression toward rationality (toward a perspectival world). Man's inertia and desire for continuity always lead him to categorize the new or novel along familiar lines, or merely as curious variants of the familiar. The labels of the venerated "Isms" lie ever at hand ready to be attached to new victims. We must avoid this new idolatry, and the task is more difficult than it first appears.

Let us again look at our example of the fusion of time and the psyche: as long as time is dredged up from oblivion and thrust into visibility in bits and pieces, our preoccupation with the past aspect of time will bring on further chaos and disintegration. But the moment we are successful, like Picasso, in wresting past "time"— that is latently present time—from oblivion via its appropriate structure and means of expression, and render it visibly anew and thus present, then the importance we accord to the earlier times and their diverse structures of consciousness will become apparent in the development of aperspectivity.

If we fail to recognize this still potent past legacy, it may at any time become critical and threaten to overwhelm us; and this would prevent us from perceiving the new with the requisite vigilance and detachment.

Because of this, we will examine in the following chapter those incisive occurrences that have manifest themselves (to use our term) as mutations of the consciousness of mankind. The results of these mutations are latent in each and every one of us in the form of the various consciousness structures and continue to be effective in us. It is our hope that this brief outline of the nature of the unperspectival and the perspectival worlds has clarified one point: the degree to which the aperspectival world must be built on the foundations of the perspectival world if it is to surpass it. And as we expand and extend the temporal breadth and depth of its temporality, the bases for the aperspectival world will become broader and increasingly supportive.

1   As we shall see later in our discussion (Part I, chapter 3), the unperspectival European world was preceded by a world we would have to call the "pre-perspectival." As a first orientation in this discussion of the European worlds, however, the three named will be sufficient, and consequently we have limited ourselves to only these three.

2   Wilhelm Worringer, *Ägyptische Kunst: Probleme ihrer Wertung* (Munich: Piper, 1927), p. 105f. It is not necessary here to examine Fritz Saxl's polemics against Worringer's conception (see the appropriate references in his publications of the Bibliothek Warburg), as his point of departure is not directly relevant to our thesis.

3   Guido Freiherr von Kaschnitz-Weinberg, *Die Grundlagen der antiken Kunst*, I: *Die mittelmeerischen Grundlagen der antiken Kunst* (Frankfurt/M.: Klostermann, 1944), particularly pp. 14ff. and 62f.

4   See also the favorable review of von Kaschnitz-Weinberg's book by K. Schefold, *Basler Nachrichten*, 38, no. 26 (Sunday edition, July 2, 1944).

5   A splendid example of the survival of this cosmological conception far into the Renaissance, as reflected in the firmament decorations on vaulted ceilings, can be found in the description of the villa of Agostino Chigi in: Arnold von Salis, *Antike und Renaissance* (Erlenbach-Zürich: Rentsch, 1947), p. 193ff.

6   See *Pompejanische Wandbilder* (Berlin: Die silbernen Bücher, 1938) and especially Ernst Pfuhl, *Malerei and Zeichnungen der Griechen* (Munich: Bruckmann, 1923), in particular vol. 3.

7   See in this connection the informative book of Karl Schefold, *Die Bildnisse der antiken Dichter, Redner und Denker* (Basel: Schwabe, 1945). Ernst Buschor's *Bildnisstufen* (Munich: Münchener Verlag, 1947), which came to our attention after the present work was in press, defends a thesis identical to ours from the standpoint of the history of art and culture.

8   It would seem that portraits were first created in Asia (in Japan) about the same time as van Eyck; see Jean Gebser, *Asienfibel*, Ullstein edition no. 650 (Frankfurt/M.: Ullstein, 1962, ⁴1969), p. 82; *Gesamtausgabe* (Schaffhausen: Novalis, 1977), VI, p. 82.

9   On this controversy of Hispanus' name, see the paper of the Paracelsus specialist K. Sudhoff: "Petrus Hispanus, richtiger Lusitanus, Professor der Medizin und der Philosophie, schliesslich Papst Johan XXI.: eine Studie," *Medizinische Welt* (1934), p. 24.

10   Pedro Hispano, *Scientia libri de anima*, ed. by P. Manuel Alonzo, S. J., under the auspices of the Consejo Superior de Investigaciones científicas, Instituto filosófico "Luis Vives," series A no. 1 (Madrid, 1941). This edition is the first complete publication of the Latin original. It was primarily the research of Martin Grabmann, Munich (1925ff.) that reawakened interest in the original text.

11   Origen, *Genesishomilie*, I, 7 (GSC Origenes IV, Preuschen, p. 164, line 21), cited in Hugo Rahner, "Mysterium Lunae: Ein Beitrag zur Kirchentheologie der Väterzeit," *Zeitschrift für katholische Theologie*, 63 (1939), pp. 311ff. and 64 (1940), p. 61ff.

12   See Alfred G. Roth, *Die Gestirne in der Landschaftsmalerei*, (Berliner Schriften zur Kunst, III; [Bern-Bümplitz: Benteli, 1945]), p. 45f. and illustrations 48/49.

13   Francesco Petrarca, *Le Familiari*, critical edition edited by Vittorio Rossi, vol. 1: Introduction and books 1-4 (Edizione Nazionale delle opere di Francesco Petrarca; [Florence: Sansoni, 1933]), pp. 153-161. Our translation of the passages cited is based on the original text of this edition written in Tuscan Ciceronian Latin. The available partial translations into Italian and French were not sufficiently comprehensive for our purpose: Giuseppe Morpurgo, ed., *Antologia petrarchesca*, trans. Carducci (Milan: Albrigi, Segati & Co., 1925), pp. 415-417, and Henri de Ziegler, *Pétrarque* (Neuchâtel: Baconnière, 1940), pp. 39-41. This was also true of the study by Paul Guiton, "Pétrarque et la Nature," *Annali della cattedra petrarchesa*, 6 (Arezzo: Academia Petrarca, 1935/36), pp. 47-82. Guiton's article did, however, furnish proof for an exact dating of Petrarch's ascent of Mount Ventoux.

14   On this subject see *Le Génie d' Oc et l'Homme méditerranéen*, a special issue of the *Cashiers du Sud* (Marseille, 1943). For more information on the *pneumatici* in the Cévennes, see Hans Leisegang, *Pneuma Hagion* (Leipzig: Hinrichs, 1922), p. 39.

15   See Albert Pauphilet, ed., *Poètes et Romanciers du Moyen-Age: Texte établi et annoté* (Bibliothèque de la Pléiade, Paris: NRF, 1938), p. 18.

16   Our italics.

17 H. de Ziegler (note 13) also renders this as "de l'espace dans le temps," but does not mention the psychic relationship.

18 A parallel description from the early Romantic period can be found in a letter of Ramond, quoted in an essay "Ramond de Charbonnières" by Fritz Ernst in his *Iphigenia und andere Essays* (Schriften der Corona iv, Munich: Oldenbourg, 1933), p. 77f., and reprinted in his *Essays* (Zürich: Fretz & Wasmuth, 1946), III, p. 107f.

19 See Augustine's *Confessions*, IX, chapters 20 and 23; in the translation of Herman Hefele (Jena: Diederichs, 1918), p. 243ff. Augustine's view goes back to Aristotle's *Physics* (IV, 14 *initio*); cf. Hans Eibl, *Augustin und die Patristik*, Geschichte der Philosophie in Einzeldarstellungen (Munich: Reinhardt, 1923), X-XI, p. 331f.

20 We should mention here that the Arabic Sufi manuscripts of the same period contain scientifically accurate depictions of the firmament and the constellations, thus antedating Western anthropocentrism by several centuries (See Roth, note 12 above, p. 191). Despite several indications to the contrary during the Renaissance, a scientific-allegorical, i.e., no longer symbolic representation of the firmament from a human vantage point on the basis of astronomy was unpopular in Europe until well into the nineteenth century. It is also of note that during the second half of the thirteenth century, Alphonso X ("El sabio") of Spain commissioned scientifically accurate pictures or miniatures that were to be made according to Arabic models. They depict the sky "from within," that is from the human vantage point, and correspond exactly to such a view. Several miniatures in Alphonso's compilation on chess also express a certain freedom in the representation of the human form; see Arnald Steiger's new edition and translation: Alfonso el Sabio, *Schachzabelbuch* (Zürich: Rentsch, 1941). And, finally, a rationalizing treatment of the cosmological background of certain chess games is evident in Alphonso's commentaries, a phenomenon previously overlooked and worthy of further examination.

21 Special issue: "Les très riches heures du Duc de Berry" of *Verve* (Paris, 1945)

22 See the well-known interpretation of Pisano in Wölfflin's *Kunstgeschichtliche Grundbegriffe* (Munich: Beck, 1915). Roth (note 12), pp. 44 and 187f., provides a perceptive analysis of the "Astronomer's relief." We would underscore his finding that the space rendered on this relief is the "space of scientific observation" clearly related to the pensive astronomer who is contemplating it (see illustration 47 in Roth).

23 See Julius von Schlosser, *Leben und Meinungen des florentinischen Bildhauers Lorenzo Ghiberti* (Basel: Holbein, 1941), a work that decisively contributed to Ghiberti's well-deserved rise in status among historians.

24* Cennino Cennini, *Trattato della pittura*, eds., G. and C. Milanesi (Florence: Lemmonier, 1959). A more reliable edition of Cennini's treatise of 1437 is that of Renzo Simi, ed., Cennino Cennini, *Il libro dell' arte* (Lanciano: R. Carabba, 1913). There is also a German edition, edited and translated by Albert Ilg, *Das Buch von der Kunst oder Tractat der Malerei des Cennino Cennini de Colle di Valdelsa* (Vienna: Braumüller, ²1888).

25 Heraclius, *Von den Farben und Künsten der Römer*, translated and annotated by A. Ilg, Quellenschriften für Kunstgeschichte und Kunsttechnik des Mittelalters und der Renaissance IV (Vienna: 1873). (The first edition of Ilg's translation of Cennini, note 24 above, was published in this series in 1871.) Further information on Heraclius and Theophilus in : Woltmann and Woermann, *Geschichte der Malerei: Die Malerei des Mittelalters*, revised edition by M. Bernath (Leipzig: Kröner, 1916), p. 83f.

26 On Cennini see also Caterina Lelj's typewritten dissertation: "Il significato della prospettiva nella pittura del primo Quattrocento fiorentino," Tesi di Laura (Milan, 1939), p. 21f. We have passed over the studies of G. J. Kern whose views have been superseded by recent scholarship.

27 In addition to the examples of early panel painting, further illustrative examples of the incorrect, emotionally tinged perspective employed at the time can be found in miniatures of the mid-fifteenth century (incorrect according to Renaissance canons), such as in the manuscript "Champion des Dames" in the Grenoble library and the "Livre du

Cuer d'amours espris" (MS 2597) in the *Nationalbibliothek*, Vienna. From the latter manuscript Alfred Hoeflinger has published several illustrations in *Graphis*, 3, no. 19 (Zürich: Amsturz/Herdeg, 1947), pp. 163-169.—In his *Indienfahrt eines Psychiaters* (Pfullingen: Neske, 1959), p. 164ff., Medard Boss suggests that we concede a certain "virtuosity" to the perspectival rendering in the cave-temple frescoes of Ajanta (ca. 500 A. D.), which he considers comparable to the perfection of perspective during the Renaissance. (The Ajanta temples are located in the Deccan plateau in Central India, northeast of Bombay.) The author has visited Ajanta himself (see note 8 above, Jean Gebser, *Asienfibel*, p. 82; *Gesamtausgabe*, VI, p. 82); there can be no question that the frescoes there evidence a rudimentary perspective, somewhat better than the germinal technique exhibited by the Pompeijan murals. But no more than that; there is nothing there to suggest a perfection of perspective, as the impartial observer can now determine for himself, since a considerable number of the relevant frescoes have been reproduced in the following recent publications: *Malereien aus indischen Felstempeln (Ajanta)*, UNESCO Taschenbücher (Munich: Piper, 1963); *Ajanta Paintings* (New Delhi: Lalit Kala Adadami, 1956); *India: Paintings from Ajanta Caves* (N. Y.: New York Graphic Society, by arrangement with UNESCO, 1954); Herbert Härtel, *Indische und zentralasiatische Wandmalereien* (Berlin: Safari, 1959).

28 See volume 4 of the *Opere volgari* by L. B. Alberti, ed. Bonucci (Florence: Tip. Galileiana, 1847), p. 95ff.

29 A. Manetti, *Operette istoriche edite ed inedite*, ed. G. Milanesi (Florence: Lemmonier, 1887).

30 See Leon Battista Albert, *Della Pittura, libro I*, translated by Cosimo Bartoli (1782), p. 293 (cited in Lelj, note 26 above, p. 2ff.): "Sarà dunque la pittura il taglio della piramide visiva secondo un determinato spatio o intervallo, con il suo centro, et con i suoi determinati lumi, rappresentata con linee et colori sopra una propostaci superficie."

31 Vitruvius, *Architettura*, libro I, chapters 2, 5, 8.

32 See von Schlosser (note 23), p. 167ff.

33 See von Schlosser (note 23), p. 170: "The 'prospettiva' is [Ghiberti's] own addition and displaces knowledge of the rules as Vitruvius demanded."

34 Since this is not intended to be a complete survey of the "history of perspective," but rather a summary emphasizing several achievements important from the standpoint of the history of the soul and mind of the fifteenth century, we have avoided mentioning early authors concerned with the optical aspects to whom Alberti, and particularly Ghiberti and Leonardo are indebted: Euclid (*De aspectuum diversitate*, not to mention the *Elementa*); Ptolemy; Pliny; Diophantes; Archimedes; the Arabians Alhazen (Ibn-al-Haitam) and Avicenna (Ibn Sina); the Pole, Witelo; and the Englishmen John Peckham and Roger Bacon. The writings of these precursors, together with those of Vitruvius, furnish the elements that later made possible the development of perspective. In like manner, the third dimension had been prefigured by Euclid, but it nevertheless had to be transformed from a plane measurement dimension into a space-creating dimension of depth.—For more on the lingering influence of these authors on late scholasticism and the later Renaissance, particularly with reference to the mathematical-arithmetic mode of thought, see Max Bense, *Konturen einer Geistesgeschichte der Mathematik* (Hamburg: Classen & Goverts, 1946). This book, which came to our attention only after the present work was in press, also includes bibliographic references to the wider aspects of this subject, including optics, by such authors as H. Scholz, K. Hasse, M. Cantor, K. Reidemeister, and others. The reader should also consult the literature on perspective catalogued there.

35 Edited by Winterberg (Strassburg, 1899), 2 volumes.

36* See Paul Wescher, *Jean Foquet und seine Zeit* (Basel: Holbein, 1945).

37 See the interesting and enthusiastic remarks made by Facius, a contemporary compatriot of Masaccio, on those pictures of van Eyck with which he was familiar (p. 46f. of the 1475 edition); they are quoted in A. Ilg in a digression on the third book of Heraclius (note 24 above, pp. 183 and 187).

38   There is a certain piquancy in the fact that the personification of perspective—this most profound expression of views and teachings of Giordano Bruno and Galileo—was not only admitted to, but complacently sheltered in such an exalted place in St. Peter's basilica.

39   The author presented a preliminary exploration of this subject in a lecture before the Psychologische Gesellschaft Basel in late February, 1944, later published as "Über das Wesen des Dichterischen," *Schweizerische Zeitschrift für Psychologie und ihre Anwendungen*, 3, 3 (Bern: Huber, 1944), pp. 216-231.

40   The particular negating quality of an initial "n" (an insight we owe to Hugo Kükelhaus, *Urzahl und Gebärde*, Berlin: Metzner, 1934) is more easily understood if we recognize, within the context of the present discussion, that the two important words *ein* (one) and *nein* (no) in German, for instance, have a reciprocal relationship [as in English]. Moreover, when rendered backwards or mirrored, *ein* has the further property of being *nie* (never), which is itself merely the negation of the original *ie* that has become modern *je* (ever).—For more on the "i-j" shift, see Kluge/Götze, *Etymologisches Wörterbuch der deutschen Sprache* (Berlin: de Gruyter, ¹¹1936), p. 257.

41   The method of amplification in psychoanalysis, where a psychic chain-reaction as it were is released, can be equated to atomic fission in nuclear physics (the difference of course being that the latter culminates in a material chain reaction).

42   See Jean Gebser, *Rilke und Spanien* (Zürich: Oprecht, 1939, ²1945), pp. 40 and 43f.; *Gesamtausgabe*, I, pp. 41 and 44f.; see also Jean Gebser, *Abendländische Wandlung* (Zürich: Oprecht, 1943), pp. 23ff., 171, and 173; ²1945, pp. 23ff., and 197ff.; Ullstein ed. no. 107, pp. 19ff. and 148f.; *Gesamtausgabe*, 1, pp. 180 and 300ff.

43   Linguistics apparently has been unable to establish a possible etymological relationship between these two words; see (inter alia) the speculations in volume 11 of J. and W. Grimm's *Deutsches Wörterbuch*, sec. 1, pt. 1, column 538, as well as the fifth of our "Remarks on Etymology" in the appendix (p. 559 below).

44*   Erwin Panofsky, *Meaning in the Visual Arts* (New York: Doubleday Anchor Books A59, 1955), p. 278. Dürer's translation, from which this is quoted is to be found in Erwin Panofsky, "Die Perspektive als symbolische Form," *Vorträge der Bibliothek Warburg*, IV, 1924/25 (Leipzig: Teubner, 1927), p. 287, source reference p. 324, note 66.—On perspective see also Ernst Cassirer, *Philosophie der symbolischen Formen* (Berlin: Cassirer, 1925), II, p. 107f. Some excellent illustrations bearing on the history of perspective can be found in the *Enciclopedia Italiana*, XXVIII, p. 350ff.

45   Panofsky, *Vorträge der Bibliothek Warburg* (note 44), p. 291, note 3.

46   As to the meaning of the word "perspective," see in addition to Lelj (note 26), p. 1, the article "Sul significato della parola 'prospettiva,' " *Cronaca delle Belle Arti*, 5, 1-4 (January-April 1918), supplement to the *Bolletino d'Arte*.

47   Panofsky, *Vorträge der Bibliothek Warburg* (note 44), p. 287.

48   Heinrich Wölfflin, *Die Kunst Albrecht Dürers* (Munich: Bruckmann, 1905).

49   Leonardo da Vinci, *Traktat von der Malerei*, new edition with introduction by Marie Herzfeld, based on the translation of Heinrich Ludwig (Jena: Diederichs, 1925). The original edition of Ludwig's translation was published in the *Quellenschriften für Kunstgeschichte und Kunsttechnik des Mittelalters und der Renaissance* (Vienna: Braumüller, 1882) mentioned earlier (notes 24 and 25). Of the countless Italian editions we would single out that of Giuseppina Fumagalli, *Leonardo omo senza lettere* (Florence: Sanzoni, 1939), which contains excellent annotations to selections from Leonardo's treatise.

50   See Gebser, *Rilke und Spanien* (note 42), p. 43; *Gesamtausgabe*, I, p. 44.

51   See Leonardo da Vinci, *Tagebücher und Aufzeichnungen*, translated and edited by Theodor Lücke on the basis of the Italian manuscripts (Leipzig: List, 1940), p. 770. Since we are interpreting this remark, in contrast to the one following, we are here citing the original: "Prospettiva è ragione dimostrativa per la quale la sperienzia conferma tutte le cose mandare all' occhio per linee piramidali la loro similitudine" (Fumagalli, note 49 above, p. 256).

52   There being no accepted chronology of Leonardo's "notebooks," the reader should consult the sequence adopted by Ch. Ravaisson-Mollien as to the conjectures for dating; see his edition of those notebooks in the Institut de France, *Les Manuscrits de Leonardo da Vinci* (Paris: Quentin, 1881/91), 5 volumes.

53   Leonardo da Vinci, edition of Lücke (note 51), p. 777.

54   The concept of "participation inconsciente" is an adaptation by C. G. Jung of Lévy-Bruhl's "participation mystique" which the latter introduced to denote the expressly soul-bound interdependence of "belonging" characteristic of so-called primitive cultures. To us it would seem that both are prefigured by Plato's *metechein*, meaning "to take part, be a part of," a central term for Plato that he uses in place of the verb "to be." This equivalence of "participation" and "being" is a good example of man's basic response to the world, both during the early period and in antiquity; and in this equation participation can be regarded as constitutive for being. All three ideas reflect the interwovenness and enclosure of man in the world, a characteristic of the unperspectival world which we have sought to underscore earlier in our discussion, and to which we will return later.

55   Agrippa von Nettesheim, *Die Eitelkeit und Unsicherheit der Wissenschaften*, ed. by Fritz Mauthner (Munich: Müller, 1913), I, p. 98. See also chapter 24, p. 99f., "De pictura."

56*   Pietro Aretino, *Dialogo della Pittura di M. Lodovico Dolce intitolato l'Aretino* (Venice, 1557). This dialogue was first published in the year of Aretino's death, and is reprinted with annotations in volume 2 of the *Quellenschriften* (notes 25 and 49).

57   See Jean Gebser, *Abendländische Wandlung* (note 42), [1]1943, p. 26. [2]1945, p. 24; Ullstein ed. no. 107, p. 19; *Gesamtausgabe*, I, p. 182, and also his *Rilke und Spanien* (note 42), p. 39f.; *Gesamtausgabe*, I, pp. 40-41.

58   See Bruno Köhler, *Allgemeine Trachtenkunde*, Reclams Universal-Bibliothek no. 4712/13 (Leipzig: Reclam, n.d.), Part 5: "Neuere Zeit: Erste Abteilung," pp. 151 and 181 for more on the transplantation of the new lace industry from Italy to France during the reign of Francis I.

59   Regarding the concept of "haptification"—making graspable or palpable—and "haptics," terms which circumscribe an attitude toward the world where only measurable quantities are valid, see Hermann Friedmann, *Die Welt der Formen* (Munich: Beck, [2]1930) and Jean Gebser, *Abendländische Wandlung* (note 42), Chapter 21 ([1]1943, p. 125ff.; [2]1945, p. 127ff. and 139; Ullstein ed. no. 107, p. 99f.; *Gesamtausgabe*, I, p. 253ff.

60   Our later discussion will show that collectivization or "the masses" is not only closely related to the expansion of space, and the consequent "being lost" in space, but also that it is conditioned by a temporal-psychic component. Needless to say, the indiscriminate use of the word *Vermassung* by sociologists, and its subsequent correction and rehabilitation in recent psychology, would seem to indicate that the use of this term should be tempered with caution.

61   With regard to egocentricity see Jean Gebser, *In der Bewährung* (Berne and Munich: Francke, 1962), p. 108; *Gesamtausgabe*, V/I, p. 255.

62   For a discussion of the original kinship of the words *schön* and *schauen* (*schön* being the adjectival derivative of the verb *schauen*), and their derivation from the identical Germanic root *sku:skau*, see J. and W. Grimm (note 43), VIII, column 2310 and IX, column 1463, as well as Kluge/Götze (note 40), pp. 510 and 539.—We would also mention that other derivatives of this root underscore its psychic character, for example Gothic *skug-gwa*, Old Norse *skugg-sja*, Old High German *scuchar*, "mirror." The same root also underlies the Old Norse *skuggi*, Old High German *scuwo*, Anglo-Saxon *scua*, "shadow." Our conjecture that the English word "sky" can also be traced back to this root is borne out by Walter W. Skeat, *An Etymological Dictionary of the English Language* (Oxford: Clarendon, 1935), who cites for all the derivatives listed above the Indo-Germanic root *sqeu* (p. 567-68) which is still evident in Latin *obscu-rus*, "dark." Outside of the Germanic branch the word occurs in Sanskrit *kavi*, "wise man, poet, seer." In our section on the "Mythical Structure" (Chapter 3, Section 4 below) we will have occasion to

note that all of these meanings of "mirror, shadow, sky, seer, *schauen*, and *schön*" affirm the basic configuration of this root and, in turn, affirm the psychic content of all concepts that they express.

63   This definition is not intended to postulate either the etymological primacy of, or judgement on, the Platonic trinity of the "true, the good, and the beautiful," but only to indicate the predominantly psychic aspect of beauty (*schön*) as well as of viewing and contemplation (*schauen*).

64   Daniel–Henry Kahnweiler has reiterated on various occasions his opposition to the misconception that Picasso derived inspiration from Negro art. Picasso painted in a "negroid" manner independently of Negro art, and thereby enabled his contemporaries to discover and appreciate it.

65   Certain "materialists" often belong to our category of "psychists" just like the "idealists," because of their coldly fanatic propensities and wild imaginings. Many so-called psychologists, too, belong in this group. We speak of "psychists" rather than of "psychics" since these have acquired their name from their opposition to the *pneumatici* in the Neo-Platonist controversies.

66   Reproductions of such portraits can be found in the following works, among others:
   a) *Pablo Pacasso 1930-1935* (Paris: Les Cahiers d'Art, ca. 1937);
   b) Jaime Sabartés, *Picasso en su obra* (Madrid: Cruz y Raya, 1936);
   c) *Picasso-El Greco*, Cahiers d'Art, no. 3-10 (Paris, 1938);
   d) Jean Cassou, *Picasso*, Collection des Maîtres (Paris: Braun, 1937);
   e) Gertrude Stein, *Picasso*, Collection "Ancien et Modernes" (Paris: Floury, 1938);
   f) Alfred H. Barr, Jr., *Picasso: Forty Years of his Art* (New York: Museum of Modern Art, [2]1939);
   g) Paul Eluard, *A Pablo Picasso* (Geneva/Paris: Trois Collines, 1947);
   h) Ramón Gómez de la Serna, *Completa y verídica historia de Picasso y el cubismo* (Turin: Chiantore, 1945);
   i) Alfred H. Barr, Jr., *Picasso: Fifty Years of his Art* (New York: Museum of Modern Art, 1946);
   j) Carl Einstein, *Die Kunst des 20. Jahrhunderts*, Propyläen Kunstgeschichte, XIV (Berlin, [3]1931); illustrations on pp. 304-41;
   k) Bernhard Geiser, *Picasso Peintre-Graveur: Catalogue illustré de l'oeuvre gravé et lithographié 1899-1931* (Bern: published by the author, 1933); as well as the numerous monographs on Picasso since 1950, and also the complete catalogue of Picasso's works edited and published by Christian Zervos, Paris.

67   Illustrations in Einstein (note 66j), pp. 318-19.

68   For illustrations see Sabartés (note 66b), Cassou (66d), nos. 37 and 40, and Einstein (66j), p. 323.

69   Reproductions of the last three portraits mentioned can be found in Cassou (note 66d), nos. 39 and 45, and Einstein (66j), p. 332.

70   The reader is referred to the easily accessible books by Stanislas Fumet, *Braque*, Collection des Maîtres (Paris: Braun, 1942), and Carl Einstein (note 66j), illustrations on pp. 342-67.

71   See Christian Zervos, "Braque et la Grece primitive," *Cahiers d'Art*, 15, 1-2 (Paris, 1940), pp. 3-13.

72   Reproductions of those works in Einstein (note 66j), p. 367, and Fumet (note 70), no. 31. For works after 1936, the reader is refered to Fumet, nos. 33, 34, 37, 38 and his cover illustration.

73   For more information on our earlier references and discussion of this process of consciousness emergence that gives our epoch its stamp, the reader is referred to our *Abendländische Wandlung* (note 42) (the natural sciences), *Rilke und Spanien* (poetry), and *Der grammatische Spiegel* (Zürich: Oprecht, 1944) (literature); all in volume 1 of the *Gesamtausgabe* (Schaffhausen: Novalis, 1975).

3

The Four Mutations
Of Consciousness

1. On Evolution, Development, and Mutation

Before we can discern the new, we must know the old. The adage that everything has already happened, and that there is nothing new under the sun (and the moon), is only conditionally correct. It is true that everything has always been there, but in another way, in another light, with a different value attached to it, in another realization or manifestation.

Let us recall, for instance, Aristarchus' incipient heliocentric world-view, Zeno's incipient theory of relativity, Democritus' atomic theory, Euclid's emergent conception of space; or other inceptions, such as the beginnings of a demythologized logic (Socrates), of autobiography (Plato's "Seventh Letter"), of historiography (Herodotus). These inceptions were all anticipations, the seedlings as it were, of later blossoms that could not flourish with visible and immediate effect in their respective ages, since they were denied receptive soil and sustenance.

Even Petrarch, though well in advance of his contemporaries, is terrified and deeply disturbed by his precipitous discovery of landscape. He bans the thought from his mind, entrusting to God a matter which for him belongs to divine, not human providence. Similarly, the first generation of our own century rejected the new discoveries, hoping to deprive them of fertile soil (a reaction discussed further in the author's *Transformation of the Occident*[1]). Acceptance and elucidation of the "new" always meets with strong opposition, since it requires us to overcome our traditional, our acquired and secure ways and possessions.[2] This means pain, suffering, struggle, uncertainty, and similar concomitants which everyone seeks to avoid whenever possible.

Yet such anxiety about suffering is not the only barrier to an acceptance of new and novel circumstances. There is also a sense of threat that results from our inability to comprehend them, since we are too firmly attached to the old consciousness structure. Seen from the old standpoint, the new seems suprarealistic or supernatu-

36

ral; and, in fact, with reference to the old consciousness structure, the new not only appears to transcend and supersede the old reality but actually does so. We are then left with what seems to us to be the only alternative: we try to adapt or assimilate the new into the old, at the expense of course of the integrity and verity of the new. It is such attempts at explaining the new on the basis of the old, using old concepts rather than allowing the new to stand out in its originality against the old background, that give rise to the misunderstandings, misinterpretations, and objections.

In order to prevent such impasses and to meet the demands of the new, we must act like anyone forced to come to grips with the unique and utter newness of a situation, if we are not to succumb to the hopelessness of our particular circumstance or attitude. But we can meet the demands only if we are able to perceive clearly what has happened. With this in mind, we can now direct our attention to the unique event of mankind that underlies, it would seem, all human endeavor: the unfolding of consciousness.[3]

Looking back on this endeavor of mankind, we can distinguish *three consciousness structures* proceeding from origin, from the *archaic* basic structure. These are the *magic,* the *mythical,* and the *mental.* If, in the course of the following discussion, we are able to establish the contents, forms of realization, and attitudes expressed by these structures, we should be able to determine to what extent the one or the other of these structurations predominates in us and predisposes our attitude to the world and our judgement of it. We could then consider the new structure and attempt to describe and evaluate it without the danger of intermingling the old with the new. We shall designate this new consciousness structure as the *integral* structure, and its emergent world modality as the "aperspectival world."[4]

Before considering these structures still latent in us today, however, we must critically examine the validity of the structural differentiations we have proposed. We must recognize that the attempt to set forth the temporal course commonly referred to as the "evolution of mankind" is merely an attempt to structure events for convenient accessibility. Consequently, we must exclude from our discussion as far as possible such misleading notions as "development" and "progress."

The comforting conception of progressive and continuous evolution has been in vogue for more than two hundred years, ever since the publication of Vico's *Principe di scienza nuova d'intorno alla comune natura delle nazioni* in 1725.[5] This evolutionary notion may well have been a good working hypothesis, but in time came to be regarded as a manifest, rather than limited, reality, and has demonstrated the familiar consequences of a biologized conception à la Spengler.

Yet no truly decisive process, that is to say, something besides a tenative and arbitrary occurrence with its provisionalities and recurrences, is a continuum. A true process always occurs in quanta, that is, in leaps; or, expressed in quasi-biological and not physical terms, in mutations. It occurs spontaneously, indeterminately, and, consequently, discontinuously. Moreover, we become aware of such presumably invisible processes only when they have reached sufficient strength to manifest themselves on the basis of their cumulative momentum (a limitation we must observe when applying this concept to psychic events[6]). The apparent continuity is no more than a sequence subsequently superimposed onto overlapping events to lend them the reassuring appearance of a logically determinate progression.

These remarks, and those that follow, are intended to clarify the fact that the mutational process we are speaking of is spiritual and not biological or historical. It would be tantamount to a misrepresentation if the concept of mutation used here were to be understood by association as biological. It is important to emphasize that biological and consciousness mutations are, indeed, similar in their spontaneous, non-temporal creation of new genera, potentialities, or structures which, having been once acquired, are hereditary. But there is also an essential difference: biological mutation leads to a specialization of functions within a particular environment— a minus mutation. Consciousness mutation, by contrast, unfolds toward overdetermination: toward structural enrichment and dimensional increment; it is intensifying and inductive—a plus mutation. Hence, we are to understand the minus attribute as restrictive and deterministic, the plus as overdetermining. It is of interest here that this notion of the plus-aspect of mutations has also been taken under consideration by C. F. von Weizsäcker.[7]

It might seem that our concept of mutation has a biologically determined anatomical basis; but it remains an open question whether we are dealing here with a step in evolution brought about by specific organic factors, or with a change "elicited" by the spiritual principle, that is, by plus mutation. Most likely we have to do here with the latter, since it is always the superordinate potentiality that seems to enable man to develop the requisite organ appropriate to the requirements of a given situation. Consequently, there was first light and then the eye, first the word and then the speaking mouth, first the thought and then the cerebrum capable of reflective thinking (or mental thought altogether).[8]

It is this basis that is required for the apparent "ex nihilo" emergence of hereditarily transmissible changes in the brain, a possibility noted (with the necessary reservations) by Lecomte du Noüy.[9] Although at one time rejected by brain physiologists (ca. 1950), this trend of thought has been recently continued in the work of Hugo Spatz (1960), which suggests that incipient modifications in the brain to permit new capacities of receptivity are demonstrable in brain anatomy.[10] (In a way this would imply a spiritually conditioned process of mutation, paralleling the above-mentioned development of the cerebrum during the mutation of consciousness from the magic-mythical to the mental structure, a modification first appearing in the human physique as the higher protrusion of the Greek forehead.)

Now with respect to a biologically based interpretation of consciousness, we should caution that as a consequence of our definition of mutations, it is as legitimate to transfer a term from one discipline to another in this instance as in all others. As Erwin Schrödinger has noted, why should only medicine and algebra share a common term, Brüche, for such differing phenomena as fractures and fractions? Bone fractures and algebraic "fractures" have no more (or less) in common than biological mutations and mutations of consciousness.[11] Since even in biology the concept of mutations has taken on metaphoric properties as a result of the distinctions made not only between micro- and macro-mutations, but even between further subspecies and related species, there seems to be no compelling reason to replace it here by another term.

We have selected the term "mutation" (and will retain it for the duration of our discussion despite possible objections by critics of a deterministic and sectorial-relativistic bent) because it best describes the discontinuous nature of events that occur in consciousness following the primordial "leap" of origin (Ur-sprung). Moreover, it allows us to maintain the very necessary detachment from such concepts as progress, evolution, and development. The rationalistic thought-cliché of "progress" (more often than not a progression away from origin), the biologizing notion of evolution, and the botanizing idea of development are all inapplicable to the phenomenon of consciousness. The concept of mutation as a discontinuous process, on the other hand, and its transposition into consciousness, underscore the originally present spiritual content latent in consciousness from origin. Every consciousness mutation is apparently a sudden and acute manifestation of latent possibilities present since origin.

In contrast to biological mutations, these consciousness mutations do not assume or require the disappearance of previous potentialities and properties, which, in this case, are immediately integrated into the new structure and overdetermined. As we noted earlier in our *Transformation of the Occident*,[12] this process seems sudden to us only because certain "processes"—to the extent that we can speak here of processes—seem to take place "outside" spatial and temporal understanding and conceptualization, thus preventing us from making a spatial-temporal cause-and-effect relationship. We know today, however, that origin, being pre-spatial and pre-temporal, presentiates itself in the respective consciousness mutations, intensifying and integrating them. The duration of such a process correlates with the extent of its given dispersal, since the mutation affects the whole of humanity at any particular time. In consequence, it is only with extreme caution that this process can be called a "major mutation," as suggested by Giselher Wirsing in his modification of our terminology.[13]

A further modification suggested by Ernst-Peter Huss is not applicable (although Huss is in agreement with us on the primordiality of spirit[14]). Instead of the time-free event of origin-bound mutation, he postulates a so-called maturation process, coming perilously close to a botanizing and biologizing notion of spirit. But again we emphasize that it is possible to relate aspects of consciousness mutations to such concepts as progress, evolution, and development; yet this has at best a certain dialectical, psychologizing or biologizing-botanizing application; and wherever it is done, it robs the process of its originary character, which is by nature spiritual.

In the consciousness mutations, there is a process of rearrangement in a discontinuous and intermittent (*sprunghaft*) form apart from spatially and temporally dependent events. These processes of relocation make it possible for the intensified spiritual origin to be assimilated into human consciousness. Origin itself comes to awareness in discontinuous mutation: consciousness mutations are completions of integration. (It is instructive to note here once again that the German language associates "origin" with suddenness and discontinuity with respect to primordial events, whereas temporal inceptions are designated as "starts" or "beginnings.")

As to the legitimacy of our terminological transfer of the concept of mutation, we would point out that various writers have recently considered or applied it to spiritual events, confirming our choice. Hermann Graf Keyserling, for example, speaks in one of his later essays of the contemporary "world mutation" (1948).[15] René Grousset, in his discussion of the sudden appearance of both the Egyptian and Sumerian civilizations that foreshadowed the equally unexpected emergence of Greek culture, poses the question: "Are Vries' and Morgan's laws of biological mutation equally applicable to human society?"(1950).[16]

Julius Glück, in turn, has underscored the mutative nature of artistic styles and phases, and the succession of discontinuous transitions toward new degrees of humanity's integration (1951-1952).[17] Hendrik de Man, in his survey of our present situation, confronts us with the alternative: "Either death or mutation" (1951).[18] Rudolf Pannwitz contemplates the possibility of a "moral mutation" as a solution to our predicament (1951), and—corroborating our views—notes that "Man as a whole is a synthesis and crystallization of all his dimensions and acquisitions . . . and is doubtless growing toward 'complex man' " (See Part I, Chapter 4, Section 5, "Man as the Integrality of his Mutations").[19] Pannwitz' notion of "complex man" is synonymous with our "integral man"; we have avoided the term "complex" because of its one-sided psychological connotation deriving from "complex psychology."

We should also mention Walter Tritsch's discussions of today's transformation of reality. He writes: "This spiritual metamorphosis or mutation can also be understood as a sudden illumination of a different segment of reality. Those who see and perceive it are always individuals, but the direction of this radiance—which makes possible or compels the perception—emanates from the society in which the individuals live and in whose structure a decisive transformation or mutation takes place."[20]

And finally, we would mention the work of Pierre Teilhard de Chardin (in publication since 1955; see above, p. xxix). Though strongly influenced by the postulate of Darwinian evolution, Teilhard insists that "there is no way of escaping the problem of discontinuity," at least within contemporary modes of thought. He also speaks of a "transition to reflective consciousness" as a "critical transformation or mutation which we have been obliged to assume on the basis of the facts at hand," and proceeds to investigate further the bearer of this mutation. Later in his discussion he speaks more specifically of this (at the very least) "psychic" discontinuity and is obliged to acknowledge it as the "most decisive constituent in the emergence of man"; hence his deduction that "such a fundamental mutation as thinking—which gives the entire species its distinctive stamp—must transcend the point of origin and the beginning of evolutionary development."[21] Thus, even this thinker, who is indebted to the teleological principle of evolution, ultimately takes recourse to the concept of discontinuous occurrence, that is, mutation, to explain the decisive events. We would hope that these examples, written after the present work was first published, further support the adequacy and justification of our term and concept of "consciousness mutations."

While these remarks have addressed the non-biological aspect of consciousness mutations, we would also caution against a further possible misinterpretation, the historistic, that can easily result from our habits of rational thought. Many people who reject a spiritually qualified mutational process will tend to seek reassurance by insisting on "technological progress" and give in to a frantic hubris which, judging from past applications of the notion of progress, has probably forfeited whatever justification it once may have had (to the extent that hubris is justifiable at all). The view that our epoch and civilization are on a higher plane of development, as propagated by defenders of the progress-thesis, has become tenuous in the light of its application and results. In any event, the results, and particularly the application of this progress concept oblige us to guard against any self-congratulation or overestimation, especially against the biologistic postulate of evolutionary superiority.

This postulate has strongly permeated the European mentality throughout the later modern era (since about the 1730s). Its roots extend back to Vico, and it was continued by Montesquieu in his *Observations on Roman Greatness and Decline* (1734), and by Voltaire in his *Experiment concerning the Customs and Spirit of Nations* (1756). The thesis was further expanded in France by Bossuet, Duclos, Volney, and Condorcet; in England by Spencer and Darwin; and in Germany by Buckle's *History of English Civilization* (1860), by Lecky's *History of the Mind of the Enlightenment* (1865), by G. E. Lessing's *Education of the Human Race* (1780), by Herder's *Ideas toward a Philosophy of Human History* (1784), and by Schelling, Hegel and

Krause. The postulate received its present form of a "three-stage law" or "three-stage theory" in 1847 at the hands of Auguste Comte.[22] According to this still widely accepted "law," the scientific world-view proceeds through successively displacing stages: the theological, the metaphysical, and the positivistic; and it is naively assumed that the displacement of theology and metaphysics by positivism precludes any possibility that theological or metaphysical thought might recur.[23]

The patently perspectival-sectorial fixity of Comte's postulate—with its almost biologized aspect and markedly teleological, finalistic, purpose-and-goal orientation, and its evolutionary thesis—underscores its incommensurability with our *"four consciousness mutations."* The apparent succession of our mutations is less a biological evolution than an "unfolding," a notion which admits the participation of a spiritual reality in mutation. Under no circumstances is this form of development to be considered "progress"; we must accept the term "progress" for what it is and not for what it has become counter to its original sense. "Progress" is not a positive concept, even when mindlessly construed to be one; progress is also a progression away, a distancing and withdrawal from something, namely, from origin.

With the unfolding of each new consciousness mutation, consciousness increases in intensity; but the concept of evolution, with its continuous development, excludes this discontinuous character of mutation. The unfolding, then, is an enrichment tied, as we shall observe, to a gain in dimensionality; yet it is also an impoverishment because of the increasing remoteness from origin. We can, of course, eliminate this negative aspect by projecting the idea of origin into the very development of consciousness; or, allowing the possibility that man can realize the idea of origin in the process of consciousness development, we can then speak of *origin's development toward self-realization* in man. As we have not yet given or discussed conclusive reasons, this question is premature and would lead at best to mindless speculation and the reiteration of Hegel's notion of the self-unfolding absolute spirit.[24]

We should also forewarn against yet a further possible misconstruction, the interpretation of consciousness mutation as voluntaristic or volitional. Since we do not know the degree to which man has power or voluntary influence over the mutations occurring in him, the anthropocentric or man-oriented theory of voluntarism, with its obvious perspectival-relativistic character, has no justification. In any event, our attempt to objectively describe the rise of perspectivity should have indicated the extent to which the generations between 1250 and 1500 A. D. were *possessed* by, and did not merely *possess*, the urge to realize space.—It is our hope that these remarks have served to preclude a historicizing falsification and misinterpretation of spiritual mutations that occur in consciousness.

The manifestation of this mutational process should not be construed as a mere succession of events, a progress or historicized course. It is, rather, a manifestation of inherent predispositions of consciousness, now incremental, now reductive, that determine man's specific grasp of reality throughout and beyond the epochs and civilizations.[25] Once more, it should be emphasized that we must remain suspicious of progress and its resultant misuse of technology (to the degree that we are dependent on it and not the reverse), as well as of the doctrines of evolutionary superiority and voluntarism mentioned earlier. The voluntarism which begins with Duns Scotus and is clearly evident since Vico, has transferred the capacity of signification from an origin presumed to be "behind" all being, into human reason and will. We would hope that Spengler and Croce were the last protagonists of this viewpoint.

Our rejection of progress and voluntarism, on the other hand, must not lead us into the Oriental position where man is degraded into a mere plaything of some power or powers. Our dissociation from the aforementioned exaggerated perspectival theories need not tempt us to Oriental resignation, to submitting ourselves to the naturalistic flow of inevitability, nor even to that regression, if only symbolic, of the cave, which for us is deadened rather than enlivened by Buddha and Eastern as well as Western ascetics. Such a regression to the unperspectival cavern embodies in its Orientalized form an unambiguous desire to suspend and reverse the cycle of birth.[26]

It is to such an Oriental attitude, in the last analysis, that Theodor Lessing's conception leads. For despite his opposition to notions of "progress" and "evolution," he has called progress the "most fruitful of all European ideas," which was "made into a real and temporally coursing process of history."[27] And yet he has not gone beyond rational-perspectival Europeanism with its teleological and finalist evolutionary thesis but rather regresses to the irrational, unperspectival and—for us—inaccessible Eastern attitude. His work *Europa und Asien*[28], and Paul Cohen-Portheim's *Asien als Erzieher* are sufficient proofs of such reversion.[29]

Mere regression is no more an alternative than it is a perpetuation of the ideas of progress, evolution, voluntarism, positivism, etc. Our task is to realize the predisposition in ourselves toward discontinuous transformation. The degree to which such transformation is successful will depend on the breadth and stability of the incipient foundations and on our awareness of them. Should the transformation fail, the present possibility of atomization will preclude any further development of the already occurring mutation.

In order to achieve the requisite basis for the transformation to which we have alluded, we wish to present as a working hypothesis the four, respectively five, structures we have designated as the archaic, magical, mythical, mental, and integral. *We must first of all remain cognizant that these structures are not merely past, but are in fact still present in more or less latent and acute form in each one of us.* Only an explication and its attendant awareness in us of the hitherto more or less ignored evidence will enable us to achieve an integral mode of understanding in contrast to the practice of, say, Hegel and Comte. We are therefore not just proposing our consciousness mutation theory in opposition to the theory of evolution. In our reflections on the presentation of the past (thus making it present to consciousness), we shall include the future as latently existent and already present in us. We not only leave open the possibility of a new consciousness mutation toward integral awareness of the aperspectival world, but also bring it closer to us, that is, effect its presentation.

In the light of this emphasis on the present, two essentially distinct facts emerge. First, consciousness is neither knowledge nor conscience but must be understood for the time being in the broadest sense as wakeful presence. Second, this presence or being present excludes as a contradiction any kind of future-oriented finality; we forfeit presence when we reduce it to a mere one-sided recollection, or possibly to a mere voluntaristic kind of hopefulness. The unintentionality and positive lack of design is therefore important since it excludes all utilitarianism and rationally conditioned, essentially perspectival corrections of the possible. Consequently, we do not share with the positivists a conviction that the contemporary positivistic stage, or any rational, perspectival structure represents the *non plus ultra* of human development. Rather, in constant opposition to Hegel and Comte, we are convinced of the continuous effectuality of the "earlier" structures in us and the incipient, i.e., present effectuality of the so-called "future" structure.

We acknowledge the effectivity of the so-called past—which for Hegel and Comte is a mere corpse—to a much greater extent than is done indirectly by Georges Sorel, for example, and, in his wake, by the ambivalent Vilfredo Pareto. Sorel and Pareto rediscovered in certain political and social theories secularized Christian mythologies, which as "mythical residua" underlay certain socio-political programs and ideologies. Just as the new ethnography has opened our understanding to the continuous effectivity and life of the magic attitude, so has the new psychology, initiated primarily by Freud and expanded by C. G. Jung, demonstrated in their investigations of myth that the mythical attitude continues in us more than just residually. Unfortunately, psychoanalysis, by its own discoveries, has reverted to perspectival exaggerations and generalizations, so that the aforementioned psychic inflation erupting from the unconscious takes on ever-increasing predominance. There is only one defense against this: our strictly wakeful being-and-remaining in the present. In the course of the following discussion we must not regress and submerge ourselves into the actively psychologized past; rather, we must consciously retain and presentiate the past. It is our task to presentiate the past in ourselves, not to lose the present to the transient power of the past. This we can achieve by recognizing the balancing power of the latent "future" with its character of the present, which is to say, its potentiality for consciousness.

Let us then proceed to deepen the temporal foundations of the aperspectival world by investigating the consciousness structures we have spoken of, which in their own way are already suggestive of aperspectivity.

2. Origin or the Archaic Structure

The structure closest to and presumably originally identical with origin we shall designate as the archaic structure ("archaic" is derived from Greek *archē*, which means inception, origin; we emphasize origin since its essence, as everpresence, is not true of "inception"). We chose the word "structure" since structures are not simply spatial constructs, while "levels" with their connotation of spatialization abet a purely perspectival view. Structures above all can be spatiotemporal, or even spaceless and timeless. We have avoided such other expressions as "position," "stage," or "stratum," which have even more spatial connotations than the term "level."

The initial, archaic structure is zero-dimensional; it is thus spatial and temporal, although our present mentality, if it grasps this at all, will see in this a paradox. It is origin; only in a terminological sense is it a "first" structure emanating from that perfect identity existing "before" (or behind) all oneness or unity which it initially might have represented. It is akin, if not identical, to the original state of biblical paradise: a time where the soul is yet dormant, a time of complete non-differentiation of man and the universe.

A search for evidence in statements on, or references to this time furnishes hardly any clues as to its structure, aside from general, essentially mythical allusions, e.g., androgyny, or the mythical life and imagery of primal man, Protanthropos.[30] The written evidence itself is fragmentary and, though not incorrect, is at least deficient regardless of the time, occurrence, event or utterance. It is important for us to note that written evidence, especially from earliest times, is itself indicative of a transitional period. The preservation in written form comes about because of a waning of genuine understanding of life, an anxiety about the loss of vital knowledge. Such anxiety may arise whenever men sense that they insufficiently retain the substance of the original force and content of life. All such texts, despite their abundant wisdom, are merely pale reflections, compiled during deficient periods, of the vital truths.

Later times, perhaps because of their increasing dimensionality, show the progressive fragmentation of basic knowledge into a growing aggregate of disparate material. Increasingly deficient attitudes seek refuge in syncretisms (religions based on random collections of "esoteric" teachings and "mystical" truths), or encyclopedic compendia (as, in the first instance, in post-Christian Roman times, and in the second, since the Enlightenment).[31] Presentiate wisdom becomes accumulated knowledge; when summarized and compiled, it yields a new sum, but no new wisdom. Wisdom is reduced from a quality of being to a quantity of possession.

We have found only two direct and precise statements in sources of the type considered adequate by our age that bear on and indirectly characterize the archaic structure. They originate at the close of the Chinese mythical era, in what is perhaps our oldest tradition. The first is Chuang-tzu's statement: "Dreamlessly the true men of earlier times slept," which may be regarded as a key to the understanding of the archaic structure of existence.[32] With reference to his own time (ca. 350 B. C.), he expressly states: "In sleep the soul engages in intercourse." On the basis of old commentaries, translator Richard Wilhelm has emended the saying to include: "And thus the dreams are born from which the holy man of calling is free." Since dreams are one of the manifestation forms of the soul, dreamlessness suggests its dormancy. In this sense the early period is that period when the soul is still dormant, and its sleep or dormancy may have well been so deep that even though it may have existed (perhaps in a spiritual pre-form), it had not yet attained consciousness. Yet a further implication of the statement cited is the emphatic absence of dualistic opposition in archaic man; only a world which has lost its identity contains the possibility of the reciprocal nature of any intercourse.

Two especially revealing words in Chuang-tzu's statement deserve particular attention. It is significant that one of the greatest sages of China does not demean early men with the words "primitive men" (as would a contemporary European, caught up in scientific hubris), but rather calls them "true men," which the commentator designates as the "holy men of calling." We emphasize this wording since the archaic structure in our sense is by no means "primitive." Anyone who regards contemporary "primitives" as representatives of this structure denies the essential basis of his own humanity. The contemporary "primitives" no longer live in the archaic, but in a more or less deficient magic structure. Their predominantly magic attunement has become to a great extent devitalized, and their magic comportment becomes deficient the moment they come into contact with Europeans.

The second item of evidence bearing on the consciousness state of the archaic structure, which from a contemporary vantage point is inaccurately characterized as a state of non-consciousness, is found in an informative observation of Richard Wilhelm. In a note to his discussion of early Chinese chromatic symbolism, he writes: "At that time blue and green are not yet differentiated. The common word Ch'ing is used for the color of the sky as well as of the sprouting plant."[33]

If the non-differentiation, indeed the non-distinguishibility of archaic man from world and universe—a non-awakeness by virtue of which he is still unquestionably part of the whole—is evident at all in any of the extremely rare sources about the beginnings of mankind, then it is surely the case with the two statements cited. Dreamlessness means, beyond doubt, an unconcerned accord, a consequent full identity between inner and outer, expressive of the *microcosmic harmony*. Identity of the sky and earth color certainly indicates unproblematic harmony and complete identity of earth and sky. (The possible objection that this may be a case of primitive color blindness is groundless. Application of such a concept here is tantamount to anachronism.) The identity of earth and sky is an expression of the macrocosmic harmony; taken together, microcosmic and macrocosmic harmony are nothing less than *the perfect identity of man and universe*.

From this vantage point, it is possible to illuminate an assertion of Plato which has baffled the understanding of not only Aristotle and Thomas Aquinas, but of a host of other thinkers, some of whom have gone so far as to suggest textual changes via freely interpretative translations.[34] As quoted in Aristotle, the statement reads: "The soul . . . [came into being] simultaneously with the sky."

The two Chinese examples adduced to characterize the archaic structures contain essentially the same Platonic thought; the sky, undifferentiated from the earth, is no more "existent" than the soul in dreamlessness. The awakening of the soul initiates the simultaneous awareness of the blue sky, since "the soul comes into being simultaneously with the sky."

In retrospect, it may seem as though this consciousness mutation occurring in man were directed toward us: toward present-day man and our consciousness structure; but we must guard against such a one-sided relativization of these events. Our present mode of thinking would insist that everything be considered from the vantage point of the present and would proceed to trace in reverse the path of events. Yet if we did this, we would draw conclusions and results from fragmented manifestations and would never reach the nearly inaccessible origin. Moreover, such a procedure would founder wherever the succession of events was interruped by mutation.

It is for this reason that we have attempted to avoid this retrograde mode of inquiry and have begun our investigations with the original structure and not the predominantly rational-perspectival structure of today (which no longer even corresponds to our actual consciousness structure). The observations of the Chinese and Greek sages which make previously unseen domains accessible, domains replete with extraordinary consequences, tell more about the archaic structure than would any of our retrospective conclusions or prognostications. Anyone capable of sensing and presentiating the significance of these utterances will at least be able to perceive some measure of the splendor of origin—the first radiance of the emergent world and man that suffuses these words of ancient times still present in us. Yet in so doing, we will fall silent.

3. The Magic Structure

We should perhaps interpose one or even two further structures between the archaic and magic, such as a "post-archaic" and a "pre-magical" structure, but the material at our disposal does not furnish any decisive evidence for precise delimitation of such intermediary structures. Consequently, the magic "epoch," as we see it, not only encompasses an extended "era" but also a variety of modes of manifestation and unfolding that are only imprecisely distinguishable from one another. In order to avoid a possible lack of clarity we shall consider all such modes to be manifestations of magic man; and he is distinguishable above all by his transition from a zero-dimensional structure of *identity* to one-dimensional *unity*. And we shall see that the representative symbol for one-dimensionality, the point, the basic element of the line, is as such of paramount significance as an attribute for magic man. On the one hand, the point is suggestive of the initial emergent centering in man (which leads later to an Ego) and is, on the other, an expression of the spaceless and timeless one-dimensionality of magic man's world.

There is a word group correlating among others the words "make," "mechanism," "machine," and "might," which all share a common Indo-European root *mag(h)-*.[35] It is our conjecture that the word "magic," a Greek borrowing of Persian origin, belongs to the same field and thus shares the common root.

The man of the magic structure has been released from his harmony or identity with the whole. With that a first process of consciousness began; it was still completely sleep-like: for the first time not only was man *in* the world, but he began to face the world in its sleep-like outlines. Therewith arose the germ of a need: that of no longer being *in* the world but of *having* the world.

The more man released himself from the whole, becoming "conscious" of himself, the more he began to be an individual, a unity not yet able to recognize the world as a whole, but only the details (or "points") which reach his still sleep-like consciousness and in turn stand for the whole. Hence the magic world is also a world of *pars pro toto*, in which the part can and does stand for the whole. Magic man's reality, his system of associations, are these individual objects, deeds, or events separated from one another like points in the over-all unity.

These points can be interchanged at will. It is a world of pure but meaningful accident; a world in which all things and persons are interrelated, but the not-yet-centered Ego is dispersed over the world of phenomena. Everything that is still slumbering in the soul is at the outset for magic man reflected mirror-like in the outside world; he experiences this outer world blindly and confusedly, as we experience dream events in sleep. Herein, too, lies the root of plurality of souls, which to magic man was a reality. (We will return later to this question.)

In a sense one may say that in this structure consciousness was not yet *in man himself*, but still resting *in the world*. The gradual transfer of this consciousness, which streams towards him and which he must assimilate from his standpoint, and the awakening world, which he gradually learns to confront (and in the confrontation there is something hostile), is something that man must master.

Man replies to the forces streaming toward him with his own corresponding forces: he stands up to Nature. He tries to exorcise her, to guide her; he strives to be independent of her; then he begins to be conscious of his own *will*. Witchcraft and sorcery, totem and taboo, are the natural means by which he seeks to free himself from the transcendent power of nature, by which his soul strives to materialize within him and to become increasingly conscious of itself.

Impulse and instinct thus unfold and develop a consciousness which bears their stamp—a natural, vital consciousness which enables man, despite his egolessness, to cope with the earth and the world as a group-ego, sustained by his clan. Here, in these attempts to free himself from the grip and spell of nature, with which in the beginning he was still fused in unity, magic man begins the struggle for power which has not ceased since; here man becomes the maker. Here, too, lie the roots of that tragic entanglement of fighter and fought: to ward off the animal that threatens him—to give but one example—man disguises himself as that animal; or he *makes* the animal by drawing its picture, and to that extent gains power over it.

Thus arose the first external expressions of inner forces—such as the cliff- and cave-paintings.[36] Leo Frobenius in his book *Unknown Africa* (first published in 1905) showed to what extent these drawings are predominantly spell-casting and magic in character.[37] He describes how, in the Congo jungle, dwarf-sized members of the hunting tribe of Pygmies (three men and a woman) drew a picture of an antelope in the sand before they started out at dawn to hunt antelopes. With the first ray of sunlight that fell on the sand, they intended to "kill" the antelope. Their first arrow hit the drawing unerringly in the neck. Then they went out to hunt and returned with a slain antelope. Their death-dealing arrow hit the animal in exactly the same spot where, hours before, the other arrow had hit the drawing.

Frobenius states that, having fulfilled its magic purpose—magic with respect to the hunters as well as the antelope—this arrow was then removed from the drawing with an accompanying ritual designed to ward off any evil consequences of the murder from the hunters. After that was done, the drawing itself was erased. Both rituals—that of drawing as well as that of erasing—were performed in absolute silence, a point of utmost significance.

These sand drawings of the Pygmies are very closely connected with the cave paintings mentioned above. This was shown by an archaeological discovery in the caves of Niaux, in the French Pyrenees. There, a prehistoric drawing from the Quaternary was found, depicting a buffalo "hit" by an arrow (fig. 4). Hugo Obermaier, in his commentary,[38] has noted their magical nature and that similar drawings have been found in other caves; this kind of hunting magic is still being practiced in a number of places, such as Viet Nam. We may therefore consider the hunting ritual observed and described by Frobenius as a late example of the magic world, even though it differs in one very basic respect from the rituals portrayed in the cave drawings. Cave drawings of the type described were found only in the very darkest parts of the caves where no light, let alone sunlight, could penetrate. With the Pygmies, however, the sun played a decisive role in the ritual. Consequently, the rites

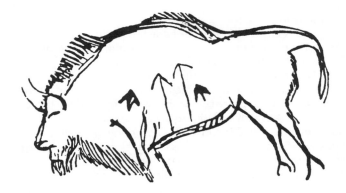

Figure 4: Prehistoric depiction of a bison (reproduced here in black and white) from the cave at Niaux in the French Pyrenees (reduced in size).

practiced in the cave must have belonged to a distinctly earlier period of the magic world.

These rites, which from the rational-psychological viewpoint of today could be called a concentration of the libido (i.e., of the psychic and vital energies) on a specific object, doubtless contributed to the formation of consciousness. For the centering of human will on an object inevitably brought about at the same time a centering of the psychic energies in man.

That this process occurred in the obscurity of the sleeping consciousness is shown by the site of the early magic ceremony. The darkness of the caves—even if a fire may have been used in the ritual to "substitute for" the sun—indicates the great remoteness from consciousness, the unawakened state of the consciousness in those early magic times.

So, compared with the cave drawings, the sand drawing of the Pygmies is "late," as the accompanying ritual shows a certain release from nature, the beginnings of a free human attitude toward nature. Nevertheless, it does express—if we may hazard an interpretation of the scene—some of the essential characteristics of magic man. These characteristics are five in number: (1) the egolessness of magic man; (2) his point-like unitary world; (3) his spacelessness and timelessness; (4) his merging with nature; (5) his magic reaction to this merging (giving him power and making him a "Maker").

In the hunting rite, the *egolessness* is expressed first of all in the fact that the responsibility for the murder, committed by the group-ego against a part of nature, is attributed to a power already felt to be "standing outside": the sun. It is not the pygmies' arrow that kills, but the first arrow of the sun that falls on the animal, and of which the real arrow is only a symbol. (Nowadays, of course, one would interpret it just the other way around and say: the sun's ray is a symbol of the arrow.)

In this linking[39] of the responsibility of the hunters' group-ego (assuming the form of four human beings performing the rite) with the sun—which, because of its brightness, must be considered a symbol of consciousness—it is clear to what extent the capacity for consciousness of these human beings is still on the outside or connected with the outside. With the Pygmies in their egolessness, the moral consciousness that they must bear responsibility, deriving from a clearly conscious Ego, is still attributed to the sun. Their Ego (and with it an essential part of their soul) is still scattered over the world, like the light of the sun.

This leads us directly to the second characteristic: *point-like unity*. This is expressed in the visible interchangeability of the real and the symbolic causative element: that is, in equating the ray of sunlight and the arrow.

At the basis of this point-like unity lies a natural *vital nexus*, not a rational causal one. This point-related unity in which each and every thing intertwines and is interchangeable, becomes apparent when the symbolic murder in a rite, performed before a hunt, coincides exactly with the actual one committed by the hunter. In the spaceless and timeless world, this constitutes a working unity which operates without a causal nexus. Hence it is "unreal"—as unreal as, for example, the purely accidental or the "pre-rational" is in "our world."

We now come to the third characteristic: the *spacelessness and timelessness* of magic man. Only in a spaceless, timeless world is the point-related unity a working reality; outside that world it is an unreality. Because of this spaceless-timeless unity, every "point" (a thing, event, or action) can be interchanged with another "point," independently of time and place (like the hunting scene) and of any rational causal connection. Every point, whether real or unreal, causally or merely symbolically connected, can not only be linked with any other point but is identified with it. One can substitute for the other completely.

Thus absolute reality is bestowed on phenomena, the fusion of which must strike us as unreal, since this fusion occurs in the realm of vegetative energy. But this character loses its effectiveness the moment it is stripped of its basic vital connections and relations; the injection of consciousness disturbs and interrupts the "unconsciously" binding vital energies.

All magic, even today, occurs in the natural-vital, egoless, spaceless and timeless sphere. This requires—as far as present-day man is concerned—a sacrifice of consciousness; it occurs in the state of trance, or when the consciousness dissolves as a result of mass reactions, slogans, or "isms." If we are not aware of this sphere in ourselves, it remains an entry for all kinds of magic influences. It does not matter whether such magic influences emanate knowingly from people or unknowingly from things which, in this sphere, have a vital magic knowledge of their own, or are linked with such vital knowledge.

Nor does it matter if this sacrifice of the consciousness is stimulated by ideas in the unconscious.[40] In such cases persons, things, or concepts are able to force us, by projection, to link a part of our unordered, and hence shadowy–negative, vital, and psychic energies to themselves. In that way, they get a hold over the part of our Ego which we ourselves were not strong enough to place under our own power.

We refer quite advisedly to these spaceless and timeless phenomena. They arise from the vegetative intertwining of all living things and are realities in the egoless magic sphere of every human being. Insight into these realities could clarify many situations, among others, those which parapsychology is trying to study. Of course, they can become consciously known only if present-day man, despite his rational and relativist attitude, realizes the power of spacelessness and timelessness and, with that realization, accomplishes what magic man was not able to do because he was still remote from consciousness and deeply immersed in this egoless, timeless, spaceless world of unconscious unity.[41]

This *merging*, as we have called our fourth characteristic, this interweaving is likewise shown in the hunting scene. It expresses unity, on the one hand, but also the discrepancy in the unity relationship contained within it. This was shown when we stressed its pointlike character. In the process of merging it becomes apparent to what extent this unity is related to the individual phenomena, events, and actions— that is, to the "points"; on the other hand, it is also related to the actual man-nature unity, in keeping with its basic spacelessness and timelessness. We will return shortly to this aspect of unitary interweaving as well as to certain examples from the magic period which vividly demonstrate this interweaving. At this point we should like to point out that unitary merging is expressed in this hunting scene, in that not a single incident in it can be treated as cause or consequence. The over-all magic event depicted in the drawing forms an inextricably interwoven unity. This unity is not destroyed by any spatiality or temporality; its equilibrium is not shattered by any undue stress on any of the participants. All of them—humans, arrows, sun, drawing, forest, and antelope—are egoless.

Nevertheless, precisely this fact clearly reveals the *contradiction* in the unity concept, namely, the unconscious discrepancy between the parts (i.e., the points) and the actual unity. Here man, or a human group, is the protagonist, even though this is extremely well concealed. Although man fits in and merges with the event, this very merger and fusion give the event a definite direction.

As we shall see, all directing implies a conscious process. To that extent this process of consciousness begins to grow visible in the struggle of magic man against nature, in his attempts to master it and thus free himself from it. The starting-point for this possibility is the revealed duality of the unity, which can be related to itself and to any point identical with it. It lies in the interchangeability of the unitary points, in consequence of which the part, as well as the whole, can stand for everything.

The concept *pars pro toto* (the part for the whole) is at the same time always a *totum pro parte* (the whole for the part)—where, curiously and without any probable etymological connection, *totum* suggests by chance *totem*. This interchangeability goes even further: the rule may be changed into *pars pro parte* (a part for a part), and in this sense even into *totum pro toto* (all for all), without losing its validity.

The effectiveness of such interchangeability is perhaps most strikingly demonstrated in the vicarious sufferings experienced in the course of ritual sacrifice. Exchange (*Tausch*)—in the realm of magic—is by no means deception (*Täuschung*); it is rather the expression of the genuine validity of "equals."

In this equal validity of the whole and the part, two additional basic features of the world of magic emerge. These consist of equal treatment and equal significance, without differentiation. Equal treatment brings with it what we may call thinking by analogy or association, which is less "thinking" than it is a purely accidental association based on analogies.

Here, too, lie the roots of sympathetic equal treatment which magic man is able to mete out to everything which is, or even seems to be, similar. Herein lies the reason why magic man feels things which seem to resemble one another as "sympathetic to," or "sympathizing with," one another. He then proceeds to connect them by means of the vital nexus—not the causal nexus.

As for equal significance, that is the first step in the process of drawing analogies. But to an even stronger degree it is an expression of the fact that the magic world is a world without values, in which everything is of equal significance or validity.[42] We need not stress that this is true solely of the early magic period. Thus the hunting scene, for example, already indicated moments of evaluation. Despite this equality of treatment and validity, however, there is latent in the magic unity that discrepancy which hastens the moment of breakthrough. This discrepancy is the decisive moment because it is the one that releases the capacity for consciousness. It becomes visible in the contradictory character of the unity relationship of which we have spoken. This discrepancy gives rise to what we have listed as the final characteristic of magic man: his magic reaction, enabling him to cope with the spell of this magic interweaving and thus escape it.

This *magic reaction* (the fifth characteristic in our enumeration) is the real content of the hunting rite. The very fact of the rite, supplanting natural chaos with a defined and directed action, shows to what extent our hunting example attests to a late period of development of magic man. Man, or the human group, is still only a co-actor in it; but he is already acting for himself. This represents a far-reaching step away from complete unity. The group, beginning to grow dimly conscious of itself as a unity (the group-ego), begins to free itself from its merger with nature, breaking that spell with a counterspell of its own.

In this shattering of the ties, in this gradual emergence of the ego, is revealed that polarization of the world, which, in the mythical structure, then becomes world-shaping and consciousness-forming. The magic reaction thus creates an opposing element and an arena of struggle or play for the individual involved.

This release from nature is the struggle which underpins every significant will-power-drive, and, in a very exact sense, every tragic drive for power. This enables magic man to stand out against the superior power of nature, so that he can escape the binding force of his merger with nature. Therewith he accomplishes that further leap into consciousness which is the real theme of mankind's mutations.

This remarkable and deeply inveterate impulse to be free from miracles, taboos, forbidden names, which, if we think back on the archaic period, represents in the magic a falling away from the once-prevailing totality; this urge to freedom and *the constant need to be against something* resulting from it (because only this "being against" creates separation, and with it, possibilities of consciousness) may be the answering reaction of man, set adrift on earth, to the power of the earth. It may be curse, blessing, or mission. In any case, it may mean: whoever wishes to prevail over the earth must liberate himself from its power.

Deep in the magic structure, at least at the outset, man is earth-bound and earth-imprisoned, natural and primal, so that he can scarcely overcome this merger with the primeval forest. (Even today we associate the forest—etymologically related, at least in German, with the word for "world"—with dark, pre-conscious life.) Then, in this magic structure, he makes the almost superhuman attempt to free himself from the jungle-like bonds and spell of his fusion with nature. Here lies the basis of all sorcery and magic, such as rainmaking, ritual, and the countless other forms by which magic man tries to cope with nature.

In the final analysis, our machines and technology, even our present-day power politics, arise from these magic roots: Nature, the surrounding world, other human beings must be ruled so that man is not ruled by them. This fear that man is compelled to rule the outside world—so as not to be ruled by it—is symptomatic of our times. Every individual who fails to realize that he must rule himself falls victim to that drive.

The skill needed in mastering and guiding our own being is still projected into the outside world. We may not have power over it, but, mindful of our forgotten heritage, we ought to maintain the right to guide it. The magic heritage—the striving for power—has not yet been overcome, in this split form as well.

Our attempt to shed light on the magic structure by means of a late magic scene bears the stigma of all such efforts. In that scene we presented in a rational way relationships which are irrational or pre-rational. We are, here too, forced to work with inadequate means. The irrational cannot be presented rationally. On the other hand, we cannot "pre-rationalize," that is, evoke what is merely emotional, affective, and vital if we are to clarify these pre-rational components of magic man. Our example is, of course, a curious admixture of rational and pre-rational elements; we have restricted ourselves to the foregoing attempt since we have to avoid both recourse to the means employed by occultists, as well as the inadmissable tricks of the obscurantists. We have limited ourselves deliberately and consciously to this one minor example, although a more powerful instance will be taken up later. We did not unleash those powers held in check; today's psychic chaos is sufficiently widespread to discourage its further activation. Moreover, it would be a fruitless and thankless task for us to open up the multitude of magic manifestations, which correspond to the multitude, indeed the infinitude of nature-related manifestations. This jungle of interconnections and amalgamations, this infinite world could not be captured in books—even in rows of books—anyway, but, if at all, perhaps only in a huge card-file.[43]

It is impossible to evoke the abundance of auditory effects, the entire field of magic-acoustic symbols. The fateful pounding of the jungle drums, that heightened beating of the heart and throbbing of the pulse of a group-ego, that concentrated and highly charged epitome of the innate vitality of the group-heart, which reduces to silence the voices and movements of the nocturnal jungle—who would dare describe just this one small yet so powerful sample of the magic forms of expression?

And, since we cannot evoke here in audible form these forms of expression, we have had to settle for the less vivid conceptual form in order to suggest something of the reflected splendor of this magic world. But we should like to recall at least those illustrations which depict magic man's fusion with nature in a purely pictorial way. We refer to the late drawings, paintings, and frescoes of magic man, in which man's merger with nature is portrayed so graphically that the entire picture is nothing but a plant-like amalgam, in which the bodies of the human beings depicted seem to merge right into the picture.

The tapestry-like nature of these pictures, which still partially survive in geometrical form in tile floors, mosaics, and tapestry designs (art nouveau has done more than its share of this), is of course most strongly expressed in tapestries.[44] We must discuss somewhat in detail the pictorial material which reveals this aspect of the magic structure. Heretofore, this aspect has never been clearly brought out; yet it may well be considered—more than a mere aspect—the basic nature of the magical.[45]

Examples of this are numerous, down to the most recent periods. Apart from the cave drawings discussed above, this tapestry-like interweaving of man and nature emerges clearly, for example, from a wall painting found in the Weserhêt grave near Thebes, depicting two noblewomen.[46] This wall painting dates back to approximately 1300 B.C. Dated about the same period is the "Nubian Battle" which decorates a chest found in King Tutankhamen's grave (fig. 5). The section we have reproduced shows this interweaving quite vividly.[47] More strongly ordered in intent, though less strikingly executed than this Egyptian example, is the fragment of a drawing on a shard of Boeotian origin, and dating from the ninth century B.C. (fig. 6).[48] This, and a "wagon journey," depicting perhaps "the abduction of Helen," and found on an earthenware bowl of Attic origin from the eighth century B.C.,[49] remind one even more strikingly of the earliest cave drawings—which have now been transferred from the inner wall of the cave to the outer wall (!) of the vessel containing the cavity.

The "Artemis as Mistress of the Animals" (fig. 7), found on a Corinthian ointment jar of the seventh century B.C.,[50] is lost on a veritable sea of flower-like rosettes and exquisite ornamentation. Expressed differently, it is woven into a tapestry. A painting of "Hercules' Wedding Journey," found on a Melian amphora of the same period, possesses this same tapestry-like character.[51] This interweaving effect is expressed with similarly graphic vividness on two Iberian vases of the third century B.C., found at Liria (near Valencia).[52]

Echoes of this magic interweaving are to be found in Arabian, Mongolian, Persian, Indian, and even in early Christian miniature paintings;[53] there are examples in many fourteenth century frescoes, such as the "Tour de la Garderobe" in the Palace of the Popes at Avignon (fig. 8).

These illustrations may give some idea of the basic character of this magic world and may round out our efforts to depict it rationally by drawing upon magic ritual. It is impossible to imagine how totally interlaced that magic world is. It in-

Figure 5: "Nubian Battle," from a painting on a chest from the tomb of Tutankhamen; 1300 B.C. (reduced in size).

Figure 6: Fragment of a Boeotian vase drawing; ca. 1000 B.C. (reduced in size).

Figure 7: "Artemis as Mistress of the Animals;" Painting on a Corinthian ointment jar of the seventh century B.C. (reduced in size).

Figure 8: Fresco in the "Tour de la Garderobe" in the Palace of the Popes, Avignon; ca. 1300 A.D. (reduced in size).

cludes everything that constitutes the essence of the magic structure: egolessness and a hint of the still unawakened, sleep-like consciousness, spacelessness, time-lessness, and merged unity. But when this merger is presented pictorially, as our illustrations show, it already contains the first glimmerings of separation, the initial consciousness of release from this fusion with nature and its overpowering spell.

If we wish to experience even the slightest afterglow of the emotions of magic life, we must be able to visualize the integral relationship—or at least the relation-ship potential—between all things and persons as operative at any time or place; and we must do this without any attempt to evaluate the individually related "points."

This merging with nature, which in its spacelessness and timelessness also connotes a remarkable boundlessness, explains the well founded powers of magic man—powers which survive today in the form of human mediums. Magic man pos-sessed not only the powers of second sight and divination, he was also highly telepathic.

Today telepathy is based on a mass of authenticated data; even the most hard-bitten rationalist can no longer deny its existence.[54] It is explained in part by an elimination of consciousness, which obscures or blacks out the ego and causes it to revert to a spaceless-timeless "unconscious participation" in the group soul. Clair-voyance may be interpreted in the same way. (Here let us note that the worlds of the ants and bees offer us a primitive form of "unconscious participation" in the group soul. The individual insect occasionally "knows" when and where an event affecting the group occurs, so that insects of the same community, far removed from each other, often show the same reaction to events at the very same time.)

Man's nearness to nature, the broad extent to which he and nature are still undivided, his more fluid situation and his sharper senses make possible these phenomena of a spaceless-timeless character. Pictorially they are expressed in cer-tain early drawings of the magic period in the dreamy, almost trancelike way in which the head, and often the whole body, merges with the surroundings. We have noted three pictures illustrating this heightened, natural, sensory apperception of magic man—superior to our own. They come from human groups widely separated in time and place and are evidence of a magic attitude and the powers arising therefrom.

The oldest picture (fig. 9) is a prehistoric cave drawing from Australia:[55] here the aura is clearly in evidence and set in greater relief by the coloring, which cannot, unfortunately, be reproduced here.[56] The second picture comes from the ninth cen-tury A.D. (fig. 10). It is of Irish origin and is a section of a full-page miniature portray-ing a crucifixion. It was found in a psalter in Dover.[57] The third drawing, like the first, comes from Australia and, in some respects, forms the link between the two others (fig. 11).[58] At any rate, from the clearly drawn radiations, appearing here on a group of no less than nine heads, it seems obvious that they do not represent head orna-ments, as Kühn maintained, or the attributes of a sun-god, the opinion of Winthuis.

Perhaps the most arresting thing about these paintings is the *mouthlessness* of the figures portrayed. In a recent study, Kühn furnishes numerous illustrations from early geological periods from geographically disparate sites. Many of the drawings and statuettes among his examples are mouthless, among them a carving in mammoth-ivory of a "female idol" excavated in western France and dating from the Ice Age (figs. 12 and 13),[59] as well as a similarly designated "female idol," a statuette in stone from an Ice Age site in Russia (fig. 14).[60] From a much more recent period are depictions of mouthlessness from Sumer and China, whereas the two statuettes illus-

Figure 9: Prehistoric cave drawing from Australia (reduced in size).

Figure 10: Irish miniature from a psalter in Dover; ninth century A.D. (section, reduced in size).

Figure 11: Prehistoric cave drawing from northwestern Australia (reduced in size).

trated in figures 15 and 16,[61] from Aleppo and Baghdad, apparently can be ascribed to the fourth and third millennia respectively. Even more recent are two Chinese examples, "masks" still in use today in the Peking Opera: one is a painted, the other a bearded mask. The painted masks, of which there are some 1,200 different examples, all painted in vivid colors, date from the period of the Six Dynasties (220-589 A.D.). The beard mask (*By-hu-hsu*), which effectively obscures the mouth, is worn only by the two highest and most powerful ministers, the secret and wise counsellors of the Chinese emperor, the Son of Heaven. Their sacral-ritual role is evident: Chang-Chian is secretary (the man of learning), Ying-Hsiung is swordsman (protector) of the Son of Heaven (figs. 17[62] and 18).[63]

What this mouthlessness means is immediately apparent when one realizes to what extent these paintings and statuettes are expressions of the magic structure—

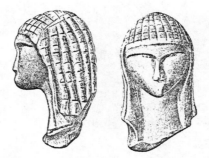

Figures 12 and 13: Profile and frontal view of a "Female Idol" of sacral character; found at Brassempouy, Dép. Landes (western France); ivory, reproduced actual size; dates from the middle or upper Aurignacian (Upper Paleolithic period, ca. 40,000 B.C.).

Figure 14: Female idol found at Gagarino (upper Don, Tambor province, Lipezk district, Russia); stone, reproduced actual size; dates from the Aurignacian-Perigordian period (Paleolithic, ca. 30,000 B.C.).

but not yet of the mythical structure. Only when myth appears does the mouth, to utter it, also appear. Incidentally, these two structures overlap even within the same cultural sphere ever since approximately the third millenium (B.C.); along with mouthless depictions from that period, we also find many which are no longer lacking the mouth, whereas the very early examples, as those from the Ice Age, uniformly evidence the magical mouthlessness.[64] The basis for our interpretation of this lack of mouth comes from the fact that the lack—especially in the early, highly schematic depictions—indicates to what extent magic man placed significance on what he heard, that is, on the sounds of nature, and not on what was spoken (we will return to this question in a moment). Adolf Portmann has established the connection between this lack of mouth, as we have portrayed it here, as a prototypical "schematic representation of the face" or a structural configuration, and the "pre-verbal social

Figure 15: Sumerian idol from the Aleppo
Museum; fourth to third millennium B.C.

Figure 16: Sumerian idol from the Baghdad
Museum; fourth to third millennium B.C.

contact" of babies.[65] The parallels between the developmental stages of mankind
and those of the individual, in the context of the various structures of consciousness,
have also been documented from another sector (Max Burchartz, Oskar Küst, et
al.).[66] In any event, the lack of mouth is a sign that, for magic man, the organ which
enables us to articulate is still irrelevant. Communication between members of the
group-ego, the "We," does not as yet require language, but occurs to a certain
extent "subcutaneously" or telepathically. The egolessness of the individual—who
is not yet an individual—demands participation and communication on the basis of
the collective and vital intentions; the inseparable bonds of the clan are the dominant principle. The extraordinary role of silence within the magic structure and its
effects has been remarked on above in connection with the ritual of the hunt (p. 47).

Figure 17: Chinese mask from the Peking Opera; dates from the time of the Six Dynasties, 220-589 A.D.

Figure 18: Bearded mask from the Peking Opera, worn by the greatest living Chinese actor, Tschu-Hsin-fang, in his role as a minister of the T'ang Dynasty (618-907 A.D.); Peking, December 1961.

Here we should also emphasize to what extent magic man's authority is effective in the struggle with earth and nature. Even today it is still effective, but, as consciousness has developed, it is now vestigial and expresses itself predominantly in a negative form.

This negativeness arises from the fact that an overstimulation of the magic components in present-day man brings a reversion to the magic structure. But today, in contrast to earlier periods, this is not the only or the dominating structure within us. In the course of time the magic structure has been transmuted into the mythical and the mental, and both have weakened the magic structure within us. Relapse into this magic structure means, therefore, a decline—that is, only when it is overactivated and endowed with a character of exclusivity. It is a dangerous act of sacrifice for us and our state of consciousness, yet it is one that is carried out in our time far more frequently than is generally supposed. We are speaking of the flight "backwards" into the vitality and unity of the magical, so frequently observed today; and this disposition to regress is brought about by the absence nowadays of these aspects in our rationalized world, as well as by an anxiety in the face of the emerging mutation. All of these negative phenomena with which present-day "mass psychology" is concerned are rooted in the reactivated predisposition to magic in contemporary man.

Gustav Meyrink, author of once widely read magic novels, has offered a good definition of what magic can be and how it can be recognized in mass reactions. His formulation is: 'Magic is doing without knowing."[67] Translated in terms of today, this phrase would read: *Magic is doing without consciousness.* Today, for example, everything that arises on this plane as a mass manifestation is at the same time irresponsible, because a return to the collective brings about a loss of consciousness and also the elimination of the responsible ego. The mass reactions and psychoses of our day are disturbing cases in point. Only where the magic structure in the individual still works through impulse and instinct does it realize its eminent, life-dispensing value in our day and age.

As long as magic man, in his own time, was enclosed by the unconscious wisdom of the archaic heritage, there was no danger in his dream-like activity, particularly as the emerging impulse and instinct consciousness could express itself without censorship of the intellect. His situation was diametrically opposed to today's magical mass attunement. He escaped danger, since the liberation from nature which he achieved became a reality; he did not succumb to the unconsciousness of nature, but instead gradually emerged from it. Today, however, it is apparent that this wisdom has been broken up into knowledge, and since such knowledge has been degraded to purposes of power ("Knowledge is Power"), we face the threat of blind activity from which we, at least we Europeans, hoped to have escaped. As long as we do not perceive these relationships, we cannot escape from the threat. It is up to each individual to achieve such insight, and for this reason we have emphasized the blind authority of the magic structure. Whether we speak of "white" or "black" magic—there is no such distinction—it is always related to the striving for power.[68] Only if we grant power to something can it have power over us. It becomes a serving and sustaining potency when we again are able to place it into the realm where it belongs, instead of submitting to it.

We can discern in the auditory aspect of several common verbs, used in their normal way, the acoustic-magic stress indicative of the extent to which power is expressed, not in a palpable but rather an auditory manner and appeals to the incomprehensible and pre-rational in us: to belong [*gehören*, derived from *hören* = to hear]; to obey [*gehorchen*, related to *horchen* = to hearken]; and, to submit [*hörig sein*, related again to *hören* = to hear]. These words and what they convey are always subordinated to power that we ascribe to things, events, or human beings, whether as possessions, authoritarian beliefs, or sexuality; and they are always connected to the loss of ego and responsibility. It is not the sun-related eye but the *labyrinthine ear that is the magic organ*; the sun represents diurnal brightness, whereas the labyrinth represents the cave-like nocturnal darkness of dormant consciousness. The vital, though lucidly receptive, is blind, and due to this blindness is destructive. Only our insight into this power that constitutes us can release us from its blindness. If we do not gain this insight, the unconsciously activated magic structure will ultimately (at least for us today) lead—via the atomization of vitality, the psyche, and the ego—to destruction.

4. The Mythical Structure

It is characteristic of the European to be dissatisfied with the mere knowledge of a fact or an event; he must also locate them in time or place, since without such location they have no real conceptual value for him. It should be evident from our discussion that this mode of observation is closely related to the perspectival attitude which is also characteristic. For this point of view, however, everything we have said up to now with respect to the archaic, and particularly to the magic structure, must, for current standards, remain deficient in one important respect.

The location in space is, presumably, sufficiently evident from our illustrations: the magic structure occurs everywhere on earth, although always at the appropriate time for any given place. From our vantage point, it occurs in prehistory. This fortunate term, which the sciences have coined to denote prehistoric time, indicates one of the essential elements of the magical: it lies *before* time, before our consciousness of time. How far back we may wish to place this magic time into prehistory is not only a question of one's predilection, but, on account of the timeless character of the magical, is essentially an illusion. One group will tend to date it back several hundred thousand years, another will be content to place it in the post-glacial period, still another will place our "four consciousness mutations" into the post-Atlantean era, that is, the last 12,000 years, admitting a pre-Atlantean dating for the archaic and the beginnings of the magic structure at the very most.

It is pure speculation if we attempt to locate something timeless in a temporal framework that we have subsequently devised. In the context of the timeless, what can such terms as "day," "month," or "year" possibly mean? Were the "years" then as "long" as those today? In all likelihood they were "slower"—a supposition that will likely have little effect on the actual passage of time.

We can, however, locate approximately the time of the mutation from the magic to the mythical structure, since a consciousness of time, however rudimentary, would have had to manifest itself before the mutation was possible. In accord with the magic structure, this would have been more a sense of time than a knowledge of it—a time-sense closely attuned to nature. When we speak of "time" we are also speaking of "soul." They both share *energeia*, and, to the extent that they are separable, they are both preforms of matter. We will return in a moment to this affinity or possible identity; here we would note that whereas the distinguishing characteristic of the magic structure was the emergent awareness of nature, the essential characteristic of the mythical structure is the *emergent awareness of soul*. Magic man's sleep-like consciousness of natural time is the precondition for mythical man's coming to awareness of soul. Wherever we encounter seasonal rituals in the later periods of the magic structure, and particularly in astronomical deliberations and various forms of the calendar, as for example among the Babylonians and later in Egyptian and Mexican civilization, we find anticipations of the mythical structure. Such forms of evidence indicate that the coming-to-awareness of nature has reached its conclusion, a process whereby the rhythm of nature with its conspicuous auditory emphasis becomes, in a purely natural way, temporal. This is the decisive step taken by magic man out of his interlacing with nature.

We find evidence in pictorial form of this step out of magical enmeshment in several select works of Occidental art dating from the second millenium B.C. It is conveyed in strikingly vivid form in a colored stucco relief, for example, which depicts a "Prince with a Crown of Feathers" from the Palace in Minos. It was discovered in Knossos, Crete, during the first quarter of our century and dates, in all probability, from the middle of the second millenium B.C.[69] (fig. 19). It expresses man's extrication from his intertwining with nature in two ways: first, by presenting terrestrial man (and not a divinity) standing out in partial relief from the background which surrounds and protects him, and thereby depicting the body in partial extrication from his surroundings; and second, by placing the upper torso against the "sky"—"the sky is simultaneous with the soul," and, we would add, is also "simultaneous with

Figure 19: "The Prince with the Crown of Feathers," colored stucco relief from Knossos (Crete); restored; ca. 1500 B.C. (reduced in size; actual height: 2.10 m).

time." (We will discuss later why "time" here is temporicity and not our mental time.) The upper torso is free, as it were, and only the actual vegetative-vital region of the body, from the waist to the feet, is surrounded by nature; and even this is no longer an enmeshment, for the "nature" surrounding him, the lilies, is a nature already illuminated. The body itself, with its almost flower-like form and natural grace, is crowned by a head which looks above and over the earth. Its eyes could already reflect the sky, and the head is not ornamented by small flowers or fruits or vines, but rather by light, airy feathers.

Pictorial representations of man's emergent awareness of his enmeshment in nature (which express this by the very fact of depicting it) are also extant, along with vase drawings, from Greece, together with other examples illustrative of man's further step out of this enmeshment into the reality of mythical consciousness. This process is visible in a detail form a Boeotian shard referred to earlier (fig. 6, p. 53)—the twining garland visible in the upper right-hand corner—as well as in later Greek vase decoration. It is presumably a part of such garlands or vines which clearly intertwine the figures with one another on a vase drawing of the earliest type which depicts Hermes in the company of the three goddesses Hera, Athena, and Aphrodite on their way to meet Paris (fig. 20). In his commentary on the drawing, Creuzer refers to these garlands as mere "foliage, drawn in the background to indicate to the viewer that the scene takes place in the open."[70]

This explanation, if tenable, is at the very least inadequate. It is our contention that these garlands, which, like an umbilical cord, link the figures into a unity, are intended to express if only unconsciously their close ties. Garlands such as these are in evidence only until the beginning of the sixth century B.C., a period when the mental structure begins to prevail. We have searched the relevant literature in vain for an explanation of these garlands, which also occur in a few other examples.[71] It would seem to us that this detail definitely admits of a significance beyond that of a perspectival-rationalistic interpretation. Neither the interpretation of Creuzer, who explains them allegorically as "foliage," nor the explanation of Pfuhl, who sees them as "loose decorative branches," can be considered to be in accord with the mythical structure of their origin. It is true that in the magic, and even mythical, period everything seemed to be "by chance" as we have said; but in those structures it was a world of meaningful accident. Everything, including the least consequential detail, had significance.

The very original meaning of the word "religion" (from *relegere*) indicates this: it means "careful observance" and is the opposite of "negligence" (from *neglegare*), "careless non-observance."[72] Since we will later deal with the Christian interpretation of the word "religion" in the sense of "tie back," "constrain," we would only mention here that within a world that paid meticulous attention to language, which was in consequence unusually nuanced,[73] nothing could have been arbitrary. This is also true of pictorial expression, to which the mythical world was even more closely tied, since imagery is the prominent mode of the soul's manifestation. To this extent, the garlands are not merely a naturalistic or decorative trimming, but rather are charged with significance. Where shortly before the tapestry-like patterns and the geometric-ritualistic interlacings were characteristic,[74] we now see the free yet interlinking sweep of the garlands against an open background. On the illustrations reproduced here, the garlands are indicative of the gradual awareness of being extricated from nature mentioned earlier; the tapestry-like interweaving has given way to a many-faceted and idolized image of the soul, an interrelated unity with which man now comes face to face and which is depicted in the very moment

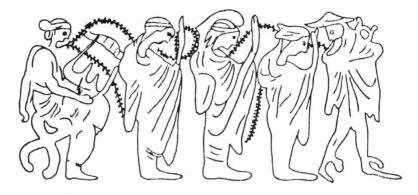

Figure 20: Early Greek vase drawing (eighth century B.C.?): "Hermes accompanied by Hera, Athena, Aphrodite (and seated Muse?)" (reduced in size).

when it comes face to face with the human being, Paris. And in contrast to the leftward movement still evident in the "Prince with the Crown of Feathers," a movement invariably indicative of an emphasis on the unconscious, the movement here is toward the right, a movement toward emergent consciousness.

This brief illustration of an extraordinarily sublime event visible from the reproductions included here would not be complete without a warning about a possible misinterpretation. This is necessary since there are numerous vase drawings from later periods, from about 650 B.C. onward, that include intertwining vines, and these must not be mistaken for the garlands we have spoken of above. They are distinctly grape vines and occur, moreover, in vase pictures of a Dionysian context. They occur exclusively in depictions of Dionysus himself, or where his immanent presence is to be evoked via the Dionysian ceremonial aspect attributed to the grape leaves, as in the depictions of satyrs dancing.[75] However, the most vivid depiction of the mythical structure is to be found in a vase drawing of the sixth century B.C.; and though the design is vaguely reminiscent of the magic structure, particularly of the Irish miniature in figure 10, it differs in one essential respect: *the muse* (in figure 21) *is not mouthless.*[76]

Ever since Homer, the muse has been invoked to begin epic or hymnic song in which mythic events have their formation in language; and the muse possesses the myth-articulating mouth. But we wish to speak here of myth, not of the muse; and in the magic period, we repeat, there is no myth. Man's inner potency is not externalized there via the singing voice, but by the emanation, the aura of the head and even the entire body which forms a seamless transition to the flux of things and nature with which he is merged. Where the mouth appears, the aura diminishes in strength and is replaced by the mouth.[77]

Consequently, the muse in our illustration lacks an aura, as the lack of mouth—signifying inarticulateness—is a characteristic of magic. In the absence of an articulate mouth there can be no myth, for mouth and myth are inseparable. This is evident from an etymology referred to by J. Ellen Harrison, who has noted the relationship between the word "mouth" and the Greek word *mythos*, which originally meant "speech, word, report."[78] But this derivation does not exhaust the wealth of connotation inherent in the word *mythos*, and our search through the available lexica[79] yielded, at first glance, a confusing and contradictory pattern with

Figure 21: The muse "Kalliope" from the so-called François vase; sixth century B.C. (reduced in size).

respect to basic meaning that was resolved only when we realized to what extent the word evidences the ambivalent nature of a primal word.

The corresponding verb for *mythos* is *mytheomai*, meaning "to discourse, talk, speak"; its root, *mu-* , means "to sound." But another verb of the same root, *myein*—ambivalent because of the substitution of a short "u"—means "to close," specifically to close the eyes, the mouth, and wounds.[80] From this root we have Sanskrit *mūkas* (with long vowel), meaning "mute, silent," and Latin *mutus* with the same meaning. It recurs in Greek in the words *mystes*, "the consecrated," and *mysterion*, "mysterium," and later during the Christian era, gave the characteristic stamp to the concept of mysticism: speechless contemplation with closed eyes, that is, eyes turned inward.

Yet we must not make the error of deciding in favor of the one or the other of these two basic meanings; only from a rational standpoint are they contradictory. From an elementary standpoint, this apparent contradictoriness is more than that, for both meanings are valid. It is not enough if we admit only the aspect of "silence," like the traditionalists who recognize only the esoteric tradition; they are obliged to do so, given their orientation to the past. This is, in fact, the position of the two leading defendants of this orientation today, Guénon and Ziegler.[81] Nor is it sufficient to emphasize only the "speaking," like the evolutionists, who recognize only the "exoteric" (secular-scientific) progress-orientation; their forward-looking orientation obliges them to emphasize the spoken word. This is the case with Harrison and Prellwitz, who support their position merely by citing the naturalistic fact of audible sounds made by the opening and closing of the lips.[82]

Only when we acknowledge both meanings of the root can we discern the fundamental nature of the mythical structure. Only when taken together as an elemental ambivalence, and not a rational contradiction, are they constitutive for the mythical structure. Yet when speaking of "constitutive," it is necessary to choose a more appropriate word, one which expresses the stronger field of tension than the term "ambivalence." We are entitled here to speak of the polar nature of the word "myth," whose primal verbal structure gives the mythical structure its effective stamp.

Just as the archaic structure was an expression of zero-dimensional identity and original wholeness, and the magic structure an expression of one-dimensional unity and man's merging with nature, so is the *mythical structure the expression of two-dimensional polarity*.

While the archaic structure led to the unity of the magic structure by a loss of wholeness and identity, providing a gradually increasing awareness of man's individuation, the liberating struggle against nature in the magic structure brought about a disengagement from nature and an awareness of the external world. The mythical structure, in turn, leads to the emergent awareness of the internal world of the soul; its symbol is the circle, the age-old symbol for the soul. The individuated point of the magic structure is expanded into an encompassing ring on a two-dimensional surface. It encompasses, balances, and ties together all polarities, as the year, in the course of its perpetual polar cycle of summer and winter, turns back upon itself; as the course of the sun encloses midday and midnight, daylight and darkness; as the orbit of the planets, in their rising and setting, encompasses visible as well as invisible paths and returns unto itself.

In the natural, temporal rhythm of the circle we again encounter the affinity of time with the soul. Moreover, if the magic structure "results" in the emerging awareness of earth's natural cycles, then the mythical may be said to establish an awareness of earth's counterpole, the sun and the sky. In this the earth, having been acquired via the magic struggle, is encompassed, as it were, by both polar psychic realities: by the sub-terrestrial Hades, and by the super-terrestrial Olympus.

Both of these realities are reflected in turn by ancient architecture. They become more comprehensible now that we begin to understand the mythical structure from within itself and not from a perspectival point of view as merely an "unperspectival world." The two fundamental architectonic forms in antiquity, however, whose origin we have traced above (p. 11) in rationalistic terms to an analogy with the uterus and the phallus, have deeper roots than in a mere superimposition of basic anatomical structures onto architecture. There is, moreover, a distinct sense of duality evident in the perpendicular arrangement of these basic forms, and every dualistic conception is a sign of a rational attitude. The true duality of these forms does not come about until they become separated in Christian architecture into nave and tower.

In antiquity, it is principally their psychic reality and polarity which are evident, for both Hades and Hell are vault-like and cavern-like; they reflect the nocturnal aspect, maternal mystery, shelter, and the parturient principle. The columnar aspect, in turn, corresponds to the sky and to Olympus: in architecture it expresses the very essence of open, in-between space. It is the diurnal aspect, paternal illumination, exposure, the seminal principle.

Thus even architecture reflects mythical man's polar conception; the cavern sanctuaries, such as those of Trophonios in Boeotia, are the complement of early Greek columnar temples and prefigure the transformation of the cavern. Freed from the earth, the cavern comes full circle in the column-borne, vaulted Roman dome.

The architectural arrangement of stone with its harmonious proportions mutely reflects the articulation of mythic word; the stones of antiquity's sanctuaries sing the latent myth, the complement of the vocalized mythical narrative.

Myth is the closing of mouth and eyes; since it is a silent, inward-directed contemplation, it renders the soul visible so that it may be visualized, represented, heard, and made audible. Myth is this representing and making audible: the articulation, the announcement, the report (*Bericht* = the "setting aright") of what has been seen and heard (again we encounter *richten* with its suggestion of an orienting consciousness). What in one instance is a mute image is, in another, a sounding word; what is viewed inwardly, as in a dream, has its conscious emergence and polar complement in poetically shaped utterance.

Thus the word is always a mirror of inner silence, and myth a reflector of soul. The "blind" or unreflective side of the mirror is necessary to produce the visible reflection. Since all psychic phenomena have an essentially reflective character, they not only evidence natural temporality but also make reference to the sky; the soul reflects the sky . . . as well as hell. Thus the circle is complete: time—soul—myth—hell and heaven—myth—soul—time.

To these remarks it must be added that there is such a thing as what we call a *speculatio animae* (of which more will be said later), and also that the closing statement of the previous paragraph is not a rational deduction, but a mythical circling: not a conclusion but a circular linkage as befits myth. And before we turn to the myths themselves, it should be mentioned that an examination of myth with respect to the emergence of consciousness, which has not been done before, will bring out many surprising and illuminating aspects.

The mythical structure is distinct from the magic in that it bears the stamp of the imagination (*imago*, Latin "image"), rather than the stress of emotion. In the magic structure, the vital connections reach awareness and are manifested in emotional forms: in actions dominated by impulse and instinct and subordinate to the demands and ramifications of spontaneous, affective reactions such as sympathy and antipathy. We have already spoken of the pre-perspectival nature of the one-dimensional magic structure; it is spaceless and timeless, and has an emotional and instinctual consciousness responsive to the demands of nature and the earth. The mythical structure, however, whose unperspectival two-dimensionality has a latent predisposition to perspectivity, has an imaginatory consciousness, reflected in the imagistic nature of myth and responsive to the soul and sky of the ancient cosmos.

Although still distant from space, the mythical structure is already on the verge of time. The imaginatory consciousness still alternates between magical timelessness and the dawning awareness of natural cosmic periodicity. The farther myth stands removed from consciousness, the greater its degree of timelessness; its unreflective ground resembles the reverse side of a mirror. By contrast, the closer its proximity to consciousness, the greater emphasis on time; and, in its highest expressions, it approaches the illumination of the sun. The great cosmogonical images in the early myths are the soul's recollection of the world's origination. In later myths, the soul recalls the genesis of earth and man, reflecting the powers of light and darkness in the images of the gods. Slowly the timeless becomes temporal; there is a gradual transition from remote timelessness to tangible periodicity. This ambivalent relation between time and timelessness, which defies our rational understanding, once again finds its expression in the polarity of the mythical structure, for both forms simultaneously exist and complement each other.

There is a breakthrough of this polarity even in mythical utterance. The spoken words in themselves are not decisive; this holds true in myth as in any other utterance. They become decisive—"de-cisive" is the elimination of separation—only when understood in conjunction with what was left *unsaid*. Only when the unspoken communicates its silent message does the spoken word convey the depth and polarity that constitute the tension of real life. Silence by itself is magical spell, and speech by itself mere rational babble. The word has value, apart from (magical) power or (rational) formula only where the speaker takes this interdependence into account. The attentive listener, moreover, will discern the affinity—perhaps not demonstrable—between "word" (*Wort*) and "value" (*Wert*).

In a certain sense myths are the collective dreams of the nations formed into words. Until expressed in poetic form, they remain unconscious processes; their mere utterance is an indication only of their latent possibility for consciousness, not of consciousness itself. Every emergence of consciousness presupposes the externalization of something that presses, or is pressed, toward awareness. Consequently, the emergence of consciousness always has a reiterative and retractive function, and depends above all on a certain formative and shaping power. In the formed myth, consciousness reveals the soul and, at the same time, an invisible and extended region of nature, the cosmos; it reveals everything that has materialized and is now manifest in the imagery of psychic processes as myth, coming to awareness in consequence of its emergent form.

Disregarding the pure cosmogonies, we see that all the previous interpretations of myth are predicated mainly on two predominantly contentual aspects of myth: the astral and the natural, the natural being interpreted mostly in sexual-erotic terms. The astral-mythological interpretation was introduced by Dupuis,[83] and its most recent exponents are Drews and Eisler.[84] The natural-mythological interpretation, which no doubt still shows here and there some magic residues, began with Creuzer[85] and numbered among its proponents such diverse investigators as Freud and Rank, Klages, Jung and Kerényi.[86] Despite the inevitable one-sided extremes, both orientations have made signal contributions toward elucidating the phenomenon of myth.

Whatever aspect is emphasized, the interpretation of myth always brings about an illumination of life. Yet it sometimes reverts to a kind of topsy-turvy obfuscation as a consequence of a hyper-vitalistic stance, as in the case of Klages, whom we might call a "metabolist." This term is applicable to those investigators caught in the spell of a deficient mythical attitude, who fall victim to a false *metabole*—a premature reversal or short-circuit upsetting the equilibrium—characteristic of our times. It represents a deficient and residual form of what was once the organic interaction and balancing between one polar extreme and the other, as in the seasonal rhythms, the course of the sun, the planets, the heartbeat, and breathing. But the present-day metabolist permanently gives up one extreme in favor of another. Two insubstantial variants are the opportunist, who acts without character, and the *rancuniste*, as we might call him, motivated by resentment. Lacking the center that makes the circle possible, the metabolist is prisoner of one segment, and, unable to shape the organic cycle, he merely adds impetus, overwinding it and destroying its momentum.

The illumination of life coming from myth interpretation is closely akin to the successful dream interpretation of modern depth psychology. Our emphasis, however, is on the "illumination" and not the "life" as the essential moment of the mythical process. For whether myth is interpreted from an astral standpoint, that is, with particular reference to cosmology, or from a vital, that is, a basically anthropological standpoint, very nearly all myths contain an element of consciousness emergence to the extent that they reflect the emergent awareness of the soul.

From the inexhaustible wealth of mythologemes on consciousness emergence (as we shall designate them), we will select five in which this fundamental trait is evident. These are the mythologemes of sea voyage, of Narcissus, of the sun, of the descent into Hades which have come down to us as "Nekyia" accounts, and finally, one of the most remarkable, the mythologeme of the birth of Athena.

These mythologemes begin to take shape as man becomes aware of his soul. They are the most visible sign of an emerging consciousness, which is of course also an emergence of the ego. This is mirrored by the mythologemes of sea voyage. Every such voyage is a symbol of man's gradual mastery over the soul; as late as Heraclitus, soul and water are still closely related.[87]

There is, for example, the "Seventeenth Rune" of the *Kalewala*, wherein the great bard Wainamoinen must find the meaning of several words before he is able to complete his boat. Only after he has learned the words from the primal giant Wipunen, only after finding expressions for all primordial phenomena (which is equivalent to a process of realization, i.e., consciousness emergence), can he complete his boat and embark on the voyage described in the "Eighteenth Rune."[88] Having traversed his own soul, symbolized by the voyage (which we understand as symbolic of emergent consciousness), mythical man finds the "other" person, the partner specifically intended for him. The awakening toward the self proceeds circuitously through the awakening toward the "Thou"; and in the "Thou" the entire world opens up, a previously egoless world of total merging.

Only someone who has learned to say "I" to himself, a self no longer dispersed over or withdrawn from the world, is capable of losing himself and regaining himself in another person. And the mystery of this "gain," which is at the same time a loss, is perhaps life's most inscrutable secret, profound and fathomless as the sea. Having withstood the voyage, Wainamoinen finds Annikki on the opposite shore, as Theseus, after crossing the Aegean, finds Ariadne on Crete (in the very palace where the "Prince with the Crown of Feathers" was excavated).[89] After a long voyage, the Greeks regain Helen in Troy, and, surviving his shipwreck, Odysseus encounters Nausicaa.[90] Gunther finds Brunhilde, "queen across the sea,"[91] and Tristan, having braved many storms at sea, discovers Isolde—and himself; for *every voyage is a discovery of self.*

The motif of the sea voyage is found in all cultural traditions: Nordic, Greek, and Germanic.[92] Even in the cultures of the Near East we encounter this manifestation of the experience and expression of emergent consciousness. It has survived, for example, in a mythical account from a Persian-Indian-Turkish collection of folktales known as the *Tuti Nameh*.[93] There, the "Story of the King of China" recounts the king's journey to the land of Medinet-el-Ukr to gain the princess's hand. Accompanied by his vizier, an aged wiseman, he arrives at the sea; the text continues: "At the seashore they embarked upon a ship and sailed many days and nights before they reached an attractive coast." Despite the innocent appearance of this statement, it furnishes the key for the following event: after they have landed, the wiseman leaves the king to himself, i.e., the king "found himself" and was no longer in need of his companion; and, having found himself, he then—after four days—finds the king's daughter, and during yet another four days, takes her back to China to be his wife.

It is noteworthy that the process of consciousness emergence here is accentuated by the significance of the Eight; the two sequences of twice four days each are specifically mentioned for the discovery and the union. In these mythical texts, we may interpret the Eight like a symbolic act, such as the enthronement of the "Eighth Muse" (p. 17 above), where the Eight also had a symbolic significance; indeed, we are obliged to do so if we wish to do justice to the mythical content, particularly if the interpretation suggested is able to shed light on structural interrelationships.

This same water aspect of the sea voyage mythologemes is also met with in the mythologeme of Narcissus. Here, too, the water-soul symbolism plays a significant part and becomes an expression in myth of the emergent consciousness: Narcissus, whose very name contains a hidden reference to the water element,[94] catches sight of himself in the water's reflection. In mythical terms: he looks into his soul and thereby sees himself, becoming conscious of his own existence. To look into the mirror of the soul is to become conscious; and to apprehend the soul, as mythical man does in the reflection of myth, is nothing less than to become conscious of the self. The *Corpus Hermeticum* has gone so far as to incorporate this mythologeme into its cosmogony; the "First Nous," the highest thought, created the divine man out of itself, the original man who then descended to the sphere of the Demiurge where the individual planets shared with him their essence. Then, he broke the circle of the spheres and manifested himself to Physis below. Having beheld his image in the water, he was enamoured of it and descended into nonrational nature and united himself with it.[95]

This cosmogonological parallel to the Greek mythologeme of Narcissus shows the reflective element inherent in all parallels, even where they do not intersect until infinity; infinity, after all, is itself expressly a conception of the soul. The parallelism between the Greek mythologeme of Narcissus and the Hermetic cosmogony clearly reflects that not only man, but also the once divine man becomes conscious of himself in reflection. This "speculation"—*speculum*, Latin for "mirror"—reveals anew the polar nature of myth.[96] In these myths we see not only a reflection of the human soul, but also one of a soul outside or beyond the human, that is, a divine soul; or so it seemed to mythical man as documented in his myths.

But there is no point in pursuing these speculations ("mirrorings") further; they only lead into the boundlessness of the soul already known to Heraclitus. While he related the soul to water, others, like Democritus, held it to be identical with fire. Now all of these speculations may appear to us as sheer superstition; nonetheless, the polarity expressed by the naturalistic equation of soul with water and fire, or with air and stone, is at least symbolically correct. Besides, it is irrelevant whether we understand these things in our rationalistic way or not, for their effectivity for their time remains unaffected. Even though we are dealing here with mere speculation or irrational knowledge, these speculations express the essence of soul, namely, that it is itself a reflection as well as a reflector, living in the ambivalence of polarity.

Let us now turn to the sun mythologemes; wherever we encounter them, we find light, the brightness of consciousness. It can be demonstrated that they took shape about the same time in both the East and the West, and that at the moment of their formation and verbalization they became an effectual reality. Earlier, such conceptions of sun mythologemes were still dream-like, as in the naturalistic Horus symbolism in Egypt (ca. 2500 B.C.); but once shaped into an account and expressed in myth, they became recollections of dreams. Seneca, most likely drawing on Plato,[97] points out that only when awakened can someone recount his dreams. This is to say that only the "awake" man is able to organize and judge them, and, in so doing, become conscious of their meaning. The first allusions to such sun mythologemes in the East are found in the Chinese "Hiho" mythologeme; which has survived only in fragmentary form in the *Kwei Tsang*;[98] in Greece, the first record of the Helios mythologeme is in the *Odyssey*; and both accounts date from about the eighth century B.C..

Another significant motif appears at about the same time in both East and West: wrath or anger. Specifically, the reference is to "divine wrath" which is often described as a fire immanent in man. The simultaneous occurrence of the sun mythologeme and "divine wrath"—particularly when viewed within the context of myth, to which we are here striving to be faithful—almost seems to suggest that the sun descended into man for the purpose of manifesting itself through wrath.

Wrath or anger is the force which bursts the confines of community and clan, to the extent that it manifests the "hero" in the individual and spurs him on toward further individuation, self-assertion, and consequently ego-emergence. We noted earlier the decisive role of the concurrent emergence of wrath in both the *Bhagavadgita* and the *Iliad*;[99] the *Iliad* begins with the words: "Menin aeide, thea, Peleiadeo Achileos," ("Sing, goddess, the wrath of Peleus' son Achilles"), words in which we can recognize a summons to consciousness.

Later on, *after* his encounter with Nausicaa—which we now recognize as being of signal importance—this wrath of Odysseus, this opening motif of the *Iliad*, leads to his moving words: "*Eim Odysseus*," "am Odysseus." These proud words herald the full magnificence of Greece and strike the keynote, as it were, of our Western culture.[100] But this "am Odysseus" is not yet an "I am"; the "I" latently present in its bearer's name is there only to the extent that it forms a part of the verb, the active part of the phrase. Even today, Italian and Spanish—whose speakers are more closely clan-oriented and more given to emotional vehemence—do not have separate pronouns; they occur only as a part of the verb, i.e., within the action itself (or in passive forms within the "being acted upon" or "suffering").

Only in acting or being acted upon does man begin to sense his individuality. This is the aspect of the individuation process that underlies the situation of Italian and Spanish noted above, languages that have retained strong verbal endings to which the pronouns are bound because of their closer ties to the languages of antiquity, whose nearness to origin they share. Other languages have removed the ego from the act where it was once depicted or described and further relativized it, and in these languages the verb endings have undergone a gradual weakening.

The "*Eim Odysseus*" rests on two characteristics repeatedly emphasized by Homer: first, that Odysseus is *polymetis* or (rationally) inventive, and second that he is also *polytlas* or an "endurer." "Metis," however is also the name of Athena's mother—Athena who was protectress of both Achilles and Odysseus. This dual aspectuation expresses an abiding accompaniment to every consciousness emergence, in which, after all, reasoning thought is a co-participant. In every consciousness emergence, no matter how insignificant or inauspicious, and including every emergence of the ego, passive suffering is also present. The passive aspect is the polar complement of the active; the suffering of endured loss corresponds to the joy of the considered act of discovery. And it is this aspect, this demand of consciousness emergence, namely being able to endure suffering, that Western man is scarcely able to fulfill today despite the favorable conditions for it that he has himself created (as in the years 1930 to 1950), for Western man has unilaterally yielded to the active and dynamic principle.

It is precisely the abundance of sorrow and suffering endured by Odysseus that enables him to save the "psyche" of his companions.[101] But only someone who has rescued himself can save others. What lies concealed behind this rescue of the *psyche*? Here, via the Greeks, an eminently significant aspect of the mythical form of expression comes to light, for *psyche* is synonymous with life and the soul; and this equivalence is to be found not only in this passage but as late as Heraclitus, Plato, and even the Gospel of John.[102] For this reason, we have spoken of the life-illuminating aspect of genuine myth interpretation, for it is a concurrent illumination of the soul, i.e., an emergence of consciousness.

We need not be disturbed by the varied meanings inherent in the word *psyche*, for its meaning of "breath" does not contradict its equivalence with life, nor does it contradict its various associations in the works of Heraclitus, Democritus, and others who equated the soul with the various elements. In whatever form, sun or water, stone or air, the soul and life are the bond between these polarities. In the mythical accounts, now the one, now the other aspect predominates, revealing in each instance its unspoken polar complement on the invisible reverse surface of the mirror. And the emergence of consciousness which effects its presence in these myths reminds us that not just the sun but also the darkness within man is thereby rendered visible.

This immeasurable darkness is expressed and made visible in the mythologemes and descriptions that have survived in the form of "Nekyia": nocturnal voyages or descents to Hades or hell. We find it for example in Istar's descent to hell in the *Gilgamesh* epic; Odysseus too had to endure such a journey, mentioned by the Orphics and alluded to by the "Y" symbol of the Pythagoreans. Later it is described by Virgil and is revealed by the Gospels; Plutarch speaks of it, Dante has furnished a description, and Don Quixote survives such an ordeal. It survives in the *Nigredo* of the medieval alchemists and has been rediscovered by modern science as the theory of the "shadow" in psychology. Since the Nekyia reveals the Hades in man and affords him the opportunity to become aware of this dark polar complement of the soul's manifest light and brightness, it represents the pre-eminent expression of the integration of the soul.

A mythical saying has recorded the rise of this new capacity in man for discerning the shadowy or dark, nocturnal part of himself (today we would call it the "unconscious"). This capacity, at first a dream-like anticipation of the fundamental character of the mental structure, in all likelihood enters the gradually awakening and later fully awakened consciousness in the form of a dream, as reported in the mythologeme. The reality of mythical dream, however, was so vivid as to be almost identical with what we today call "reality"; myth was the polar complement of life, dream the polar complement of waking consciousness. It is via the polarity that mythical man, as he becomes aware of dream in myth, comes to an awareness of consciousness; standing in the circle, he courses through the cycle of dream and wakefulness, a cycle of awakening.

This process, scarcely comprehensible and conceivable in rational terms (aside from recollections of our own childhood), has been articulated by Chuang-tzu with the uncertainty of a seeker: "Are not you and I perchance caught up in a dream from which we have not yet awakened?"[103] And at almost the same time in Greece, Sophocles formulates the identical thought in his *Aias*: "I see that all of us who are alive are but the figment of dream—no thicker than the thickness of a shadow." Two thousand years later, this question of awakening reappears at the outset of the seventeenth century in Spain, the "unperspectival" country lacking a renaissance and existing on the outer fringe of Europe. There Calderón wrote his *La vida es sueño*, "Life is a dream." About the same time, Shakespeare reveals the same thoughts in the *Tempest*.[104] This expression and mythical attitude, still utterly confined to the soul, recur in Novalis and, in our day, in Hofmannsthal's *Der Tor und der Tod* (Death and the Fool); and in the novels of Virginia Woolf, *The Years* and *The Waves*, it finds almost literal expression. It is indicative of her preoccupation with circularity and the mythical constellation, not only in the titles of her works but even more clearly in their theme and structure.

Wakening and the capacity for seeing in darkness were anticipated, as if in a dream, and rendered visible in the firm outlines of the mythologeme of Athena's birth. She springs forth (i.e., a leap, a mutation) from the head of Zeus; she is the image of thought, of conscious thinking capable of perceiving once unseen relationships, as well as realities hidden by darkness. Athena is owl-eyed, and her attribute, the owl (which as a bird is a polarity symbol of the soul) sees in darkness and perceives night as day. And it was Athens which was destined to become the site of Western man's awakening to truly rational thought,[105] Athenians whose voice determined our world and whose thought determined our notion of time, whose sagacity gave our mental, perspectival world its shape and countenance: Socrates, Euclid, Plato, Aristotle.

In this "voiced determination" (*Bestimmen*)—and in the very fact that we are justified in using a term reminiscent of the acoustic undercurrent of the magic-mythical heritage—the completed transition from the magic world of the ear and hearing to the mythical world of the speaking mouth is evident; and the "shape and countenance" heralds an essential characteristic of perspectivity: it is a visual world.

Everything that "belongs" to us (gehören), with its connotations of the auditory (hören = to hear) is an expression of our power or might; it belongs to the magic structure and is "attuned to its unity," i.e., in accord with its nature. Everything that corresponds to, or conforms with us is an expression of our psyche or soul, and corresponds to the mythical structure (see also p. 220 below). Everything we see is an expression of our understanding; and this "seeing" and "conceptualizing" are commensurate with the mental structure.

And it would be well for us to be mindful of one actuality: although the wound in the head of Zeus healed, it was once a wound. Every "novel" thought will tear open wounds. When recalling mythical man and his achievements, we must not forget the infinite pain and agony, even though, as the "infinite" may suggest, they may be only irrational grief or anguish in the soul. Everyone who is intent upon surviving—not only the earth but also life—with worth and dignity, and living rather than passively accepting life, must sooner or later pass through the agonies of emergent consciousness.

5. The Mental Structure

In our description of the "perspectival world" we have already given a partial outline of the mental structure; but in so doing, we were more or less compelled to view everything from the vantage point of the emergence of perspectivity in the decisive year 1500, when the perspectival European world finally mutated from the unperspectival European world of the Middle Ages. In order to describe the mental structure at this juncture in our discussion, we shall have to proceed from a different point of departure.

Rather than attempting to describe retrospectively the rise of the perspectival world from our present time, we shall endeavor to follow the path which leads *from origin to our time*, which begins with the Occidental or Western structuration of our consciousness. This choice of a point of departure may well pose obstacles to our understanding, but they will vanish when we clarify the connections between our remarks on the unperspectival world and the (also unperspectival) mythical structure. We must bear in mind that the unperspectival world represents only one part of the mythical structure, the European part, as it were. We must also remember a fundamental fact, namely, that the events of 500 B.C. in Greece had to be repeated around 1250 A.D. by European man; and his basis was considerably broadened because of three major achievements, all containing an element of incipient perspectivity: the Greek theory of knowledge, the Hebrew doctrine of salvation, and Roman legal and political theory.[106]

If we were to proceed in our discussion exclusively from the standpoint of this perspectival European world, we would be justified in defining it, even at this stage, as "rational"; the Latin notion of *ratio* already gives it its direction. Even in scholastic terminology, which is derived from Aristotle, man is called an *animal rationale*, an animal with the gift of rationality. And in the word *ratio*—which means "to reckon" as well as "to calculate" in the sense of "to think" and "understand"—we meet up with the principal characteristic of the perspectival world: directedness and perspectivity, together with—unavoidably—sectorial partitioning.

We are, however, dealing here with the deficient phase of the perspectival world. Just as we were able to discern an efficient as well as a deficient phase of the magic structure where the one was distinguished by spell-casting, the other by sorcery, so too are we able to discern two such phases in the mental structure; the efficient or mental phase and the deficient or rational phase which resulted from it. It is the efficient phase which gives this perspectival world its distinctive stamp, which even today is, or at least could be, valid. The European perspectival-rational world represents, in this sense, only the deficient and most likely ultimate phase of the exclusive validity of the mental-rational structure.

Now the reader will immediately associate the term "mental" with the notion of "mentality," and the German reader in particular will understand it in a more circumscribed sense than the English, French, Italian, or Spanish reader, for whom the word "mental" still has a more vivid or vital connotation. Such a one-sided association unconscionably limits the range of significance contained in the word "mental," for even the word "mentality" expresses more than the mere moral or ethical component of a mental predisposition or attitude, while the terms "predisposition" and "attitude" already show a definite perspectival character.

We have chosen the term "mental" to designate the consciousness structure still dominant today for two reasons. In the first place, its original meaning—still preserved in the Sanskrit root *ma-*, with secondary roots such as *man-*, *mat-*, *me-*, and *men-* —shows an extraordinary wealth of interrelationships; even more importantly, the words formed from this group all express the specific characteristics of the mental structure. And in the second place, this word is the first or initial word of our Occidental culture; it is the first word of the first verse of the first canto of the first major Western utterance. I refer, of course, to the word *menin* (accusative of *menis*), the opening word of the *Iliad*, in which the word "mental" is present.

In manifestations originating in the mythical structure nothing is accidental; everything has its corresponding meaning and significance. Thus there is apt to be a corresponding significance in the fact that this earliest among the accounts of our Western world begins with this word, particularly since the *Iliad* does not only evoke an image but rather describes an ordered course of action by men (and not just gods) in a directed, that is, causal sequence.

The Greek word *menis*, meaning "wrath" and "courage," comes from the same stem as the word *menos*, which means "resolve," "anger," "courage," and "power"; it is related also to the Latin word *mens*, which has an unusually complex set of meanings: "intent, anger, thinking, thought, understanding, deliberation, disposition, mentality, imagination."

What is fundamental here is already evident in the substance of these words: it is the first intimation of the emergence of *directed or discursive thought*. Whereas mythical thinking, to the extent that it could be called "thinking," was a shaping or designing of images in the imagination which took place within the confines of the polar cycle, discursive thought is fundamentally different. It is no longer polar-related, enclosed in and reflecting polarity from which it gains its energy, but rather directed toward objects and duality, creating and directing this duality, and drawing its energy from the individual ego.

This process is an extraordinary event which is literally earth-shaking; it bursts man's protective psychic circle and congruity with the psychic-naturalistic-cosmic-temporal world of polarity and enclosure. The ring is broken, and man steps out of the two-dimensional surface into space, which he will attempt to master by his thinking. This is an unprecedented event, an event that fundamentally alters the world.

This event is recorded in the myth of the birth of Athena, and its imagery and allusions are unmistakable. Zeus has wedded Metis, the personification of reason and intelligence, who, being one of the daughters of Oceanus ("the river encircling the world"), had the power of transforming herself.[107] Fearing the birth of a son more powerful than he, Zeus devours Metis, who is already pregnant with a daughter, thereby transporting her into his own body. When Hephaestus (or Prometheus or Hermes) splits Zeus' head with an axe, this daughter, Athena, is born. Pindar has described this birth brought about by the blow of an axe as having taken place accompanied by a terrible tumult throughout nature, as well as by the astonishment of the entire pantheon. The sea (the all-encompassing soul) surges forth, and Olympus and earth—until that moment polarly related—tremble and shake; the carefully preserved balance is destroyed; even Helios interrupts his course. The circle is indeed interrupted, and, from the breach, the wound, a new possibility of the world emerges.

In the name "Athena" the root *ma:me-* is not visible; yet, as befits the mythical, it is invisibly present in the name of her mother, *Metis*; in the names of her *accoucheurs*, *Prometheus* and *Hermes*; and also in one of Athena's attributes (besides the owl and the well-aimed lance), the head of *Medusa*. In the Roman tradition, Pallas Athena is called *Minerva* (originally *Menerva*), while the earliest Etruscan names for her are *Menerfa* and *Menrfa*.[108] And this goddess, variously described as pugnacious, bellicose, and yet bright, ethereally clear-thinking, knowledgeable of darkness, and of never-failing aim, is the protectress of Achilles, whose *menis* is sung by the *Iliad*; and it is she who stands by him in battle: battles unleashed and successfully fought by this very wrath.

In yet another culture that has been constitutive for our own we have an example of this decisive consciousness mutation which took place in Greece about 1225 B.C., in which the element of anger had an important role; we refer of course to the anger of Moses, the awakener of the nation of Israel. Bearing himself the guilt of murder, he confronts the Israelites with the vengeance of the one God; it is the birth of monotheism, counterpart of the birth in man of the awakened ego. And it is also the birth of dualism: man is here, God is there; they are no longer polar correspondences or complements, but stand opposite one another as a dualism. The individual is not a polar complement of God, for if he were, he would have no need of a mediator; and so the trinity, too, is born, a further characteristic of the three-dimensional, mental structure.

Here we have discovered the link between thinking and wrath, between Greek *menos*, Latin *mens*, and Greek *menis*. Anger—not blind wrath, but "thinking" wrath—gives thought and action its direction. It is ruthless and inconsiderate (*rücksichtslos*), that is, it does not look backwards (*Rück-sicht*); it turns man away from his previous world of mythical enclosure and aims forward, like the lance or like Achilles poised for battle. It individualizes man from his previously valid world, emphasizing his singularity and making his ego possible. We deliberately emphasize the "man" as an individual, for *mens*, *menis*, and "man" derive from the same root.

If we pursue these etymological interrelationships further,[109] we find the following basic pattern which constitutes the mental structure: from the root *ma*, meaning "thinking" and "measuring," the secondary roots *man*, *mat*, *me* and *men* are derived. From the root *man-* comes the Sanskrit word *manas*, which means "inner sense, spirit, soul, understanding, courage, anger"; and from this same root the Sanskrit word *manu* has come, meaning "man, thinker, and measurer," as well as Latin *humanus*, English "man," German *Mann* (from whose adjectival form, *männisch*, "manly," the word *Mensch*, "human being" derives), to name only a few.

Even if we overlook the fact that Latin *humus*, "earth," belongs here, we must nonetheless emphasize that in addition to the name for the Indian lawgiver *Manu*, the names for the Cretan King Minos and the first "historical" Egyptian King Menes are most likely derived from the root *man*.[110] It has in any case been proven that *Minos* also means "deliberator" and "measurer," thus effectively establishing its connotation as being related to the Indian *Manu*.[111] We are justified here in recognizing that this almost simultaneous emergence of the three legendary figures, who embody a mutational principle for mankind, is a first manifestation of the mental consciousness structure.

Wherever the lawgiver appears, he upsets the old equilibrium (mythical polarity), and in order to re-establish it, laws must be fixed and established. Only a mental world requires laws; the mythical world, secure in the polarity, neither knows nor needs them.

In early Greek culture, the mental principle appears not only in the names Menerfa, Metis, Hermes, and Prometheus, but conceivably also in the name of the Mycenaen King Agamemnon, and certainly in the name of Spartan King Menelaus. In all these names, the mental principle is visible from the root *ma:me*, or its secondary roots. And it is perhaps not accidental that the Trojan War, which we might interpret as the triumph of the patriarchal over the matriarchal principle, came about because of Menelaus' wife Helen, sister of Clytemnestra and sister-in-law of Agamemnon (see p. 160, notes 42 and 43).

Let us consider for a moment some other secondary roots; we have already mentioned *mat* as a second root, from which the Sanskrit words *matar* and *matram* are formed. *Matar* becomes Greek *mater* and *meter*, both meaning "great mother," and has given rise to such words, among others, as our word "matter"; *matram*, or "musical instrument," reappears in the Greek *metron*, from which our word "meter" is derived.

We should note here something that we will consider later in greater detail, namely that the original root *ma:me* contains the female principle in complementary and latent form: the Greek word for "moon" (*men*), for example, is derived from this very same root. And in the patriarchal world of today, the secondary root *mat* undergoes its apotheosis in the dominance of rational man by "matter" and "materialism."[112] Where the moon was for early man the measure of time, matter is for present-day man the measure of space.

And finally, from the roots me- and men- we can trace a large number of Greek verbs, all of which connote more or less "being angry or rancorous" on the one hand, and "demand, desire, intend, aspire, have in mind, and devise" on the other.[113] (In all of these, it is of note that they express an aspiration, an intent and contriving directed against someone.) And to this same root we can trace the English word "mind," Latin *mentiri* (meaning "to lie," i.e., to tell an untruth!), German *ermessen*, in the sense of both "measuring" and "pondering or considering," and also Greek *medomai*, which means "to think of or about" (that is, definitely directed thinking), and so on throughout all of the Germanic languages.

It is also worth noting that the Greek interrogative *ti* in the phrase *ti men* ("why?") is an intensifier, a kind of co-creator of the question—the question which stands at the very outset of the sciences; and, it will be remembered, both Athena and Minerva became the patronesses of the sciences.[114]

The root, then, on which the word "mental" is based, carries within itself the germ of an entire world which takes on form and shape, and becomes an effective reality in the mental structuration. Even if we recall only the most important of the words and ignore any additional examples, we can circumscribe the essence of this mental structure: it is a *world of man*, that is, a predominantly human world where "man is the measure of all things" (Protagoras), where man himself thinks and directs this thought. And the world which he measures, to which he aspires, is a material world—a world of objects outside himself with which he is confronted. Here lie the rudiments of the great formative concepts, the mental abstractions which take the place of the mythical images and are, in a certain sense, formulae or patterns of gods, i.e., idols: anthropomorphism, dualism, rationalism, finalism, utilitarianism, materialism—in other words, *the rational components of the perspectival world*.

When compared to the mythical structure, with its temporal-psychic emphasis, the transition to the mental structure suggests a *fall from time into space*. Man steps out of the sheltering, two-dimensional circle and its confines into three-dimensional space. Here he no longer exists within polar complementarity; here he is in confrontation with an alien world—a dualism that must be bridged by a synthesis in thought, a mental form of the trinity. Here we can no longer speak of unity, correspondence, or complementarity, not to mention integrality.

To be sure, traditionalists, religious persons, those who tend to turn toward the past, and even present-day mystics are able to experience, or have experienced occasional sparks, stars, or suns of a manifestation—experienced, sensed or imagined and now vanished—of completion or unification; yet even this in the form of an afterglow, and not in its original form. And this is even less so with wholeness itself. The transition takes place at the turn from the sixth to the fifth century B.C. and is mirrored in the image of Athena's springing forth from the head of Zeus. Parmenides, who "promulgated" his fragmentary didactic poem around 480 B.C., spoke the words destined to become the principal motif of the Western world: *to gar auto noein estin te kai einai*, "For thinking and being is one and the same."[115] The mythical world breaks apart, the equivalence of soul and life manifest in the word *psyche* gives way to the equality of thinking and being. Here the first philosophical statement is formulated: the first spatializing, mental manifestation.

It was prefigured by many things which become meaningful and lose their accidental and puzzling appearance when viewed from the context of consciousness emergence. This manifestation is evident in sculpture, in architecture, in vase drawing and painting, in writing, in legislation, in the Orphic mysteries, and in Ionic naturalistic philosophy. Restricting our survey to these areas, let us briefly examine the principal features and their changes, for it is here—in Greece during these centuries—that our world came into being, our world which is now perhaps coming to a close. Anyone who perceives the end and shares in its agonies should know of the beginning.

Three characteristics are evident from the Greek sculpture of the period (we are speaking here chiefly of the seventh and sixth centuries B.C.). First there is an awakening sense of the human body expressed in this sculpture, which forms a precondition of the later conscious realization of space. Second, there is the so-called archaic smile, a mysterious smile still remote from pain and joy, but reflecting the awakening and dawn of the emergent radiant human countenance. And third, there is the gradual appearance of the free and clear forehead, which, in the earliest sculpture, is covered by artfully plaited hair almost down to the eyebrows—a protection, as it were, of the still dreaming forehead. Even today, this forehead, unawakened from dream with hair loosely combed over it, can be seen among male peasants in the Balkan regions and in Spain, and even more universally in Latin America and the Far East.

But as early as the sixth century, and definitely by the time of Praxiteles, the forehead had emerged unrestricted, clear, and awake; the sleep [Schlaf] of the temples [Schläfen] is no longer protected by the natural fullness of hair. This awakening to the human countenance—and it is exclusively the human countenance and no longer the image of a divinity that is being shaped—is surely one of the most moving events of man, particularly as it is carried out in silence. Step by step, agony after agony, the emergence of consciousness, this awakening-to-himself, can be discerned in man's countenance.

It could only have been to such a countenance that Thales of Miletus turned at the beginning of the sixth century—Thales, last of the Seven Sages of early Greece and first of the Ionic natural philosophers—to have his exhortation inscribed on the temple of Apollo in Delphi. The lapidary sentence gracing the temple of the sun god, itself a manifestly spatial articulation of singing columns and stones, even today has lost none of its validity: gnothi seauton, "Know thyself."

These two words inscribed on the sun temple have yet another significance. Since time immemorial man had written either from top to bottom, as to some extent in China even today, or from right to left, as for example in the Islamic countries. But this exhortation to emergent consciousness, "Know thyself," is written from left to right. If, as we might say, the first manner of writing connects the heavens with the earth, and the second repeatedly turns the vital connection towards the left, the unconscious and past side, we find here for the first time—under the auspices of the wakeful god—the motion toward consciousness emergence, a movement commensurate with the sense of the words themselves.

Thus, even this "minor detail," otherwise merely considered a curiosity, has its sense; and let us not forget what it means to grant a phenomenon sense or significance—it is to give it direction. This is expressed in German even today in the locution Im Uhrzeigersinn, that is, "clockwise"; but it is even more emphatic in other European languages, such as French, where *sens* has the dual meaning of "sense" and "direction," and the same holds true of English, Italian, and Spanish.

In this connection we should return to the question of our repeated use of the word "direct" (*richten*). Since ancient times, the left side has stood for the side of the unconscious or the unknown; the right side, by contrast, has represented the side of consciousness and wakefulness. The degree to which this valuation has been reinforced over the years is evident from the fact that in the present-day European languages "right" does not mean simply "to the right" or "the right side" but also "correct" and "direct," in the sense of leading toward a goal; French *droit* and *à la droite*, Spanish *derecho* and *a la derecha*, and even Greek *orthos* are all further evidence of this. It is also evident here that law or jurisprudence (*Recht* in German), as well as the administration of justice (*Rechtsprechung*), are, in this sense, exclusively "directing" acts—acts of consciousness unilaterally dependent on waking, mental consciousness, a fact apparently overlooked until now by the "Philosophy of Right." Wherever we find "rights" and the first intimations of a formalized legal code, an act is taking place that can only be brought about via an awakened consciousness.

"In this sense" the law of Moses is more than the mere handing down of laws; and in Greece it is Lycurgus who establishes the austere laws of Sparta, and later Solon who enacted his legal code in Athens. A natural concomitant—natural if we remember that the right side represents the masculine as well as the wakeful principle—is the emphasis on the paternal aspect inherent in every legislation and act of judgement. The directed words over the temple in Delphi are under the protection of Apollo; Mosaic law under that of God the Father. Moses and Lycurgus open the age of patriarchy; matriarchy—the sheltered world protected by darkness—is supplanted by being exposed in wakefulness. From this moment on, *man had to direct and judge himself*; herein lies the almost superhuman grandeur of the age that became a reality around 500 B.C. in Greece via the mutation to the mental structure.

We have already alluded to the fact that these events correspond to a law of the earth; and since we are about to digress, let us first mention that reply which the shade of Enkidu brings to Gilgamesh from the realm of the dead as recorded at the close of the Gilgamesh epic.[116] "Speak, my friend, speak! Tell me the law of the earth which you have seen!" pleads Gilgamesh, as he addresses the shade of his departed friend. The reply: "My friend, I cannot tell you, for if I proclaimed to you the law of the earth which I have seen, you would sit and weep."

This law of the earth inexorably comes to pass, but this should not be cause for anxiety or fantasies of impending doom; only those who permit themselves the injustice of surrendering to the earth, from which they should have disengaged themselves via the magic structure, will perish in the maelstrom of blind anxiety. The words "law of the earth" are in any event an appeal to us so that we may correctly perceive the event or events, and with this, to see how the earthly law is fulfilled. This law of the earth becomes clearly evident within the space of about five hundred years between the age of Moses and that of Lycurgus. It is evident in the simultaneous formation of the sun mythologeme in both China and Greece, and the simultaneous appearance of wrath as a consciousness-awakening power in both India and Greece, setting the direction of the two great accounts, the *Bhagavadgita* and the *Iliad*.

But there are further parallels: In China, Confucius introduces patriarchy only slightly later than Lycurgus in Greece; and, at almost the same time, Chuang-tzu in

China and Sophocles in Greece are formulating their respective statements relating to life and dreams and reflecting the awakening from the mythical structure (see above p. 72f.). And in Persia, Zarathustra asserts the dualism which, although differing from the Platonic and Manichean, underlies Parmenides' notion of a Being opposed to Non-Being; and this is ultimately an insoluble problem, as it is an incomplete attempt undertaken from a too close proximity to myth, and an insufficient detachment from the mythical world. Parmenides' Non-Being is essentially measureless and spaceless, that is, mythical, whereas his notion of Being is emphatically spatial: an incipient mental, measuring *concept*.

But to return to our discussion: the most famous code of laws in India, the *Mānava-Dharmasāstra*, whose authorship is attributed in legend to the divine protoman Manu, contains a law forbidding the Pariahs to write from left to right.[117] Every prohibition, however, particularly when it prevents the fulfillment of what we called the law of the earth, is also subject to this law, although it seems to contradict it. And like every prohibition, this one fulfills its significance because it restrains and intensifies tendencies that once they have become self-secure and thus directable, ultimately effect their breakthrough and consequent detachment from their chaotic origins.

Such an alteration of direction, or more accurately, appearance of direction (only a turn toward the right is a di*rec*tion) is evident in a vase drawing to which we have already called attention (Fig. 20, p. 64). And the more this emphasis on the right breaks forth—as in the legal directions of Lycurgus, the direction of writing, in the upright positioning of columns, in the directive, "Know thyself"—the lighter the background becomes in the vase decoration of these centuries, until the figures depicted are completely removed from their undirected amalgamation with the ground and are placed against a monochromatic backdrop. From the seventh to the fifth centuries, all instances of Greek vase painting bear witness to this process which culminates in the first style of representation suggestive of space and perspective, which are realized only much later.[118] We can discern intimations of this perspective both in the "Odyssey landscapes" in the Esquiline area from the first century B.C., and in the murals and frescoes of Pompeii spoken of earlier (p. 11).

But before turning to this question of space, a question of decisive significance to an understanding of the mental structure, we should once again descend to the fathomless depths of spacelessness; for only if we are able to trace the emergence and extrication from the psychic spacelessness of the mythical structure will we "understand" it and be able to recognize the actual significance of this supersession of the spaceless.

The relationship between discursive, directed thought, emergent consciousness, and space is, we would hope, by now evident, above and beyond the fact that space can exist only where there is the possibility of directing and direction—a consideration previously overlooked. The process of divesting the residua of spacelessness was notably strengthened by the "Dionysia" and "Lenaea," as they are sometimes called, which took place in Athens ever since the sixth century B.C. In these celebrations, besides the frenzied release of the remaining vestiges of darkness via dance and drinking, a certain disenchantment was effected; and there the drama came into being. The word "drama" means "a thing done" or "performed," but this refers to the ritual presentation to Dionysus and not to the work of art embodied by the drama. In such drama, the chorus stood *in opposition*, as it were, to the individual performers, criticizing or explaining their actions.

This means that in the drama we have an *individual* who acts in contrast to a "common psyche" and distinct from it, even where he is acting in the name of the god; even the leader of the *choros* was depersonalized by having to wear a mask. Only the individual was a *persona*, one "sounded through," one through whom the god sounded; *per-sonare* means "to sound through." This derivation is a conjecture, but one which had currency even in antiquity; this presumably Etruscan word *persona* was most likely etymologically related to Greek *prosopon*, "mask."[119]

The origin of our word "person" in the sense of "an individual" from the word for "mask" is, however, of utmost importance if we are to understand the implication of today's lack of mask, particularly if we accept the thesis of J. Gregor that the mask is to be considered a "phenomenon apart from time and space."[120] In any event, we can see in the mask a vestige of magic: magic because of its spacelessness and timelessness, but vestigial as early as the Greek theater where the performer wearing the mask is placed in opposition to the chorus. The performer was called a *Hypokrites*, which meant essentially "the responder"; and in the early Greek period he co-responds mythically, as the responding individual soul, to the common soul and forms its reciprocal pole. He re-sponds or reciprocates the words of the chorus, subsuming it and establishing the polar equilibrium and polar complement.

But even in tragedy this process undergoes a change. The performer is no longer a "responder" in the mythical sense; rather, as an individual (one becoming conscious), he represents the opposite or antithesis of the chorus (the "unconscious"). The mask as an expression of magic egolessness gives way to the mask in our modern sense which depersonalizes or obscures the true ego: the ego concealed "behind" it in the newly acquired dimension of depth, which is as inaccessible to the magic structure as a spatial "behind."

In this connection we should mention to what extent the magic component appears in the very structure of the theater; it is visible in the earliest form of the theater which, not without justification, has been defined as a stone shell or conch. But the ear, too, is conchoidal; and this acoustic-labyrinthine magic emphasis is the basis for all theater.

Yet this magic root is enriched on the one hand by mythical polarity, and on the other by the directedness of the mind. The mythical element is expressed in the polarity created by the (passive) spectators and the (active) performers; the mental element is expressed by the mental direction of the dramatic action that results in spectators and performers, those acted upon and those acting, becoming involved in the same expectation of a goal or end despite their opposing attitudes.

True theater, like all genuine representational forms of man, is a cross-section of at least three structures; and like every other expressive form, it becomes spurious and consequently inhuman whenever one of the structures is overprominent. A one-sided overemphasis is not commensurate with our present-day consciousness structure and represents, accordingly, a falsification. The roots of the frequent falsifications today are already present in the ancient theater, where the polarity was transformed into a duality which in turn leads to rational isolation.

Nonetheless, it was this same theater in which the shift of emphasis resulting from mutation took shape that gradually displaced the importance of the chorus in favor of the individual. And this meant that man stepped out of the shelter of the group which previously surrounded and protected him like a cave. This group spirit attains a kind of awareness of itself for the first time in the Greek chorus, where it became voice and word. Stated differently, the self-contained group began to express itself, to press its inherence outward; it began to act and separate, and in this separation placed the ego outside of itself.[121]

This brought about a further stabilization of the mental structure. The actual awakening to the mental consciousness took place in the Dionysia. There, under the patronage of the male god, the process of integration was completed: the emergent consciousness of its polarity initiated by *menis* which made possible directed thinking. And we would note that this process can only be represented as integrative if we observe it (as we are) from the standpoint of the mental structure, that is, in retrospect. Viewed from the archaic structure, it may seem to be a process of disintegration and dissolution; the psyche relinquished its polar incontestability, its certainty, and undiminished effectivity when its dominance was displaced by mental thought.

But when we observe this process in retrospect, as a process of integrating the consciousness, we shed light on one of the most obscure utterances of Heraclitus, the "obscure thinker": *outos de Haides kai Dionusos, hoteoi mainontai kai lenaisousin* ("Hades and Dionysus are one and the same, for whom they rage and celebrate their Lenaea").[122] These Dionysia are not at all what the Klages' circle makes them out to be; their interpretation merely demonstrates their own metabolist lack of character. They maintain that this Dionysian movement in Greece was a return to the "undercurrent of life" from "spirituality"; it was in fact precisely the reverse.[123] It is the disengagement from this primal ground of life and soul, as evident in the statement about the polar character of Dionysus being also Hades. This is the reason why frenzy, where "they rage" (the verb is the not unfamiliar *mainomai*, with the root *ma:me*) and drama, the formed and directed action, occur and unfold together in the Dionysian rites, complementing and creating the awareness of each other.

A similar process must have taken place in the Orphic mysteries, as evidenced by the *lamellae orphicae* or "Orphic tablets" found in graves of the cities Thurioi and Petelia (southern Italy), as well as in Eleutherniae (Crete). These date from the fifth to the fourth centuries B.C., a time when the Pythagorean mystic communities connected with Eleusis were flourishing. The tablets reveal in words the meaning of the great secret sign of the Pythagorean mystery, the Greek letter "Y" or ypsilon;[124] it is the image of conscious and knowing decision, of distinguishing thought. It is the symbol for the situation expressed by "the choice of Hercules" or "Hercules at the parting of the ways"; in abstract form it captures the essence of the mental structure, the conscious differentiation of the duality of left and right. Hercules correctly took the right path.

It was this knowledge which was given to initiates of the mystic cult in the form of "unspoken words" (*aporreta*) whispered into their ear that was engraved on these gold tablets for the departed mystics as a kind of passport to the realm of the dead. Among others, there are inscriptions as: "There in the realm of Hades you will find on your left a spring, and nearby a white cypress; be careful not to approach it. There you will also find a second source with cold water flowing from the lake of memory. To the watchmen guarding it you should say: 'I am the son of the earth and the starry sky.' "

All of these aspects—the secret knowledge; the relation to the watchmen, i.e., the wakemen (watch=wakefulness) who are guarding a primordial faculty of consciousness, memory (the Greek verbs for "remember," as in English, clearly show the root *ma:me: mimnesko* and *memnemai*); and the distinguishing between left and right, a result of knowing the terrestrial-celestial, psychic-polar relationship of man—all of this is expressed in yet a further sentence of the *lamellae*: "If your psyche departs the light of the sun, go to your right as befits the wise man. Rejoice, rejoice! Go to your right. . . . "[125]

This emphasis on the right is also expressed in Pythagoras' precept: "Enter the sanctuary on the right side, and remove first the right shoe,"[126] which places the accent of the initial act on the side of conscious emphasis. Corresponding to this awareness, the speeches in Plato's *Symposium* celebrating Eros make their rounds to the right,[127] an act commensurate with the nature of Eros since he represents consciously emerging intention (and consequently directedness). The *Symposium*, however, already belongs to the realm of the awakened mental consciousness; the *lamellae*, by comparison, still reflect processes indicative of the awakening of this mental consciousness.

Even though these processes are still clothed in myth or mystery, it is no longer merely the pictorial or imaginative element of the mythical structure which suffuses them but rather the outline of thought and directed conceptualization which they reveal. The difficulties against which conceptualization struggled are more intelligible if we recall the psychic and vital profusion inherent in every word at that time;[128] each word was the flaring up of an aspect of the psyche and the visible psychic reality which, undifferentiated, includes the one or the other aspect of the same word as a kind of sympathetic vibration. This wealth of connotation in each word, which to us appears like an irritating hyper-fertility where even the unspoken aspect is conveyed, posed nearly insurmountable difficulties of expression to early philosophical attempts.

This is most clearly evident if we examine the surviving texts of the earliest natural philosophy, that of the Ionian school, of which Parmenides' theory of Being is an eloquent example.[129] It required centuries to sufficiently devitalize and demythologize the word so that it was able to express distinct concepts freed from the wealth of imagery, as well as to reach the rationalistic extreme where the word, once a power and later an image, was degraded to a mere formula.

Let us observe for a moment Parmenides, and especially his pupil, Zeno, who defended the ontology of his teacher in Athens around 450 B.C. What is the result of this defense? The conception of Being attendant upon thought includes also the question of space. W. Capelle entitles a summary of these fragments of Zeno "Zeno's comprehension of being as only spatially extended being";[130] but the decisive fact is that space assumes form in conceptual thought and philosophical statement and formulation. And it was Zeno who was instrumental in this in Athens around 450 B.C.

This far-reaching and extremely complex question as to the connection between thinking, being, and space—which could expose several considerations of present-day existential philosophism as mere pretention since they have "fallen for" mere empty formalism (and "fallen" in more than one sense)—led Zeno to those arguments that mark him as being the first relativist. They prompt him to the incisive formulations that give rise to dialectics, which in turn lead via Socrates to logic just one generation later; and with logic, we step out into the clarity of thought where we can breathe freely after having been only too long devoted to magic darkness and mythical twilight.

To be sure, we cannot yet speak of complete mental clarity at the moment when Plato becomes a pupil of Socrates and makes his indelible impression on the Athenian Academy. Clarity is where there is no further search; yet it is precisely this search for truth which supplants truth itself that was characteristic of Socrates and even of Pythagoras. One of Plato's maxims derives from Pythagoras, the first "measurer" of Western civilization. (He was not only the first geometer, but notably the first to establish the connection between magic sounds and mental visibility and enumeration by measuring tones on the monochord. This is the origin of the theory of harmonics which is being revived today.[131])

The maxim which Plato ostensibly inscribed over his door reads: *Medeis ageometretos eisito mou ten stegen*, "No one unversed in geometry shall enter." In order to estimate or adjudge something, we must be able to measure it; and more particularly: whoever would gain patriarchal supremacy over the mother and mentally establish man, that is, the human being, as the measure, must be able to measure the earth; geometry is, after all, "earth measurement."[132]

Here we find the clear and still qualitative expression of that relationship between man, discovering his mentality and the earth, a relationship which has reversed itself since the definitive victory of the deficient mental, that is, rational structure (around 1790). Since that time, the primacy has passed from man back to the earth; it is the earth's red which glows on the revolutionary flags. Having once ordered the chaotic mass and detached himself from it—a process mirrored by the image of the human head on ancient coins—the individual now threatens to resubmerge into it.

In the mythical structure, the form of expression was the mythologeme; in the mental structure, it is the philosopheme. But while the mythologeme has universal validity, each philosopheme has merely an individual or specific validity. The proliferation of philosophical systems is accompanied by a proportional decrease of mythical elements which survive in weakened form in religion and legend, and in diffuse form in the fairy tale; they disappear almost completely in the saga, after having attained a highly rationalized form.

Yet the first important philosophemes—those of the Ionians and Pythagoreans, as well as those of Heraclitus and even Plato—are still distinguished by their proximity to myth; and we have already spoken of Parmenides' attempt to place the new element, thought, and Being—because it is identified with thought—into opposition with Non-Being. And this Non-Being is definitely a reference to the mythical context whose spacelessness is henceforth mentally defined as Non-Being.

This transition from the mythical form of utterance to the mental form of thinking, a process that can be clearly demonstrated merely on the basis of Heraclitus, Plato, and Aristotle, will be examined in detail in Part I, Chapter 7, sections 3 and 4; for the moment, then, let this reference suffice. The same is true of the space-time question, to which we will return in Part I, Chapter 5, although the one-sided spatial and dualistic emphasis in the deliberations of Parmenides is already evident here. We will return to these questions since it is necessary to examine carefully the earlier modes of thought and statements on time and space if we are to make evident the foundations of the aperspectival world.

The question remains as to what took place in the interval between the two "spans" of some two hundred years each, the period of Pythagoras and Aristotle (ca. 550-350 B.C.) and the time of Petrarch and Leonardo da Vinci (ca. 1300-1500 A.D.), for there is an underlying correspondence between both epochs. We hope that the reader will not be unduly unsettled by our temporal demarcations, which are merely intended to establish some order and will have to be extended in both directions. As far as they go, such contrived limits are merely an aid to assist our synoptic view. In the present instance the interconnections extend well beyond the two periods, as will be evident later in our discussion when we note the links between Zeno and Einstein, between Plutarch and modern psychology, and between the Ionic School, Herodotus, Plato and St. Augustine. The reason for this close affinity is partly a result of the decisive stamp made on the centuries after Christ by both Greek epistemology and especially by the Jewish doctrine of salvation, in which the consolidation of the ego, already apparent, was further strengthened by Roman law and the use of Latin, a language less ambiguous and more directive than Greek.

However, before turning our attention to the so-called *rinascimento* of antiquity—which was in fact less a *rinascere*, a rebirth, than a *riannodare* or *riannodamento*, a reconnection with the characteristic inceptive manifestations of the mental structure—we should first take note of several essential traits of the mental structure.

The directedness inherent in the mental structure, which around 1500 gave rise as a measure of its "sense" and "right" sequence (i.e., logically and consequently) to perspective as the distinctive mark of our perspectival world and initiated its sectoring, its specialization, and ultimately its spatialization, bore from the beginning the one-sidedness that embodies the greatness as well as the ominousness of this structure. The one-sidedness is to be found in the *identification of rightness with directionality and judgement.*

It is true that this identification greatly strengthens everything pertaining to the conscious, i.e., everything measurable or moderated by consciousness, but it takes place at the expense of what we call the unconscious: the immeasurable and immoderate. The unmeasured and autonoetic, that is, self-thinking world of mythical images has no place in the world measured and thought by man; at best, it is assigned a place in opposition, for there is no bridge to the inestimable in the world of measuring thought; in terms of measurement, it does not exist, or at the very most it exists as "Non-Being."

Moreover, the thinking man turns away entirely from the past and is supported in this by religion with its notion of redemption: religion, which in faith or belief furnishes the last remaining tie to the world of the immeasurable and irrational, is in consequence placed in dualistic opposition to knowledge. To the thinking person, the past exists only to the extent that he can measure it or fix its outlines with dates. As for himself, he one-sidedly sets his sights on the future, particularly as he thinks—from his anthropomorphic attitude—that he can shape this temporal sector at will, as if it were dependent on him. In view of the one-sidedness, this error of judgement is unavoidable. Furthermore, there is the extensive web of relationships linking the mental structure with the magic, which in our day is visibly breaking through in its deficient form and is evident in the conviction of present-day man that he is the maker of the future.

The partial negation of the past—the extent that is unmeasurable—, a result of the directedness striving toward the future for its own sake, is one of many dualistic manifestations of the mental structure. Duality is characteristic of this structure to the same extent that polarity is a hallmark of the mythical structure. But duality differs in one essential respect from polarity: in polarity, correspondences are valid. Every correspondence is a complement, a completion of the whole. Whatever is spoken is corroborated by the invisible and latent unspoken to which it corresponds; in the polar, unperspectival world of the mythical structure, both the voice (*die Stimme*) and the muteness (*das Stumme*), appropriate to myth—what is spoken and what is left unsaid—are correspondences and complements to each other. They suspend and supersede the polarity, returning it to near-integrality, to an identity that nonetheless remains diminished, since its archaic authenticity seems to be irrecoverable; it is a re-completed, not a complete, identity.

Despite this fact, a profound system of relationships is expressed in this identity between the archaic and the mythical structures, like that existing between the magic and the mental structures. But with respect to duality, we cannot speak of correspondence or complementarity as we could in the case of polarity; in the mental realm, we can never "speak of something," but only determine something or conceive of it. *Duality is the mental splitting and tearing apart of polarity*, and, from the correspondences of polarity, duality abstracts and quantifies the oppositions or antitheses. Whereas there is a totality, even though deficient, which can be recompleted in the form of complementarity within the mythical structure, from duality only a deficient, because unstable, form of unity can be realized as the unification of opposites in a third aspect.

Here we encounter again the relation of the mental to the magic structure, inasmuch as the mediating or reconciling (*versöhnend!*) third aspect aspires to a *unification*. This unstable form of unity is expressed by the fact that the antitheses or contraries are only able to beget a third element in a temporary for-better-or-worse union, a *tertium* which is again separated at the moment of its birth. Accordingly, it does not represent a new unity but merely a quantity that becomes dependent on its antithesis or opposite, with which it in turn creates once more a momentarily unifying *tertium*. In this we see a further characteristic of our civilization: quantification— for the unification or synthesis via a third element can never be completed in time, only in the moment. The third element, freeing itself, becomes the procreator and carrier of one of the contraries able to engender a new unification and synthesis.

Viewed as to creativity (and not from a religious standpoint), we can say that consciousness of the Son, the creative trinity, proceeds from dualism; and that the most valid form of this is the birth of the Son of Man. With this are given both he-who-is-to-come [*der Zukünftige*] and everything of the future [*die Zukunft*]. This is most clearly expressed in the aversion to the past which begins thereafter, the renunciation of ancestor worship in favor of worship of the child of Bethlehem; ancestors are always those of the past, while the child represents those who are coming, those of the future. Seen as speculation, we could say that the speculative trinity proceeds from dualism and is expressed in what we shall later call triangular or pyramidal thinking when we discuss forms of thought; and such pyramidal thinking, which is characteristic of Plato, has its most trenchant expression in the Hegelian axiom of thesis, antithesis, and synthesis (see below p. 257).

Although Hegel's axiom represents the rationalistic form of trinity, and therefore can be mentioned in the same breath with the mental Christian Trinity only with reservations, we must still emphasize that the mental trinitary form is not to be confused with pre-mental ternary forms. Stated differently: there is a fundamental distinction between triadicity and triunity; that is, between trias and trinity. Only the trinity has mental character; the unification of previously polar elements does not take place as in the mythical structure, but must employ the "third" element to effect the union.

Accordingly, trinity or triunity must not be confused with the trias which is in evidence in early, supposedly religious conceptions. The trias must be considered to be chiefly a ternary preform of the trinity. All ternary forms are distinguishable by the basically free interchangeability of their three elements, and by their ability to exist independently as whole principles (as the Hindu Trimurti) despite their homogeneity. The repeated depictions of three-headed divinities in pre-Christian "re-ligions" furnish vivid examples of this.[133]

There is yet a further basic distinction; our conjecture is that ternary forms are predominantly lunar in character, the trinitary forms essentially solar. The solar nature of the trinitary forms should be readily evident, while the lunar character of ternary forms is exemplified by the trident of Poseidon and the three-horse chariot of Dais (see below p. 175f.), as well as by the three phases of the nocturnal moon presumably reflected in the trias.

In this distinction it is important to stress that we are not advocating a one-sided naturalistic interpretation of the symbolism; the naturalistic aspect of the symbol is always one among several, for the full extent of any symbolic expression cannot be plumbed merely by a naturalistic simile. This is true particularly as we can assume, although we do not know absolutely, that specific basic forms such as the point, the circle, the triangle, and the square very likely existed before nature, as if these symbols were prethought (or pre-thinking) prototypical patterns visible transiently in the phenomena which they structure (see p. 221). Such "preconception," however, does not require us to conclude that there is a demiurge associated with it, nor that we have to populate the world magically with spirits or sublunar and cosmic entities as carriers or agents of these proto-forms.

Earlier we ascribed the point or dot to the magic structure as being its most characteristic sign because of its evident one-dimensionality and lack of relation to space and time. Similarly, we assigned the circle to the mythical structure because of its polar and planiform nature, which contains the moment of temporicity in the form of expansion or extension, or in the form of the circle reverting upon itself. Since we have done so, it is only logical that we now assign the *triangle* to the three-dimensional structure as its identifying mark. Mental directedness is contingent upon dirigibility, the possibility of direction at an opposing or antithetical object in confrontation. This is a dual relation, one which, however, leads logically to the trinity: the base of the triangle with its two points lying in opposition represents the dual contraries or antinomies which are unified at the point or apex.

Having determined the characteristic attribute of the magic structure to be emotion, and the characteristic attribute of the mythical to be imagination, whereby the emotional attitude corresponds to magic man's relation to nature, the imaginative attitude of mythical man to his relation to the psyche, we now define *abstraction* as being the identifying characteristic of the mental structure. It corresponds to the relation of this structure to man, inasmuch as everything is in relationship to human measuring thought; and this thinking removes man from the impulsive world of emotion, as well as from the imagistic world of the imagination, replacing them with the world of mental thought which inevitably tends toward abstraction.

To what extent the triangle, by being measured or plotted, is a considerably more abstract symbol than either the dot or the circle—and thereby more appropriate to the mental structure—is evident from the fact that it is unknown even today in Chinese symbolism, unlike the circle and the square. The triangle is basically foreign to Chinese culture, which is still today predominantly mythical and best symbolized by the square, whose four points suggest the liberation from the one-point, uniform world of magic. As a symbol of the earth, the square is the terrestrial complement to the circle, the symbol of the sky and the psyche; and the degree to which the circle eludes rational comprehension is evident from the fact that it cannot be measured by rational means unless we employ such immeasurable numbers as π.

The implications of the trinity mentioned above—its tendency toward abstraction, as in the instance of the synthesizing act of thought, or toward quantification, an act which gains continuity only via repetition or reiteration—implications which at first glance seem incompatible, are in fact, a result of duality which measures the opposite and the contrast; a duality which makes the trinity possible at all. Every act of abstraction results from the presence of measuring thought in the ostensible invisibility of what is being calculated, while every quantification results from the presence of measuring thought in the semblance of what is actually measured.[134]

This process is reflected in the reality of our world of thought; the symbol, always inherently polar and imagistic, is reduced to allegory, then to mere formula, as in the formulas of chemistry or physics and even in the formulas of philosophy. In its extreme form of exaggerated abstractness, it is ultimately void of any relation to life and becomes autonomous; empty of content and no longer a sign but only a mental denotation, its effect is predominantly destructive.

The process is also reflected in the reality of our objective world; the duality which destroyed polarity is compelled to bring forth the *tertium* just to assure its dualistic continuity. And this progression from the originally qualitative moment of monotheism, which is subsequently divided into the duality with its quantitative emphasis, merely begets the qualitative third which must be ever created anew; thereafter only what can be enumerated or dealt with statistically is of importance.

It is surely no accident that this turn from qualitative valuation to quantitative judgement took place during the fifteenth century A.D., the period of the formation of perspective. The destruction of the Order of the Knights Templar was most likely carried out because of their resistance to the mere quantification of gold, as they had recognized the last vestiges of the polar effectivity inherent in money, i.e., minted gold, as it was in antiquity. The gold coins kept in the Thesauros, the Greek treasury (which was not a bank but rather a shrine to Zeus and Apollo), were in antiquity effectual symbols of the brightness of solar consciousness; the gold coin was identified with the sun's disk, and the polar unity was reflected in the complementary nature of the two sides.

On these coins were imprinted the thinking heads of the gods, and later those of the rulers.[135] At that time gold still retained its qualitative character that became quantitative following the end of the Knights Templar. That event abetted the process of quantification which has become gradually more pervasive ever since, and the invention of double entry bookkeeping by Luca Pacioli is only one of the milestones in that development. Pacioli, incidentally, was the friend of Piero della Francesca and Leonardo da Vinci, and the panegyrist of perspectivity of whom we spoke earlier.

Apart from the fact that an isolating perspectivation is inherent in every abstraction, and that perspectivation leads to sectorization (whereby the phenomena, be they real in a mental or in a material sense, are not only divided and made measurable, but also quantified by a progressive subdividing and subsectoring), both abstraction and quantification ultimately lead to emptiness, indeed to chaos. At the point where they overstep the clarification appropriate to their nature, they revert metabolistically to the opposite of clarification, where they result in "absolute void" and absolute chaos (and not mere obscurity), as befits their quantitative character. From this particular point on, that is, from hyperdistinctness, either as mental illumination or as the measurable rendering-visible of objects and things, the inexorable downturn into the quantitative mass begins: the gradual decline to where the contentual void—now autonomous—releases those chain reactions incongruous with the earth that engender complete disintegration.[136] This atomizing process does not occur only in the physical reality of atoms, which is only the more tangible form of a process of mental atomization already underway, and whose disintegrative nature is recognizable in the formalistic jargon of pseudo-philosophizing where nothing remains of philosophical language.

Let us, however, return to the starting point of these implications: the observation that the initial directedness of the mental structure includes duality—something essentially distinct from polarity—duality from which the trinity necessarily comes forth.

Earlier we spoke of the creative as well as the speculative trinity, avoiding mention of the dogmatic trinity which belongs to the religious sphere, a form of the trinity with a magic and not a mental emphasis. It is the sole form of the trinity which has been raised by dogma (itself a mental act) to *unity*; and *unity always has an innately magic character*. This magic character is further accentuated by the conception of the creator-god or demiurge who makes or fashions the world (also mentioned by Plato). Here the terrestrial-magic structure (as befits the religious standpoint) is transcendentalized into a cosmic-magical structure. Yet it is of fundamental importance to note that wherever we meet with ternary forms, whether in mythologemes, in the morphology of language, or wherever, they are prototypical and precognitive indications of the possibility of mental consciousness.

We also spoke of the symbol of the mental structure, the triangle, as well as of the essential characteristic of this structure, abstraction and also quantification. We could easily lose sight of the basic subject of our discussion, the emergence of consciousness, if we were here to examine further the dogmatic trinity. The creative trinity, however, is a part of the emergence of consciousness because it renders visible what is to come; the speculative trinity is also a part of the emergence of consciousness because it renders visible "man thinking," by confronting him in what is thought. But more important than these partial manifestations is their effector; and this effector or agent, the bearer of consciousness, is the ego. With this we are fully in the mental structure, the anthropocentric structure where consciousness becomes centered.

We have already encountered this ego that proceeds from the sea voyage, from the integration of the psyche, in "Am Odysseus." The mythological bearer of consciousness was Helios, the sun-god; the attribute, also applied to the Roman emperors (*sol invictus*), later came to be used for Christ;[137] and it was Christ who was the actual bearer of consciousness (and thus empowered to lead the soul). Even today, those who act in his name, particularly the Catholic clergy, stress this essential and salutary hermeneutic aspect; for while the state numbers individuals, the church counts the number of souls. Christ is the first to be immune to the threat of resubmersion and regression into the depths of the soul or psyche, a regression against which Plato constructed the first mental network of philosophy.

Christ's immunity to resubmersion into the psyche is symbolically expressed by his survival of a shipwreck; but he was not carried by the sea onto land as Odysseus had been delivered onto the shores of Phaeaces. (Or are we to think that the "world soul," so to speak, "spit out" Odysseus? This aspect too is visible: the dark side together with the bright aspect indicative of consciousness.) Odysseus, upon awakening, found himself on the rescuing shore; and in this sentence, every word is in its attendant place: Odysseus "found himself"; "Awakening" from sleep, from unconsciousness to consciousness, "on the rescuing shore," on the new brink where, literally, with "firm ground under his feet," he could look back on the sea, the ever-wavering psyche. Only after this finding of himself, only after the sea, the great Heraclitean psyche, had given him up was he able to utter—still deeply moved himself—that word which moves us even today: "am."

Christ survives a shipwreck, however, and is able to *walk on the water*; with this deed he overcomes the depths of chaos and is entitled to say not "I am Christ" but "I am the light of the world." With that declaration the first wholly self-assured resplendence of mankind breaks forth, a resplendence venturing to state for the first time that it will assume the burden of the world's darkness and suffering. It is at this point where the paths of mankind, East and West, are to diverge—although there is in India a mythological parallel of Christ's sovereign deed: one of the designations ascribed to Vishnu is Nârâvayana or, literally, "He who walks on water."[138]

There is little point for us to pursue the magic possibility of something which, from a non-magical standpoint, seems miraculous, for even if the magic reality of this deed had been equally efficacious for Nârâvayana as well as for Christ, Christ's deed was to a great extent divested of its magic character because of his historicity. Of more significance than a clarification of this event in terms of magic is its obvious consciousness-intensifying aspect. The identical deed that prompts Christ to accept suffering via his conscious ego, leads, in Buddhism, to the negation of suffering and to the dissolution of the ego, which, transformed, returns to the original state of immaterial Nirvana. In Buddhism the suspension of sorrow and the Ego is held in esteem; and this suspension of sorrow and suffering is realized by turning away from the world. For Christianity, the goal is to accept the ego, and the acceptance of sorrow and suffering is to be achieved by loving the world. Thus the perilous and difficult path along which the West must proceed is here prefigured, a course which it is following through untold hardship and misery.

Since the strength of the Mediterranean region is diminishing, the region of dominance is shifting further toward the northwest, as once the vital center moved from Mesopotamia and the Nile region to the Greek Islands; and allied with the strength from the regions surrounding the Jordan, this Greek dominance infused new strength into Rome, later moving again to the West in the course of the centuries and culminating in the Frankish kingdom. But here we are speaking already of the European world; and before we return to this perspectival-mental world which we have already portrayed, we must follow those lines which converge in the Patristic Age and effect the last definitive major mutation, that to perspective.

Our subject in this discussion is the history of consciousness emergence, and as such, our task cannot be to provide a history of philosophy, even in outline, suggestive as this thought is if only because the philosopheme is the most important expressive form of the mental structure. In the last analysis, however, it is not so much a question of the various philosophies but rather of the philosopheme itself, a question which we do not intend to avoid.

But first we should address the question of the subject of consciousness as represented in the symbolic liberation from the bondage of the psyche in Christ's walking on the water and its relation to specific sayings of Christ himself. It is not our intention to play the role of exegete and interpret various passages of the New Testament; but we would like to refer to a minor incident on the fringe, as it were, of canonical scripture recorded in the apocryphal passages ascribed to St. John and entitled "St. John and the Partridge."[139]

In this scene, where he rebukes a priest for being annoyed by a partridge running ahead of him, St. John demonstrates his sovereign knowledge of the soul; he says to the annoyed priest: "The partridge, you know, is your own soul." This clarity of insight and knowledge about projection—as we might express it in modern albeit inappropriate terms—bears witness to an extraordinary illumination of consciousness and distancing from the psyche; here is a mental reality able to survey the mythical and psychic reality of symbol. (We will have more to say about birds as symbolic representations of one psychic pole when we examine the symbolism of souls and the spirit.)

This same lucid understanding of psychic processes, which in itself presupposes a considerable degree of wakeful consciousness and ego-centering, comes to the fore repeatedly toward the close of the first century A.D. in the Writing of Plutarch. Plutarch rejects wrath and *menis* on two different occasions, once in one of his longer treatises and once in his "Table Talk."[140] The object of his denunciation, in which he attempts to judge and direct the regressive tendency of his contemporaries toward the instinctual and psychistic, is not the original holy wrath, but anger in its deficient form: the anger which destroys what someone else has ventured to build.

As if this twice-repeated warning were not enough, Plutarch also writes a passage in his *Erotikos* which more than clearly reflects that mental superiority able to judge and direct the psyche, and anticipates the entire theory of projection in modern psychoanalysis. Plutarch writes: "Chrysippos. . . , for example, traces the name of [the god] Ares to *anhairein*, meaning 'to kill,' thereby lending support to those who would call the belligerence in our nature, our quarrelsomeness and irascibility 'Ares.' My father replied: 'Do you then consider Ares to be a god, or one of our emotions?' To this, Pemptides responded that, in his opinion, Ares was a god who formed the irascible and masculine components of our nature."[141]

During the centuries following Plutarch, which were marked by the increasing strengthening of Christianity in the wake of the persecutions, Christianity was forced to defend itself against the last great magic-mythical incursion inundating Rome from the East, as well as against the syncretistic assimilation of deficient mythical and mystical residua. Once again the mental structure detaches itself from the mythical; the result is the new interpretation of the word "religion" that became current in the age of the church fathers. From here on, the word is given an arbitrarily mentalized etymology based on the verb *religare*, "to tie back, constrain." This change reflects the growth of Christian man out of the polar mythical structure characterized by careful observance, or *relegere*.

The capability for such careful observance becomes vestigial because the structure demanding it is no longer dominant. *Relegere* is supplanted by *religare*, the attempt of the church for the next two thousand years to constrain man—or at least his soul—to the archaic-magic-mythical zones which he has for the most part mentally outgrown.[142] Here the demand of faith is created and placed into dualistic opposition to knowledge. This *religio* is the sole attempt to maintain a tradition which was to have duration in the West, and it survived in all probability because the magic element, the element of might, was perhaps too strongly maintained by the church even to the point of bloodshed in its struggle against all other traditional communities. Yet this concern for the constraining bond had its legitimacy, as we can see if we recall that the measuring and experiencing of the psyche that create a distanciation from it are accompanied by a growing knowledge of its nature. But all knowledge is ever in danger of being forgotten, and all distanciation is imperiled by the ever-present possibility of isolation; today, many people have forgotten their heritage, if indeed they have not lost it altogether.

Let us disregard the contributions outside of Europe toward the consolidation of Christianity, i.e., the Syrian and Coptic as well as Celtic and Irish achievements, despite their uncommon interest, and limit ourselves to discussing a figure central to European civilization: St. Augustine who, like St. Paul, his spiritual mainstay via a certain "elective affinity," was a metabolic (not a metabolist) and had experienced more intensely than others the polarity of the psyche; from the *metabole* which he had undergone he remained able to extend his insight into the limitlessness of the psyche. As a convert who not only knew but had experienced the "other side," he was compelled to justify again and again to himself his conversion from Manicheism to Christianity in order to assert his new attitude.

The continual psychic tension evident in his inflamed zeal, again like St. Paul, gave him his tremendous effectiveness—a trait common to all true metabolics. The enormous expenditure of energy required to maintain the new attitude demands the utmost mental intensity to enable the metabolic to grow out of the psychic *metabole*. Only those compelled to sustain themselves in this way gain converts and form communities; the words that issue forth from the anguish of the heart to fortify oneself also strengthen the hearts of the listeners.[143]

Augustine was the first to clearly perceive the relation of the soul or psyche to time. Since we will return to the question of this relation to time, we shall confine our remarks here to determining what made Augustine and his unique achievement the focal point of the Patristic Age where the inceptual rays of consciousness from past ages converged and radiated forth to the following generations.

In Augustine the three major components of our civilization come together: the Greek, the Judaic, and the Latin. Though an African, Augustine was native to the Latin tradition and was instrumental in ultimately fusing the two "monologies" into a Christian realization: Judaic monotheism, with its doctrine of an "other worldly" god, and the monistic one-element theory of origin, held by Ionian natural philosophy. This fusion is the ultimate source of the expanded dualism later driven by Descartes and the Enlightenment into its most radical form in the diametrical opposition of "spirit" and "matter."

It should be noted that the elemental theory of the Ionic School was decidedly monistic, inasmuch as these first philosophers derived the origin of the world from *one* single element: for Thales of Miletus the primordial element was water; for Anaximenes it was air; and for Heraclitus fire. The directed line of thought imputes origin to a single (terrestrial) element, one moreover with a distinctly numinous character; and it is not merely fortuitous that this word "element" contains in its Latin form the root *ma:me*.

In the monotheism of Mosaic law, the origin is numinously directed to a single god, who also has a certain "this worldly" character, as he is placed into a dualistic opposition to his antagonist Satan in later Christian teaching. And while the basic Ionic concept contains in its Latin form the root *ma:me*, the initial Hebrew concept in its Greek form in the word *monos*, "the monarch," i.e., the sole ruler, has yet a further polar undertone corresponding to its religious moment; the root of *monos* is the proto-Indo-European root *me/mo*. We have therefore in two respects a synthesis of faith (to the extent that it is a psychic-mythical tie or restraint) and mental knowledge brought about in Christianity by Rome and the use of the Latin language.

Nonetheless, no synthesis has duration; it must be created ever-anew. From this compunction to re-create there is a natural progression to a culminating point, a more definite directedness and fixity which lead first to Petrarch's discovery of landscape (in which Augustine had an important role), then to perspective, and ultimately to perspectivity.

With this we have arrived at the starting point of our initial informational remarks about the perspectival world. However, we have yet to discuss the *riannodamento* and how the perspectival inceptions of antiquity established a connection with the Renaissance, from whence their problematic sectorial-perspectivistic constriction and limitation resulted. We will limit ourselves to mentioning only a few names since we have previously alluded to some of the many representatives.

There is, for example, the lyric monologue first employed by Sappho which does not recur until Dante's *Vita nuova* and the songs of the Minnesingers, where (it goes without saying) it reappears in a different form against a different background, as we have tried to indicate. There is the notion of Pythagoras that the earth is a sphere, an idea which had currency among the Greek philosophers from Aristarchus to Aristotle, and is re-thought by Copernicus (Thales, it will be remembered, held the view that the earth was a disk floating on the primordial waters, that is, within the context of mythical symbol, a view still maintained today among the Jainists[144]). The dissection of the brain and the human body begun by Alkmaion was continued in the anatomical studies of Vesalius. Euclid's geometry, constructed in planes, was spatialized through the discovery of perspective.

This perspective—to continue our enumeration—first suggested by a vaguely spatial sense evident in Greek vase painting of the fifth century B.C., and further developed from the merely landscape-depictive intent of the Esquiline landscapes from the *Odyssey* to the actual attempts at a spatial perspective in the Pompeian murals, culminated in the achievement of Leonardo da Vinci. Plato, the first great consistent dualist, is surpassed in this respect by Augustine. Aristotle (and in his wake the major significance of Islam to which we have only alluded) is interpreted anew and elaborated by Albertus Magnus and St. Thomas Aquinas in Paris; and, together with Augustine, they laid the foundations of a Christian Renaissance. Historiography, which had begun with Herodotus, evolves a directed and secured Christian awareness on the basis of historical Christianity and its roots in the Judaic history of the prophet Amos (again Augustine is instrumental in this development). And Augustine wrote his personal *Confessions*, unlike Plato with his biographical epistles whose authenticity is once again being questioned.[145] But the most imposing arch— is it perhaps the link from a beginning to an end?—spans the distance between Zeno and Einstein, between the first design of relativity and its realization in our day.[146] And in this enumeration we have not even named the Atomists, the Sophists, and countless others.[147]

This completes our attempt to indicate the connections between the period of Pythagoras and Aristotle and that of Petrarch and Leonardo. Leonardo's development of perspective with its emphatic spatialization of man's image of the world marks the beginning of the deficient phase of the mental structure. We have already defined it as the phase characterized by *ratio*; and while the word pair *menis:menos* at the outset of the mental consciousness structure had a definitely qualitative accent, the word *ratio* is definitely quantitative. Whereas the Greek world of the classic period is a world of measure and moderation *par excellence*, the late European world and particularly its derivative cultures, the American and the Russian, are worlds of immoderation.

We noted earlier a deficient form within the magic structure analogous to this rational phase of the mental structure: spell-casting still retains the character of moderation, while witchcraft or sorcery is immoderate and unmeasured. Just as spell-casting directs nature—and man's organic nature consists, after all, of directed organic functions justly able to support the spell-caster out of his own substance—so too *menis* directs *menos*, or thinking. And just as sorcery in immoderation oversteps the established limits of mere spell-binding, employing extraneous means and foreign substances to attain its ends, the *ratio* immoderately oversteps the bounds of measured direction and moderation which *menis* and *menos* have established, "rationing," that is, dividing and dissecting everything and using extrinsic and extraneous substances to attain its purposes.

The very act of setting aims or purposes emphasizes the negative effect of these two deficient forms of the magic and mental structures; every set purpose is always charged with might and is, moreover, emphatically self-serving. Thus it is the very antithesis of the wholeness of the world. Here we can discern the reason that both of these deficient forms, witchcraft and ratiocination, or intellectualizing, which substitute ritual or organization for the organic processes, can be regarded as demonic forces. The connection is already evident in the root of the Greek word *daimon*, da-, which in its Sanskrit form in the word *dayate* means "he divides or severs." The cognate Greek verb *daiomai* means in fact not merely "to divide," but "to split apart, dissect, tear asunder, mangle."[148]

But let us return to the question of perspective. If we draw upon the main implications of our discussion (in Chapter 2 above, as well as in our intervening survey), we can see how the negative aspect of the mental structure begins to emerge with the Renaissance. This emphasis of the negative is not our personal, emotionally-charged reaction, but merely an objective assessment of what is implicit in the nature of the mental. Nor have we forgotten that the mental is still a psychic function, despite its partial emancipation from the psyche.

Every emancipation, for that matter, is a process threatened by a latent perspectivization and sectorization; these become acute whenever the emancipation is deficient; that is, when it does not merely aspire to a re-arrangement or an equalization of emphasis, but to dominance or predominance. The degree of slackness or tautness of the bonds between the psyche and the mind depends on the intensity of the mind; as long as the mind moderates and directs the psyche, the psyche is to a certain extent dependent on it. But whenever the mind in its intellectualized form loses its moderating ability and is dispersed without direction, the relationship is reversed: the negative aspect of the psyche imperceptibly gains dominance over the rational. Because the potentiality of the mental world grew out of the mythical world with its psychic emphasis, it necessarily evidences the dual aspect of everything psychic as a latency within itself, if only in the diminished and mentalized form of duality.

By mentioning the term "duality" we again focus on one of the consequences of perspective, and in the present instance on a dualism that is considerably stronger than the dualism of the earlier centuries. Then it was still in flux whereas now it is uncompromisingly fixed. Perspective fixes the observer as well as the observed: it fixes man on the one hand, and the world on the other. Compelled to emphasize his ego ever more strongly because of the isolating fixity, man faces the world in hostile confrontation. The world in turn reinforces this confrontation by taking on an ever-increasing spatial volume or extent (as in the discovery of America), which the growing strength of the ego attempts to conquer. This strengthening of the ego (which later culminates in its hypertrophy) is revealed in the sense of self-importance manifested by the *condottiere*, the Renaissance man, as well as in the many diaries which were then very much in vogue.

This dualistic opposition of contraries, whose positive aspect is the concretion of man as well as of space, includes at the same time the negative component recognizable in the fixity and sectorization. The fixity led to isolation, the sectorization to amassment. These developments are the conclusion of a process in our day that was already prefigured as a negative possibility in the very beginnings of the mental structure. Its roots can be traced to the inadequacy of the synthesis of duality, an inadequacy manifest in abstraction and quantification. As long as the moderating quality of the mental consciousness was still effective, abstraction and quantification were only latently capable of negative effects. But when moderation was displaced by the immoderation of the *ratio*, a change most clearly evident in Descartes, abstraction began to transform itself into its extreme form of manifestation (best defined by the concept of isolation), while the identical process led from quantification to amassment and agglomeration.

These consequences of the perspectivization of the world evident in the isolation and mass-phenomena of our day are patently characteristic of our time. Isolation is visible everywhere: isolation of individuals, of entire nations and continents; isolation in the physical realm in the form of tuberculosis, in the political in the form of ideological or monopolistic dictatorship, in every-day life in the form of immoderate, "busy" activity devoid of any sense-direction or relationship to the world as a whole; isolation in thinking in the form of the deceptive dazzle of premature judgements or hypertrophied abstraction devoid of any connection with the world. And it is the same with mass-phenomena: overproduction, inflation, the proliferation of political parties, rampant technology, atomization in all forms.

All of these consequences are sufficiently obvious as to absolve us from the effort of adducing further examples. Yet it is eminently worthwhile to inquire as to what sustained or reinforced the "development" over the past four centuries which led to these results. And to this we have indirectly furnished an answer: it can be found in the notion of technology that brought about the age of the machine with the aid of perspectival, technical drafting; in the notion of progress that spawned the "age of progress"; and in the radical rationalism that, as we are surely justified in saying, summoned the "age of the world wars."

Some readers may be dismayed that we have placed immoderation into the context of *ratio* or rationality. But *ratio* must not be interpreted in a perspectivistic sense as "understanding" or "common sense"; *ratio* implies calculation and, in particular, division, an aspect expressed by the concept of "rational numbers" which is used to designate fractions and decimals, i.e., divided whole numbers or parts of a whole. *This dividing aspect inherent in* ratio *and Rationalism—an aspect which has come to be the only valid one—is consistently overlooked, although it is of decisive importance to an assessment of our epoch.*

This is not to pass a judgement, but rather to point out a fact, a fact of perhaps even greater import inasmuch as we do not view the efficient form of the rational structure—the mind or the "mental"—in any sense negatively, and have expressly emphasized its extraordinary qualities and illuminative capabilities. These positive qualities of the mind able to convey illuminative insight into the world are still effectual today, although it would seem that they are distinctly diminished in strength in proportion to the effectivity of the rational. Only the very few summon the courage to speak their own mind and not the rationally circumscribed and mass-produced attitude or viewpoint, against philosophical authorities or popular opinion. It is easy to speak one's own mind only after the particular opinion has become common currency; beforehand it is a distinctly thankless undertaking, unless of course what must be said is plainly visible to the open mind and can be hinted at or suggested. Regrettably, open minds have seemingly become rare in our age of perspectivistic tunnel vision.

The rational phase of the mental structure has not yet come to an end, and its actual end is not yet in sight. None of the structures we have described ever completely "ended." There are still unsuspected, although probably merely one-sided technological and dehumanizing "progressive" developments within the realm of possibility. If the destructive might of such "progress" is not weakened, these developments, according to their degree of autonomy, will automatically fulfill the law of the earth. Depending on various factors, this can require decades or again centuries. If the law of the earth is not yet to be fulfilled, the process of outgrowing and mutation from the old and deficient mental structure will extract or sublimate sufficient energy, strength, substance—or whatever we may call it—so that the structure that is overcome will have no greater destructive effect than, say, the deficient mythical or deficient magic residues in us or in the world.

It is true, of course, that such residua are having greater effect today because the temporal phase in which they are at work is itself deficient. No one should entertain the slightest illusions as to the consequences of this fact. If a new mutation does not take effect—and only a completely new attitude will guarantee the continuation of the earth and mankind, not some sectored partial reforms (reforms are always merely efforts to revive something)—then the consequences of the deficient residua of an age such as ours, which is itself deficient, will soon assume forms, will necessarily assume forms that will make the previous events of our time look like mere child's play. If we are soberly prepared for this, then there is nothing terrifying about it; it will be terrifying only to those who feel threatened, and they will be the ones affected.

With reference to the subject of this section we should like to discuss in conclusion the three most familiar definitions or statements on thought and thinking. The first, that of Parmenides mentioned above, would seem in philosophical terms to inaugurate the mental consciousness structure; we refer to his sentence: "For thinking and being is one and the same." This statement equates, giving moderation and balance. The other two definitions, which may be considered to initiate the rational phase of mental consciousness, are quite different. The one is by Hobbes and reads: "Thinking is calculation in words." The measuring aspect of thinking, its quality, has been changed to a quantity via the pluralizing inherent in the statement as well as by the numerical "calculation." The third statement, by Descartes, is *Cogito ergo sum*, "I think, therefore I am"; here the isolated thinking by an individual is alone valid, and the spatial Being of Parmenides comes to be identified, as a consequence of thinking, with the being of a person.[149] What takes place here is typical of all "thought processes" that result in extreme abstraction: they denature and invert the genuine interdependencies. The inceptual "am" of Odysseus becomes a result of a faculty of the ego, an ego with the faculty of thinking in addition to its vital and psychic capabilities.

That such statements such as this axiom of Descartes are amenable to various interpretations is demonstrated by the interpretation of Bertrand Russell, which is partly in contradiction to our own. In Russell's view, Descartes' statement is evidence that the mind is more certain than matter. But if we take into account, as Russell does, that *cogito* for Descartes includes also the meaning of one who doubts, understands, conceives, affirms, denies, wills, imagines, and feels ("for feeling, as it occurs in dreams, is a form of thinking"), we still do not eliminate the problem of ambiguity.[150] But if we compare Descartes' axiom with Augustine's query in his *Soliloquia*, "You, who wish to know, do you know that you are? I know it not," we can see that the Cartesian dissociation that we spoke of above is not yet crucial for Augustine. We should also bear in mind that Descartes' sentence represents a reply to Gassendi's *Ambulo, ergo sum*; this "I walk about, therefore I am" is an expression of that manifestation of the ego or "I" whose consciousness rests primarily in action or deed. As we noted earlier, this form is recognizable as to its structure in the conjugation without separate pronoun in both ancient and modern Latin, as well as in Italian and Spanish (see p. 71). Descartes, with his premise of *cogito*, transposes the action or movement confirming or substantiating the existence of the ego essentially from the psychic-vital realm into the psychic-mental; and this is merely a kind of hypergradation that does not eliminate the *ergo*.

We have deliberately selected Russell's commentary from the many similar individualistic interpretations of Descartes' axiom. The fact that such varied interpretations are possible at all and remain at variance even if we take into account the particular definitions of each individual philosopher, can be explained if we remember that all such axioms are in part determined by the psyche. In the rarified air of abstraction, they regain a certain ambiguous or sometimes merely equivocal aspect, a formalistic, stereotyped ambiguity and equivocation inherent in the psyche. How could this not be true also of Descartes who limits his inquiry in *Discourse de la Méthode* to the rationalistic calculation of the "verities," the truths alone?

Here we can discern the tragic aspect of the deficient mental structure (and there will be further instances): Reason, reversing itself metabolistically to an exaggerated rationalism, becomes a kind of inferior plaything of the psyche, neither noticing nor even suspecting the connection. Although the convinced rationalist will be unwilling to admit it, there is after all the rational distorted image of the *speculatio animae*: the *speculatio rationis*, a kind of shadow-boxing before a mirror whose reflection occurs against the blind surface. This negative link to the psyche, usurping the place of the genuine mental relation, destroys the very thing achieved by the authentic relation: the ability to gain insight into the psyche.

In every extreme rationalization there is not just a violation of the psyche by the *ratio*, that is, a negatively magic element, but also the graver danger, graver because of its avenging and incalculable nature: the violation of the *ratio* by the psyche, where both become deficient. The authentic relation to the psyche, the mental, is perverted into its opposite, to the disadvantage of the ego that has become blind through isolation. In such an instance, man has become isolated and his basic ties have been cut; the moderating, measuring bond of *menis* and *menos* is severed. Cut, severed: what was again the meaning of the root *da-*? It is this "cut off, severed, divided," the "demonic." The gates to the "demonic forces" have been opened; nothing exists out of itself, everything follows upon something else, everything has become a consequence. We may well ask: a consequence leading to what?

6. The Integral Structure

But not everyone followed; not all acquiesced to the separation postulated by Descartes, his division of mind and matter that are linked together in primordial kinship. This is of decisive importance with respect to the manifestations of a new consciousness structure, for these manifestations indicate that the specific consciousness mutation is occurring in man from which the aperspectival world can take shape.

This is not yet the place to describe this world in detail. We will first have to gain some insight into its foundations, for without a survey of the site, as it were, our description would be unconvincing and non-committal. And, too, we are reluctant to postulate or outline the aperspectival world in a relativistic-perspectival manner. For the time being, then, we can only hazard a cursory glance at those initial indications which in our opinion could lead to a new mutation, even though they can be recognized as indications only from the "standpoint" of the integral structure, that is, in retrospect.

Yet even mention of these indications can give rise to misunderstandings, since the relationship of each individual inception to the integral consciousness structure now emerging is not immediately apparent from our discussion so far. It is, nonetheless, our intent to outline the foundation of the integral structure with sufficient distinctness so that its nature, like any foundation, reveals itself as the specific basis of the structure under construction. In this instance, however, it does not evidence merely a spatial but also a specifically temporal character that renders it quite distinct from the traditional notion of a structure, even from a purely structural viewpoint. This is especially true as the mental process of time-concretion may be said to "go beyond" a mere synthesis of time and space. We cannot speak here of a synthesis of any kind, whether as the unification of space and time or as their identity (both instances being unconscious tributes to the unity of the magic structure). Our attempt to effect any kind of synthesis here, with or without attempted unification, would, in light of what has already been said, lead only to a duality.

The new structure, moreover, cannot be realized by a re-activation of those structures underlying it. This contradicts, it is true, the two basic conceptions current today that form the polar field of tension of our contemporary perspectivistic world: the natural and human sciences, on the one hand, and the occult sciences on the other. It is regrettable that each of these sides maintains a claim of exclusivity and, equally regrettable, that they lack insight into their mutual duality and antagonistic interdependence. Their dualistic antithetical character is patently obvious; on the one hand the natural sciences, with the human and social sciences closely modeled on their example, and on the other the sciences of the occult. The one group is exclusively forward-directed, the other almost exclusively backward-oriented; the one emphasizes today the quantitative aspect, the other ostensibly the qualitative; the one is predominantly materialistic, the other psychistic; the one is intent on fragmenting everything, the other on unifying.

Then, too, the one side seeks salvation in synthesis or in some kind of "third" entity, as in a "Third Reich," or a "Third Way" (Röpke), or a "Third Humanism" (Thomas Mann); the other envisions salvation in a retrogressive unification, thereby activating deficient mythical and magical forms to a degree that most adherents of Western traditionalism are devalued into a psychistic and magical "state" (and this word is definitely symptomatic) as a result of their mentality, a state "at best" of complete engulfment in the cosmos. And there is on the one side a surrender of the sovereignty of the mind via a kind of rational dissolution that, in suprarational form, has an atomizing effect on matter; on the other, a surrender of the mind's sovereignty—a sovereignty appropriate to our civilization that has been acquired in the course of millenia—via a return to the irrational, an irrational dissolution that in de-mentalized form has an atomizing effect on the psyche and the mind.

None of these routes is passable; all paths lead only to where they have led away from. Either we run in a circle, inexorably confined and imprisoned, or we run to and fro from one opposite to the other in the belief that in this compulsive back-and-forth we will find a synthesis. What is needed, then, is not a way or a path, but a "leap." Is the general insecurity of today an indication that we are "on the mark," or about to leap? The depths of the abyss are visible only when one leaps across (and surely we have seen enough of the abyss during recent decades). But it is no longer enough to reach or jump to the "other side."

The inceptions of a new consciousness mutation represent the outward boundaries of what can be intimated and described in a "contribution to a history of emergent consciousness" such as ours. We indicated some of these points of departure some years ago;[151] here we shall limit our discussion to a further inquiry into the subject of time-concretion, with reference to our remarks in the third section of the second chapter above where we described it in connection with our example of Picasso as a fundamental trait of the aperspectival world.

The concretion of time is one of the preconditions for the integral structure; only the concrete can be integrated, never the merely abstract. By integration we mean a fully completed and realized wholeness—the bringing about of an *integrum*, i.e., the re-establishment of the inviolate and pristine state of origin by incorporating the wealth of all subsequent achievement. The concretion of everything that has unfolded in time and coalesced in a spatial array is the integral attempt to reconstitute the "magnitude" of man from his constituent aspects, so that he can consciously integrate himself with the whole.

The integrator, then, is compelled to have not only concretized the appearances, be they material or mental, but also to have been able to concretize his own structure. This means that the various structures that constitute him must have become *transparent* and conscious to him; it also means that he has perceived their effect on his life and destiny, and mastered the deficient components by his insight so that they acquire the degree of maturity and equilibrium necessary for any concretion. Only those components that are in this way themselves balanced, matured, and mastered concretions can effect an integration. The difficulty—and we will return to this in the next chapter—is that in every instance we are necessarily dealing with the ability of our faculty of consciousness to adapt itself to the different degrees of consciousness of the various structures. Now, as the state of deep sleep is characteristic of the archaic structure, a sleep-like state for the magic, a dream-like state for the mythical, and wakefulness for the mental, a mere conscious illumination of these states, which are for the most part only dimly conscious, does not achieve anything; in fact, to illuminate these states from consciousness is to destroy them. Only when they are integrated via a concretion can they become transparent in their entirety and present, or diaphanous (and are not, of course, merely illuminated by the mind).

There are two important consequences that indirectly result from these observations. One is that consciousness is not identical with intelligence or rational acuity. The other is that the completion of integration is never an expansion of consciousness as spoken of today particularly by psychoanalysis and certain "spiritual" societies of a quasi-occult kind. The expansion of consciousness is merely a spatially conceived quantification of consciousness and consequently an illusion. Rather, we are dealing here throughout with an *intensification* of consciousness; not because of any qualitative character which might be ascribed to it, but because it is by nature "outside" of any purely qualitative valuation or quantitative devaluation.

Let us, however, by way of conclusion return to the indications of the integral structure mentioned above. It was none other than a pupil of Leonardo da Vinci who went beyond the limitations of perspectival spatialization; we refer, of course, to Jacopo da Pontormo, and specifically with reference to some of his portraits. Here we can define more intensively than before the distinguishing aspect of the portraits.[152] Despite Pontormo's use of perspectival techniques, the gaze of the people in his portraits does not correspond to the perspectival age; their gaze is not fixed within spatial limits, but is, on the contrary, depicted with reference to time. It goes beyond the spatial confines of the picture rather than being focused or turned on an actual or imaginary point within the picture. In this reference to time, which we should note occurs simultaneously with reference to space, is a point of departure for a possible temporic concretion of time.

Further temporic indications become evident among those of the generation following Pontormo, to which Descartes belonged, notably in the case of Desargues, a friend of Descartes. In 1636 Desargues published his *Traité de la section perspective*, followed significantly by his "Theory of conic sections" in 1639. This was tantamount to abandonment of a purely three-dimensional space in favor of spherical solid or "filled" space, leaving behind the "emptiness" of purely linear space and touching that dimension of fulfillment that is a precondition of, at the very least, the latent presence of the temporal.

Here, too, we encounter for the first time the striking symbol of the integral structure, the sphere. It is in fact a kind of signature for the four-dimensionality of this structure which we are to understand as a sphere in motion. It is, significantly, the sixteen-year-old Blaise Pascal who continued the conics of Desargues in his *Essai pour les coniques* of 1640. The two treatises of Desargues were of great consequence, as they established projective geometry at the very time that Descartes was setting down his analytic geometry. This projective geometry was freed by Christian von Staudt (1798-1867)—he called it "positional geometry"—from the last vestiges of debt to the old metric geometry remaining in the theories of Desargues and Pascal which was based in part on da Vincian perspective, in part on Euclidian geometry. Metric geometry, once reigning supreme, became a mere appendix of projective geometry, which in the words of M. Zacharias "set the elements in motion: points intersect lines, revolve around fixed points or roll as tangents around curves, [and] planes revolve around fixed axes. . . . "[153] It is the procedure of projective geometry that took into account the position of the elements and their respective motion to each other, and not the calculating process of analytic geometry that gained currency and validation. In this too we can see a further indication and point of departure for a later concretion of time.[154]

And following upon Descartes and Desargues, after yet another generation, is Leibniz, who counters the dualism postulated (albeit ambivalently) in Descartes' treatise *Les passions des âmes* in which the soul and the body, or the mind and matter respectively, were said to constitute their own worlds independently of each other.[155] To this Leibniz responded: "There is an exact correspondence between the body and all thoughts of the soul, whether they are reasonable or not; and dreams have their traces in the brain just as much as the thoughts of men awake."[156] If we recall what we said regarding the interdependence of the soul or psyche and time in the section above on the "Mythical Structure," then this interdependence of soul and time as granted and established in mental terms by Leibniz may be considered evidence that the very recognition of the temporal-psychic constituents constitutes a temporic point of departure for the later concretion of time. This holds true even though Leibniz conceives of the soul in terms of the prevailing *Zeitgeist* as being attached to matter (in this instance, to the brain).

Still another generation later, a new sense of time becomes evident with the advent of Mozart. We have mentioned in another context to what degree this is expressed in *Don Giovanni* and in the second movement of the "Jupiter" Symphony.[157] Here we would point to one of his unfinished later works, the C minor Fantasy for Piano, as well as to his *Variations on a Theme of Gluck* based on Gluck's opera *Der Pilger von Mekka*. In the C minor Fantasy, in particular, a harmonic as well as rhythmic-melodic "loosening up" can be discerned that is far removed from the hierarchic strictness and dominance of the classical tradition.

In order that the significance of this fact can be grasped we should perhaps point out the significance of a basic rule of classical composition; namely, that every movement of a piece of music was supposed to close in the same key as it began. This requirement clearly demonstrates the relation between such music and the course of natural cosmic events: the circle must be completed. The principal subject ties the beginning and the end together by the same key; consequently, every sonata movement was a reflection or image of a divinely created day or year, or of a planet returning upon itself in its orbit, or of the path of any other God-given celestial body. This late music of Mozart simply breaches the naturalistic regularity that corresponded to the precepts of the law-giving creator-god lauded and celebrated in tone, both as to the inner structure of the music as well as to its incompleteness and pervasive anguish (the Fantasy is written in the minor key). Is Mozart moving here from the ostensible realm of the perspectively fixed personified God into the realm of the Divinitary? Is this the source of his early death? A contemporary of Mozart with similar audacity, Hölderlin, died even before his physical death. Be this as it may, the elimination of the purely natural-time orientation in music, a (literally) "unheard of" achievement, bore the possibility of a temporal point of departure for a time-concretion to be later fulfilled.

Again following the span of a generation, we meet up with a phenomenon in the works of Leopardi that has been traditionally misunderstood but that seems to make sense in this context: Leopardi, as is evident from his *Zibaldone* and his diaries, is the thinker who elevates *noia* or boredom and celebrates it in his works. But this presence and acceptance of boredom could be said to be the negative manifestation—today we would call it the "unconscious" manifestation—of the psyche pressing to manifest itself in time. This is the same individualistic psyche to which his contemporary Stendhal, the "egotist," pays tribute via his "psychological realism." Stendhal was one of the very first to take the positive step out of isolation and to discover his own "inner" world, the isolation described in his *Armance* having become effectual via his own ego-banishment. Here once again, although in a different form, the creation of a new kind of relationship is evident, one which connects to the timeless-temporic aspects of one's own psyche and not to the general or collective natural-temporal soul. Once more we find the point of departure for the possibility of a later time-concretion.

After yet another generation there is the work of Heinrich Schliemann, a contemporary of Christian von Staudt whose completion of projective geometry we mentioned earlier. Schliemann's excavation of Troy during the years 1870 to 1883 (a kind of cultural-historical parallel to the importance of Freud's "excavation" of the psyche) is still predominantly an examination of time from a spatial viewpoint, particularly if we consider it from the standpoint of its relevance to a temporic inception. Yet the layers uncovered in Troy convey neither a purely naturalistic perception nor a purely abstract notion of time. They expand the historicity of European man and enrich that faculty of consciousness that enables him to perceive time forms other than those bound to the psyche or to the abstract measurement of natural time. Again we encounter a temporic point of departure and yet another inceptive moment towards the possibility of a later time-concretion.

And to the extent that this concretion of time leads to a *diaphanous present* and to a *transparent presence,* some words of Hölderlin are appropriate—Hölderlin, who encountered the sun on his journey home from Bordeaux.[158] Like Dante's teacher, Brunetto Latini, and, later, van Gogh, he too encountered the great measure-ess of time; and we are perhaps justified in relating his words to the consciousness structure then emerging which he anticipated in many respects. Hölderlin wrote: "Behold! it is the eve of time, the hour when the wanderers turn toward their resting-place. One god after another is coming home. . . . Therefore, be present. . . . "

1   See Gebser, *Abendländische Wandlung* (Zürich: Oprecht), [1]1943 and [2]1945, p. 216ff.; [3]1950, p. 194ff.; Ullstein ed. no. 107, p. 163ff.; *Gesamtausgabe,* I (Schaffhausen: Novalis, 1975), p. 313ff.

2   It would be a worthwhile and rewarding task to trace the likely kinship or at least the remarkable affinity of the two words *neu* (new) and *neun* (nine); cf. note 103, p. 246 below.

3   The discussion in this and the following chapter, as well as in Chapter 3 of the second part, formed the basis of lectures held by the author on the subject of the "History of conceptions of Psyche and Spirit" presented in courses on applied psychology at the Psychologische Gesellschaft, Basel, in July of 1946, and later in the psychological seminar of the Institut für angewandte Psychologie, Zürich, during the summer term, 1947, the full text of which is now reprinted in the *Gesamtausgabe,* V/I, pp. 7-100.

4*   Sri Aurobindo was the first to propound in detail the thought that the fundamental and signal event of our time was the present-day transformation of consciousness. The genial articulation of this thought first appeared in the years 1914-1916 in articles entitled "The Life Divine," which he published in the journal *Arya* (Pondicherry, South India). They later appeared in English in book form under the same title, *The Life Divine* (Calcutta, 1939-1940), and in complete form in 1955 in Pondicherry. An abridged German edition came out in 1957 (Sri Aurobindo, *Der integrale Yoga,* Rowohlts Klassiker no. 24), which first introduced the present writer to his world of thought. Other publications in German include his *Der Zyklus der menschlichen Entwicklung* (München-Planegg: Barth, 1955); *Stufen der Vollendung* (Weilheim: Barth, 1964); and *Der Mensch im Werden* (Pondicherry: Sri Aurobindo Ashram; Zollikon bei Zürich; Sri Aurobindo Verlag, 1964).—From a different point of departure (the principles of Darwinian evolution), Teilhard de Chardin has developed lines of thought closely akin to the basic conception shared by Sri Aurobindo and the present author. He has recorded these thoughts in his *Le Phénomène Humain* (Paris, 1955); English translation by the title *The Phenomenon of Man* (N. Y.: Harper & Brothers, 1959); German translation: *Der Mensch im Kosmos*

(Munich: Beck, 1959), as well as in his subsequently published writings. We have noted earlier this concurrence or "co-incidence" in our *In der Bewährung* (Bern/Munich: Francke, 1962), p. 132; *Gesamtausgabe*, V/I, p. 279; *Asienfibel* (Frankfurt/M.: Ullstein ed. no. 650, 1962), pp. 96 and 165; *Gesamtausgabe*, VI, pp. 95 and 181; and "Parallele Ansätze zur neuen Sicht," *Die Welt in neuer Sicht* (München-Planegg: Barth, 1959), II, pp. 110-14; *Gesamtausgabe*, V/I, pp. 267-81.

5   Giambattista Vico, *La scienza nouva seconda* (Bari: Laterza, 1942), II. This is a new edition of the second version; cf. the German edition edited by Erich Auerbach based on the edition of 1744: Giambattista Vico, *Die neue Wissenschaft über die gemeinschaftliche Natur der Völker* (Munich: Allgem. Verlagsanstalt, 1924).

6   See our discussion in *Abendländische Wandlung* (note 1), [2]1945, p. 46; Ullstein ed. 107, p. 35ff.; *Gesamtausgabe*, I, p. 196. Since acceptance or rejection of the mutational theory is also a question of determinism or indeterminism, it should be noted that all exclusively natural phenomena (and this would include for the most part psychic phenomena) have a determinate character, while extranatural phenomena can be said to have an indeterminate character; this would include such phenomena as the marginal zones of the material universe that are perceptible in the volatilization of matter (elemental particles) as discovered in nuclear physics. We will return to this question in our discussion of freedom and its attendant aspects, as well as in the chapter on Mathematics and Physics (Part 2, Chapter 5, Section 1).

7   Carl Friedrich von Weizsäcker, *Die Geschichte der Natur* (Zürich: Hirzel, 1948), p. 117.

8   See also Gebser, *In der Bewährung* (note 4), p. 120; *Gesamtausgabe*, V/I, p. 268.

9*   Lecomte du Noüy, *Human Destiny* (New York: Longmans, Green, 1947), p. 224ff., and *L'Homme et sa Destinée* (Paris: Colombe, 1948), p. 180. For more on Lecomte du Noüy, see Part 2, Chapter 7.—The extent to which the mutations in the brain posited by Noüy, and referred to on page 224 of his book, can be scientifically proven today, and whose existence can be demonstrated in material terms at all, we do not know; on the basis of the current state of brain research in Switzerland (1952), we were informed at that time that such mutations could be surmised, but not organically proven. See also the next note.

10   Hugo Spatz, "Gedanken über die Zukunft des Menschenhirns und die Idee vom Übermenschen;" Ernst Benz, *Der Übermensch: eine Diskussion* (Zürich/Stuttgart: Rhein, 1961), pp. 315-83, and pp. 366 and 374f., in particular; see also Hugo Spatz, "Vergangenheit und Zukunft des Menschenhirns," *Jahrbuch 1964 der Akademie der Wissenschaften und der Literatur* (Wiesbaden: Steiner, 1965), p. 228ff. The results of Hugo Spatz' research seems to bear out the assumptions of Lecomte du Noüy; see below, Part 2, close of Chapter 7.

11   Erwin Schrödinger, in defending our concept of mutations, used this example during a discussion after a lecture by the present writer at the "Sixth International University Week" held in 1950 under the auspices of the *Europäisches Forum Alpbach*. That particular lecture has now been published (*In der Bewährung*, note 4), pp. 39-51; *Gesamtausgabe*, V/I, pp. 189-200.

12   (Note 1) [2]1945, p. 46; [3]1950, p. 40; Ullstein ed. no. 107, p. 35; *Gesamtausgabe*, I, p. 196.

13   Giselher Wirsing, *Schritt aus dem Nichts* (Düsseldorf and Köln: Diederichs, 1951), pp. 54 and 345, note 14.

14   Ernst-Peter Huss, *Das Gesetz des Seins* (Stuttgart and Köln: Kohlhammer, 1951), p. xii.

15   Graf Hermann Keyserling, *Gedächtnisbuch* (Innsbruck: Rohrer, 1948), p. 37 ff.

16   René Grousset, *Bilan de l'Histoire* (Paris: Plon, 1946), p. 6; German edition *Bilanz der Geschichte* (Zürich: Europa, 1950), p. 9.

17   Julius F. Glück, "Die Gelbgüsse des Ali Amonikoyi," *Jahrbuch des Museums für Länder- und Völkerkunde: Linden Museum Stuttgart 1951* (Heidelberg: Vowinckel, 1951), pp. 61f. and 71, note 81. See also Julius F. Glück, "Zur Soziologie des archaischen und des primitiven Menschen," *Soziologie und Leben*, ed. Carl Brinckmann (Tübingen: Wunderlich, 1952), p. 160.

18   Hendrick de Man, *Vermassung und Kulturverfall* (Bern: Francke, 1954).

19   Rudolf Pannwitz, *Der Nihilismus und die werdende Welt* (Nürnberg: Hans Carl, 1951), p. 20.

20   Walther Tritsch, *Die Erben der bürgerlichen Welt* (Bern: Francke, 1954).

21*   Pierre Teilhard de Chardin, *The Phenomenon of Man* (New York: Harper, 1959); German edition (note 4), pp. 158, 183. Teilhard's discussion is centered more on the development of mankind than on consciousness as such.

22   Auguste Comte, *Die Soziologie: die positive Philosophie im Auszug*, ed. Friedrich Blasche (Leipzig: Kröners Taschenausgabe 107, 1933).

23   In this regard see also Hans Leisegang, *Denkformen* (Berlin: de Gruyter, 1928, p. 35f.

24   The most recent attempt at salvaging this theory of Hegel was made by the Neo-Hegelian J. Hessing, in his *Das Selbstbewusstwerden des Geistes* (Stuttgart: Fromann, 1936). See the critique by Paul Schmitt, "Von der Grundform des Geistes in seiner Geschichte," *Neue Zürcher Zeitung* 1740 (November 2, 1941), 23, sheet 3 (supplement), later reprinted in Paul Schmitt, *Religion, Idee und Staat* (Bern: Francke, 1959). p. 486ff.

25   We wish to particularly emphasize this fact, since it underscores the requisite detachment from the principle of evolution—a point we deem important. It would be incorrect if our presentation of the emergence of consciousness were understood as an evolutive process, since our discussion has demonstrated the basic structure of time as a world-constituent and a timeless intensity that is time-free with respect to consciousness. See also Gebser, *In der Bewährung* (note 4), p. 106f.; *Gesamtausgabe*, v/ɪ, p. 254ff., particularly as the entire question of the ego is important in this connection.

26   We have repeatedly referred to this question, particularly with regard to cultures with a matriarchal emphasis, and notably in our *Asienfibel* (note 4).

27   Theodor Lessing, *Geschichte als Sinngebung des Sinnlosen* (Munich: Beck, 1919), p. 217.

28*   Theodor Lessing, *Europa und Asien: Untergang der Erde am Geist*, fifth completely revised edition (Leipzig: Meiner, 1930). This is the definitive and most complete edition of the book which was first published in 1914; the second edition bore the subtitle: "Man and the Immutable: Six books against History and Time" (*Der Mensch und das Wandellose: Sechs Bücher wider Geschichte und Zeit*). Lessing's identification of spirit with intellect—and he presumably meant intellect when he speaks of *Geist*—is regrettable, particularly since this same confusion has resulted from Klages' widely read book, as well as from the title itself (*Der Geist als Widersacher der Seele*, ɪɪɪ, 1929-1932).

29   Paul Cohen-Portheim, *Asien als Erzieher* (Leipzig: Klinkhardt, 1920).

30   From among the multitude of these conceptions we would mention only the Vedic "Purusha," the Mandaean and Manichean "Adam Kadmon," and the Pauline "Old Adam." Iranian conceptions are discussed in O. G. von Wesendonk's *Urmensch und Seele in der iranischen Überlieferung* (Hannover: Lafaire, 1924), p. 153 ff., as well as in R. Reizenstein's *Das iranische Erlösungsmysterium* (Bonn: Marcus & Weber, 1921), particularly page 39. For a discussion of Hellenistic (Egyptian-Gnostic) conceptions, see Josef Kroll, "Die Lehren des Hermes Trismegistos," *Beiträge zur Geschichte der Philosophie des Mittelalters*, xɪɪ, nos. 2-4 (Münster i. W.: Aschendorff, 1914), pp. 64, 136f.; as well as R. Reizenstein, *Poimandres: Studien zur griechisch-ägyptischen vorchristlichen Literatur* (Leipzig: Teubner, 1904). The extensive source material on which these last two works are based has been recently made available: A. D. Nock, A.-J. Festugière, *Hermès Trismégiste, Corpus Hermeticum: Poimandres, Traités ɪɪ-xvɪɪɪ, Asclepius*, text and translation, Collection des Universités de France (Paris: Les Belles Lettres, 1945), ɪɪ. This edition replaces partial translations such as those of Georges Gabory, *Le Pimandre d'Hermes Trismégiste: Dialogues gnostiques, traduits du grec*, Petite Collection Mystique (Paris: La Sirène, 1927), and Reno Fedi, *Il Pimandro di Ermete Trismegisto*, Breviari Mistici no. 7 (Milan, 1942).

31   In contrast to the rationalistic encyclopedias which address themselves to "perspectival" man, we now have some recent "irrational encyclopedias," as it were, directed at only unperspectival man. The most significant of these works, estimable in their own way, are Ernst von Bunsen's *Die Überlieferung: ihre Entstehung und Entwicklung* (Leip-

zig: Brockhaus, 1898), II; and Leopold Ziegler's *Überlieferung* (Leipzig: Hegner, 1936). It should be noted that Bunsen's is essentially speculative, while Ziegler's is mainly evocative and pathos-ridden; both, in other words, have a predominantly psychistic mode of presentation resulting from their psychistic bent, which would seem to exclude any claim to spiritual validity. We will have occasion later to examine the extent to which both the speculative and the pathetic are both decidedly psychic-dominated forms of expression.—It is beyond the scope of the present work to examine the recent syncretistic attempts to salvage "tradition," theosophy, and in its wake, anthroposophy.

32 *Dschuang Dsi: Das wahre Buch vom südlichen Blütenland,* trans. Richard Wilhelm (Jena: Diederichs, 1940), pp. 12, 226. Dschuang Dsi (Chuang-tzu) is sometimes transliterated as Tschuang Tse.—In connection with the passage cited, see the French version of Henri Borel, *Wu Wei* (Paris: Monde Nouveau, 1931), page 43, who translates according to the sixth chapter of Nan Hwa King: "Parmi les Anciens, ceux qui étaient vraiement hommes dormaient sans rêves, et la reprise de conscience ne les troublait point." The same passage is also quoted in Arthur Waley and Marcel Granet (see note 98 below).

33 Richard Wilhelm, *Geschichte der chinesischen Kultur* (Munich: Bruckmann, 1928), p. 57 and note 12 to that page.

34 Aristotle, *Metaphysics*, XII, 6, 1072a; in the translation of E. Rolfes (Leipzig: Meiner, 1904), II, pp. 94, 182, note 37.

35 Cf. Menge-Güthling, *Griechisch-deutches Wörterbuch* (Berlin: Langenscheidt, ²⁸1910), I, p. 374, as well as Friedrich Kluge-Götze, *Etymologisches Wörterbuch der deutschen Sprache* (Berlin: de Gruyter, ¹¹1936), p. 368; for *mögen* see p. 396.

36 For illustrations, see among other sources, the following: (a) Eckart von Sydow, *Die Kunst der Naturvölker und der Vorzeit*, Propyläen Kunstgeschichte I (Berlin: Propyläen, ³1932), pp. 203-06, 282, 469-74, and plates vii and xxiv; (b) Hugo Obermaier, "El hombre fósil," *Memoria número 9* (serie prehistórica, num. 7) de la Comisión de Investigaciones paleontológica y prehistóricas (Junta para Amplición de estudios e investigaciones científicas) (Madrid: Museo Nacional de Ciencias Naturales, ²1925); (c) Hugo Obermaier, Antonio García y Bellido, *El hombre prehistórico y los origines de la humanidad* (Madrid: Occidente, ²1941); (d) (L. Baltzer), *Schwedische Felsbilder von Göteborg bis Strömstad* (Hagen i. W.: Folkwang, 1919); (e) Leo Frobenius, Hugo Obermaier, *Hadschra Máktuba: Urzeitliche Felsbilder Kleinafrikas* (Munich: Wolff, 1925); (f) Hugo Obermaier, Herbert Kühn, *Buschmannkunst: Felsmalereien aus Südwestafrika* (Leipzig: Pantheon, 1930); see also the publications since 1954 by Abbé H. Breuil, Herbert Kühn, and the numerous publications of the past decade on cave drawings.

37 Reprinted in Leo Frobenius, *Kulturgeschichte Afrikas* (Vienna: Phaidon, 1933), p. 127f.

38 Hugo Obermaier, "El hombre fósil" (note 36b, pp. 273, 251f.; our figure 4 is taken from his figure 121.—The cave of Niaux is in the Département de l'Ariège, France, on the Andorran frontier. Similar reproductions and cave drawings can be found in Herbert Kühn, *Die Felsbilder Europas* (Stuttgart: Kohlhammer, 1952), p. 20, fig. 11; p. 21, fig. 12; p. 22, fig. 13 and plates 3 and 24. All of these depictions date from the Ice Age (Kühn ascribes various dates from 60,000 to 10,000 B. C.) and are from caves in Spain as well as in Western France: Trois Frères (Dep. de l'Ariege); Pindal (Asturia); El Castillo (Prov. de Santander); Lascaux (Dep. de la Dordogne).

39 We use the word "linking" deliberately to avoid any associations which may be awakened by the psychological term "transference" whenever we are dealing principally with the vital nexus or connection.

40 German Vitalism was a similar conception of pervasively magical character, and has been dealt with at length in our *Abendländische Wandlung* (note 1), chapters 19 and 20 of the first, chapters 19, 20 and 23 of the later editions. To the extent that it could be described as "blind dynamism"—a blindness which includes the lack of consciousness—vitalism was regressive and, thus, deficiently magical. Its deficiency is patently obvious from the chaos and collapse which it brought forth.

41 It is perhaps redundant to note here that the aspectual reality, and the stage, for this

magic unity of the world is the *cavern*. The spacelessness of the cave is still expressed in modern German: the house—the most recent form of the cave—has a *Boden*, an undifferentiated term denoting "floor" as well as "attic," i.e., an emphasis on the lack of spatial orientation where the identical word means both lower and upper. For more on the relation between cavern and house see Jean Gebser, *Lorca oder das Reich der Mütter* (Stuttgart: Deutsche Verlags-Anstalt, 1949); *Gesamtausgabe* (note 1), I.

42   This equal validity furnishes evidence of the relation between the magic world and the Christian "realm of the angels," a world which is also of powers and not values. As such, it is perhaps partly a projection of the magic structure onto the heavens, a structure which Christian man in his ego-emergence sought to externalize. We have referred in another context to the equal validity of angels and mention it here only because of its magical component; see Gebser, *Rilke und Spanien* (Zürich: Oprecht), ¹1939, p. 48; ²1946, p. 48 and 90 f., note 61a; *Gesamtausgabe* I, p. 47, as well as Gebser, *Das Wintergedicht* (Zürich: Oprecht, 1945), and *Gesamtausgabe*, VIII, pp. 131-32, verses 188-208.—The fact that angels are arranged in hierarchies does not deny them their power or might, as hierarchy here is clearly a gradation of powers, evident in the very names for the angelic realm: "dominions," "majesties," "powers," "thrones." Moreover, power excludes value, and greater power does not in any event include greater value.

43   To give at least some idea of the manifold nature of the manifestations of magic, we should like briefly to discuss some of the best known ones. At the same time we must emphasize that we are dealing, for the most part, with forms of once valid magic that have become deficient: magic activity (hunting magic, rain magic, magic of the seasons, expulsion of the winter demons, etc., all of which are based on sympathetic effect, that is, on the similarity between the phenomenon and the magic means used); picture magic (fetishes, totems, taboos, amulets, jewelry superstitions, etc., based on the sympathetic action between picture and reality); word magic (oracles, taboos, forbidden names, etc.); touch magic (based on the vital connections between those things which were once linked—for example, parts of the body such as nails, hair, and the like); and sex magic (love sorcery, fertility magic, and the like).—Nor must we fail to mention all those manifestations resulting from mediums, mediumistic and hypnotic states. At present they are being studied by parapsychology and depth psychology. Attempts are being made to distinguish between the subconscious and the unconscious; and as a matter of fact, it might be better to employ here the term "interconsciousness," for it is illogical enough to designate spaceless phenomena by means of spatial concepts.—From among the innumerable studies devoted to this subject, we would cite here only five works; several others will be mentioned in the course of our discussion. (a) J. J. Meyer, *Trilogie altindischer Vegetationsmächte* (Zürich: Niehans, 1937); (b) Eduard Renner, *Goldener Ring über Uri, ein Buch über Erleben und Denken unserer Bergler: von Magie und Geistern und von den ersten und letzten Dingen* (Zürich: Metz, 1941); (c) S. Seligmann, *Geschichte des Aberglaubens aller Zeiten und Völker: Der böse Blick und Verwandtes* (Vienna: 1909), II; (d) H. Driesch, *Parapsychologie* (Zürich: Rascher, ²1944); (e) E. Moser, *Der Okkultismus* (Zürich: Orell Füssli, 1936), II.

44   Good illustrations of this can be found in the tapestry illustrations reproduced in Heinrich Glück, Ernst Dietz, *Die Kunst des Islam*, Propyläen Kunstgeschichte, V (Berlin: Propyläen, ²1935); on pp. 384-403 are examples of Egyptian, Near-Eastern, Persian, Chinese, and Spanish tapestries.

45   Although we cannot go into great detail here, it is of note that ornamentation belongs predominantly to the magic realm, even in those instances where it can be interpreted as being purely geometrical; for ornamentation inevitably reflects an intertwining or interlacing, as well as inextricability and confinement which are inherent in everything cavern-like. Even where noted mathematicians have attempted to incorporate ornamentation into their mathematical and geometrical conceptions, they are at best rationalizing it; and they remain unaware of their basic (and unconscious) magic predisposition; cf. Andreas Speiser, *Die mathematische Denkweise*, Basel: Birkhäuser, ²1945, p.

17ff.). —In Part Two we will return to the predominantly magical component in present-day mathematics, with its belief in the potency of its formulae, since there is in every formula an inherent remnant of magic-ritualistic character.

46   See the illustration in J. H. Breasted, *Geschichte Ägyptens: grosse illustrierte Phaidon-Ausgabe* (Zürich: Phaidon, 1936), fig. 265.

47   Reproductions of the entire picture, as well as a similar "lion hunt," can be found in Howard Carter, A. C. Mace, *Tut-ench-Amun: ein ägyptisches Königsgrab* (Leipzig: Brockhaus, ²1924), I, plate 42, pp. 233, 235, as well as in Georg Steindorff, *Die Kunst der Ägypter* (Leipzig: Insel-Verlag, 1928), p. 242-43.

48   For information on the datings of this drawing, see Ernst Pfuhl, *Malerei und Zeichnungen der Griechen* (Munich: Bruckmann, 1923), I, section 65, p. 73; the illustration itself is in vol. 3, no. 17.

49   For three different treatments of this scene, see Ernst Buschor, *Griechische Vasen* (Munich: Piper, 1940), illustrations, pp. 18-20; see also Pfuhl (note 48), III, nos. 15 and 84.

50   Buschor (note 49), fig. 41, p. 34f.

51   Buschor (note 49), fig. 67, p. 58.

52   Illustrations in Obermaier/Bellido (note 36c), fig. 45 A and B, p. 283.

53   Illustrations in Ernst Kühnel, *Miniaturmalerei im islamischen Orient*, Die Kunst des Orients, VII (Berlin: Cassirer, 1922); examples of Arabic art on pp. 15 and 17; of Mongolian on pp. 26, 28-32 and 47; of Persian on pp. 55f., 58f., 60, 71ff., and 98; of Indian on pp. 103f. and 115. In addition to the numerous publications relating to early Christian miniatures, we would note expressly the depiction of the "Fall of Man" from the *Jakobuskodex* reproduced by Heinrich Glück, *Die christliche Kunst des Ostens*, Die Kunst des Orients, VIII (Berlin: Cassirer, 1922), illustration on p. 71.

54   See chapters 14 and 15 of Gebser, *Abendländische Wandlung* (note 1).

55   See J. Winthuis, "Das Zweigeschlechterwesen bei den Zentral-Australiern und anderen Völkern," *Forschungen zur Völkerpsychologie und Soziologie* 5 (Leipzig: Hirschfeld, 1928), plate 14; this is a reproduction of plate B in volume 2 of the *Proceedings of the Royal Geographical Society of Australasia-Adelaide*, 1890. G. Grey, who discovered these drawings, has described them in his *Journals of two Expeditions of Discovery in North-West and Western Australia* (London, 1841), I, p. 203. - On page 197ff. of his work, Winthuis interprets the depiction as representing the sun-god, whereas Herbert Kühn has called the aura "in all probability, a head ornament," a point of view quite acceptable then (Herbert Kühn, *Die Kunst der Primitiven*, Munich, 1923, p. 63).

56   We would mention in this regard the work of two English doctors who have apparently been successful in capturing the human aura on supersensitized photographic plates prepared with dicyanin. Walter Kilner has successfully used these photographs for diagnosis at St. Thomas Hospital, London; see his *The Human Atmosphere: the Aura* (London: Redman, 1912), II; (London: Kegan Paul, ²1926). References to Kilner's work can be found in G. Contenau, *La magie chez les Assyriens et les Babyloniens* (Paris: Payot, 1947), p. 37; and Oscar Bagnall's *The Origin and Properties of the Human Aura* (London: Kegan Paul, 1937) is a continuation of Kilner's work.

57   A full-sized reproduction can be found in O. Elfrida Saunders, *Englische Buchmalerei* (Leipzig: Pantheon, 1928), I, plate 13. Two similar drawings, also without commentary, are in *Cahier d'Art* 22 (Paris: 1947), pp. 272-73.

58   These drawings, which accompany Jean Guiart's article "Art et Magie," *Les Lettres françaises*, no. 164 (Paris: July 11, 1947), p. 3, are published there without commentary. Herbert Kühn, however, has furnished a description and designates these *Wondschina* figures as representations of "primordial men from whom the rain, the earth, the rivers, the mountains, the great plains originate"; (*Die Frühkulturen*, Knaurs Welt-Kunstgeschichte I [Munich: Droemer, 1964], p. 41); see the illustration on p. 42 which corresponds to ours.

59   See Herbert Kühn, "Das Problem des Urmonotheismus," *Abhandlungen der geistes- und sozialwissenschaftlichen Klasse*, Akademie der Wissenschaften und der Literatur,

22 (1950) (Wiesbaden: Franz Steiner, 1951), p. 1663, fig. 24a and 24b. With respect to the dating, see the following note.

60 Herbert Kühn (note 59), p. 1666, fig. 37; on p. 1672 there are further source references (Piette, 1895 and 1907; Salmony, 1931). —The datings by various scholars diverge by as much as ten to twenty thousand years (or more); Kühn (p. 1662 and 1666, and in his *Die Kunst Alt-Europas*, Stuttgart: Kohlhammer, 1956, p. 15) dates the beginnings of the Aurignacian period some 30,000 years earlier than Paolo Graziosi, for example (*Die Kunst der Altsteinzeit*, Stuttgart: Kohlhammer, 1956, p. 14f.). The works of Herbert Kühn cited here furnish numerous other examples of early magical man's "mouthless" depictions.

61 See André Parrot, *Sumer* (Munich: Beck, ²1962), fig. xv, a and b; unfortunately no exact datings or details as to the size and material are given for these two statuettes. In comparison to other idols and "fertility goddesses" reproduced in his book, these two would seem to date from the fourth to the third millenium B. C. . They are apparently made of clay, and their height would seem to be about 30 cm. There are also reproductions in *Das Kunstwerk* 14, 8 (Baden-Baden and Krefeld: Agis Verlag, February, 1961), p. 28.

We would also mention the marvelously distinct feminine idols of the same period (third millennium B. C.), from the so-called Cyclades culture of the Aegean. In these idols (made of marble from the islands) we again see the mouthless prototype of the "Great Mother." Unfortunately, there are almost no reproductions of these statuettes, some of which are as large as 76cm in height; and even in the collection of the National Museum in Athens they seem to be all but completely lacking. A very rough sketch is included in Friedrich Matz, *Kreta und Frühes Griechenland*, Sammlung "Kunst der Welt" (Baden-Baden: Holle, 1962), p. 58, fig. 9; also p. 60. Although found in several private collections, these statuettes are lacking in all but a few museums in Europe and North America, one of the exceptions being the Folkwang Museum (Essen); see *Die Welt* (Hamburg) 285 (December 7, 1963), p. 7.

A pharmacologist, Sigrid Knecht, has furnished evidence that the lack of a mouth is a prototypical configuration in the earliest period, and still latently present in the present-day European. She has described "mouthless masks" which she observed during a mushroom ceremony in a Mazatec mountain village in Mexico, worn during the "mushroom frenzy." The "sacred mushrooms" brought about a change of consciousness which freed, as it were, the otherwise buried lower level of awareness and revealed this proto-configuration inherent in the natives (as in all of us); see Sigrid Knecht, "Das Phänomen der Mundlosigkeit in menschheitsgeschichtlicher Sicht," *Transparente Welt: Festschrift für Jean Gebser* (Bern: Huber, 1965); also her "Gesichter ohne Mund und Farbe," *Farbenforum* 15 (Ludwigsburg, August 1964), pp. 16-21, and "Magische Pilze und Pilzzeremonien," *Zeitschrift für Pilzkunde* 28, no. 3-4 (1962), pp. 69-78. The latter article contains references to masks (!) of mouthless gods worn by dancers over their heads (in northeastern New Guinea), as well as to mouthless figures among "very early Peruvian and Mexican idols."

62 Photograph of a small clay copy of a Chinese make-up mask of the type currently made in Taiwan (Formosa); in the possession of the author.

63 Reproduced from the (color) title page of the journal *China Reconstrūcts* 9, no. 6 (June, 1962) from Peking. —It would be a mistake to assume that the magical component, visible in these make-up and bearded masks still in use today, was merely a vestige or an expression of a one-sided magical attunement on the part of the Chinese. The Peking Opera unquestionably represents a breathtaking example of synthesis or integration of modes of artistic expression appropriate to the various structures of consciousness. We, in our rationalization (=division) have separated artistic expression into sacral and ritualistic representation, ballet, opera, theatre, cabaret, and circus; but the Peking Opera includes all of these varied types in each and every performance. It is, consequently, an extremely vivid reflection of all basic human structures and modes of expression: the magic (ritual, mouthlessness, dance, music); the mythical (imagery, dream); the mental (deliberate, conscious and purposive-oriented statement and action)—all of these are brought to expression.

64   This paralleling and overlapping of the still-magical and just-mythical attitude is particularly evident in the many illustrations of artifacts from the two early Sumerian cultures from the third millennium onward; see André Parrot (note 61).

65   See Adolf Portmann, "Die Urbilder in biologischer Sicht," *Eranos Jahrbuch* 18 (Zürich: Rhein, 1950), as well as in his *Biologie und Geist* (Zürich: Rhein, 1956), p. 143f.

66   See Max Burchartz, *Gestaltungslehre* (Munich: Prestel, 1952), p. 20 ff. Oskar Küst has shown children's drawings from his school classes at various exhibitions, notably in Karlsruhe; the spontaneous drawings of preschoolers as well as those of pupils in the early grades characteristically lacked the representation of the mouth.

67   Gustav Meyrink, *Der Engel vom westlichen Fenster* (Bremen: Schünemann, n. d.), p. 426.

68   T. Campanella, around 1600 A.D., has already noted this power aspect of human nature in his *Del senso delle cose e della magia*, translated from the Latin by A. Bruers (Bari: Laterza, 1925), p. 121ff. On the other hand, Jacob Böhme speaks of the volitional aspect inherent in all magic in his *Sex Puncta Theosophica* (Leipzig: Insel-Bücherei No. 337, n.d.).

69   A reproduction of this relief showing a reconstruction differing from the one on which our illustration is based can be found in Gerhart Rodenwaldt, *Die Kunst der Antike*, Propyläen Kunstgeschichte, III (Berlin: Propyläen, ³1927), p. 119; see there also, on plate 1, the fragment of a mural from Knossos from the same period, depicting a boy picking saffron which shows considerable intertwining and enmeshment in nature.

70   Friedrich Creuzer, *Deutsche Schriften* (so-called to distinguish them from his Latin writings), zweite Abteilung I (Darmstadt: Leske, 1846), p. 238, and also the plate at the close of the volume.

71   The vase paintings illustrated in Ernst Pfuhl (note 48), III, nos. 279, 284, 285, and 297, exhibit similar garlands.

72   See G. van der Leeuw, *Phänomenologie der Religion* (Tübingen: Mohr, ²1933), as well as Karl Kerényi, *Die antike Religion* (Amsterdam: Pantheon, 1940), p. 131.

73   See Gebser, *Der grammatische Spiegel* (Zürich: Oprecht, 1944), p. 10; ²1963, p. 14; *Gesamtausgabe*, I, p. 150.

74   It would be interesting to pursue the relationship which undoubtedly exists between geometricizing forms and ritual, but such an investigation goes beyond the scope of the present work, as would many others that we have had to forego as they stray too far from the essential line of our discussion. Moreover (to continue the same image), they would only serve to underscore our thesis. One observation, however, should be made here: it is undoubtedly incorrect to view the geometric forms of magic art as abstractions; on the contrary, they are a kind of vital condensation of essential proto-forms. It is only in (later) formulas and concepts that we meet with abstractions appropriate to, and inherent in the rational, and not the magic, structure.

75   Drawings of such vines are reproduced in Ernst Buschor, "Satyrtänze und frühes Drama," *Sitzungsberichte der Bayrischen Akademie der Wissenschaften*, philosophisch-historische Abteilung, 1943, no. 5 (Munich: Beck, 1943), figs. 38 and 80, as well as in Pfuhl (note 48), I, p. 40 and 315f.

76   For details on the so-called Françoise vase and the depiction of the muses, see W. H. Roscher, *Ausführliches Lexikon der griechischen und römischen Mythologie* (Leipzig: Teubner, 1894-1897), II, Part 2, column 3243 f.

77   The connection as well as the distinction between the magical aura of our illustrations and the halo are best explained if we distinguish between colored and golden halos. Saints and holy men of both early Buddhism and early Christianity have colored halos; in the Buddhist tradition they are depicted with a blue, yellow, red, or green nimbus according to the region of the earth to which they have been assigned (North, South, West, and East respectively). Medieval stained glass windows show Christian saints with a halo of the color which corresponds to their nature. In this phenomenon we are most likely dealing with a more sublime form of manifestation of the saint's transfigured radiance, who in contrast to profane men, is aware of mouthless silence. The golden halo,

on the other hand, is particularly appropriate for the figure of Christ, as it illuminates his transfigured earthly form and expresses a more conscious brightness (*Hell*igkeit) and sanctity (*Heil*igkeit). —Reproductions of colored "halos" are to be found in Otto Fischer's *Die Kunst Indiens, Chinas und Japans*, Propyläen-Kunstgeschichte iv, (Berlin: Propyläen, 1928), and in Fridtjof Zschokke's *Mittelalterliche Bildfenster der Schweiz* (Basel: Holbein, 1946).

78   Jane Ellen Harrison, *Themis: A Study of the Origins of Greek Religion* (Cambridge: University Press, ²1927), p. 328.

79   See Menge-Güthling (note 35), pp. 380, 382, as well as the etymological reference by Prellwitz (*Etymologisches Wörterbuch*, 1905) cited in Harrison (note 78).

80   Residual examples in modern German for the ambivalence created by vowel quantity in a given root are evident in the word pairs *der Wēg* and *wĕg, das Māss* and *die Māsse*, and *die Mūsse* and *das Mŭss*; in each instance both words come from the identical root; see Kluge-Götze (note 35), pp. 379, 380, 405, and 576f., as well as our remarks in Chapter 4, Section 2 below.

81   René Guénon, *Aperçu sur l'Initiation* (Paris: Les Editions Traditionelles, 1946), p. 126ff., and Leopold Ziegler (note 31), p. 261.

82   See Harrison (note 78) and the interpretation there by Prellwitz.

83   Dupuis, *Origine de tous les cultes ou religion universelle* (Paris: Agasse, 1792), x; (Paris, ²1822), vii; an abridged edition was also published under the title: *Abrégé de l'origine de tous les cultes* (Paris, Tenré, 1820).

84   Arthur Drews, *Der Sternenhimmel* (Jena: Diederichs, 1923); Robert Eisler, *Weltenmantel und Himmelszeit* (Munich: Beck, 1910), ii.

85   Friedrich Creuzer, *Symbolik und Mythologie der alten Völker, besonders der Griechen* (Darmstadt: Leske, 1810, ²1819, ³1836).

86   We would single out the following as random examples: Sigmund Freud, *Der Mann Moses* (Amsterdam: de Lange, 1939); Otto Rank, *Psychoanalytische Beiträge zur Mythenforschung* (Vienna: Psychoanalytischer Verlag, 1919); Ludwig Klages, *Vom kosmogonischen Eros* (Jena: Diederichs, 1930, ⁴1941); C. G. Jung, *Wandlungen und Symbole der Libido* (Vienna: Deuticke, 1910, ³1938); C. G. Jung, K. Kerényi, *Einführung in das Wesen der Mythologie* (Amsterdam: Pantheon, 1941).

87   The fragments of Heraclitus to which reference is made here, and which we will examine later in greater detail, are to be found in Diels-Kranz, *Die Fragmente der Vorsokratiker* (Berlin: Weidmann, ³1934), i, p. 150ff.

88   *Kalewala* (Berlin: Schneider, n.d.), i, p. 220ff. and 240ff. —We should note here the interesting parallelism with the Nausicaa scene: Wainamoinen meets Annikki on the shore washing her laundry, Odysseus meets Nausicaa engaged in the same activity, and one surely of symbolic nature, since its reality is open to question: laundry is not washed in salt water, but in the mouth of a nearby river or stream. Yet it is dried (as well as bleached) on the ocean beach, to which there is specific reference made in the *Odyssey* (vi, 85-95; ix, 19). This contention is borne out by the fact that the alchemistic *Ars Magna* mentions laundering as a symbolic act: *purificatio, mundificatio, leukosis* in the sense of purification, bleaching and whitening. One of the most reknowned hermetic-alchemistic parchments (Codex 87 D 3, Berlin, Kupferstichkabinett), "Splendor solis oder Sonnen-Glanz" (1532), contains a washerwoman scene and references to its symbolic character. For a reproduction as well as an interpretation, see Gustav Friedrich Hartlaub, "Signa Hermetis," *Zeitschrift des deutschen Vereins für Kunstwissenschaft*, 4 (Berlin: de Gruyter, 1937), pp. 144, 149, fig. 3.

89   See Plutarch, *Vergleichende Lebensbeschreibung* (Leipzig: Reclam, n.d.), i, p. 9ff. (the first description, "Theseus").

90   *Odyssey*, vi.

91   *Das Nibelungenlied*, 6th Adventure: "Wie Gunther um Brunhild gegen Isenland fuhr."

92   See also Jean Gebser, *Das Ariadnegedicht* (Zürich: Oprecht, 1945), and *Gedichte* (Schaffhausen: Novalis, 1974), pp. 103-112.

93   *Tuti-Nameh: das Papageienbuch*, Bibliothek der Romane, XVII (Leipzig: Insel Verlag, n.d.), p. 370ff.

94   The name "Narcissus" has a reference to water: *nar* in Greek denotes "water"; see J.J. Bachofen, *Versuch über die Gräbersymbolik der Alten* (Basel: Helbing, ²1925), p. 347f.

95   See the *Corpus Hermeticum*, ed. Nock, Festugière (note 30), I, 11 (Poimandre, Traité I, 13/14), as well as the commentaries: Kroll (note 30), pp. 136-37; Reitzenstein (note 30), pp. 81f., 114; Ménard, Hermès Trismégiste (Paris, ²1868), p. 85 (cited in Kroll). —They all, however, uniformly overlook the Narcissus aspect, as well as its inherent symbolism of consciousness emergence.

96   We would recall here the psychic mirroring of "contemplation" [*Schauen*] (see note 63, p. 34), as well as our remarks on the reflective nature of myth; Hades and Olympus are reflected by man in myth, a psychic process visible from the correspondence of the words for "shadow/shade," "sky," "mirror," and "contemplation/reflection" in several Germanic languages, where these words share a common root.

97   Plato, *Timaios*, 45f.

98   Marcel Granet, *La Pensée Chinoise*, Collection L'Evolution de l'Humanite xxvbis (Paris: Michel, 1934), p. 121f.; German edition: *Das chinesische Denken* (Munich: Piper, 1963); also Marcel Granet, *Danses et Légendes de la Chine Ancienne*, Bibliothèque de Philosophie Contemporaine (Paris: Alcan, 1926), I, p. 312ff.

99   See Gebser (note 1), ¹1943, p. 25; ²1945, p. 23; ³1950, p. 21.

100   *Odyssey*, IX, 19.

101   *Odyssey*, I, 9.

102   For example, John 12:25 and also Matthew 10:39; Luke 9:24 and 17:33; Mark 8:35-36.

103   *Dschuang Dsi* (note 32), IV, Chapter 5, p. 53.

104   Shakespeare, *The Tempest*, IV, 1; Prospero's words are: " . . . We are such stuff/As dreams are made on; and our little life / Is rounded with a sleep." In a performance at the Schauspielhaus, Hamburg (1961), Gustav Gründgens rendered these lines as: "Wir sind vom gleichen Stoff / aus dem die Träume sind; und unser kleines Leben / Umfasst ein langer Schlaf."

105   A depiction of the birth of "Athena of acute vision" (*Athenās oxuderkoūs*) from the head of Zeus, is reproduced in Fr. Creuzer (note 85), ²1819, atlas, plate 39, no. 5; the description is on p. 17, no. 17.

106   We noted this crucial date in Chapter 2 and passim. of our *Abendländische Wandlung* (note 1). Coincidentally, during the same year that the first part of the present work was published (1949), Karl Jaspers spoke of the period around 500 B.C. as an "axial time" (*Vom Ursprung und Ziel der Geschichte*, Zürich: Artemis, 1949, p. 76ff.).

107   Our interpretation follows the principal version of this mythologeme, based on various sources and variant readings, in: Preller-Robert, *Griechische Mythologie* (Berlin: Weidmann, ⁴1894), I, Part 1, p. 184ff. From the wealth of interrelationships in this mythologeme we have singled out only the most important which bear on the process of consciousness emergence. We have not undertaken to examine the cosmological aspects underlying it, nor have we concerned ourselves with the age of the mythologeme, which, in its earliest form (in the *Vedas*) exhibits a definite and striking naturality in the form of the "Aurora" mythologeme. As to this early aspect of the myth, see F. Max Müller, *Die Wissenschaft der Sprache* (Leipzig: Engelmann, 1892), II, p. 592ff.

108   See L. Preller (-Köhler), *Römische Mythologie* (Berlin: Weidmann, ²1865), p. 258ff., as well as F. Max Müller (note 107), II, p. 594.

109   The etymological kinship of the roots and attendant words cited in our text have their scholarly-scientific basis in the following sources, on which we have based our remarks throughout the present work; they are: Kluge-Götze (note 35); J. and W. Grimm, *Deutsches Wörterbuch*; and Menge-Güthling (note 35) under the respective entries. See also F. Max Müller (note 107), I, pp. 5, 266, 499, and II, pp. 445, 594ff., as well as his *Sanskrit Grammatik* (Leipzig: Engelmann, 1868), under the respective roots and words cited.

110*   Walde-Hofmann has shown the root kinship of the words *humus* ("earth") and *homo* ("man") in his *Lateinisches Etymologisches Wörterbuch* (Heidelberg: Winter, ³1938), I, pp. 655 and 663f. But for both words, in contrast to the etymological sources listed in note 109, Walde-Hofmann has conjectured the Indogermanic root *gdhem* (gdhom) or *ghem*, from which he derives Gothic *manna*, Old High German *man* (*mennics*), Old Indic *mánuh* and *mánus*, all of which have the meaning "man" (*Mann* and *Mensch*). We are not able to say to what extent the root *ghem* can be considered an extension of the root *ma:me*; we have mentioned Walde-Hofmann's conjecture merely for the sake of completeness; it does not identify a proto-root such as *ma:me* very likely is.

111   See Robert Eisler, *Weltenmantel und Himmelszelt* (Munich: Beck, 1910), I, p. 268, note 2. Basing his derivation on the investigations of E. Assmann (*Philologus*, 1908, p. 165ff.), Eisler establishes the relationship between the Cretian name *minos* and Latin *mina* (a sum of money), Greek *mna* (coin, weight), and Aramaic *mene* (weight). Incidentally, the German word for "coin," *Münze*, deriving from Latin *moneta* (cf. Kluge-Götze, note 35, p. 403) very likely can be traced to the same root on which Latin *mundus*, "earth, man, humanity, world" and later even "universe" were based; and it will be recalled that, according to the old conception, the earth was round and flat, i.e., a coin-shaped disc. The Homeric view, still held by Thales of Miletus, that the earth was a disc surrounded by water (the ocean), is also to be found in the Vedic literature of India (see W. Kirfel, *Die Kosmographie der Inder* [Berlin: Schroeder, 1920], p. 9) More than any other, this example underscores the two-dimensional nature of the mythical world image.

112   See Gebser, *Asienfibel* (note 4), p. 102f.; *Gesamtausgabe*, VI, p. 101.

113   Some examples: *maino, menio, meneaino, menoinao* (related to Old High German *meina*, "intent" and modern German *meinen*, "to be of the opinion"), *maiomai, maomai*. Relevant in this connection and also worthy of note is the verb *manthano*, meaning "to learn, inquire"; modern German *munter* ("awake, watchful") derives from it via Old High German *mendan*, "to be glad," and *muntar*.

114   As to this "why?," a mode of questioning that first surfaced in Greece on which all science is predicated, see Gebser (note 1), 1942, p. 19; ²1945, p. 17; ³1950, p. 16; Ullstein ed. no. 107, p. 15; *Gesamtausgabe*, I, p. 177. This form of questioning is unknown in the Orient.

115   Diels-Kranz (note 87), I, p. 231; fragment 28 B 3.

116   See the *Gilgamesch*, Insel-Bücherei no. 203 (Leipzig: Insel, n.d.).

117   See Robert Saitschick, *Schöpfer höchster Lebenswerte* (Zürich: Rascher, 1946), p. 111.

118   The inceptions inherent in these examples have been summarized from the abundant pictorial material in Pfuhl (note 48), II, paragraph 668ff., p. 618f. See also the references to the abundant secondary literature on this subject (p. 633ff. in Pfuhl). References to the Odyssey landscapes are in vol. 3, section 969ff., p. 883ff., and the illustrations in the same volume, beginning with no. 721.

119   See Alexander Mitscherlich, *Freiheit und Unfreiheit in der Krankheit* (Hamburg: Goverts, 1946), p. 97f., and note 1. See also H. Rheinfelder, *Das Wort "Persona": Beiheft 77 zur Zeitschrift für romanische Philologie* (Halle: Niemeyer, 1928), p. 18ff.; and also H. C. Dowell, "The Word 'Person,'" *Times Literary Supplement* 47, no. 2, 414 (May 8, 1948), p. 268.

120   See J. Gregor, *Die Masken der Erde* (Munich: Piper, 1936), p. 6.

121   According to Menge-Güthling (note 35), the etymology of Greek *choros*, rendered variously as "rondel, choral dance, group, chorus," is still unclear. We would surmise that it is based on the Indo-Germanic root *ker*, meaning to "cut" or "divide"; and this root, in turn, we would surmise to be the "active" form of the root *kēl* (see p. 171 and our "Second Remark on Etymology," p. 550 below.) Since the names Kronos, Kore, and others, as well as the word for "sheaf" in German, *Garbe*, appear to have derived from the root *ker* (see p. 171 and the "First Remark on Etymology"), while those words associated with the central concept of "cavern" have derived from *kēl*, it may not be amiss to recognize the cavern-principle in the word *choros*. In this it would have assumed the

"active" form, becoming thereby a precursor of the mental mutation, or its expression; this mutation burst the enclosed cavern and later the perpetually closing circle, magical as well as mythical.

122   Fragment 22 B 15 in Diels-Kranz (note 87), p. 155. Because of the "D"-element, the initial and formative letter of his name, it is apparent that Dionysus is not only the god of frenzy and darkness (on the importance of division, and diurnal brightness in the "D," see our "Fifth Remark on Etymology," p. 558); and Arthur Drews has exhaustively documented Dionysus as the god of fire in his *Geschichte des Monismus*, Sammlung Synthesis, v (Heidelberg: Winter, 1913), p. 140ff.

123   G. van der Leeuw (note 72), p. 279, note 3, has expressed an opinion parallel to ours, a rarity in the wide-ranging literature on this subject.

124   This important symbol is mentioned by Xenophon (*Metamorphoses*, II, 1, 20), Hesiod (German edition of his works, p. 287ff.), Plato (*Republic*, II, 364c), Virgil (*Aeneid*, VI, 540), and Lactantius (*Institutiones divinae*, lib. VI, cap. 3), cited in Albert Dieterich, *Nekyia: Beiträge zur Erklärung der neuentdeckten Petrus-Apokalypse* (Leipzig: Teubner, 1893), p. 192f.

125   For the entire text, as well as its sources, consult Hans Leisegang (note 23), p. 83; Leopold Ziegler, *Apollons letzte Ephiphanie* (Leipzig: Hegner, 1937), p. 242; D. Mereschkowskij, *Das Geheimnis des Westens* (Leipzig: Grethlein, 1929), pp. 442f., 552, note 65; and Albert Dieterich (note 124), p. 122, where he points out the correspondence between these texts and the myths in Plato. For further source references, see the works cited (references to Foucart, Reinhardt, *et al.*).

126   Quoted from J.J. Bachofen, *Das Mutterrecht* (Basel: Schwabe, ²1897), p. 377, col. 2. As to the name of Pythagoras, it must be remembered that it contains the pythian, i.e., a mantic-magical element. Moreover, Pythagoras was the first to mentally measure the magic element *par excellence*: tone.

127   As it more or less persists in the pre-Platonic attitude, the Orient (Asia) is less aware of this direction. As a curiosity, it might be mentioned that even today, medicinal massage in Asia is carried out in counter-clockwise motion, i.e., toward the left, while this same motion is done clockwise in the West.

128   A brief remark of Paul Schmitt (note 24) furnishes an extremely revealing indication as to the depth of meaning of individual words in antiquity. He states that the apostle Paul knew precisely the numinous connotations and associations that the word *ploutos* (in a Christian sense) would elicit among members of his Greek-speaking congregation.

129   Besides Diels-Kranz (note 87), the edition of Wilhelm Capelle, *Die Vorsokratiker* (Kröners Taschenausgabe vol. 119, Leipzig: Kröner, 1928), p. 163ff. should be consulted.

130   Capelle (note 129), p. 171ff.

131   See the books on this subject by Hans Kayser, as well as Gebser (note 1), ¹1943, ch. 23, ²1945-⁷1965 (Ullstein ed. no. 107), ch. 24; *Gesamtausgabe*, II, pp. 266-72. See also Kayser's article "Eine neue Wissenschaft: die Harmonik," *Die Weltwoche* (Zürich), 655 (May 31, 1946), 2.

132   Our emphasis on the geometric world-image of antiquity should not in any way alter the fact that this image was also pervaded by an arithmetic one; Pythagoras, the "measurer," was also an "enumerator" (see Gebser, note 131, the chapter entitled "Harmonik," where a discussion of the arithmetical world-image may be found). We would again stress that we do not deny that late antiquity had a sense of space, but only emphasize that it was preeminently body-related. —See also Max Bense, *Konturen einer Geistesgeschichte der Mathematik* (Hamburg: Classen & Goverts, 1946), p. 21f.

133   Instructive pictorial material can be found in W. Kirfel, *Die dreiköpfige Gottheit* (Bonn: Dümmler, 1948).—On the trinity, see Fr. Chr. Baur, *Die christliche Lehre von der Dreieinigkeit* (Tübingen: Ossiander, 1841-1843), III, and G. A. Meier, *Die Lehre von der Trinität* (Gotha: Justus Perthes, 1844), ii. There is a brief summary of the "development" of the doctrine of the trinity in Walther Köhler, *Dogmengeschichte* (Zürich: Niehans, ²1943), section 31, p. 269ff.

134   The particular use of the syllable *men* as a suffix for abstract words in Indo-European, a root which we were able to identify as the secondary root of the mental structure, should indicate to what extent abstraction is inherent in that structure; see Walter Henzen, *Deutsche Wortbildung* (Halle/S.: Niemeyer, 1947), p. 119, section 76, 4. Walde Hofmann, on the other hand (note 110, I, p. 323f., entry "daps"), designates this Indo-European *men* as a mere *formans* (see the entry "time" in our "Fifth Remark on Etymology," p. 558 below). A comment by H. Usener is enlightening; in his words, "nouns are generally formed by 'm' suffixes from verbal roots." Such nouns are invariably designations of measuring and quantification: the material aspect of language as opposed to the temporal aspect expressed in the verb.

135   Reproductions of the coins can be found in L. and M. Lanckoronski, "Das griechische Antlitz in Meisterwerken der Münzkunst," *Albae Vigilae* 3 (Amsterdam: Pantheon, 1940), and in Karl Kerényi, L. and M. Lanckoronski, *Der Mythos der Hellenen in Meisterwerken der Münzkunst* (Amsterdam: Pantheon, 1941).

136   The impropriety of releasing atomic energy processes— which are solar and are induced artificially on earth by technological means, and consequently improper on the earth— reflects both the immoderation and the addiction to hyperillumination of the consciousness of modern man evident in this man-made release or production of solar energy. For further discussion on this subject, see the author's *Abendländische Wandlung* (note 1), the augmented ninth chapter in the third and subsequent editions, and also his article "Atomenergie und kosmische Strahlen," *Die Weltwoche* (Zürich), 656 (June 7, 1946), 9.

137   See Hermann Usener's interpretation of the *sol invictus* from the standpoint of religious history in his *Das Weihnachtsfest* (Bonn: Cohen, ²1911), I, Part I, pp. 359-78; see also the work of Paul Schmitt (note 24), p. 198ff., a discussion from the vantage point of the history of religion and of government that takes into account the syncretistic moment.

138   See René Guénon, *Les états multiples de l'être* (Paris: Vegas, 1932), p. 97, note 5.

139   See Edgar Hennecke, ed., *Neutestamentliche Apokryphen* (Tübingen: Mohr, ²1924), p. 180, 56/57.

140   Plutarch, *Vermischte Schriften*, trans. Kaltwasser (Munich: Müller, 1911), I, p. 171ff.: "Table Talk," fifth book; and III, pp. 1-30: "On the Taming of Wrath."

141   Plutarch, *Erotikos*, trans. Paul Brandt (Dresden: Aretz, n.d.), p. 62f. A careful comparison of translations with the original will demonstrate the superiority of Brandt's version; it is a more modern reading in contrast to the versions of Hediger (Munich, Heimeran) and Kaltwasser (note 140), II, p. 23f. We would note in passing that there are passages in Cicero—who had considerable influence on Petrarch—that come from an attitude closely akin to Plutarch's. We would also mention that we have refrained here from citing numerous other witnesses so as not to burden the text, since we do not intend it to be an encyclopedia or compendium.

142   Even "Mosaic Law," the divine instruction about observance of *relegere*, is, as pre-Christian law, predominantly *relegio*, and contains only the germ of *religio*; consequently it is "attention to" (Beachtung) and not yet a "bond to the past," as in the church fathers.

143   The effectiveness and thrust of all "metabolics" (and, unfortunately, of the "metabolicists,", i.e., those caught up and rigidifying in a *metabolé*) results from the fact that they not only preach and defend an idea, but are also compelled to maintain it against themselves, i.e., against their original psychic constitution or disposition. This struggle against the ties to their own past, against themselves as it were, and what they once were, gives them an additional intensity; they must ever negate what they were in order to affirm what they became. Converts have always been the most zealous advocates of what they have—or have been—converted to.

144   See Gebser, *Asienfibel* (Frankfurt: Ullstein ed. no. 650, 1962), p. 86; *Gesamtausgabe*, VI, p. 86.

145   The authenticity of these letters was recently called again into question by the noted authority on the history of autobiography, G. Misch. But whether several of these letters

of Plato are authentic or not, their real significance lies in their form as biographical missives, particularly in view of the time when they were written.

146 See the remark on the fourth proof of relativity by Diels-Kranz (note 87), I, p. 254, note, where they state: "Zeno furnishes the most primitive form of Einstein's theory of relativity." See also Capelle (nóte 129), p. 180.

147 These brief remarks would seem only to skirt that vast period between the close of antiquity and the later Middle Ages when the northern countries were preparing to reconnect to the thought and forms completed in the Riannodamento, or Renaissance. We have had to forego a more detailed description of this intervening period, since our main emphasis is on the mutative junctures in the historical continuum.

148 See Menge-Güthling (note 35), p. 126, and our "Fifth Remark on Etymology" under the entries "time" and "daimon." We have since learned that O. Kern, in his *Die Religion der Griechen* (Berlin: Weidmann, 1926), I, p. 263, speaks of the *daimonen* as "dividers," and that von Wilamowitz remarks that "a *daimon* is, as we know, a severer" in his *Der Glaube der Hellenen* (Berlin: Weidmann, 1931), I, p. 363. Neither, however, mentions what is "divided" or whose "divider" the demonic is supposed to be.

149 We have based our remarks on the causal structure of Descartes' statement, occasioned by the *ergo*; we do not wish to get involved in a discussion of its syllogistic intent, particularly as it would have to have an *atque* as a middle term to be a true syllogism (on the syllogism, see below p. 257). We also wish to refrain from an existential interpretation such as that of Jean-Paul Sartre in his *Descartes* (Paris: Trois Collines, 1946); his attempt would seem to be misguided as long as he uses the original Latin text, since the axiom gains its problematic individual character through the separation in French of the pronoun *je* ("I") from the verbal action: *je suis* instead of *sum*.

150* Bertrand Russell, *Western Philosophical Thought* (London: Allen & Unwin, 1945), pp. 586ff., 374; *A History of Western Philosophy* (New York: Simon & Schuster, 1945), pp. 564ff., 355.

151 See Gebser, *Rilke und Spanien* (note 42), p. 43ff.; *Gesamtausgabe*, I, p. 44ff.

152 Further details as well as sources for the illustrations in Gebser, *Rilke und Spanien* (note 42), p. 43 and note 54.

153 Max Zacharias, *Einführung in die projektive Geometrie*, Mathematische Bibliothek, VI (Leipzig: Teubner, 1912), 1; see also pp. 2, 25, 47, and 50.

154 Our estimation of Desargues recognizes what is symptomatic in his work from the vantage point of intellectual history. For more specialized estimations the reader is referred to the discussions of mathematicians such as M. Zacharias, M. Cantor, and others whose investigations are necessarily more exhaustive than ours.

155 Descartes, *Oeuvres et Lettres*, Bibliothèque de la Pleiade XL (Paris: N.R.F., 1937), p. 556ff.

156 G. W. Leibniz, "Neue Abhandlungen über den menschlichen Verstand," *Philosophische Werke*, III, trans. Ernst Cassirer (Philosophische Bibliothek vol. 69 [Leipzig: Meiner, ³1915]), p. 92.

157 See Gebser, *Rilke und Spanien* (note 42), p. 43f.; *Gesamtausgabe*, I, p. 44ff.

158 Gebser, *Rilke und Spanien*, pp. 49f., 48f.

4

Mutations as an Integral Phenomenon: An Intermediate Summary

1. *Cross-sections through the Structures*

Having attempted to present the various consciousness structures in their temporal sequence, in "longitudinal section" as it were, we should now, before addressing the most important attendant problems, turn to a summary that presents them in "cross-section" from a different vantage point. Besides ensuring an orderly survey, this will also demonstrate that, when speaking of the structures which constitute us, we are dealing with an integral phenomenon. Each and every one of us is not just the sum or "result" of the mutations described, but their embodiment as a whole—a whole that also contains latently the possible further mutation to aperspectivity (which we will describe in Part II below).

Two considerations are fundamental to this provisional summary, one with respect to its manner of presentation, the other to its main organizing principle. We must bear in mind that the cross-section in its entirety which is to organize the material we have discussed so far will necessarily consist of various thematically ordered sections. Our task, then, is to summarize the various mutually interdependent characteristics of the individual structures in their respective unfolding throughout the course of the mutational sequence. This will provide the main point of departure for our summation: we shall have to inquire into the unfolding of the individual characteristics, forms of manifestation, and interrelationships of the respective structures.

Basic to this mode of consideration is the circumstance that we can ascribe to the individual structures certain characteristics within their given relationships to space and time. We have found two categories that serve to express these relationships: dimensions and perspective. When we summarize our previous discussion of the individual structures in the form of a cross-section, the following structuration becomes evident for each of the categories mentioned. When read from the top down, it indicates an unfolding structuration, when read across a complementary structuration:

Structure	1. Space and Time Relationship		
	a) Dimensioning	b) Perspectivity	c) Emphasis
Archaic:	Zero-dimensional	None	Prespatial Pretemporal
Magic:	One-dimensional	Pre-perspectival	Spaceless Timeless
Mythical:	Two-dimensional	Unperspectival	Spaceless Natural temporicity
Mental:	Three-dimensional	Perspectival	Spatial Abstractly temporal
Integral:	Four-dimensional	Aperspectival	Space-free Time-free

We are now able to see how every mutation of consciousness that constituted a new structure of consciousness was accompanied by the appearance and effectuality of a new dimension. This clearly underscores the interdependence of consciousness and a space-time world; for each unfolding of consciousness there is a corresponding unfolding of dimensions. An increase in the one corresponds to an increase of the other; the emergence of consciousness and the dimensioning imply and govern each other. What we have defined as perspectivity is accordingly only one, although essential, aspect of the respective space and time relation—an aspect which only stands out when viewed from the present-day perspectivally rigidified world. This shows that consciousness-unfolding and -dimensioning are accompanied by an increasing reification or materialization of the world. These two facts beget further new facts, suggesting thereby a kind of symmetry which in a remarkable way underscores the complex problem we can define as the problem of measure and mass. This in turn will illuminate a fourth actuality, namely the symmetry evident in the succession of the mutations, a regularity that is revealing with respect to the mutations in their entirety, as well as to the relationships of the individual structures in themselves, and can, accordingly, shed light on our present-day situation.

This should indicate that our intention is *not to systematize but rather to elucidate* the living and working interrelationships, and to convey vividly the vital and effective facts that result from these interrelationships.

Before directing our attention to the cross-sections of further unfolding characteristics of the structures, whose next grouping includes their respective sign, essence, and properties, we must consider for a moment the ascriptions made above for the integral structure that result from their particular relation to space and time. Its four-dimensionality represents ultimately an integration of dimensions. It results in a *space-and-time-free* aperspectival world where the free (or freed) consciousness has at its disposal all latent as well as actual forms of space and time, without having either to deny them or to be fully subject to them. To what extent this space-time freedom can be realized in life, to what extent it is compatible with the occurrence of presentation, and to what degree it can be related to what we call the *diaphainon*[1] —these are questions which are resolved to the degree that we become aware of further elements that make up the individual structures.

Let us now turn our attention to further cross-sections. If we recall the previously mentioned sign, essence, and properties for each individual structure, the following new cross-section results:

Structure	2. Sign	3. Essence	4. Properties
Archaic:	None	Identity (Integrality)	Integral
Magic:	Point	Unity (Oneness)	Non-directional unitary Interwovenness or fusion
Mythical:	Circle O	Polarity (Ambivalence)	Circular and polar Complementarity
Mental:	Triangle △	Duality (Opposition)	Directed dual oppositionality
Integral:[2]	Sphere ●	Diaphaneity (Transparency)	Presentiating, diaphanous "rendering whole"

As in the case of the dimensioning, it is again evident from the sequence of signs that we can observe an increase or expansion in the course of the mutational series. Our choice of signs is not arbitrary but rather an organic outgrowth of our exposition of the individual structures. The signs do not distort or denature the objectively given state of affairs any more or less than in any instance in which we describe or represent something; every description or representation contains an alien factor not present in what is described, inasmuch as we are compelled to impose an order on something undeniably organic that confronts our linguistic and conceptual means, and to arrange sequentially an obviously complex event.

The signs convey the extension of the point to a circle, the break-up of the circle by the triangle, that is, the division of the circle into sectors—the quantitative increase and extent of the mutations. Conversely, we can see in the rearrangements that determine the given essence of the structures a countermovement; the increase of dimension by which consciousness gains extent and scope is inversely proportional to the qualitative character of the individual structures, which undergo in each instance a reduction or diminution of value or intensity. The incrementation of consciousness does not correspond to an increase within the relationship to the whole, even if that were possible, but rather to a lessening or weakening of this relationship.

In qualitative terms, then, the expanding consciousness reduces its own system of interrelationships. Unity is only a reduced wholeness; yet an inceptual consciousness in man is possible only once this unity has been achieved. Polarity further expands the arena in which consciousness operates, providing the tension necessary for everything that lives and unfolds. At the same time, the originary presence of the whole is lessened or dimmed. It can no longer be experienced to its original degree as wholeness but only through an act of completion or complementarity. And, as noted earlier, the further dimensional increment that drives polar self-complementarity into the dualistic division and measurability of oppositions does not even allow for an act of completion but at most for an act of unification which is always fragmentary. (These reductive "Potentialities of the Structures" will be presented in the very next cross section below.)

There seems, therefore, to be a qualitative reduction of wholeness that corresponds to the quantitative augmentation of consciousness which, by dimensioning, creates its own system of interrelationships. The increasing expansion, extension, or growth of consciousness evident in the mutations is inversely proportional to the reduction of the integral system of interrelationships which it has apparently lost. When viewed in this way, the dimensioned world seems to be one split off from the whole. The quantitative spatio-temporal system of relationships increases to the degree of the growth of consciousness and is recognizable in the increase of dimensions and reification. Yet there is at the same time a proportional decrease of the pre-spatial and pre-temporal presence of origin; man is no longer in the whole. Henceforth he is to an ever-greater degree merely a participant in the whole, although the whole ultimately cannot be lost since the archaic structure or origin is irrevocably present.

What takes place here is perhaps less a weakening or distantiation from origin than a remarkable kind of rearrangement. To us, accustomed as we are to thinking in terms of subject and object so as to be capable of mental thinking, this presents itself as a rearrangement of intensities similar to consciousness, in which what is rearranged is carried over from the objective world—or universe, i.e., world in its entirety—into man. Man becomes the bearer or agent of the originary "consciousness" (or whatever we may wish to call it), and his earthly conditionality, via his spatializing and temporalizing, renders terrestrial that which is integral and related to the whole.

Man, however, is not just a creature of earth; he is also a creature of heaven, if only because he breathes this heaven with every breath (if one will permit the somewhat loose physical description). In every breath the "substance" of even the most remote heavens is present if only to an infinitesimal degree. Now, to the extent that he is a creature of the heavens, what we have just observed to be a diminution or an augmentation, a loss or a gain, may seem for the moment somewhat perplexing; but it would be even more perplexing if man were *only* a creature of earth and heaven. Since he is more than this—and, because quantitative terms are irrelevant here, we could also say: less than this—we could perhaps, in the further course of our discussion, extricate this state of affairs from its dualistic cul-de-sac or, in mental terms, its statement of gains and losses, particularly as we will be able to verify a number of inceptions including some that free us from the compulsion of dualism.

If we are to summarize in a third grouping those aspects which can bring us a step further toward resolving the questions that have arisen, this cross-section will have to make evident what we have designated as the "Potentialities of the Structures." To the extent that these are potentialities which consciousness opens up through its mutations, we must be aware of the particular aspects of world with which the respective potentialities of consciousness associate, that is, which aspect takes on the nature of consciousness for a given structure. In addition we must also become aware of the energy—the movement and dynamism—which is the agent or initiator in man of the particular consciousness emergence. If we do this, we can in mental terms note the particular accentuations of consciousness in the familiar categories of subject and object which result in the following cross-section (the ascriptions in parentheses cannot be discussed until later):

Structure	5. Potentiality	6. Emphasis	
		a) Objective (external) (Aspect of World)	B) Subjective (internal) (Energy or Initiator)
Archaic:	Integrality	Unconscious Spirit	None or Latency
Magic:	Unity by Unification and Hearing/Hearkening	Nature	Emotion
Mythical:	Unification by Complementarity and Correspondence	Soul/Psyche	Imagination
Mental:	Unification by Synthesis and Reconciliation	Space - World	Abstraction
Integral:	Integrality by Integration and Presentation	(Conscious Spirit)	(Concretion)

From this it will be evident that the incrementation of consciousness goes hand in hand with a "diminution" of the relation to the realizable whole; we do not lose this relation to the whole completely only because the presence of origin cannot be lost, and consequently, it lends to all of the structures which mutate from it and constitute us this same imperishability.

The next cross-section, by contrast, shows how an increase occurs in the sequence of the aspects of world realized in consciousness, which is accompanied by a simultaneous increase in the powers of emergent consciousness by which consciousness is increasingly able to become a reality. Whereas the tenor of the magic structure is definitely one of nature realized in emotion, and that of the mythical structure is one of the psyche realized in imagery, the tenor of the mental structure is one of a spatial world realized in thought. Now it is true that the powers which make possible these realizations increase in number and become conscious and usable; but there is a simultaneous narrowing of the realized aspect of world which at first glance appears incongruous: nature and the psyche, both incommensurate, are more all-encompassing than the spatial world apprehended by the measuring thought which culminates in perspectivity.

The dilemma can perhaps be resolved if we turn to a summary of aspects that can be brought together under the headings of the degree and the relation of consciousness of the respective structures. Here we encounter the symmetry spoken of earlier that may provide some assurance where the apparent inconsistencies of the phenomena could tend to become confusing. This symmetry will be apparent from the following cross-section:

Structure	7. Consciousness- a) Degree	b) Relation
Archaic:	Deep sleep	Universe-related: Breathing-spell
Magic:	Sleep	Outer-related (Nature): Exhaling
Mythical:	Dream	Inner-related (Psyche): Inhaling
Mental:	Wakefulness	Outer-related (Spatial world): Exhaling
Integral:	(Transparency)	(Inward-related: Inhaling? or Breathing-spell?)

Our inclusion of deep sleep and sleep under the rubric of consciousness in this cross section may be justified by the fact that we do not attribute consciousness to these two states (which might be designated as a somnolent and somniative, i.e., dream consciousness respectively), but only a form or degree of consciousness in view of their function in the awakening process reflected by the mutational series. This also renders invalid the prevalent dualistic pairing of an Unconscious as opposed to Consciousness (see p. 204f.).

The symmetry to which we have just referred is evident in what we might call the pulse or the breath rhythm inherent in the mutations when considered as a whole. The archaic structure might be thought of as the silent pause before breath; and when we apostrophize this structure in a somewhat unilateral manner as a "silent pause," we should also bring to mind the inaudible singing latent in every pause: the *musica callada* or "silenced music" of which St. John of the Cross once wrote. The magic structure in turn, inasmuch as it is definitely outer-related toward nature, is a first exhalation, one which we do not wish to postulate for the moment as also a form of "being exhaled," as this could immediately elicit the undeserved reproach of being animistic, a likely charge by the dualistic and anthropocentric mentality prevalent today.[3] But the mythical structure—definitely inner-, i.e., psyche-related—is by comparison to the magic structure definitely suggestive of exhalation; here we find the psychic equivalence of the "inhaling of the heaven" to which we referred earlier. And this "inhalation," as it were, in the mythical structure is even more evident if we consider the mental structure which "follows," for it is again decidedly outward-related to the world and thus shows a distinctly exhaling character.

These conclusions based on the inner-outer relationship of the various structures parallel the data presented in the preceding chapter: the opening up and mastery (and consequent consciousness emergence) of nature by magic man, of the psyche by mythical man, and of the objectified world of space by mental man. In this way the mutational series closes to form a living whole in the symmetry recognizable in the alternation of breath, the organic succession of inhalation and exhalation, as well as in the pulse of the structures.

We have, to all appearances, lent to this symmetry an organic character, giving the mutational process a one-sided biologistic aspect which, to the extent that the biological is predominantly natural, necessarily takes on a magic taint. But we can also understand this symmetry as a polar event, thereby emphasizing its complementary rather than unitary moment. In so doing, however, we run the danger of mythologizing and will have to strive to understand the regularity in terms of our still dominant state of consciousness, comprehending mentally in a sequence what would be diaphanously apprehended as a whole. Since this state of diaphanous consciousness and its form of realization have only been initiated and not yet achieved, we will of necessity have to agree on the mental basis.

We can fathom this symmetry in mental or rational terms and extricate it from the biological-natural magic as well as the psychic-polar mythical spheres by viewing inhalation and exhalation not as a unitary process (specifically as undifferentiated breathing) or as a complementary process (although it is also that), but by understanding it as an antithesis. Yet even this is not sufficient in itself; we must be able to measure the antitheses or antipodes. Only what is measurable can be posited as an opposite, or for that matter posited at all. And, as will be evident, we have taken the first step toward a mental positing and measuring at the very first mention of symmetry. In order to comply adequately with the demand of conceptual measurability as required by the mental structure, we can examine this symmetry in question in terms of the conceptual pair of measure and mass.

We have selected this pair of terms in the first place despite its apparent antithesis, because it is still able to demonstrate its rarely fathomed character as a primal word in the root common to both words. And although everything subsumed by such a conceptual pair bears the stamp of mental antitheticality, it does so only to the extent that it is articulated. In inarticulate form such a pair also embraces polar, unitary, and originary elements. We have selected this pair in the second place because it allows us to observe other revealing phenomena; we would recall in this connection the increase of consciousness and dimensioning, the reification of the world (p. 118f.), as well as the apparent contrary movement of the incrementation of consciousness viewed against the diminishing relationship to the whole (see p. 119).

Here we have arrived at a particular juncture: all of the questions and problems that have surfaced in the previous cross-sections come together and are united in the common denominator of the conceptual pair of "measure and mass." This result provides a natural conclusion to the present discussion and forms the link between our previous deliberations and the inferences that remain to be drawn from them. We shall, accordingly, interrupt for the moment our summation of individual characteristics begun above in order to establish a provisional statement of account.

To facilitate this, we shall summarize all of the previously worked out cross-sections schematically in a form that should be understood not only in vertical cross-section (from the top down), but also in horizontal cross-section (that is, from left to right). We shall also have to extend our "synoptic survey" by an additional cross section (no. 8, p. 142, and also the synoptic table at the end of the volume) which serves to illustrate a further aspect of the problem of measure and mass as it relates to the efficient as well as deficient phases of the particular consciousness structures, and expresses their respective qualitative and quantitative forms of manifestation. To be able to clarify this problem of measure and mass with a view toward our first provisional statement of account, we must digress for a moment to clarify the matter of primal words and the particular background unique to the conceptual pair "measure and mass."

2. A Digression on the Unity of Primal Words

We have already pointed out above (p. 1-2) that we intend to draw particularly on linguistic evidence to elucidate our inquiry. Speech or language is not only fundamental to the life of every individual, it is also a compelling and linking factor. The success of our exposition will depend to a considerable extent on how we approach and incorporate language into our discussion. This is particularly true of our attempt to present and describe new circumstances and conditions by means of traditional language.

The present work is concerned with new or at least novel actualities; because of this we do not restrict ourselves to treating a clearly circumscribed thesis with rationally placed subdivisions and a consequently invariable and predetermined terminology. In order to reveal an integral structure in which the pre-rational and irrational elements have a role equal to the rational, it is essential for us to maintain an attitude toward language cognizant of its wholeness. Just as every person represents and lives the entire mutational series of mankind through his structures, so too each word reflects its mutational exfoliation within language itself.

We have refrained from the common practice of imputing to words, particularly to our key words, a mental or rational connotation with a rigid and unilateral definition. Rather we have endeavored to ascertain what the word itself denotes and articulates; we have, in other words, not restricted our understanding to the gradually obdurate conceptual meaning in each instance as if it were the word's only valid sense. This procedure will undoubtedly offend some, particularly those who believe they can function entirely within the confines of the "rational" structure in their pursuit of scientific "objectivity," oblivious to the limitations imposed by their objectivation of their own vital and psychic makeup.[4]

This does not necessarily place our procedure into a value-opposition over against contemporary modes of inquiry. We merely wish to indicate how and why our procedure must differ. The task that has posed itself to us of revealing the world as an entirety necessarily differs from that of the exclusive rationalist who divides and subdivides—indeed is compelled to do so—in order to obtain his specialized and partial results. Like a purely rational approach with its weaknesses and limitations, ours too has its shortcomings, limitations and, above all, temporal restrictions in the form of temporal boundaries.

It is this very fact of temporal boundaries that induces us to begin our discussion of language with a temporic moment. We must let the words—at least those central to our discussion—reveal whatever their temporal aspect holds. This temporal aspect resides in the primordial meaning of the word-root which even today gives the word in latent and potential form its distinctive stamp. It is the original meaning that is still luminous throughout the unfolding changes of meaning taken on or attributed over the years. Every word, after all, is not only a concept or a fixed equivalent in writing; it is also an image and thus mythical, a sound and thus magic, a root and thus archaic, and thus, by virtue of this root meaning, still present from origin.

The perils inherent in such an approach to language are of course legion and can be avoided only when an equilibrium prevails in the actual form and structure of the language used to describe the integral structure—an equilibrium corresponding to that which must be maintained among the various structures that constitute us and tend to be dominated by the mind when we describe this integral structure. We must, in other words, go back to the word-roots, as we have been doing, and listen to those words that belong together; we must complement these with others that seem to correspond to each other until an image appears, and we must allow ourselves to be directed by the criteria imposed on us by our thinking, or which we impose on it. Then we can be certain that we remain within the respective framework of the data of each individual structure, and that these data, viewed from our present mental standpoint, are effectual.

But merely avoiding the danger of overemphasizing one aspect—magic, mythical, or rational—in our interpretation of a given word is not enough; we must guard against the greater danger of not recognizing the temporal boundaries of even the integral approach. These boundaries—or more precisely, limits—are found in the "furthermost" or "deepest" past where a beginning starts to mutate from origin, and they are also found in the present, since it too has the character of origin. But if we for the moment were to look "back," particularly as we are proceeding mentally via measurement and method and not diaphanously, we discover this beginning located where the individual word-roots mutate from their nocturnal amalgamation with the world in its entirety.

Our inability to trace this decisive process of word formation to a specific point is analogous to our inability to determine precisely when and where the root hairs of plants, already invisible, merge and coalesce with the surrounding soil, or the soil, in turn, assumes the form of the root hairs. Indeed the very obscurity, dormancy, fusion, and undifferentiated texture of the primal sounds and roots give us at the very most an intimation of what takes place beyond that temporal limit which exists between the archaic and the magic structures and had to be surmounted during the formation of the primal words.

With these remarks we hope to have dispelled some of the apprehensions which may have prompted some readers to question our approach. By remaining cognizant of our attempt to proceed integrally, we can avoid the over-emphasis on the one or the other structure; and if we recognize that there is even a limit to this integrality (with respect to its manifestations), we have the further protection from being submerged into abysses and obscurities which the illumination of our mind and our diurnal wakefulness are ill-equipped to counter.

There are also deficiencies in our mode of inquiry evident here that result from our need to single out and order mentally the particular strands of the roots from the thicket of the root context whenever we wish to trace back the root meanings—strands which must correspond both to the function we shall have to grant the particular root, and to the aspect of world which they are to illuminate. This is how we have proceeded in our discussion of roots for the words magic, myth, and menis. Thus what at first glance appears to have been a possibly arbitrary interpretation may be justified if we recognize the given relationship as the valid initiator of our respective selection and emphasis.

Yet we must not assume that the discovery of irrational and prerational contexts necessarily leads to irrationalism. Every attempt to recover the roots summons forth in us at least one defense: their obscurity and unfathomability run counter to the mental attitude, and the very proximity of the non-rational structures tends to activate negatively pre-rational, affective-emotional responses.

This is particularly true unless we are able to some degree to view these matters from the "aperspectival" vantage point alluded to (though not elaborated) earlier, thereby protecting ourselves from sliding into the prerational or irrational stances, rather than to attempt to "rise above" them, particularly as the rational attitude cannot do this of itself. And it may be appropriate here to note that the present work has nothing in common with what we might term "life philosophies," although we take vital and psychic relationships into account. Such "philosophies" are the work of Vitalists, among whom Klages and Spengler are notable representatives, and also of "Emotionalists," as we should like to call them, who disport even more luxuriantly in the waters of irrationalism; representative of this tendency are Ernst Bergmann and Fritz Klatt, among others.

In spite of these complications, let us turn our attention to the task of examining roots which even today show the greatest vitality in the primal words. Karl Abel, in his monumental study cited earlier (p. 8, note 3), has demonstrated that these primal words are "contrary in sense," prompting Sigmund Freud to speak of them in his review of Abel (also cited above) as being "antithetical." To us it would seem that this definition, while not inappropriate, is at least one-sided; it is valid only if we are content to describe the phenomenon of primal words in mental-rational terms. The words "contrary in sense" clearly demonstrate the purely rationalistic attitude of its author, both in the "contrary" and in the "sense," which in this instance clearly reflect that sense of direction inherent in the word "sense," as we noted earlier (pp. 78-79).

But in dealing with primal words, as with all primal phenomena, it makes no sense to speak of antithesis and direction unless we were to content ourselves, contrary to our human inclinations, with explaining only the rational sector of our world and dispensing with the presentiation of the whole. To the extent that all primal phenomena are manifest in, and belong predominantly to, the efficient phase of the magic structure where the emphasis lies on the magic unity and not on conceptual antithesis or mythical complementarity, we must define a rational conception of the "contradictoriness" of primal words as their "unity." We speak here of "unity" because it is *one* syllable, *one* root, or *one* word family that expresses something nonantithetical and unitary which only later is polarized and even later still undergoes a modification by our thinking into an antithesis.

The beginning of the process that leads to polarity and antithesis presumably occurs as early as the deficient phase of the magic structure, or at least has its preparatory stage there. At the outset the primal words testify to the very directionless, "senseless" undifferentiation which we find characteristic of the magic structure. And it is not true as Abel apparently maintains, if we are to judge on the basis of Freud's review, that the positive or negative "meaning" or sense was conveyed via signs or gestures accompanying their utterance (among the Egyptians or the Greeks for instance); rather, this sense was expressed, in any event before the Egyptian and Greek periods, by lengthening or shortening the stem vowel, that is, by a phonic distinction.

The root *mu* on which the word "myth" is based (see pp. 64-65) can serve as a representative example, with its vowel pronounced long or short, thereby giving rise to its later "antithetical" meaning. For it is this auditory aspect, not the imagistic or pictographic, which we will have to attribute to the initial phenomena if we are to remain consistent with the results of our findings. In its beginnings the magic structure is definitively auditory; the ear is the magic sensor, not the eye with its images and signs. Sonority and music, not image or sign, are the inceptual and coincident manifestational and realizational forms of the magic structure, where they still form a unity. Nowhere is timelessness more evident than during those moments when we abandon ourselves to the power of music, becoming nearly as timeless as magic man.

Magic man, however, had a keener and more nuanced sense of hearing; and languages such as Chinese that are less rationalistic, and therefore closer to the magic realm than the European tongues, are distinct in their phonetic nuances which are able to confer completely different meanings on otherwise identical stem syllables or phonemes. The meaning of a particular word in Chinese, for example, is determined by the pronunciation of the stem vowel; a lengthened or shortened vowel, a rising or a falling intonation, conveys in each instance a different meaning.

We could conceivably speak here of an auditory orientation on which magic man's "confrontation with nature" is similarly based (to which we addressed ourselves earlier). Even in Old Greek, and as late as Latin, where meter or the mental quantifying moment is manifest as an opposition to the organic presence of rhythm (we need only recall Homer and Virgil), we meet up with this auditory ability which we have nearly lost. It enabled the Greeks in their declamation of a hymn or an epic poem to express not only the meter—hexameter—but also to emphasize the individual words of a given verse according to their natural accentuation, a remarkable auditory achievement particularly as the metric accent rarely coincided with the stress of the individual words.[5]

It is this primordiality of hearing that enables us to find an adequate definition for the phenomena of primal words. Perhaps the auditory sense is not the first from a physiological standpoint, but it is definitely more prominent in the magic realm than the visual sense. Or, to be more exact: both were undifferentiated; and to the extent that the eye reacted, it was more receptive to the tone colors in what it perceived, as is evident in the aura depictions which show in the original a relatively greater differentiation of colors than of contours. Speaking of the age before the influence of the earliest founders of religion, Creuzer observes that "auditory symbolism . . . was not yet distinguished from visual symbolism."[6] He senses, in other words, the still-evident undifferentiation of eye and ear, at least with respect to what we have called the efficient phase of magic. Indeed, this lack of differentiation is valid for that structure in general, particularly as the sharp contours of the prehistoric cave paintings were presumably executed only toward the close of the deficient phase of the magic structure.

Yet even today in our intellectualized languages there are word pairs which manifest the polarity or ambivalence of the primal syllable that in itself expresses and represents a unity. An instance of this is the word pair that formed the point of departure for this digression, measure and mass, or *Māss* and *Măsse*; they bear the same relationship to each other as the words *Wēg*, "way" and *wĕg*, "away," and *Mūsse*, "musing" and *Mŭss*, "compunction," cited earlier (p. 110, note 80). In all three instances, the lengthening or shortening of the stem vowel echos the ambivalence of what was once an undifferentiated unity.

This is also true of yet another word pair which has a signal role in our discussion, particularly as we are concerned throughout with the question of consciousness and, of course, the unconscious: the pair *Höhle*, "cavern," and *Helle*, "brightness." Both words derive from the Indo-Germanic root *kel* to which are related from earliest times the Latin words *clam*, "secretly," and *clamare*, "to scream," as well as the German words *hehlen*, "to conceal," *Halle*, "hall," *hohl*, "hollow," *Hülle*, "cloak, shell," and *Hülse*, "hull, husk," among others.[7]

The root of the word pair "measure" and "mass" is *ma:me*, a configuration at the basis of the mental structure. From this root it should be evident that at the outset primal words are neither contradictory nor ambivalent (nor in consequence, polar), but rather became so; their unity became polarized and later antithetical. We must not overlook the effects of this cleavage in our attempt at an integral mode of understanding and presentation, for it is in effect a dimensioning of the primal words. The initially unitary and later polar nature unique to these words can no more be rationalized away than man's instinct, emotion, and imagination can be explained away without denying and destroying man's very humanity. Rational analysis, it is true, can explain some things; but it is powerless to come to terms with phenomena such as unity or polarity. Moreover, our concern here is with clarification, not with explanation.

Let us then keep in mind that the presence of origin manifest in the inceptual unity—and in the successive mutations to polarity and then duality—is still recognizable in the principal words. If we remain cognizant of this origin and employ the words in a manner that manifests their integrity, they will at least lend the lustre of wholeness to those phenomena which they denote. Then, too, our sense of hearing, our heart, and our mind must be equally awake; within the natural measure of things none of these faculties must dominate to a degree greater than that commensurate with our given state of consciousness.

Since our capacity for regarding things in the way just mentioned may well be a preliminary stage of what we have described as aperspectival perception or concretizing, that is, integrating transparent sight, we should adduce some additional examples to illustrate the function of such words as those already cited toward achieving an integral mode of realization. For the world—at least to us—is not just a concept but at the same time always a sound and an image. "Behind" these the presence of origin "resides," and can be diaphanously present for us only when we presentiate these aspects of our world as a whole.

There are relatively few word pairs such as those cited (Māss-Măsse, Wēg-wĕg, Mūsse-Mŭss or Höhle-Hĕlle) that illustrate the initial unity which is later polarized and ultimately rigidified as an antithesis; and those that are extant are difficult to locate since we have only etymological dictionaries which trace the modern words back to their Indo-European roots. What is lacking are dictionaries which we should like to call "root dictionaries" in which the development or exfoliation of the roots throughout the various languages is recorded.[8]

A dictionary such as this would also have to consider what we shall call the "mirror root." By this we mean the inversion of the root sounds that express the "other side" of the basic meaning; as an example of this we would like to describe how we came to discover the mirror root in connection with the pair Höhle (hēhlen)-Hĕlle.

We had been preoccupied for some time with the likely root kinship of the words "Logos," "light," and "lie" (untruth); now the Indo-Germanic root of Logos (from the Greek verb lego) is leg, that of "light" is le(u)k, and that of "lie" is presumably this same root, leg:le(u)k.[9] But this is of course merely the inversion of the root kel; in other words, in the mirror sound—where everything is reversed—obscurity and concealment (das Verhehlte, "what is hidden," die Hölle, "hell," and die Höhle, "cavern," which are all silent) become light (and also voice). That is, when inverted, kel, "darkness," is leg.

The effect of this law of mirroring inherent in the unity of the roots is consistent with what we have called the speculatio animae; whatever is "inside" becomes visible "outside" in the mirror image. One meaning is expressed directly in the word, while there is an additional latent and unexpressed "inner" meaning that is directly expressed as a complementary (and thus unitary) rather than antithetical meaning. The mirroring thus renders this complementary meaning expressible and audible.

The allusion to "silence" and "voice" in the next to last paragraph above[10] brings us to another pair of words which expresses the former unity of primal words, *Stimme* (voice) and *Stumme* (silent, dumb). This unity is not only echoed in the modern words by the shortening or lengthening of the stem vowels, as in the word pairs *Māss-Măsse* and *Wēg-wĕg*, but also by modification of the vowels, as in the shift from the verb *hēhlen* to the noun *Höhle*, "cavern," which have the same root as *hĕll*, "bright."

A further pair we have noticed is *Tat* ("deed") and *tot* ("dead"); what we first found remarkable was the shift from the initial *A* to the concluding *O*—the Alpha and Omega of Greek—as well as the pair's occurrence with the *T*, which long before Greek tau was a symbol for life among the Egyptians. But such an interpretation is not adequate for our present thinking because of its symbol-based mythologization,[11] and we accordingly sought after the roots of both words, only to discover that they in fact share the same root despite their "antithetical" denotations. The verb *tun*, or "do," from which *Tat* (and in this case "deed") is derived can be traced back to the Indo-Germanic root *dhe:dho*, while the word *Tod*, "death," goes back to the Indo-Germanic root *dheu:dhou*. And there is almost a final confirmation of the primal unity of these words in the fact that their double root has given rise to the word *dad*, which in Old Saxon means "to do" and in Old Frisian "dead."[12]

Our reasons for emphasizing this pair are neither fortuitous nor accidental, and we will return to the basic or original conception contained in it, namely that life also embraces death. This conception is of the same importance to our discussion as that which is evident in the initial unity of *Höhle* ("cavern") and *hell* ("bright").

Finally, let us mention the more familiar form of that "unity of primal words" which is evident in the antitheticality of our intellectualized European languages, for instance in the word "cold" which as *caldo* in Italian and *chaud* in French mean "hot" and not "cold." This interplay, emphasizing in the one language now the one, in another language now the other or "contrary" aspect of the once unitary signification, is more frequent than commonly realized.[13] It may be worth pondering that this process holds true of a fundamental word in the Western conceptual hierarchy: Latin *deus* and French *dieu* (God) can be traced to the same Sanskrit word *deva* as English "devil" and German *Teufel*.[14]

Among the implications which urge themselves on us from this consideration of the unity of primal words one is pre-eminent: within the medium which we must employ to present the whole or the integral, that is within language, we can discern integral echoes which emerge from "behind" the unity of primal words and restore to language the integral character indispensable to the success of any attempt to represent this integrality.

A further implication, resulting primarily from the auditory predisposition of the magic structure, can be found in our ability to find in language itself some enlightenment about certain primordial interrelationships if we are willing to listen to language and respond to it in the same degree that we believe it to be under our "command." Some words manifest an identity, others a correspondence, others a complementarity in image; still others establish a logical-antithetical relation to each other. Consequently, it is no accident that we speak of a plea or a prayer being "heard" by something or someone able to "answer" it; this auditory process shows that it too, like everything else connected with this form of utterance, has a magic character.

Nor is it accidental that wishes are "fulfilled"; fulfillment requires something that can be closed or completed, such as a circle or the psyche that responds to a wish. And the fact that we speak of ideals as "ideal images" (*Wunschbilder*) and "wishful thinking" and "pipe-dreams" as *Wunschträume* or "wish dreams," and even equate the notion of "dream" with "wishes" ("dream home," etc.), shows the degree to which all aspects of wishfulness correspond to our psychic-mythical structure with its imagistic and dream-like character. And it is surely no coincidence that language relates the word "will" or volition with "attaining a goal" rather than with being heard or fulfilled, since such goal-orientation definitely relegates it to the mental structure.[15]

If we consider these primordial interconnections, recalling the close kinship between the words "think" and "thank,"[16] as well as "live" and "love,"[17] our suggestion that we "attend" to language will bring about a greater "wakefulness" than mere "attention" (for a discussion of the expressive force of the number eight which occurs in the words for "attend" and "attentin," *achten* and *Achtsamkeit*, see p. 17 above); it will result in the "supra-wakeful" diaphany to which not only what is past but perhaps also what is yet to come could be present.[18]

Let us conclude this digression with the sole example of a primal word still intact in modern German: the word *All*, whose importance for the archaic structure is evident in the previous cross-sections. This word in everyday speech, which is less intellectualized than formal writing, presents us with the pure primal word and its expression of unity or identity without any modification of vowel or vowel quantity. This word, which denotes the most encompassing existence of everything, can at the same time mean utter non-existence, since when speaking of something we look for and find used up we say: *Es ist alle*, "It is all (gone)."

3. A Provisional Statement of Account: Measure and Mass

The cross-sections ensuing from our discussion in the first section of this chapter, which we summarized in the first part of the synoptic table, led to various questions and "symmetries" which can be dealt with under the uniform heading of "measure and mass." We noted in particular four "symmetries" or "laws":

1) There is an interdependence of the incrementation of consciousness and the increase of dimensions that results in a growing reification of the world. Thus the problem of measure and mass presents itself in the form of a transition from moderation to augmentation and (material) aggregation; as it appears here as an aspect of mass, it is a seemingly rational problem;

2) There is an interchange of moderation and immoderation evident in what we have described as the breathing character of our structures. This questions does not present itself with a one-sided emphasis on one aspect as in the case of mass, but rather as a polar question where exhalation is a natural consequence and complement of inhalation. It also appears as a biological question, inasmuch as it relates to breathing as a biological function; but to this we may, in turn, attach psychic polar values. Here we are faced, in other words, with a predominantly psychic problem (see p. 71f.);

3) A certain equalization (always a prerequisite of any unity) takes place be-

tween the diminution of the relationship to the whole, as we have defined it, and the increase in the powers of consciousness which create their own texture of interrelationships and apparently compensate for the diminution. Here the problem of measure and mass manifests itself as an aspect of unity and therefore essentially as a question of magic;

4) Each individual structure has an inherent and recurring symmetry in that the qualitative (moderate) and efficient form is superseded by the quantitative (immoderate) formlessness which is deficient; measure and mass, then, are characteristic of these two phases of each structure. Since we can place this symmetry into the causal context, the problem poses itself in an essentially mental form; we shall see, however, that the causal nexus is manifest here as an expression of wholeness or integrality. Only an aggregation or quantification—an indication of an exhausted qualitative potency—can guarantee a new mutation which seems to emerge from "the whole" that forms the decisive element in each mutation. We can assume on the other hand that the mutations occurring in man "strive toward" or enable the integration into the whole.

From this enumeration it will be evident why we could not approach this discussion of the four "symmetries" directly in terms of our antithetical pair "measure and mass," for we would have achieved only the partial results characteristic of mental quantification and distorted the actual effective agency. Since we now know that the terms "measure and mass" not only embody the antithesis that is expressed in rationalistic terms, but the polar moment and the basic unitary element as well, we can convey—through the conceptual pair as a whole—individual aspects as well as the integrality of those things and problems which, in mental terms, present themselves to us as symmetries.

If we are able, then, to keep in mind that this pair "measure and mass" is definitely not just an expression of antithesis, but also of a complementary and originally a unitary phenomenon, we shall be in a position to consciously effect the integrality represented both by the conceptual pair and by the sum of its individual aspects, even though we can deal with only one of these aspects at any given time.

Yet it is surely not sufficient here to merely recount certain "symmetries," particularly as we are dealing predominantly with the "-metries" or measures that we have imposed on things, and things which we have described in such a way as to make possible this imposition of measure. We grant these symmetries a value only to the extent that they are able to bring something to bear "in time"; our spatial thinking will have to be complemented and integrated by the intensity of time (see Part II, chapter 1, section 1). If we can effect this, we again come near to integration of the whole; let us then venture a provisional statement of account to determine what conclusions can be drawn from the individual symmetries and observe them one after the other as to their possible consequences.

We are today, perhaps more than ever before, prone to take stock and inquire into our gains and losses; consequently the gain or increment in dimensions of which we spoke earlier leads us directly to a consideration of the consequences of this increment of consciousness and dimensions that we have identified. We saw how each new mutation was accompanied by a new dimension that began to take effect; each new mutation, in other words, "accrued" a gain in dimension. And this increase of a dimension in each instance unquestionably represents "progress," a progression we might define as one from measure or moderation to a gradual measurelessness or immoderation of (the) mass, particularly if we deemed an ever-expanding dimensioning and expansion of consciousness to be desirable. But: every-thing depends on an *intensification*, not on an expansion or extension of con-sciousness.

We have just spoken of a "gain" in connection with the word "progress" or progression, which terms, as we noted earlier, also express a loss. This particular configuration expresses something that from a dualistic vantage point we could con-sider positive, inasmuch as it contains an increase. But it also expresses a negative aspect since the increase is faced by a decrease or loss on the ledger: the predomi-nance of this progressive increase leads to disintegration and ultimately even to atomization.

Here we arrive at the particular juncture where the anxiety of our age is so much in evidence. The "either-or" of dualism comes into prominence as an un-bridgeable alternative and threatens to place everything in doubt. We are presented with the choice: either we must have progress as advocated and promised by the "exoterics" (i.e., the technicians and technocrats)—more of the quantification and progression away from origin—or we must undergo a return to origins as preached by the "esoterics" (i.e., the occultists). In either case—forcing the wheel forward or turning it back—we are confronted with an illusion as illusory as any mere forward or backward motion as such.

This alternative, a symptom of the predicament of the mental structure in its quantitative, rationalistic phase, can have accordingly only a limited validity. Its va-lidity can extend no further than that of dualism itself; from an integral standpoint it is merely a pseudo-alternative, a "solution"—if at all—only in the form of a synthetic compromise whose effect is almost entirely restricted to the mental-conceptual world. It is, in a word, ultimately no solution at all.

Here the dualistic-trinitary conception of the world reaches its own limits; even the attempt to transcend this conception, as is recurrently undertaken by phi-losophy, is illusory to the extent that any transcendence is inseparably bound to spatial and measurable criteria. Only phenomena that are spatially limited can be transcended, that is, crossed over or "gone beyond"; and temporal limits or fixed terms can be exceeded only in the language of banking and finance. The spatial character incident to any attempt at transcendence "adjusts" the very attempt in both senses of the word: it aims toward a further emphasis on mental consciousness and "being in the right," and thus toward further perspectivistic rigidity, and also adjudges or passes final judgement and condemnation on itself.

This dimensioning of the structures encompassed by the problem of measure and mass is not a question of gains or losses, then, unless we wish to remain in the cul-de-sac of dualism with its extremes. Nor—if we consider the increment of dimensions as an illustration or an expression of mankind's development—is it concerned with either a descent or an ascent of mankind, positions held by the traditionalists and the evolutionists respectively, who in the one instance cite the demonstrable loss of certain capabilities in man and in the other point to the demonstrable new technical triumphs.

Both parties, however, ignore the fact that this is not a question of gain or loss but of restructuration. At one time man himself, or, more precisely, the human body, was the instrument of sight or thought across distances—tele-vision and telesthesia—or the perceptor of the faint radiation of the aura, while today man fashions instruments for such purposes.

This is not an opinion as to the value of the natural, or the lack of value of the artificial instruments. Yet the very fact of the quantity, indeed the quantification of the constructed artifacts could well cause us to reflect on the phenomenon even where we are speaking of valuable precision instruments. Detractors of such instruments will decry them as being substitutes, defenders will point to the enhancement they bring, and both will be able to marshall weighty arguments to defend their positions. But this conflict of opinions does not resolve the problem; it merely achieves the temporary triumph of the one or the other opinion.

Yet to the extent that the machine is an objectivation or an externalization of man's own capabilities, it is in psychological terms a projection. We have already spoken of the decisive role of projection in the emergence of consciousness: it is only because of these projections, which render externally visible the powers lying dormant within man, that he is able, or more precisely, that it is possible for him to become aware of this intrinsic potentiality which is capable of being comprehended and directed.

All "making," whether in the form of spell-casting or of the reasoned technical construction of a machine, is an externalization of inner powers or conditions and as such their visible, outward form. Every tool, every instrument and machine is only a practical application (that is, also a perspectival-directed use) of "inherent" laws, laws of one's own body rediscovered externally. All basic physical and mechanical laws such as leverage, traction, bearing, adhesion, all constructions such as the labyrinth, the vault, etc., all such technical achievements or discoveries are pre-given in us. Every invention is primarily a rediscovery and an imitative construction of the organic and physiological pre-given "symmetries" or laws in man's structure which can become conscious by being externally projected into a tool.

This is equally true of the natural capacities at the disposal of magic man we spoke of above such as telesthesia and telepathy; but it is not true of our radio and television. Today, European man supersedes, that is, excludes time and space by utilizing such contrivances since he is caught up in the consciousness-sustaining world of space and time and is scarcely able to achieve this supersession any longer by himself. Magic man does not need this exclusion at all since he lives and moves and is absorbed in a spaceless-timeless world of which he is a part. In this respect the acts of yogis are not miracles but natural occurrences;[19] the miracle would be if such phenomena or events unbound by space and time did not have their place in the spaceless-timeless world.

The European has for the most part forfeited these capacities through the unfolding of consciousness and has replaced them by their projected objectivation or externalization into television and radio. (The giant telescopes belong to this same context inasmuch as magic man "saw" and "knew" those phenomena which we "discover" via such instruments, though in a merely optical and sectoral form.) We might also say that we would not have such instruments if we did not possess within ourselves the genuine capability of such achievements as they permit.

This consideration also points up the limits of technology, for technology is definitely unable to bestow on man the omnipotence which he imagines himself to have. On the contrary, technology necessarily leads to an "omn-impotence" to the extent that the process of physical projection is not realized.[20] It is, for example, a requirement of a projection that it not be left without temporal limits; it must be integrated. But such integration is possible only if the projection is retracted, and retraction can be realized only out of a new consciousness structure. Psychic projections can be undone only by conscious mental understanding. Does this perhaps suggest that material-physical projections can be resolved through the integrating spiritual capacity of diaphany? Be that as it may, we have in any event a possibility of resolving the problem of technology, a problem which cannot be solved merely by further technological advancement.

It should be emphasized that the retraction mentioned above does not necessarily lead to the annulment of the *ratio* and technology; that would not be a solution but a dissolution. And indeed the retraction of psychic projections does not bring about the annulment of the psyche in this sense but rather the establishment of a new equilibrium which the psyche is able to achieve on the strength of the additional structure that is realized. The need for this new equilibrium is surely evident.

The rearrangement of certain capacities in man from the qualitative, natural instrumentality of early man into the externalized instrumentality of the machine entailed more than mere quantification. The objectivation should free, and has freed, energies for new tasks. Early man, for instance, with his merely vital or magic powers was not able to think in our sense. And yet it would be an injustice to regard this as a negative or deficiency, as traditionalists generally do, for this is equivalent to questioning the sense or meaningfulness of life: a struggle between the senseless (and thus undirected and irrational) and the meaningful and directed which, not being solely mental-rational but rather embedded in the organic event, comes to awareness in the mental structure.

None the less, the present-day inquiry into the "sense" of our modern world is justified inasmuch as mere quantification and isolation lead to a material insignificance; indeed, they have already led to a considerable degree to such a state. But the very fact that the question as to the sense or significance can be posed may well mean that the sense is "open to question" —the language, as usual, revealing more than we realize in our rigidified and sectoral manner of thinking.

Be this as it may, of interest here is the observation that the evolutionistic conception which is forward-directed toward the future is, in its one-sidedness, just as illusory as the traditionalistic attitude which, by responding only to the once-dominant unity, turns toward the past. This way of approaching things, which today elicits an anxious response in mankind and drives it ever further into the "narrows," is itself an outgrowth of this very anxiety.

Let us pause for a moment and turn our attention to this question of anxiety as it is immediately illuminating for our discussion. In particular we would point out the connection between "anxiety" (*Angst*) and "narrow" (*eng*), since the concept of *Urangst* bandied about is a puffery of partly magic and partly mythical components that unnecessarily activate in us deficient powers rather than efficient energies of the magic and mythical consciousness structures, and confuse rather than clarify our present situation.[21]

Those who foment this anxiety are, depending on their predominant structural constitution, of a vitalist and emotionalist, or psychistic and even "nothing-but-psychological" bent respectively. They are abetted by those occultists who indiscriminately activate the basic powers of these structures which they have failed to perceive. In the wake of their agitations, these individuals—if they come to a realization of what has occurred—are amazed whenever their non-conscious deeds (inevitably magic) menacingly turn back upon them, making them victims of their own actions. Incapable of withstanding the powers they have unleashed alone, they are now the hunted who dispense *Urangst* and feign leadership, if only the leadership of the herd.

Anxiety, whether in the life of the individual, the clan, the nation, or of humanity itself, inevitably comes about where the lack of alternative becomes consciously or unconsciously evident in a particular attitude or stance where it reflects the impotence rather than the potency of the particular attitude. Anxiety is always the first sign that a mutation is coming to the end of its expressive and effective possibilities, causing new powers to accumulate which, because they are thwarted, create a "narrows" or constriction. At the culmination point of anxiety these powers liberate themselves, and this liberation is always synonymous with a new mutation. In this sense, anxiety is the great birth-giver.[22]

Thus even the confines of the cavern, with their latent brightness, are a part of anxiety, as is the wish inherent in all anxiety that its cause is merely the passage to its counterpole, expanse and light. It is no accident that the anxiety orgies of the Renaissance, the dances of death and the doomsday extravagances come to an end precisely when perspective became an effective force through the efforts of Leonardo da Vinci. These orgies of anxiety have a causal connection with the breakthrough to the requisite new dimension of the world which constituted the three-dimensional perspectival world in its final form.

The orgies of anxiety, the doomsday phantasmagoria, and the mass psychoses of our day may well be phenomena that parallel those of the Renaissance.[23] The ancient Dionysia too, at least to the extent that they elicited ecstatic states and had detached themselves from the original awe-struck numinous shudder which has nothing to do with anxiety (see Part I, chapter 6, section 2), would seem to have arisen from the same anxiety that wanes at the very moment the new structure is secured in classical Greek tragedy.

The line of questioning pursued earlier that calls into question progress on the one hand, as well as any reattachment to the past on the other, both elicits and is elicited by anxiety; and to the extent that the problem is posed today in terms of alternatives, any unilateral solution is an illusion because it is temporally and mentally, even mentalistically, conditioned. The advocates of one solution adjust their sights to quantitative steps, advocates of the other place their hopes on unfathomables; but positive or negative, both sides are addicted to a mental-rational conception of the world, which is one-sidedly quantitative, dualistic, and fragmenting as well as being transitory—a fact that only very few seem to consider.

What is at stake here is *neither a loss nor a gain, neither an ascent nor a descent, but a re-arrangement or restructuration, a mutative unfolding* that is both positive and negative in the terrestrial arena, in other words, in the space-time world where it appears and is fulfilled. But "outside" this battlefield, arena, scene, and proving ground (to the extent that we can even speak here in inappropriate spatializing terms of an "outside"), is located that "core" which is scarcely touched by terrestrial matters because it is itself only tangential to them. And this "core" or "nucleus" is in all likelihood identical to the presence of origin, and as such also forms, shapes, and directs each and every individual human being.

This "core"—to use our tentative designation so as to avoid such concepts as essence, essentiality, substance, superego, self, divine spark, and the like—we should like to describe more appropriately with the term "the itself." The "itself" can become visible in the reflexivity of the ego without succumbing to the autism of a "self" and the psychic coloration inherent in the mystical "divine spark," which shows its indebtedness to the psychic-mythical structure by virtue of the fire-spirit symbolism (see below, Part I, chapter 6, section 6). Both the impersonal aspect—which in the reflexiveness of the pronoun also shows a bond to the personal sphere

—and the detachment from self characteristic of the "itself" in our sense, have prompted us to use the term.

Between the ego and the "itself" exists the same degree of difference visible in the distinction between the expressions "I see" and "to see oneself/itself." This is accurate inasmuch as there is a dependence, in a grammatical sense, of the "oneself" and the ego or "I," for the grammatical structure reflects inner data and events to which it gives expression. Among such inner events in our sense we would have to include the so-called "extraplanetary" phenomena as well, since we are here dealing with "invisible" phenomena.

The fact that the grammatical structure is also a mirror of "inner" data serves to express and indicate that the ego, in order to function effectively in its sphere, is dependent on the "itself." We can, indeed, discern here a possibility of mutation, a mutation from the hypertrophied ego-consciousness that is today either submerged in the "we-(non)consciousness" of the masses, or hopelessly isolated in self-aggrandizement to a consciousness of the itself which relates not only to the ego but to every Thou, to every "it," and to every We.

Regarded in this way, the itself is that which pervades or "shines through" everything in which the diaphanous spirituality, in its originary presence, is able to become transparent. This presence of origin, in itself pre-spatial and pre-temporal (not merely magically spaceless and timeless), anticipates by this pre-spatiality and pre-temporality the space-timelessness of magic in the same way that space-timelessness in turn—despite its apparent formlessness—anticipates space and time. It is in and by the human itself that the presence of origin which "corresponds" to it could become diaphanously visible.

This rendering visible is perhaps the decisive element by which to "bring about" the "new": it would elicit or it would itself be the expression of the new mutation. And here we would again mention that the *diaphainon*, "that which shines through," has nothing to do with things circumscribed by the mental terms essence, existence, substance, and the like; by such psychic phenomena as images or symbols of fire, the sun, the "divine" spark, and light; or by magic expressions of any form of unity or identity. All such concepts, images, and "identities" manage their limited pseudo-existence in each instance by rationalization, by their appeal to myth or to magical unity. Concepts in particular have their spatial limitations since they must proceed from a world of being, space, and thought which makes them possible and which, in turn, is not only temporally but also spatially limited.

The diaphainon, then, cannot be classed either as a form of symbolism or as a methodology; it is neither psychic nor mental, nor does it bear the stamp of magic. Rather, becoming co-visible in and through man it attests to the new mutation by which all previous spatio-temporal unfoldings represented by the increments of dimensioning in consciousness are integrated and made "meaningful." And as these spatio-temporal unfoldings or exfoliations open the possibility for the conscious emergence of the presence of origin, this presence diaphanously enters the realm of conscious and visible effectiveness from its unconscious and invisible state. It mutates in man himself—or is it that he mutates in its "direction" or from within the originary presence? It mutates in man from its pre-spatiality and pre-temporality to a space-free, time-free presence of origin that is manifest as an effectuality of the human itself.

Attempting to define it in rational, antithetic terms we can say, then, that the itself is on the one hand the central or "deepest" core, the intensity "in" us that is time-free and corresponds with the pre-spatial, pre-temporal presence of origin. It is, on the other hand, this identity of origin itself which pervades and suffuses everything and, if we are able to mutate from the spatio-temporal limitations of the purely ego-centered consciousness, becomes transparent even for us just as the world itself—even the "non-world" as it might be called—becomes diaphanous.

This definition—although the very word "definition" expresses a notion of finiteness that is incongruent with diaphaneity—may have served to indicate by the rationalistic division into "on-the-one-hand, on-the-other" how inimical the dualistic compulsion of our present-day language is to an approach to the whole. At the same time, a mode of expression reductively employing psychic (polar) or magic (unitary) elements rightly seems dubious to modern man because of its irrational, and thus one-sided character.

In the course of these remarks we have already intimated potentialities inherent in the aperspectival world. This form of anticipation is intended as an initial orienting glance at a new landscape whose contours are only gradually becoming distinguishable and amenable to description. But while examining the question of ascent or descent we also touched upon man's—and possibly not just man's—mystery and destiny.

But what do such words as mystery and destiny in fact signify, and what is the extent of their validity? In the first instance the word denotes non-freedom, in the second an absence or lack of freedom; the words actually belong to two different structures of consciousness, whose respective character they describe. Mystery is an outgrowth of the magic realm; it is the indissoluble relation to the concealment and shelter of the dark cavern-world—the covert world that is displaced by the inscrutable world of destiny. Destiny in turn is associated with the mythical structure, for it has nothing covert or secret in its nature; characteristic of destiny is the expulsion from, not the shelter of the cavern world. Destiny is the inscrutable fulfillment of events that seems irrevocable since mythical man has no will of his own and is consequently bound to the fateful course of events which relentlessly presses toward fulfillment.[24]

For the integral structure such words as these are as irrelevant as the (mental) judgement on man's ascent or descent, or the question of gains or losses. Ascent and descent signify directedness; gain and loss denote in a polar sense life and death, in antithetical terms measure and mass. All of these terms, however, ascent or descent, gain or loss, are valid only within the structures of consciousness from which they sprang. Their reality or efficacy in us is present only to the degree that these structures are co-constituents of our integrality. This means that *they lose their former exclusive claim and validity at the moment of a new mutation.* None the less, it is fitting that we recall from time to time the pains which we experience because of the tensions of these realities, for without them there could be no preparation for the birth of a new mutation capable of liberating us from the earlier sufferings.

With these remarks we have perhaps ventured too far beyond the present realities since we cannot as yet make fully evident those elements of tomorrow which are beginning to be visible today. But one thing is certain: these observations should give no cause for new or additional anxieties even though it may seem to some that we are addressing uncertainties. On the contrary, our remarks definitely warrant a liberation from anxiety, assuming as always that we are able to demonstrate in the remaining course of our discussion the manifestations of a new consciousness built on the foundations of those structures of consciousness that we have here attempted to describe in summary. And even if we cannot comprehend and grasp the certainty of the freedom from anxiety, it is perhaps possible to allow it to "shine through."

Once again the word "anxiety" forms a point of departure for continuing our discussion along the lines we have chosen for our description of the mutations. Anxiety is, after all, a force dammed up primarily in the "unconscious" which only takes on the negative character of might where its origin remains unconscious and thus causes it to manifest itself in the form of panic or psychosis, that is, as forms of impotence.[25] Since we are concerned here with the history of consciousness-emergence the question of consciousness is pre-eminent in our discussion.

This question of consciousness can also be posed in terms of measure and mass, inasmuch as the immoderate or immeasurable unconscious is commonly placed in opposition to the calculating consciousness. We have been able to show that each consciousness mutation went hand in hand with a gradual strengthening of consciousness which culminated in the ego-consciousness of the mental structure. This increase in consciousness parallels the increase in dimensions, and the dimensions themselves are nothing more than the gradual appearance of everything spatial and temporal. There is, in other words, a mutual and even interdependent relationship of consciousness to the spatio-temporal world.

Here we again encounter the question of measure and mass. To the extent that consciousness is an intensity and thus intangible, the space-time world represents the corresponding tangible phenomenon as an extensity; the space-time world is the stage, as it were, on which consciousness itself is capable of being actual and efficacious. The reification attendant upon this is evident because the increasing consciousness summons forth an increasing materialization.

Whereas in the magic realm there is a shaping and substantive forming of nature, there is in the mythical realm an imagistic and pictorial substantivation of the psyche, evident from the imagery of even the most finely-wrought texture of dream and mythical images which in their own way are reified in man's emergent consciousness. This substantivation becomes tangible in the mental zone, where the world becomes comprehensible by means of the emergent awareness and manipulation of the third dimension as well as by the substantivation of thought and by perspectivation. This process of increasing substantivation and materialization is alarming, yet it loses its alarming character when we recognize that it is a process confined to the terrestrial sphere, which is to say that it occurs on earth where it necessarily exhibits a creative and creaturely tension of polarities and antitheses appropriate to the earth and its nature.

If we follow this train of thought to its conclusion, it leads to a further "leap" based on the fact that today a space-time unity is becoming increasingly evident within fourth dimensionality that could effect the concretion of time. Time—previously understood to be merely measured or abstracted natural time and as such perceived only in its partial aspects—is energy, and is thus able to bridge the dualistic conceptual antithesis of an "unconscious" opposed to consciousness. In this opposition, consciousness is generally understood to comprise little more than the illuminated part of the so-called unconscious; and this very partiality serves to indicate the purely rational basis of this mode of understanding oriented toward the psyche.

Now anyone, like the modern psychologist, who thinks in terms of the alternative of the brightness of consciousness and the darkness of the unconscious—although this is merely a kind of conceptual transposition of the images of the column temple and the cavern—will doubtless greet these ventures into strange territory with amazement and mild disapproval. At best he will wish us good fortune in our audacious attempt to integrate the "unconscious," which he naturally associates with the notion of making conscious. But the immoderation inherent in the "unconscious" is devouring, even though it is thus, in a negative way, integrating. If this reciprocal functioning is known, which must occur in an active as well as passive form, one can dispense with a discussion in dualistic terms, inasmuch as everything depends on the knowledge that an integration takes place. Whether or not it takes place actively or passively, whether we as humans on the earth are active or passive, only the knowledge of this process affords us the detachment as well as the guarantee that in it we are neither the hero nor the victim.

What is decisive for us is to "know" in any given instance where and how to act passively or actively, where and how to make things happen or let things happen to us; to know, in other words, to what extent our natural, magic creatureliness permits and commands us to hearken to and obey the natural flux of events; to what extent our mythical and psychic being is permitted and charged with co-responding to the psychic flux of formative images; to what measure our observant, mental-abstracting nature is permitted to direct the natural and psychic flux of instincts and sensations, that is, to orient as well as pass judgement on them and ourselves.

Everything hinges on this knowledge of letting-happen and making-happen. Only this attitude can protect us from the inescapable anxiety experienced by the dualistic-minded psychologists who fear being dazzled or even blinded by consciousness, or being devoured by the unconscious at the moment when one is forced to come to terms with the development and emergence of consciousness that has been worked out conceptually. But if we maintain the attitude appropriate and commensurate with the individual structures, this problem should not even arise.

A coming-to-terms is a purely rational process that is inapplicable to psychic processes, and leads at best to either a magically-accentuated unification or to a rationally-directed reconciliation, which is in each instance a retrogression. For this reason we again emphasize that integration—whether of four-dimensionality, of time, of mythical temporicity, or even to a certain degree of the unconscious itself—is not contingent upon our activity or passivity but on our knowledge of the occurring process that we have gained by our detachment from it.

This knowledge is nearly synonymous with the phenomenon we have called the diaphainon which is not bound to activity or passivity, light or darkness, but rather pervades or shines through them all. For it is irrelevant to speak of day or night, consciousness or the unconscious, action or acquiescence. Proper to the essence of the diaphainon (to the extent that we may speak here of essence and propriety) is that it shines through and is unfettered by the forms of appearance.

It is, accordingly, neither a tertiary or third component that unifies opposites, nor a secondary or polar complement, nor a primary, unitary and self-contained state from which it can emerge. It is the originary presence that has itself attained consciousness because one of its bearers, man, has undergone the spatio-temporally conditioned unfolding of consciousness, which he has enjoyed but also had to suffer through. Only someone who has integrated the past as well as the future—with their inevitable psychic emphasis on joy and suffering—and freed himself from the tensions and prepossessions of the once-unconscious psychic structure (for every integration is a form of prevailing) is able to realize the present.

Now, it might seem that the act of freeing oneself from this tension is the same as death. This is true in the sense that it brings about a realization of death; but it is not the same as death itself. Those who deduce that the resolution of tensions is tantamount to death forget two actualities: one, of which we have spoken earlier, is the certainty that as life cannot be lived apart from tensions, so too does life encompass death and death life. The second—overlooked by those who would object that the dissolution of psychic tension brought about by presentiation necessarily leads to death, as well as by those who forget their own foundations (foundations which sustain their lives as long as they are part of the earth)—is that none of the structures excludes the others.

To the extent, then, that this natural structure too is a co-constituent of our being, it precludes the danger of a fatal effect of presentiation, or of the diaphainon. The danger is precluded, however, only where we are aware of the individual structures and their commensurate effectiveness. Any disequilibrium at the moment of mutation is fraught with the danger of ego-loss and destruction. But, as may be assumed, the leap will be ventured—or more accurately, will venture itself—only in those who are themselves capable.

As for those who from rational hubris believe or calculate (calculated in the form of rational belief) that they can make this leap voluntarily, they will be swallowed up by the abyss which they must cross (since their dualistic belief compels them to assume an "other side," a mere mental construct, that they must reach). We have already noted this form of untimely leap: it is atomization. It expresses the negative aspect of the tension which, when overstretched, destroys rather than creates life, bringing not death but annihilation. Such overstretching is always present where one extreme comes to an end: the dead end that evokes anxiety.

Every dead end or lack of recourse is not only an indicator that the course has run out and that a given development has attained its greatest (quantitative!) extent and may at any moment give way to a loss of tension and consequent annihilation. It is also a sign that only a leap, that is, only a mutation, can bring about a solution. Without a doubt we are at such a moment today, not only with respect to the mental structure predominating in us, but also with respect to all the previous structures that make up our integral constitution. The incrementation of consciousness reflected in a material sense in the increase of dimensions effects an increasing objectivation of the reality unlocked by consciousness on what we have called the stage of dimensional gains.

The effect, however, is an ever-increasing reification of the world, causing an increase in tension even with respect to the whole, that is, throughout the mutations. There is a corresponding increase in consciousness for each increase in the discovered world that precipitates the further reification or materialization. The error made today, which results from the quantitative emphasis of the rational attitude, is the notion that this material increase must be countered by an increase of consciousness.

Such an increase must always be understood as one of reflective cognition with its quantitative character, and never one of consciousness itself which is qualitative. For this very reason we emphasized earlier (pp. 99-100) that we must not lapse into the error of aspiring to an expansion of consciousness, since everything depends on an *intensification* of consciousness. Mere expansion of consciousness leads to decline and destruction in exactly the same way as material quantification; it corresponds on the non-material plane to the atomization on the physical or material. Ultimately it would be nothing else than the psychic atomization which to a certain degree has already begun to show its negative effects, as amply demonstrated by Surrealism, Dadaism, existential philosophistry, and especially by certain trends in contemporary psychoanalysis.[26]

By returning to the subject of consciousness-intensification, we have again emphasized the question of measure and mass. The preceding discussion of the subject based on the established fact of dimensioning was able to indicate the many facets of the question that arise when we attempt to approach it from an integral standpoint rather than merely consider in terms of an antithesis. In any event it has furnished us with a general view, an insight, and a prospect: a general view of what we might call the significance of mutation when we view the events in a fixed, mental way, a significance which is rendered recurrently illusory by the question of mankind's ascent or descent; an insight into the partner of consciousness, the "unconscious"; and the prospect of a possible new mutation whose landscape we have initially and tentatively attempted to describe in terms like the diaphainon, the itself, and the *originary presence*. (We will see later in chapter 6, section 2 of this first part, that the concept of the "unconscious" does not hold up in our form of discussion because of its specific dualistic character. There is no unconscious which negates consciousness, but only pre-forms of consciousness as such with respectively fewer dimensions.)

Let us turn now to the other three symmetries, and specifically to the second which we have designated as the breathing character of the mutations (see p. 121 above). We have systematically incorporated it into the problematics of measure and mass because in this case too the polar nature of the conceptual pair is evident and we are dealing with the complementary interchange of a life-sustaining event. From the seemingly rhythmic symmetry or regularity pulsing through the mutational series as a whole the next question arises: What will be the nature of the new mutation? Will it, like the mythical, be "inner"-related, and if so, what will be the nature of this "inwardness"? Or will it be a new breathing spell? Let us stop with this question,[27] for it would be hubristic to attempt at the moment to postulate an answer. Such questions as these will nearly all have answers, as the foundations of the New, and the points of departure deriving from them, take on more distinct forms.

The questions presented by the third symmetry, however, are more easily answered. This symmetry presented itself on the one hand as a decrease in the relationship to the whole, and on the other, as an increase of the powers of consciousness. Here the unitary moment of the measure-mass question becomes visible inasmuch as we shall have to treat it as a unitary event, and not as a divergent process, as we have done by rationally dividing it in order to make it comprehensible.

We have already mentioned the key word in this context: we are here dealing with a *restructuration* within the unity. The apparent decrease of our relationship to the whole (to the extent that we are justified in speaking of a relationship) is compensated, in other words, by the increase of the conscious relationship partaking in wholeness; there is a transposition from the so-called objective sphere into the so-called subjective. By virtue of the irrevocability of the archaic structure within us—which is not tied to temporal beginnings but is originary—all mutations that proceed from it are equally irrevocable.

Viewed from our present structure of consciousness, we are human beings only to the degree that we are aware of this integrality, for otherwise we are only partial aspects of the whole. This is to say, without this awareness we are out of balance, or, in mental terms, "out of measure" (proportion), and form a part of its negative counterpart, the "mass(es)," an impersonal state bordering on the inhuman.

As in the case of the dimensions, it is not a question of an increase or a diminution when we are dealing with the integral point of view. It is, rather, a question of our ability not just to take in the measure of phenomena, to experience them in image or in their vital unity, but to see through them in their entirety. And how do we arrive at such an attitude? The question must be posed, for experience suggests that rarely is it, or has it been possible, to alter what we call "human attitudes" by means of rational considerations or arguments. It is not difficult to discover the reason for this, inasmuch as the basic human attitude, and therefore that of each human being, has its roots predominantly in the vital and psychic spheres (in what we have called the magic and mythical structures). Petition and wish, whose basic character as a demand gives any attitude its essentially unconscious stamp, can be only partially directed by rational will, that is, unless we become aware of them.

We have, then, an indicator as to whether a given person has attained this awareness or not: someone who has learned to avoid placing blame or fault on others, on the world itself, on circumstances or "chance" in times of adversity, dissension, conflict, and misfortune and seeks first *in himself* the reason or guilt in its fullest extent—this person should also be able to see through the world in its entirety and all its structures. Otherwise, he will be coerced or violated by either his emotions or his will, and in turn will himself attempt to coerce or violate the world as an act of compensation or revenge. The adage that "how we shout into the woods is how the echo will sound" is undoubtedly accurate—and the woods are the world.

Everything that happens to us, then, is only the answer and echo of what and how we ourselves are. And the answer will be an integral answer only if we have approached the integral in ourselves. One path toward this goal is for us to try for once to take the blame ourselves in a given instance in its entirety; after a dispassionate examination we will see to what extent we are to blame, and the equalization and equilibrium appropriate to wholeness (to the extent that anything can be appropriate) will restore themselves. We will be surprised at the conclusion of this frequently difficult process to discover that our perceptions—and this includes self-perception—of the world as well as of ourselves have become a few degrees more transparent.

It is only when we permit the integral point of view to prevail, or to become prevalent are we in a position where we can realize in a "positive" sense the apparently negative process mentioned in connection with the fourth symmetry or regularity—negative when we consider it in a mental sense as a unidirectional process. It is apparently characteristic of every structure that its beginning is qualitative, after which an increasingly quantitative devaluation sets in, as is evident in cross-section 8. Within the magic structure we first find spell-casting as a qualitative manifestation which later becomes deficient in witchcraft with its quantitative emphasis. We find a parallel process occurring within the mythical structure: the ineffable, primordial myth begins to be fragmented into the multitude of individual, spoken myths,[28] which disintegrate in turn into new and partial aspectuations until the vast quantity of psychic manifestations and realizations makes their very significance doubtful, and—in the wake of a new structure of consciousness—gives way to the "sense" of directive thought (*Menis* and *Menos*).

Viewed in this context, the acquisition of the new structure by the Greek

| Structure | 8. Forms of Manifestation | |
	a) efficient	b) deficient
Archaic:	None	Presentiment, foreboding
Magic:	Spell-casting	Witchcraft
Mythical:	Primal myth (envisioned myth)	Mythology (spoken myth)
Mental:	*Menos* (directive, discursive thought)	Ratio (divisive, immoderate hair-splitting)
Integral:	Diaphainon (open, spiritual "verition")	Void (atomizing dissolution)

thinkers protected Western civilization from what we might call "psychic atomization." (This will be more meaningful after we consider in greater detail the forms of realization and thought, Part I, chapter 7, below.) But *menis*, too, did not escape quantification, as we noted earlier in our discussion of this process mirrored in the rationalization of the world. Since in our present consciousness structure it is mainly a question of the spatial world, it is this spatial world that is principally affected; but it equally affects all other aspects of the world as well, that is, including also the psychic and vital. The present threat is accordingly one of an atomization of the material-spatial world, and there is no great difficulty in determining that this atomization has already taken on tangible and palpable forms.

If we consider from a strictly rational viewpoint this symmetrical succession of the deficient following the efficient phase within each individual structure, we are compelled, in accord with rational thought, to speak of a natural process rushing toward its inevitable conclusion. In this, destiny, anxiety, and lack of an avenue of escape are givens, particularly since the only possible result—annihilation—affords no escape. But it must be evident on the other hand that our present state is one of *exhaustion*; that is, what was at the beginning of our structure its constituting strength or energy has become exhausted in the course of the exfoliation of consciousness.

Exhaustion, however, does not bear within itself the possibility of continuation or evolution, unless perhaps in the sense of progress. This will perhaps emphasize again why we have disavowed the concept of evolution and prefer instead to speak of mutations. The sequential aspects or character are limited to the individual structures, whereas the integrality is embodied in the mutations. No new structure proceeds from an exhausted one, but a mutation can readily spring forth from the originary presence of the whole.

"Behind" the antithesis, the polarity, and the unity expressed by the conceptual pair "measure and mass" is its original, integral content. Only when we take this into account do we avoid, and are "wared"—sustained "in truth"—from the error of subscribing to today's mass-phenomena and further rational quantification with their one-sided consequences. And only if we are able to keep ourselves from such error can there be any certainty of our prevailing over the atomization, in a material sense as well, which would otherwise befall the world.

4. *The Unique Character of the Structures* (Additional Cross-sections)

Two difficulties present themselves in these deliberations with which we must contend. The first is inherent in the demand of any treatise for a sequential presentation, which is necessarily contrary to the simultaneity of an integral mode. In a given moment where we must deal with various strata of the problems at hand, not merely the various aspects but the very problems themselves tend to intersect. If we isolate only one aspect for discussion, the ordered and sequential presentation is undoubtedly beneficial; but only in part, for we shall have had to forego in the meantime the integral perception and presentation of the particular question in all its aspects.

We have attempted to resolve this first difficulty by immediately pointing to the multiple aspects or strata of a question as we discussed it, a procedure that has uncovered and established a considerable number of interrelationships. Accordingly, constant reference has been made to matters already discussed in other contexts; but we have also had to anticipate certain things lest we find ourselves caught in the dualistic cul-de-sac.

This stratiform multiplicity inherent in our questions in which their entirety becomes visible has necessitated a stratiform and multiple mode of presentation. But as such a method can be considered inherently inconsistent—a method is only able to assess and evaluate one matter at a time—we have designated our approach as "diaphany" which, in contrast to method, at least allows the integral simultaneity to be made transparent. It defines, then, how the integral simultaneity can be made diaphanous despite the necessity of a sequential presentation and the impossibility of its being presented in customary expository form.

The second difficulty rests in our attempt to elaborate something "new" within the framework and limitations of "old" language. The words and concepts of our present-day language are to a great extent rigidified along the lines of the perspectival world.[29] It is true that the language of poetry (as we indicated in our book *Der grammatische Spiegel*) at least attempts to accommodate itself to the new and novel phenomena striving to take shape, but this is confined mainly to initial indications which, moreover, remain mostly unnoticed. We have endeavored to overcome this obstacle by attempting to "loosen up" language, taking into account not only the present-day perspectivistic conceptual connotation of the words but also their integral nature.

Once again we would like to summarize various specific characteristics, attributions, and qualities of the respective structures in cross-section in four groupings. The necessity is particularly acute here since we have been repeatedly forced to allude to certain matters whose clarity and scope become evident only in summary or retrospect. Let us, then, proceed to recapitulate those things which were not immediately evident from our sequential presentation, and for this the "synoptic view"—complemented and supplemented by the following cross-sections—will afford us the integral view, the simultaneous presence which is necessarily more or less lacking in our mode of exposition.

We shall attempt once more to organize the material under some specific headings, summarizing it in the following four groupings:

1) the basic attitudes of the individual structures, as well as their psychic and physical-organic emphasis;
2) the forms of realization and thought;
3) the forms of expression and manifestation; and the forms of assertion or articulation;
4) the temporal, social, and general interrelationships which distinguish the individual structures.

If we arrange the material discussed above with respect to the basic attitude of the respective structures, noting what we might call the bearer or agency of energy in the first instance as well as the organ emphasis in the second, the following summary emerges (the attributions for the integral structure are in anticipation of their discussion and verification which come only in the course of our further discussion, and are placed accordingly in parentheses; see also p. 156, note 2, below):

Structure	9. Basic attitude and agency of energy		10. Organ emphasis
Archaic:	Origin:	Wisdom	--
Magic:	Vital:	Instinct Drive Emotion	Viscera -- Ear
Mythical:	Psychic:	Imagination Sensibility Disposition	Heart -- Mouth
Mental:	Cerebral:	Reflection Abstraction Will/Volition	Brain --- Eye
Integral:	(Integral:)	(Concretion) (Rendering diaphanous) ("Verition")	(Vertex)

This summary will present few surprises in the light of what has been said earlier. It will be unnecessary, for example, to elaborate on the vital basis of magic and its guiding force in the conscious-weak instinct, its support in drives which can become conscious, and its expression—notably of identity or identification—in emotion. Nor will we need to comment on such attributions as the psychic accentuation of the mythical or the cerebral emphasis of the mental structures.

Cross-section 10, on the other hand, may at first glance be surprising, although our ascription to the magic structure of the auditory organ, the ear (which also corresponds to the labyrinth and the cavern), is perhaps evident by now. But the ascription of the viscera to the magic structure is understandable only if we recall several facts. The divining of entrails as a means of foretelling events belongs to the time we have designated as the magical, and its labyrinthine aspect is palpably evident.[30] And the homogeneity of the viscera, as well as their essentially non-directional arrangement, definitely place them in relation to the magic vital consciousness.

The viscera simply have a more eminent position within the larger unity of organs in the magic structure; their functions are more decisive than those of the other organs.[31] How decisive may be discerned from the fact that they served as the source for divining destiny and events for the magicians and medicine men.[32] We can comprehend this curious procedure—which is only seemingly a nonsensical superstition—by remembering that the viscera represent the intertwined unity which we have ascertained as characteristic of the magic structure of consciousness. Magic man, actively partaking and completely intertwined in the magic vitality, was surely able to sense a disturbance or indisposition—the immediate occasion for such oracles and prophecies—within the visceral texture as it lay spread out before him, for such a display was not only coincidence, since indeed, in magic everything is co-incidental.[33]

The importance of the ear, on the other hand, derives from the primordial notion of the "receptivity of the ear."[34] Sound or tone is procreative; the ear, the projected likeness of the cavern and the labyrinth, is receptive and, consequently, is also parturient: it gives birth to the magic world.

We can discern the degree to which tone is a primordial force that works via the magic structure to shape the world if we observe the meaning of the Latin word *carmen*. It signifies a "song" or "poem," but originally meant a "religious and magical incantation."[35] Singing in this sense is a charm for spell-casting, which is to say an effecting by tone or sound. Even today such words as French *charme*, Spanish *encantado*, English "charming" are imbued with this basic sense which expresses the "charm" or "spell" that men or objects are able to cast on us.[36]

Since the relation between tone and spell indicates their inseparability as well as their pre-eminently magic character, it will not be surprising that we feel justified in ascribing the predominant role within the magic structure to the ear as well as to the inner "vital" organs. The magic world, as well as an essential part of our present constitution, came forth from the magic tone which—becoming effective via the ear—evoked a world. It is this same tone, like that of the jungle drums, whose rhythm is one of the most vital expressions of magic man, that gave birth to *dance*. Dance is tone become visible: the medium of conjuration and of "being heard" by the deeper reality of the world where man is united with the rhythm of the universe.[37]

Whereas the viscera or intestines are evidence of unity or identity—the prefix "in-" means not only "in" but also "one"—the pulse of the heart is an expression of polarity, like the mouth which can both speak and remain silent. (In its unitary function the ear can only hear.) We have already spoken of the root kinship of the words "myth" and "mouth." And although etymologists have not as yet demonstrated whether the German word for mouth, *Mund*, can be traced to the same root (*mu*), we believe nevertheless that we have sufficiently established the primacy of the mouth with respect to the mythical structure.

As for the heart, the Gospel of St. Luke (2:19) records, in an appropriately mythical manner, that "Mary pondered these words in her heart," while the Gospel of St. Matthew (12:34) clearly expresses the mythical correspondence and relation between the heart and the mouth: "Out of the abundance of the heart the mouth speaketh."[38] Even today we refer to the heart as the organ of courage and disposition, and such phrases as "take heart" when we mean "have courage" and our synonymous use of "stout-hearted" and "courageous" are not just coincidences. Even apart from this, Creuzer's somewhat willful etymology which relates *mythos* with the German word *Gemüt*, "mind, heart, disposition," is not entirely far-fetched.[39]

Whereas in the mythical structure one "ponders" or "holds" something in one's heart, we speak today in the mental structure of "keeping an eye on something," again an expression that is most likely not just coincidental. This turn of speech is merely one of the subtle hints suggestive of the primacy of the eye which comes to dominate the mental structure. The perspectival world is primarily visual, just as the unperspectival is primarily sensorial and the pre-perspectival primarily emotional.

But the perspectival world is at the same time the world of thought, just as the unperspectival was a world of contemplation and the pre-perspectival one of hearing.[40] In the world of thought, in the mental structure, it is the brain which is the primary inner organ. Once again the close relationship of the mental to the magic structure is evident, for the brain too has the nature of a labyrinth. As long as its functions remain dominant, thinking will be unable to escape from its ambiguity, despite its attempts to elude it (see chapter 7 of Part I, below).

In the ninth and tenth cross-sections we have made only tentative ascriptions for the integral structure, and those that we are able to make here will acquire their legitimacy only in the course of our further discussion, particularly in the light of the manifestations which remain to be discussed in the second part of the present work. But we can perhaps venture to make several ascriptions for the integral structure in the next grouping without causing misunderstandings. This eleventh grouping is a cross-section through the forms of realization and thought of the respective structures which will be emended and completed in the course of the remaining discussion (notably in chapter 7 of this first part, below). A summary of the discussion up to this point yields the following cross-section:

Structure	11. Forms of realization and thought	
	a) Basis	b) Mode
Archaic:	———	Originary
Magic:	Empathy and Identification Hearing	Pre-rational, pre-causal analogical
Mythical:	Imagination and Utterance Contemplation and Voicing	Irrational: non-causal, polar
Mental:	Conceptualization and Reflection Seeing and Measuring	Rational: causal, directed
Integral:	(Concretion and Integration "Verition" and Transparency)	(Arational: acausal, integral)

It will be found that these ascriptions hold true when they are also read horizontally and considered together with the other attributions, a task which is facilitated by the "Synoptic Table" printed at the end of the volume. The magic structure is more or less characterized by the unitary empathy and sense of identification and identity basic to it, just as the mythical structure is characterized by the polar complements of imagination and utterance, contemplation or "vision," and vocalization or "voicing" inherent in myth. The basis of the rational form of thought is expressed by the antithesis of conceptualization and reflection, as in *Vorstellen* and *Nachdenken* with their respective suggestion of "before" and "after," as well as by seeing and measuring. As for the attributions for the integral structure presented above, they have presumably been discussed in sufficient detail so that we can forego further comment here, at least with respect to cross-section 11.a; the attributions in 11.b for the integral structure are best understood when read together with those of the other structures.

It is of fundamental importance that we clearly distinguish between "irrational" and "arational," for this distinction lies at the very heart of our deliberations. Arationality has nothing to do with irrationality; their only connection exists in the fact that arationality is not possible without irrationality, or for that matter without the pre-rational or the rational. All three form the basis of arationality. Our entire endeavor of making the individual structures distinguishable in the course of making them visible is primarily intended to prevent the possible confusion of arationality with irrationality.

It is only natural that the rational mind will find it difficult to grasp this basic distinction between the two, for its quantitative means are hardly applicable to the realization of the transparent, arational structure. The rationalist will perhaps mistakenly confuse the lack of measurability characteristic of diaphaneity with the unfathomability of the irrational. There is of course no proof that we are even justified in speaking of a lack of measurability with respect to the diaphainon, for it may well be that diaphaneity is free of measure.

However we may wish to define it, arationality is never identifiable with irrationality or prerationality. There is a fundamental distinction between the attempt to go beyond the merely measurable, knowing and respecting it while striving to be free from it, and rejecting and disregarding the measurable by regressing to the immoderate and unfathomable chaos of the ambivalent and even fragmented polyvalence of psychic and natural interrelations. Projective geometry has long since demonstrated that the rejection of measurability can by no means be equated with chaos. And so this suggestion may perhaps serve to anticipate what we hope to clarify gradually in the succession of these pages and those of the second part so that it may be transparent and thus evident.

The third grouping which summarizes the forms of expression and manifestation can be represented as in cross-section 12 and 13 on the following page. With regard to these attributions it should be noted that those of the magic structure are not to be understood in any way pejoratively. The denigrating characterization of "idols" today, for example, which proceeds from a one-sided religious viewpoint, despoils the sacred intensity of what such idols originally represented. We have no right to look disparagingly at this form of an awakening religious consciousness, particularly as we ourselves are still "superstitious," if in no other sense than in our rejection and persecution of superstition.

The natural succession in cross-section 12 of idols-gods-God is not a value judgement but rather an illustration of the formation and increasing objectivation of the perceptive faculty of consciousness. The centripetal direction towards one God prefigures the centering of the human ego that takes shape in the mental structure as ego-consciousness. A similar process of formation is evident in the gradual supplanting of idols by symbols which are in turn displaced by dogma. Whereas the idol

Structure	12. Forms of Expression		13. Forms of Assertion or Articulation
Archaic:		—	—
Magic:	Magic:	Graven images Idol Ritual	Petition (Prayer): being heard
Mythical:	Mythologeme:	Gods Symbol Mysteries	Wishes (Ideals: Fulfillment "wish (pipe-) dreams")
Mental:	Philosopheme:	God Dogma (Allegory, Creed) Method	Volition: attainment
Integral:	(Eteologeme:)	(Divinity) (Synairesis) (Diaphany)	(Verition: Present)

has an unlimited unitary validity, the symbol is always polar and ambivalent, that is, ambiguous as well as equivocal; and dogma—rigid and one-sided—creates an antithesis between adherents and those who reject it.

Commensurate with the fragmentation into separate sectors that takes place in the mental structure, dogma has currency and validity only within a single sector, the religious-theological. Other fragmented and intellectualized sectors, in the instance of the symbol, are recognizable in allegory as a rationalized form of conceptuality already dissociated to a great extent from the psyche. As such, allegory forms an antithetical and intellectualized expression of the imagistic-didactic rather than religious sphere. The fragmentation is also evident in the formula and the formalistic tendency which are constitutive for the rationalistic stamp of the natural sciences and the sciences of the mind.

This process of consolidation of consciousness, finally, is mirrored in the transposition that takes place from ritual through mysteries to ceremony and method; each is preceded by its earlier pre-form, which is in every instance of lesser consciousness intensity and dimensions. When understood in this way, the interrelationship between these various instances should prove instructive with respect to various phenomena and their examination.

Since we have ventured to make several partial attributions for the integral structure we must hasten to add that the term "divinity" appearing under the rubric of forms of expression (p. 101) must not be taken to be a reference to the religious sphere. We will see later the degree to which "the divinatory" is not a religious term in a strict sense but is rather based on what we described as the "preligious." And we would also mention that *praeligio* represents neither a form of religious antipathy, nor a type of substitute religion. The preligious aperspectival world can no more dispense with the religious than the religious can do without *relegio* or its magic preform, *proligio*.

Preligion is merely an expression of the aperspectival form of "religion" which integrates the archaic *presence*, and its presentation is neither forward- (or future-) directed, nor backward- (or past-) oriented; but religion forms an irrevocable constituent of its foundations. And when we recall in this connection our discussion of both presentation, which is a realization or effectuation of presence, and the diaphainon or diaphaneity, this reference to the preligious character of the divinitary will come as no surprise. (We shall return to this question in our discussion of cross-section 16 in chapter 7 of Part I below.) Nor will the material in cross-section 13 which is discussed above in the second section of the present chapter (p. 128-129) evoke any astonishment.

The material contained in the fourth and concluding grouping has also been discussed for the most part above. The three cross-sections which summarize this grouping deal with the temporal, social, and general relationships of the respective structures and provide the following survey:

Structure	14. Relationships		
	a) temporal	b) social	c) general
Archaic:	—	—	universal or ["cosmic"]
Magic:	undifferentiated	Tribal world [clan/kith and kin] natural	egoless — terrestrial
Mythic:	predominantly past-oriented [recollection, muse]	Parental world [Ancestor-worship] predominantly matriarchal	egoless "we"-oriented psychic
Mental:	predominantly future-oriented —— [purpose and goal]	World of the first-born son, individuality [child-adulation] predominantly patriarchal	egocentric — materialistic
Integral:	(presentiating)	Mankind neither matriarchy nor patriarchy but integrum	ego-free amaterial apsychic

The temporal relationships in cross-section 14.a have been in our estimation sufficiently explored above, and the same is true of those in cross-section 14.b. We wish, nevertheless, to make some additional supplementary remarks concerning patriarchy. We noted earlier (p. 79 above) the connection between the patriarchal and emphasis on the "right," directed thought, and "rights" and law-giving in our discussion of Lycurgus and Solon (who, incidentally, was the first to have coins minted). It is the mental structure which first places emphasis on the principle of *masculinity,* and there is a causal connection between Solon's legislation and the matricide documented in the *Oresteia* which even touched the realm of the gods: Zeus devoured a mother, Metis, who was pregnant with Athena.[41]

Or, stated another way, both legislation and matricide proceed from the same newly-forming consciousness structure. The tremors and shock unleashed by this murder must have been overwhelming; they can be felt in Greek tragedy, in Aeschylus' trilogy of the *Oresteia* as well as in the aftershocks that appear even today. Indeed, the consequences are today more distinct than ever before.

Matricide is synonymous with the elimination and collapse of matriarchy. Yet we must not forget that matriarchy had by then become deficient. Bachofen, for instance, has written, "Mankind has not forgotten that the time of feminine dominance visited experiences of the bloodiest kind over the earth."[42] The matricide extensively reduced, although not quite destroyed, what was once the sanctity that had turned into atrocity within the once-valid mythical structure, along with the remaining foundations of that structure itself.[43] Orestes' actions bring on the collapse of one world and the dawn of another with the full force and attendant circumstances of such cataclysms.

A downfall of the soul such as man then experienced must have been horrendous, particularly as the new structure could not fully unfold before this collapse. The demands and the pains placed upon man by this emergent structure are reflected in the exertions and struggles of the ancient heroes to assert themselves in the world.[44] The demeanor of Odysseus—or of any other Greek hero—which manifests his boastfulness and self-adulation, is symptomatic of his compulsion to bridge the gap rent by matricide, as well as to assert himself.

Those vainglorious monologues of the Greeks, which have always seemed embarrassing because of their boastfulness and exaggeration, are accordingly an expression of the mania and compulsion of these heroes to regard themselves as seriously as the already emerging mutation demanded. Only a man still unsure of himself is given to boasting as the only way of establishing his status; this is why the ancient Greek had to assure himself by swaggering: he had destroyed the security of his maternal world and stepped out into the diurnal brightness of the columnar solar temple.

What was then taking place in moderation, counterbalanced by the cults of Demeter and Artemis (and later by the worship of the Virgin Mary), became increasingly and perilously one-sided with the onset of rationality. It is almost as though the *mater*ial-crazed man of today were the ultimate victim of the avenging mother—that *mater* whose chaotic immoderation is the driving force behind *matter* and *mater*ialistic supremacy. Besides, a world in which only the man or the father (or his representative, the son) has status and worth is ultimately inhuman.

Here lies the root of the most dangerous phenomenon of the so-called humanistic age: militarism. Patriarchal inhumanity exists particularly because the father is viewed only as, and nothing but, father; *the emphasis is on his paternity and not on his humanity.* The woman of this age, to the extent that she has any status at all, is seen correspondingly as only a woman and not as a human being. The "humane" age, notably the era beginning with perspectivity, is most likely the least human, and the most inhumane ever.

Yet despite this assertion we do not wish to join Mereschkowski or Bergmann in proclaiming a return to a new matriarchal world.[45] This would be tantamount to turning back the wheel of time. What must happen is rather a change in attitude by the male, who will have to forego many of his presumptions such as the arrogance that everything, including wife and child, belongs to him. He will have to give up this presumption in order that a world can come to be without maternal or paternal dominance, that is a non-masculinized world where man and woman together honor the human, and think not merely in terms of the human but of humankind in its entirety. This would mean that as matriarchy was once succeeded by patriarchy, patriarchy should be succeeded by an "integrum," as we have designated it. In this integral world neither man nor woman, but rather both in complement as human beings, should exercise sovereignty.[46]

Negligent propagandists of Heraclitus' phrase "War is the father of all things"[47]—such as the power-obsessed paternalistic militarists and politicians, and some interpreters of Heraclitus infected with this same mentality—have failed to realize because of their one-sided patriarchalism that the sentence might well be only fragmentary. It has never occurred to them that—as in the case of all statements by Heraclitus—the phrase makes sense only when completed by its polar complement. What we have is apparently only a fragment of a larger writing that is not extant, and it is symptomatic that only this part has survived. The partial sentence, "War is the father of all things," may, in one version or the other, have been originally completed by such words as "Peace is the mother of all things." And even if this or any other complementary thought had never been written by Heraclitus, such a complement was still present in its silent meaning, for he dedicated his book of famous fragments "On Nature" to Artemis of Ephesus, the "Great Mother." It was her image that Orestes once brought from Tauris to Greece at Apollo's behest to release himself from the Erinyes.[48]

We have dwelt on this mother-father problem because of its importance for contemporary Western humanity, as any father-confessor or psychologist could attest at length. Moreover, the problem of the son previously addressed (p. 86) is equally inseparable from this context. The son can become human only when he desists from killing others in the name of the father or the son.[49] For centuries Western civilization has burdened itself with this shameful offense which, like any deed, sooner or later reverts to its doer.

Anyone with ears to hear can already discern the approaching echo sounding from the (unillumined world of) the "woods." We are beginning to ask: "Have there been as many deeds for life as for its destruction?" And most of all we are beginning to inquire whether the question can even be asked in such measured, dualistic, and irresponsible terms, for irresponsible means unanswerable unless we were to invest some father-god with renewed avenging power.

But with that we limit the answer to a mere response, placing the problem into an insoluble causal and dualistic context. An answer that "does away" with our questions and deeds[50] will definitely never emerge from this context. This is only the ego, fearful of itself—the ego querying itself, the reflection of the mass (or amassed) "We." This ego will never receive an answer, only a dark muteness: a silent echo more terrible than a sounding one.

With this mention of the "ego" we have temporarily come to the last of our cross-sections, 14.c. It may serve to illustrate our description of how man's ego emerges and increases from mutation to mutation, culminating in the deficient mental phase with its overemphasis of ego and its pendulation between isolation and rigidification (egocentricity), as noted earlier. It will, consequently, not be unexpected that we speak of the integral structure as being "ego-free."[51] As for the two concepts "apsychic" and "amaterial" (to which we shall return), they express the aperspectival manner of considering the psyche and matter much in the same way as the term "arational" served to convey the nature of aperspectivity with respect to the rational.

The cross-sections 1 through 11.a/b, and 12–14 discussed above have been included in the "Synoptic Table" at the end of the volume, without any claim to completeness (which is, in any event, unattainable). Nonetheless, they may serve as a basis for the deliberations that follow and can shed some light on the further course of our investigations.

5. Concluding Summary: Man as the Integrality of His Mutations

It should by now be evident that in showing the structures which constitute us we have also gained a theoretical as well as practical means for clarifying our own lives. All of the deliberations (*Überlegungen*) we have advanced are to begin with what the word suggests: namely, the spatializing superimposition of thought onto phenomena and objects. Viewed in this way they are partly a blanketing, partly a superstructuring. And if we go, as we must, a step further we shall have to take into account that such deliberation, which in this sense is merely a spatializing construct, does not of itself achieve anything.

We have, accordingly, repeatedly emphasized that the structures we have outlined exist not only on paper but are in fact part of the phenomena and actualities which constitute us. To be sure, these actualities in the way we have presented them have an inherent organizing scheme, as does any form of representation, which contains an element of distortion or violence. And yet our organizing scheme applies to living processes which of themselves correct the schematic rigidities where they would be too powerful. We have already considered this corrective force inherent in all life in the gradually expanding design of our "Synoptic Table." The table is intended to be, not a straitjacket of rationalistic patchwork, but, in its demonstrable overlappings, an attempt in mental fashion to show man viewed in terms of his principal components as an entirety.

It is with such elucidation and clarification that we are concerned, not with explanations or deliberations. Nor are we inclined merely to interpret, since interpretations imply a one-sided relationship to the imaginary or imagistic and the mythical-psychic in us. And we are equally disinterested in presenting conceptualizations which unilaterally relate to the measuring and measurable spheres in us and in the world—that is, to the rational and material aspects.

But even assuming that our discussion were actually to provide us with a survey of ourselves—our reactions and actions—as we might hope for: what is gained thereby? This is a rational, that is a perspectivistic, goal-oriented question, and this is precisely why we are raising it. For even when viewed from the one-sided utilitarian viewpoint such a survey of those things that give our life its main emphasis can have a clarifying effect. If we apply the knowledge and insight laid out in the "Synoptic Table" directly to ourselves and to others, we will gain a better understanding of many actions and reactions since we will have come to see their roots and conditionalities.

The significance of this becomes evident when we realize that in every human being the one or the other structure predominates over the others. This brings about extremely obstructive consequences for us since we respond to certain events inadequately without noticing the inadequacy of our reactions and their negative effect on us. For example, someone at home in a predominantly magic attitude will find it difficult to cope with the demands of life posed by the mythical, not to mention the mental, structure. Instead of responding to a rational demand in a disciplined and directed way, and to a mythical demand in an encompassing and equalizing manner, such a person can only react to the dictates of drive and instinct, that is, in emotional, non-committal, and chaotic or predominantly magic responses. This means that he or she will founder in the face of important questions of life (such foundering is mainly expressed in major, protracted, and chronic illness).

In addition, life has a tendency to find its equilibrium. Since we live in a consciousness structure pervaded, as ours is, by conceptions of perspectivity, we must bring this structure into balance with the others if we are to act against life itself. The fact that we achieve such an equilibrium by living an integral and not merely a fragmented life is the basic condition that makes possible the mutation which could possibly surmount the dualistic dead-end into which we have maneuvered ourselves.

Let us note the decisive fact that *man is the integrality of his mutations.* Only to the extent that he succeeds in living the whole is his life truly integral. But we should go one step further: only if life is integral in this sense of equally living-to-the-full the structures which constitute us does it encompass the emerging structure not only potentially, but in an actual and acute sense.

By this time it should be evident that we are not merely toying here with thoughts, but are turning our mind to the prime difficulties that face the realization of an integral life. For life, after all, is not just a sum of vital aspects; the Vitalists failed to realize the fundamentally one-sided and magic nature of their vitalist preoccupation.

We must again approach here, by way of summary, a phenomenon that is truly terrifying so long as we remain unenlightened about it. We refer to the *incursion of deficient magic phenomena into our world*—the regression noticeable everywhere of our rational attitude to one of deficient magic. It is not as if the mythical attitude alone is over-activated today, although the imagistic aspect of the cinema or the inflation of psychic imagery made conscious are clear testimony of a process of unbridled and uncontrolled regression to the deficient mythical structure. Far stronger than this is the regression to the deficient magic structure. The relation of both the magic and the mental structures toward something outside of themselves— that of the magic to nature and of the mental to the world—results in a stronger affinity between them than between either and the mythical.

We have pointed out this regression to the magical several times; we would recall here our discussion of the basic component of Vitalism (p. 105[49]), as well as our indication of the parallel deficient forms of sorcery and utilitarian thinking with their goal and purpose orientation (pp. 93-94). We would also recall the remarkable correspondence between the labyrinthine aspects of the viscera and the brain (p. 146) which T. S. Eliot has also pointed out. [52] And lastly, even if we disregard the emphasis on "making" and power inherent in both structures in their deficient phases, we find an indication of deficient magic forms of manifestation in the tendency noted earlier toward collectivization or mass-phenomena in the one instance, and isolation in the other, whose antithetic tension threatens to tear apart our perspectival world.

Collectivization and mass-phenomena, for that matter, may well be nothing other than a reactivated magic clan-attunement in deficient form. Political parties are a compelling example, particularly the extreme ones dominated by the fanatically blind point-relatedness of the magical. And isolation or individuation may well be nothing more than the reactivated magic point-like unity become deficient.

While the beginnings of individuation and the clan formed a unity in the magic structure, they are today rationally torn asunder and, driven to extremes, have in their deficiency a destructive effect.

Or, stated differently, we might say that the hyperobjectivation achieved by the *ratio* brings about isolation, whereas the hypersubjectivation—the over-emphasis of the Ego—leads to the limits of Ego-capacity where the ego, reverting to its psychic conditionality rather than mastering the psyche, is itself ruled and condemned by it: it is absorbed by the unconscious, by immoderation, by the mass.

All remedies proposed to combat this danger turn out to be unsuitable. Political parties of "unity" or unified states attempt to regulate the problems of isolation or collectivization, although they reveal their own deficient character by their one-sided demands for power. The attempt is made to improve the circumstances of deficient magic by means of deficient magic, an attempt, as it were, to drive out the devil by invoking Beelzebub.

Let this one example suffice to show the basic point: wherever we encounter a predominance of insistent requests (and fanaticism is a request blindly elevated to a demand which not only petitions but compels); wherever we find a prevalence of the idea of unification in whatever form—a doctrine of unity, the establishment of an association, a huge organization, a one-party state and the like; wherever we encounter a stress on the concept of obedience, as in an overemphasis on the military, or of belonging and belongings, as in the property claims of capitalistic trusts or family patriarchies; and in general wherever we meet up with overweening emotionalism as in mass assemblies, propaganda, slogans, and the like, we may conclude that we are dealing mainly with essentially *deficient manifestations of magic.*

Their deficiency can be recognized by their very claim to *exclusivity*, as if they alone had validity or worth in contrast to the validity of other structures and forms of manifestation. Yet one may well ask what is to be gained by our classification of these phenomena as being deficiently magical. The answer is that because we know how they come to be, and recognize their conditionality, we no longer have to face them unaided. Even though we may be unable to do anything against such phenomena, we can at least avoid becoming submissive to them. We can view them with a certain detachment, secure in the knowledge that a deficient acquisition of unity does not lead to strength but rather of necessity, and naturally, to brutal power and, ultimately, to impotence.

After what has been said, examples of an overly mythical conception come easily to mind. Wherever we encounter an immoderate emphasis on the imagistic, the ambivalent, the psychic—on unbridled phantasy, imagination, or power of fancy—we may conclude the presence of a *deficient mythical attitude* that threatens the whole or integrality.

And, too, wherever we are caught up in the labyrinthine network of mere concepts, or meet up with a one-sided emphasis on willful or voluntaristic manifestations or attempts at spasmodic synthesis (trinitary, tripartite, dialectical), isolation, or mass-phenomena, we may assuredly conclude the presence of a *deficient mental,* that is, extreme rationalistic source.

This manner of observing the manifestations which we encounter must not, however, be applied mechanically or indiscriminately; only their *immoderation or excess* are deficient. Where they emerge in moderation these phenomena are today still efficient and effective. We must not lose sight of this fact, for if we do we place ourselves into question. It is not the measure alone which is decisive; it is the moderation contained in measure along with the immoderation, the measured as well as the immeasurable as expressed in the root of the words measure and mass.

This summary, then may have served to illustrate that:

1) All structures constitute us;
2) All structures must be lived commensurate with their constitutive values if we are to live a whole or integral life;
3) No structure may therefore be negated; negation enters when one structure or the other is overemphasized, whereby this accentuation is transferred to its deficient manifestations, which are always quantitative;
4) Certain designations, ascriptions, and characteristic concepts attributed to the individual structures render their effectuality evident.

With this result we come to the end of our chapter. The foundations that constitute each of us and thus also a possible new mutation may by now have become apparent at least to a certain extent. Nonetheless, before we can turn to the possibilities and first manifestations of the new consciousness or the new mutation, we must address in three short chapters some additional measures in order to preclude misunderstandings.

We cannot forego these measures since among the new and modern phenomena there are too many that, though forgotten, are merely reactivated manifestational forms. Inasmuch as they have been forgotten they give the appearance of being new and are erroneously valued as such. Certain modern artistic trends are a good example: surrealism and dadaism, for instance, are only regressions and not inceptions of a new mutation. They are to a certain extent the rubble covering the foundations; and on occasion they are even deliberate and conscious efforts to destroy these foundations.

We must, therefore, establish some additional means for distinguishing with certainty the seeming from the actual "new." For this we append three additional considerations to supplement our discussion so far. The first addresses the question of space and time, the second the question of soul/psyche and spirit, and the third the forms of realization and thought. Without having clearly demonstrated the conditionality of space and time, without having established what is psychic and what is presumably spiritual, and without having gained insight into the forms or types of realization and thought processes within each individual structure, we will be unable to make evident the "new."

Without such clarification we would be constantly in danger of reverting imperceptibly to the merely unitary space-timelessness of the pre-rational, or to the immoderation of purely psychic irrationality, or would remain confined in mere quantitative, rational thought. If we wish to gain insight into the arational and the aperspectival, this must be strenuously avoided. Only such insight into the mutation to the integral structure that is in process can transform our consciousness and our humanity into an effective whole. It is this structure, after all, that also encompasses what is to come: the future, which even today is our co-constituent. For not only we form it; it shapes us as well, and in this sense the future, too, is present.

1*   The term "diaphainon" (emphasis on the syllable *phai*) is the (present) participial noun from the Greek verb *diaphainomai*, an intransitive verb meaning literally as well as figuratively "that which shines through," and thus also "that which is transparent." Its particular emphasis is that something is or becomes visible or perceptible through something else, without implying that what is visible or perceptible necessarily has to shine or be resplendent; compare English "diaphane," *OED*, III, p. 318.

2   The attributions made here et passim for the integral structure represent indications of the possibility or potentiality that the full course of our discussion intends to make evident. They are, in other words, suggestions or indications and not postulations or preconceived (=mentally fixed) concepts; moreover, concepts as such would be alien to the integral structure and thus irrelevant. The "attributions," then, should be understood and estimated at the very most as tentative orientations which have yet to be made more precise; and the attributions made for the archaic structure are to be understood within the restrictions discussed on p. 43.

3   The one-sided anthropocentrism of the mental structure is also expressed by a loss of mythical polarity, since a center knows only the field of might that surrounds it and to which it belongs, and not its complementary pole. The result is an antithesis that gives rise to the dualistic principle.

4   The grave peril courted in the past by the sciences because of their observance of objectivity, of which we once spoke with pride just as we now are justified in speaking of its partial dubiousness, is manifest in the non-committal detachment and consequently in the threat of dehumanization in the sciences. The results of this objective and, from a human standpoint, non-committal attitude have turned against man and his continuation. This is true in spite of the numerous responsible scientists who have either rejected or begun to reject the coercion by objectivity. (A mere rejection does not bring forth a new attitude!) But it is not our intent, when speaking of the "objectivity of the sciences" and the alarming consequences in its wake, to lend support, say, to a "subjective science." Nevertheless, there ought to be an attitude possible that can rise above this dialectical alternative with a certain detachment and function responsibly with respect to the whole.

5   This ability has not been lost even today, as was demonstrated by my experience while in Florence. In school we observed only the metric accents when reciting Virgil's *Aeneid*, and so I was greatly surprised years later when I heard an educated Italian convey the individual emphasis of the words as well as the metric accentuation while reading the same verses.

6   Friedrich Creuzer, *Symbolik und Mythologie der alten Völker*, selected by G. H. Moser (Darmstadt: Leske, 1822), p. 8. The accuracy of the sequence tone-image-sign is borne out by the development of writing. It was first hieroglyph, that is, mythically stressed writing and only later a script of sign or letter, that is, mental and abstracting. The meaning, in other words, had to be first expressed most likely by sound and intonation—acoustic characteristics of the magic structure—and only later in pictograph or sign.

7   According to Kluge-Götze, *Etymologisches Wörterbuch der deutschen Sprache* (Berlin: de Gruyter, ¹¹1936), pp. 239 and 244, entries "hehlen" and "hell." Unintentionally Kluge has lent support to our contention that in the early period greater import was placed on auditory than on visual phenomena. In his discussion of the word *hell*, he notes that the word first refers predominantly to the brightness of sounds, rather than to the modern meaning of "brightness" or "brilliance"; this modern connotation is still lacking as late as the Old High German period. -The following borrowings can all be traced to the root *kel* (from Latin): cell, from *cella*, "chamber," related to *celare*, "to conceal, disguise"; cloister, from *claustrum*, "closure"; chalice, from Greek *kalyx* via Latin *calix;* and in addition, our word "cellar," Sanskrit *Kali*, the Indian goddess venerated in Hinduism for her dark, black aspect, and *Kalypso*, the Greek nymph, as well as German *heilig* which will be discussed below in chapter 6. See Kluge-Götze, pp. 294, 295, 309, and 707, and also Menge-Güthling, *Griechisch-Deutsches Wörterbuch* (Berlin: Langenscheidt,

[28]1910), p. 296. We shall have to return to a discussion of this root and its effects; see the text, p. 171, as well as our "First Remark on Etymology," p. 549.

8   It would surely be a distinguished achievement if one of the many philological seminars at a university, or one of the various academies, were to prepare a dictionary of this type on the basis of the "unity of primal words." It would certainly accomplish more for the awareness of mankind's "belonging together" than for example a superorganization founded on the power (or impotence) of its members, which in its unitary character represents only a magical attempt. It might be said that everything depends on the demonstration of *strengths* or *energies*, since they always possess a binding, cohesive character, and not on the establishment of new might or forces, which are perpetually locked in combat. *Any might or potence is usurped strength,* and thus always threatened by impotence.

9   See Kluge-Götze (note 7), p. 357, and Menge-Güthling (note 7), pp. 344 and 350. Neither Kluge nor Grimm, in *Deutsches Wörterbuch*, VI, column 1272, indicates the Indo-Germanic root of the word *Lüge*, "lie, untruth," although Grimm cites the word *Lug* (vi, column 1266) which originally meant "lookout cave" or "lurk cavern"(!). (We have already met up with the Latin word for "lie," *mentiri* (p. 77 above) in which the "other aspect" of the root *ma:me* is expressed.) An indication of the possible kinship of the words *logos* and *Licht*, "light," can be found in Ferdinand Ebner, *Das Wort und die geistigen Realitäten* (Innsbruck: Brenner, 1929), p. 35 note. See also our "Fourth Remark on Etymology," p. 557.

10   We have alluded to this primordial word-content on p. 85 and should point out that Abel already noticed the fundamental kinship of these words, as is evident from Freud's paper (see p. 8 above, note 3).

11   In regard to the Alpha-Omega symbolism, which contains the polarity of beginning and end, the active as well as passive element, and the father-mother symbol, see the author's *Der grammatische Spiegel* (Zürich: Oprecht, 1944), p. 46 note; [2]1963, p. 10 f; *Gesamtausgabe* I, p. 148, where we have ventured a brief discussion of these connections as they are represented in the mythical realm.

12   See Kluge-Götze (note 7), pp. 613, 620, and 623, under the respective entries for these words, as well as our "Fifth Remark on Etymology," p. 558.

13   To describe this as a process of repression would be to indulge in a one-sided psychologizing interpretation fashionable among such psycholinguists as Karl Terebessy in his *Zum Problem der Ambivalenz in der Sprachentwicklung* (Trnava: Urbánek, 1944). The fact that the more recent languages express for the most part only one aspect of the former polarity does not indicate a repression, but rather a process of rationalization that has affected language. Rational language is no longer able to mirror the irrational (ambivalent-psychic or pre-rational (unitary-vital) valuations of primal words. Hence it must rend these valuations asunder and quantify them into antithetical pairs in an attempt to make them rationally comprehensible as "opposites." It may well be such a compulsion to tear apart, as in logic, that Socrates called his "demon" (daimonion). We would recall in this context our remarks on the root *da* on which *daimonion* is based; its basic meaning is "to tear apart, tear to pieces." It is revealing that it occurs together with the root *mu*, the basis for the words *monos* and *mythos*; myth, i.e., the polarity of the soul, is rent asunder. This is the inception of the "demonic." (For a discussion of the various conceptions of the second syllable of *daimōn*, see note 134 of the previous chapter, p. 113 above, as well as our "Fifth Remark on Etymology," p. 558.)

14   Terebessy p. 10; his example is from Abel.

15   We have already indicated (pp. 46 and 60, as well as note 68, p. 109) that "will" or volition has also a magical character. Magic will, however, in contrast to mental volition, is emotional; it springs from the vital and not from thought. Its efficient form is in spell-casting, its deficient form in sorcery, and it is more appropriately described as "impulse" or "drive" rather than "volition."

16   On this subject see the author's "*Über das Wesen des Dichterischen*," in *Schweize-*

rische Zeitschrift für Psychologie und ihre Anwendungen, 3, no. 3 (Bern: Huber, 1944), 219; Gesamtausgabe, V/I, pp. 82–100.

17   Jean Gebser, Das Ariadnegedicht (Zürich: Oprecht, 1945), p. 15, verse 106; Gesamtausgabe, VII, p. 117.

18   An unconscious presence of the future is expressed by the Hindi word Kal which means "yesterday" as well as "tomorrow." In this state of undifferentiation there is a magical element still evident in the present-day Hindi-speaking Indian. The "superwakeful transparency" of which we have spoken excludes this magic component, and guarantees that the once undifferentiated content of the somnolescent consciousness is henceforth "superawarely" accessible to consciousness; see Gebser, Asienfibel, Ullstein ed. No. 650, (Berlin and Frankfurt/M.: Ullstein, 1962), p. 20 f.; Gesamtausgabe, VI, p. 24 f.

19   On this subject see Gebser, Abendländische Wandlung (Zürich: Oprecht), 1943, p. 92; ²1945, p. 96; Ullstein ed. No. 107, chapter 15; Gesamtausgabe, I, p. 230 ff. In addition to the works cited there, notably the books of Tucci and Seabrook, see also the writings on Tibet by Alexandra David-Neel, Meister und Schüler (Leipzig: Brockhaus, 1934), and Heilige und Hexer (Leipzig: Brockhaus, 1936).

20   Regarding "physical projection" see Jean Gebser, In der Bewährung (Bern: Francke, 1962), p. 86 ff.; Gesamtausgabe, V/I, p. 235 ff.

21   The etymological derivation of "anxiety" (Angst) is "narrow" (eng); see Gebser (note 19), 1943, p. 172; ²1945, p. 199; Ullstein ed. 107, chapter 29; Gesamtausgabe, I, pp. 289–304. See also Kluge-Götze pp. 18 and 132, entries "Angst" and "eng."

22*   Further remarks on the anxiety question can be found in Jean Gebser's Anxiety, tr. Peter Heller, illus. Heiri Steiner (New York: Dell Books, 1962).

23   See also Jean Gebser, Rilke und Spanien (Zürich: Oprecht, 1940), pp. 85–86, note 48; ²1945, p. 86 f.; Gesamtausgabe, I, p. 77. These doomsday feelings that are recognizable today in psychoses of atomization, war, or destruction, are to a certain extent justified; in each instance a world—the world valid up to that moment—perishes. The Renaissance was the conclusion of the unperspectival world; today's era is perhaps the end of the perspectival. The danger inherent in such doomsday feelings is that they beget a lack of self-control as well as a confusion of ideas in the minds of their victims: it is not "the" world which threatens to perish, but merely "their" world. It is common to both the Renaissance and our own era that the most terrible exterminations take place: then those of the Inquisition, now those of which the dictatorships were, and are, guilty. The gas ovens of the "Twelve Year Reich" (perhaps only a harbinger of what is to come) are the stake of the Inquisition with the horror quantified into larger dimensions, befitting the general and progressing quantification of our day. (Most likely it was the "same" people then as now who were guilty.)

24   Numerous examples are cited in Gebser, Asienfibel (note 18).

25   We are here speaking of "anxiety" and not fear, disregarding the organic causes of fear as well as most of those forms manifest as birth trauma. Birth trauma can, in fact, result in death anxiety, since both birth and death are closely related if we consider them as passages through the narrows. - It is not possible in the limited space here to deal with Kierkegaard's idea of metaphysical anxiety, or H. Keyserling's juxtaposition of a "primordial anxiety" (Urangst) with a "primordial hunger." Nor can we deal with the response of anxiety as a hormonal reaction (release of adrenalin into the blood stream) as is done in recent psychophysical and psychosomatic research (Rudolf Brun, Allgemeine Neurosenlehre, [Basel: Schwabe, ²1946], p. 112); these findings would suggest fright or alarm rather than anxiety. Nor will we examine anxiety as a primordial feeling without an object, the main finding of the genial von Monakow. We would, however, expressly emphasize that trust is the positive form of anxiety, while hope is the positive form of fear; both fear and hope are phenomena of insecurity which the mind relates to the future. Thus only a dialectician can justifiably speak of a "principle of hope" (Ernst Bloch). But anxiety and trust are inceptual phenomena, latent in themselves and in us when we are conscious of them; at least in the Christian view, anxiety can turn to trust

and consequently to innermost security, rendering hope and fear superfluous. Hope and fear, moreover, are both "principles," preventing and undermining every freedom. See also Jean Gebser, "Vom spielenden Gelingen," in *Jeder Tag ein guter Tag* (Weilheim /Obb.: Barth, 1961), pp. 151–156; *Gesamtausgabe*, VI, pp. 396–400; also in Gebser, *Ein Mensch zu sein: Betrachtungen über die Formen der menschlichen Beziehungen* (Bern: Francke, 1974), pp. 45–48.

26   See Gebser, *Abendländische Wandlung*, (note 19), ²1943, p. 233, note 12; Ullstein ed. 107, p. 174, note 12 *Gesamtausgabe*, I, p. 323.

27   It is not just a question of the fate of our world, but of the world—a question of destiny that can come about with finality during the very next generation. And it should be noted that for the author, the "next" generation is the one born between the two world wars.

28   An indication of the existence of this unspoken primordial myth is probably also evident from the fact that the Pelasgi, the presumed aboriginal inhabitants of Greece, knew only nameless gods (see Creuzer, note 6 above, pp. 1–2 of the 1822 edition).

29   Werner Heisenberg and Adolf Portmann have also pointed out the present inadequacy of language to deal with the new discoveries and modes of inquiry; cf. Gebser (note 20), p. 147. Notes 21 and 22 of that source also document the respective works of Heisenberg and Portmann where they comment on this question; (*Gesamtausgabe*, V/I, p. 294).

30   Karl Kerényi has noted the connection between the labyrinth and the viscera in his *Labyrinth-Studien*, Sammlung Albae Vigiliae 25 (Amsterdam: Pantheon, 1941). T. S. Eliot also mentions it in his *Family Reunion* (N.Y.: Harcourt, Brace, 1939).

31   Numerous examples of the visceral emphasis of the magic structure can be found in Gebser, *Asienfibel*, (note 18), passim; *Gesamtausgabe*, VI, pp. 11–187.

32   See, among others, Paula Philippson, *Griechische Gottheiten in ihren Landschaften*, Symbolae Osloenses, Fasc. suppl. 9 (Oslo: Brogger, 1944), p. 14.

33   As evidenced by a reference in his poem "Die heiligen drei Könige," Rainer Maria Rilke most likely also senses this magic organ relationship; there he imputes to the wise men and magicians from the East *Magenkraft*, "visceral strength," literally, "stomach power" in the sense of "magician's power"; poems of the *Buch der Bilder, Gesammelte Werke* (Leipzig: Insel, 1930), II, p. 75. Moreover, this particular poem has a notable "charm" of diction, a charm suggestive of the magical attunement and effect that emanates from it.

34   The notion that Mary conceived Jesus via the ear was still widely held among the Catharii; see F. Chr. Baur, *Die christliche Kirche des Mittelalters* (Tübingen: Fuess, 1861), p. 190. This conception is indicative of the magical frame of mind of the late Gnostic sect expressed also by their use of caves during times when they were most likely not persecuted. These caves and grottos were discovered a number of years ago in the Pyrenees by Charles Rinderknecht of Bern; one of the caves was called the *gleisa santa*, an echo of the root *kēl*; see Déodat Roché, *Le Catharisme* (Toulouse: Institut d'Etudes Occitanes, ²1947), p. 118.

35   See Hans Lamer, *Wörterbuch der Antike* (Leipzig: Kröner, ²1936), KTA vol. 96, p. 114 f.: "Carmen, (Lat.: "poem"), more appropriately an ancient cult-song sung during the ceremonial procession through the fields [spell-casting] and accompanied by rhythmic dance. Its purpose was for expiation of the plantings and imploration of the gods for prosperous crops."

36   The words *carmen, charme, canto*, and "charming" are all traceable to Latin *canere*, "to sing"; see Alois Walde, *Lateinisches etymologisches Wörterbuch* (Heidelberg: Winter, 1906), p. 91 f.; Walde-Hofmann, *Lateinisches etymologisches Wörterbuch* (Heidelberg: Winter, ³1938), I p. 169, f.; *Diccionario de la Lengua Española* (Madrid: Espasa-Calpe, ¹⁶1939), p. 505; Emile Boisacq, *Dicionnaire étymologique de la langue grecque* (Paris: Klincksieck, ²1923), pp. 413–414 and 451, entries "karkairo" and "keryx." Walde-Hofmann rejects the possibility of an Indo-Germanic root *qar*; Boisacq postulates *qer*. We will encounter this root *qer* again (p. 171), as it, together with the root *ker*, may well be the phonetic element for the awakening cavern world of magic.

37   Indirect corroboration of our thesis is furnished by Marius Schneider in his *El origen*

musical de los animales-símbolos en la mitología y la escultura antiguas, Consejo Superior de Investigaciones Científicas (Barcelona: Instituto Español de Musicología, 1946). This study came to our attention only after the present work was in press. Schneider's remarks are also an inadvertent contribution to Hans Kayser's "Harmonics," for they echo sounds that give evidence of the magical-mental emphasis of modern harmony. Senghor, the statesman-poet of Senegal, in a speech in Frankfurt in 1963, emphatically underscored the primordial role of dance and rhythm for the cultures of Africa which still today are predominantly magical; see Gisela Bonn, "Botschaft aus Afrika," *Christ und Welt* 16, No. 14 (Stuttgart, April 5, 1963), 17.

38*   The Bible, which presents us again and again with people living in the mythical world and moving toward the mental, is replete with indications which point to the role of the heart; see for instance the numerous examples listed in the *Bremer Biblischer Hand-Konkordanz* (Zürich: Gotthelf, 1941), pp. 387–389. The Bible is particularly full of examples linking the heart with the word, for it is the heart and no longer exclusively the ear that hears; some examples: Deut. 6:6: "And these words . . . shall be upon thine heart;" Deut. 11:16: "Take heed . . . lest your heart be deceived"; 1 Sam. 1:13: "Now Hannah spake in her heart"; Isa. 35:4: "Say to them that are of a fearful heart"; Jer. 15:16: "Thy words were unto me a joy and the rejoicing of my heart"; and 1 Thess. 2:4: "God, which proveth our hearts." An echo of this "knowing" and speaking through the heart is preserved in French *savoir coeur* and English "to know by heart"—both languages more rational than German.

39   Creuzer (note 6), p. 18.

40   As may be clear from our usage, the word "contemplate" denotes the psychic ability of "inner vision," of images in which the soul is reflected or depicted, whether in the form of dreams, myths, fantasies or mystical visions. Inasmuch as even the instincts "become visible" in them, they were considered for a time to be psychic factors.

41   See Jean Gebser, *In der Bewährung* (note 20), p. 99; *Gesamtausgabe,* V/I, p. 247.

42   J. J. Bachofen, *Das Mutterrecht* (Basel: Schwabe, ²1897), p. 64, column 2, where he adduces several examples from antiquity to support his statement.

43   The conquest of Troy by the Hellenes may also be understood as an expression of the destruction (or supersession) of the early Greek matriarchal-mythical world (see p. 76f.), and in this the role of Helen seems to be decisive. (For a discussion of the etymology of the name "Helen" see the "First Remark on Etymology," p. 549.)

44*   We use the word "assert" here deliberately (in German, *behaupten*), for it is the head (*Haupt*), the bearer of the brain, that plays the decisive role in the mental structure. This, then, does not only refer to Alkmaion, who first dissected the brain (see Gebser, note 19 above, 1943, p. 20; ²1945, p. 18; ³1950, p. 17; Ullstein ed. No. 107, p. 15 f.; *Gesamtausgabe,* I, p. 177); Athena, it will be recalled, sprang forth from the head of Zeus. We might also mention that the thought has its source in the psyche, insofar as the head of Zeus can be considered as a symbolization of the sky; see F. M. Müller, *Die Wissenschaft der Sprache* (Leipzig: Engelmann, 1892), II. And yet this birth of Athena is a tragic awakening reflected in the sundering of the heavens, which is at the same time a sundering of the circling soul.

45   Certain circles of analytical psychology, too, are dreaming of a restoration of matriarchy, particularly since the United States of America give clear indications of this tendency. To us, this seems unlikely; see Gebser (note 20), p. 101; *Gesamtausgabe,* V/I, p. 249. We have indicated that the matriarchy did not completely disappear during the era of patriarchal supremacy but survived in *materialism;* see Gebser (note 18), p. 102; *Gesamtausgabe,* VI, p. 100 f. It should be apparent that the matriarchal element, at least in Europe, has been reduced to a shadow existence, having survived only residually and surfacing only rarely. These occasional surfacings are evident particularly in several expressions, notably in French: in the phrase *cherchez la femme,* for example, used with reference to important events (significantly, *negative* events), and in the pejorative sense of "mistress," that is, the paramour of a married man who is called *sa maîtresse,* literally "his governess."

46   For a detailed discussion, see the essay "Mensch oder Apparat im modernen Staat," in Gebser (note 20), pp. 87-110, particularly pp. 101 and 109; *Gesamtausgabe*, v/ı, pp. 235-258, particularly pp. 249 and 256. Wolfgang Schwarz has extended our concept by his term "anthroparchy," which he suggests in his book *Hoffnung im Nichts: Radhakrishnan, Gebser und der westöstliche Geist* (Krailing: Müller, 1961), p. 119; but this is somewhat less than adequate since *anthropos* means not just "human being" but "man" in the sense of a male human and "soldier," and the corresponding feminine form, *anthrope*, means "woman"; see Menge-Güthling (note 7), p. 53. For this reason we prefer the term "integrum" to indicate the integration of woman and man.

47   The entire fragment is printed in Diels-Kranz, *Die Fragmente der Vorsokratiker* (Berlin: Weidmann, ³1934), 22 B 53.

48   In venturing an interpretation of the *Oresteia* one should not overlook the circumstance that Orestes, the perpetrator of matricide, rediscovered his sister Iphigenia, believed dead, at the very place where his expiation began, that is, in the sanctuary of Artemis. This discovery of his sister after he had released himself from his maternal attachment may impart a purely humane touch to this tragedy of consciousness emergence.

49   It is indicative of our times that killing is inevitably carried out in the name of the father: in the name of God the father in heaven, in the name of the king (father of the people), and in the name of the fatherland.

50   The word "answer" or *Antwort*, with its modified prefix deriving from *ent-*, "de-", is always expressive of suspension and dissolution, and suggests in consequence "dewording," a suspension of the (questioning) word. A similar sense underlies the word "correspondence," *Entsprechung*, literally "de-speaking" whatever "corresponds" either mutually suspends, or in its positive form, completes itself. It is such a fitting expression of the mythical process that we have striven to use it mostly with reference to the mythical structure.

51   Regarding this "ego-freedom," which we use to indicate both the liberation from egolessness as well as from mere egotism, and overemphasis on the ego, egocentricity, see Gebser (note 20), p. 104 and p. 107 f.; *Gesamtausgabe*, v/ı, pp. 251-252 and 254.

52   See note 30.

5

The Space-Time
Constitution of
the Structures

1. The Space-Timelessness of the Magic Structure

Whenever we speak of space and time we must remember that these are concepts worked out by our consciousness—concepts which are the primary constituents of consciousness and make possible its effectuality. Yet the point of departure for this achievement was space-timelessness. And this space-timelessness which we have attempted to render comprehensible as being characteristic of the magic structure—which is, indeed, of basic and decisive import for this structure—this space-timelessness is not amenable to depiction or representation. To represent or depict is to spatialize something; but how are we to render something spaceless in spatial terms unless we forego its non-spatial character?

We are compelled accordingly to look for another procedure. We could for example attempt to evoke or invoke or conjure up the prerational events—an approach which we suggested earlier (p. 51). This would result in our being transported back to the magic state where we could experience it; but it would also mean that upon re-emerging from this state we would be unable to give any account of it, since the somnolent, trance-like state of this consciousness with its weakly developed awareness would have sufficiently infected or lowered our own awareness that we could not count on its deliberative capabilities. We would have had an emotional experience, it is true, but would be unable to account for what actually happened, not to mention being able to make any kind of judgement on it.

Therefore this avenue too cannot be traversed; but perhaps there is another way to the goal. If we were able to evince clearly the positive effect resulting from such a submersion into space-timelessness, we could at least convey some idea of the nature and the genesis of space-timelessness. For as long as we merely point to the deficient manifestations of this basic phenomenon we have accomplished little towards its clarification. Let us, then, disregard here the deficient manifestations of today's "machine magic" such as the effects of the radio (with its almost space-timeless functioning and its exclusive tie to the auditive which indicate its magic roots, just as the imagistic effects of the cinema are an indication of its mythical source). Deficient applications or effects of the magic structure will not furnish us with information about the efficient efficacy of space-timelessness.

To discover this efficacy we must turn to a positive manifestation. We have noted in an earlier context[1] a phenomenon which could not be explained on a rational basis by rational means, namely, the miraculous healings of Lourdes. In that connection we quoted a remark by the physician Alexis Carrel, who observed that "the only condition indispensable to the occurrence of the phenomenon [of healing] is prayer."[2] We also pointed out that certain aspects for which we had then no explanation could be designated as being akin to "communion."

We have seen that prayer is a magic form of manifestation in addition to being a *communio*, that is, a "being one with" (the Latin word is built upon *con-*, "with," and *unio*, "unity, oneness"). Genuine prayer, which is an outgrowth of a need (in the case of the mortally ill, a vital need) and is not therefore purpose- or goal-oriented, has the nature and function of communion. It restores the inceptual unity or oneness; the absorption of the suppliant in prayer is an immersion into the natural unity of everything in this state at that moment. The individual is, as it were, extinguished and forms a true unity with the hundreds of others who are united with him in prayer.

In this the location itself—Lourdes—where the healing takes place is of decisive importance. Its mythical configuration, to which we shall return in a moment, makes possible the transition from the diurnal wakeful awareness via the dream-like mythical consciousness to the weakly-conscious somnolent and trance-like state of magic space-timelessness. The magic-mythical configuration of Lourdes is evident on the one hand in the primordial aspect of the grotto, the sheltering cavern; on the other, in the figure of the saint, the protectress and "Great Mother"; and also in the source from which the living water springs forth. These are all magic and psychic fundamentals administered by the church in the name of the one God.

The healing process is a descent whereby the believer in the one God descends down to the darkness of the source ruled over by the sheltering mother: a descent to the unity "below," where the individual loses his individuality and is united with everything. When the diurnal or wakeful consciousness is sufficiently depressed so that the surroundings are no longer present to the suppliant, and he "sinks" even deeper where even the psychic reality of dream and image vanish, his individuality is obliterated in the magic realm (of the grotto or cavern) and he becomes one with the unity to which all differentiation is unknown. There spatial boundaries and temporal limits are suspended. One thing affects the "other" with which it is united; individual organs, even individual afflicted organs, are effaced and are, say, henceforth hand or arm inasmuch as the hundreds of arms and hands are now undifferentiated and unbounded, comprising *one* arm and *one* hand.

This power of natural healing—and because of the vital need it is efficient strength, not the deficient might of magic which reponds—which the individual body is unable to summon for the afflicted organ is marshalled by the *unity* of all organs. The power which was individually lacking in the afflicted hands flows from the healthy hands with which they are united. A unifying flux, a communion streams through and equalizes this unity of those united in prayer who recover as a single body. Of itself nature furnishes the equilibrium to this organism of suppliants which has become a unit, an equilibrium that the individual organism was no longer able to establish. When the suppliant reemerges from the depths of meditation and returns to his rational wakeful consciousness, he brings along from the magic depths his recovery and health.

Such places as Lourdes are truly religious, for they establish the *religio*, the bond to the past which in this case extends back to our beginnings in the magic structure. Let this example suffice to illustrate the efficacy of space-timelessness to those who are able to free themselves from the confines of rational rigidity without necessarily plunging into the depths of irrationality.

This particular example is perhaps successful in "describing" the effect of space-timelessness, and yet it must not be overlooked that the healing processes that take place at Lourdes can also be interpreted in other ways. But however they are interpreted, their principal character is one of proximity to the "state" of space-timelessness. It is generally recognized that the irrational and prerational nature of these cures which occur in the non-measurability of space-timelessness has enabled the modern rational sciences to speak of occult or parapsychic phenomena.[3]

Instances of such phenomena are legion; we would mention an instance cited by E. Bozzano because of its relevance to Lourdes.[4] In his example there is a transfer of psychic and vital energy: a transfer of the vitality from a healthy to a sick person which occurs unconsciously and is fostered by the ambiance of the location. The result is that the sick person is healed while the healthy one—in this case an attendant—suffers for several days from psychic as well as physical exhaustion. In this instance an individual accomplishes a transfer of energy which otherwise would take place as an exchange of energy among the "congregation."

The psychic *participation inconsciente* is indicative of a process which occurs far removed from space and time but which leaves its visible imprint nonetheless in the spatially and temporally-bound body. This one instance of processes which can be described in parapsychological terms may be sufficient in itself, but there are numerous others. All such phenomena interpreted along the lines of parapsychology, however, are liable to the danger of a psychologizing misinterpretation, particularly because a mostly misconstrued magic element plays a decisive part in such interpretations, an element which is beyond the grasp of psychic experience.

Such phenomena remain one-sided whenever they are explained in a psychologizing manner. We are, however, interested in the condition and process in their entirety, and for this reason the example of Lourdes can serve for all similar and identical instances. Moreover, the nature of prayer[5] has furnished a convenient and unquestionable point of departure. A conscious reversion to the effectivity of the magic structure which in fact occurs hour by hour in us, sustaining us as proof of its power, would make "sense" (for we live in the mental structure) only if it led us to expect a strengthening of the direction of our lives in the mental structure. But such is rarely the case; to the mental structure the magic appears to be mostly chaotic. Whenever it breaks into consciousness it subordinates consciousness to its might, thereby not strengthening consciousness so much as confounding it. For this reason alone the rational defenses vis-à-vis the magical are justified. Everything depends on the individual's constitutional bent and whether he is able to see through the variegated texture in which he is at once seedling, flower, and fruit.

There is some risk in speaking of such matters, for at the very least they endanger (*Gefahr*) the "soul"; and every peril is either a demise (in the oceanic reaches of the psyche) or an enduring experience (*Erfahrung*). The experience of where the magic structure begins and how it works must be made by every person individually, and the peril lies "behind" the experience and threatens anyone unprepared with the loss of self. For unity does not just unify; from the standpoint of the individual[6] it disintegrates: unity is a process and state of dissolution in the spaceless and timeless.

Someone unsure of himself should not approach or be led into these matters. For this very reason we have referred to the well-known example of Lourdes. It cannot be treated exhaustively, for within the magic structure which we have touched upon here a dense network of associations begins where everything commences to coincide with everything and everyone else—a situation extremely dangerous for the rational consciousness. Moreover, here we approach that powerful attraction of the earth from which every supplication (*Flehen*) tries to flee (*fliehen*).[7] But one can escape a force—and this is the "secret"—only by passing through it. (Other forms of this "passage" are the alchemistic *unificatio*, the *chymische Hochzeit* of the Rosicrucians, and many others, and the decisive role of magic space-timelessness is not limited only to them.)

But now let us leave this spaceless-timeless world which our rational awakened consciousness finds so disquieting and turn to that world characterized by temperament, disposition, and courage; by the pulse of the heart; and by the mute as well as singing mouth, that is, the world of myth and its incipient temporicity.

2. The Temporicity of the Mythical Structure.

With the advent of polarity came the phenomenon of complementarity: day and night, brightness and darkness, heaven and earth, pillar and cavern. As we have observed in the myth of Athena, later myth is no longer a form of pure dreaming but rather a type of dream-of-awakening in which the mental image of world is anticipated. If we are to discover the apparently natural contingency of temporicity we should therefore not rely too heavily on these myths; rather, we shall have to go back to the unspoken myths. But as these unspoken myths elude the grasp of our quantifying rationality, we are compelled to seek a different approach to the problem.

When speaking of the temporicity of the mythical structure we must not lose sight of its residual spacelessness. In the undifferentiated brightness and darkness man begins to discern forces which slowly disengage themselves from movement and become animated primal images. These primal images are reflections of the inner dark and unfathomable forces in man which we call the powers of the soul or psyche. The initial dimly-lit consciousness is pervaded by darkness; only with the gradual increase of conscious intensity is there a proportional illumination of those powers represented as movement. This process takes place on a surface which is spaceless or at least remote from space, like the night, with its dark, two-dimensional planiform ground devoid of spatial depth.

There must have been a far-reaching connection between the discovery of the first perceptions of regular, that is, periodic movement and the discovery of the soul. These movements were first discerned from the night sky, and the correspondence between its movements and man's own rhythm and dynamics may have brought about man's first sensation of time. Plato has obliquely revealed this in his obscure statement that the heavens and the soul simultaneously came to be. The dark, spaceless confines from which movement slowly emerges is evident from the fact that the earliest mode of telling time was based on nocturnal and lunar periodicity.[8] Vestiges of this are still preserved in our modern languages: English for example speaks of a "fortnight," that is, fourteen nights instead of fourteen days, and "sennight" for "eight days"; and German *Fastnacht*, "Shrove Tuesday," and *Weihnacht*, "Christmas" are further examples.[9]

We must not lose sight of this dark background, although in fact it is very commonly overlooked, perhaps because it is confined to the darkness of spacelessness. There is an emergent awareness of the autonomous motility of the point—whether in the form of a star, of a person, or a falling leaf—which begins in man following the discovery of the punctiformity of nature and of man himself; and we are using the abstract terms here deliberately since it is difficult to apprehend this process concretely. With this autonomous motility of the point, unity is transformed into polar movement: into an event of correspondence which is reflected by the heavens as well as by the soul. And toward the close of the mythical age these components—movement, eventuation, soul, and also the heavens, all of which are in a certain sense identical—give birth to Chronos and the form of time which makes possible the experience of spatiality.

Let us for now, however, avoid a premature discussion of the problematics involved in the progression from eventuation via conceptual time to their cleavage into becoming and being, particularly as these are mental thought processes that were anticipated in imagistic form in the Greek lore of the Titans. Our concern here is with the temporicity of the mythical structure and its probable genesis in the spacelessness of the punctiformal consciousness. This temporicity is based on movement or kinesis, a movement still apart from space. It is the movement of Greek gods who with the swiftness of thought were able to conquer unimpeded an as yet unconscious and hence nonexistent space (much as we experience spacelessness today in our dreams).

It is a form of movement that leads from one phase of the moon to another, from new moon to new moon, nine moons to nine moons, birth to death, spring to winter; from the tides of the earth to the tides of the body which blossom forth, bear fruit, and attain completion, just as the year unfolds, bears fruit, and completes its cycle, like the stars which ascend, reach their zenith, and descend. In this the cosmos itself forms a circle, rotating and drawing the energy for its rotation from the polarity.

For mythical man the movement of his own soul became visible in the reflection of dream and myth, and in this way he became aware of the actual movement of the world. If we are to discover something "outside" ourselves, we must first discover it "inside" ourselves. The prevailing identification of the soul with number and star in Plato's later works, which he derived from the Pythagorean school, is an indication of the nocturnal birth of the temporal consciousness that was at first in step with natural as well as cosmic time. The cyclic motion of inner forces which began to be represented in myth had a complementary and polar-reciprocal relationship to the natural and cosmic forces outside man.

This world of virtual yet still sheltered movement, which was motionless, as it were, since every movement returned upon itself and cancelled its effect,[10] burst apart when oriented thought temporarily halted the course of the sun: when Helios interrupted his course because of his indignation at the birth of Athena, when thought, severing the equilibrium of phenomena, severed the circle. With this, our "time" and "space" were born: orientation and direction, which the circle, being without beginning and end, was lacking. Only movement, that is, directed motion, could give rise to what we today call "time."

When we speak of the temporicity of myth we are employing a term which is not entirely adequate to the given data. We have, accordingly, attempted to lessen this error by restricting the definition to "natural and cosmic" time which circumscribes both the movement and the agitation or eventfulness of the heavens and the soul. It is this form of movement which is common to both temporicity and the soul, the former being represented in days, months, years, and eons, the latter in the proliferation of inner images and their transitoriness. However we may regard the soul, it will always be viewed in the image of movement, in the image of water or air; its tides or breathing are life-giving and life-sustaining to the same degree as the daily and annual tides and cycles of time.

It is this constant movement of temporicity which reveals the true time-form of myth. This same time-form, with its self-completing occurrence and constancy, also reveals the undifferentiated state of what is now separated into the two parts of the word pair *Weg:weg*. This pair, or the word for "movement" itself, *(Bewegung)*, is derived from the common Indo-Germanic root *wegh*, which means "to move, to bear or carry." From it, along with many others, came the word *gaieochos*, "earth-mover," an attribute of Poseidon. And it was Poseidon who ruled in the procreative depths and nocturnal darkness of the sea,[11] that same sea whose tides are determined by the nocturnal moon, itself a reflection of the sun which forms what we may call the erstwhile heart of our universe and awakens the images and animates the thoughts once pondered in her heart by Mary, whose cloak was the starry firmament.

This seemingly associative manner of observation is in fact an attempt to report and direct events and phenomena as they occur in the spaceless temporicity of the closed and dynamic image-world of myth. By merely describing and thereby intellectualizing it, we would sever its self-complementarity and two-dimensional intermeshing, reducing the pure eventfulness and dynamism to mere temporal sequence or succession. To the extent that they are successful, these whimsical attempts to illustrate some of the intermingled events from the living cycle and to suggest the invisible nascence of temporicity will create an image not unlike that visible to mythical man. We will not have described anything but rather will have remained faithful to the imagery (one might say that we've "got the picture") as befits the corresponding demands of this world of kinesis and temporicity.

Let us now take leave of the mythical twilight. We have seen that the inceptual element of temporicity remained dormant until reflected by the awakening consciousness, which thereby gave rise to the two-dimensional mythical world of movement and near-temporality and went "beyond" the point-like one-dimensional world of space-timelessness. It is without question difficult for us to imagine how this mutation took place, but in the light of what we have just described it will at least be possible to see that it happened and, indeed, had to happen. And although the process unfolded in a world which our present-day thought can scarcely grasp, inasmuch as the third dimension, the indispensable constituent of our mental thought, did not yet exist in it, we must nonetheless make an attempt to make the phenomenon vivid and comprehensible.

There are only limited ways and means for accomplishing this; indeed it may appear at first glance that there are none at all. If we are content, however, to stay within the framework of visual means as befits the imagistic nature of mythical phenomena, there is the possibility that we will at least be able to imagine if not to conceptualize this process.

Indeed there is an image with which we can perhaps illustrate the temporicity of the mythical structure in our attempt to describe it. And even beyond this there is even the possibility that we can discover a tone or sound from whose echo we can discern the kind of process which led to the mutation from the space-timelessness of magic to the non-spatial temporicity of the mythical.

Let us first consider the image and then the sound, observing first what came to be and then its genesis. The image we are speaking of is that of Kronos, one of the Titans. We are cognizant that we are dealing here with a late mythological account of the images, but it would appear that a recollection has here taken on the nature of imagery which is itself already a manifestation of temporality. Moreover, the figure of Kronos also bears traits of a definitely mental stamp. Consequently, the account is not merely a dream-like reminiscence whose imagery portrays a past or present event, but is also a kind of prescience or pre-dreaming. That is to say, the mythologeme of Kronos is not just an expression of mythical temporicity but in its mythologizing, dream-like, anticipatory form is also the germ of the notion or concept of time. It is essential to note that what it conveys to us as an image of temporicity must not be confused with our present-day concept of time (which will be discussed in the next section).

We owe our earliest knowledge of the Kronos mythologeme to Hesiod whose account already reveals utilitarian aims. By investigating all available sources of the mythologeme we can single out several important attributes from the complex series of images and events which signify the essence of mythical temporicity and suggest, or rather echo, its genesis in magic timelessness.

Kronos is the son of Uranus and Gaia and thus a child of heaven and earth. As we know from later Orphic times, as shown by the lamellae tablets and their inscriptions (see above p. 82), such knowledge is not merely imagistic but will come to be a kind of integrated personal and conscious knowledge. Kronos is the youngest of the Titans and father of Hera and Zeus as well as of Demeter, Hades, Poseidon, and Charon. He is, in other words, father of those gods and demigods who populate the world's nocturnal sphere. To prevent the fulfillment of a prophecy that one of his children would gain ascendance over him, Kronos devoured them; but none other than Metis, the mother of Athena, prepared him a potion causing him to disgorge the devoured children. In the subsequent great struggle of the Titans with the gods, Zeus conquered his father, and Kronos was banished to the realm of the shades.[12]

This clearly represents the triumph of wakefulness over the nocturnal darkness of the cavern. And the banishment to the nether world is banishment only if understood within the context of Zeus' world, that is, as a condemnation to remain in the nocturnal cavern world as viewed in terms of the magic-mythical configuration. From the extant descriptions and illustrations it is evident that Kronos belongs pre-eminently to this realm; figure 22 depicts him holding a sickle, a symbol for the moon, and in figure 23 he is shown wearing a veil,[13] the veil being of course a symbol of the covering cloak of the night sky.[14]

Curiously, the attribute of the half-covered head has never been satisfactorily explained, although Hild for example speaks of the head draped from behind *en forme de voile*.[15] Now since the night as a symbolic figure is also depicted as being draped or veiled, the drape or veil symbolizing the night sky, we are surely justified in interpreting Kronos' cloak as nocturnal symbolism. Such night-symbolism of the

Figure 22: Kronos with Sickle (from a Hellenistic copper bowl)

Figure 23:   Veiled Kronos (after a Mural in Pompeii)

veil is apparent from yet another source. In the very earliest representations, Kronos is depicted without a veil; rather, his head is surrounded by a border which, so far as it is still intact, contains two rows of bright dots against a dark circular background (the lower part is perhaps damaged or eradicated). We can in all probability assume that the circle represents the starry night sky, which in later representations appears as a veil or cloak covering the head. And this interpretation is further supported by the fact that this particular representation is a design from a shield, the shield being a pre-eminent example of circular form (see figure 24).[16]

Figure 24: Kronos (on a shield); from an archaic clay pinax found in Eleusis (after a tracing by Roscher)

The mythical account of Kronos clearly shows his nocturnal relationship. It not only portrays his essence as temporicity, (pro)creating and destroying as symbolized by his devouring and later disgorging his children, but also specifically locates his activity in the nocturnal realm dominated by the moon where it increases and decreases as the moon waxes and wanes. This moment of movement as well as those additional moments—Kronos' emergence from the mythical polarity of heaven and earth; his receipt of the impulse of temporicity by Metis, whose potion made him a life-giver and not just a life-devourer since the disgorged children all lived—these moments place Kronos into the configuration of the awakening temporicity which is reflected in his deeds and sufferings. With it mythical polarity becomes visible, a polarity which awakens the soul; or, as we might say, here the soul awakens, its circle-closing movement giving polarity its effect and efficacy.

The Kronos mythologeme is a manifestation of what we attempted to clarify at the outset of this section, namely, that temporicity is not just of nocturnal origin but is itself nocturnal in nature. Again we can discern the close relationship between the dynamism of the soul and the movement of temporicity. This is also expressed in the audible resemblance between the Greek word for time, *chronos*, and the name of Kronos the Titan, even though not all etymologists are willing to trace these near-homonyms to the same root (undoubtedly *gher*). The root *gher* means "to desire, strive for, need" and therefore evidences a tendency toward movement which in a more goal-directed form is inherent in the root *ma:me*, the root which forms a part of the name *Metis*. And Metis, it will be remembered, was the one who, as a result of her potion, elicited polar-reciprocal action.[17]

The Kronos mythologeme, then, is pre-eminently a sequence of images of nocturnal events which makes visible to us the temporicity of the night. From this example we can be said to have inferred the nature of "mythical time"—a perpetual self-completion of the circle which is itself a symbol of the soul—and thereby provided a vivid illustration of mythical temporicity.

But how are we to obtain a glimpse of the genesis of this temporicity? What means are at our disposal for distinguishing the mutation of magic timelessness to mythical temporicity? We should mention here that we are referring specifically to the pure import of the word for genesis, *Ent-stehung* or de-stasis, for the process of becoming conscious of temporicity is one of disrupting the state of timelessness by the movement which gives rise to temporicity. This abolition of stasis via movement is then a true "de-stating" or de-stasis.

As we come closer to the magic structure, the images fade away, for its space-timelessness is not only remote from imagery but from the imagination itself. Only one means remains for approaching it more closely: sound. Or, if you will, we must attempt to render audible certain specific and highly differentiated primordial sounds, for only hearing and the auditory values perceptible to it are basically able to unlock for us the magic world. The question is, How do we find these values?

It would not be amiss if we were to seek them in the sound of the word-roots. And such a venture will disclose audible interconnections and events which we will be unable to account for in any other way. For this reason a consequential sound shift in one of the primordial roots can be illuminating in the best sense of the word, inasmuch as it discloses events of the magic structure that cannot be imagined or conceptualized. Yet our no longer sensitive hearing will be unable to evaluate the original nuances and distinctions of sound, and this lack of auditory sensitivity to re-experience these nuances will prevent many from realizing the mutation as it is represented by the particular sound shift we will speak of in the following discussion.

We will have occasion to observe that the root group *gher:ger:ker:qer*, which even Walde has characterized as being closely related because of their guttural initial sound,[18] is of an extremely complex nature and expresses a very specific aspect of life. Before we turn to this we must, however, interpolate an important consideration by way of clarification and information.

We have previously dealt with the root *kĕl* meaning "to hold, shelter, conceal (in the earth)" (see above p. 126).[19] The wealth of words proceeding from this root is characterized by the aspect we can circumscribe as being "shelter" or "security" as well as "darkness" and which is conveyed in the image of the self-contained and static cavern, the cavern being of course also symbolic of the magic structure. (A compilation of the most important words derived from the root *kĕl* is contained in the first of our "Remarks on Etymology" below, p. 549.)

The root *ker*, as well as the roots *gher*, *ger*, and *qer*, are quite different inasmuch as they all express movement, in part, as Walde-Hofmann indicates, a "vehement agitation of the temperament." And more important, all of the words derived from these roots circumscribe a very specific form of movement, namely, rotation. Whereas the root *kĕl* is a reflection of the self-contained cavern with its space-timelessness, the root *gher:ker* is a reflection of the dynamic circle. At the moment of formation of the Kronos mythologeme the mythical world of dream and the night springs forth from the cavern world of magic, giving rise later to the mutation to the diurnal mental world. (See the second and third "Remarks on Etymology" which treat the root grouping *qer:ger(gher):ker* as well as the related *kel:gel:qel*.)

In other words, at the moment when the *l* of the root *kĕl* changes into the *r* of the root *gher:ker*, temporicity—which is a form of movement or kinesis—is born. It is as though the static cavern were set in motion, a motion which in order to be represented needed a dimension which the one-dimensional cavern did not possess. This dimension becomes visible in the circular motion of the nocturnal sky—in the words *choros* and *kyklos* ("circle, disk") which proceeded from the root *gher* and its close relative *qel*—in which spacelessness was transformed into surface. Choric and cyclic movement—*choros* means not just "roundel and dance" but also "roundel of the stars," that is, regular sidereal movement—carve polar surface (if we may be permitted a paradox) out of spacelessness.

Although to us today this sound shift from *l* to *k* may seem insignificant, it is still an echo of the birth of temporality. For there can be no doubt that *l* preceded *r*; even today, peoples closer to the magical realm than we of Western civilization have difficulty articulating the *r*. The Chinese, for example, pronounce it as an *l*.

If we closely observe the qualitative distinctions between the three (con)sonants *k*, *l*, and *r*, we can discern the mutation which gave birth to the reality of the mythical structure. The guttural *k* is formed at the most secluded, deepest, and darkest part of the oral cavity.[20] When joined by an *l* the composite sound (assuming the vowel e) formed by the guttural *k* is completely contained within the mouth; *kĕl* is a static sound, as it were, which occurs within the confines of the oral cavity.

But if the *k* is joined by an *r*—which from the very outset is a dental and not a guttural—the entire sound generated by the initial *k* vibrates toward the outside. We might say that the *k* is a sheltered, the *l* an enclosing, and the *r* an agressive, egressive sound. The consequential distinction between the *l* and the *r* was noted as far back as Ebner, who had a keen ear for such details: "The 'R,' a phonetic opposite of the affricative 'L,' appears in fact to be the phonetic symbol for the experience of a resistance or its overcoming."[21] And the terminology in German to denote the tonalities in music—to cite but one example—attributes to the dark or minor tonalities *l*-character (Mo*ll*tonarten), to the brighter or major tonalities *r*-character (Durtonarten).

With the genesis of the *r* a counterpole is created to the unitary *kl*; *r* can therefore be heard as the polar sound of the *l*. Transposed to our image, Kronos forms the awakened counterpole to the static, secluded darkness; as such he is none other than the motion of the night. That is to say, he is mythical temporicity, the image of the reciprocating, self-complementary circle which creates and destroys, again creating and destroying like the roundel of ascending and descending stars, whose rhythm is still represented in many folk dances such as the Catalonian *sardana*, a roundel which like many others still manifests today the presence of mythical temporicity.

It may appear from the foregoing that we have lent inordinate weight to the relationships of the word-roots; this is correct only if it implies that we attribute to them a valuation since their genuine or true valuation cannot be measured. In doing so we are merely recognizing the auditory valences inherent in the magic structure, and attributing to them an adequate role.

It is for instance not just a coincidence that the formation of the *r*, in which, or by means of which a new dimension is constituted, first makes possible the two-dimensional, polar, and imagistic character of myth. This is evident from the circumstance that those words which convey an opposite or "mirror" meaning in the mirror form of their root come from the word-root *regh*, which is the mirror root of *gher*. And what is the significance of this inversion, or more precisely this antonym of the rotary movement and expanding circle inherent in the root group *qer*: ger(gher):ker, if not to indicate straight or linear movement? So it comes as no surprise that the mirror-root *regh* designates in fact "straight linear movement"[22] in contrast to the undirected temporicity of circular movement characteristic of the original root-group. And those words which signify "right" and "direction, orientation" in the Western languages are derived from this particular mirror-root *regh* (see the fourth "Remark on Etymology," p. 557).

By referring to this mirror root (which definitely points towards the masculine principle characteristic of the mental structure) we are already moving beyond mythical temporicity and approaching the mental conception of "time" with its definite directionality. And this particular mirror root *regh* does not of course become active until the inception of right-handed or clockwise movement which we described in the second chapter.

With this we leave the rhythmic temporicity which sustains and encloses the stars as well as our hearts: the zone in which the inexorable course of events harnesses man's fate to the periodic tides, the inescapable destiny of ascent and decline. Let us rather return to the attempt by Western man to extricate himself from the restrictions of destiny and the confines of the soul. When we view this struggle henceforth from a temporal aspect, we will perhaps better understand how the step from the circular or cyclic image of temporicity was able to usher in the predominance of the rational concept of time.

3. *The Spatial Emphasis of the Mental Structure*

In order for us to demonstrate the temporicity of the mythical structure, it was necessary to go back to the question of its spacelessness. Similarly, if we wish to describe the spatial preoccupation of the mental structure, it would be necessary for us first of all to inquire as to its form of time. Yet the question of "time" is one that has resisted philosophical attempts to resolve it for some two and one-half thousand years, despite the many individual solutions, explanations, or abstractions which it has brought to light. Now, it is not our intent to provide a philosophical solution to this age-old question, nor seek one out in the results of discoveries in the sciences, for even a psychological point of departure would be irrelevant here in that it represents only a partial aspect: partly philosophical, partly scientific. We shall accordingly have to find a different point of departure.

The temporicity of myth differs from the temporality of the mind. The temporistic movement of nature and the cosmos is unaware of the temporal phases of past, present, and future; it knows only the polar self-complementarity of coming and going which completely pervades it at all times. It is devoid of directionality, whereas the past and the future, viewed from the present of any given person, are temporal directions. It is this directional character of "time" which underscores its mental nature and therefore its constitutional difference from natural-cosmic temporistic movement which is mythical in nature. Or, we might say that time differs from temporicity because of its directedness, and hence a retrogression into mythical movement can neither answer nor resolve the question as to the nature of our mental time.

Let us, rather, proceed along a route which we have taken before and inquire into the root of the word "time." When we do this we discover that all of the words of our familiar languages for "time"—English "time," German *Zeit*, Latin *tempus*, French *temps* and so on—can be traced back to the Indo-Germanic root *da*.[23] We have encountered this root before: it also formed the Greek verb *daio*, which in the Ionian dialect, the original language of Greek philosophy, meant "to divide, to take apart, to lay apart, to tear apart, to lacerate." In Sanskrit the root forms the words *dayate* and *dayati*, that is, "he divides, he cuts;" on this the German word for "part" or "share," *Teil*, is based. And the root is also the basis of the word "demonic" as was discussed earlier (see p. 94 and p. 157, note 13).

"Time," in other words, conveys the idea that it is a divisor, separating as well as cutting asunder. But a divider of what? We may be permitted the question although we know today that time—and we will discuss this in detail below—has become an abstraction. The word has shared the same fate as other concrete mythical images which have without exception become transformed into rational concepts in the mental realm.

As to our question of what "time" in fact divides, we have an answer if we remain cognizant of the mythical configuration. We have noted repeatedly that magic occurs in the dark, indeed in darkness itself, while myth occurs in the night and dreams where a twilight is already evident. But the mind or the mental presents itself in the brightness of daylight. There was once a close relationship between the "day" and "time," indeed there was a certain degree of identity between them inasmuch as both words can be traced to the same root. But, in a pre-eminently nocturnal world, what can the significance be of utilizing a root with the inherent meaning of "to divide, to sever," to form a word expressing the day (Latin *dies*), if not to convey at the outset of the mental structure that the "day"—as opposed to our present-day sense—was a *divider and partitioner of the night*.

With the awakening of the mental structure, as diurnal things gradually assume a greater importance than those of the nocturnal and twilight realm, the "every-day" world comes into greater prominence. Not only does right-handed movement take precedence over left-handed or leftward movement (which always reverts toward darkness), as we have seen, but there is an ascendancy of directedness and direction as the "right" usurps the non-directional nature of circularity. Those things which man prepares for himself predominate over things that simply lie in readiness for him. In this connection it is no accident when we speak of preparing "meals" (*Gerichte*, originally from *richten*, "to direct, orient") whenever we mean "mealtime." Meals are day-to-day things, accomplishments or actions determined by time; mealtimes are the pre-eminent daily affairs: "the time for eating was time *kat' exochen* (time as such)."[24] Our very word "mealtime" is revealing in this respect as it is formed on both the root *ma:me* and on *da:di*, that is, it measures and divides, and the affairs of the day are oriented around it.[25]

In this same connection we can note a significant passage from the research of Claude-Sosthène Grasset d'Orcet which refers to a sacrificial act. (We shall only mention in passing the important fact that the sacrifice and the sacrificial act were originally a part of the mealtime, whereas today a "sacrifice" refers mostly to an act of renunciation.) D'Orcet writes: "The Hebrews, like other peoples of antiquity, levied a death-penalty on prisoners of war which they called *doush*. The captives were laid on the threshing-floor among the sheaves of wheat, after which stone sleds with razor-sharp stones (*silex tranchants*) were driven over them. These sleds, which are still used throughout the orient even today for threshing and cutting the straw, were called in Greek *tribolos* and in Hebrew *doush*. Purification by *tribolos* was one of the principal dogmas of the cult of Bacchus (Dionysos); and for the adepts of the cult *tribolos* and Hades were synonymous. On Greek vases the *tribolos* is depicted as a wagon drawn by three horses and steered by a goddess named Tis or Dais which is to say the "Dividing one" [celle qui divise]."[26]

We have quoted this passage since it affords insight into a process that is essential to the concept of time: the genesis or, more accurately, the mutation of time from temporicity which can be discerned from this account. We attempted to elucidate the genesis of mythical, nocturnal temporicity from the self-contained dark and timeless cavern world by using the mythologeme of Kronos and particularly the sound shift audible in the roots *kel* and *gher*; and it will be evident from the remarks of d'Orcet—which incidentally make no mention of the word or subject of "time"—

what the nature of the process was which brought forth "time" from mythical temporicity.

Before we examine this extraordinarily revealing text word for word it should be noted that in Greek *dais* means "portion, meal, mealtime, share." Unfortunately it is not possible to determine where d'Orcet obtained his knowledge of the goddess *Tis* or *Dais*; from the available reference material we consulted, only two complementary facts emerge. First, the word or name of this goddess is derived from the root *da:di* from which, it will be recalled, the word "time" can be traced; and second, the significant fact that a goddess of this name can be dated back no farther than late Greek antiquity. A fragment of Sophocles, for example, reads: *elthen de Dais thaleia presbiste theon*, which means "Dais, the eldest of the gods, came forth in all her beauty."[27]

The interpretations by Roscher and Pauly-Wissowa, as well as that of Gruppe, which suggest that Dais had merely been elevated from the rank of a personification of the mealtime to that of a divinity, overlook the fact that she is here invested with the stature of being the eldest of the gods. What is significant, then, is not the personification but rather what is personified. Sophocles, by giving her such prominence despite her apparent lack of an obvious role in mythology (her covert role is certain from the discussion by d'Orcet as well as from the remark by Harrison that Dais, like Thalia, represented a demonic principle in the magic ritual of sacrifice), shows that he either knew of her Kronos-destructive role, or he considered the time of the mealtime—time *kat' exochen*, a directed as well as directing time—to be the most significant form of time in his mental conception of the world.

We can at least infer from the remarks of d'Orcet that Dais conquers Kronos and is thus the prototypical image of the mental structure overcoming the mythical. This is indicated by the form of sacrifice. It is not a genuine sacrifice, or the complete surrender of a vital element of one's own constitution, but rather a form of ransom showing, in its cruelty, evidence of the deficient sacrificial rituals characteristic of all rituals, including even certain mystical rituals of the gradually exhausted mythical structure.[28]

In the case of this particular sacrifice, it is apparent from the context that we are dealing with the struggle between the awakening mental time and mythical temporicity. Dais, symbol of the partitive principle, imitates in one sense Kronos, representative of the circular principle, while she destroys at the same time the power of the Kronos principle by virtue of the strength of her dividing. In the ritual it is not the sheaves which are sacrificed ("threshed") but rather the living humans, the captives.[29]

The configuration itself, being nocturnal, is Kronos-like and indicated by the presence of three horses. As we noted above (p. 80), the number three has a definitely lunar character; a solar character does not come until the conception of a trinity.[30] This Kronos aspect is accentuated by the location of the sacrifice, the threshing floor, and as noted above, by equating the victims with the sheaves. Moreover, the Kronos aspect is further emphasized by the equivalence accorded to the tribolos and Hades in the Orphic tradition; Hades was the realm of Kronos after he had been banished there. It is that realm through which Acheron flowed; and this is another way of saying that the nocturnal underworld or realm of the shades, with its incipient temporicity, owed its life and source to timelessness. For Acheron means "nontemporistic," or to quote Grasset d'Orcet (who offers no further explanation), it is a realm "where one does not count time."[31]

The cart or wagon (Greek *harma*), on the other hand, which later becomes the tribolos in the Orphic ritual, is indicative of the inceptual nature of the sacrificial rite, for its root is ar:(r).[32] This sacrificial rite was one of purification and among the most significant for the Orphics whose lamellae, as we noted earlier, clearly manifested the mental principle. But what was the guilt that had to be atoned for through purification, if not the transgression against the mythical world—the world of Kronos and the world of tradition which they left behind by their turn toward the right?

Since they no longer lived in accord with mythical temporicity, they sacrificed to it the captives whom they had subjugated: those who were thus "beneath" them by still belonging to the mythical world that they had left behind. With these captives—their "possessions" as it were—they sacrificed their mythical structure as a form of purifying themselves (a sufficiently ambivalent act). In the mythical tableau, however, it is Dais who carries out the sacrifice which they have presented as an offering; it is Dais who is the principle who prevails whenever the Kronos sacrifice is repeated. Here the protective circle is disrupted, and the partitive principle comes into evidence: "time" supersedes temporicity. And we ought not to forget that Dais *steers* the three horses, that is, the three phases of temporicity. This is tantamount to a triumph of awakened "time" over mythical temporicity: the victory of the day, with its mental brightness, over the night of twilight myth.

Once again there is evidence that "time" and the "day" are essentially the same, for the root from which Dais and "time" are derived is identical to that for "day" (Latin *dies*) and Zeus, the (bright!) god who dwells *on* Mt. Olympus and not *in* the mountain (cavern). Both are dividers of the night. At the outset, day and night are not opposites; we make them antithetical by our way of thinking. The partitive brightness of the day is merely a principle, expressing attentiveness (*Acht*samkeit) and wakefulness; the complement of the night was "eight" (*acht*) (see above, p. 17), just as sleep was the complement of wakefulness.

This also explains the interrelationship between Zeus and "day" which scholarship has been hitherto unable to elucidate; beyond this, it affords insight into the connection between Dais and "time." And since we can consider the day and time in this manner, we can also think of mythical temporicity as being "nocturnal" and mental time as being "diurnal" time. But as we do not wish to imply that they are antithetical it is perhaps best if we stay with the terms "temporicity" and "time," particularly as they have the further distinguishing characteristic that the one is rhythmic, the other metric, i.e., measured and measuring.[33]

With the irruption of the mental structure, the Dais-principle, as the divisor or partitioner, is not only destructive but has also a pre-eminently constitutive aspect. The word-root *da:di* has at the beginning the dual denotation of "giving" as well as "dividing." And the moment this dual principle becomes effective, the mental structure with its temporal character is also present; but it divides and thus destroys the *image* of the world which is replaced by a *conception* of the world.[34]

Let us now step forth from the mythical realm and its images of Dais, or Athena, or Metis or Zeus, in which time is foreshadowed in dream. In attempting to describe the dream-like texture from which time mutated we have endeavored to transpose the tableau surrounding Dais into language amenable to our rational understanding and to suggest what might conceivably lie "behind" the nocturnal veil of that other Dais, the goddess from Sais: the unfathomable mystery of magic unity. Having again touched upon the darkness and obscurities, let us not lose sight of the illuminating point of departure for our journey over the previous several pages: that all words in our familiar languages expressing "time" go back to the word root *da:di* (see the compilation of the relevant words in our fifth "Remark on Etymology," p. 558 below).

Time, we reiterate, is a divider which partitions as well as severs. It severs, not itself, but rather the *ker-gher* principle: the temporistic and mythical image of the world. We have witnessed this same process in the shift from the equilibrium of the *Mu-* principle to the acuity of the *Me-*. Just as the demonic is at first nothing other than the "severance of myth"—not without good reason does Harrison speak of the demonic character of Dais—so is time, in the sense of a directed course of events, something utterly different from the non-directed and autonomous reversional movement of myth with respect to dimensions. Time, that is, our mentally oriented conception of "time," the divider of mythical movement and the partitioner of the circle, severs its two-dimensionality and thereby creates the possibility of three-dimensional space.

Immeasurable and "lasting"agitation is a form of expression of the mythical structure; timelessness is another form of expression, that of the magic structure. Time—as a conceptualization and concept, and as a measuring element—is yet a further form of expression or conceptualization, that of the mental structure. The mythical form of expression evidences an increase in dimensions over against the magic, the mental an increase over the mythical, since magic timelessness is pre-dimensional, mythical temporicity non-dimensional, and only mental temporality one-dimensional or dimensional in the strict sense.

These increments in dimensionality must be borne in mind, just as we must not lose sight of the fact that mythical agitation, temporicity, and "duration" must not be placed in opposition to our conceptual time, as this would account for only the mental factors and leave out our awareness of the structure of integral data and events. If we make antitheses of mythical temporicity and mental temporality or conceptual time, we are guilty of creating an inappropriate dualism, inappropriate because these terms are not antithetical but rather different in their constitution.

Ever since Plato such dualizing has been a favorite intellectual pastime of philosophers. Plato, for instance, makes the distinction in *Timaeus* between the mythical accentuation of "unity" of *aion* (i.e., "time"), and the various parts and forms of *chronos*, and thus initiated the falsification of mythical-cosmic time into a form of time defined as "universal time." It was then possible to place it into an antithetical relationship with so-called "individual time." But even the basic concept of *aion*, which is usually rendered as "duration, era, epoch," has a rational character inasmuch as it is derived from the root *ai-*, which means "to divide."[35] The word itself survives in such words as "eternity" and in German *Ewigkeit* (from a medieval word, *ewe*).[36] Eternity is only a large section or portion of what we described as temporicity with its emphasis on Kronos.

At the beginning of the mental world "time" retained a certain connection to temporicity and agitation. Aristotle, for example, speaks of time touching the soul,[37] and Plotinus says: "Time is the life of the soul."[38] And as we have seen (p. 15 above), Augustine recalled this connection as well. For all three the soul is, however, also the individual soul, and the time they relate to it is consequently actually "time," the partitioning and severing "individual time."

This connection and interdependence of the soul and time were perhaps most clearly perceived by Nicolaus Cusanus, who defined time in a sense appropriate to its nature as a mental phenomenon. In his dialogue *De ludo globi* he writes: "Therefore time, the measure of movement, is an instrument of judgement and understanding. The understanding soul [*ratio animae*] therefore is not dependent on time, but rather the understanding measure of movement, which is called time, is dependent on the understanding soul. For this reason the understanding soul is not subject to time but precedes time [*ad tempus se habet anterioriter*] just as sight precedes the eye. Although sight requires the eye, it does not proceed from the eye since the eye is merely the instrument."[39]

The "understanding soul" spoken of here may be understood as describing the process of thought or that "logos of the soul" (*logos psyches* mentioned by Plato). Plato has also postulated a tripartition of the soul,[40] which like any trinitary form is characteristic of the mental structure and may be seen as a direct connection to the tripartition of time effected by Parmenides, who was the first to posit the three-phase nature of time. This gave rise not only to the problematic aspect of the future, but also to the question of becoming and the entire problem of the dimensioning of time, which later loomed so large in the philosophy of Romanticism in the works of Baader, Schelling, and Fichte. The dimension of the future necessarily lends a forward thrust to spatiality, giving both space and time the semblance of direction.

Let us take note of this result: our conceptual time is not a psychic but a mental phenomenon which proceeded from the psychic; it is the line that severs the circle and thus forms the basic dimension of a four-dimensional space. By virtue of the fact that it was itself divided, time became measurable; but it thereby forfeited its original character. In the course of philosophical speculation it was to a great extent spatialized and, as it has a spatializing tendency, was to a considerable extent dementalized. This transposition or reversal is a typical *speculatio rationis:* the divider, instead of being treated as such, is itself divided. Commensurately with this transposition there is necessarily a devaluation of the concept of time which engenders a manifest debasement of time, particularly in the wake of the discovery of perspective and the complete spatialization of the world.

This brings us to the *spatial emphasis of the mental structure* which we discussed in considerable detail in our remarks on the perspectival world. As this spatial emphasis is particularly characteristic for the rational phase of the mental structure, we would also point out the corroboration of our discussion on this spatial emphasis in the remarks of W. Gent, a distinguished authority on the time question.[41] He has repeatedly called attention to the "modern tendency" to devalue time, as in the following statement: "It is really not surprising that even in the work of Thomas Hobbes we can discern a disdain of anything having to do with time, for to him also the spatial world . . . is immeasurably closer." And with respect to Descartes he writes: "When he describes time as *ens in anima* he is unquestionably devaluating it over against space. This represents naturalism as a world view. Time has no proper place within his system." And again: "For such men as William Gilbert, Johann Kepler, and G. Galilei, time does not represent a special problem; it surfaces in their work merely as a numerical quantity in the form (say) of infinitesimal time segments."[42]

The spatial emphasis of this mental structure is also expressed in its dualization of time. From Duns Scotus to Volkelt, including Locke, Kant, and Bergson,[43] it is separated into the objective time of things and the subjective time of the soul, or into some other conceptual dualism. As we have said, this is a *speculatio rationis.* But it is precisely these recurrent attempts to dualize time—whether as Bergson's antithesis of time versus natural "duration," or understood as being in opposition to itself as begun by Aristotle and continued down through Volkelt[44]—which are in danger of a deficient psychization or mythologization. It is not our intent to adduce the numerous examples which any history book of philosophy can furnish as proof of this psychization, but only to note a symptomatic example from Aristotle. He proceeds from the point of view that the "Now" does not exist, since it is at once the end of the past and the beginning of the future; consequently he considers it to be merely a kind of "in between" which interrupts or interlinks as a fixed point in space a time without beginning or end.

This apostrophe may well be an unconscious reversion to the mythical attitude, one whose impact is not lessened by the fact that Aristotle implicitly places past and future into opposition and thereby dualizes them at the same time he attributes to them a psychistic lack of beginning and end. By this dualization, or as Volkelt has called it, "two-dimensionality," time is linearly spatialized. As soon as the Now is interposed as an "in between" between past and future, it ceases to be a purely mental modality of time and becomes a spatialized modality. It is no longer merely oriented, but has the additional (and deficient) aspect of spatiality. In this sense of "in-betweenness" the Now is a conceptual positing as a part of time, a definitely spatializing and rationalizing act of consciousness applied, not to space, but to time which spatializes space.

This spatializing aspect is evident also in language, evidence of the pervasive grasp of spatialized thought on the European mentality. In French, for example, *maintenant* ("now") suggests literally "holding in hand"; German *Augenblick* ("moment") means literally "glance of the eye." The measured aspect of time is expressed in Spanish *ahora*, "on the hour," while German *jetzt*, "now," reflects a certain abstractness because of the abstract nature of the adverb in general.[45]

This setting–fast of time as "in-betweenness" is a perversion of time, since time thereby acquires spatiality and ceases to be the initiator and function of space as a result of its partitive and severing characteristic. Time, and with it the temporal as well as the timeless, is a basic constituent of space; it is not a part of space, that is, a disqualified dimension, but its very basis and basic dimension. (We shall see farther on that it is more appropriately defined as an "a-mension" because it reaches beyond dimensionality; see pp. 340, 383, and 458 f. below.) This "dimension" is only today coming to awareness, or, more exactly, is only able to come to awareness when it is no longer conceived of as "time," "movement," or "timeless being," but as the presence of origin. One point of departure for this kind of time concretion today is the fact that time is considered to be "reversible," a manifestation of a pervasive departure from the rationalistic and perspectivistic attitude, since time is then no longer divisive and directionally oriented in only one "sense."

The division of measurable time into past and future is a form of deficient spatialization and psychization, if only because past and future are invariably characterized by their emphasis on joy and suffering. It is this characteristic of experiential tension that reveals the deficient and psychistic nature of the dualism. Anyone who indulges in this manner of thinking is confined to the psyche right down to the very level of his abstractions. He is a *psychist*, the unknowing counterpart of the materialist.

This is manifest in the case of Volkelt who devises an "experiential time" in his defense of the two-dimensionality of time. "Experiential time" is of course merely a fiction. A phenomenon of the magic sphere, vital experience, cannot be merely coupled with a mental phenomenon, time, without rendering both phenomena and their respective spheres deficient. And this deficiency leads inevitably to a rational destruction of time, to that amorphous nothingness into which man in Heidegger's view is "thrown" out of a worrisome "now."

If we take Heidegger at his word—since he delights in taking statements at their word to the point of rationalizing them into formulas devoid of any content—this "being thrown" is itself evidence of the inhumanity of his philosophy (earlier only animals were "thrown", i.e., brought forth). Heidegger's philosophy is a clear example of the consequences of such psychistic deficiency, for his positing of a "nothing of nothingness" in opposition to a "being of being" is surely nothing else than a rebellion of the one-time interpreter of Duns Scotus.[46]

By abandoning the religious sphere surrounding the work of Duns Scotus in a mood of resentment, and seeking to escape from its protective polarity by making it into a rational antithesis, Heidegger necessarily went astray in the wake of the incomplete transition: he did not realize in his psychic confinement that he was already operating in a different structure, substituting in his confusion a negative caricature of the mythical, with its religious bond, for the mental. Instead of transcending his point of departure, he negates it by his deficiency. And this means that at best there is a negative transcendence of his point of departure; it is the naught, the zero, the activated amorphous dust that triumphs in the negatively activated "nothing of nothingness." It is no wonder that Heidegger accorded to "care" and "worry" such a crucial place in his philosophy.[47]

Let these brief remarks suffice to call attention to the perils inherent in the improper view and application of the purely mental conception of time to our spatial world and our lives. Dividing time, which is itself a divider, leads to atomization, whether of the *ratio* or of the spatial world; a psychistic mode of understanding leads to a deficient mythologization in the guise of an abstraction; and spatialization divests space itself of its foundation.

The degree to which the labyrinthine entanglement of rationality can be manifest is evident from the fact that, since Parmenides, and notably since Plato, now space, now time, and yet again duration have been equated with being. We have repeatedly pointed out this basic error which led to the postulation of non-being or non-beings (p. 80 among others), a self-destructive antithesis because it lacks a congruent counterpart. This antithesis, moreover, is able to activate this non-being into a nullifying nothingness. Athena's well-aimed lance which overtakes space threatens to dissolve into dust, thereby bringing to an end the space which it has opened up and dominated.

It should by now be evident from the above discussion that the spatial emphasis of the mental structure is threatened with the destruction of its laboriously achieved three-dimensionality. This threat lies in the amorphous nullity which occurs whenever the concept of time is spatialized in a psychistic and deficiently mentalized manner. This spatialization is subject to dissolution because it destroys the very basis for space. We will see later on the degree to which *our rational thought is a spatializing act and the expression of this spatialization.* Here we would only note once again that the phenomenon of "lack of time" is characteristic of our material, spatially accentuated world: How is anyone to have time if he tears it apart?

It is sufficient for us to know that time ruptured the mythical circle and thus made possible our world of thought and detachment. Let us take care that the inappropriate manipulation of time does not bring about its destruction and the destruction of what is dependent on it. Let us ensure that it is used effectively according to its nature in the four-dimensionality where it can establish a new possibility of the world: concretized and integrated, and superseding the mere spatial emphasis of the mind.

Wherever time is able to become "the present," it is able to render transparent "simultaneously" the timelessness of magic, the temporicity of myth, and the temporality of mind. There are already signs of this inceptual mutation that can be demonstrated (and it is the task of the second part of the present work to make this demonstration). What has been said up to this moment has endeavored to give evidence of the spatial emphasis of the mental structure on the basis of its principal component, time, and not as before on the basis of perspectivity.

Space will change, indeed, it is already changing. In this change it will lose its conceptualized material emphasis when presentiality shows through. Our exposition of the dimensional aspects was addressed to the foundations of a new mutation of consciousness from which the capabilities of diaphany and presentation can come forth. This presentation will appear impossible only to those who are caught up exclusively in their magic, mythical, or mental spheres; and they will necessarily react with fanaticism, emotion, or sophistry to our discussion as a result.

But these are only conditionalities, inevitabilities, and limitations; what is more important is the attempt to establish that mankind is able to catch sight of values and inceptual events precisely at that moment when it faces bankruptcy and suicide. Are there visible inceptions which point "beyond" this Western civilization? The answer is positive: nowhere does the "new" seem so visible as where something is going to "rack and ruin": the ruins which themselves contain the basis for the new.

1   See Jean Gebser, *Abendländische Wandlung* (Zürich: Oprecht, ¹1943), p. 93 f.; ²1945, p. 97; Ullstein ed. no. 107, pp. 77; *Gesamtausgabe*, I, p. 234.

2*   Alexis Carrel, *Man, the Unknown* (New York and London: Harper, 1935), p. 149.

3   It is symptomatic of the psychic prepossession to which even well-known contemporary psychologists are subject that they do not distinguish between "parapsychological" and "parapsychic." Yet only the phenomena can be termed "parapsychic," and only their interpretation called "parapsychological."

4   Ernesto Bozzano, "Popli Primitive e manifestazioni supernormali," in *Collana di studi metapsichici*, I (Verona: Albero, 1941), 239. See also the German edition: *Übersinnliche Erscheinungen bei Naturvölkern*, Sammlung Dalp (Bern: Francke, 1948), p. 201 f.

5   To what measure prayer is related to nature and magic is evident from the actual or unconsciously imagined attitude in prayer: kneeling, folding of the hands, and bowing the head. The knees—the most intensely radiating vital zone of the body—make contact with the ground, uniting so to speak the body with the earth. The folding of hands not only expresses a renunciation of activity but completes and unifies, as it were, the circuit of the body. And the bowing of the head is an expression of self-renunciation, of the suppliant's surrender of self-assertion, and of his submission to those powers that sustain him.

6   The Latin word *individuum* is composed of *in*, "non," and *dividuus*, "separable, divided," which is in turn derived from *dividere*. The *di-* is based on the root *da;* the stem

videre means, of course, to "see." The meaning of *individuum* would therefore be "someone divided and dividing by seeing." In this light it would seem risky to demand "individuation" or "coming-to-self" as is currently done in analytical psychology. See Gebser (note 1), chapter 29; *Gesamtausgabe*, I, p. 291 f.

7   "To implore" (*flehen*) and "to flee" (*fliehen*), despite inconclusive etymological derivation, can be considered akin to one another; see Kluge-Götze, *Etymologisches Wörterbuch der deutschen Sprache* (Berlin: de Gruyter, ¹¹1936), pp. 164 and 165.

8   For numerous examples see Juliet Bredon and Igor Mitrophanow, *Das Mondjahr: Chinesische Sitten, Bräuche und Feste* (Vienna: Zsolnay, 1937). This is one of several works on the subject.

9   See Kluge-Götze (note 7), p. 408 under the entry "Nacht."

10 In this world within the mythical structure, Lao-Tzu's demands that we "act without acting" can be fulfilled; see also Gebser, *Rilke und Spanien* (Zürich: Oprecht, 1940), p. 91, note 65; ²1946, p. 92; *Gesamtausgabe*, VI, p. 207 f.

11 See Kluge-Götze (note 7), pp. 54 and 676. From the same root *wegh* come the words "weight," "wagon," *wichtig* (important), *Wiege* (cradle), and *Woge* (billow); see Kluge-Götze, pp. 205, 665, 688, 696. Not only Latin *vehiculum* but also Greek *ochos* mean "wagon" and have the same root; see Menge-Güthling, *Griechisch-deutsches Wörterbuch* (Berlin: Langenscheidt, ²⁸1910), I, p. 420.

12 Regarding the attributes of the Kronos mythologeme, see Hesiod, *Theogony*, verse 137 and 452 ff.; see also the *Iliad*, VII, 479, and XIV, 203 and 274, as well as Gottfried Muys, *Forschungen auf dem Gebiete der alten Völker-und Mythengeschichte* (Cologne: Heberle, 1856), I, p. 101 ff., section 155; K. W. Ramler, *Kurzgefasste Mythologie* (Vienna: Haas, 1794), pp. 1 and 13; K. Eckermann, *Lehrbuch der Religionsgeschichte und Mythologie* (Halle: Schwetschke, 1845), II, p. 12 f.; H. W. Völcker, *Die Mythologie des Japetischen Geschlechts* (Giessen: Heyer, 1824), p. 120 and passim; W. Vollmer, *Vollständiges Wörterbuch der Mythologie aller Nationen* (Stuttgart: Hoffmann, 1836), p. 1416 f., and p. 973 ff. of the second edition (Stuttgart: Scheiblin, 1851), entry "Saturnus"; E. Jacobi, *Handbuch der griechischen und römischen Mythologie* (Leipzig: Brauns, 1847), p. 553; Preller-Robert, *Griechische Mythologie* (Berlin: Weidmann, ⁴1894), I, p. 45 ff. and passim; O. Seemann, *Mythologie der Griechen und Römer* (Leipzig: Kröner, ⁶1924), p. 8; Walter F. Otto, *Die Götter Griechenlands* (Frankfurt/M.: Schulte-Bulmke, 1934), p. 170; W. H. Roscher, *Ausführliches Lexikon der griechischen und römischen Mythologie* (Leipzig: Teubner, 1894–1897), II, 1, columns 1452–1573; Pauly-Wissowa, *Reallexikon der Altertumswissenschaften*, 22. Halbband, columns 1982–2018.

13 The two illustrations are taken from Roscher (next to last entry in note 12 above), II, columns 1557–58, figures 6 and 9 respectively. It would lead too far afield here to pursue the symbolism of the stone (Kronos is holding a stone in his *right* hand in figure 23), which can be considered to overlap the area of phallic symbolism. For the phallic significance of the stone see among other sources, M. von Zmigrodzki, *Die Mutter bei den Völkern des arischen Stammes* (Munich: Ackermann, 1886), paragraph 187, p. 281 f.

14 Further illustrations of the veiled Kronos in Roscher (note 12), II, column 1558 ff.; also in the article "Saturnalia" by J.-A. Hild in Daremberg-Saglio, *Dictionnaire des Antiquités grecques et romaines* (Paris: Hachette, 1908), IV, 2, p. 1089, fig. 6123; Guigniaut-Millin, *Nouvelle Galerie Mythologique* (Paris: Didot, ²1831), II, p. lx, fig. 240; also in Millin, *Mythologische Galerie* (Berlin: Nicolai, ³1848), II, pl. 1, fig. 1.

15 See Daremberg-Saglio (note 14), IV, 2, 1089, a description by Hild of a bronze statuette representing Kronos from the Gregorian Museum. Pohlenz (Pauly-Wissowa, last entry in note 12 above), column 2017, refers to the "inexplicability of the so-called veiling of the head, a peculiar motif in men's clothing," but like Löschke or Preller, he is at a loss to furnish a suitable explanation. - For more on the *nyx* (night) representations of the type mentioned, see A. G. Roth, "Die Gestirne in der Landschaftsmalerei des Abendlandes," *Berner Schriften der Kunst*, III (Bern-Bümplitz: Benteli, 1945), 193, as well as F. Piper, *Mythologie der christlichen Kunst* (Weimar: Comptoir, 1851), I, 1, p. 350.

16   Our illustration is taken from Roscher (note 12), column 1550, fig. 2. The interpretation there by M. Mayer, that this is a depiction of Kronos, is most likely correct; J.-A. Hild also considers it to be a representation of Kronos. Pohlenz, however (note 12), column 2015, rejects this interpretation without further explanation. As for our interpretation of the "dots" as being stars, it must be noted that this is a frequent form of depicting them; see A. G. Roth (note 15), p. 180, and his list 90, p. 327, as well as his illustrations 48–50. Roth's illustrations, to be sure, date from the fourteenth century A.D., but as we have seen, this era shows evidence of the awakening to the mental, and specifically in this instance to the definitely rational consciousness, not unlike the era encompassing the last few centuries before Christ. It is noteworthy, we might add, that during the fourteenth century the still non-spatial yet resplendent gold ground had displaced the dark background of vase painting in antiquity, a reflection of the Christian illumination of the world as over against the darkness of antiquity.

17   With respect to the meaning adduced of the root *gher*, see Menge-Güthling (note 11), as well as Emile Boisacq, *Dictionnaire étymologique de la langue grecque* (Paris: Klincksieck, ²1923), p. 1072. Pohlenz, on the other hand, maintains that the "assimilation of *chronos* and *Kronos* are late syncretistic speculations" (in his article "Kronos" in Pauly-Wissowa, note 12 above, column 1986 f.) Döhring, quoted in Pohlenz, considers the root *ker* likely (*Jahrbuch für Philologie* CLIII, 107), although Pohlenz himself cites fragment 832 (Nauck) of Sophocles which clearly relates *chronos* to *Kronos* (column 2017). For further conjectures regarding either the relationship between *chronos* and *Kronos*, or the respective etymologies, see: Ph. Büttmann, *Mythologie* (Berlin: Mylius, 1828/29), II, pp. 28, 33, and 230; C. A. Böttiger, *Ideen zur Kunst-Mythologie* (Leipzig: Arnold, ²1850), I, pp. 11, 219, and II, p. 15 f.; F. G. Welcker, *Griechische Götterlehre* (Göttingen: Diederich, 1857–1863), I, pp. 140–160, 265, and 272 ff.; H. Usener, *Götternamen* (Bonn: Cohen, ²1929), p. 25 ff., where Kronos is described as the "maturer of fruits," underscoring the harvest aspect; H. Usener, *Sintflutsagen* (Bonn: Cohen, 1899), p. 204; O. Gruppe, *Griechische Mythologie und Religionsgeschichte*, Handbuch der klassischen Altertumswissenschaft, V/II (Munich: Beck, 1906), II, p. 1104 ff.; Preller-Robert (note 12), I, pp. 51–63, M. Mayer, in Roscher (note 12), II, 1, column 1548; E. H. Meyer, *Indogermanische Mythen* (Berlin: Dümmler, 1883–1887), particularly volume 2, pp. 270 ff. and 280 ff.

18   Alois Walde, *Lateinisches etymologisches Wörterbuch* (Heidelberg: Winter, 1906), p. 143 f., entry "cornix"; p. 151, entry "crimen"; p. 126, entry "clepo." In the last entry, Walde remarks that in the shift from *k* to *q* we find a "shift in series." For a discussion of final *g*, *gh*, and *q* see Walde, p. 525, under "rigo." It should be noted that only *g* and *k* are gutturals, strictly speaking, whereas *q* is a labio-velar, i.ė., a guttural shifted toward the front of the oral cavity.

19   Menge-Güthling (note 11), p. 296, entry "kalypto"; Walde-Hoffmann, *Lateinisches etymologisches Wörterbuch* (Heidelberg: Winter, ³1938), p. 195 f., entry "celare."

20   *K* is probably a primordial sound, at least one of the very first and in any event "earlier" than those sounds formed farther front. Not fortuitously, though without stating reasons, Karl Abel begins his index I with *k*; this index lists Egyptian roots and furnishes supporting evidence for our elementary etymological remarks; see Karl Abel, *Einleitung in ein ägyptisch-semitisch-indoeuropäisches Wörterbuch* (Leipzig: Friedrich, 1887). Languages with prominent guttural sounds, such as have survived in modern Arabic, Chinese, Spanish, and several Swiss dialects, permit certain conclusions about the psychic and vital structure of the respective peoples, and their closer proximity to the inceptual *k* and the magic world. It is not accidental that the cavern culture is, as Spengler has pointed out, symptomatic of Islam. And in Spain, as well as in Switzerland, a strong clan feeling survives along with the labyrinthine-cavern component recognizable in bullfighting.

21   F. Ebner, *Das Wort und die geistigen Realitäten* (Innsbruck: Brenner, 1921), p. 126. It is not possible here to pursue the question of the "death-relationship of the 'R' " implied by Ebner, but it is worth mentioning inasmuch as the consciousness of death does not

come about until the mythical structure. It is as unknown to the unproblematic, vital magic structure at the outset as life itself, hence its weak conscious resonance; the magic structure knows only "being." In Indo-Germanic, the protoroot for our concepts of "being" and "becoming" is identical; see Menge-Güthling (note 11), p. 616, entry "phua," root *bhu/bo.* We would also allude in this connection to the curious circumstance that the Chinese cannot pronounce the *r* and say it instead like an *l.*

22   A. Ernout and A. Meillet, *Dictionnaire étymologique de la langue latine* (Paris: Klinck-sieck, 1932), p. 816; the root *reg (regh)* "indiquait un mouvement en droit ligne," emphasizing the *droite* by placing it before the noun.

23   For substantiation of this derivation, see our "Fifth Remark on Etymology," p. 558.

24   Kluge-Götze (note 7), pp. 370 and 372, entries "Mahl" and "Mal."

25   As to the words "meal" (*Mahl*) and "time" (*Mal*): in Old High German, *mâl* meant "point" and "point of time"; in Gothic *mél* meant "time" (as in English "meal"); see Kluge-Götze (note 7), p. 370 and 372. The coincidence of the root *ma:me,* with which we began our discussion of the mental structure, and *da:di,* which visibly express not only the orienting but also the severing (rational) element, is not accidental. The two roots most likely also coincide in the name "Metis," as well as in that of the Egyptian goddess of law (right) and Justice, Me'et (see our "Fifth Remark on Etymology," p. 560).

26   Grasset d'Orcet, "Les Fouilles d'Utique," in *Revue Britannique* (Brussels: Lebègue, October, 1881), pp. 367–398; our reference is to p. 384 ff. (D'Orcet makes no reference to the time question.) We owe our knowledge of this work to Mme. M. Loeffler-Delacheux, who has revived interest in his work via her study *Le Circle: un Symbole,* Collection Action et Pensée, 38 (Geneva: Mont Blanc, 1947).

27   Steuding, quoted in Roscher (note 12), i, 1, column 939, remarks only that *Dais thaleia,* the abundant meal personified as a goddess, is mentioned in a Triptolemos fragment of Sophocles (cited in Hesych) as the *presbiste theon.* Waser merely states: "*Dais thaleia,* the bountiful feast personified by Sophocles in *Triptolemos* and designated as *presbite theon;* frag. 544 . . . " (Pauly-Wissowa, note 12 above, IV, 2, column 2014). O. Gruppe speaks of Dais only in a footnote: "There is a clear instance of the imitation of theogonic poetry where an idea is converted into an eldest (most honored) or a youngest divinity, as was done frequently . . . ", and then quotes in full the passage cited in our text (O. Gruppe, note 17 above, II, p. 1068). And finally, there are two references to the goddess in J. E. Harrison: "The speaker in a fragment of the *Triptolemos* of Sophocles says more truly than he knows . . . " (followed by a translation of the fragment, with the original in a footnote); and also in another footnote, Harrison relates Dais to Thaleia: "Like Dais, Thaleia is no mere goddess of banqueting and revels, she is the daimon of the magical fertility-feast" (*Themis: A study of the Origins of Greek Religion* [Cambridge: University Press, 21927], pp. 146 and 372 respectively). Aside from a reference in d'Orcet (note 26), we can find nothing about a goddess *Tis* whose name is strikingly reminiscent of "Metis."

28   One example of this type of sacrifice was prevalent in old Mexico, where a prisoner's heart was torn out of the living body and, still beating, was consumed by the priests. Since the heart's power is the preeminent mythical power, deficient mythical man, when threatened by the loss of this power, seizes, in this disreputable act, the heart of another—in this instance the heart of the prisoner who is already in his possession. Parenthetically, it could be mentioned that the atrocities committed in our own day are in part an expression of the exhaustion of our mental-rational structure. This is not to be construed as an excuse or in any way a reduction of guilt, but only as a further indication that this now deficient structure must be superseded.

29   This Kronos-sacrifice still survives today in various harvest customs. Seen in this light, descriptions like that of W. Mannhardt take on new meaning. Mannhardt, for example, writes of the prevailing custom in Europe of "Binding into a sheaf a stranger, or the lord of the manor [the "old man"!]—representatives of the grain-spirit—who are taken captive by the peasants and then symbolically killed by scythe and flail" (*Mythologische Forschungen* [Strassburg: Trübner, 1884], p. 28 ff.).

30 The three-faced Hecate is not the only instance of an expression of nocturnal triadicity (Friedrich Creuzer, *Symbolik und Mythologie der alten Völker*, ed. by Moser [Darmstadt: Leske, 1822], p. 51, no. 83); the ancients also recognized three dream genies (see plate vii, fig. 1 in Creuzer). Cerberus, who guards the nether world, also has three heads (root *ker:gher!*); see the illustration in Creuzer, plate xxxix, fig. 4, as well as in A. L. Millin, *Mythologische Galerie* (Berlin: Nicolai, ³1848), ii, pl. xlvii, fig. 342, "Pluto and Proserpine" and "Hades and Kora." Poseidon bears the trident, an attribute of the night (and not, as Adalbert Kuhn maintains, in *Die Herabkunft des Feuers und des Göttertrankes* [Berlin: Dümmler, 1859], p. 237, a symbol of lightning which is solar). The original number of the muses was three, and later increased to nine (three times three); threefold is also the number of the Gorgons (root *ker:gher!*), of whom Medusa was one; her head was the emblem on the shield of Athena (see note 34 below). The primordial giant Geryon (root *ker:gher?*), whose cattle were stolen by Heracles, had three bodies; see illustration in Werner Schmalenbach, *Griechische Vasenbilder*, (Basel: Birkhäuser, 1948), pp. 40, 41, and 67. We would also mention Varro's demand that the number of those dining together be not less than three (the number of the graces), nor greater than nine (the number of muses). These meals were taken in a reclining position on couches called *triclinia* which were arranged in threes alongside each other; see Hans Lamer, *Wörterbuch der Antike* (Leipzig: Kröner, ²1936), p. 462, entry "Mahlzeit." The name *triclinia* conceals within itself not only the nocturnal "tri-" but also the root *kel*; see Boisacq (note 17), p. 470; Walde-Hofmann (note 19), p. 235, and also our "Third Remark on Etymology." *Cline*, to be sure, originally designated the bed or death-bed; see Ziebarth's article "Kline" in Pauly-Wissowa (note 12), 2. Halbband, 1921, column 851. Therefore, the evening meal—with which we are dealing in most of these source references—preserved well into late antiquity the kronos-character from which "time," i.e., the "daily" or "daytime" meal mutated. This temporicity of the triad survives, it would seem, as a recollection of the nocturnal-mythical realm and a complement of the trinity principle in the Christian church. The altar, the ancient sacrificial stone, is surrounded by the triptychon; on the altar in front of the triptychon the *Abendmahl*— literally, "evening meal"—or Lord's Supper is served; and the triptychon represents the nocturnal triadicity.

31 Grasset d'Orcet, "Les Cabires et la Vénus mutilée," *Revue Britannique* (Brussels: Lebègue, February, 1880), p. 451. Two modern examples of an acherontic nature are cited in Gebser, *Lorca oder das Reich der Mütter* (Stuttgart: Deutsche Verlags-Anstalt, 1949), and *Gesamtausgabe*, i, pp. 85–144. That *Acheron* can be considered as a negation or exclusion of the Kronos element is evident from the "negated" (i.e., *alpha privatum* "a-") noun *cheir, cheiros* = "hand, deed," which can be traced to the root *gher* (see Menge-Güthling, note 11 above, p. 621); a-cheron, means, then, "no hand, deedless," hence "timeless."

32 According to Menge-Güthling (note 11), entry "ararisko," pp. 86 and 82 f., the root is *ar*. *Harma*, in contrast to latin *carrus*, does not contain the *k* element. This root survives today in the call of the Spanish mule drivers, "¡arre!," used to spur on the animals. K. Faulmann records a German interjection *har!* used by drayment to signal their draft animals for a left turn; he traces it to the same root as Germanic *hëran*, "submerge, demise, conceal," and thus to *hehlen* itself ("to conceal, make secret") (*Etymologisches Wörterbuch der deutschen Sprache* [Halle: Karras, 1893], p. 157). It is interesting to note that "turning left" is equated with "submerging" or "demise," and also that the corresponding interjection can be traced to the root *kĕl*. Understood in this way, "downfall" or "demise" is not an end but a sinking back or submerging into the magic beginning, into somnolence and darkness.

33 We would recall here the ability of the early Greeks to erect an orienting, regulating metric structure onto the rhythmic "slope," let us say, of the words, evident in the verses of Homer. In them the mental world visibly emerges from the mythical without in any way denying it.

34 It is perhaps unnecessary to remark that the process exemplified in the instance of Dais

could have been equally demonstrated in the case of Dike or Thalia, or with the aid of the son of Kronos, Poseidon (with his trident). And even another son of Kronos could have served in this capacity: Zeus himself (whose name can be traced to a *d* root), or Chiron, the mentor of Achilles, whose protectress, let us not forget, was Athena, daughter of Metis and leading figure in the Kronos mythologeme. We would also mention that the dividing element presumably inherent in the name Metis (Dai = Tis, and Me-tis) also pervades the name Athena. Also belonging to this group are most likely Medea (Me-de-a), and above all, Medusa (see note 30), "Me-du-sa," the Gorgon whose head was the emblem on Athena's shield (see our "Fifth Remark on Etymology"). It is noteworthy that (mental) Athena employs, like Dais, the *gher* or *ker* element as her defense and security ("Gorgo," it will be recalled, can be traced to the root *gher*). It was, of course, Medusa who was the devouress. We have chosen the figure of Dais for our discussion because she most clearly illustrates the time aspect, and supported our interpretation of the roots without taking us too far afield. It is well to remember that in addition to the *m, k, r,* and *d* principles on which we have based this account, it could have been equally illuminating on the basis of *p* or *s*.

35   See Menge-Güthling (note 11), pp. 16, 18, and 20, under the entries "aisios" ("to come at an opportune time"), "ainymai" ("to seize"), "aisa" ("share"), and "aion." For more on these roots, see also Julius Pokorny, *Indogermanisches etymologisches Wörterbuch* (Bern: Francke, 1949), p. 10 f. Because of this independent publication by Pokorny, we have omitted reference to his revision of Walde's dictionary in our etymological deliberations. For a discussion of "aionic" and "chronic" time in Plato's *Timaeus*, with particular regard to Hesiod, see Paula Philippson, *Untersuchungen über den griechischen Mythos* (Zürich: Rhein, 1944), pp. 43–56, where she treats the time question from the vantage point of "genealogy as a mythical form." On the Aion-Chronos question, see also Heinrich Junker, "Über iranische Quellen der hellenistischen Aion-Vorstellung," *Vorträge der Bibliothek Warburg 1921/22* (Leipzig: Teubner, 1923), pp. 123–178. As a final note on the root *ai*, we would mention that the Spanish interjection *¡ay!* ("woe be!") is most likely derived from this root.

36   See Kluge-Götze (note 7), p. 140, entry "ewig"; this word is itself related to *je* (see note 40 for chapter 2, p. 33 above).

37   Aristotle, *De anima*, 433 b 5 ff. (cited in the edition of A. Busse [Leipzig: Meiner, 1911], p. 88 ff.); see also 408 B, where the circular motion is mentioned, and Aristotle's *Physics*, δ, 10–14, where he speaks of time as a circle.

38   Plotinus, *Enneads*, IV, II, 1; III, VII, 13, cited in the French edition of E. Brehier (Paris: Les Belles Lettres, 1924–1938), IV, p. 7 ff.; III, p. 127 ff. See also the German edition of R. Harder (Leipzig: Meiner, 1930–1937), I, 49 f., IV, p. 199 f. This formulation, incidentally, recurs in a modernized form in Gestalt psychology, as in D. Katz's remark: "All psychic processes occur in time" (*Gestaltpsychologie* [Basel: Schwabe, 1944], p. 410.

39   Nicolas Cusanus, *De ludo globi*, II; cited according to the edition of F. A. Scharpff, *Des Kardinals und Bischofs Nicolaus von Cusa wichtigste Schriften in deutscher Übertragung* (Freiburg i. Br.: Herder, 1862), p. 255. We would note that it is not accidental that Cusanus speaks of the eye and sight in this regard. We would add that it is not only sight which existed before the eye; the thought was there before the brain that thinks it, and breath was there before breathing, just as there was being before essents—a fundamental fact rediscovered by Heidegger. His preference for essents, however, for the divided, is revealed in this fragmentation of language.

40   Plato, *Republic*, XI, 580b–588a; cited here in the edition of Schneider (Berlin, n.d.), II, p. 344 ff. With regard to Plato see Aristotle, *Nichomachean Ethics*, I, 13, 1103a 3 (Leipzig: Meiner, ²1911), p. 21 f.

41   As to the numerous conceptual explanations of time, see the compilation in the works of Werner Gent: *Die Philosophie des Raumes und der Zeit* (Bonn: Cohen, 1926); *Die Raum-Zeit-Philosophie des 19. Jahrhunderts* (Bonn: Cohen, 1930); *Das Problem der Zeit* (Frankfurt/M.: Schulte-Bulmke, 1934). In the second part of our book, in the chapter on

"Temporics," we will have more to say about the many recent definitions of time, such as that from the standpoint of biology (Lecomte du Noüy), Christianity (O. Cullmann), psychiatry (E. Minkowski), psychopathology (von Monakow), physics (Einstein, Jeans, and others), psychophysics (J. W. Dunne), mathematics (Speiser), psychosomatic medicine (W. von Weizsäcker), and others. We omit a discussion of them here since their specialized partial definitions do not go to the root of the problem, as we are attempting to do, but merely reveal in each instance certain incomplete aspects which we have defined as magic timelessness, mythical temporicity, and mental time.

42 See W. Gent, *Die Raum-Zeit-Philosophie* (note 41), pp. 22–24, 311–318, 357, and 383–395; *Das Problem der Zeit* (note 41), pp. 8–13 and 72. It seems doubtful whether one should reckon Leibniz among the detractors of time as Gent does. See the mathematical-philosophical study by René Guénon, *Les Principes du Calcul infinitésimal* (Paris: NRF-Gallimard, 1946), which represents a tendency of an otherwise qualitatively-inclined philosopher toward quantification.

43 See Gent, *Die Raum-Zeit-Philosophie* (note 41), p. 357. Husserl, incidentally, ascribes to space a dependency on time as we have done here and in the previous passage, though from a non-phenomenological position (see Gent, *op. cit.*, p. 368). According to Husserl, "space-thing-constitution" presupposes a "temporal constitution."

44 See J. Volkelt, *Phänomenologie und Metaphysik der Zeit* (Munich: Beck, 1925), pp. 75 and 157; there is also a reference to Aristotle's *Physics*, VIII, 251 B, 20 ff.

45 See Grimm, *Deutsches Wörterbuch*, IV, column 2317 f., and Kluge-Götze (note 7), p. 267 f., entries "je" and "jetzt." As to the German word for "hour," *Stunde*, it should be noted that it is derived from the verb *stehen*, "to stand"; see Kluge-Götze (note 7), p. 604. The inadequacy of the mental-rational mode of expression is clearly evidenced by this definition since "standing time" is a contradiction in terms, at least unless we were to take the word for what it is, namely, for a rational fixation.

46 Heidegger's dissertation is on the categories and semantics of Duns Scotus (1915); (Tübingen: Mohr, 1916).

47 Heidegger's later turn toward mythologization, notably of Hölderlin, is an indication of the dead end of "Being and Time." Nonetheless, the book has at least shown the cul-de-sac of this type of philosophy.

6

On the History
of the Phenomena
# of Soul and Spirit

1. Methodological Considerations

Our exposition of the question of space and time, particularly with respect to their constitutive role in latent or nascent form appropriate to the individual structures, indicated that further consideration of this question was needed if we are to understand the foundations of consciousness.

The discovery that "time" in our sense is an instrument we have created with which we are able to shape the three-dimensional, perspectival world and permit it to become a reality presents us with several suppositions. Inasmuch as the "soul" has a certain particular affinity to mythical temporicity, while thinking has an affinity primarily to space, it should be possible to infer certain conclusions with respect to the soul and thought that might parallel those which we drew for time and space. This is not to suggest that they are in any way identical; but we can expect none the less that those bearing on the soul will correspond to our conclusions about temporicity, those on thinking to our conclusions about space.

The conditionality of any multidimensional world concept is directly proportional to the possibilities which can be realized in it. Thus the mythical, paradoxical as it may seem, is tied to its lack of boundaries; expressed in rational terms, it is the negative form of limitation which gives it its stamp. Consequently, the mental is tied to its limitation, although this does not prevent it from the perennial temptation to burst out of these boundaries in the form of a regression to irrationality or prerationality, or from a flight "forward" into the expanses of transcendentalism, or from a lack of knowledge as to its own temporal constitution (that, despite its clock-like nature, demonstrates a certain focused dynamism and energy which, when not perceived, has a destructive effect). This dynamism is destructive whenever left to itself and not treated commensurately with its nature as a directing factor that gives a spatial orientation to the spaceless. Wherever it is itself divided instead of being a divider, or is too markedly sectored, it destroys space, resulting in a negative space-lessness rather than an ordered direction.

There are, therefore, good reasons for undertaking in this first part of our study the task of clarifying several important questions: first, the question as to "soul and spirit," and, the question of "forms of realization and thought." Beyond this it is imperative to show the conditionality, temporal restrictions, and limitations of the individual structures, particularly of our present-day mental-rational structure, if we are to gain a general view of the possibilities of the new consciousness. And, after our description of the predominantly spatial conditionality of the mental structure and the genesis of its spatial emphasis, it will surely have become obvious that there can, indeed there must be, a freedom from space-time in a new integral structure of consciousness.

It is also our desire to clarify the extent and nature of the effects of the psyche, and to examine the possibility of an *apsychic* world, that is, *a world freed from dependence on or enslavement to the psyche* in which the psyche is in consequence not negated but rather becomes transparent. It is also our intent to discover the nature and extent of the effects of rationality and materialism, and the possibilities of an arational-amaterial world where the same holds true as in the case of the psyche, that is, where matter is not negated but in fact becomes transparent.

This may also make evident the order of our chapters and thus the sequence of presentation; whereas the first three chapters presented the structures, beginning with their dimensioning and consequently their respective space-time constitutions, the fourth chapter was a summary of the structures which also provided some tentative conclusions that may be drawn when they are viewed from an integral standpoint. These in turn showed the decisive importance of our conceptions of time and space because of the particularly close relationship between psychic manifestations and time, and between mental-cognitive manifestations and space. The fifth through seventh chapters, which are devoted to these questions, supplement the general description of the structures which preceded them.

It is our hope that by dealing with these particular topics we have sufficiently laid bare the foundations, so that when approaching essentially "new" manifestations we will be able to distinguish those which are truly new from those of previous structures which are merely disguised in modern dress. To be able to do this we must clarify for ourselves in each instance the specific dimension, vital conditionality, psychic temporal restrictions, and mental limitations inherent in them, otherwise we shall find ourselves wandering aimlessly in a labyrinth. Both the psychic and the mental structures (leaving aside the definitely entangling tendency of the magic-vital structure), and particularly the rational structure, that is, the deficient form of the mental, are predisposed to delusions and will-o'-the-wisps: the psychic because of its ambiguities and the mental because of its sector-like multifacetedness. Apart from this we are all subject to the temptations of our vital experience, of our visions, of our views; without these forms of realization we could not survive even for a day, since the structures on which they are based along with these forms of realization make up our integral constitution. It is the degree of our insight into and encompassing perception of them—or, more exactly, the degree that they become transparent for us—that transforms them into our instrument and prevents us from being their plaything.

Any attempt to describe the problematics of soul and spirit is fraught with risks, since we know that the soul eludes to a great extent a calculative rational description, and that such an approach is incommensurate with the soul's immeasurable nature. But this is not the major difficulty; more significant is the difficulty posed by this immeasurability itself. Manifestations of the psyche are infinite; the material which must be sifted through is, in the final analysis, beyond our grasp, comparable to the flow and flux of the ever-changing water which runs through our hands or to the incessant gusts of wind in the air.

Here then, particularly here, it is necessary for us to make modest claims and not be taken in by the fascinations and enticements of the will-o'-the-wisps and the sheer wealth of manifestations even though they give every appearance of revealing the explanation of their contexts. It is at that very moment when we are groping for a definite and specific result that such explanations imperceptibly elude our forceful grasp and revert to the darkness of their counterpole. From a rational standpoint, nowhere else is the possibility so great that a given statement will be so easily and quickly refuted by the appearance of its polar complement. We must therefore remain cognizant that what *seems to us in rational terms to be an antithesis is in psychic terms a polarity*. This polarity must not be severed by a rational approach, nor should we allow ourselves to succumb to its ambiguity.

There are, then, two dangers inherent in any involvement or debate relating to this aspect of the world: the danger that we will destroy it by approaching it from a rational-antithetical standpoint; and the danger that we become captive to it by our submission. What sort of possibility remains for us to gain an awareness of this aspect without the attendant perils? It is above all necessary for us to be cognizant of those structures which constitute us; that is to say, we need an approach of not only vital and psychic, but also mental discipline and confidence, if we are to avoid the imminent perils.

Such self-discipline—which is more than mere wakefulness—provides the assurance or the chance to survive the adventure inherent in every previous attempt to measure oneself against the immeasurable. Simple hearty courage is not enough to assert itself against the unfathomable depths or the Icarus-like flights of the soul; and we must be equally on guard against mere half-hearted involvement. Our aid can be found in the discipline and assurance which, though generally only attainable from time to time, enable us to place the phenomena to be described in their proper place and order, as well as to incorporate them into their corresponding events and actualities. We are speaking of that self-discipline for which the somber lament of all creatures, the ambivalent imagery of the psyche, and the dissecting antitheses of thinking become transparent.

The very fact that we can discover a point of departure which might be adequate to cope with the problems indicated is beneficial even if it should prove difficult to make it effective at all times, for the assurance spoken of is effective only when it works of itself. Whenever we strain to make it work and thereby violate the phenomena and things under consideration, activating the one-sided ego-emphasis of the will and overactivating the mental structure, we place into question the other structures that constitute us and should be the source from which our self-discipline comes.

It is from this point of departure that we wish to examine the immeasurable material at our disposal; and what is important is not the seductive multiplicity of phenomena but rather the clarity of our range of vision. In order to avoid the dangers of intellectualization we shall present the phenomena of soul and spirit from the standpoint of their history; thereby these phenomena will find their appropriate place and order in our sense, in what is inherently a circular structure. We shall, then,

examine the phenomenon "history," in the hope that we will be able to clarify afterward the phenomena of soul and spirit. If we are attentive above and beyond this to
the perils which can emerge from the other structures, our integral attentiveness will,
in the best sense of the word, truly "sustain" us in the face of their danger.[1]

2. The Numinosum, Mana, and the Plurality of Souls

The first part of this study bears the subtitle, "A Contribution to the History of
the Awakening of Consciousness." But wherever we encounter historical topics we
are definitely in the mental structure. Magic, even mythical, man is without "history"; the Egyptians of old knew only of annals or chronicles, not of historicity.[2] If we
are to speak, then, of a "history of the phenomena of soul and spirit" as we spoke
earlier of a "history of perspective," we must be clear as to the meaning of the word
"history."[3]

Over the past several decades the philosophy of history has furnished a
number of approaches whose rationalistic speculations are not devoid of a certain
charm; but in the last analysis they turn out to be one-sided. Karl Joël's conception,
for example,[4] definitely borders on a biological-mythical attitude since he maintains
that for history to be history it must elapse in periods. A different approach is
pursued by Vitalists like Spengler, who place the power principle at the forefront of
their conception of history—evidence of their predominantly magical thinking. And
Benedetto Croce,[5] whose conception derives mainly from Vico and Hegel, divorces
history in a strictly intellectualized manner from any connection with irrational
events while at the same time basing it on the unity of thought and deed. Yet every
thought (as an active intention) is primarily mental, and every deed (as a unitary act
resulting from a union) is predominantly magic. For this reason alone they cannot
undergo a synthesis in the intellectualized history à la Croce, as such a synthesis is a
suspension of thought and deed in favor of "history"—that is, unless one would err
by assuming that these three components—thought, deed, and history—are in
their interworkings merely a kind of continuous process. By its denial or exclusion of
the mythical reality (so important to Vico) such vitalism or voluntarism results in a
falsification or simplification of a theory of history.

These and similar theories of history appear to have individually only a partial
validity. It does not matter whether we speak of a history of nations or peoples, of
philosophy, or of the soul, for in every instance the visible or invisible events which
in some way determine one another are arranged in one time sequence. As a result,
even contemporary political historians frequently make the error of relying on the
inevitably power-oriented events, and ignore as inconsequential the "uneventful"
periods in which the truly eventful actions occur. Essential to such "history" are the
coronations, abdications, wars, treaties, and revolutions—an extremely one-sided,
perspectivistic, and materialistic emphasis.

This common and widespread form of historiography is dominated primarily
by the masculine point of view of power; even where it inquires as to "strengths" or
"forces" it reifies the non-substantial factors. Its approach is appropriately perspectivistic, and in spite of all calculations, it does not take this form of calculation into
account. The same may be said of historical writing on subjects from the sciences of
the mind or the humanities where dates—particles of time— have the principal
role.[6]

In an inquiry into the "history of the phenomena of soul and spirit" it may at first glance seem contradictory that these phenomena are linked to the word "history," especially as the soul in particular is a temporistic and not a temporal phenomenon, and temporality would seem to be the first requisite for anything having to do with history. None the less it is permissible to speak of a "history" of these phenomena; as the word itself may suggest, history (Geschichte) is not just "occurrence" (Geschehen) but also what has occurred. Inasmuch as we base our interpretation on both these aspects, it has a validity conferred on it by Theodor Lessing. The title for his book on history was suggested by a friend, and this friend has furnished us with a key: his title is "History as the Attribution of Sense to Senselessness."

As we noted earlier, such attribution of "sense" includes also a direction; in this sense, history gives—or we allow it to give—direction to the directionless. If we perceive history in this way it becomes integral rather than one-sidedly magic, mythical, or mental; it does not exclude directionlessness as a phenomenon and is based not only on comprehensible and palpable dates, but also on the dateless. There is, accordingly, more than one affinity between history in our sense and what we have defined as the awakening of consciousness. In this, history is divested of its mere temporality and sequential nature, and assumes its place within the mutational structure.

This circumstance can be even more strongly "integrated." For instance, the meaning of "giving direction" is originally inherent in both the word "history" and the German word, Geschichte, without restricting this directing to man as an agent. The word "history," which is derived from the Greek historia, is based on the Greek verb historeo,[7] meaning "to inquire after something" and thus conveys a clear expression of being directed. The German word Geschichte conveyed originally the sense of "providence, coincidence, event" and is an emphatic form of Old and Middle High German gesciht, a derivation of scehan, meaning "to occur by means of a higher providence."[8] The word Geschichte is thus clearly an intensified form of a participle of the root word geschehen, "to occur." This intensified sound is accompanied by an intensification of meaning, that is, it addresses not just any occurrence but a very special one. And this intensification of meaning points to a noteworthy fact: something which of itself is directed at us (since it is "sent by providence") is not just a common but rather a special providence; and behind this sense of something special we can detect a numinous background.

Recollection has a decisive role in the formation of history. Let us for the moment disregard the role of memory within the emergent awareness of what we call history; we will have occasion to speak of the memory symbolized by the muses in the context of another kind of history called "poetry." But both these forms of "history," to the extent that they are qualitative history and not merely a sequence of dates or words, have in common an immanent quality of recollective internalization (Er i n n e r u n g, "memory") and the corresponding "externalization" of utterance (Ent ä u s s e r u n g, "giving up, getting out"). A process of the awakening of consciousness with mythical overtones is discernible in this reciprocal interplay of recollection and its externalization; whether they are visible events as in history or invisible events of poetry, if yo:˙ will, they must be re-collected, that is, mutely absorbed and internalized before they can be externalized in the form of speech or report. (The internalization of memory and the externalization of utterance as constituents of the poetic process in its broadest sense will be examined in the second part of the book.) It would seem that the creative process (hitherto predominantly psychic) is beginning to undergo a transposition or displacement to another zone.

Here we should introduce a term at least as important for the phenomenon of history as recollection, namely the *numinosum*. It was coined by the Moravian Pietist Zinzendorf who first used it in his treatise "Natural thoughts on the Nature of Religion" (*Naturelle Gedanken vom Religionswesen*, 1745) where he spoke of the *Sensus numinis*. The concept was later reformulated in 1917 without mention of Zinzendorf by Rudolf Otto in his book *Das Heilige*, and further developed in his later work, *The Sense of the Transcendent* (*Das Gefühl des Überweltlichen: sensus numinis*).[9]

This latter work is a discussion and critique of the positivistic theory of religion of Wilhelm Wundt as elaborated in his monumental *Völkerpsychologie*, as well as of the animism which began with the work of E. B. Tylor (1875) and of the preanimism formulated by R. R. Marett (1909). "Numinous," derived from Latin *numen*, "divine power or rule," is an articulation of the prerational and irrational components of religious "holiness" and is primarily concerned with the vital experience rather than with any valuative or ethical category.

On the other hand we must take note of the fact that the adjective "holy" (German *heilig*) is related to the word for "heal" (*heilen*) and to its adjective *heil* which have close ties to English "whole"; all of them are most likely traceable to the same Indo-Germanic root *kěl*, source of the word pair *Hölle-Helle* (i.e., "hell"-"brightness").[10] The expression "numinous" circumscribes a very specific sphere of vital experience: religious "trembling," *tremendum*, the awe and thrill of man's encounter with the "completely other." Let us for the moment remain with this definition as a useful working hypothesis; its limitations will be discussed at the close of the section.

The concept of the numinous is an attempt to grasp and define a primordial experience, and this experiential character places it not only within the context of mythical-psychic experience but particularly within the sphere of the pre-rational vital sphere of magic. Both realms are responses to the *numinosum*. It expresses man's predominantly emotional reaction to experiences which he cannot comprehend or understand. In a sublimated form the numinous experience still exists within our culture, as many a devout Catholic or Protestant can attest: the feeling of religious awe, the "pious shiver" which overwhelms him or her during the sacramental rites.

But the concept is not just restricted to the religious sphere; we have noted above that its effectuality is still visible in the original sense of the word "history." What we might call its numinous background is the residuum of historical events and experiences beyond our understanding and frequently inexplicable in causal terms. The religious attitude of our forefathers predisposed them to experience such events as "completely other," that is, as numinous; and they would have believed in the participation of this *numinosum* in what we call history. This attitude, of course, has as little validity for enlightened Europeans or pragmatic Anglo-Saxons as it does for Russians trained in the dialectic tradition who are all convinced (although unmindful of the warning of over-conviction inherent in the word "convinced," *überzeugt*) that they can with impunity explain all historical phenomena in terms of ideology, social structure, economy, or the like.

If we inquire into the history of soul and spirit we are setting out to discover the genesis of the concept of soul. As a concept, it already belongs to the mental structure; but as an effectual potency, the awakening awareness of a soul has, as noted earlier, left its imprint on the mythical structure. And the presence of this "soul" appears to be irretrievably lost in the darkness of the magic structure, since it becomes visible only with the dawning of myth.

It is primarily to the researches of comparative anthropology that we owe our knowledge of manifestations of "primitive" tribes and cultures. There we find a key term which has afforded a basis for redefining the notion of the *numinosum* and which will be useful for our discussion. It is the Melanesian-Polynesian word *mana*, first mentioned in a letter of R. H. Codrington published by the noted Oxford Indologist F. Max Müller in 1878. In the letter, as well as in his book *The Melanesians* (1891), Codrington defined *mana* as ". . . a power or an effect in a certain sense supernatural and definitely not physical which manifests itself in strength of body or in any kind of power or ability of which man is capable. This mana is not restricted to objects but can be transmitted by nearly any object. Spirits possess it and are able to transmit it. . . . The Melanese religion as a whole is based on this fact that man can obtain mana for himself and is able to apply it to his own advantage." G. van der Leeuw has commented on this revealing definition on the basis of parallel information from other cultures: "Wherever something unusual, something enormous, potent, or successful is found it is spoken of as mana. Natural, that is predictable events never serve as the basis for mana. 'Something is mana if it has an effect, and if it doesn't, it isn't mana' remarks an inhabitant of the Island of Hocart. . . . Mana can mean good fortune, *veine* [French for "luck," "vein"] as well as power."[11]

To these definitions we would also add Rudolf Otto's comment on this "power": "Whatever is grasped as 'power' is also grasped as a *tremendum*. It renders its objects 'tabu.' "[12] This shows that the concept of power or might is not to be interpreted as being intrinsically one-sided and deficient since it serves primarily to express effectivity or an effect. It is a power which renders something holy by being "tabu," that is, by making things "untouchable, ineffable, holy." It is predominantly this effect, arising from the already lost shelter of wholeness and belonging to the arcane, which because of this mystery is always something "completely other." The idea of the "holy" contains this effect just as the sheltering cavern or the surrounding and protective circle—which is a "whole"—are also intact and embody a healing effect.

It is early man's primordial experiences and experience of the *numinosum* that prompt him to impart mana-character to those things, events, or actions which form the basis of the concept of soul. We emphasize this since E. B. Tylor's theory of "animism" still enjoys today a certain currency.[13] But its validity must be restricted in the sense that "animism" is, in psychological terms, in all likelihood merely a "psychic projection," as contemporary psychologists would call it. As such it conveys only one—albeit essential—aspect of the emerging consciousness of the soul since, as we have already noted, no awakening of consciousness can take place without projection.

The objections which can be mounted against the correctness of the theory of animism—which from our viewpoint account primarily for early mythical manifestation, less for magic—have been stated particularly by J. G. Frazer and later by R. R. Marett who introduced a preanimism and also animatism in opposition to animism.[14] Lévy-Bruhl extended these theories in 1910 with his idea of *participation*[15] (see above, p. 34, note 54), providing recent psychology with a useful working hypothesis, particularly after C. G. Jung reformulated the decisive *participation mystique* into a concept of *participation inconsciente*.

These three theories on the origin of man's awakening of soul and religion underwent a further clarification and refinement in the work of N. Söderblom,[16] as well as in the previously cited works of Rudolf Otto (since 1917). The two most recent major studies recapitulating and emending the results of these predecessors are G. van der Leeuw's *Phänomenologie der Religion* mentioned above, written from the standpoint of religious history, and Herbert Schmalenbach's article on the origin of the concept of soul, written from a humanistic-scientific point of view.[17] These works in the religious-historical tradition of Rudolf Otto are clearly indebted to the psychology and philosophy of Cartesianism, whose equation of soul with consciousness is as untenable in the light of recent research as the identification of consciousness with knowledge.

Having briefly surveyed the most important attempts of ethnology and the psychology of religion to clarify the question of the origin of the soul, we would like to examine more closely the nature of the numinous experience which may have been favorable to this origin. We shall follow the resume of Schmalenbach from his paper noted above, for despite his pronounced rationalistic position and philosophical approach, it is a most useful summary as it includes most of the discoveries and conclusions by ethnographers and psychologists of religion. He writes: "Anything can be the object of numinous experiencing, although certain objects have a particular propensity for it. As the experience as such is a withdrawal from the familiar, because of its nature as the 'completely other,' it shows a preference for objects outside the range of daily events. On the other hand, certain things have a heightened ability to evoke numinous attraction and feeling because of their particular constitution: spurting, coagulating, surging, and smelly blood, for instance, or the pulse and breathing of someone asleep; shadows in the midday sun, at dusk, at night; a dead man, the rigid, immobile corpse, the phallus; the entire sphere of the phallic; dream images and names; the metallic body of lizards and snakes, the primordial eye of cattle; nocturnal animals like owls and bats, the whole animal realm more than the human, death more than life. Then there are the disc or crescent of the moon with its uncanny light; phosphorescent tree-trunks, will-o'-the-wisps haunting the swamps, and many sounds and noises, especially the crackling or rustling of branches or twigs . . . drums, cymbals, and fifes . . . ; in short, everything is suitable for numinous experience . . . even the most commonplace items: my door-step on which I always tread, familiar from long use with no other apparent import than as a path-leveler at my threshold. Then one day in the noon-day sun something mysterious begins to stir within it; it glistens at me in a strange, half-covert, precarious and enticing way. I am seized by awe and shudder, and run away in fear perhaps, hair on end. But if the very opposite, a vital attraction, triumphs in me, drawing me back although not completely dispelling my misgivings, I take the object to me, knowing that I hold something precious replete with wondrous powers in which I, as its possessor, share to the fullest."[18]

From these findings of the history of religion (notably the discriminating work of Söderblom and van der Leeuw) we know that all of those earlier concepts which until recently were rendered by the terms "soul," "spirit," and "god" are more accurately explained in terms of mana and power. In all these instances we are faced with primary, numinous phenomena in various forms. These include Egyptian *ba* whose plural *baw* denotes now "soul," now "power," and even sometimes "divine being or predecessor"; they also include other Egyptian designations for soul, *ka* and *iachw*,[19] Old Iranian *frawaschi* or *ferwers*, guardian spirits or genies of light and life which are depicted in Persian art as a "spiritual ego," a Doppelgänger hovering over man.

The same is true of Mexican *muitsix*, of the innumerable forms of soul and spirit found among various "primitives," or of the wealth of numinous designations to be found even in Homer, where *psyche* is not the only designation for soul but is merely one alongside such words as *etor, kēr, noos, thymos, boule, menos,* and *metis. Etor* refers not only to the "heart," but also means "life, vital force, courage, disposition, spirit and soul," and originally the viscera in general.[20] This change of meaning again reflects the shift of organ emphasis spoken of earlier: *etor* in the sense of viscera belongs to the magical sphere, while in the sense of heart and disposition it is already a part of the mythical. *Kēr*, with nearly the same range of meanings as *etor*, emphasizes the soul, and *kér* has the attendant meanings of death and dying and derives from the Indo-Germanic root *ker* with the sense of "to injure, strike." This root is contiguous to the roots *quer* and *gher* which were involved in the formation of the name of Chronos and of his son, Chiron (see p. 170). *Ker* also forms the basis of the names for the Greek goddesses of misfortune and death, the *keres*.

To this group of Greek designations for the soul which all have a numinous character are the further words mentioned above *noos, thymos, boule, menos,* and *metis*, each of which we should like to examine in that order. [21] *Noos* meant originally "sense, disposition, heart, divinity" and later "power of thought, understanding, reason." *Thymos* had the general meaning of "soul," and the "vital force" localized in the diaphragm, as well as "will, instinct, disposition, feeling, heart," and finally "anger" and "sense." It is an outgrowth of the verbs *thymoo* and *thyo* which mean "to anger," as well as "to move violently, roust about, sacrifice, butcher" and "murder." The Indo-Germanic root of all three words is *dhew:dhu*, "to move violently, breathe, sacrifice," and is closely akin to the root *dhe:dho–dheu:dhou* from which our word pair "death–deed" derives.[22]

Boule has the meaning of "will, wish, opinion" and is associated with the verb *boulomai* which expresses "wishing, enjoyment, intention" and comes from Indo-Germanic *g(w)el*[23] which is in turn closely related to *kel* on which the word pair *Höhle-Helle* (cavern, brightness) is based. And it will be no surprise that we again encounter the words *menos* and *metis*; together with the word *menis* they formed the point of departure for our observations on the mental structure, and express the directed psychic force embodied in the mythologeme of Athena or the directed anger of Achilles. Having entered awareness, this anger enabled man to direct the psyche, such "direction" being of course the principle characteristic of the mental structure.

These "concepts," these primary numinous forms, are all distinguished by one characteristic: movement. It is either polar or then again partly severing; a movement of the heart or relating to life or to death; or a movement from within itself or aiming out of itself and becoming visible where volition and intent appear, superseding mere wishfulness. Moreover, it expresses the shift or upward trend of organ emphasis which we were able to observe in the shift of meaning in the words *etor* and *kēr*. A similar shift occurred in those words mentioned in the preceding two paragraphs, which at first denoted the visceral-magic zone, later the polar field of tension localized in the heart, and ultimately the emergent reason of thought.

If we return to the non-Greek words characterizing "soul" and consider those expressing the multitude of soul-forms dispersed throughout the world and time, we find that the gradual conscious awareness of the inner, psychic-dynamic movement expressed in these words begins to take on an outward shape. In proportion to their propensity for projection, they denote souls, gods, demons, or spirits; they are personified—or at least reified—imagistic forms of intangible forces that make up man and the world. They can be essences, that is, potencies, or more correctly effectualities that function as the departed vitality or life force only after man's death, as seems to be the case with *ka* and *frawaschi*. This connection between numinosity and the vital forces, which underscores its inherent dynamism, is of particular significance; as Söderblom writes: "The close proximity of power and soul can be seen also in Hebrew *nefesch*, the word for soul, the life-giver in man. . . . "[24]

This discussion of previous scholarship on the *numinosum* and mana has necessarily required us to quote definitions that show a bewildering array of terms like "potency, power, effectuality." We are hopeful that our use of these words in the discussion so far has been sufficiently careful so that the quoted definitions at least do not cause any confusion as to terminology. And we wish to note with particular emphasis that the terms strength or power and might or force are not identical since might is always usurped, that is, misused strength.

There has been until now no successful attempt to discover or trace with precision the emergence of soul from the jungle of various "representations of soul." The most penetrating and systematic to date is that of van der Leeuw who has brought some order into the nearly impenetrable thicket and overwhelming wealth of numinous representations. Some primitive tribes ascribe to a person up to thirty souls, and texts from the pyramids indicate the dead king—as such more powerful—possessed up to fourteen *kas*. These souls are not merely souls of name, blood, breath, and shadow; there are also those which depart the body only at death, others during life, still others which depart for intermittent periods. Some assume a separate existence after departing from the body, some seem to lead a separate existence altogether; and there are also human, animal, vegetative souls, souls of mountains, caves, waters, objects, stars, and constellations.

From this enumeration we can gain some idea of the dynamism, of the potency and vitality which, unchecked by mental capacities, held their spell and movement over the world of magic, as well as of mythical, man and call forth the counterspells and countermovement of magic and myth. Only if we recognize the potent abundance of numinous content can we estimate the enormous step necessary for the detachment and exteriorization of psychic energies before the sudden first quantum-like appearance of mental capacity around 500 B.C. evident in Parmenides' sentence, "Thinking and being is one and the same"; (every sentence is a rigidifying positing). The *noein*, "thinking," of this sentence, for whose initiation we have named responsible *Menis* and *Menos*, has in a way placed itself "above" the *psyche*, which for Homer still retains the meaning of life itself, not just of soul.

We can now recognize the concordance of these two termini. Even in Aristotle's teaching on the soul, the soul is still vital, and its vitality is emphasized although Aristotle himself sought without success to discount the inherent dynamic principle, the *autokineton* or self-mobility of the soul. His wrestling with the problem is clearly mirrored in his treatise *De anima*, where, in the third chapter of Book I (406a–407) he states his "objections to the movement of the soul," followed by the definition in Book II, chapter 2 (413b), that "the soul is determined by four capabilities: by memory, perception, cognition, and movement."[25] From this we can see that even at the mental inception of Western philosophy the original numinous and dynamic character of the concept of soul is still effective.

What, then, is the relationship of soul to spirit? Originally, a concept of spirit was no more in evidence than one for soul; the numinous mana-like "representations" gradually gave rise to souls and spirits, not to the soul or the spirit. The first truly recognizable concept of soul is the Greek *psyche*, the first notion of spirit the Greek *nous* of the pre-Socratics and the *logos* of Heraclitus which is also present in the Gospel of St. John.[26] In its meaning of "word," however, this *logos* has a breath-character which reveals its psychic rather than "spiritual" derivation. The same is true of *pneuma* which shows clear evidence of a breath soul; its "spiritual" connotation, which has prompted Leisegang and others to think of it as spirit,[27] most likely was first acquired via the *hagion* ("holy") of the New Testament. This in turn definitely shows mythical-magic and even numinous, that is, predominantly dynamic characteristics.[28]

There is a clear significance which shines through this configuration if we think of the fact that at one point a single god emerged from the many gods. Parallel to this process of monotheization, which initiated dualism and the trinity and reflected a centering of the ego, another process was underway: the soul emerged from the plurality of souls; spirit emerged from spirits; the demon (the devil) emerged from demons, just as man, bearing his ego, emerged from men. Man assimilates this trinitarian form by attributing to himself a triune soul (as formulated by Plato) corresponding to the triune God, and conceiving of himself as being in three parts: body, soul, and spirit. Is this paradoxical route to trinitarian unity (where plurality is suddenly less than singularity since for mental man spirits are less than spirit, gods less than god, souls less than soul) perhaps more than just a perspectival finite goal toward the self-discovery of the entity "man"—a man who can come to awareness of his essence only as an individual, and therefore projects everything else in terms of individuation, separation, and perspectivation?[29] What if there is another world "behind" or "before" this individually conquered world—a spatial world as much as a universe of space? Is there another world in wait, accessible only through individuation and its supersession, just as individuation was brought about by surpassing the clan? What if behind man humanity, behind god divinity, behind spirit spirituality, were to become "attainable" to man, or more exactly, become transparent to him to the degree that he could divest himself of individuality and cancel his exclusive and patriarchal ego-confinement by freedom from the ego,[30] just as mythical man abandoned the secure enclosure of the maternal, magic man the unity of the mere clan world?

Construed in this way, rational-mental individuation would make "sense" after all, a sense that would not only make sensible the mental structure—inherently "sensible" because of its directedness—but also a sense capable of revealing the significance of the previous mutations. We are using the term "significant" or "sense-ful" here in an aperspectival manner so as to express the full-fillment of direction and directedness; if this process of projecting what is centered in man, that is, his triune individuality, were to be transformed into a retraction of this projection, it would achieve a mutation that would reveal the "divinitary" and the "humanitary." Understood in this manner, would this projection then still remain "correct" in the light of the increasing absurdity of its deficient and extreme ego-hypertrophy, specialization, and sectorization? It is, or at least was, correct for the mental structure since "correctness" is there identical to rectitude and right-handedness. But this also implies a one-sidedness: the mental structure emphasizes only the one bright, right, conscious, masculine, active side just as it accentuates one god, one soul, and the individual human being, culminating in the deficient, rational phase of the uomo singolare of the Renaissance. And it should be noted that this mental one-sidedness and unidirectionality are not to be confused with the unity and unitary interrelatedness of the magic structure, a confusion to which the mind is unconsciously prone in the course of becoming deficient.

To preclude any misunderstandings let us emphasize here that potentially future mutational forms are present in all those phenomena which we today define in singular terms such as god, man, soul, spirit, devil. Their potentiality derives from the originary presence which is "at work" within them. This means that the true believer may be numinously touched by their efficacy, since he does not confront a rational, perspectivist representation of "God" or its conceptualization, but instead turns to the numinous abundance of the name itself. From his irrational attitude, or more exactly, from his irrational sustenance, the believer participates in the abundance and forgets the strictures imposed on the word-contents by intellectualization and perspectivization. But this is a matter for believers; and besides, participation is not yet integration.

Let us return to our starting point. We began by clarifying the concept of "history" which led to a consideration of its numinous aspect; and this in turn led to the question of the numinosum itself. Our understanding of numinosity was made possible via the word "mana," whose efficacy served to indicate the genesis of the soul. We must now ask to what extent mana and soul might be equated.

Representations—to the extent that we are justified in speaking here of "representations"—that are associated from the very earliest time with mana point to a certain duality of the soul, for on the basis of the abundant ethnographic evidence we are compelled to distinguish between a mana of the living and a mana of the dead, that is, between life-souls and death-souls. We see how basic this distinction originally was if we read Erwin Rohde's book *Psyche* with this in mind; the study deals with "the cult of the soul and the belief in immortality among the Greeks," and is devoted primarily to elucidating the nature of the death soul and the attendant notions of immortality and metempsychosis, or migration of souls.

In the representational world of "primitives," mana of the dead takes effect whenever the living encounter the dead in a dream, for example, or when the dead appear in recollections. But especially in the continuing presence of his name as heard, recalled, dreamt, and echoed, the mana of the dead man (or his soul) remains effective and thus lives on. Names in particular have an inherently strong numinous character; even today a name can take the place of the actions and effectiveness of a person; we can act in someone's name, whoever he may be, "in the name of God," or "in the name of the law." And here we might mention the probable kinship of the words *numen, nomen,* and *name.*

But life and death souls should not be considered to be antitheses, as is frequently done in rationalistic discussions. Originally life and death are an entirety, a whole; in the earliest magic period they unquestionably form an undifferentiated unity, and in the mythical age they are complementary and mutually interpenetrating poles. Only in the mental conception are life and death opposites. But where an uneasiness about death or the dead intrudes and "confronts" early man as the "completely other," we see that mana is not only power as traditionally defined, but also powerlessness. Mana of the living is power over life, indeed life itself; but it is powerlessness in the face of the mana of death!

Undoubtedly both magic and mythical man groped to find a resolution of this tension, and their endeavors brought about not only spell-casting, but sorcery, mystical contemplation, and myth in the form of poetry. Man's response to the numinous encounter with the "completely other" was the attempt to subjugate it to his own power, his own mana. In this way he attempted to compel the rainfall by his rain-making ritual, or animals of the hunt by his hunting spell; or to command the vital forces of his enemy—which too are mana and soul—to do his bidding; or to protect himself from inimical mana with charms and defense rituals. Even early Greek drama, although emerging from myth, was still essentially a sacral rite: an attempt to force the "completely other" into man's own power and mana.

Having established the "antithesis" between the life and death soul, ethnographers and others such as Schmalenbach went on to inquire how "primitives" were able to bridge this dualism in such a way as to create the soul. This approach is one-sided, rationalistic, and consequently untenable, for it completely skirts the actual problem. For the "primitive," for magic or mythical man, no such antithesis exists, and it is senseless to inquire into its resolution. (Even today believers "return to the fold" in death [heimgehen] in the belief that they are returning to the cavern. But the magnificent ancient cosmogonic conception of a "world egg" was shattered long ago, irrevocably precluding man's return.) For magic man, life and death formed a dark somnolent unity; for mythical man they were the polar intermingling and movement of dream image. Only for us, with our European mental orientation, are life and death antithetical.

Whenever we inquire into the connection between life and death, we are already at the beginnings of the mental structure, where consciousness awakens to one-sided brightness, and brightness alone first takes on spatial significance. This mental consciousness, by means of its measuring propensities, places all darkness and thus death (which at best is "transfigured" into brightness) into an opposition with its brightness. As Rohde has shown, it is the death-soul which mainly preoccupies the awakening Greeks in the late mythical period.

Not yet awakened to ego-consciousness, man responds through magic or myth to the intuitively sensed tension of life and death. Magic man, himself intertwined with life and death, links them together and thus establishes their unity. Mythical man, enclosed by them, carefully preserves their equilibrium and submits to their inherent movement. As long as man's mana-attunement sustains the balance between life and death, life-mana and death-mana, life-soul and death-soul, and is not overwhelmed by them, he is not impelled toward a new mutation: a new mutation which increments consciousness and would transcend these forces and powers by virtue of a new capability, permitting man either to polarize mythically or to antithesize mentally the phenomena by measuring. The overpowering dominance of rationalistic materialism today is compelling man toward a new structure and a new reality, as mythical man was once impelled by the superabundance of psychic-laden mana to a new mutation.

Returning to the rationalist attempt at resolving the connection between the two mana conceptions they have established, we can say that it presents a plausible explanation. The association between the "antithetical" life-soul and death-soul for the "primitives" is supposed to have resulted from the sight of a dying person.[31] We can well imagine how the immediate experience of dying—the transition from breathing, pulsating life to rigor mortis, and the numinosity of an immobile facial expression—can prompt an association between the life- and death-soul. In the transition that occurs in death the "same mana" or "same soul" has obviously lost its numinous, vital force which was potent just moments before, while the other, the diminished yet "heightened" soul gained in death an increased numinous power.

The situation stated here in antithetical terms is, however, not an antithesis but a *self-complementary phenomenon*. The rationalistic separation of this irrational matter is not to be taken as fact but only as a working hypothesis. When investigating the death and life symbolism of the soul we shall have to bear in mind that we are not considering a rational opposition but rather attempting to retrace first one then the other pole, in order to determine how the perpetual movement enables the one pole to flow ever-anew into the other.

However, before we turn to this symbolism of the polarity of life and death, we must first subject the concept of the *numinosum* to a brief concluding critique. The concept of the *numinosum* is not a very ancient notion like mana, but a true concept coined by our age for the purpose of comprehending a non-conceptual and irrational phenomenon. Now insofar as the *numinosum* is defined as the "completely other," it is not an antithesis; yet as a third element it already suggests more than an echo of trinitarity and thus its dependence on mental thought. For this reason we may well have misgivings that whatever it designates will take on mental overtones unless we take into account its conditionality.

We have already intimated that the concept of the "holy," closely tied to the *numinosum*, belongs to the inceptual sphere of the undifferentiated unity of cavern and brightness. This in itself brings it within proximity to the distinctly "other" because of its mystery and unfathomability. The word actually circumscribes the sphere that is not yet, or no longer, accessible to the particular consciousness structure. As a result, the concept formulated as the "completely other" already falls into the subject-object dichotomy of mental thought; the very formulation attests to this conditionality that divides the whole. Since a whole is always entire, a "completely other" is "nonsensical." There cannot be such an "other"; something is either a whole or a part, and only as a part can it be a "completely other."

This is not a play on words but rather a "taking it at its word" to show that the concept of the "completely other" is untenable. Neither the objection that "completely" means here "absolutely," nor the assertion that the concept refers to "another whole," is acceptable. The absolute is an expression of rational conceptuality, not of the numinous world of vital experience. It is as absurd to speak of "another whole" as it is to consider the concept of the "completely other" as an ultimate explanation. The structure within which this type of interchangeability holds true clearly shows that the "whole" excludes any "other," and hence the connection between these words is merely a makeshift or stop-gap.

Thus even the concept of the "completely other" can serve only as a temporary hypothesis, and even then it raises several questions that demand explanation to prevent extraneous elements from impinging on our central concern: man as an entirety, or *whole man*, as we have presented him in his previous manifestations via the mutations of the various structures.

If we were to approach the question of the *numinosum* from a religious standpoint, then the concept formulated by the theologian Rudolf Otto would be seen to include a supernatural divine power to which man in his belief subordinates himself. As long as we are concerned only with considering manifestations and the unfolding of soul we will be unable to counter the possible objection of a theologian that power and mana are not just force or might manifest in the *numinosum*, but a power of divine rule.

In order to shed light on the background(s) of the *numinosum* we must remember that it was for good reason defined as a primordial experience. Its experiential character places it within the magic realm (see p. 250). If we separate the magic unity of vital experience from the one who experiences it, as is the custom today, then of course we can discover a dualism to the effect that—from the viewpoint of man—the *numinosum* is a primordial experience. But this discovery immediately elicits the logical question: What is the experience viewed from the standpoint of the *numinosum*? Is it a spontaneous release and manifestation of objective powers, or is it in fact nothing else than what we define in psychological terms as a psychic projection, the energizing of external objects, events, or actions by the dynamism or psychic energy inherent in man?

Perhaps we can come to a suitable answer if we examine two mutually illuminating considerations. The first is that the capacity for numinous experience loses its energizing intensity in proportion to the increment of consciousness: the greater man's ability for conscious awareness, the lesser is his experience of actions, events, and things as numinous. Early man and even children today experience a thunderstorm, for instance, as a *numinosum*: as an expression of the power of the "completely other"; but the rational knowledge of the physical conditions of the storm divests it of any numinosity.

But here we encounter a remarkable fact: as the possibility diminishes for numinous experiences from nature there is a proportionate increase for such experiences from art as created by man. The emotional upheavals which can be evoked by (say) Mozart's *Requiem*, or by a poem of Hölderlin, or by a philosophical reflection are most likely no less powerful than the original emotional response to a natural numinous experience. And since the basis for music is found in the magic structure, for poetry in the mythical, and for philosophy in the mental, all of them representing in a certain sense man's employment and mastery of these structures, man is thus able to elicit the numinous effect that resides primarily in the magic and mythical structures.

The result of our first consideration, then, is that numinous experiencing diminishes with the increasing awakening of consciousness, and that the *numinosum* is transposed from nature into art, or if you will, from the respective active structure into the particular reality expressed by man.[32] The second point with regard to the *numinosum* has to do with the *visual perception of early man*. All ethnographers who have heretofore written about the *numinosum* or mana have not considered that early man saw in a different way, and saw different things from those we do today, not only in numinous experiences but in general. The aura drawings clearly show that early man's visual perception took in at once more and less than ours. He perceived in any event an emanation—the energy in motion—and saw a portion of a person's mana. In this sense his numinous experience is more realistic and more palpable than ours of a composition by Mozart, a poem of Hölderlin, or a statement by Leibniz.

This more realistic mode of perception of early man is expressed not only in the aura drawings; an examination of the Chinese colored prints from the sixteenth and seventeenth centuries reveals that, despite the clearly executed contours of the branches, blossoms, stones, and the like, they are suffused by a radiance which seems to emanate from them. Similar phenomena are much in evidence in the so-called "Colored drawings from the Ten Bamboo Studio," edited by Jan Tschichold, or in those of the "Textbook on the Mustard-Seed Garden."[33]

It is a phenomenon in art similar to the color relationships or transitions which connect one object with another in the art of Impressionism. They illustrate that even when still predominantly bound to myth, man sees the energy that emanates from objects. And since everything that affects us is to a greater or lesser degree present within us, although our senses are limited, anything that affects us above or below these limitations will affect us numinously. Of course the degree of our insight into these interconnections would proportionately reduce their numinous influence.

We are now free to resume our deliberations at the point where we paused for our two digressions. These showed us the transposition of the numinous experience and the effect of our degree of conscious awareness on our susceptibility to numinous experience. These two points provide a fortunate clarification of the basic question about the background of the *numinosum*. As we are more concerned with insight or transparency than faith, we could not be content with the religious component of the *numinosum* that was sufficient for R. Otto. Accordingly we have had to inquire into the constitution of the *numinosum*. Is it the spontaneous release of objective powers, or merely a projection of human psychic energy into objects, appearances, or actions which carry a psychic charge of this dynamism?

This question would now seem to be more or less answerable. Our purpose in seeking out the background of the *numinosum* is not to foster any regressive tendencies toward irrationalism but rather to leave its structure intact while laying bare the foundations capable of supporting an inception or of representing the point of departure of a new structure.

Answering our question remains, however, a hazardous venture. If we consider the adaptable and versatile nature of the *numinosum* and, because of this, its relative permanence, as in its transfer from thunderstorm to poem, as well as the dependence of numinous experience on our degree of consciousness and psychophysical constitution, our two findings might suggest the following. The *numinosum*, in psychological terms, is a projection; in psychic terms, it is an over- or understimulation of our capacity for "resonance." As long as we lack insight into the *numinosum*, it remains a correspondence between the inner and outer, between man and the world, the soul and power; either man incorporates it, or he subordinates himself to it.

Yet to the extent that we have insight into this process, even where it over- or underinfluences our capacity for "resonance" and places in doubt its temporal limits, the *numinosum* makes transparent inner and outer, man and the world, soul and power. And from this constellation we see that the power immanent in us—the soul— and the power which resides in things—the *numinosum*—resolve and balance each other as complements at the same time that they engender a kind of mutual insight in a sense that reveals to us, indeed renders transparent, the basic structure and providence of the world.

The role of consciousness in this process is evident: consciousness makes it possible to retract the projection that once took place. In more exact terms, the reintegration of the projection is itself an act of the awakening consciousness. Thus consciousness always has a reintegrative capability because it can reveal a lesser-dimensioned structure whose events can be realized in us only through the directive ability gained from an additional dimension. Consciousness is therefore a function which reacts to the visible course of events in reality. These events are able to manifest themselves within the world of dimensions which correspond to the particular consciousness structure and are thus accessible to our perception.

We can therefore dispense here with several of the previously proposed definitions, notably the most rationalistic of them all, the Cartesian, which equates consciousness with soul. Recent psychology, especially psychoanalysis, has demonstrated that this equivalence is untenable. Consciousness has also been equated with the contents of knowledge; in this sense, a historical or a moral consciousness and the like were posited on the assumption that the knowledge of historical or moral matters or values is tantamount to their actuality. To us this definition seems equally untenable; consciousness is more than mere knowledge, recognition, or cognitive faculty.

By its postulate of the "unconscious" as an antipode to consciousness, present-day psychology has perpetrated a falsification of primordial psychosomatic actualities. Such terminology and the consequent false structuration of phenomena is a classic example of the error which follows from a radical application of dualistic principles. *There is no so-called Unconscious. There are only various modalities (or intensities) of consciousness*; a one-dimensional magic, a two-dimensional mythical, a three-dimensional mental consciousness. And there will be also an integral four-dimensional consciousness of the whole.

This immanent four-dimensional consciousness is the original zero-dimensional consciousness as such, which is represented in man and in the transposition of its mutations in man. Just as breath is present before breathing, the thought is present before thinking, sight before seeing, being before entities, so is awareness present before the variously dimensioned modes of consciousness. There is no question here of the "unconscious."

It is of interest to note that even today the literature of psychology extensively identifies the unconscious with the "repressed," the forgotten, and thus frequently devalues its own antithetic conceptualization. The "unconscious"—if one insists on using this misleading term at all—is the structure of consciousness one dimension less than a particular or given structure; and it is the next "higher" or incremented consciousness structure which makes the "unconscious" amenable to its mode of understanding. This is not to establish any kind of general oppositionality between the unconscious and the conscious, and even less to negate the conscious, but a way of indicating a unique aspect of consciousness itself: its differentiation because of the various mutations, and its various possibilities of manifestation and realization as determined by the respective or given set of dimensions. G. R. Heyer has given this fact additional meaning by his suggestive and pithy remark on the "mythical frequency" of consciousness.[34]

Consciousness is the ability to survey those interconnections which constitute us: it is a continuous act of integration and directing. And we must observe the fundamental point that there is more to consciousness than mere formal or reflective knowledge. Consciousness is not identical with the process of thinking, nor is it limited to awareness of the ego. Its illuminative function is definitely not restricted to spatialization and temporalization. It is not a mere counterpart of objects and appearances; rather, it is an observant onlooker and an active agent with regulatory functions.

Since consciousness is subject to (and co-initiator of?) the mutations which seemingly transfer a pre-given originary presence to man, it expresses with each new mutation that this presence of origin can be realized through man. Thus consciousness does not depend only on the ego, but also on the itself, although it does not for this reason take on the nature of numinosity (unlike the mythical structure where there is no insight into the effectivity of recollection). Consciousness, because it is bound to both the ego and the itself (which are neither a unity, nor a complementarity, nor an antithesis), is *the intensity capable of integrating the mutations in their entirety in man.*

Only where consciousness itself has overcome its numinous and temporic conditionality is it able to avert the danger of dividing the whole into an antithesis or division alien to it. Our way of perceiving the world depends entirely on the nature of our consciousness, for it establishes the boundaries and temporal limits of our world. To the degree that we are able to integrate these boundaries and limits with the help of an *intensification* (and not an expansion) of consciousness, we presentiate the itself. This means at the same time that our *entire constitution becomes proportionately transparent;* and not merely the "part" that is already manifest which we have endeavored to make vivid by our exposition of the individual structures, but also the "part" that is still latent in us which, together with the part already manifest, becomes accessible to integration.

One of the preparations for this integration is that we withstand the power of the *numinosum* without rationalizing it. By this we do not intend to foster any kind of hubris; we have emphasized again and again that everything depends on "knowing" when to respond actively and when passively, when to let things happen and when to make them happen, while hearkening to the magic events, correlating to the mythical, and taking into account the mental, thus giving an appropriate degree of direction to these magic and mythical events.

If we react in this way, it is possible for us to become aware of certain types of reaction that reveal how the one or the other structure in us predominates, ever threatening our integrality; that is, we become aware that we have our own specific emotional reaction to certain phenomena, reactions charged with a superabundance of psychic power or energy. And we become aware that the echo which returns to us will be appropriately disproportionate—indeed of hyperproportions—to our too-violent reactions. This echo unleashed by incongruous, non-correspondent, or "unheard of" and inappropriate behavior is the striking-back of the so-called strokes of fate, missteps, misfortunes, and the like. Even if only temporarily, such reactions and their echoes deflect us from our true direction. It is the balancing of such reactions by consciousness, our insight into the interconnections of vital and psychic potencies immanent as well as extraneous to us, that is capable of establishing the equilibrium in which our life as a whole can sustain itself and stand the test ("of truth").

Let us now go on to observe those potencies which are represented by mana, souls, and spirits, which became "soul" and "spirit" in response to the centering of our ego. In so doing, we shall avoid two pitfalls: we will neither rationalize these events, nor will we permit ourselves to be irrationalized by them. Cognizant of the polar nature of the soul, we shall endeavor to obtain insight first into the one, then into the other pole. This will not be easy since what is revealed to our quantifying reason in a symbolic-imagistic form is not in fixed imagery but rather in constant flux and movement in accord with its mythical nature, and, as in other instances, its unbounded spacelessness is an obstacle to the spatial predisposition of our understanding.

3.   *The Soul's Death-Pole*

The two poles which we have designated as the life- and the death-poles of the soul represent a design of relations for the psychic dimension. This design encompasses in its fixed categories of death and life the indeterminate and fluid movement

Figure 25: A Soul, emblem of Osiris as Ba-neb-Tattu, that is "Soul, Governor of Tattu" (Budge, VII, 2, p. 272) [see note *36* on p. 239].

of both powers. The bipolarity and ambiguity which have also been defined as ambivalence[35] are characteristic of everything directly or indirectly relating to the soul. This explains why each individual pole is also bivalent and ambiguous. Since this dual aspectuality does not occur as an antithesis but as a complementarity, it poses obvious difficulties for rational comprehension, as noted earlier; the energy and agitation inherent in the soul simply defy understanding.

Then there are the potencies inherent in the soul, efficacies which unleash the energies of life and death. When we point to the dangers attendant upon an examination of the soul, it is not meant as an idle remark. Not all who have ventured out onto the sea of the soul, and trusted its flight, have returned. We are all closer to the abyss than we would wish to admit. But it is fortunate that we have an insight into the fact that we are the abyss. In particular, each of us must have this insight in order to prevail over the abyss, at the very least in the hour of our death; and if such insight is not gained until then, this hour will be one of bitterness and anxiety.

Let us carefully note the aforementioned configuration of the soul: it contains the essential words: sea and flight, water and air. Both the water and the air symbolism of the soul have come down to us in pictorial representations. At the very outset of the magic structure (and extending well into our Middle Ages) an auditory and acoustic symbolism must also have existed for them, expressed presumably by gong-like instruments on the one hand, and by whirring sticks on the other, followed later by percussion instruments of all kinds.

The pictorial symbolism—restricting our discussion as before to the forms of expression primarily from our Mediterranean cultures—has survived both in the texts from the Egyptian pyramids, collected in the so-called "Books of the Dead," and in Greek drawings. The vignettes in this and the following sections are from the papyrus scrolls preserved in the British Museum and reproduced in the books of E. A. Wallis Budge and, in part, of Ќolpaktchy.[36]

This symbolism has, however, survived in linguistic as well as in imagistic form. We find it as pure utterance in the mythical accounts or the numinous attributes such as that of the "owl-eyed" Athena or the "twittering souls" mentioned in Homer.[37] But the symbolic element fades away soon after Homer; in Heraclitus we can discern symbolic references to the soul, although the symbolism tends to be a definitional symbolism. With the advent of philosophy such symbolism is even more markedly mentalized and later rationalized; in this form, in part deliberately, in part "unconsciously," such symbolism survives into our day in religious as well as poetic utterance.

Given the immensely rich material devoted to the symbolism of the soul, our decision to bring to discussion only that part relating to the symbolism of life and

Figure 26: The Soul standing before a doorway to the tomb (Papyrus of Ani, Budge, VII, 2, p. 283).

death was based on its suitability as an essential constellation for demonstrating the basic character of the psyche. At the same time we must bear in mind that even this approach is a partial violation of psychic events since the death-pole of the soul is always simultaneously the life-pole, and vice-versa. Every symbol, then, which we adduce (say) as a representation of the death-pole will always contain the other aspect. Nevertheless, we shall attempt to seek out the characteristics first of the death-soul, or soul of the dead, and second of the life-soul, with the aid of such one-sided symbolic attributions which emphasize in each instance only one aspect or expressive valence. And we shall ascribe water with its pre-eminently "living" attribute to the life-soul, air—which has been visualized in the form of breath, a sail, or something in flight—to the death-soul, although breath of course contains the living element as well.

Let us first examine the symbolism of the death-soul or soul of the dead. The researches by the Egyptologists noted above have revealed the significance of texts from the pyramids which are in fact instructions to the soul of the departed as to its behaviour in any of the possible metamorphoses encountered in the "beyond" or afterlife. From these texts we have learned that the *ba* of the Egyptians, of which we spoke earlier, was a winged creature or soul-bird which departs man at the moment of death and later returns to visit the mummy.[38]

Greek mythology either borrowed the idea of the soul-bird—to the extent that we may speak of a borrowing, since such motifs are primordial images which need not be derived—or else they undoubtedly came under the influence of Egyptian symbolism. Various small terra cotta birds with human-like heads similar to those in our illustrations have been unearthed in Greek graves, and there are others on tombstones and elsewhere.[39] *Thanatos* or death himself has been depicted with wings on several surviving drawings.[40] All of the winged creatures which pervade Greek mythology in the form of Keres, Erinyes, Harpies, Stymphalian birds, Sirens, Striges, Moirai, and Lamia are death-souls or spirits of the dead. Moreover, the Greeks also considered the nightingales, eagles, bats, ravens, doves, and swans to be soul-birds.[41]

Turning once again to the Egyptian *ba*, we find that it later became an angel and assumed an almost human form.[42] This form of Egyptian *ba* is clearly recognizable as the prototype of the later Harpies. They, together with the harpy-footed

Sirens, are in our opinion most likely complementary images for the Muses who, as we will examine later, express the other pole of the soul, the water aspect: whereas the song of the Muses invigorates the poet, that of the Sirens entices him to death. Symbolizing the reapers of death in the form of demons, the Harpies or Sirens survive in the Christian idea of the angel of death, and their singing has an ambivalent sound even in the song of the heavenly host.[43]

Here we should point out a connection which is able to shed light on our subject as a whole, the background of which has been previously overlooked. We refer to the struggle between the Muses and the Sirens and what it represents. It should be evident that the struggle expresses the mythical Greeks' attempt to come to terms with the two aspects or poles of the soul. This should not be surprising if we consider that the account of this struggle of previously "numinous" powers makes vivid the awakening consciousness of the soul which we can only perceive, tragically, in the form of a quarrel. Goethe speaks of these "two souls" or potencies in us in *Faust;* the aspects which we have underscored in this discussion will be immediately apparent in the verses quoted below:

"Du bist dir nur des einen Triebs bewusst;
O lerne nie den andern kennen!
Zwei Seelen wohnen, ach! in meiner Brust,
die eine will sich von der andern trennen;
die eine hält, in derber Liebeslust,
sich an die Welt, mit klammernden Organen;
die andre hebt gewaltsam sich vom Dust
zu den Gefilden hoher Ahnen."

["One instinct only are you conscious of,
Oh, never learn to know its counterstate!
Alas! two souls within my breast abide,
And each from the other strives to separate;
The one in love and healthy lust,
The world with clutching tentacles holds fast;
The other soars with power above this dust
Into the domain of our ancestral past."]   (tr. Alice Raphael)

In connection with these verses we would call attention to an empirical-scientific statement of our own day whose inherent profundity and greatness are evident when viewed in the context of the present discussion, although there has been an unwillingness in many quarters to concede this profundity. We refer to the formulation by Sigmund Freud which asserts both a "life-impulse" as well as a "death-impulse" in man. It is unnecessary to explain this assertion here for it is plain from the exposition of the mana nature of the soul and its particular vital-lethal dynamism that Freud's term "impulse" corresponds precisely to these characteristics of the soul.

In this context it should be noted that the psychology of Freud can be understood primarily as a coming to terms with the magic-vital structure of man. To this realm belong the instinctual drives and thus sexuality; and we have already alluded to the magic emphasis on the vital-erotic in our discussion of the root kinship of the words "live" and "love." This is not to imply that life as a whole is magic, but only that the instinctual and vital sphere is a primary constituent of the magic structure.

Figure 27: The Scribe Ani holding his Soul in the Stream of his Breath (Papyrus of Ani, Budge, VII, 2, p. 206).

Figure 28: The Soul of Ani visiting his mummified body, bearing in its claws the emblem of the sun's orbit (Shen), a symbol of eternity (immortality) (Papyrus of Ani, Budge, VII, p. 2, 279, and II, p. 113).

Figure 29: The Scribe Ani walking out of the tomb with his Heart-soul (hovering above his head) and his shadow (Papyrus of Ani, Budge VII, 2, p. 285, and II, p. 115).[44]

209

It is of interest that modern science shares with Freud and psychology a common point of departure: the magic sphere, for the *unity* of space and time is a magic conception. In both disciplines it was superseded by a mythical conception; in psychology, C. G. Jung built what we might call a mythicizing superstructure on Freud's theory of "drives" and in physics N. Bohr discovered the principle of complementarity. This made comprehensible the dual nature of light as being both wave and corpuscle, light (or the speed of light) being in Einstein's theory one of the universal constants (i.e., a unity); but complementarity is only another expression for a "self-completing polarity." This reflection of vital as well as psychic constituents in the exact sciences is not only of interest but also instructive as to the conditionality and temporal limitations of their exactness.

But let us return to our earlier topic. The notion of the soul as being a winged being is evident from numerous Greek representations, predominantly from vase paintings. The soul is frequently depicted as a butterfly,[45] and in a treatise by Porphyrius it is depicted in the symbol of a bee.[46] Then there is the late, almost allegorical representation which also transforms the word *psyche* into an image: the winged Psyche found in Greek depictions of the scenes of death, where, like *ba*, it departs from the mouth of the dying person who literally gives it up with his last breath. "To exhale, expire" is of course one of the many meanings of the word *psyche* clearly recognizable in the verbal form *psychein*. (To "expire" or breathe one's last are words predominantly relating to exhalation and are thus related to death.)

It is in this sense of expiring and breathing—themselves components of the air—that we can undoubtedly interpret the Egyptian symbol for soul represented by the sail recognizable in the vignettes (figures 30, 31, and 32). These vignettes accompany the instructions to the dead mentioned earlier which instruct them in breathing in the waters of the nether world so as to gain dominance over both powers of soul. There are extensive circles of conceptions surrounding and intertwining this symbolism of the soul as a being of breath or air, and they are in turn linked to the infinite series of conceptions based on the immortality of the soul. These again are interwoven with the numerous strata of "conceptions" on which the idea of metempsychosis is based, and these in turn are related to the others of astral nature which have to do with the soul-related aspect of the stars and the astrological conceptions based on the mana-nature of the planets. No less a man than Plato himself has left detailed theories in *Timaeus* on this notion in connection with the teachings of Pythagoras and his own initiation into the Egyptian mysteries.[47]

The death-pole of the soul reveals yet another relationship which will be of considerable help in our deliberations on the phenomenon of spirit. This relationship centers on the kinship between the death-soul and the moon. The lunar character of the soul is already manifest in Vedic literature, where we find the words in the Upanishads: "All who depart from this world go to the moon; their lives cause its waxing side to swell, and on the strength of its waning side it ushers them into a new bi. th. But the moon is also the portal to the heavenly world, and whoever is able to answer its queries is permitted to proceed further. Those, on the other hand, who are unable to answer are transformed by the moon into rain and they fall down on the earth. Here they are reborn as a worm, or as a fly, or as a bird, or as a lion, or as a boar, or as a tiger, or as a human being, or as something else, at this place or that, according to his works and according to his knowledge. That is to say, if someone comes to the moon and the moon asks him: Who are you? he should reply: I am you. If he replies in this way the moon will let him pass beyond."[48]

Figure 30: The Scribe Ani arrayed in white apparel holding in his right hand a sail, symbolic of air or breath [soul] (Papyrus of Ani, Budge, VII, 2, p. 197).

To complement this passage from the Upanishads let us quote another from the Brhadaranyaka Upanishad, third Adhayaya, second Brahmanam: " 'Yajnavalkya,' the son of Ritabhoga spoke, 'when the speech of this man enters the fire after his death, his breath goes to the wind, his eye to the sun, his *manas* to the moon, his ear to the pole, his body into the earth, his atman into the *akasa* (space), his body hair into the plants, the hair of his head into the trees, his blood and semen into the water. What remains, then, of the man?' "[49]

This text from a different cultural context is of particular significance because of its numinous complements, particularly as the blood and the semen, forces bearing the life-mana, are attributed to the water while the *manas* corresponds to the death-mana and is attributed to the moon. This Sanskrit word *manas*, by the way, has nothing to do with the word "mana" and is variously and ambiguously rendered as "inner sense, spirit, understanding, soul." We would surmise that it is akin to the Greek *men (mene)* or *menas*, which mean "moon" and "month," as well as with *menos* (also Greek) which connotes among other meanings "drive, instinct, force" and is, as we noted earlier, one of the constitutive words of the mental structure.

At first glance, the resulting constellation from the lunar aspect of the root *ma:me* may seem confusing, especially since the emphasis of the mental structure is on its function of illuminating consciousness and giving direction. Yet if we recall the source of the mental structure in the twilight and nocturnal realm we can see that the first form of counting or enumeration—the initial calculative direction— occurred, indeed had to occur, according to lunar phases.[50] And if we recall further that the phases of the moon are reflected by the tides of the sea, we are face to face with the mythical interpretation in which thinking is a reflection of the soul, a reflectivity exemplified by Bohr's "principle of complementarity" and by C. G. Jung's analytical or "complex" psychology.

This close connection between the death-pole of the soul and the moon is not restricted to the Upanishads. The Egyptian Book of the Dead is full of references to the soul as coming to the earth from the moon. In the Pythagorean tradition the moon is the abode of souls and the home of ghosts and spirits,[51] while the same assumption is prevalent in Gnosticism as evidenced by a passage in the apocryphal

Figure 31: The Deceased holding the symbol for air [in his left hand] (Papyrus of Nu, Budge, vii, 2, p. 199).

"Writings of Thomas," and by Manichean texts.[52] In Plutarch there is also a Nekyia-description recounting Thespesius' journey to Hades in which the souls of the dead arrive on the moon,[53] a remarkable agreement with the many passages in Vedic literature where the moon is the gate to heaven.[54] And according to Theophilus of Antioch, the sun is "the image of God, the moon the image of [mortal] man."

The moon (masculine only in German) is not, however, merely the portal of death; it is also parturient, giving birth to the souls.[55] This ambivalent symbolization expresses of course the circumstance which we noted at the beginning of this section and to which we will return shortly, namely, that the symbolism of each pole of the soul also inherently encompasses its complement.

In these interrelated aspects of the breath-soul or death-pole of the soul and its connection to the symbolism of birds, air, or the moon, we are dealing with a more or less universal phenomenon. Such symbolism is evident not only among the peoples from the Mediterranean civilizations but can be found among cultures everywhere independent of each other. Abundant examples of this are documented in the studies of Frazer and Frobenius.[56]

Two references to the inveterate potency of the numinous resonance latent in the lunar aspect will furnish additional evidence. First there are the medieval allegories which depict death, in which connection we should recall that *every allegory is a kind of rationalized and atrophied symbol* in a frozen, torpid, and vacuous form as it were. Why, in medieval representations, is death depicted carrying a scythe? The plausible rational allegory would contend that the scythe cuts the life-giving grain which is equivalent to the vital energies of man, and hence death is allegorized as the reaper. This allegory seems to all appearances to be somewhat empty and superficial in its rational, contrived form; but this shallowness is quickly charged with psychic potency when one realizes that the scythe is none other than the sickle of the moon.[57]

To be sure, all of these somewhat confusing affairs, interrelationships, and symbolizations seem to be "senseless"; and senseless they are, since they lack "direction." The possible "sense" of the symbolizations quoted above does not become evident until we also consider the complementary pole. When we are able to treat or embrace both poles together, then we will be able to recognize them as being even today an effective potency (which we are attempting to describe here in irrational terms, that is, in terms which correspond to their nature).

Enlightened rationalists will not take this potency seriously, while idealists

Figure 32: The Deceased holding the air symbol in
both hands (Papyrus of Nu, Budge, VII, 2, p. 198).

will perhaps find it amusing. It is possible, of course, to ridicule and deride all of this.
But anyone who does so is ridiculing his own soul and deriding what he or she
cannot fathom and consequently denies; and such denial is only the result of a lack
of courage and strength for another kind of measurement, the contemplation appropriate to the nature of the soul.

The idealist will at best join the legion of imitators, associative "thinkers," psychists, and emotionalists who fail equally to do justice (to the extent that one can do
justice) to the soul, since they do not direct their soul but rather are themselves
directed and confused for the most part by its unperceived powers. Idealists and
materialists are both like two children on a seesaw who have been teetering back
and forth for two thousand years. Now one, now the other is on top and shouts
"Hurrah!" while the other summons all his weight and strength to be able to do the
same; and thus the game goes on. Each thinks that his own weight and strength is
decisive, and neither considers the fulcrum in the middle which, from its point of
rest, is what makes their movement and the game itself possible at all.

The second reference to the lunar aspect relates to several verses of a poem by
Goethe. The poem is one of despair, of Romantic *Weltschmerz*, a lament on the
misfortunes of love where the river—to a certain degree a water symbol and therefore implying "life"—flows on, passing him by. It is titled "To the Moon" (*An den
Mond*) and begins with the verses,

> Füllest wieder Busch und Tal
> still mit Nebelglanz,
> lösest endlich auch einmal
> meine Seele ganz.

> [You once again enclose the vale
> with still and misty sheen,
> and free at last my soul entire
> from its terrestrial dream.]

In the hour of grief, the "power" or mana of the moon breaks forth to release the
soul from life.

213

We turn now to the other pole of the soul, the life-pole, which we will attempt to render with the aid of water symbolism since the living aspect of the soul is also symbolized by water. But we remind the reader that our approach does not quite correspond to either the substance or the mythical structure of consciousness where it originates; for our procedure, if not rationalistic, is at least mental in its ordering, estimating, and construction of the material at hand, and our undertaking is a construct to the extent that we are being selective even though already dealing with a selection of available evidence.

It is also important for us to bear in mind that the polarity we are attempting to bring out does not allow us in any way to speak of a dualism, and that our procedure has severe limitations when we approach, even with reservations, a decidedly irrational subject matter from a discursive, mental standpoint. We should therefore emphasize that we are necessarily trying to evince the ambivalent character of the psychic sphere with means inadequate to it. The sole adequate means here would be the mythical attitude: we should have to let a pre-dream run its course, rather than to elicit a series of conceptions. By endeavoring to retrace something dream-like in descriptive terms, we all too readily transform the ambivalence of things in the mythical sphere into a dualism.

Nevertheless, let us proceed without succumbing to the irrational (as would happen if we think ourselves able to rise above the "nonsense" of such symbolizations) and without severing or segmenting it. The ambivalent character of the soul must continue to be present even if we seem to be speaking in favor of a dualism. As must be evident by now, we have no other avenue of approach than a discursive one; and we must even guard against pointing to facts which emphasize the ambivalence we have spoken of. It is precisely because of their boundless ambivalence that they exceed or undermine our rational capacities for comprehension and expression. We have addressed this extremely confusing state of affairs since we can grasp it in its entirety if we remember that the mythical structure is still present in us, even though we do not consider it advisable to activate it too strongly.

The fathomless ambivalent character of everything psychic is by no means restricted to the polarization of the original life- and death-soul, or to its symbolic configuration in the symbolism of air and water. Since both the life-soul and the death-soul have ambivalent aspectuations, the ambivalence lies at a deeper level. It is evident, for example, from the fact that other symbolizations for the death-soul are extant besides those which we found with relatively patent corresponding images or symbols (and which we will point out for the life-soul), in which a symbolic representation of the death-soul unexpectedly shows attributes characteristic of the life-soul.

Thus we find representations of the death-soul as a (soul) bird like the Sirens, who also have attributes of water, namely, the fish-like lower part of the body and Egyptian water jugs—both attributes, of course, of the life-soul. Then there is the bee which, as a winged being, was associated with the death-soul but which appears as an attribute of the Muses. They in turn stand closer to the life-soul because they are water nymphs. Indeed, water itself has a death aspect, notably in the Greek myth of Lethos and the river of forgetfulness, Lethe.

From these references it should be sufficiently evident that everything pertaining to the psyche, as manifest in image, myth, and dream, is ambivalent. In particular we should not forget that we have (re)called attention to this sphere of mythical-psychic realities precisely because they are even today actual energies which, in times of semi-wakefulness, dream, and sleep—more than half of our lives—give our lives their effective imprint and coloration. This is true even if our reason may disclaim or dismiss them; such rejection or defense merely heightens the tension, and therefore the effectivity, of these essentials.

Rather than to dismiss them, it would be better if our reason were to gain insight into their workings whereby they then become an effective reality. Our capacity to think can also strengthen the innate tendency of the soul toward senselfulness: oriented thought, it will be recalled, sprang forth from the mythical structure. Only if these conditions are met are we no longer a plaything of our unperceived wishes and stirrings, and of our emotions and imaginings.

4.   The Soul's Life-Pole

Having entrusted ourselves to the flight of the soul, perceiving some interrelated aspects of an unsettling and confusing rather than clarifying nature, we would now venture out onto the sea of the soul. (This manner of speaking may be dis-

Figure 33: The Deceased scooping up water into his mouth with both hands from a stream [the T-shape of the stream is symbolic of the stream of life] (Papyrus of Nebseni, Budge, VII, 2, p. 207).

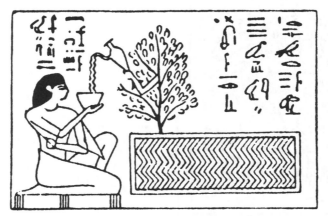

Figure 34: The Deceased kneeling beside a pond or stream of running water which the goddess of the sycamore (Hathor) pours into a vessel (Papyrus of Nu, Budge, VII, 2, p. 208).

counted by the rationalist, for he will also be skeptical of the phenomena under consideration.) It is not our intent to awaken the slumbering irrational latencies but rather to reveal the broad zone within us and in the world pervaded and dominated by the effectivity of these images and interrelationships. And we would recall our observation at the outset of this chapter that the overwhelming and confusing energy and effectiveness of this irrational world of images demand from us our utmost vital, psychic, and mental discipline to maintain our detachment from it.

We can, however, survey these images and their interconnections without submitting to their spell if we remember that many of those described have today been divested of their numinous content because we have learned to regard them in conceptual terms. This holds true, of course, only for our waking state and periods of awareness, for the moment we surrender our attention we are afloat amidst the images and unable to account for them, images we regarded only moments before as mere pictures or passed over in our minds. The more clearly we recognize them and admit the validity which is their due as symbols vividly revealing our constitutive powers, the greater our guarantee of insight into that segment of our lives outside our mental wakefulness.[58] Such insight would also show to what extent our wakefulness is constantly pervaded by daydreams and associative reveries, for *even during the clarity of daylight our wakeful, mental consciousness is not continuously effective.*

We meet up with the life-pole of the soul and its water aspect whenever we utter the word "soul" itself, notwithstanding our reservations as to water symbolism as a means of elucidating the nature of the soul. The etymology of the word reveals the following: "Soul, or German *Seele*, is a word common to the Germanic languages; its basic form is *saiwalso* or perhaps *saiwlo*. The exact origin and kinship are still unclear. It was previously associated with the word 'sea' (Proto-Germanic *saiwiz*); although a reasonable conjecture from a phonetic standpoint, this semantic derivation is possible only by artificial and implausible elaborations."[59]

Although the Brothers Grimm here dispute its semantic if not phonetic deriva-

Figure 35: The Deceased kneeling beside a stream or pond of running water from which the sycamore (fig) tree seems to be growing. In the tree is the goddess Hathor who is giving him water (and bread) (Papyrus of Ani, Budge, II, p. 105).

tion, recent scholarship has shown it to be correct. We would note further the importance of this derivation of "soul" from the image of the "sea," for it provides at the very least an explanation of its polar complement: there is a mirror aspect immanent in the sea. We may conclude from this that the soul reflects physical nature and is, in turn, reflected by it, which gives the notion of the so-called unity of body and soul—which is also a polarity of body and soul—a certain plausibility.

We have already alluded (and will return) to the paradox of linguistic mirroring. This aspect of psychic phenomena is of interest in any case, for it not only discloses the intensely psychic nature of religiosity, whose most succinct message is always paradoxical but, if truly understood, also goes beyond speculation.[60] The word *speculatio* derives from *speculum*, "mirror," which is, as we have shown, a component of our civilization's central concept, perspective. Here we do not wish to speak of perspective, however, but of perspectives that are a part of the mirror aspect of the soul and provide an aid to its understanding.

The question as to whether the word soul comes from "lake" (*der See*) or from "sea" (*die See*) is only incidental;[61] what is of interest here is that we once again encounter the ambivalent character of the life-soul. If it is the "sea," we have moving, active, and living water; if it is the "lake," then we are speaking of stagnant, "dead" water as described by Maurice de Guerin in his diary: "Il y a au fond de moi je ne sais quelles eaux mortes et mortelles comme cet étang profond où périt Sténio le poète." [In the ground of my very self are—I know not what—dead and fatal waters like the deep pond in which the poet Stenio drowned.]

This quotation recalls a fragment of Heraclitus: *psycheisin thanatos hydor genesthai,* "it is death for souls to become water."[62] This idea must be deeply rooted in our psyche, for it is still at work today. Shipwrecked seamen do not radio the Morse signal "S. O. L.," "save our lives," but rather "S. O. S.," "save our souls." When we are faced with drowning, our reaction and utterance as in all decisive moments of life emerge from the origin of our inner depths. This "save our souls" still distinctly echoes the ancient Greek equation of life and soul that is inherent in the word *psyche.*

A further quotation can shed light on the words of Heraclitus; Montesquieu has written: "Enfin, l'opinion des Anciens, que l'âme de ceux qui se noyoient dans la mer, périssoit parce que l'eau en éteignoit le feu, étoit très propre à dégôuter de la navigation. Il y avoit des gens qui, dans ce danger de naufrage, se tuoient d'un coup d'épée." [In short, antiquity's notion that the soul of those drowned at sea perished because the water extinguished their fire, could well account for their dislike of ship-travel. There were those who, fearing imminent shipwreck, took their own lives by dagger.] In a footnote to this entry—and any annotation is an apostrophe—Montesquieu comments: "je crois que cela se trouve dans Pétrone" [I believe this passage is found in Petronius].[63]

Yet the quotation from Heraclitus, "It is death for souls to become water," seems at first glance to express precisely the opposite of our contention, namely, that water symbolism expresses the living aspect of soul's life-pole. Here again we observe the ambivalence. But another fragment of Heraclitus affords a resolution: *ek ges de hydor ginetai, ex hydatos de psyche,* "But water proceeds from earth, and from water soul."[64] If the soul is born of water it must not drown therein, for that would be a reversion to the unborn state, to death.

Above all we must emphasize that water is the primordial element in all of the very ancient representations; and the statements of Heraclitus may be considered to be among the very first precise formulations in language. Even in rational terms this can be understood, for we know that the earth in its earliest state, as recounted in Genesis, was completely covered by water. The first forms of life, the first organisms, were aquatic; even the embryo is surrounded in the womb by amniotic fluid. And all organic life went forth from the waters. On the basis of scientific discoveries at the time of the First World War, Marcel Proust could state that "On prétend que le liquide salé qu'est notre sang n'est que la survivance intérieure de l'élément marin primitif" [It is said that the saline fluid in our blood is merely the survival of the primordial sea element in us].[65]

In this connection we should also call attention to Sigmund Freud's paper "The Oceanic Feeling" (Das ozeanische Gefühl) in which he records that the recollection of the primeval sea—and thus the primordial soul—repeatedly manifested itself as the basic element in his patients' dreams, a movement which he appropriately named the "oceanic feeling."[66] The extent to which these notions and sensations correspond to the primal events present in the pre-mental state of awareness can be inferred from Bachofen's summary remark in his Mutterrecht ("Matriarchal Law," 1861).[67] There he notes in his discussion of the vowel a that it is the vowel of water, dominant in Latin aqua, Sanskrit apa (water) and German Wasser. He goes so far as to consider this a to be the materia prima, the aquatic birth sound, the beginning of the saga of the world.

We might add that this a is still echoed by many words for "blood," as in English, or in French sang and Spanish sangre. The accuracy of Bachofen's interpretation is borne out by the many designations for rivers in Switzerland and elsewhere, such as the Aa, Aach, Ach, Ache (from Old High German aha, "water"), for example, the rivers Aa in Engelsberg, Sarn, Wäggital, and even Livonia, and also by the many names for settlements situated on rivers such as Aarau, Aachen, Fulda, and others.[68]

As a further illustration of this inceptual life-element that appears in the a of water we would recall the effect elicited by the initial poem in Rilke's "Book of Hours" (Das Stundenbuch). The poem is built around the a-sound, achieving its effect not only by its repetition within verses, but particularly by the emphasis on the masculine verse endings which are all in a. The opening stanza of this pre-eminently primordial poem is as follows:

> Da neigt sich die Stunde und rührt mich an
> mit klarem, metallenem Schlag:
> mir zittern die Sinne, ich fühle: ich kann—
> und ich fasse den plastischen Tag.[69]

> [Departing, the hour bends toward me to touch
> with vibrant clarion stroke
> all senses atremble, I summon my power
> and grasp onto the formable day.]

Fewer depictions of water symbolism[70] have survived than those of air and flight symbolism unless we include—and rightly so—the depictions personifying divinities of rivers, sources, and seas, as well as those of Nymphs and Muses. We have, however, restricted our illustrations here to reproductions of the vignettes from the Egyptian Book of the Dead.

None the less, it should be emphasized that water symbolism is visible not only in these Egyptian vignettes but also in examples of Greek vase painting and Hellenistic art. The difficulty in recognizing their symbolic value lies in part in the obscure and covert form in which this symbolism is expressed within Greek culture. It is most often found in depictions of dolphins who symbolize waves as well as the sea, and consequently life itself.[71]

We cannot claim to have exhaustively examined water symbolism here, for such symbolism, corresponding as it does to the nature of water, is inexhaustible. We have, for instance, made no mention of cosmogonic accounts, deluge traditions, Stygian waters (streams of forgetfulness and recollection), nor of the extensive realm of baptismal and initiation symbolism.[72] And we have passed over the Christian as well as Islamic and Mediterranean traditions and conceptions which are closely tied to the symbolism of the soul's life-pole.[73] Despite this, the powerful role of water should be evident: water is an element in which the dynamic, energic moment is equal to that of the air. It is an element which corresponds to the symbolism of soul, and enters into a natural relationship with the soul or precipitates its inception. When we consider the enduring effect of this soul-revealing, soul-depicting element, it would seem that *water is one of mankind's traumas.*

In conclusion, let us cite yet another fragment of Heraclitus: "Souls, however, emerge as vapor from dampness."[74] Anyone who considers this far-fetched should recall Goethe's verses in *Faust* which coincide with the words of the fragment:

"Und steigt vor meinem Blick der reine Mond
Besänftigend herüber, schweben mir
Von Felsenwänden, aus dem feuchten Busch
Der Vorwelt silberne Gestalten auf—
Und lindern der Betrachtung strenge Lust." (3235–39)

[And when the pure moon rises into sight
Soothingly above me, then about me hover,
Creeping from rocky walls and dewy thickets,
Silver shadows, phantoms of a bygone world,
Which allay the austere joy of meditation.]　　　　(tr. Alice Raphael)

Surely we too may be permitted a glance at the assuaging images of the soul, and perhaps be entrusted with the task of transforming them (as the continuing mutations of consciousness tend to indicate) so that they may recast their twilight into crystal, or like crystal, become transparent. For this reason we have endeavored to view them in a form which corresponds to their nature. Now that their contradictory nature, as seen in mental terms, and their mutually complementing polarity, in psychic terms, have become transparent to us, we must in turn contemplate the soul as something self-complementary, whereby one pole suspends or complements the other and renders the inconsistent consistent, permitting its mysterious and sheltering character to shine through—the secret and sheltering aspects of the irrational which is something ir-rational, un-rational, and as such indivisible.

5.　The Symbol of Soul

If the two words "deed" and "death" (*Tat:Tod*) are for us today primarily antithetical (since our measuring thinking divides phenomena which correspond in the mythical region, belong together in the magic, and form a pre-conscious whole in the archaic), we also know that they reveal the two complementary poles. Thus the word-pair reflects the life and death poles of the soul for which we were able to establish a series of various symbolizations.[75] Many of these openly bear the stamp of not yet retracted projections, others are patently recognizable as analogues of the primordial processes of nature, and still others appear simply as accidental speculations, that is, reflections of an undirected image world.

Whatever we may think of them, these symbolizations share a common trait: they make visible the effectuality of the soul and still retain this efficacy today in one form or the other. Equally important, their efficacy is such that never is only one pole activated; even if "negatively," the other pole is also active. This means that they continually act in tandem as complementary powers, flowing into each other undivided by any boundaries.

These are relationships which require less "sight" on our part than "contemplation" (we have already noted the psychic nature of contemplation above, note 62, p. 34), as these matters are more difficult to depict than to envisage. This psychic or mythical structure was earlier the proper domain of the poets, and it is not fortuitous that the co-presence of the life-death poles is only rarely expressed or symbolized in imagery.

In the exceedingly vast literature on this subject we find very few pictorial representations; of the few, we have selected three as illustrations (figures 36 to 38). The oldest of these is the Chinese *T'ai-Ki* (figure 36). In accord with our mental consciousness, our reproduction shows this Chinese symbol for origin oriented to the right side; in China it is always presented with the light (for us, right-conscious) side toward the left and the dark (for us, left or unconscious) side to the right. It is a prototypical symbol, expressing in a complementary way the polar powers—dark as well as light—*Yin* and *Yang*.

A true symbol always encloses two complementary poles; it is always ambivalent, ambiguous, and indeed polyvalent, particularly if we focus on only one of its values or poles. We could not avoid this ambiguity in our *successive* presentation of the polarity of the soul. The ambiguity is inherent in all psychic articulations even when we consider only one of their possibilities. The oracular answers of the Delphic Pythia express this same ambiguity which is latent in all psychically-tinged manifestations.[76] Consequently, our individual presentation of both poles must have had a similarly ambiguous effect.

The T'ai-Ki itself expresses this ambiguity: each half of the symbol contains the other pole, the dark containing a light spot and the light containing a dark one. Darkness and light, in other words, are not just complements of one another, but, seen in itself, each also contains the other. The soul's death-pole, which we have

Figure 36: The Chinese T'ai-Ki.

found in symbolic form in the imagery of air, flight, birds, and the moon, always symbolically included the death-pole, just as the soul's life-pole—symbolized predominantly in water imagery—includes the death-pole. Only when we proceed from their complementarity and not from the individual poles, recognizing in each pole its polar complement, will the true symbol and self-complementarity of the soul be revealed.

The symbol as a fusion of two complementary events is thus always ambivalent and becomes ambiguous when we regard only one of its values. We must not forget that the word "symbol" comes from the Greek verb *symballo* meaning "to roll together, join, unify."[77] Every symbol is latent with two main possibilities which rationally speaking are antithetic; only in psychic terms do they form a complementary whole. This complementarity represents only a psychic and thus always ambivalent "unity."

Seen in this context, the obvious circular, self-enclosed energic field of the T'ai-Ki is one of the consummate representations of the mythical world-image and, consequently, of the psyche. It is a graphic expression of the fragment of Heraclitus quoted earlier (p. 82): "Hades and Dionysus are one and the same." It is further illuminated by yet another of his fragments: "Life and death are in our lives just as in our dying."[78] The dark and, in a rational sense, barely comprehensible nature of these fragments becomes clear when we examine them in terms appropriate to their domain—in this instance, the mythical realm. In view of the T'ai-Ki, where light and shadow, life and death, Hades and Dionysus are visible as homogenous psychic energies, where the di-valence appears as an unusually distinct polarity, the words of Heraclitus certainly seem to be not dark, but rather "twi-lit."

From the abundance of the symbolic energy of the T'ai-Ki we have selected for our interpretation of this sign that effectuality related to the essence of the soul. It is, of course, more than just a soul-symbol and lends itself to a more encompassing interpretation as one of the manifest original configurations of the primal and invisible cosmic-universal structure and formation. Precisely in the case of the T'ai-Ki, if we ascribe to it this more encompassing sense, can we see to what extent an authentic symbol is an efficacious originary element, a preforming and primal paradigm of Being, beings, and what is already formed: in short, the whole of reality. Like all original symbols it is in all likelihood not just pre-human, that is, pre-mankind, but pre-tellurian, emerging from a "time" when the earth did not yet "exist"—from the pre-terrestrial time alluded to in an apocryphal saying of Christ: "I chose you before the earth came to be."[79]

We point to this origin since it is customary today to interpret or locate symbols and symbolism in a rational way as though a symbol, though unbound to space, could be ascribed to a particular location. Since symbols do not originate in the mental structure it is wrong to interpret them in mental terms as happens in any attempt to explain the occurrence of the same symbol in various times and places by a process of migration. Migration is already a space-time conception commensurate only with the mental structure; it is not applicable to the symbol because symbols are not spatio-temporal at all but originary, and as such would be pre-spatial, pre-temporal, and perhaps even *pre-archaic*.[80]

For this contention, of course, no rational proofs can be furnished. Demonstrable knowledge, that is, the rational-mental capacity alone, is not sufficient to reveal this presumed truth. To reason such expressions appear "twi-lit" or possibly as hyper-illuminated; twi-lit if they are rooted in the mythical attitude and have a definite psychic-irrational emphasis; hyper-illuminated if they are grounded in an attitude that has mutated from the previous structures and acquired an apsychic-arational emphasis. In this too it will become clear that the new mutation can open up "new" interconnections to our consciousness.

There is a silent law according to which anyone who perceives certain inter-connections cannot merely contemplate them with impunity. In other words, when certain of these interconnections come into our purview, they begin to affect and oblige our consciousness. The emergence of such interconnections is, after all, for the structure under consideration here a coming-into-view of recollection which demands a complementary externalization and includes a vital action or deed. Or, restated in rational terms, our estimative knowledge about the given and visible interconnections is insufficient unless it is transformed into living knowledge. Estimative knowledge makes itself known to us conceptually, living knowledge via experience; and every experience as a psychic process is a traversal (*Erf a h r e n*) of the sea (p. 69 f.) as well as an externalization of inner knowledge relocating itself in consciousness.

Today, those of an exclusively rational turn of mind resist this necessary act of integration. At best they will use understanding where, to employ a metaphor, they should act only with the heart: with the moderation and tact which are oriented to the heartbeat and not in such a way as to force understanding onto the heart. Understanding cannot achieve the requisite integration; reason would be more likely able to achieve it, for despite its affinity to understanding, it has not lost its connection with the heart, whose measured pulse it is still able to sense.[81]

At all times and in all places, many and diverse ways have led to the living knowledge of the soul's polar complementarity. Yet we must not mistake this bi-unity for the unity of the soul, since such unity would require something opposed to it. The Chinese numerical-symbolic interpretation attached to the T'ai-Ki recognizes the polar self-completion of the soul and strongly emphasizes the notion that the number one cannot be associated with the T'ai-Ki.[82] Our description of the mutations which have taken place has taught us not to impute to psychic events a magic unity; the psychic realm, being itself polar, forms in turn a pole to the physical.

The soul and the body, in their mutually conditioning and complementing tension, have the same relationship to one another as time and space. Bodily space and the spatialized body are materialized time and materialized soul which require the formation and rigidification of space and body for their unfolding. The acute energy of the soul corresponds to the latent energy of the body (see p. 25); one is the latent form manifesting the other, and the measurability of space and body corresponds to the immeasurability of time and the soul. Whatever we can understand on the one hand we must sense or experience on the other; and this sensing or experiencing is the living knowledge required to complement our calculative, estimative knowledge. Without this process and achievement, no life is capable of achieving conscious integration.

Since ancient times the most diverse avenues have led to this living knowledge according to the degree of awareness of the respective structures. Jacob Boehme, the great German mystic, intuitively became aware of this knowledge when he gazed at night in his shoemaker's workshop into the glass ball suffused with light.

As for Eastern civilization, D. Suzuki's descriptions of Zen Buddhism[83] afford us a view not only of the Eastern experience of the soul, but also of the mental, waking structure which is intentionally realized in the practice of Zen. Yet, because of the rational consequences, Zen students seek to free themselves from it in order to attain, ultimately, a sudden leap or mutation to a *satori*, an elevated supra-wakefulness of consciousness evoked by one of the seemingly "senseless" *koans* (a kind of paradoxical sentence). We have defined this consciousness structure of integrative effectiveness as the "arational-integral."[84]

Within our own culture we meet up with various forms of psychic experience which emphasize the dark or death-pole of the soul. Rational man considers everything that appears in light and clarity, even if only his own good characteristics, to be—without any particular justification—in no need of further experience. But even in ancient Egyptian civilization we find this constellation, and there is abundant documentation relating to the dark side of the soul. There man—still predominantly magical and similar to the deficient magic (rational) man of today—is more closely tied to the dark than to the light, with this difference: in magic the dark affords shelter and concealment, while today it works mostly as a destructive force and indeed must be so since its denial of the strength latent in its darkness and depths reacts negatively on present-day man.

The great Egyptian literature on death is an endeavor to master the death region of the soul. Its difficult texts radiate a knowledge about this realm which is already recognizable in the vignettes (figures 37 and 38). What the T'ai-Ki presents as a pattern or design is here represented in graphic or image form: man's complementary unification of both poles. The life-pole is symbolized by water, the death-pole by a sail; and the deceased, caught up in both poles, which in rational terms are mutually exclusive, bears and endures both.

These texts and pictures, we must not forget, were given to the dead by those still living as instructions for the death journey; both "knew" and were supposed to know about the subject matter represented. It is surely no accident that the figures in the vignettes are almost without exception turned toward the right; this implies that the living, who rendered the drawings, had experienced the dark death-pole and were thus more able to turn consciously toward life, toward the light, right pole of the whole. Our description of the ancient Greeks' emphasis on the right at the inception of the mental structure is sufficient proof, we feel, that this interpretation is not merely a speculation. Further corroboration can be found in a passage from the *Acta disputationis* of Archelaus: "The Manicheans, when meeting each other, extend their right hand as a sign that they have been released from darkness."[85]

Figure 37: The Deceased standing in a stream, holding in his left hand the sail, symbol for air or breath (Papyrus of Nu, Budge, VII, 2, p. 200).

Figure 38: The Scribe Ani and his wife Tutu standing in a stream or pond of running water and holding in one hand the symbol of air or breath while the other—the right—scoops up water into their mouths [the right hand—the living side—draws the living water while the left holds the symbol of death] (Papyrus of Ani, Budge, VII, 2, p. 202, and II, p. 106).

In Greek mythology the Nekyia descriptions offer an expressive account of what we have called the path of revelation and the experience of living knowledge. Modern psychoanalysis attempts to deal with this same area although its rationalistic treatment divides into "conscious" and "unconscious" something "deeper" or more profound than this antithesis: something not only dark or light but a complementarity of life and death, whose polarity includes a question as well as a response.

Before returning to the Nekyia descriptions which express the experience of death in life, we must point out two other particulars which give us some idea of the once-familiar "knowledge" of the complementary nature of life and death.

In one of the books of the *Mahabharatam*, which also includes the *Bhagavadgita*, we find a passage in the philosophical texts of the *Sanatsujata Parvan* that is surely not unique. Since only a few parts of this gigantic work have been translated, we are familiar with merely this passage; but the statement to follow certainly expresses a basic conception of one of the oldest traditions: " . . . (death) is the inner soul fraught with delusion; truly it is death that inhabits your body."[86] Since "body" here (*Leib*) may be considered as a synonym for "life," and since a rational dualism was not yet valid then, this utterance may well be equated with the pictorial manifestations of the T'ai-Ki and the vignettes from the *Book of the Dead*.

This basic truth that *life and death are not opposites but complements*, that they are not a perspectival succession but a *polar coexistence* in which we at all times participate, has been rediscovered by more than one present-day poet at the outset of the "aperspectival epoch." Rilke, for instance, speaks of "death in us," an indication that this apparent reconnection to expressions of truth surviving from premagic times (or timelessness) can be said to manifest an attribute of the "aperspectival." (This will be discussed further in the second part of the present work.) Here we would only note the apparently fundamental difference between the Vedic sentence and the modern-day expressions: what was once an immediate wisdom is today mediated by consciousness. This consciousness is the pre-condition for the integration which may occur in the integral structure of the "aperspectival world."

This complementarity of life and death can also be observed within the Greek tradition. To be sure, it is no longer recognized as such in our day since rational dualism is unable to realize the polar experience expressed in those representations. We refer in particular to two symbolic representations which are equivalent in their expressive validity to the Chinese and Egyptian symbols. One is from a Greek representation of the year 500 B.C. decorating a dish (see figure 41); we see a figure bearing a shield which depicts a winged dolphin enclosed by three circles. Since the dolphin symbolizes the sea and water, as noted earlier (p. 219), we find here both the life-and the death-poles represented by the symbols of water and air, complementing one another and enclosed in a circle.

A bronze from the Hellenistic period also impresses on us this image of soul. The representation of the "winged Ephebe" (Rabinovitch) carried by a dolphin is not only an attractive work of art (figure 40); it is the handle of an ash urn found in the excavations of Myrina.[87] In this example fish and wing, sea and flight, water and air (and thus the life- and death-poles of the soul), close the circle in an unquestioning intermingling rhythm. Once again, as if frozen in metal, the complementarity of the soul's image shines forth, for the youth is not only at one with the wings but also with the dolphin. It is the same rhythm which is manifest in the T'ai-Ki, and here flows through wing and fish.

Yet there is a fundamental difference between the Chinese and the Greek symbols: man appears in the center of the Hellenistic soul-symbol; he is not represented in the more encompassing symbol of the T'ai-Ki and appears in only schematic form in the vignettes from the Book of the Dead. In the Hellenistic version, which dates from the period when the mental consciousness structure was unfolding and consolidating, man has already become the spatialized center. The soul is no longer the sole recipient of symbolic expression.

Although this representation has to do with contents bound to the cult of the

Figure 39: Winged Dolphin (section from fig. 41, p. 227).

Figure 40: Winged Ephebe with Dolphin; bronze, Hellenistic period.
It is the handle of a funeral urn from the graves at Myrina.

dead, since they represent a symbolic allusion to the fate after death like the Egyptian vignettes, we must not overlook the fact that in both instances the soul is depicted as a polar complementarity. As Usener writes, the boy is not just a "winged Eros" or (in Rabinovitch's words) a mere "winged Ephebe"; he is the winged soul-likeness of man who "knows" both poles, and for whom both are present at the moment of death. The entire soul is visible: its dark as well as its light pole, or in the words of the *Mahabharatam*, its "blinded" or blind (and thus dark) "inner part" silently evokes the implicit co-presence of the sightful, light part.[88]

In our exposition of the awakening of consciousness within the mythical structure we mentioned several extant Nekyia descriptions (p. 72). These accounts which describe sea voyages or the descent into the nether world all have an inherent element of discursive thought since they are presented in descriptive form. The actual experiences were transmitted to the early Greeks via the Orphic mysteries, which were undoubtedly based on the ritual experience of the mythologeme of Demeter and Persephone. This myth conveys in image and in an appropriately vivid form the message of Heraclitus' terse statement: "Hades and Dionysus are one and the same" (late sixth century B. C.).

Barely a generation later (early fifth century B. C.) this was stated in antithetic terms by Euripides in the question, "Who knows whether life is not being dead, or being dead is life?" Yet whereas the mysteries underscored the feminine aspect, Heraclitus, who already belongs to the patriarchal era, emphasizes the masculine. In the mysteries the matriarchal dimension is expressed in the elevation of Persephone, daughter of Demeter, to goddess of the nether world. But inasmuch as she is presented as Demeter's daughter, we can discern the basic polar structure of the soul. In the mythologemes, sons and daughters represent none other than the image of an aspect of the parents emerging into consciousness. Thus when Demeter, goddess of fertility and life, symbolizes the mother of Persephone, while Persephone becomes the goddess of the nether world, this expresses the unfolding of the soul into an ambivalent polarity.

Figure 41: Drawing on a Greek bowl; ca. 500 B.C..

We know today that this mystic rite ended with a reunification, although only temporary, of mother and daughter. The myth itself was presented in its entirety to the initiates during the ritual in which they participated. It is evident from this that at least some form of imagistic awareness of the Hades or death aspect of the soul entered consciousness during these mysteries. The extent to which this experience of the dark side of the soul represents a process of consciousness emergence, and to some degree a process of integrating what is today inadequately called the "unconscious," is discernible in the mythologeme of Narcissus which we examined earlier (p. 70 f.).

Like the mythologemes of sea journey and of the sun, the myth of Narcissus is a pre-eminent expression of the awakening of consciousness. Narcissus was the Greek name for one who had caught sight of himself in the reflection of the water, that is, of the soul. Persephone picked Narcissus flowers after being tempted by Eros, and thus surrendered herself to the nether realm. But for Persephone, this surrender is the same as an experience of the underworld; and here again we encounter the great mystery of the context of the whole which can only be suggested by the words love, life, and death. This Hades, realm of Persephone, the protectress of the golden apples, this realm of darkness in ourselves, was still considered as the realm of chaos as late as the third century A. D. In the final pages of the *Pistis Sophia*, a Coptic-Gnostic text, is the following unusually revealing statement: "Thereafter they [the demons] lead it [the soul] before Persephone to chaos."[89]

This description does not in any way exhaustively treat the mythologeme or the mysteries, for they are inexhaustible. If they were not, they would not have their source in the mythical realm of the inexhaustible and unfathomable soul. It is of fundamental importance to observe that each mythologeme, like nearly every symbol later on, *contains everything,*—in any event, *everything related to the soul.* And everything which appears in them to be unspoken is like the reverse of a carpet

227

whose negative image normally does not enter our awareness when we look at the side turned toward us, woven for our wakeful consciousness.

We have attempted here to emphasize the visual rather than the representational aspects. All our efforts are aimed at integrating the polarity and ambivalence of the soul in order to create an awareness in the individual of the soul's polarity from an awareness of its ambivalence. In this endeavor the visual can clarify more than the conceptual.

Psychological concepts represent at best an attempt to approach the soul rationally. They can be helpful and assist in ordering our knowledge of the soul if we become aware, and can divest ourselves in due course, of their inadequacy. Just because we learn to describe certain psychic processes does not of itself accomplish anything. In any case such processes cannot be brought under control by this modern form of discussion. On the contrary, this train of thought has inadvertently regressed to the magic structure where it was possible to gain power by the use of magic formulas of name-giving and name tabus.

Our task is not to bring psychic phenomena under our spell, nor to grasp them conceptually; and it goes beyond the attempt to give them a definite direction, since direction is only a continuing emphasis on the right-aspect. Rather, our task must be to form and shape their inherent sensefulness by integrating them. By integrating we mean the process of making, as well as letting, events happen. Applied to the psychic realm it means a realization of the pre-given "senselessness" as well as "sensefulness" of the psychic realm. Its inherent sensefulness seems to contradict the lack of directedness proper to circular motion; such motion is without direction because this direction (a curvature) immediately completes, and hence eliminates or suspends itself. Moreover, two-dimensional space can never sustain direction, and the circle is two-dimensional.

When we speak none the less of the "sensefulness" and directedness of psychic phenomena and processes, the contradiction is resolved because each of its forms of expression must have its polar complement in accord with the polar nature of the psychic. The manifest lack of direction corresponds to its hidden directedness, as the latency corresponds to the acute function of the psychic. Activation of this latency as manifest in oriented thinking, itself a mutation from the psychic, has corresponded ever since to the continuous deactivation of the once directionless enclosure of the psyche which today retains only a latent function and hence so often manifests itself negatively. In an integrative fashion we must perceive that "lack of direction" is not a negative reality but rather a complementation and correspondence. By such insight even the present state of the world, with its obvious psychic vexation and torment, could be superseded.

It was necessary for us to consider first each pole of the soul independently of the other before we could approach their complementarity; only now are we in a position to form an image of this self-complementarity of the soul. Its polarity cannot be conceptualized but only experienced. And we must accept this in an almost literal sense since the words for "experience," erfahren and Erfahrung, echo an aspect of the soul: the aspect of water. Only the journey (Fahrt) through the zones of life and death in one's soul, only this literal experience enables the individual in some way to gain the living knowledge of what we have described as the bi-unity of the soul.

But we should be particularly wary of any pathos in the face of these problems.[90] As long as we are caught up in pathos we are slaves to our soul, and prisoners of our psyche—"psychists," as we have called them. And psychists are merely coun-terparts to the materialists who feel empowered to judge the psyche although as judges they fail to notice the one-sided and one-sensical direction of their judge-ment, unsuspecting of a possible "senseful" shape of this direction.

If we contemplate this polarity as soberly and clearly as it is depicted on the imprint of an early Christian glyptograph (figure 42),[91] we find the image of death sur-rounded by the living circle which encloses both poles of the soul: above is the butterfly, symbol of air and of death; below is an Egyptian water vessel, symbol of life. Here is a symbolic expression of the thought clothed centuries later in Omar Khayyam's words: "Like water I came, only to depart like the wind."[92] Both the gem and these words signify the entirety of soul as manifest in the complementarity of its poles. If the words of Omar Khayyam suggest that life is a transformation, the gem suggests that death, too, is a transformation; one complements the other as before-birth complements after-death, while both remain within the whole. But the gem in particular reveals the soul's perpetual process of complementation as both a living and as an experienced knowledge.

Figure 42: Glyptograph, Early Christian Period.

6. On the Symbolism of the Spirit

From our deliberations in the preceding sections it should be clear that the term "symbol" circumscribes and expresses *eo ipso* a psychic configuration. The symbol is not merely a form of representation but also a form of expression or mani-festation of the psyche; and the psyche is by nature polar and ambivalent. When we now turn to the history of the phenomenon of spirit, it will not be surprising that we must here too speak of symbolism, since what has been traditionally defined as "spirit" is primarily a psychic phenomenon.

In our conclusions about the *numinosum* and mana we found that there was originally neither a concept of spirit, nor one of soul. The numinous, mana-laden "conceptions" gradually gave way, not to the soul or the spirit, but to souls and spirits. Thereafter the gradual cleavage of the concept of soul became evident in the expressions of ambivalence of the life- and death-souls. From the death-soul there is a fragile conceptual link to the spirits of the dead; and in these souls of the dead, or "demons," the notion of spirits takes on the character of a concept. These "de-mons" are mana with a negative effectuality around which all kinds of apparitions, ghosts, spectres, and spooks come into play.

Yet the concept has also its positive aspects, such as the tutelary spirit or angel which, from a psychological standpoint, is nothing more than the outward projection of the individual's inner sense of security. The visibility of this inner security which works from a secure presence of unrecognized "knowing," this making-visible or becoming-visible of security within us is recognizable in our realization afterwards that we have reacted correctly in a given situation. Even today this misleads us into projecting this inherent power—which to the understanding seems to be a superpotency—into an external power like the personification of the guardian angel.

Not only did this unrecognized power occasion early man's belief in ghost-like entities, but also the propensity of certain objects for mana which were then embodied as elemental spirits. These include noises charged with mana which, as parapsychological research has demonstrated, do not necessarily have their so-called "causes" in physical events. There is more truth in a statement of Otto Weininger than would be readily conceded by contemporary materialists or psychologists: "The rapping noises in the room are an inner shattering buried in the unconscious."[93]

We would here emphasize that in the case of these "spirits" we are dealing with psychic potencies that are actually able to manifest themselves in persons having a strong psychic predisposition. And for anyone who reflects for a moment, this fact explains a whole series of so-called "occult" phenomena. Actually there is more evidence of such phenomena than complacent average persons and even less secure solid citizens find tolerable. Our interest, however, lies in the connection between the concept of spirit and the originally mana-laden soul and not with the so-called "occult" side of such manifestations. Until well into the Middle Ages the phenomenon called "spirit" was for the most part nothing other than the mana-charged psyche.

We have good reason, therefore, to maintain that wherever we can find ambivalent traits in a "concept" of spirit we are not dealing with spirit but with preeminently psychic phenomena. This includes also interpretations which falsely attribute unitary or unified characteristics to the spirit. The univalence of magic, the ambivalence of psychic, the trivalence of the mental consciousness are not, in themselves, valid expressive forms of the spirit. Very few of those who speak of the "knowledge of the spirit," for instance, seem to sense their strong attraction to magic.

All forms of "recognition" and "knowledge" in our European languages have strong sexual overtones characteristic of the Biblical expression itself. Even in a metaphorical sense such knowledge is a vital act and as such recognizable as magic in nature. It is today a most "primitive"—and hence mostly deficient—manner of avoiding the demands of the world and coming to terms with it to speak of "Universal knowledge," the knowledge of everything as an object in opposition to the subject. The perils of such one-sided attunement to the world lie in the presumption of such "knowledge," which can only yield valid results if the person with such knowledge is aware of the conditionality of his actions and of the zones in himself and in the world to which he must restrict them.

Let us now examine some of the early expressions associated with the conception of spirit. First of all is the Hebrew word *ruach*, a feminine noun rendered in versions of the Old Testament mostly as "spirit," sometimes as "wind." Martin Buber and Franz Rosenzweig have furnished a detailed etymological description and analysis of this concept of spirit which is most likely the oldest in our cultural heritage. The Hebrews, according to this analysis, conceived of *ruach* as an oppositional principle to *nefesch* or "soul."[94] It has the same meaning as other concepts of spirit, like Greek *pneuma*, "wind, breath, spiration." The Greek word *logos* has similar denotations to the extent that it is translated as "speech," and later "word": a "breath become sound," as it were.[95]

As we observed earlier (p. 196 f.), the Greek concept of spirit, *noos* or *nous*, is of numinous origin, and its meaning shifted from "heart" to "power of thought." The earliest Greek doctrines about the sun ascribe a solar origin to *nous*, naming the sun as its "source."[96] It was not until Aristotle that *nous* became hypostatized or objectivated.[97] Latin *spiritus* initially meant "breath of air, air, wind, breath"; like *anima* it acquired later the sense of "soul," and only much later the sense of "spirit" as opposed to *anima*.

All of these conceptions are still present today in the modern derivatives of Latin *spiritus*: English "spirit," French *esprit*, Spanish *espirito*, all of which echo the earlier conceptions. The German word *Geist*, "spirit," has been traced by Rudolf Hildebrand in his notable and informative article in Grimms' *Deutsches Wörterbuch* to its basic denotation of "breath, respiration, wind,"[98] along the lines of Wilhelm Humboldt's discussion in the postscript to his "Über den Geist der Menschheit." This derivation has been challenged by Trübner who traces the word to Indo-Germanic *gheizd* and its root, *ghei*, meaning "animated movement."[99] From all this one could with justification define the basic meaning of "spirit" as the "life force" itself, thereby placing it into the context of the realm of mana that is also expressed by the word "psyche."

It is evident from these particulars that all of those words which for us convey today a denotation of spirit rather than of soul are derived from the realm of mana and soul; this would also include Latin *mens*, which has the same root as Greek *menos*. Originally there was no distinction between the content of the words "soul" and "spirit"; their meanings were identical. A definite distinction began only with the inception of mental thinking in Greece with Anaxagoras and Parmenides. It has its first formulation in Parmenides' axiom, "Thinking and Being is one and the same." Thus the character of spirit was ascribed to the most recently acquired—and hence highest—capability of man; and this capability is thinking, *noein*, and *nous*. It is, as we know, a capacity of the soul, the "most exalted" capacity of soul in the mental structure, which, in the course of the further awakening of consciousness, becomes more and more emancipated.

It is therefore not surprising that ultimately the *ratio* and even the intellect come to be addressed as "spirit," as for instance by Klages. Nor is it surprising that philosophical and religious, notably Christian, speculation projects this new capacity into the cosmos (or finds it reflected by the cosmos) or believes that it has actually rediscovered there a potency corresponding to this new capability in man. We refer to the birth of the *pneuma hagion*, the Holy Spirit of the New Testament whose psychic conditionality we spoke of earlier (p. 197 f.). The *mens divina*, the *spiritus sacer*, and the *animus divinus* or "divine world spirit" of Cicero, derived not only from Seneca but also from the Church Fathers, particularly Augustine, correspond to a great extent to this idea of spirit.

Here we must note a fundamental point: we must bear in mind that the "existence" of a spiritual principle even for the early age is beyond question. The fact that it cannot be distinguished for that time in an isolated conceptual form does not speak against its existence. It has without a doubt its effectuality; indeed, it seeks to find expression in its own form of symbolic and imagistic language, which as a result of the fusion with nature by magic man is first expressed as idolatry, and later in the mythologemes of the sun. For there is a very early tendency of the symbolism of the phenomenon of spirit to unfold from the rest, an indication of the first readying of a mutation of consciousness (and thus of the separation of spirit from the soul); and this illustrates its unique position, one which is for the most part still effective today despite all attempts to hypostatize it.

This symbolism unique to the spirit is at first glance identical to that which we have observed for the soul. Although the water symbolism is similar, the symbolism as a whole differs by a preponderance of symbols for fire and light. The major distinction, however, is that the spirit is not exclusively depicted in a feminine form like the soul, but, notably in the case of the Holy Spirit, is predominantly masculine. Because of this it can be looked upon as the other pole of the soul; and in any event this particular constellation abetted, if only unconsciously, the later conceptual dualization of the two phenomena.

The inexhaustibility of the question of spirit—analogous to that of soul—and the persistent endeavors over the past two-and-one-half millenia to resolve this problem, which was viewed as the pre-eminent problem of thought, are two indications of the enormity of our task. Moreover, if we mention the sheer overwhelming mass of philosophical, theological, psychological, and psychic speculations, dogmas, and theories attached to the problem, it will be apparent why we must be content to work out merely the basic structure of the question, and even then be satisifed with only the most important points. We are aware of the grave dangers inherent in such a concentrated description of this problem, particularly where even the most innocuous remark can unleash legions of emendations, contradictions, sublimations, differentiations, and other speculations.

We began by examining the origins of the phenomenon of spirit and proceeded to delineate its basic structure: a structure conditioned by, yet differentiated from the psyche. We also noted the symbolizations which illustrated the initially irrational phenomenon of the spirit. These symbolizations are of many and diverse forms.

The symbolism of light and fire is well known, as it forms the general store of imagery of the religious interpretation of spirit. In this the light–symbolism is the later form, representing the "heightened" or "elevated" form of fire symbolism.[100] The bird symbolism is equally familiar. It exists not only in the singular form as the Holy Spirit symbolized in the dove; the *logos* as well as *pneuma* is pluralized and conceived as winged beings comparable to birds. This is particularly true in the case of Philo, for whom the *logoi* are definitely souls—a conception which may well go back to the Egyptians.[101]

The masculine aspect of spirit comes about via the identifrcation of the spirit with God, which in turn goes back to his identification with the sun.[102] This sun symbolism explains also the identification of spirit with constancy, a characteristic which forms a natural opposite to the periodicity and change expressed by the lunar symbolism which reflects the waxing and waning of the soul's powers. The association of the moon with the soul is an expression of the soul's powers. The association of the moon with the soul is an expression of the soul's natural affinity to spirit (to the extent that the latter is symbolized by the sun). The power of the spirit shines only dimly as an indirect light through the lunar soul. This lunar soul, then, is not just the mirror of Narcissus or awakening man; it is also the mirror of the spirit as symbolized by the sun.

The objection could be raised—and we must dwell a moment on this objection—that this mode of observation is only a hypothetical construct: hypothetical because such interpretations of the symbol could not be correct inasmuch as non-mental man would have lacked the bases for such conceptions or deliberations. In order to have perceived things our way, one might object, he would have had to know that moonlight is only indirect reflected sunlight, and it is a proven fact that he did not know this. Consequently such an interpretation will not hold up.

It would surely be an error if we were to draw such a conclusion. Consider for example the following. It is well known to those familiar with manifestations of so-called "primitives" that the number nine has a particular significance in their views and utterances. The importance of the number nine is also the fact that it is the significant number for human gestation, inasmuch as a human pregnancy lasts nine months. But the "primitive" lacks any knowledge of the causal interconnection between conception and birth, as various scholars have shown.[103] In magic and mythical man a different kind of "knowledge" is at work. He does not know something; rather, it knows *him*, and, consequently, the circumstances and things affecting him. In psychological terms—remembering that they do not fully encompass this context—it is not he, but the "Id," i.e., the "it" (Freud), the "unconscious" in him, that knows.

This is also the probable explanation for the fact that the measurements of the Cheops pyramid reflect with surprising accuracy "cosmic" dimensions (the earth's circumference, the distance between the earth and the sun, and between the earth and the moon, and so on). The profound affinity of man, particularly magic man, to the world, his deeper "inherence" in and attunement to it, are mirrored by this context of knowing, just as for mythical man his correspondence with the mythical events guarantees the world's coherence.

The dynamism of the spirit which even today is conceded to it, particularly in Catholic doctrine, is also an outgrowth of the sun symbolism. This is a further expression of the spirit's essentially psychic emphasis. There is on the other hand also a de-dynamization of the spirit, notably in Protestant theology where even the Holy Spirit is conceived of as a person.[104] Translated into macrocosmic terms, this rigidification is a reflection of the rigidification and fixation of thought in the conceptualized *ratio*.

An entirely different situation exists with the demonstration by C. G. Jung that from a psychological standpoint the spirit manifests itself in psychic events as an archetypal image of the father, the wise man, and similar aspectuations.[105] We would tend to perceive this less as a manifestation than as a reflection or *speculatio animae*. Whereas Jung is entitled on the basis of his experience to place primary emphasis on this manifestational form, we must point to the opposite conceptual sphere which is more widespread than commonly supposed. We refer to water symbolism and its feminine form, both of which appear primarily in the Holy Spirit; and even Christian theology does not acknowledge a purely spiritual manifestation of the Holy Spirit.[106]

The water symbolism is vividly expressed in the "outpouring of the Holy Spirit" at Pentecost (cf. Acts 2:3). The spirit is poured out as only fluids, especially water, can be treated. The emphasis is on the image, that is, on the soul rather than on the spirit, although fire is of course also a natural symbol for the spirit. In baptism too, which has come down to us in the form of both fire and water, the "spiritual" aspect has an important role in invigoration and rebirth. It is perhaps the "living spirit" inherent in water and characteristic of this maternal element which fostered a feminine conception of the spirit. In any event the Holy Spirit was also represented as a living stream of water, and was conceived in Gnosticism to be a feminine being who is addressed as "mother" in Gnostic doctrine.[107] This view is not, however, limited to the Gnostics. Origen has recorded an apocryphal saying of Christ in his "Commentary of John" which reads, "My mother, the Holy Spirit, has just seized me and brought me to the great mountain Tabor."[108]

Usener's explanation of the feminine form of the Holy Spirit as an analogy to the feminine Hebrew word *ruach* does not touch on the basic questions. His explanation is strictly philological and leaves unanswered the more important issue of why "spirit" was expressed by a feminine term in Hebrew at all, and why spirit is symbolized by a female dove. Already a symbol of soul to the Greeks, the dove indicates the psychic accentuation of this feminine manifestation of spirit. The patriarchal attitude of the Hebrews most likely determined the feminization of their word for spirit, since an equalizing and counterbalancing force of a "maternal spirit" was a necessary pole of the active and vengeful paternal god. We see this psychic polarization even today, although in deficient form; the overly patriarchal, authoritarian European experiences a compensatory obsession and seizure by the "spirit of *material*ism."[109]

There is a further criterion for the feminine conception of spirit which has not been sufficiently taken into account—and we must not forget that from 500 B.C. onward, only the male or patriarchal world has held validity, a one-sidedness all too frequently forgotten or overlooked. We refer to the fact that thought—which sprang forth from the head of Zeus and was raised by philosophy to spirit during the course of increasing mental consciousness—was symbolized by Pallas Athena, that is, by a goddess. Here too we find an expression of compensation by the psyche which has left its imprint on thought.

It must be emphasized that we have in no way endeavored to provide a new definition of spirit on these few pages. Our concern is rather with clarifying the source of its psychic emphasis or *at least its psychic conditionality* via the medium of its symbolism. All symbolism is inevitably conditioned by the psyche; and with respect to the phenomenon of spirit (though not the spiritual)[110] we can observe that the divine spirit "moved over the face of the waters," and was therefore not symbolically identified with the water but was above or beyond such equating.

It is today of particular urgency that we recognize this distinction, for the psychic component still attached to the phenomenon of spirit (though again not to the originary principle of the spiritual) is still effective today, even though mostly unnoticed, and pervades the definitions, hypostases, abstractions, and absolute pronouncements pertaining to spirit. This psychic aspect is clearly visible when we consider the "source" of the concept; and its continuing force right down to our day is evident when we recall the closing words of *Faust*, "The eternal feminine draws us ever onward," which have a remarkable affinity to the apocryphal saying of Christ quoted by Origen.

Here we leave the realm of symbol, so unsettling to thinking because of its ambiguity. Let us only bear in mind the results we have recurrently sensed, deduced, or postulated and which are summarized in the laconic sentence of the alchemist Zosimos: "Soul is distinct from Spirit."[111] This distinction is clearly expressed in a vignette from the *Book of the Dead* (figure 43). The most striking proof of the difference is most likely that the spirit was given quite early attributes (besides that of polarity) which emphasized its opposition to the soul. This began the dualization of

Figure 43: Anubis, God of the embalming chamber (death) embracing the mummy of Ani; at the doorway of the tomb, about to leave, are Ani's soul and his spirit, the latter in the form of a Benu bird or phoenix (Papyrus of Ani, Budge, II, p. 114).

the soul that followed later. And to the extent that luminescence becomes a prominent attribute of spirit, its various forms are associated with conscious processes and erroneously equated with thinking or reason, understanding or intellect, most notably in philosophical discussions.

The theological tradition has subordinated spirit to God, and the Catholic church has thus retained the power over souls and spirits, fully conscious that the maintenance of the spiritual would be entrusted to a later time. Thus the church opposed the untimely defenders of the spiritual, knowing that the physical eradication of its defenders more than likely strengthened the "spiritualistic-psychic" power of the persecuted viewpoint. The decision to subordinate the spirit to the trinitary God came at the Council at Nicaea in 325 A.D. and resolved the feud between the Athanasians and the Arians in favor of the former.[112] The Arians, who placed *the Spiritual* above the trinity, were exterminated by fire and sword along with many other heretical religious groups who came after the Manicheans and Arians. The Catharii and the Knights Templar were the most recent to suffer this fate.[113]

The difficulties posed for philosophy by the problem of spirit are apparent from the manifold and ambiguous interpretations reflected in its speculations. Commensurate with the mental structure, spirit was first singularized, whereby the many spirits became one spirit. Second, the spirit underwent an abstraction, becoming conceptualized and later rationalized and perspectivated. Third, the spirit was absolutized (*ab-solutum*, "separated") and isolated, and lastly, as a reaction to this isolation, was for the most part negated.

Philosophy very nearly sustained its major and incontrovertible achievement in the wake of its most extreme results, namely the liberation of thought from its magic and mythical fetters and conditionalities. Only the ultimate attempt to transcend its own limitations, the limitations of thought, or to dissolve dialectically the subject-object relationship, was doomed to fail—for thought can only function within itself while directing this relationship. The recently postulated "pure act of thought" which is already prefigured in Plato's *dianoia*, "pure thought," is death-oriented, and coincides remarkably in its consequences with the psychistic and anti-spiritual teachings of the Vitalists.[114]

(This would suggest that both of these extreme movements have reached the limits of their positions where "les extrêmes se touchent," thus, in case of living extremes, reclosing rather than transcending the mythical circle. And if these extremes are in fact supervitalized or devitalized, then their own annulment has already begun. Both attempts to attain an open world have failed, and the merely empty world is now beginning to threaten everything with atomization.)

If spirits were a manifestation form of the *spiritual*, spirit is at best its refined or clarified manifestation. And if spirits are psychic projections, the spirit is a mental, that is, a thought projection, although illuminated by the spiritual like all projections and manifestations. The spiritual, having appeared in the form of idols in the magic sphere, in polar form in the psychic, and in trinitary form in the mental, will possibly—indeed probably—luminesce in man and the world if we consider that the mental structure, now in its deficient phase, has attained the limits of its own possibilities. This opens up the possibility of a mutation, and as a consequence of an actual and real mutation, the spiritual will not be approached in unitary, polar, or dualistic-trinitary form but can be truly perceived as the energy which effects itself transparently and diaphanously throughout the whole.

1*   It should be noted that *Gefahr*, "danger," and *bewahren*, "keep, preserve," or "sustain in truth" in our sense, show an extensive etymological congruence since they both derive from the same Indo-Germanic roots *per* or *bher*; see Kluge-Götze, *Etymologisches Wörterbuch der deutschen Sprache* (Berlin: de Gruyter, [11]1936), pp. 144 and 666 f., entries "*fahren*" and "*wahr*," and also Menge-Güthling, *Griechisch-deutsches Wörterbuch* (Berlin: Langenscheidt, [28]1910), I, pp. 443 and 604, under the related words "*peiro*" and "*phero.*"

2   See W. Worringer, *Ägyptische Kunst: Probleme ihrer Wertung* (Munich: Piper, 1927), p. 11.

3   We wish to emphasize that inasmuch as the subject of this chapter is "The History of the Phenomena of Soul and Spirit" we are not concerned with the psychiatric question which we have already addressed in our discussion of modern psychology in our *Abendländische Wandlung* (Zürich: Oprecht, 1943 ff.); *Gesamtausgabe*, I, pp. 173–323. We are here inquiring into the soul or psyche and the spirit, and how their "history" is to be considered, not into the sufferings or maladies of the psyche and their treatment. This approach may seem naive or antiquated, but it has not been pursued or explained, even by psychiatry. Moreover, the simplest questions and approaches are often the most difficult; the more complex are more easily answered, as they are restricted to more specific areas.

4   Karl Joël, *Wandlungen der Weltanschauung: eine Philosophiegeschichte als Geschichtsphilosophie* (Tübingen: Mohr, 1929–1934), II.

5   Benedetto Croce, *Die Geschichte als Gedanke und als Tat* (Bern: Francke, 1945); *Theorie und Geschichte der Historiographie* (Tübingen: Mohr, 1930); *Die Philosophie Giambattista Vicos* (Tübingen: Mohr, 1927).

6   We again encounter the root *da* in this word "dates"!

7   Menge-Güthling (note 1), p. 285.

8   See Grimm's *Wörterbuch*, IV, column 3857 ff.

9   Rudolf Otto, *Das Heilige* (Munich: Beck, [23]1936); *Das Gefühl des Überweltlichen* (Munich: Beck, 1932).

10   As yet, etymological research has not been able to determine with certainty the root for the group of words to which *heil*, "whole, healed" and *heilig*, "holy," belong; however, on the basis of the available conjectures and the connotation of the words, we can conclude that their root is *kĕl*. Kluge-Götze (note 1), p. 240 f., traces *heil* and *heilig* to pre-Germanic *kailos*; Grimm (note 8), IV, 2, column 815, points to Greek *kalos*, "beautiful, good," while Grimm, Menge-Güthling, and Boisacq, *Dictionnaire étymologique de la langue grecque* (Paris: Klincksieck, [2]1923), p. 399, all trace *kalos* to Sanskrit *kalyas*, "healthy," as well as to Sanskrit *kalyanas*, "beautiful," although Grimm and Menge-Güthling make no mention of the root, and Boisacq assumes the root *qe:qa*, noting the possible kinship with Latin *carus*, "dear, valuable." Alois Walde, *Lateinisches etymologisches Wörterbuch* (Heidelberg: Winter, 1906), p. 101, and Walde Hofmann, *Lateinisches etymologisches Wörterbuch* (Heidelberg: Winter, [3]1938), p. 357, adduce the root *qa:qe* as a conjecture for Latin *carus*; Kluge-Götze, however, surmises a relationship between *heil* and Greek *chaire* (p. 240), which according to Menge-Güthling has the root *ger* (p. 617, entry "chairo"). Kluge-Götze, on the other hand, points to the demonstrated kinship between *heil* and English "whole," which is corroborated by Skeat in his *Etymological Dictionary of the English Language* (Oxford: Clarendon, 1935), p. 714. Both Skeat and Trübner, *Deutsches Wörterbuch* (Berlin: de Gruyter, 1937), III, p. 381 f., trace both words to the Indo-European *koilos*, "whole, entire"; since Kluge-Götze as well as Skeat also relate it to English "heal," presumably akin to Greek *holos*, "whole," we can presume the root to be Indo-Germanic *kĕl*. Menge-Güthling does not mention a root, but does list the following cognates of *holos*: Sanskrit *sarvas*, "unscathed, whole"; Latin *salvus*, "whole," and *solidus*, "solid"; Gothic *sels*, "good, useful"; Old High German *salig*, "blessed, blissful"; New High German *selig*, with the same connotations of "blessed" and "blissful." Sanskrit *sárvas* (çarvas?) could perhaps be traced to the root *kĕl* on the basis of the Indo-European sonant shift; on this subject see Ernout/Meillet, *Dictionnaire étymologique de la langue latine* (Paris: Klincksieck, 1932), p. 157 ff.

11   G. van der Leeuw, *Phänomenologie der Religion* (Tübingen: Mohr, [2]1933), p. 5, from which the quote from Codrington is taken.

12   Rudolf Otto, *Das Gefühl des Überweltlichen* (note 9), p. 55.

13   E. B. Tylor, *Primitive Culture*, 1872; German edition: *Die Anfänge der Cultur* (Leipzig: Winter, 1873), II.

14   J. G. Frazer, *The Golden Bough* (London: Macmillan, [3]1920), XII; abridged ed. (London: Macmillan, 1922), on which the German translation was based: *Der goldene Zweig* (Leipzig: Hirschfeld, 1928). We have not had access to R. R. Marett, *The Threshold of Religion* (London, 1909), but have quoted it from van der Leeuw (note 11) and Schmalenbach (note 17 below).

15   See particularly L. Lévy-Bruhl, *Les fonctions mentales dans les sociétés inférieures* (Paris: Alcan, [9]1928).

16   N. Söderblom, *Das Werden des Gottesglaubens* (Leipzig: Hinrichs, 1916); it was first published in 1915 in Swedish.

17   H. Schmalenbach, "Die Entstehung des Seelenbegriffes," *Logos*, 16 (1927), pp. 311–355.

18   Schmalenbach, p. 318 ff.

19   See van der Leeuw (note 11), p. 261, note 1. For more on the Egyptian designations for the soul (of which there are seven, most likely corresponding to the seven planetary spheres), see E. A. Wallis Budge, *The Book of the Dead* (London: Kegan Paul, [2]1923), I, as well as his *Egyptian Religion: Egyptian Ideas of Future Life*, Books on Egypt and Chaldea 1 (London: Kegan Paul, 1899). To the extensive scholarship on Egyptology by Lepsius, Erman, Maspero, Kees, Moret, Jecquier, Petries, Breasted, Naville, and Sethe, among others, we would add the study by Gertrud Thausing, *Der Auferstehungsgedanke in ägyptischen religiösen Texten* (Leipzig: Harassowitz, 1943), which examines the functioning of *ka*.

20 Menge-Güthling (note 1), p. 264, also refers to the kinship of this word to German *Ader* "vein, artery," which is further related to Greek *etron*, meaning "belly, lower abdomen."

21 This enumeration of the eight originally numinous terms is taken from Schmalenbach (note 17), where they are mentioned without further comment.

22 Menge-Güthling (note 1), p. 275 f., and our "Fifth Remark on Etymology," p. 558.

23 Menge-Güthling (note 1), p. 113, and our "Third Remark on Etymology," p. 555.

24 Söderblom (note 16), p. 81.

25 Aristotle, *De anima*, trans. A. Busse (Leipzig: Meiner, 1911), pp. 11 f. and 31 ff. On the sentence of Parmenides, see among others Paul Natorp, *Über Platons Ideenlehre*, Philosophische Vorträge veröffentlicht von der Kantgesellschaft 5 (Berlin: Reuther & Reichard, 1914), p. 4 ff. Aristotle further emphasizes the element of movement by associating the soul with breath (pp. 11 and 98, note 36); (exhalation expresses the soul's death-pole, while breath is identified in Greek with the soul). This fundamental interrelation of breath and soul is still widely ignored in contemporary European medicine and psychology, despite the fact that the verb *psychein*, from which the word psyche is derived means "to breathe, aspirate" in Greek, whereby "aspiration" shows a tendency toward exhalation.

26 A. Dyroff has furnished evidence that the well-known opening of the Gospel of John, "In the beginning was the word," (*en arche ēn ho logos*), not only bears the stamp of Heraclitus but most likely derives from him; see "Zum Prolog des Johannes-Evangeliums," *Antike und Christentum: Festschrift für F. J. Dölger*, Ergänzungsband I: Pisiculi (Münster: Aschendorff, 1939), pp. 86–93.

27 Hans Leisegang, *Pneuma Hagion* (Leipzig: Hinrichs, 1922).

28 Even the most important early Christian hymn, *Veni creator spiritus*, can be said to underscore this *psychic*-dynamic content of the notion of spirit.

29 The fact that we can speak of this path as being a paradox is further evidence that this individual conception of man, God, soul, spirit, the devil, etc., even with respect to man, shows its irrational, religious emphasis despite, or even because of, its rational fixity. Paradox and paradoxical facts are always the expression of at least a mythical state of consciousness, as we will see from our discussion in the next chapter.

30 See Jean Gebser, *In der Bewährung* (Bern: Francke, 1962), pp. 107, 117 et passim; *Gesamtausgabe*, V/I, pp. 254, 265, et passim.

31 See among others Schmalenbach (note 17), p. 327.

32 We are not overlooking the fact that man as an artist has a decisive role in this process since it is man who has the ability to shape from within himself this pre-given numinosity in accord with the scope of conscious intensity (or dimensioning) that has been attained in any given instance. Art, then, in these terms is that expression of man with which he bestows human validity and reality, and thus efficacy, on the numinosum in accordance with his respective consciousness structure.

33 See also Jan Tschichold's *Neue chinesische Farbendrucke der Zehnbambushalle*, published, as were the other two works mentioned, *Farbendrucke aus der Zehnbambushalle*, and the *Lehrbuch des Senfkorngartens*, by Holbein in Basel (1943–1946).

34 With this phrase we mean to counter the erroneous terminology that refers to "layers" of the unconscious. Our use of the term "levels" in the first edition of Part I of the present work was merely an expedient to define the variously dimensioned types of consciousness, and we expressly noted its inadequacy. In a literal sense, only the two-dimensional mythical "plane" has the nature of a "level"; the magic structure is punctiform, the mental spatial. In the present edition, as well as in the first edition of Part II (1953), we have replaced the term "level" by "structure." For a discussion of the term "consciousness frequency" or "vibrancy," see G. R. Heyer, "Umgang mit dem Symbol," *Kritische Psychotherapie*, ed. Ernst Speer (Munich: Lehmann, 1959), later published in Heyer's *Seelenkunde im Umbruch der Zeit* (Bern: Huber, 1964), p. 117 ff., and particularly p. 130.

35 The term "ambivalence" to denote the bi- or di-valence of psychic events and expres-

sions stems from E. Bleuler and was used by him primarily to designate psycho-pathological behavior in his *Lehrbuch der Psychiatrie* (Berlin: Springer, [7]1943), p. 72 et passim. See also his *Naturgeschichte der Seele* (Berlin: Springer, [2]1942), p. 186 et passim.

36   E. A. Wallis Budge, *Egyptian Magic*, Books on Egypt and Chaldea 2 (1899); *The Book of the Dead II*, same series, VII, 2 (London: Kegan Paul, 1899 and [2]1909). The first edition of the *Book of the Dead* by Budge was issued in 1898 (minus vignettes); the third edition (1920) is an unaltered reprint of the second (1909). The complete edition of the Ani-papyrus furnished additional material: E. A. Wallis Budge, *The Book of the Dead: The Papyrus of Ani, Scribe and Treasurer of the Temples of Egypt about B.C. 1450*, (New York: Putnam; London: Medici, 1913), II. There is a French version of the texts by Naville and a German by Sethe; a more recent German translation is that of Gregoire Kol-paktchy, *Das aegyptische Totenbuch* (München-Planegg: Barth, 1955). A valuable com-plement to these works is A. Dieterich's *Eine Mithrasliturgie* (Leipzig: Teubner, [3]1923), p. 100 f. The legends under the vignettes we have used for the present work are from Budge; our emendations are in square brackets. Fig. 25 is from the Ani-papyrus, Budge, vii, 2, p. 272, and Kolpaktchy, p. 28.

37   *Odyssey*, XXIV, 5, 6, 9.

38   Regarding the "Celestial journey of the soul and its conception," see the *Vorträge 1928–1929 der Bibliothek Warburg* (Leipzig: Teubner, 1930), and the articles by Kees and Reitzenstein on the Egyptian and Christian views, respectively. A Rüegg's work repre-sents a Catholic standpoint: *Die Jenseitsvorstellungen vor Dante* (Einsiedeln: Benziger, 1945), II.

39   Georg Weicker, *Der Seelenvogel in der alten Literatur und Kunst* (Leipzig: Teubner, 1902), p. 38.

40   For illustrations of the few surviving representations of this type see Carl Robert, *Thana-tos* (Berlin: Reimer, 1879), and also *L'Art Grec* (Paris: Ed. Cahiers d'Art, 1938), plate 299. There are also descriptions of similar representations in G. Rathgeber's monumental *Nike in hellenischen Vasenbildern: zusammengesetzte und geflügelte Gestalten in den Denkmälern der Kunst der Babylonier, Assyrier, Phoiniker* (Gotha: Müller, 1857). There is also the recent work by Werner Schmalenbach, *Griechische Vasenbilder* (Basel: Birk-häuser, 1948); see particularly p. 140.

41   See G. Weicker (note 39), pp. 1, 5, 28 f., and 31 f.

42   From the voluminous literature on angels we would mention the following interpreta-tions: van der Leeuw (note 11), p. 123 ff., considers angels to be the embodiment of "special power"; A. Neander refers to the Gnostic conceptions of the Ebionites, who saw the angels as "nature spirits," in his *Genetische Entwickelung der vornehmsten gnostischen Systeme* (Berlin: Dümmler, 1818), p. 404 f.; in this regard, see also A. Schliemann, *Die Clementinen nebst den verwandten Schriften und der Ebionitismus* (Hamburg: Perthes, 1844), p. 520, and E. H. Schmitt, *Die Gnosis* (Jena: Diederichs, 1903), I, p. 525; also, from a Catholic viewpoint, Georg Köpgen, *Die Gnosis des Christentums* (Salzburg: Müller, 1939), p. 175 ff. F. Cumont, in his "Les Vents et les Anges psycho-pompes," *Festschrift für F. J. Dölger* (note 26), p. 70 ff., emphasizes their aspect as guides of the soul. Hahn refers to the ancient conception prevalent also among Albian Catharii that Christ was an angelic being in his *Geschichte der Ketzer im Mittelalter: Geschichte der neumanichäischen Ketzer* (Stuttgart, 1845), p. 65. Martin Werner's *Die Entstehung des christlichen Dogmas* (Bern: Haupt, 1941), is a large-scale attempt at an angelic Chris-tology; see the response to Werner's book by W. Michaelis, *Zur Engelchristologie im Urchristentum* (Basel: Majer, 1942). Of the more important "angelologies" we would mention those by Philo (Dionysius Areopagita, *Über die beiden Hierarchien*, Bibliothek der Kirchenväter [Kempten: Kösel, 1911], new translation under the title *Die Heirar-chien der Engel und Kirche* [München-Planegg: Barth, 1955]; Thomas Aquinas, *Summa theologica*, I, 44–65; in the German edition, volume 4, *Schöpfung und Engelwelt* [Leip-zig: Pustet, 1936]), as well as the grand angelic visions in the apocryphal "Shepherd of Hermas" (*Neutestamentliche Apokryphen*, ed. Edgar Hennecke [Tübingen: Mohr, [2]1924], p. 327 ff.). We can only allude here to the Sohar and the Islamic conceptions that

strongly influenced Dante, but we do wish to mention a further study of the Islamic tradition that elaborates on the double nature of angels; see, in addition to the works mentioned earlier, L. H. Gray, "The Double Nature of the Iranian Archangels," *Archiv für Religionswissenschaft* 7, 3/4, ed. A. Diederich/Th. Achelis, pp. 345-372.

43   See G. Weicker (note 39), pp. 84 and 88, as well as p. 56 ff., where he elaborates on the Pythagorean-Platonic equation of Sirens with the stars (which were considered the abode of the souls), as well as the resultant equation of the harmony of the spheres with the song of the Sirens. The demons of death, which are parts of the soul, are reinterpreted as benign spirits, which would not be possible if this aspect had not been inherent in them from the very outset. What Weicker fails to see is that they are merely the counterpole of the Muses. We must also consider the fact that the Sirens in Plato recover that aspect which they had as *baw*, for the demonic aspect of abduction is characteristically and singularly Greek. We should also not forget that Plato was, according to tradition, initiated into the mysteries in Egypt. Regarding the equivalence of souls, Muses or Sirens and the stars, see especially Plato's *Timaeus*, 41 D ff. As to the "harmony of the spheres" and conceptions of "harmonicality," see (besides the works of Kepler, von Thimus and H. Kayser) the relevant remarks of F. Piper, *Mythologie der christlichen Kunst* (Weimar: Comptoir, 1847–1851), II, p. 245 ff., and A. Böckh, "Über die Bildung der Weltseele im Timäos des Platon," *Studien*, ed. C. Daub and F. Creuzer (Heidelberg: Mohr, 1807), III, p. 1–95.

44   For a similar representation showing the deceased with his soul above him, see Kolpaktchy (note 36), p. 57, fig. 10.

45   Around the time of Alexander the Great the word *psyche* came to denote the "butterfly" in addition to "soul, life, breath." It was applied mainly to the moth; see C. A. Böttiger, *Ideen zur Kunstmythologie* (Leipzig: Arnold, 1850), II, pp. 418 f. and 457 f., as well as S. Reinach, *Orpheus* (Paris: Picard, ⁶1918), p. 118, and in the German edition (Vienna: Eisenstein, ²1910), p. 78. As a curiosity we would mention that R. M. deAngelis speaks of Brazilian moths which "have on their wings depictions of the skull" in his *Brasilianisches Tagebuch* (sections translated into German by Hedwig Kehrli), *Neue Zürcher Zeitung* 719 (May 20, 1947). For depictions of the butterfly as a symbol of soul or psyche, see Creuzer, *Symbolik und Mythologie der alten Völker, bes. der Griechen* (Darmstadt: Leske, ²1819), Atlas, plates xxxvii and lvi, fig. 3, and the description p. 25, no. 39, and p. 27, no. 47.

46   F. Creuzer (note 45), III, p. 365, and I, p. 375; see also F. Nork, *Andeutungen eines Systems der Mythologie* (Leipzig: Dyk, 1850), p. 175, note 61; and Georges Lanoe-Villène, *Le Livre des Symboles* (Paris: Bossard/Librarie Générale, 1927–1937), I, p. 11 ff.

47   L. von Schroeder points to the survival of this mythic-psychic relationship between the soul and the star on the basis of a Russian gravestone inscription mentioned in Gorky's novel *Die Drei* (Leipzig, 1902), II, p. 262: "The earth is poorer by one flower . . . the heavens richer by one star"; see L. von Schroeder, *Arische Religion* (Leipzig: Haessel, 1914), I, p. 75, note 1.

48   Paul Deussen, *Sechzig Upanishad's des Veda* (Leipzig: Brockhaus, ³1921), p. 24; also in Deussen's *Die Geheimlehre des Veda* (Leipzig: Brockhaus, ⁶1921), p. 139 f., as well as in the *Mythologische Bibliothek* (Leipzig: Hinrichs, 1907–1916), VII, 4 (1916), p. 51 f. Regarding this passage from the Kaushitaki-Brahmana Upanishad, see also Chantepie de la Saussaye, *Lehrbuch der Religionsgeschichte* (Tübingen: Mohr, ²1925), II, p. 57, as well as Wilhelm Bousset, *Hauptprobleme der Gnosis*, Forschungen zur Religion und Literatur des Alten und Neuen Testaments 10 (Göttingen, 1907), p. 345, and F. Chr. Baur, *Das manichäische Religionssystem* (Tübingen: Ossiander, 1831), p. 308, which furnishes further parallels from Manichean and Indic religions.

49   Paul Deussen, *Sechzig Upanishad's des Veda* (note 48), p. 433.

50   According to F. M. Müller, not only "man," "human," and "measure," but also "moon" and "month" as well as the Latin word for "month," *mensis*, and even *Maya* can be derived from the root *ma;* F. Max Müller, *Die Wissenschaft von der Sprache* (Leipzig:

Englemann, 1892), I, p. 5. F. Cumont refers to a Phrygian moon-god *Men* who symbolizes the relationships mentioned in the text; see his *Die orientalischen Religionen im römischen Heidentum* (Leipzig: Teubner, ²1914), p. 23 ff.

51 See Karl Kerényi, *Pythagoras und Orpheus* (Amsterdam: Pantheon, ²1940), pp. 53 and 59; see also Roscher, *Ausführliches Lexikon der griechischen und römischen Mythologie* (Leipzig: Teubner, 1894–1897), II, 2, column 44 f., particularly the references that associate *Selene* with water.

52 See F. Chr. Baur (note 48), pp. 226 f., 277, and 311.

53 Plutarch, "Über den Vollzug der göttlichen Strafen," *Vermischte Schriften*, trans. Kaltwasser (Munich: Müller, 1911), III, p. 487f.

54 See Deussen (note 49), pp. 24, 128, and 143.

55 Both references cited according to Hugo Rahner, S.J., "Mysterium lunae," *Zeitschrift für katholische Theologie* 63 (1939), p. 311 f., and 64 (1940), p. 61 ff., where Rahner discusses a "theology of death" in connection with patristic "lunar theology."

56 With reference to the American continent, see in particular the *Annual Reports of the Bureau of American Ethnology to the Secretary of the Smithsonian Institution* (Washington, 1882-). See also J. G. Müller, *Geschichte der amerikanischen Urreligionen* (Basel: Schweighauser, 1855); L. Schultze-Jena, *Indiana* (Jena: Fischer, 1933, 1935, 1938); and H. Leicht, *Indianische Kunst und Kultur* (Zürich: Füssli, 1944). For the continent of Africa see, among others, L. Frobenius, ed., *Atlantis: Volksmärchen und Volksdichtungen Afrikas* (Jena: Diederichs, 1921-), XII.

57 It is noteworthy that this lunar crescent, represented as a waxing force along with the hammer, reappears in the most rational emblem of our day, where the sickle and hammer serve as allegorical representations of the farmer and the laborer. But this allegorization does not prevent them from retaining an ambivalent and lasting symbolic valuation. From time immemorial, the hammer has served to express the creative, solar-masculine principle and not merely to symbolize destruction, whereas the moon, at least among the ancients, was identified with the psyche. The two symbols, moreover, are depicted as being complementary by their intersecting, and are placed in or under the five-pointed star, a symbol for man as well as for the five-continent earth. We have here a clear symbolic indication of the way in which one sector of humanity intends to go: as far as possible along the exclusively tellurian-anthropocentric route. The two primordial forces, sun and moon, are here related only to the earth and man, thus creating a complete identification between man and the earth. This furnishes an explanation for the Marxist maxim that "history" is, or had better be, a creation of man. But even with respect to this earth the maxim cannot prove itself, for it remains a star among stars which share its destiny and history. - This allegory also admits a certain prognosis for those who are allegorizing it; wherever, as in this case, an attempt is made to dispose of and negate the symbolic- and psychic-energy-laden content of a symbol by a fanatically rational stance, the irrational character of the chosen symbol one day breaks through, sweeping away the skeleton-like scaffolding of the *ratio*, as the storm tides wash away the docks. Regarding the symbolism of the hammer, see J. J. Bachofen, *Versuch über die Gräbersymbolik der Alten* (Basel: Helbing, ²1925), p. 365, as well as his *Mutterrecht* (Basel: Schwabe, ²1897), p. 64, column 1. On p. 40, column 2, there is a discussion of the equivalence of moon with the psyche in antiquity, spoken of earlier.

58 Our often-repeated contention that all imagery is primarily psychic is also supported by the fact that "many peoples have only one term or expression for the three notions of soul, image and shadow"; Negelein, "Bild, Spiegel und Schatten im Volksglauben," *Archiv für Religionswissenschaft* 5 (1902), cited in Martin Ninck, *Die Bedeutung des Wassers im Kult und Leben der Alten* (Leipzig: Dieterich, 1929), p. 58.

59 See Grimm, *Deutsches Wörterbuch*, IX, column 2851 ff.

60 See also Jean Gebser, *Abendländische Wandlung* (note 3), p. 170 f.; ²1945, p. 196 f.; ³1950, p. 175; Ullstein ed. No. 107, p. 174; *Gesamtausgabe*, I, p. 298.

61 Spanish provides a parallel phenomenon: both *el mar* and *la mar* mean "lake" as well as

"ocean"; in German, however, there is a distinction made between *die See* (f., "ocean, sea") and *der See* (m., "lake") lacking in Spanish.

62   Diels-Kranz, *Die Fragmente der Vorsokratiker* (Berlin: Weidmann, ³1934), I, fragment 22 B 36.

63   Montesquieu, *Cahiers* (Paris: Grasset, 1941), p. 217.

64   Diels-Kranz (note 62), fragment 36, conclusion; the entire fragment is cited below in the context of the next chapter, p. 252.

65   Marcel Proust, *À la Recherche du Temps perdu*, x, *Sodom et Gomorrhe*, part 2 (Paris: NRF, n.d.).

66   Strangely enough, this particular work has been omitted from the London edition of the *Gesammelte Werke chronologisch geordnet* (London: Imago, 1941 ff.).

67   J. J. Bachofen, *Urreligion und antike Symbole*, selected and edited from his works by C. A. Bernoulli (Leipzig: Reclam, 1926), I, 50, 171, and 345; see also his *Gräbersymbolik* (note 57), p. 345 f.

68   *Schweizer Lexikon* (Zürich: Encyclios, 1945), I, column 1.

69   The primordial element (most certainly magical) is expressed by the musicality of these verses, as well as in the vital-sexual overtones of the "ich kann," emphasized by the following dash.

70   The water symbolism of the soul has definite echoes in two of the most famous poems of German Romanticism, whose widespread familiarity is symptomatic; in Goethe's "Gesang der Geister über den Wassern," ("Song of the Spirits over the Waters,") which concludes, "Soul of man mortal, how art thou like water! / Fate of man mortal, how art thou like wind!" both poles of the soul are recognized; and in Hölderlin's "Hyperions Schicksalslied," ("Hyperion's Song of Destiny,") the "breathing of the heavenly host" is juxtaposed with water to which human life is compared.

71   Salomon Reinach has pointed out this symbolic content of the dolphin in his *Répertoire des vases peints grecs et étrusques* (Paris: Leroux, 1899–1900), II, p. 309, legend for figure 3. On the basis of ancient sources, Melitta Rabinovitch recalls this content in her book *Der Delphin in Sage und Mythos der Griechen* (Dornach Basel: Hybernia, 1947), pp. 8 and 37, note 2; see also p. 32, as well as Martin Ninck (note 58), p. 159 ff., for a discussion of the water symbolism of the fish. This type of symbolism, incidentally, may well be an anticipation of certain Christian character traits already known in antiquity. We should on the other hand point to the relationship between the dolphin and Delphi, to which M. Rabinovitch alludes on p. 20 of her book, while Menge-Güthling (note 1), p. 131, traces both words to the probable Indo-European root *gelbh*, meaning "to hollow, scoop out, arch." From this same root Sanskrit *garbhas* and Greek *delphys* derive, both with the meaning of "(mother's) lap." We might also note that this root resembles the sound of the frequently mentioned root *gel:kel*. It is also worth noting in connection with this relationship between the oracle at Delphi and the dolphin as a symbol of the sea, that in Delphi sacrifices were offered in remembrance of rescue from the flood of Deukalion, a circumstance noted by H. Usener, *Sintflutsagen* (Bonn: Cohen, 1899), p. 40. See also our "Third Remark on Etymology," p. 555.

72   See in particular R. Reitzenstein, *Die Vorgeschichte der christlichen Taufe* (Leipzig: Teubner, 1929).

73   On the Kabbalistic-hermetic tradition, consult the entry "Azoth" in Dom Antoine-Joseph Pernety's *Dictionnaire Mytho-hermétique dans lequel on trouve les Allégories Fabuleuses des Poètes, les Méthaphores, les Enigmes, et les Termes Barbares des Philosophes hermétiques expliqués* (Paris: Delalein, ²1787), p. 52, based principally on Arnaud de Villeneuve.

74   Diels-Kranz (note 62), 22 B 12.

75   A "separation" of the aspects of the soul similar to ours, although emphasizing the dualistic rather than the polar nature of soul, can be found in the two books of Gaston Bachelard, *L'Air et les Songes: Essai sur l'Imagination du Mouvement* (Paris: Corti, 1943), and *L'Eau et les Rêves: Essai sur l'Imagination de la Matière* (Paris: Corti, 1942). Both

books contain a wealth of information relevant to the two aspects of soul discussed here. Unfortunately, they became accessible to us in 1949 only after sections 3 and 4 of this chapter were already written, having formed the basis of our lectures held in 1947, as is true also of the following sections (see note 3 on page 102).

76   The most celebrated oracular utterance of this kind is the response given to Croesus by Pythia before his war with Cyrus: "You will destroy a great empire," she said; it was to be his own.

77   The root of this word is *g(w)el*, meaning "to throw"; see Menge-Güthling (note 1), p. 106, entry "ballo." It too may be regarded as a mirror root of *leg*, on which the word "light" is based. We take this opportunity to emphasize that in view of the concentrated value accorded to each root sound, even the slightest nuance is significant; consequently every approximation of similar roots necessitates the utmost care in analysis. Our various remarks on such root affinities or kinships should be understood with this caution in mind. And there is one further point: a mirroring, or reversal of the sound sequence undoubtedly applies to the auditory as well as to the visual aspect; in the earliest period the reversal was not limited merely to the visual process but also to the auditory which at that time was hardly differentiated; see our discussion above, p. 127.

78   In this regard see Diels-Kranz (note 62), fragment 22 B 88, as well as the *Heraklit-Fragmente*, trans. B. Snell, Tusculum–Bücherei (Munich: Heimeran, ²1940), p. 23.

79   Cited according to *Die versprengten Worte Jesu* (Munich: Hyperion, 1922), p. 104, which includes a source reference.

80   This pre-archaic "existence" of the primordial symbol excludes from the outset any identification with, say, "archetypes" (C. G. Jung). From the standpoint of primordial symbols, the archetypes are psychic elaborations and aspectuations of the non-psychically bound primordial design.

81   *Vernunft*, "reason," is derived from *vernehmen*, "to feel or sense"; see Kluge-Götze (note 1), p. 652.

82   See Marcel Granet, *Pensée chinoise* (Paris: Michel, 1934), p. 281, where he speaks of an "interdiction de prêter une valeur à 1" for the T'ai-Ki. Our vignette is found there on p. 280 (vignette 12). A German translation of this important work was published under the title, *Das chinesische Denken* (Munich: Piper, 1963); see note 98 on p. 111 above.

83   D. T. Suzuki, *Zen und die Kultur Japans* (Stuttgart: Deutsche Verlags-Anstalt, 1941), and *Die grosse Befreiung: Einführung in den Zen-Buddhismus*, with a foreword by C. G. Jung. We are familiar with the manifold paths of Hindu Yoga; they "correspond" to the Hindu who does not think rationally and still lives predominantly in the mythical structure. These paths are inappropriate for Europeans, in our estimation, or even detrimental within the European milieu, if for no other reason than because the complete suppression or exclusion of volition is possible only for the few. The contemporary European can scarcely distinguish any longer between effort of will, intensive concentration, and true meditation, since he attempts to direct all of them by his rationality—an attempt that necessarily leads to unfortunate results. For more on Suzuki, see Jean Gebser, *Asienfibel* (Berlin and Frankfurt/M.: Ullstein ed. 650, 1962 ff.), pp. 79 ff. and 166 ff.; *Gesamtausgabe*, VI, pp. 80 ff. and 161 f.

84   In a conversation in Kitakamakura, Japan, in 1961, the aged Zen-master Daisetzu Teitaro Suzuki emphatically agreed with me that "Satori" must in no way be confused with Indic "Samadhi!" Satori is one possibility inherent in the arational (integral) consciousness structure for entering or participating in time freedom; Samadhi, on the other hand, is a means of reverting to magic-mythical timelessness, appropriate to the corresponding irrational consciousness structure. We have indicated this distinction in our foreword to *Die Zen-Lehre des chinesischen Meisters Huang Po* (Weilheim/Obb.: Barth, 1960), p. 7 ff., where we emphasize that "Zen has nothing in common with vague mysticism since Zen, despite opinions to the contrary, is not mysticism." If the Satori experience of Zen were not of an arational nature, it would then of course be equivalent to the irrational-mystical-vital experience of Samadhi. But we again remind the reader that this is not so,

and the same opinion is shared by Zen-master Shizuteru Ueda (Kyoto); see his contribution "Der Zen-Buddhismus als 'Nicht-Mystik' unter besonderer Berücksichtigung des Vergleichs zur Mystik Meister Eckharts," *Transparente Welt: Festschrift für Jean Gebser* (Bern: Huber, 1965).

85   See E. H. Schmitt (note 42), I, p. 596 f., who cites the translation of this passage from the *Acta disputationis cum Maneto* of Archelaus, chapter 7, quoted in Gfrörer, *Kirchengeschichte*, I, p. 467.

86   Paul Deussen, *Vier philosophische Texte des Mahâbhâratam* (Leipzig: Brockhaus, 1906), p. 6.

87   The illustration is taken from M. Rabinovitch (note 71), fig. 8, and is also in P. Hartwig, *Die griechischen Meisterschalen der Blüthezeit des strengen rothfigurigen Stiles* (Berlin: Speemann, 1893), plate xiii. A reference to this bronze not mentioned in Rabinovitch can be found in H. Usener (note 71), p. 221; he also reproduces an additional illustration similar to this of a medallion relief, as well as several of the many coins bearing the dolphin motif. In these representations Usener sees indications of a "myth" of the "journey of departed souls to the blessed isles"—a conception shared also by F. Piper, *Mythologie der christlichen Kunst* (note 43), I, p. 222, but this would account for only one aspect of the symbolic representation. The author has in his possession a small Chinese bronze from the mid-nineteenth century depicting the "god with the blissful smile"; he holds a dolphin, and on his back wears a wing-like bow. The author also has an early Hellenistic figurine from Tanagra. It depicts a dolphin on which a winged child—symbol of the human soul—is riding, holding in its left arm a grave stela.

88   Representations which, on the basis of our interpretation, may be considered equivalent to our illustrations can be found on a vase drawing which depicts a goddess driving a wagon drawn by two winged horses (*Pegasoi*). Under these horses a dolphin is depicted. Still another amphora shows Athena with a shield bearing the image of a dolphin, with a Siren near her head; reproductions are in S. Reinach, *Répertoire* (note 71), II, p. 309, fig. 3, and I, p. 214, fig. 4. In addition there is a reproduction of an ancient cameo depicting a winged boy, judged to be Eros, riding on a dolphin; illustration in J. D. Guignaut-Millin, *Nouvelle Galerie Mythologique* (Paris: Didot, ²1835), plate cxxii, no. 511, as well as in Millin, *Mythologische Galerie* (Berlin: Nicolai, ³1848), plate xlii, fig. 177. A Hellenistic sculpture entitled "Eros with Dolphin" is illustrated in Giacomo Prampolini, *La Mitologia nella vita dei popoli* (Milan: Hoepli, 1937), I, p. 405.

89   *Pistis Sophia: Ein gnostisches Originalwerk des dritten Jahrhunderts*, translated from the Coptic by Carl Schmidt (Leipzig: Hinrichs, 1925), p. 278 ff. For further Gnostic Nekyia reports, see Wilhelm Bousset, *Hauptprobleme der Gnosis* (note 48), p. 255 ff.

90   "Pathos" comes from *pathein* which originally meant "to suffer, endure," and is related to the word "passion."

91   Reproduced here three times actual size; from F. Creuzer (note 45), ¹1810, I, table vii, fig. 3. It is also reproduced in Creuzer (²1819), *Tafelband*, plate vii, fig. 3, with the description on p. 63 f; it is missing in the third edition of 1836 and in the abridged edition of 1822, although it is reproduced in Guigniaut-Millin (note 88), plate cclxii, fig. 959. Creuzer, who mentions neither the importance of the illustration as a symbol for the soul, nor its syncretistic nature, obtained it from Bishop F. Münter, but it is not included in Münter's *Sinnbilder und Kunstvorstellungen der alten Christen* (Altona: Hammerich, 1825), II. We would also mention that the same symbolism can be seen in a Greek drawing which depicts a boy at sacrifice with a dove and font of holy water; illustrated in Creuzer (note 45), *Tafelband*, plate xi, description p. 47, no. 75. We cannot consider here the fire symbolism present in some of the representations, although it is a natural complement to the water aspect of soul present there, and should be evaluated accordingly although it is more a symbolization of the psychified aspect of the spirit. Its complementarity comes as a natural result of the polarity inherent in the soul, and is evident in the pictorial representation of the multifarious polarizing and complementary elements. One such

example will have to suffice here: a (winged) Siren holding a water jug in one hand and a torch in the other (reproduction in Guignaut-Millin, note 88 above, plate cxxviii, no. 527, and Millin, also note 88, plate lxxx, no. 312.

92* [Cited according to the German edition, Omar Khayyam, *Die Sprüche der Weisheit* ed. and tran. Hector G. Preconi (Zürich: Rascher, ²1946); English readers are familiar with the lines in the version by FitzGerald: "Into this Universe, and *Why* not knowing / Nor *Whence*, like Water willy-nilly flowing; / And out of it, as Wind along the Waste, / I know not *Whither*, willy-nilly blowing" *Rubaiyat*, xxix.]

93   See Otto Weininger, *Taschenbuch und Briefe an einen Freund* (Leipzig: Tal, 1920), p. 59. Needless to say, not every "rapping" or "shattering" sound is meant. Weininger speaks of a certain materialized exteriorization of psychic energy which can no longer be maintained by the body during the process of its dissolution, or during extreme weakness, and is thus manifest outwardly. The frequently observed "coincidental" stopping of the clock at the moment of death is a parallel phenomenon.

94   See Martin Buber and Franz Rosenzweig, *Die Schrift und ihre Verdeutschung* (Berlin: Schocken, 1936), p. 160 ff.

95   From a saying of Sextus Empiricus based on Heraclitus, we know that the early Logos-"concept" was psychically stressed and represented, as it were, a counterpole of the psyche, whose breath-character was manifest primarily in expiration and exhalation (see text above, p. 210). Sextus writes, "According to the teaching of Heraclitus, we take in this divine Logos through our breath and thereby gain understanding" Diels-Kranz (note 62), 22 A 16. Western psychology has generally overlooked the influence of breath and breathing on psychic events, although admittedly the European, given his expectation or living-towards-something and never just living, would find it hard to take seriously. On the other hand, the Yoga techniques appropriate to the Orient are most likely not in accord with our consciousness structure (see notes 25 and 83 above).

96   See K. Kerényi, *Pythagoras und Orpheus* (note 51), p. 53.

97   See Paul Schmitt, "Studie über Logos, Nous and Psyche bei Heraklit und Platon und über einige späte Nachwirkungen dieser Begriffe," printed under the title "Geist und Seele" in his *Religion, Idee und Staat* (Bern: Francke, 1959); in its original form it was first printed in the *Eranos-Jahrbuch*, 13 (Zürich: Rhein, 1946).

98   See Grimm's *Wörterbuch*, IV, 1, 2, columns 2623–2741. This article, revised by Rudolf Hildebrand, also appeared separately as an offprint in 1926.

99   Trübner, *Deutsches Wörterbuch* (note 10), III, entry "Geist."

100 With regard to the *phos-* (light) and *pyr-* (fire) character of spirit, see among others Leisegang, *Pneuma Hagion* (note 27), p. 76 et passim, as well as E. Wetter, *Phos* (Upsala and Leipzig, 1915), p. 49 ff. The light characteristic of spirit is particularly emphasized by Dionysius Areopagita (note 42) and Joachim von Fioris; see also Thomas Aquinas, *Summa contra gentiles*, III, l; in the edition of Nachod/Stern (Leipzig: Hegner, 1937), III, p. 202; in the translation of H. Fahsel (Zürich: Fraumünster, 1946), III, p. 284. With regard to Fahsel, see also Robert Fast, *Geist und Geschöpf: Studien zur Seinslehre der rein geistigen Wesen im Mittelalter* (Lucerne: Stocker, 1945). For more on the pre-Christian god of light in general see L. von Schroeder (note 7), I, p. 328 ff. On fire symbolism, see particularly Adalbert Kuhn, *Die Herabkunft des Feuers und des Göttertranks* (Berlin: Dummler, 1859).

101 See Leisegang (note 100), p. 28; Weicker (note 39), p. 4 f. On the theology of logos, see J. Pascher, *Der Königsweg zur Wiedergeburt und Vergottung bei Philon von Alexandria* (Paderborn: Schöningh, 1931); on the concept of logos, see M. Heinze, *Die Lehre vom Logos in der griechischen Philosophie* (Oldenburg, 1872), pp. 220 and 278 f. under "Logoi"; Gustav Teichmüller, *Neue Studien zur Geschichte der Begriffe* (Gotha: Perthes, 1876), I, chapter 2, paragraph 6, p. 167 ff.; Ludwig Noiré, *Logos* (Leipzig: Engelmann, 1885); and H. Leisegang's article "Logos" in Pauly-Wissowa, *Reallexikon der Altertumswissenschaften*, xxv (1926), column 1035 ff.

102 The fact that in German the sun and moon, the pre-eminent ruling symbols and representatives of the basic psychic powers, have reversed genders (*die* Sonne, feminine, and *der* Mond, masculine) undoubtedly permits us to conclude that the Germans have a certain compensating function vis-à-vis the other European nations—a function which, if activated in proportion to its inherent value could be of decisive import in constituting an integrated Europe.

103 J. G. Frazer, for example, makes reference to this: "The natives themselves openly deny that children result from sexual intercourse"; *Mensch, Gott und Unsterblichkeit* (Leipzig: Hirschfeld, 1932), p. 75. The role of nine in the psychic realm is evident from an unusually significant discovery of C. G. Jung based on an extended series of dreams over a long period. He noted that almost exactly nine months were required to the day from the first intimation of a vitally important perception in a dream to its full realization in an integral dream. Further experiences seem to suggest that the process of death begins nine months before its actual occurrence; the author has mentioned earlier one such example he has observed in his *Lorca oder das Reich der Mütter* (Stuttgart: Deutsche Verlags-Anstalt, 1949), and *Gesamtausgabe*, I, p. 100. For more on the kinship of *neun*, "nine," with *neu*, "new," see Alois Walde (note 10), p. 419 f., who assumes the kinship from Indo-European times and establishes it on the basis of *novem* and *novus*; it also holds true of Sanskrit *náva-s*, "nine," and *náva*, "new." Old Egyptian gives evidence of the identical word stem for "nine" and "new," the former being related to the moon; see K. Menninger, *Kulturgeschichte der Zahlen* (Breslau: Hirt, 1933), p. 110. In view of the general uncertainty as to the root of the Latin word *ovum*, "egg," according to Walde, we are unable to prove our supposition that *novem:novus* are etymologically related to it.

104 This is also true of the Catholic interpretation; but it must be borne in mind for both the Protestant and Catholic interpretations, that the theological understanding of the term "person" is fundamentally different from the present-day conception. See the respective articles and bibliographies in *Die Religion in Geschichte und Gegenwart: Handwörterbuch für Religion und Religionsgeschichte*, ed. A. Bertholet, H. Gunkel et al. (Tübingen: Mohr, ²1930), II, column 938 ff.; IV, column 1089 ff.

105 C. G. Jung, "Zur Psychologie des Geistes," *Eranos-Jahrbuch*, 13 (Zürich: Rhein, 1946), 385 ff.

106 See van der Leeuw (note 11), p. 15. An extensive selection of textual and pictorial material on the subject of the Holy Spirit can be found in Lothar Schreyer, *Bildnis des Heiligen Geistes* (Freiburg: Herder, 1940). Some remarkable facts on angelology are contained in W. Menzel, *Christliche Symbolik* (Regensburg: Manz, 1854), I, p. 321 ff.

107 See W. Bousset, *Hauptprobleme der Gnosis* (note 48) on the relationship of spirit and water, p. 279 ff., of *pneuma* and *meter*, p. 91 ff. See also Leisegang, (note 100), pp. 38 and 65 f., and the passages cited there from Wetter, *Der Sohn Gottes* (Göttingen, 1916), p. 55 f. For a "Gnostic description of the birth of Christ" see H. Usener, *Das Weihnachtsfest* (Bonn: Cohen, ²1911), I, p. 35, where he discusses the statement, "a source of water unceasingly makes the source of spirit stream forth," the stream in this instance being represented by Mary.

108 Cited according to *Die versprengten Worte Jesu* (note 79), ed. B. Godeschalk, p. 54, and Usener (note 107), p. 118. The two versions are in some respects different. This saying may shed some light on the other mother-related utterance of Jesus: "Woman, what have I to do with Thee?" (John 2:4), particularly if both are examined from the psychological viewpoint of a shift of anima projection (for more on the anima-animus theory of Jung, see note 17 on page 265 below). In any event, the apocryphal saying mirrors in the religious sphere the overpowering emotional response evoked in poetry by the Muse.

109 In addition it should be noted that in the Kabbala the spirit is represented as a celestial woman, at least on the basis of a Sohar commentary in manuscript in the Munich library cited by Windischmann, *Philosophie der Geschichte oder über die Tradition* (Münster, 1834), II, p. 259. And according to W. Bouset (note 48), p. 82, the secret Simoniac cult

revered the lunar goddess Helene-Selena in place of the Gnostic Sophia, both of whom embody the principle of the *spiritus sanctus* and *ruach*.

110   In Part II of the present work we will deal extensively with the basic difference between "spirit" and the "spiritual." This second part is devoted to an attempt at a "concretion of the spiritual," the concretion being in all likelihood the precondition of the integral consciousness structure. Needless to say, our differentiation between the psychically-tinged phenomena of "spirit" and the principle of the spiritual is not the postulation of a new dualism, where the phenomenon would be classifiable, say, as immanent, and the primordial principle as transcendent; rather, we should understand the phenomenon of spirit as a reflection of the primordial principle of the spiritual.

111   See M. Berthelot, *Collection des anciens Alchimistes grecs* (Paris: Steinheil, 1885–1888), fascicle 2, *Les Oeuvres de Zosime*, p. 152: "L'âme diffère de l'esprit."

112   See the version of the Nicene creed in H. Denzinger, *Enchiridion Symbolorum*, 8th-10th editions, (Freiburg: Herder, n.d.), p 29–30.

113   See F. Ch. Baur, *Die christliche Kirche des Mittelalters* (Tübingen: Fuess, 1861), p. 191 ff., as well as S. Pétrement, *Le Dualisme chez Platon, les Gnostiques et les Manichéens* (Paris: Presses Universitaires, 1947), which present the so-called "dualistic" component in heresy in early times; actually, this component is polar rather than dualistic, and as such was a barrier to mental ego-realization. This polar-mythical component, it must be said in all fairness, was necessarily opposed by the Catholic church if it wished to act in accord with the mental consciousness structure which was to be realized: it could only manifest itself in monotheistic-trinitary form, and consequently the polar-mythical component was "rightly" opposed. Moreover, the Gnostic conception of spirit, barring some exceptions, presumably bore a predominantly magic accent in addition to its mythical emphasis, which the church could not tolerate; we find evidence of this in the notion held by the Catharii, mentioned earlier, that Mary conceived by her ear—a magical notion. See the extensive material on heresies from the Catholic standpoint in M. Menéndez Pelayo, *Historia de los Heterodoxos Españoles* (Madrid: Libreria Católica, 1877), III; it has been reprinted in his *Obras Completas* (Santander: Aldus, 1945–1948).

114   The same is true more recently, despite the critical position vis-à-vis Heidegger; see Hans Kunz, *Die anthropologische Bedeutung der Phantasie* (Basel: Recht und Gesellschaft, 1946), ii. See I, p. 175 ff., and II, p. 137 ff., for a summary of the philosophical definitions of the concept of "spirit."

7

The Previous Forms
of Realization
and Thought

1. Dimensioning and Realization

Nothing would be easier than to give in to the lure of employing in this discussion the abstracting descriptive form of writing so esteemed today with its deficient, quantitative modes of expression. But an ever-increasing division, dissolution, and separation will never yield a whole, nor even its opposite, which might at least represent it negatively. We have endeavored, accordingly, to avoid mere evocation in our presentation of the magic, and mere mythologization in our description of the mythical structure, and have shunned by the same token mere ratiocination in our attempt to make the mental structure comprehensible.

Anyone who is at home in the three-dimensional coordinate system whose enclosure affords him security will find our deliberations unwelcome; some might even be indignant. But what emerges in indignation if not the rationally restrained psychic content? The indignant are aroused by something that breaks through the rational confines and irrupts with natural and emphatic force in negative manifestations that reveal the depths within themselves about which they become indignant. Yet these "depths" reach only to the perspectival point, and where this becomes questionable, the indignant also believe the protective walls of their three-dimensional world to be in question. They imagine—and the imagery exposes them once more to the mythical realm from which reason had freed them—that the walls they erect could provide the necessary security. Every wall (*Wand*), however, has the inherent possibility of transformation (*Wandlung*).[1] Thus the indignant, despite all willful exertions, are still housed in a rather fragile world.

Given this insecure security, it is no wonder that the indignant should find it disagreeable to bother with other coordinate systems, such as the two-dimensional outlined in the previous chapter. In the two-dimensional structure the third or space-constituting coordinate or dimension was missing, and where in the rational world a wall exists there was an actual and continuous transformation.

Today too many people are uncomfortable whenever they are reminded of transitoriness and change. But it is undoubtedly necessary to point out that this firm-walled, three-dimensional world is subject to the possibility of change. Someone who dares to approach these matters will, however, seem to threaten the hard-won security, and we can hardly be surprised that the reaction to his diagnoses will either correspond or be commensurate to the threat. Besides, what else has he to offer in place of this security? The journey made in the last chapter to the dead and living waters, to the wellsprings?

It is doubtful whether these wellsprings could bring much joy since they apparently offer little of the security sought so insistently by rational man. It is more likely that they may be, in the first place, a form of torment. We should not find this surprising since "wellsprings" (*Quellen*) and "torments" (*Qualen*) stem from the same root.[2] And even such a return to the roots may turn out to be disquieting for it precipitates a loss of dimensions where even the painful and tormenting twilight of the mythical fades away, leaving us to grope in darkness.

The essence of the "roots" (*Wurzeln*) is irrefutably expressed by its own Indo-Germanic root which is *war* and means "to enclose, cover." It is the source of our word for "true, veracious," *wahr*.[3] So precisely where we think we are in the dark we find that it not only "wares" (*wahren*) and protects us (*bewahren*), but also shelters the "brightness" of truth—the undivided brightness which is doubtless closer to the whole than is our one-sided mental brightness.

Our endeavor in the present work is not to glorify the past. We do not advocate a return or a regression any more than a "progression" forward. Our concern is with the Ever-present. Far be it from us, in other words, to disqualify our mental illumination in favor of the brightness of the roots. What matters to us is showing their constitutional differences, and this is possible only with the help of our mental illumination. And we are also concerned with the particular dimensional conditionality, temporal limitations, and restrictions of the individual modes of illumination as they are respectively lived, experienced, and conceptualized in the darkness of the magic root, the twilight of mythical agitation, and the illumination of the mental space world.

If we realize and integrate these conditions, limitations, and restrictions we shall sustain the world and the world will "ware" us "in truth": the verity of the whole will be perceptible (*wahrnehmbar*), present and transparent through integration, since it then shines through and suffuses all things.

To avoid being held fast in darkness, tortured in twilight, and possibly blinded by brightness, we must convey with clarity the forms of previous realization by whose aid we not only recognize and comprehend, but also live, experience, and conceptualize the world.

As a means of clarifying the various thought structures it has been customary to speak of "thought forms." These definitions relate in part to actual thinking and for the rest to what we should like to call "pre-forms" of thought. If we base our observations on the mutations we have discerned, "thought forms" are valid only as they pertain to the mental structure. Only the mental structure, because of its consciously formed directedness, recognized thought as being distinct from all previous realizational forms. If we wished to attribute "thought forms" to the other structures we would not be able to speak of "thought" in the mythical structure, but only of "being-thought"; and with respect to the magic structure, not even "being-thought" but only of "being-in-thought."

It is assumed in these definitions that *there was thought before the thinker,* as

249

there was breath before the breather, and sight before the eye. To explain this in rational terms we must suppose that the power of a possible manifestation itself creates an organ able to manifest this power. As applied to our own lives this statement shows that it is our inherent possibilities which shape the circumstances and the way we lead our lives in such a way as to allow these possibilities to become effective. In other words, the components in us which are to enter our mental awareness also create the preconditions for their own effective realization.

As long as we fail to see this, we attribute our disposition and unrealized latency—which strive toward their necessary unfolding—to an intrusion of "chance" or "destiny." But chance and destiny are merely the agencies which release the intensities in ourselves which are ready for manifestation. It is these intensities that cause the decisive events to "happen by chance" or "destine" these events for us. The intensities manage the chance and destiny so that the possibilities for their own manifestation occur. In a word, *we are our chances and destiny*. (As long as "positive" events are understood, no one will quarrel with this definition; but where we speak of "negative" ones, only relatively few will admit to having brought them about.)[4]

The question of the forms of realization is therefore a question as to the form, kind, or manner in which reality is realized in each individual structure. If we continue to hold to the characteristics and attributes which distinguish the individual structures in us, it follows that the realization form of the magic structure is living, that is, vital experience; of the mythical structure an undergone or psychic experience; and of the mental structure a form of comprehending, conceiving, and representing. This definition would seem to us to be more distinct than the form selected above of "being-in-thought," "being thought," and "thinking." Such a differentiation is conceivable only in perspectival terms as a view backwards from the standpoint of the mental structure, whereas the one chosen here is more in keeping with the increasing dimensionality of the respective structures.

Let us then turn first to the realization forms of the magic and mythical structures, particularly as we will be compelled to make certain distinctions for the realizational form of the mental structure (conceptualization), inasmuch as thinking plays the principal role. The directional character of thought emerges only gradually as will be apparent from the thought forms used by Heraclitus, Plato, and Aristotle. Since the three forms of realization or thinking are still effective today alongside each other, we cannot otherwise recognize what kind of "thought form" (if we can call it such) would represent a fourth and new form of realization.

2. *Vital Experiencing and Undergone or Psychic Experience.*

Vital experiencing belongs to the vitally-accentuated magic structure. Such experience is entirely univalent, incomprehensible in conceptual terms, and inexplicable—all of which does not diminish its effectiveness but perhaps even increases it. It may have once had extensive ties to the *numinosum* which at the outset of this consciousness structure was presumably not yet a unilateral projection of man, but rather together with man formed a unitary phenomenon. Magic man was, it will be recalled, indistinguishably bound to all things, and this *pars pro toto* is expressed in the power or potency of all genuine vital experience; it is the united and unitary background which becomes acute in each vital experience.

This will also explain how magic man interprets things: from within his own merging with events he immediately places any occurrence, event, or object that for him has the nature of a vital experience into a unifying context. Such a mode of establishing a context of relationships by experiencing, a vital nexus as we have called it, is not only pre-rational and pre-causal as befits the spaceless-timeless magic world; it elicits above and beyond this a still sleep-like consciousness of being inter-woven with events and is recognizable by its associative, analogizing, and sympathetic treatment of things that cannot be considered "thinking."

It is in the vital experience that the first inkling or dawning awareness takes on a point-like contour; from the bountiful effectualities dispersed throughout the world (and also because of magic man's fusion with it) this awareness is able to make one of these effectualities experienceable. Since in the magic structure the part always represents the whole, magic man can experience himself as well as the world. Here are the reasons for the overwhelming power of such experiencing even today: every true vital experience manifestly "realizes" the unity of the world and the fundamental unity of the individual with the world. Although only dimly conscious, such realization is consciousness-forming and prepares at the very least the mythical and mental consciousness. *Every vital experience is the unbeknown realization of unity*, and the emphasis on unity suggests that such experiencing is a *form of realization of the magic structure.*[5]

Undergone or psychic experience is something quite different. Its psychic emphasis always includes the polar-ambivalent moment since it manifests agitation and not just the point-like vital dynamism that shapes the character of vital experiencing. "Undergone" experience is always experienced by the soul; it is polar because it is not just something we endure passively but is at the same time a twilight, half-conscious act since we experience ourselves and the world (or the sea!). In such experience the world, and its counterpart the soul, move toward the threshold of mental consciousness. *Truly "undergone" experience is always irrational*; the soul teaches us what our understanding cannot grasp or estimate. As the adage suggests, experience is the best teacher.

The insight of such experience, that is, insight into psychic polarity and reality, distinguishes every "undergone" experience from both point-like vital experience and causal understanding. Since it is always an *inner* process it makes possible consciousness-forming recollection (*Erinnern*). While vital experience creates our initial awareness of the world's contours, "undergone" experience opens up the first temporally bounded images of the soul. Each experience is a partially known realization of polar complementarity. And inasmuch as the polar moment is accentuated, *every undergone experience is a mythical form of realization*, and as such a prefiguration of mental understanding.

Since we have explored these two forms of realization earlier in our discussion (chapter 4, section 4), both as to their foundations and their modalities, they can be summarized here. In the light of our discussion of the problems of space-time and soul-spirit we would again emphasize that the magic structure is characterized by unity, the mythical by polarity. Vital experiencing is based throughout on empathy (*Einfühlen*) and identification; it is univalent and one-dimensional. "Undergone" experience by contrast has as its basis the polarity of the soul, and this polarity becomes expressible because it has been imprinted on us in image and through the internalization of memory. Inasmuch as it represents and realizes the relationship and the interplay between the soul's poles, undergone experience is ambivalent and two-dimensional.

Conceptualization or ideation on the other hand is trivalent and three-dimensional. We may legitimately regard this third conceptual form of realization, appropriate to the mental structure, as a "form of thinking." It is, however, important that we subdivide it into three essentially different forms: oceanic or circling thinking, paradoxical thinking, and perspectival thinking.

3. Oceanic Thinking

Oceanic thinking could also be described as oceanic circling. But inasmuch as it also posits and postulates—immediately modifying the posited by a new postulation, and ultimately returning to the point of inception—it is more than a circular combination of images or representations. Leisegang has designated it as "circular thinking" or "chain thinking"[6] as opposed to conceptual or "pyramidal thinking," a form of thought which Julius Stenzel attributes to Socratic-Aristotelian dialectic.[7] We will return to "pyramidal thinking" in our discussion of perspectival thinking.

We have deliberately chosen the term "oceanic" because it is reminiscent of mythical image, and because it is a form of thought closely tied to the mythical structure.[8] The mythical image of Oceanus as the flowing river that encircles the earth and returns unto itself is a vivid image of the active circle as well as being a symbol expressive of the tendency of all terrestrial striving toward consciousness. For the Greeks the earth represented an island encircled by Oceanus, the actual primordial sea. An island, however, symbolically expresses a tendency toward awakening consciousness, inasmuch as this tendency toward consciousness rises forth from the "sea," from the Heraclitan soul.

This mythical Greek view of the river Oceanus is based in all likelihood on ancient tradition, according to which there was once only a single continent and continuous land mass, encircled by a world-sea. Recent geological findings suggest that this may be in any event a real possibility. It is only with the various deluges (the Indian as well as Mexican traditions speak of three)[9] that the primordial continent or island became individual continents.

Heraclitus furnishes numerous examples of oceanic thinking. We must not overlook, however, that Heraclitus already formulated expressly *directed* (mental) statements, a fact apparently ignored by Leisegang.[10] If we follow Leisegang's concise and literal translation of fragment 22 B 36, the oceanic thinking appears as follows (it should be noted that the translation by Diels-Kranz which is adapted to our word order reads: "For souls it is death to become water; for water it is death to become earth. But from the earth comes water and from water, soul"):

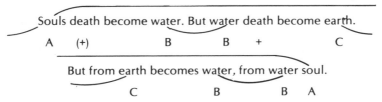

This can be represented even more vividly if we show the cyclic motion of thoughts beginning with one "concept" to which others are added before the return to the initial concept. In this diagram we must not overlook the fact that this thought movement circles about a central content: in this particular example, death.[11]

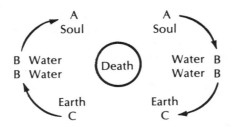

No less a figure than Dionysius Areopagita (ca. 500 A.D.) alludes to this form of thought when he writes: "The souls also have rational knowledge by their discursive endeavor in a circular motion to achieve the truth of things."[12]

A further instance of oceanic thinking is the beginning of the Gospel of St. John. Here too we find a polarization of "concepts" in a circular process (Leisegang speaks in rationalistic terms of "opposites"): concept A is associated with pole B; B is then repeated and related to a new pole, C; the process is then reversed from C to B, until B is once again related to A, thus completing the circle:

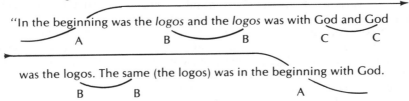

Here we again notice the circular movement of polarizing thought in the series AB/BC/CB/BA. The silent beginning forms a pole to the spoken beginning, the *logos;* this forms a pole to the speaker, God, and from there a reversed return to the silent pole. It is a process of self-complementation, and the central concept—here *circum*scribed rather than *described*—is "God."[13]

The fact that oceanic thinking circumscribes something is a vivid demonstration that the mythical circular world has a content. By destroying the circle with directed thinking, man, to the extent that he is mental man, has lost this content; for space is without content. This lack of content, which initially appears as openness, became obvious in the deficient rational phase (of the mental structure). This openness has been described ever since as emptiness, and indeed since then it is emptiness. For that reason any mere description is today empty and noncommittal. In this sense, descriptions are rational, flattened, and quantified attributions that initially had a *mental value* and made our conceptual world possible. Circumlocutions, on the other hand, as in the examples of Heraclitus and St. John, suggest the close proximity of oceanic thinking to myth.

Yet a further point should be made to set off oceanic from mental-rational thinking. In oceanic thinking, the "not-only-but-also" always holds true, while in mental thinking, only the "either-or" is valid. Vaihinger, with his "Philosophy of the As-If," and Kierkegaard, with his "Either-Or," have provided prime examples of these thought forms, Kierkegaard having proceeded along the lines of paradox (see p. 260 below). The "not-only-but-also" is not only indecisive but also inseparable, like the soul itself; owing to its ambivalence, its polarity, and its propensity for symbol, it is itself "not-only-but-also." The "either-or," by contrast, contains that "decision" or decisiveness known only to the mind which must take a one-sided position. And we should not assume that it can be opposed to the "not-only-but-also," because it expresses a form of thought which is constitutionally different from the oceanic.

We can define this thought form as "thinking in the soul," which is most likely what Dionysius Areopagita meant when he wrote, "To the soul circular movement means its entry from outside to the inner self. . . . The linear movement ultimately belongs to the soul when it does not enter into itself and moves in single-minded intellectuality [i.e., thought capacity]."[14] With the concluding sentence Dionysius Areopagita is already alluding to the other thought form which we call perspectival-directed thinking—singular as opposed to polar oceanic thinking.

In the oceanic thought form there is still a preponderance of the *relegere*, or "careful attention" characteristic of the mythical structure; it is a thinking process that still shows "re-gard," and is careful to neglect nothing so as not to disturb the balance by mere positing or postulation.[15] This is accomplished in mythical *relegio* by a constant regard for the respective complementary pole. There is even an echo of the magic moment in the auditory aspects, that is, in the rhythm and musicality of the expressive language, as well as in the endeavor to uphold a unification which in a manner corresponding to myth occurs through complementation.

These same auditory and unifying moments which we are attempting to make evident for oceanic thinking have been identified by the Jewish religious philosopher Ben Joseph in the thought and expression of the *Torah*.[16] Oceanic thought is also characteristic of Lao-Tzu, and is also found in sentence after sentence as the typical form of thought and expression of Buddha. It is also the predominant form in the writings of the Gnostics, the mystics, nature philosophers, and, not least, poets.

Among its adherents, oceanic thought can number not only oriental sages and rabbinical scholars, but alongside Heraclitus and St. John even to a certain degree Sts. Paul and Augustine, and by all means the Neo-Platonist Proklos, Dionysius Areopagita, Johannes Scotus Erigena, and Nicolaus Cusanus. Others include Eckhart, Suso, Giordano Bruno, and Jakob Boehme; Schelling, and, to some extent, Hegel as well as Goethe; and two recent poets—Strindberg, who in his play *To Damascus* has the scenes unfold backwards from the middle of the play, thus returning to the beginning with the final scene; and Platen, who was a master of the roundel, a form later revived and reshaped by Georg Trakl:

> Verflossen ist das Gold der Tage,
> Des Abends braun und blaue Farben:
> Des Hirten sanfte Töne starben,
> Des Abends braun und blaue Farben:
> Verflossen ist das Gold der Tage.

> [Subsided has the gold of day,
> The evening's brown and bluish hues
> The shepherd's soft intoning died,
> The evening's brown and bluish hues:
> Subsided has the gold of day.]

This unperspectival flux of thoughts and images is the strength as well as the weakness of this form of thought. It is strong because it is still intact, weak because it is inadequate to the demands of the mental structure. It is irrational where the other is rational; unperspectival where the other is perspectival; it circumscribes where the other describes; it is (am)bivalent where the other is trivalent. Above all, the mental-rational-perspectival thought form is directed, whereas oceanic thinking is a self-contained and enclosing self-complementation which was reduced to rubble by perspectivity. There are today more than enough psychic ruins ravaging the world ever since thought lost its immediate directedness and qualitative mental character, and became deficient in the fragmentation of rationalization, sectorization, and perspectivation. Let us now turn to this nearly formless form of thinking.

4. Perspectival Thinking

Let us here recall the closing part of the second quotation from Dionysius Areopagita cited a moment ago: "Linear movement ultimately [the 'ultimately' is particularly fitting here] belongs to the soul when it does not enter into itself [i.e., has 'left itself' or in Erasmus' words, is 'outside or beside itself'] and moves in single-minded intellectuality [as the capability of directed, and not just circular thought or 'being thought']."

This sentence conveys, in its own way, what is expressed in the mythical image of Athena's birth from the head of Zeus. We must not forget the extent to which heaven and the individual soul are correspondences, nor that the head of Zeus symbolizes not just the heavens but, at least in this particular myth, the womb. Lucretius, in turn, expresses the content of the mythologeme by praising "a man of Greece who dared first to raise his mortal eyes" against the "crushing weight of the deities of heaven," who was also the "first to burst through the closed portals of mother nature." After this mention of the directed, storming wrath of the Achillean Menis, and the "unconscious" allusion to the matricide perpetrated earlier, Lucretius continues: "And so it was that the lively force of his mind won its way, and he passed on far beyond the fiery walls of the world."[17] These lines are a moving expression of the fact that the conquest and overcoming of the soul is a violent act, and that nature itself was violated when the masculine principle assumed its autocratic rule. *Mental thought is still estimation (ermessen), while rational thinking is arrogant calculation and presumption (Anmassung)* which ultimately lead to the destructive fragmentation of human nature itself.

We first employed the term "perspectival thinking" to suggest a distinction between this form and what we called the "aperspectival form" of realization.[18] But it later became evident that the concept of perspectivity has been applied in a variety of ways, as for example by G. Teichmüller who refers to "perspectival time" as being primarily false time and for his part aims at a restoration of timelessness—that is, a retrogression.[19] Jaspers also touches upon this issue while speaking of an individual's "world image" as a given "individual perspective" or "individual enclosure." Graumann has recently defended a "psychology of perspective" (1960) although his critique of our concept fails to recognize that the concepts should not be psychologized since it is an expression (or phenomenon) of the mental structure.[20] Ortega y Gasset, speaking as an *espectador* or "spectator" associates his *perspectiva particular* (personal perspective) with truth, subsuming it into the trinity of a visual, intellectual, and evaluative perspective where not just real and imagined, but also particularly desired and dreamed of things are united.[21]

Our concept of perspectivity has as little to do with such a definition—and its application of spatializing concepts to mythical-psychic phenomena—as with Jaspers' "enclosure." And there is yet a further concept of perspective that could give rise to misunderstandings, namely Louis Locher's introduction of the concept into projective geometry to explain the Moebius strip. His concept deals with projective interrelationships between several figures of a single plane that represent "perspectivities" by being "semblances of a punctiliar sequence or sections of a plane cluster which have their "center of perspectivity" in a surface intersection or are intersectable by a "chain of perspectivities."[22] Since there is no evidence here of isolating sectorization this multi-perspectivity is suggestive of a-perspectivity in our sense.

Our formulation and description of the concept of perspectivity began with the perspective of Leonardo da Vinci. A detailed discussion of the perspectivation and consequent sectorization of the world that results from it is contained in the second chapter of the present work. There we have called attention to Leonardo's concept of the "visual pyramid." The fundamental symbol of this mode of perception is the triangle which is largely an expression of the form of our epoch's thinking. When regarded as one surface of a pyramid, this triangle can be vertical, and when seen as the perspectival depth-surface, horizontal.

Without losing sight of the vertical, let us confine our observations to the horizontal form since it lends itself more readily to a graphic depiction. In this visual triangle the eyes form the base and complete the synthesis of their simultaneous perception at the perspectival vanishing point. This synthesis is possible because of the trivalent or triadic relationship of the triangle which not only "opens up" but also closes space at the vanishing point. In this process the points formed by the eye become antinomies in the wake of an increasing intellectualization, and these antinomies meet their opposites at the vanishing point like two statements completed by a third.

This description brings us close to the simplest form of pyramidal thinking, the conceptual pyramid of J. Stenzel. Leisegang makes a case for Plato as being its creator, noting that Plato was also the creator of "logical judgement, and thus of logical thinking as such in its rationalistic sense."[23] Leisegang also observes that: "here at the source we see the intimate connection between the conceptual pyramid and what we even today consider to be logical thinking as such. The logos is for Plato the interconnection of concepts which subordinate and superordinate each other and thus unite in a pyramidal classification system to form a coherent whole."

This pyramidal thinking is the efficient thought form of the mental structure, while perspectival thinking represents its deficient form; both are extensions of what has been called Plato's method of diaresis. Diaresis today is generally understood to be conceptual hair-splitting. We come closer to the actual essence and original significance of this method, however, if we observe more carefully the word diaresis itself. The basic verbal form is haireo, meaning "to take," while the prefix di- means "apart." Diaresis is, then, a "taking apart," a separation or severing. It is in a word the method (measuring procedure) capable of separating or dis-rupting the self-contained circle. The polar constellation is no longer valid; what is valid are the parts which can be made into opposites.

This method permitted Greek man to bring under control the increasingly conscious energy of the soul that threatened to overpower him by its diversity of mythical imagery; he was compelled to direct these images lest he succumb to them. The quantifying tendency of the deficient mythical structure threatened man with psychic fragmentation. Here lies the origin of the Platonic ideas which were able to stabilize and order the increasing masses of psychic manifestations and projections. In this sense, the primal image and its likeness are no longer a polarity, but a duality "united" in the idea, the third component, the synthesis above both.

The twilight, ambiguous nature of myth had gained ascendance to the extent that the awakening of consciousness revealed its increasing self-manifestation in ever-larger quantities of ambivalent and ambiguous images. Greek man was able to escape the ambiguity and its lack of stability by positing parts which could be opposed so that in any given instance each part was unequivocal and unambiguous, and directed rather than polar. By positing the concept, Greek man reached a judgement; and judgement consists of a connection of ideas grouped together according to the categories of assertions. Since these ideas are posited assertions and not agitated images, then only one of two assertions—one affirming what the other negates—can be correct.

In the imagery of polar, mythical, and symbolic expression, both were possible: the "not-only-but-also" was valid until Aristotle's premise of *tertium non datur* annulled its force for two millenia in favor of the unambiguous "either-or." (In the second part below we will examine the recent displacement of the "either-or" by quantum logic.) An example of Aristotle's *tertium non datur* is the statement that a horse is either white or not white; a third statement or possibility does not exist. The result is the principle of noncontradiction or antinomy which no longer admits the possibility of polarity. Of any two judgements (fixed statements), determinations, or partitionings where one affirms what the other denies, only one is true; abstraction of a concept from an image eliminated the polar possibility.

This theory of judgement leads to the theory of inference.[24] Aristotle has declared that the syllogism is the fundamental form of all inference and deduction. The conclusion results from two premises, each having a common term:

First premise:	All men are mortal.	A = B
Second premise:	Socrates is a man.	C = A
Conclusion:	Therefore, Socrates is mortal.	C = B

Yet this conclusion is convincing only because it is based on a pyramidal pattern of organization.[25] The first two propositions are "premises," and the three terms contained in them, "mortal," "man," "Socrates," are called respectively major, middle, and minor terms. Once again we encounter the expression of trinitary form, opening as well as delimiting the three-dimensional space. This dual-trinitary pyramidal form of thinking can be illustrated even more vividly as follows:

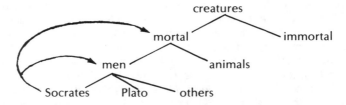

Along with Plato and Aristotle, the predominant representatives of pyramidal thinking are Democritus, Epicurus, Philo, the Neoplatonists, Plotinus, and to some extent, Augustine. Others are Thomas Aquinas and the Scholastics; later Bacon,

Descartes, Kant, Hobbes, and the Encyclopedists and Comte, as well as their follow-ers, the materialists; and present-day scientists who are still unable to accept inde-terminacy. But already the works of Bacon show evidence of perspectival thought, the deficient form of pyramidal thinking.

Let us stop with these examples, although additional and more complex in-stances, such as those cited by Leisegang for pyramidal thinking, could further illustrate our remarks.[26] Let us note here only the main characteristics of perspectival thinking: it coincides to a great extent with directed, sectorial vision; it fixes the object to be grasped; and two identical lines of vision take in the object as a third item in the same manner that two equations result in a third.

An additional example clearly shows to what extent this form of thought has an inherently exclusionary nature inappropriate to oceanic thinking, and reveals the loss of a stable, self-sufficient basis. Perspectival, discursive thinking yields correct results only if it proceeds by narrowing from the general to the particular or to what is to be excluded. It must create its own basis, somewhat like the demiurge, without knowing or being able to determine whether this basis actually is, or can be, valid. The moment the rule is not observed, or the moment it becomes impossible to determine whether the thought is aimed from the general toward a particular, we find logical errors as in the following syllogism:

A man fell into the water.
We are all men.
Consequently, we will all fall into the water.

This example is a clear instance of the reduced validity of perspectival think-ing: it is valid only where the conceptual field can be narrowed so as to permit deduction of the particular from the general. In this respect also it is similar to per-spectival vision: if a single sector is to be perceived, it must be separated from the general field of vision. The necessity of this thought form was (and is) as apparent as its one-sidedness and limitation. A consequence of its one-sidedness is perspectival-thinking-man's need for recourse to *religio*, to the ties back to a church-adminis-tered religion; and to the extent that he no longer has blind faith he tries to establish religion by using a mixture of oceanic and perspectival thinking: paradox (discussed in the next section). A consequence of the limitations of discursive, perspectival thinking is that it has itself restrictions and in turn must also impose limitations. The result of this spatial restriction is that such thinking both opens space and is confined by it.

Perspectival thinking spatializes and then employs what it has spatialized. All inferences or deductions are expressed in language by spatial concepts. Language speaks of "transcending" or "overriding" or "exceeding," and philosophic thought of this kind "represents, conceives of" (*vorstellen*, literally "places before"); it "proves" (*nachweisen*, literally "points to"); it "grasps" and "com-prehends"; it "grasps conceptually" (*auffassen*, literally "catches"); it "considers" (*überlegen*, lit-erally "turns over"); it "imputes" (*unterstellen*, literally "places under"); it "de-bates" and "argues" (*auseinandersetzen*, literally "takes apart").

Leisegang has observed and underscored this spatiality of our philosophical language and thinking which, as we noted, knows only walls and selective, divided objects, having lost its binding content and self-complementarity in favor of the comprehended spatial world: "Philosophical language is laced with expressions which point to a visible order in a conceived space. When we speak of *sub-* and *superordination, counter-* and *juxta*-posed concepts, *higher* and *lower* types, we find that these designations are based on the conception of a spatial up and down, right and left. . . . When Plato in the Symposium leads us *up* step by step to the ideas, but designates matter as the *under*lying (*hypo*keimenon, Latin *sub*stantia), we have to visualize a vertically constructed world image and philosophical system. Kant's dualism on the other hand, where appearances *confront* cognition and reason as their object and the thing in itself is to be sought *behind* the appearances, presupposes a horizontal arrangement of basic concepts and their content. There is surely a basic distinction between Platonic and Kantian philosophy inasmuch as Kant's ideas no longer reside *above* man, but are *points* of orientation lying in the same *plane* with man."[27]

Leisegang expands on these remarks in a quotation from Kant which we will cite at least in part because it expresses precisely this form of thinking which we have called "perspectival thinking": "(The ideas) have on the other hand an admirable and indispensable regulatory use in *directing* and *understanding toward a particular goal*, in view of which the lines of direction of all its regulations merge into one point" (our italics). And only a few pages farther on Kant adduces the image of the *"horizon"* of concepts in contrast to the vertically structured, conceptual pyramid of Plato.[28] The conceptual pyramid breaks through the circle, whereas Kant treats it like a horizontal triangle that has been severed from its original relationship; this is the triangle referred to above (p. 256).

But this has made thinking itself spatial and static, permitting the materialization of "spirit" and even the spatialization of time which, as we pointed out in chapter 5, was once related to inceptual thinking. With this space, time, and thinking—which as, we indicated early in our discussion, are interrelated—are driven to their extreme formulation and valuation. To a considerable degree they represent the exact opposite of their original situation; indeed, they threaten to lead themselves—and this means primarily us—*ad absurdum*.

With respect to this last remark we would again emphasize that we are in no way against this form of thinking, although we do regard its extreme forms and manifestations as damaging. At the same time we see them as the involuntary predecessors of the leap toward a new and not merely possible, but necessary mutation.

5. *Paradoxical Thinking*

The bond which diaresis has severed—a bond which man dispenses with only at the peril of denying a part of himself (the irrational)—cannot be restored either by pyramidal or, even less, by perspectival thought. Yet it is possible to propose a previously unrecognized form of thought that reveals the co-validity of the irrational in a form reminiscent of a rational mode of formulation. We have called this thought form the paradoxical and described paradoxical statement as the pre-eminent form of religious utterance.

From the mental point of view, paradoxical thinking actually establishes the bond or *religio* to the irrationality and pre-rationality of the mythical and magic structures. It is a form that mediates between oceanic and perspectival thinking and contains both rational and irrational elements. A good example of paradoxical expression is the well-known statement of Pascal: "Tu ne me chercherai pas, si tu ne m'avais trouvé" (You would not seek me if you had not found me).[29]

This statement contains the very elements we have mentioned: it employs the "if" and hence draws an inference, which shows that it belongs to mental thinking; at the same time it contains a psychic reversal since in rational terms the second part is not a result of the first but rather the opposite. Despite the irrational element, it nevertheless withstands a determined critique by perspectival thinking, which it takes beyond the fixed perspectival point.

This can be illustrated on a geometric thesis known as the axiom of parallels; it states that two parallel lines intersect at infinity. This can be shown in graphic form by crossing two lines at acute angles. The *Chi* (X) mentioned in Plato's *Timaeus*[30] is suggestive of this configuration; in the Chi or X formed by these intersecting parallels the perspectival "vanishing" point is neutralized; the elongated lines of the lower triangle of vision form a mirror triangle to the original one. Whatever lies "beyond" the spatial-perspectival point in "infinity"—that is, in the immeasurable—verifies in its reverse image what is posited in rational terms as a result:

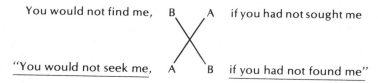

In other words, a statement of irrational character in the rational sphere has in the irrational structure a rational character, that is, "beyond" and "on the other side" of the point "behind" the spatializing horizon. This re-establishes in an unusually clever and effective manner the bond or *religio* to the past.

As befits its religious character, this form of thinking is found primarily in religious authors of the mental consciousness structure, notably hymnists such as Symeon.[31] Yet it can also be found even among rationalists, as for instance in Aristotle's statement about the "unmoved mover," right down to (or up to) the core statement of present-day nuclear physics regarding the polarity inherent in the complementarity principle. This form of thought even re-emerges now and then in its deficient form as witty psychic reflections, as in the paradoxical style of Oscar Wilde, whose genuine religiosity is first evident in "De Profundis." Or it is also suggested by statements of a mythical character such as the "silent music" of the Spanish mystic, St. John of the Cross.

Although it may veer now more toward the oceanic, now toward the rational, it exists nonetheless in its own right, particularly in the work of Kierkegaard, thinker par excellence of paradox. His mental "Either-Or" is further proof of the paradoxical uniqueness of his thought. It is, moreover, commensurate with the rational structure: it is a synthesis or compromise, a third form of thought in which there is a (consistently unsatisfactory) effort to unify opposites.

We can further clarify this state of affairs if we consider that parallels intersect at "infinity" only if their path is curved. This implies that there is at least a tendency toward circularity inherent in them although the point of intersection also gives them the character of a triangle. In this respect paradox represents on the one hand a deficient form of symbol, and thus oceanic thinking, while on the other it is a kind of mentalistic or intellectualized *religio*; for only a purely rational statement is absolute, that is dis-united and consequently cut off from religion. In any event, paradoxical thinking is a form deserving of further consideration. This is not to advocate it or give it a preference in any way; we are simply ascertaining a fact. But there is an apocryphal saying of Christ: "If you do not change low to high, left to right, back to front, you shall not enter my kingdom."[32]

If we can clearly perceive what paradoxical utterance actually represents, contains, and realizes, as in the picture of the intersecting parallels (where even the "intersecting" or severing is not negative and is thus itself a paradox), we can in part perceive what is expressed by the apocryphal saying with its relation to the whole. There is at the very least a valid left-right shift or substitution in paradoxical statement which, inasmuch as we are dealing with a thinking process, still occurs primarily in our conceptualization.

But what are the implications of a shift from left to right? It may well be synonymous with a dissolution of the mirror aspect which is an essential element of the psyche; indeed, even the polarity principle itself may be regarded as a reflective or mirror principle, whose dissolution is the final retraction of a projection. Hölderlin suggests that this process is already accomplished in the verse: "Soon one God after another returns home."[33]

The dissolution of this principle is nothing other than the supersession and concretion of the soul, and thus the first step towards its integration. This integration cannot be effected by mere thinking or contemplation, but requires another capacity which we shall call "verition" or "waring" and encompasses the "sense" of perceiving as well as imparting verity or truth. *Only through this reciprocal perception and impartation of truth by man and the world can the world become transparent for us.* This is still to be discussed in Part II, and we would not have mentioned it here if the left-right interchange were limited solely to the paradoxical form of expression and thought, where its latency was long effective and functioned for the most part unconsciously.

This shift from left to right has been underway in various areas now for a considerable time, roughly one hundred and fifty years. As we have indicated, it is an inception toward the integration of the soul; and inasmuch as the soul is "temporal," this shift also represents a concretion of time. Certain religious sects have practiced since ancient times what could be called an interchange or "transposition of lights" where the right-hand light is shifted to the left and the left-hand light is shifted to the right.

The fact that both sides uniformly have lights suggests a certain inadequacy manifest in the practice, since the unification via this interchange is magic. A further result of such interchange is that these sects can also effect an erroneous interchange of "above" and "below," as in the inversion of the pentagram or five-pointed star—an ancient symbol for man—by placing it on its point or "head." And we would mention without further comment the so-called "black masses" practiced by certain Gnostic sects. There is, incidentally, a false inversion of up and down in our own day where one might least suspect it: the "bringing to earth" of particles of cosmic radiation, since we now make "down here" on earth something of "above" while sending in turn the ultra-high-frequency radiation originating here into interstellar space.

However, we do not intend to dwell on these mistaken attempts but rather on the inceptual shift from left to right which, in its materialistic ballast, masquerading, and emphasis, still bears the stigma of its time. Because of this materialistic pretence or pretext such inceptions will remain ineffective until this pretence gives way, since it presents an obstacle, as it were, to their unfolding.

We would like first to point to four such inceptions which can be recognized in totally separate areas of our lives or civilization in the political, social, scientific, and artistic spheres.

In the political sphere it is the rise of the "left" that not only demands to a great extent the position of the "right" but is already usurping it. The expression "the Left" as applied to the mass movements of the "underprivileged" and the fact that we speak of the "awakening left" indicate the kind of process involved here. The "left" as a party establishes itself precisely when the previously "suppressed" "left" aspect—which we today also call the "unconscious"—first surfaces in the earliest psychologizing writings of Stendhal and Leopardi. During the first three decades of the nineteenth century the originally liberal party is assigned to the left side in the French parliament—surely a profoundly significant placement or "positing."

This placement, like all expressions connected with the political "left," represents the "masses," "the suppressed," "awakening," "movement," or the process of the awakening consciousness of a significant part of mankind in quantitative terms. It is an awakening which strives to equalize left and right: at first under the negative sign of a class conflict, magic attempts at uniformity, and the deficiently tinged magic claim to power, or the deficient mythical wish for power. And because of its irrational source, it is a process which evoked anxiety among its supporters who sought safety in an extremely rationalistic, that is, specifically materialistic doctrine.

The doctrine spared the left from chaos, but not everyone else. The left too, if it does not come to its senses, will succumb to the chaos it brought to light just as much as its enemies bound to it in opposition, particularly as the left threatens to deteriorate into a rigid fanaticism.[34] In any event the presence of the left mirrors an inception of a left-right shift, even if at first negatively, which will be genuine only if an integration and not merely a change of place occurs; and this refers to the integration of mankind.

From a sociological standpoint, this inceptual shift is manifest since 1792 in the negative form of the one-sided demand of the "women's question." The implications affect not only the social position of women but that of men as well. Since the feminine from time immemorial has been identified with the left and the masculine with the right, this indicator of the present-day status of women should come as no surprise. As long as women have only a one-sided striving after the "rights" of men without granting them their "lefts" in a manner of speaking (an attribution which would change men's "rights"), this inception of a left-right shift will remain negative.

Only when the one-sided will to displace one part of humanity and the (magically accentuated) demand for equal rights are abandoned in favor of an integration will the *human* be able to emerge. Just as matriarchy was once displaced by the patriarchy still in force today (in which negative residues of matriarchy are still dominant because of patriarchal-rational man's lapse into *materialism*), so too can this patriarchy be dissolved in turn by the *Integrum* where neither mater- (mother) nor pater- (father) but the human being in both will prevail: a human being integrated by man and woman who will then have acceptance and worth.[35]

In the scientific sphere the tendency toward a shift is manifest in the efforts of psychoanalysis (Freud) and analytical psychology (Jung). Each in its own way endeavors to realize in us the process of transposition between the "conscious" or directed right and the "unconscious" or undirected left. These endeavors, too, are only inceptions which are still pervaded by a rationalistic dualism, and which are for that reason still unaware of the partially magic (Freud) and partially mythical (Jung) conditionalities and limitations. As a consequence of this failure to recognize its own roots, much that sails or swims under the name of psychology is a lesser but nevertheless destructive demonology, for as long as phenomena remain unintelligible and unrecognized, their effect on us today will be disruptive. Yet despite all kinds of erroneous attempts and results, this does represent an inception of a left-right shift—however dubious—that dates back to the statement of the concept of an "unconscious" toward the end of the eighteenth century.

And finally let us mention in passing one of the many inceptions visible in the artistic sphere. So far as we are able to judge the situation, these artistic inceptions are the only ones which cannot be evaluated either in a positive or in a negative sense because they are already integral. For this reason they will be discussed in detail in Part II. We refer among other things to a style of representation in modern painting (particularly following Picasso and Braque) in which definitely "left" values, as we would call them—symbolized by a skull and similar things—are for the first time depicted on the right side of the canvas or picture.

The paradoxical form of expression, with its left-right interchange, is still partially bound to conceptualization. Yet it cannot be achieved through thinking, or at least not by thinking itself even with the forms of expression of the other consciousness structures in lived events, or experience, or conceptualization, but only through the addition of what we have called "waring" or "verition." The actual effectuality of the apocryphal words of Jesus does not take place in the conceptual and representational spatio-temporal world, nor in the two-dimensional, nor in the one-dimensional world. Only where the world is space-free and time-free, where "waring" gains validity, where the world and we ourselves—the whole—become transparent, and where the diaphanous and what is rendered diaphanous become the verition of the world, does the world become concrete and integral.

1   The antithetical terms *Wand*, "wall" on the one hand, and *Wandel, wandeln*, "change," *Wandlung*, "transformation" and *wandern*, "to wander," on the other, are derived from the same Germanic root; see Kluge-Götze, *Etymologisches Wörterbuch der deutschen Sprache* (Berlin: de Gruyter, ¹¹1936), pp. 670 and 692.

2   Both words derive from the Indo-European root *g(u)el:g(w)el*; see Kluge-Götze, (note 1), pp. 461-462. We have frequently met up with this root, which is audible in such words as *Helle: Hölle*, "brightness," and "hell," and in sym-bol; see note 77 above, p. 243.

3   For this derivation see Kluge-Götze (note 1), pp. 666, 667, and 700, as well as Menge-Güthling, *Griechisch-deutsches Wörterbuch* (Berlin: Langenscheidt, ²⁸1910), pp. 236 and 633, entries "wahr," "wahren," "Wurzel," and *eryomai*, "preserve, attend," and *hora*, "proper or correct time"; a primordial kinship also exists between these words and Latin *vereri*, "shun, honor, fear," Gothic *tuzwerjan* and *allawerei*, "to doubt" and "sincerity" respectively, and Middle High German *ware*, "peace." There can be little doubt that the latter word is a primal "opposite" of English "war"; see Skeat, *An Etymological Dictionary of the English Language* (Oxford: Clarendon, 1935), p. 701, and Kluge-Götze, (note 1), p. 693, entry "wirr," in conjunction with German *verwirren*, French *guerre*, and English "worse" (Skeat, p. 723). Skeat traces these words to a Germanic root *wers*, Kluge-Götze to an Indo-European root *wers*, which is most likely an extension of the root *war*.

4   See in this connection Jean Gebser, *In der Bewährung* (Bern: Francke, 1962), p. 109; *Gesamtausgabe*, V/I, p. 257.

5   As to the justification for considering vital experience as the expressive form of the magic structure, see chapter 8, section 1 (p. 267 f. below), as well as p. 269, cross-section 11 d.

6   Hans Leisegang, *Denkformen* (Berlin: de Gruyter, 1928), p. 35 f.

7   Julius Stenzel, *Studien zur Entwicklung der platonischen Dialektik von Sokrates zu Aristoteles: Arete und Diairesis* (Breslau: Trewendt, 1917); also his *Zahl und Gestalt bei Platon und Aristoteles* (Leipzig: Teubner, 1924). See also Leisegang (note 6), p. 208.

8   We have not defined this mode of thought as "mythical"; rather, it might be considered a "mythologizing" form of thinking. This would prevent it from being placed into opposition to the mental forms of thought. Our usage of the term "mythical," in contrast to Leisegang's (note 6, p. 17 ff.) is not ambiguous; he does not sufficiently differentiate between mythical "reporting" and ancient tragedy, which, though still bedded in a mythical subject matter, already gives evidence of inceptive mental traits. We have omitted any mention of Cassirer's *Die Begriffsform im mythischen Denken*, Studien der Bibliothek Warburg (Leipzig: Teubner, 1922), as well as of his *Philosophie der symbolischen Formen* (Berlin: Cassirer, 1925), II, because he presents such thinking from a one-sided rational standpoint, and his discussion consequently indirectly affords more insight into rational thinking than into the mythical thinking that forms the subject of his book.

9   In the Indic and Greek traditions there were four eons, called Yughas in India, whose length corresponded to the proportions of Pythagoras' key of 4:3:2:1, which totals ten. The first and oldest lasted for four "time units," the last, in which we live, one "time unit." This Indic and Greek tradition is unexpectedly corroborated by a footnote to the ancient Mexican Codex Tellerianus Pemensis, a calendar of seasonal holidays. There, under the date of the 12th of Uzcalli (January 30), it states: "Once every four years an eight-day fast in memory of the three-fold destruction of the world," and later; "O Tlaloc, god of the water, have mercy on us, do not ruin us!" See R. Dévigne, *Un continent disparu: L'Atlantide, sixième partie du monde* (Paris: Cres, 1924), p. 98; cited also in Mereschkowski, *Das Geheimnis des Westens* (Leipzig: Grethlein, 1929), pp. 131 and 534, note 7.

10   Assuming that these sentences are complete in themselves and not parts of once complementary fragments, we can also discern indications of oriented mental thought in Heraclitus. He emphasizes, for instance, law or rule, and prefers the comprehensible to the incomprehensible. In the following fragments he accentuates the "I": "Law is also to follow the will (advice) of an individual"; "I prefer everything that can be seen, heard and known (*mathesis*)"; and, "I examined myself"; see Diels-Kranz, *Die Fragmente der Vorsokratiker* (Berlin: Weidmann, ³1934), 22 B 33, -55, and -101; in Snell's translation, *Heraklit-Fragmente* Tusculum-Bücherei (Munich: Heimeran, ²1940), pp. 15, 21, and 31.

11   See Leisegang (note 6), pp. 61 and 72 f.; from this distinguished study we have taken our illustration, although we have adapted and expanded it. Leisegang represents the movement as counterclockwise; ours (clockwise) is the more correct since it has to do with a "righting," directing sequence expressing an emergence of consciousness. We have also added the rubric in the center which Leisegang overlooks and which is clearly evident in this example.

12   Dionysius Areopagita, *Über göttliche Namen*, trans. J. Stiglmayr, Bibliothek der Kirchenväter, Ser. II, (Munich: Kösel, 1933), II, p. 116. See also the more recent version by Walther Tritsch, Dionysius Areopagita, *Mystische Theologie und andere Schriften* (München-Planegg: Barth, 1956), p. 114 (Migne 868 C).

13   Numerous other examples are cited in Leisegang (note 6), pp. 61 f., 64 ff., and 256. His interpretation differs from ours in that he synthesizes and conceptualizes matters which have a polar, that is, not yet sequential but rather linking nature.

14   Dionysius Areopagita (note 12), Stiglmayr ed., p. 68 f., Tritsch ed. p. 68 (Migne 705 A / 705 B).

15   It is symptomatic that contemporary man, rational and one-sidedly materialistic, is lacking awareness of *Rücksicht*, "consideration," "regard," "retrospection," which brings about his inconsiderateness. He knows only *Vorsicht*, "caution," literally "sight ahead," and consequently if he regards anything, he regards only that which lies before him and forgoes the presence of what lies at his back.

16   Ben Joseph, "Die Struktur der jüdischen Religions-Philosophie," the initial chapter of his "Die Stimme der Prophetie und der Geist der Musik," *Jüdisches Jahrbuch der Schweiz 1919-1920*, pp. 1–24, particularly p. 8.

17*   Lucretius, *On the Nature of Things*, trans. Cyril Bailey (Oxford: Clarendon Press), with slight modifications. Compare also the translation of Diels: "Also geschahs. Sein mutiger Geist blieb Sieger, und kühnlich / Setzt er den Fuss weit über des Weltalls flammende Mauern." Lukrez, *Von der Natur*, trans. Hermann Diels (Berlin: Weidmann, 1924), p. 3, and the Latin-Italian parallel edition: Titi Lucreti Cari, *De Rerum Natura libri sex*, versione poetica di Camillo Giussani (Milan: Monadori, 1939). We would point out that Lucretius was most likely the first to relate *anima* and *animus*; the distinction, though not stated, is implicit in Weininger's interpretation in his *Geschlecht und Charakter* (1903); see in this connection Jean Gebser, *Abendländische Wandlung* (Zürich: Oprecht, ²1945, p. 183; Ullstein ed. No. 107, p. 136 f.; *Gesamtausgabe*, I, p. 288 f. In his lecture "Über die Archetypen des kollektiven Unbewussten," C. G. Jung has demonstrated that the "anima" is the archetype which dominates the masculine psyche, the "animus" that which dominates the feminine, and has observed the disastrous consequences resulting from the unconscious projection of these archetypes (*Eranos-Jahrbuch 1934* [Zürich: Rhein, 1935], p. 211 ff.).

18   See Jean Gebser, *Rilke und Spanien* (Zürich: Oprecht); a Spanish version was written in 1936 and the German edition published in the autumn of 1939; now in the *Gesamtausgabe*, I, pp. 9–84.

19   See Michael Schabad, *Die Wiederentdeckung des Ich in der Metaphysik Teichmüllers* (Basel: Helbing, 1940), particularly pp. 42 f., 78 f., and 84 ff.

20   Karl Jaspers, *Psychologie der Weltanschauungen* (Berlin: Springer, ²1922), pp. 143–144; also C. F. Graumann, *Grundlagen einer Phänomenologie und Psychologie der Perspektivität* (Berlin: de Gruyter, 1960), p. 136.

21   José Ortega y Gasset, *El Espectador* (Madrid: Occidente, ⁴1933), I, pp. 24–25.

22   Louis Locher, *Urphänomene der Geometrie, Erster Teil* (Zürich: Füssli, 1937), p. 134 ff.

23   Leisegang (note 6), pp. 214 and 206 f.

24   See H. Leisegang, *Hellenistische Philosophie von Aristoteles bis Plotin* (Breslau: Hirt, 1923), p. 42. Leisegang does not take into consideration the antimythical attitude inherent in judgement.

25   The "heightened," so-called "spiritual" paternity and father-emphasis of this form of thought is suggested by its "convincing" results: *überzeugen*, "to convince," is an intensified form of *zeugen*, "to sire," hence "over-sire." It should also be recalled that the triangle is a masculine symbol as opposed to the circle.

26   Leisegang (note 6), p. 202 ff.

27   Kant, *Critique of Pure Judgement*, cited in Leisegang (note 6), p. 11; it is on p. 672 of the original edition of the *Kritik der reinen Vernunft* (1787).

28   Kant, p. 686 (cited in Leisegang).

29   Blaise Pascal, *Pensées*, L'Oeuvre de Pascal, Bibliothèque de la Pléiade 34 (Paris: NRF, 1940), p. 1016, and Pascal, *Gedanken* (Leipzig: Dieterich, n.d.), p. 301.

30   Plato, *Timaeus*, 35 B; cited according to Platon, *Sämtliche Werke*, ed. Schneider (Berlin, n.d.), III, p. 114.

31   Symeon, *Hymen* (Hellerau: Hegner, 1930).

32   See *Die versprengten Worte Jesu*, ed. B. Godeschalk (Munich: Hyperion, 1922), p. 43, based on Acta Philippi, cod. Oxon. c.34.

33   Nietzsche's statement that "God is dead" is misleading; even the idols and gods who "died" to make room for God did not die, they "went home." Wherever this "returning

home" is not realized, they return in revenge, so to speak, in the idolatry of conceptualizations and "isms." This is clearly the case with Hegel who was the first to mention the "agony" in the "harsh statement that 'God is dead.' " Hegel also speaks of his "anguished feeling of the unhappy realization that *God himself has died*"; (Hegel's emphasis). See G. W. F. Hegel, *Phänomenologie des Geistes*, ed. by J. Hoffmeister, Sämtliche Werke II (Leipzig: Meiner, ⁴1937); vol. 114 of the Philosophische Bibliothek, pp. 523 and 545. The statements quoted were written in 1807. Heine resumed discussion of this topic in his *Geschichte der Religion und Philosophie in Deutschland* (1834), in which he concludes the second book with the statement, "The sacraments were brought to a dying God" (Heinrich Heine, *Sämtliche Werke* [Leipzig: Tempel, n.d.], VI, p. 366 ff.).

34   This is to emphasize again the decidedly rationalistic and deficient antithesis which we attempted to underscore in our exposition of the two basic tendencies of our time, agglomeration and isolation (chapters 2 and 3 above, pp. 22 f. and 94 f.). The split into the "Right" and the "Left" is a political phenomenon with deeper roots, as we have indicated, than the material claims of the "Left" make evident. A lack of knowledge of these roots leads to repeated misunderstandings, and it is hoped that our remarks can serve to illuminate them. That in itself would accomplish something, were it not that the very mention of this subject immediately evokes strong feelings on both sides. Such an emotional response is perhaps not surprising, at least not from the "awakening" side since considerable discipline is required by those living in hunger if they are not to react emotionally, inasmuch as the question strikes at the very roots of their predicament. And much of mankind, it must not be forgotten, is in this situation. Yet these roots are not the original source of the problem, but merely its inception, a fact that ought not to be ignored.

35   Again we emphasize that it is the human being in man and woman who is to gain standing and dignity. We cannot speak, therefore, of a new matriarchy or of a modified patriarchy, and we can think even less in terms of the type of androgyny envisaged by Novalis and Baader as the origin and *telos* of human development. Their error, which was the error of countless others before and since, was that they coupled origin and telos, which are mutually exclusive realities. Temporally determined telos is as inherent in the ever-present origin as is the temporally conditioned beginning. (These lines were written in 1948 before the publication of Karl Jaspers' *Vom Ursprung und Ziel der Geschichte* [Zürich: Artemis, 1949].) Only that which has a beginning can have a telos; but androgyny is not a beginning; it is rather an originary phenomenon that excludes any teleological intent. If we fail to distinguish mentally between origin and telos, and like Novalis and Baader trace "development" back to a beginning, we are engaged in mythical circling (or in the case of Novalis, magical unifying). Androgyny, incidentally, finds its expression relatively late in Egyptian scarab symbolism. We have already referred to cosmological-androgynous conceptions in the text, p. 43 above.

8

The Foundations of the Aperspectival World

1. The Ever-Present Origin (Complementing Cross-Sections)

One difficulty which to some will seem insurmountable is the difficulty of "representing" the aperspectival world. This world goes *beyond our conceptualization*. By the same token, the mental world once went beyond the experiential capability of mythical man, and yet this world of the mind became reality. Anyone who objects that the aperspectival world is, in spatial terms, unimaginable, incomprehensible, impalpable, inconclusive, and unthinkable—and there will be no end to such objections—falls victim to his own limitations of comprehension and to the visual representation imposed by his world. Some will undoubtedly also be irritated by the talk of *arational* possibilities which are not to be confused with the irrational or pre-rational.

From our deliberations it will have become evident that we reject neither rationalists nor irrationalists. We leave such a mutual rejection to the antagonists themselves since it is nothing more than homage to a dualism that must be overcome. While rationalists regard everything non-rational as being merely objectionable irrationality, irrationalists regard the rational as being merely irrational—as irrational as our spatial world is in the eyes of Indians who regard it as "Maya" (appearance). We are not speaking in favor of this antithetical negation and rejection, but we have called attention to their respective deficient manifestations. Indeed we have gone even beyond this and shown that even the pre-rational was not just valid at one time but rather that its structure continues to be effective in us as one of our co-constituents, and further, that the archaic structure is ineradicable and remains ever-present even today as a consequence of its originary presence.

Just as the magic structure cannot be represented but only lived, the mythical structure not represented but only experienced, and the rational structure neither lived nor experienced but only represented and conceptualized, so the integral structure cannot be represented but only "awared-in-truth." This perception or "verition" is, then, not an impossibility if the fourth-dimensional coordinate system receives a consciousness character. (It will be the task of Part II to bring this out and make it perceptible.) Here we would only recall that the *aperspectival world, which is arational, does not represent a synthesis.* To be a synthesis it would have to attempt to unite two worlds—for instance, the rational and the irrational—an attempt which paradoxical thinking undertakes. But here we are concerned with *at least four worlds or structures,* each of which is valid as well as necessary; and the *fifth* is absolutely required.

In the face of these four structures and the fact that not only originality but also lived events, experience, conception, and thinking or cognition must be achieved in and through us, a fifth cannot be attained by synthesis but only by *integration.* And one of the "avenues" toward this integration is for us to concretize the previous structures that constitute us. This means that they must at the same time become present to our awareness in their respective degrees of consciousness. Only what is present is perceptible, just as "awaring-of-truth" is also a truth-imparting act of pre-sentiation or making-present. Perception-in-truth or "verition" is not bound to our capacity of sight, which primarily shapes the mental structure; but without in any way going beyond the senses, it presentiates forms of appearance or manifestation and is thus able to perceive diaphaneity, which cannot be realized by simple seeing, hearing, or sensation.

Again it should be emphasized that *perception is not a super-sensory process.* Concepts such as intuition and the like are definitely out of place when characteriz-ing it. It is an integral event and, if you will, an integral state of the "itself." It is presential and itself renders diaphanous; and this diaphaneity can neither be heard, intuited, nor seen. That is to say: through perception or verition the merely audible, intuitable, and visible world will be present in its entirety or wholeness. What is necessary is that this integrity and integrality be actualized.

The actualization of this entirety or wholeness is possible only when the parts which form together merely an aggregate can, by the decisive act of perception and impartation of truth, become a whole. For this to happen there is one basic prereq-uisite: the parts must be heard or experienced, intuited or endured, seen or thought in accord with their very essence. Only concretized parts can be integrated; the ab-stract, and especially the absolute, always remain separated parts (although this is not to deny the clarifying and epistemic capacity of abstraction within its commensu-rate mental structure).[1]

The deliberations of the last three chapters were devoted to the concretion of parts (chapters 5, 6, 7). They form a complement to our first summary chapter (4) and were arranged in accord with the mutations. These chapters should have brought to perception the conditionality of the magic structure as manifest in its point-like nature, and the temporal boundaries of the mythical structure that are a counterpole to its limitlessness and are expressed by the fact that thought emerged from myth.[2] In addition, the mythic-psychic world required this temporal limitation otherwise the necessary left-right interchange which was attempted would have re-mained unachievable. Finally, besides revealing the conditionality and the temporal boundaries of the magic and mythical structures respectively, these chapters may have suggested the limitation of the mental-rational structure as reflected in the consequences of its one-sidedness, that is, in its emphasis on the right, which to a great extent was substituted for all other forms of directionality and directedness—a limitation visible in the three-dimensional violation of time.

On the basis of these findings we were able to clarify implicitly that the previous "time" was a degraded time. Instead of being left as a functional and constitutive dimension, directing and spatializing, it was itself directed and spatialized. This error was unavoidable in a purely spatialized world-conception. And with regard to spirit, we were also able to clarify implicitly that what has hitherto been called "spirit" was a degraded spirit seen either in psychistic or in abstract terms, an error possible only in a world-view entangled in the psyche. In a world representation, spirit has no place since it is an arational "magnitude"; as "spirit" it was necessarily excluded and separated from the world and absolutized. Just as time is a degraded form of "coming-to-time," so is the spirit a degraded form of the "spiritual." Both can be actualized only within the amateriality of the integral structure, just as space is realized only within the material and soul in the immaterial structures.

In order to present an annotated, though incomplete, survey of the fundamentals of the aperspectival world as well as some of the findings in chapters 5, 6, and 7, we would like to include them in several complementary cross-sectional tables. We begin with those cross-sections which complement the ones already given earlier (p. 146 ff.) for the forms of realization and thought in cross-section 11.a) and b). This results in the following additional summary:

| Structure | 11. Forms of Realization and Thought | | | | |
	c) Process	d) Expression	e) Formulation	f) Limits	g) Valence
Archaic:	Presentiment	Presentiment	World-origin	------	------
Magic:	Associative, analogizing, sympathetic interweaving	Vital experience	World-knowledge, the "recognized" world	condi-tioned	univalent
Mythical:	internalized recollection, contemplation -- externalized utterance, expression	Undergone experience	World-image or *Weltanschauung*: the contemplated and interpreted world	temporally bound	ambivalent
Mental:	Projective speculation: oceanic, para-doxical, then perspectival thinking	Representation Conception, Ideation	World-conception: the thought and conceptualized world	limited	trivalent
Integral:	integrating, rendering diaphanous	Verition	World-Verition: the world per-ceived and im-parted in truth	open, free	multi-valent

In this connection let it be noted that the attributions for the integral structure in these and subsequent cross-sections present only suggestive indications and not perspectival postulations or positings. As we have summarized these cross-sections on the preceding pages, we believe their reiteration here to be unnecessary. Cross-sections 15, 16, and 17 by contrast will be treated differently:

Structure	15. Localization of the soul	16. Forms of bond or tie	17. Motto
Archaic:	(Universe)	------	(All)
Magic:	Semen and blood	Proligio (*prolegere*) emotive and point-like	*Pars pro toto*
Mythical:	Diaphragm and heart	Relegio (*relegere*) observing, internalizing (recollecting) and externalizing (expressing)	Soul is identical to life (and death)
Mental:	Spinal cord and brain	Religion (*religare*): believing, knowing and deducing	Thinking is Being
Integral:	Cerebral cortex, humoral	Praeligio (*praeligare*): presentiating, concretizing, integrating	Origin: Present Perceiving and Imparting Truth

We consider cross-section 15 necessary here since it complements the cross-sections 9 and 10 (p. 144); moreover, it is not unimportant that we take into account the "numinous" role played by our organs in the awakening of consciousness, particularly as a residue of this once-numinous or mana-like efficacy is still effective in various places today. (The deficiently magic blood-and-earth slogan of the "Thousand Year Reich," which was defeated after only twelve years, is merely one example among many.)

We have designated semen and blood as the sole localization of soul in the magic structure because they most clearly express the original point-like dispersion of the soul over all "points" experienceable by magic man. Blood and semen were vehicles of the soul since these substances are the pre-eminent vital forces. The numinous property of such substances and fluids has remained effective down to our own mental era: the blood of Christ is administered in symbolic, sacramental form in the wine; and the semen has a major role, notably in the writings of the Gnostics in the notion of the *logos spermatikos*. In Greece Hippias still called semen the locus of the soul, while Critias located it in the blood.[3]

With the mythical structure an upward relocation of emphasis on the organs considered numinous becomes evident: a shift from the vital to the emotive sphere symbolized and designated by the diaphragm and the heart. We observed this shift as we examined the changes in the individual Greek numinous concepts, as in *etor* which originally denoted "blood" and later "heart." The diaphragm, moreover, is related to breathing, and like the heart-beat, is a polar occurrence. In the mythical sphere it is the heart that hears and is spoken to; sight does not yet play a decisive role. Hence there are good reasons why mythical bards like Homer are represented as being blind; their view of the soul does not require an eye to view the visible world, but a sight turned inward to contemplate the inner images of the soul.

And finally it is generally known that as a consequence of the mental structure the locus or organ of so-called psychic processes is considered to be the spinal cord and the brain. The first to make this claim was Alkmaion,[4] and present-day materialistic psychologists will be the last, for this they can always invoke the support of Descartes.

The attributions in cross-section 16 will likely be comprehensible without further explanation. As to mythical *relegio* and mental "religion," they provide a basis for us to infer the existence of the *proligio* of the magic structure, a term which expresses more accurately the essence of so-called "primitive religion." It is the tie to the "point" that has validity "for" (*pro*) magic man in the sense of the *pars pro toto;* and magic man's closeness to origin makes it illusory to speak here of "religion," which presupposes in any event the mental consciousness structure. In the same sense we cannot speak of mere "religion" with respect to the integral structure. *Presentation is "more" than a tie to the past;* it is also an *incorporation of the future.*

Inasmuch as presentiation integrates the presence of the past as well as the presence of the future, the ties of the integral structure are ties to *praeligio.* This *praeligio* excludes all delusions and prepossessions; it is without expectation, without hope of something, since everything to be hoped for is latent in us and is realized through *praeligio.* The same is true of recollection and of the interchange between the conditioned above and below, between the temporally limited left and right, as well as the bound before and after. Praeligio is thus a commitment to the emergent transparency of the presence of origin, which, as soon as man becomes conscious of it, enables him to perceive as well as to impart the truth of integrity or the whole. The *praeligio* does not exclude any of the other forms of tie or commitment; rather it integrates them "into" the whole.

Finally, with regard to cross-section 17, we have repeatedly referred to the magic *pars pro toto*. We also remind the reader of the characteristic ambivalence of the Greek term *psyche* which signifies not only "soul" but also "life" within the mythical context. That life, symbolized by mythic-psychic images, always contains its complementary death pole. The first "motto" expresses the unifying moment; the second, the polar. In the third we find Parmenides' sentence, the positing "is"; and in the fourth the intimation that verition is neither a unification, a polarization, a postulation, nor a synthesis, but rather an integration by means of which origin— which places its imprint on the whole—becomes the perceived present.

2. Summation and Prospect

Here we conclude our attempt to exposit the foundations of a new mutation.

To the extent that we have been successful in making this mutation evident it will be apparent that *the four structures which constitute man* must be perceived in their entirety *as a whole*. The mutations are an awakening of consciousness, and their "history" as we have presented it is a contribution toward the understanding of this awakening of consciousness. This history makes us aware of the vitality and plenitude with which these structures function.

To live these structures together, commensurate with their respective degrees of conscious awareness, is to approach an integrated, integral life. And there can be no doubt that our knowledge of the particular structure from which a specific event, reaction, attitude, or judgement originates will be of aid in clarifying our lives. But it must be a clarity aware of the obscure, and a wakefulness that knows of somnolence, for these are prerequisites demanded by the transparency of the integral structure.

During our deliberations on the foundations we have already made reference to those things able to actualize a new mutation. This entailed some risks since these references were without binding force and "proof." They are to be understood as intimations or suggestions in the same way as if they were a description of a still unfamiliar landscape, a description that appears strange rather than helpful until one has seen the landscape for oneself. Nevertheless, we believe that we have been correct in pointing repeatedly to the "new landscape" of the aperspectival world. What is needed is not a representation but an intimation of this landscape. In any event, initial manifestations of this new landscape can be identified. This landscape is not so much a promise as *a task or challenge*.

Whatever the nature of this landscape, it cannot be a repetition of what has been. At the very outset (or the conclusion) of this "new landscape" four major and encompassing modalities of the world from which we have come forth, lived, experienced, and thought, and from which we continue to go forth, live, experience, and think—four encompassing and intensifying realms of possible and actual forms of manifestation are eliminated. This surely does not simplify our task, but it does serve to clarify it.

The mutations as presented also make clear that something not experienceable did come to be experienced; something inconceivable did come to be conceived of; something unthinkable did come to be thought. For magic man cannot realize the experience or thought of the mental structure. For merely mental man, the perceptibility of the integral structure will not be conceivable; nevertheless we are already in the inception of this integral structure—a circumstance that provides support for events which still seem unrealizable.

Events of the past several decades have surely revealed that a new mutation is necessary if the dire situation of the present is to be changed. The extent of general destruction of materialized and false values today no longer requires a description. At this turn it may be well to recall that once, when the mythical structure began to pale, Greek man was faced with a proliferating chaos similar to ours today. The chaos then affected the mythical world which had burst apart, and the threat was a destruction of the psyche. With the aid of directed thinking the Greeks were able to master this chaos.

Our chaos today pervades our material-spatial world; perhaps we can master it by "verition." The ideas of Plato gave a fixed form to the thought contents of the soul without which the Greeks would never have been able to extricate themselves from soul and myth. This fixation which made the spatial world possible was itself fixed by Leonardo's perspective. Without it European man would have been lost in space just as the Greeks would have been lost in the soul without the set, idealized points.

Now that this spatial world threatens to come apart because the forces it has unleashed are more powerful than man who realized them, the new capability is being formed in him which is awakened by precisely those seemingly negative powers and forces. Just as *sense-directed thought*—which was able to prevent the Greeks from perishing in the inner world of awakening consciousness (the soul)— was awakened by the ruptured mythical circle, so too could "senseful awaring" be awakened by the bursting spatial world: a "perception" able to sustain us against perishing in the consciously realized external world of matter.

We must not forget that the splintered spatial world of our conceptualization is the assurance of the possibility of a space-free aperspectival world. If we succeed in regarding events from the vantage point of mutation, it will be evident that the comparison made above is not a question of repetition, but of a *"new"* event. From the earliest times until the present the structures have increased, and it is our task to achieve the latest incrementation for the time being by integration.

When the Mexicans in their deficient mythical-magic structure encountered the mentally-oriented Spaniards, the magic-mythical power failed in the face of mental strength; clan consciousness failed in the face of the individualized ego-consciousness. If an integral man were to encounter a deficient mental man, would not deficient material power fail in the face of integral strength? Would not the individual ego-consciousness falter in the face of the Itself-consciousness of mankind? the mental-rational in the face of the spiritual? fragmentation in the face of integrality?

It is today no longer a question as to whether "reforms" are of use; this is evident from the course of our discussion. Yet one question remains: what can man do to bring about this mutation? To this we have already hazarded an answer: we must know where we are to effect events, or to let them take their course; where we are merely to "be aware" of truth, and where we may "impart the truth." For we too presentiate the whole by realizing that we are to the same degree active as well as enduring and passive, past as well as future. Man is in the world to sustain it as well as himself "in truth," not for his or its own sake, but for the sake of the spiritual present. It is this spiritual present which elevates wholeness to transparency and frees us from our transient age, for this age of ours is not the present but partiality and flight, indeed, almost a conclusion. Only someone who knows of origin has present— living and dying in the whole, in integrity.

---

1   In his address "Die Abstraktion in der modernen Naturwissenschaft," Werner Heisenberg has eloquently demonstrated the eminent value of the free application of abstraction; it is reprinted in *Orden pour le merite für Wissenschaft und Künste: Reden und Gedenkworte,* IV (1960–61) (Heidelberg: Schneider, 1962), p. 139–164.

2   It is only natural that temporal limitation provided the "gap" or caesura whose possibility or eventuality was suggested by Helios' interruption of his course at the birth of the mental world. Moreover, mythical occurrence is not a closed eventuation, and the psyche is not a self-contained unit but rather a self-complementarity. If mythical occur-

rence were closed it would be spatial, but it is in fact non-spatial and therefore space-creating, and as such not closed but a perpetual self-closing. If this fact is not observed (*relegiert*) but rather neglected, the sheltering world disintegrates, as it indeed was broken up. And the temporal limitation, that is, the temporal gap occurs within circular mythical occurrence at that "place," or more accurately, in that term where every event closes upon, or complements itself. How deeply our "knowledge" of this circumstance is rooted in man is evident from a brief reference to weaving by Navajo women: "Quando una donna Navajo sta per finire uno di questi tessuti, essa luscia neela trama e nel disegno una piccola frattura, una menda: affinché l'anima non le resti prigioniera dentro al lavoro" (When completing one of these weavings, a Navajo woman leaves an interruption, a mistake in the warp and design, "so that her soul doesn't get caught in her work"), Emilio Cecci, *Messico* (Milan: Treves, 1932), p. 42.

3   On this and other localizations, see Aristotle, *De anima*, 408 B ff.; Aristoteles, *Über die Seele*, trans. A. Busse (Leipzig: Meiner, 1911), p. 18 ff.; see also Weicker, *Der Seelenvogel in der alten Literatur und Kunst* (Leipzig: Teubner, 1902), p. 31, for evidence on the equivalence of head and soul; Erwin Rohde, *Psyche, Seelenkult und Unsterblichkeitsglaube der Griechen* (Tübingen: Mohr, [10]1925), I, p. 23, Note 1, where the eye and mouth are indicated as localizations. Leisegang, in *Pneuma Hagion* [Leipzig: Hinrichs, 1922), p. 38, names viscera, kidneys and genitalia; see also Leonard Schneider, *Die Unsterblichkeitsidee im Glauben und in der Philosophie der Völker* (Regensburg: Coppenrath, 1870), particularly p. 53 f., as well as the relevant sections in Frazer, *The Golden Bough* (London: Macmillan, [3]1920), and Wundt, *Völkerpsychologie* (Leipzig: Engelmann, [3]1912), II, p. 2, 12 ff. and passim. As an example of the continuing existence of such effects, we would mention that for Cavalcanti the heart is still the seat of the soul; see Jean Gebser, *Rilke und Spanien* (Zürich: Oprecht, 1940, [2]1946), p. 86, note 47; *Gesamtausgabe*, I, p. 77. See also the compilation by Béla Révész, *Geschichte des Seelenbegriffes und der Seelenlokalisation* (Stuttgart: Enke, 1917).

4   See Gebser, *Abendländische Wandlung* (Zürich: Oprecht, [2]1945), pp. 17 ff., 23 f., and 25; Ullstein ed. No. 107, p. 15 ff.; *Gesamtausgabe*, I, p. 176 ff.

PART TWO:
Manifestations of the Aperspectival World
An Attempt at the Concretion of the Spiritual

"The second part of my 'Ever-present Origin' is the attempt to answer the question: What is to come? At first glance it may seem that this is only a question about the future, but in fact it is primarily one about our present situation. The events of tomorrow are always latently present today. Tomorrow is nothing other than a today which is not yet acute, i.e., is still latent. Every manifestation of our lives inevitably contains the sum of what is past as well as what is to come. If, however, we have an approximate notion of how the events of today came about—if we know their basis (which I attempted to present in the first part)—there is perhaps the possibility that we can discern in the movements of our present minute in time and in the world those of the next as well.

Thus it is not a question of analysis or diagnosis, nor even of prognosis, but rather a matter of discerning in the manifestations of our age in what respects they differ from those of earlier epochs. I have called such new or novel manifestations 'aperspectival' manifestations because one of their characteristics is that they are neither unperspectival nor perspectival; rather, they are free of that form of thinking which, since the Renaissance, has characteristically been aimed at some goal or telos and bound to space.

In order to discern the novel nature of these manifestations it has been necessary to examine the largest possible number of the various areas of inquiry and creativity. This examination has extended over nearly twenty years and has included the forms, statements, and expressions of the natural sciences, the humanities, and the arts. Only by demonstrating, which I believe to have done, that in all of these areas there is a common (and for the most part hidden) concern, would our discerning have a binding character. Thus the attempt had to be made to examine not only contemporary physics and biology, but also present-day jurisprudence and sociology, even interdisciplinary and dual sciences such as quantum biology, psychosomatic medicine, and parapsychology, and of course the principal arts—architecture, music, the pictorial arts, and literature.

This in itself was almost more than one person could reasonably take on, even when well-known representatives of the various areas gave the author their friendly assistance. But there was additionally the consideration that the discussion could not be carried on in the specialized terminologies of the various disciplines without being largely incomprehensible to the layman (although I attempted on the other hand to avoid the highly suspect 'popularizing' style frequently met with). It is my hope, to the extent that such demands can actually be fulfilled, that this second part will convey at least to the unprejudiced reader the impression that these demands have not been lost sight of. If our age were not replete with insecurity, anxiety, confusion, despair, and resignation such an attempt as this one would not have been necessary. But the complexity of our situation has required a correspondingly complex examination; even the specialists will be willing to concede this necessity. I am aware that this involves some risks, and it was of comfort, when correcting the page-proofs of this part, to read the words of Chuang-tzu: 'The sense is obscured whenever we focus only on small, finished segments of being.'

What is to come? I believe that I have given some indication of the answer to this question. As in any crisis there are two possible answers to the question of its outcome: demise or transition. It is my hope that the examination and the supporting evidence which I have presented may clarify for the reader that we can solve such an alternative in a positive way. To be sure, this requires co-operation; for this reason the book itself has been written in such a way as to require a certain participation of the reader. Anyone who takes to heart the solution to our problems, and who has not forgotten that we partake every moment of our lives in the originary powers of an ultimately spiritual nature, will be willing to participate in this task. The subtitle 'An Attempt at the concretion of the spiritual' (and not merely the psychic and the intellectual) is addressed to those who do not wish to forfeit in their lives the humility and dignity that are only then granted to us when we recognize spiritual values. To them our profoundly troubled age will reveal the new awareness that today's events have meaning and can lead to a meaningful tomorrow. It is the basic concern of the present book to demonstrate this possibility without indulging in modernism or pandering to optimism. The strengths of origin, and our own strength in bringing this origin to effectivity are the factors that will decide our fate."

> The author's comments on the second part of 'The Ever-present Origin' when it was first published in 1953.

Interim Word

Wo aber Gefahr ist, wächst das Rettende auch. (But where
there is peril, deliverance too gains in strength.)
—Hölderlin

L'esprit doit l'emporter, ou c'en est fait du genre humain.
(Spirit must tip the scales, or mankind is doomed).
—Paul Valéry

The first part of the present work was devoted to the foundations of what we
have designated as the "aperspectival world." In this second part we are concerned
with the manifestations of this aperspectival world, and in order to make these manifestations evident we have had to be somewhat daring and have included in our
discussion a wide variety of scientific disciplines, artistic manifestations, and general
phenomena of our epoch. This thankless task has been exacerbated by the present-
day fragmentation of the sciences into specialized and sub-specialized disciplines,
as well as by the attendant diversity of terminologies.

Notwithstanding these obstacles and the risk of being accused of meddling in
"areas outside of one's specialty" in this extensive undertaking by a single individual, we have had to take into account the most diverse areas since otherwise the
validity of our demonstration could well be questioned. Only if the attempt is
made—for once—to consider the most diverse areas of knowledge and manifestations of art and their underlying and common basic concern, *with reference to the
mode of thought and particular terminology of each discipline*, will it be possible to
make this basic concern evident. Or more exactly, only in this way will it be possible
to demonstrate the initial aperspectival manifestations which have become ever
more insistent in recent decades.

A further complicating circumstance in the realization of our stated task is
inherent in the natural condition of our epoch. Since a restructuration of our form of
realization is now taking place, all of its manifestations are "Janus-faced." On the

one hand they are still bound to the consciousness structure in force until now which, to the extent that it is deficient, is now threatening to collapse. Yet they are already indebted to the new yet only gradually emerging consciousness structure which is in process of formation. As a consequence a certain confusion comes to the fore because the weakened foundations of the old manner of thinking are not yet sufficiently counterbalanced by the consolidation of the new mode of perception.

If the first part of this work had not attempted to describe the "foundations" and to emphasize the permanent or lasting values, it might be charged that we are concerned here with mere modernism and not with demonstrating what will be seen to be a transposition of genuine values. Much of what goes on today is a dissolution; but it is not just a dissolution, for "dissolution" also contains a "solution." An example is the incursion so evident today into the minus or negative realm of events.

Because the zero, which we inherited via the Arabs from India, acquired particularly during the Renaissance the character of a cipher and limit and became a determinant of our manner of thinking and realization which tends toward dualism, we have been caught up in a process during recent generations which in a definitely tragic way led to the dissolution and annulment of this very mode of thought—to a dissolution, however, which prepared the way for the solution to our predicament. The incursion into the negative or minus domain that lies below the zero, of which we spoke, has come about in all areas of human endeavor.

Physics, for example, has discovered the tiny "magnitudes" or quanta whose ever-increasing refinement threatens to abet a substanceless crypto-materialism.[1] Psychoanalysis has unleashed psychic residua and encouraged the revitalization of factors previously sheltered in forgetfulness. Philosophy, notably existentialism and basic ontologistic philosophy, has escaped into mere existence or "ex-sistere," that is "being exposed." Modern art has destroyed and annulled the old forms of expression and perception. And the everyday life of the individual has been subjected to the increasing terror of an invasion of "minus" or negative values in the perverted, quantified, and degrading form of rampant automation and mechanized senseless "spinning of wheels."

Although unbeknown to most, this negative aspect of our era represents, in its unrecognized overvaluation of the "minus" realm, the very essence of modernism; and this modernism must not be identified with the new structure of consciousness. It is only the necessary side-effect of its restructuration and can only complicate the clarification of our epoch and our situation at first glance, particularly as there is no "going back." We emphasize this point because mere modernism or love of novelty must not be mistaken for the new aperspectival structure of awareness. The justice of this observation will be borne out in the course of the first four chapters of this second part. Without them, the following chapters, devoted exclusively to the "manifestations of the aperspectival world," would cause misunderstandings even at the terminological level in our estimation of these manifestations.

Let us once again note in passing above and beyond these clarifications our central thesis: with each mutation of consciousness, origin acquires an intensified conscious character of present-ness; origin, which bears the imprint of the whole and of the spiritual and "is" before time and space, becomes time-free "present." It is the aperspectival world that acquires this ever-present origin and thereby supersedes the perspectival world.

Even Karl Jaspers, despite his existential and thus one-sided, fixed mode of thinking, refers in passing to a "life from ever-present origin" on the last page of his

Origin and Aims of History, which was published in the same year as the first part of the present work.[2] And during the past few years, notably in the English-speaking countries, the idea has gained acceptance that, in physical-cosmogonical terms, origin is present. It has gained currency through Fred Hoyle's cosmogony (theory of world origins) where he has stated that the world is a "continuous creation" that proceeds from what he calls the "background matter" which continuously effects the requisite uninterrupted new creation of matter that "does not come from anywhere . . . [but] simply appears."[3]

Origin is present. Anyone who is able to perceive this spiritual state of affairs has already overcome the confusion of our epoch and maintains the greater and more decisive reality of the whole: that unique entirety and integrity which is always both origin and present.

---

1   An example of such crypto-materialism is the neurotic denial of the immaterial origin of matter, an origin now evident from developments in nuclear physics. Russian scientists are forced into this rejection for the sake of keeping the Marxist ideology intact which traces everything to matter. Two instances are cited in Kurt A. Körber, *Gespräch mit sowjetischen Wirtschaftspraktikern*, privately printed for the "Bergedorfer Gesprächskreis zu Fragen der freien industriellen Gesellschaft" (Hamburg-Bergedorf, 1962), p. 20, and in Gebser, *In der Bewährung* (Bern: Francke, ²1969), p. 150; *Gesamtausgabe*, V/I, p. 297; cf. the quotation from *Kommunist*, the official ideological organ of the Kremlin.

2   Karl Jaspers, *Vom Ursprung und Ziel der Geschichte* (Zürich: Artemis, 1949), p. 309.

3*   Fred Hoyle, *The Nature of the Universe* (New York: Harper, 1950), pp. 110 and 123.

1

The Irruption
of Time

1. *The Awakening Consciousness of Freedom from Time*

The irruption of time into our consciousness: this is the profound and unique event of our historical moment. It presents us with a new theme and a new task, and its realization—which comes about through us—is attended by a wholly new reality of the world: a new intensity and a freer awareness which supplant the confusion that seems to give our world its most characteristic stamp. Wherever we encounter this theme in the manifestational forms of our lives we are face to face with the initial manifestations of the aperspectival world. It is the task of this second part to evince and order these manifestations and to acclimate our consciousness to them.

Where today we seem to discern only shrieks and dissonance we will find a new tone, a new form, a new perception. The more the manifestations of our age of transition and decline make known their desperate and furious struggle, the greater will the vitality and intensity of the new world-transforming manifestations stand out. Every one of us today in his or her own way, wherever we may be, is not only a witness but an instrument of what is to be reality—hence the necessity for us to create the means with which we ourselves can jointly shape this new reality.

We will have made a decisive step when we are able to realize the full complexity of the question of "time"—that is, when we have actualized the "new" to the degree that we can consciously avail ourselves of it. What is occurring today is occurring almost of itself, or more exactly, of the Itself. It is essential that everyone, each individual "I", know how to conduct himself so that the new for which he is co-responsible can have a constructive effect. It is the second task of this second part to describe this—a task of which we must not lose sight even where the complexity and novelty of the subject compel us to proceed with restraint and caution.

As our deliberations in the first part have shown, "time"—that is, mental-rational time—is a partitioning principle as well as a concept. When we speak here within a broader context of "time," we are not referring merely to the concept of time; nevertheless we must begin with this diminished form.

Among all the possible time forms, the mental-rational concept of time is most closely akin to our traditional consciousness. Only when we take this temporal fragment into account as being a divider do we become aware that it can merely *initiate* a world-transforming consciousness structure. The concept of time is only an inceptual motif for the awakening consciousness of the aperspectival world. As long as it remains in force, the dividing, disrupting, and dissolving aspects remain dominant; and yet such division, disruption, and dissolution prepare the way for a new reality. What is prepared for is more than a mere concept of "time"; it is the *achronon*, or time freedom, a freedom and liberation from every temporal form.[1]

Our present consciousness is one of transition, a conciousness in the process of mutation which is beginning to unfold new forms of realization. At the moment when consciousness became able to account for the essence of "time," time irrupted. The sense of "irruption" is ambiguous just as the moments of transition are ambiguous and Janus-faced. The term "irruption" signifies both the intrusion as well as the collapse of time for our consciousness.

But what is "time"? It is more than a mere clock time which was previously considered to be reliable and constant. It is symptomatic for our predicament that today in the light of the most recent research even astronomy has brought into question the constancy of clock time. The topic for discussion at a general meeting of the Swiss Astronomical Association in Lausanne (Spring, 1951) was, "Is time constant?" It is in fact not constant but decreases by 5.3 seconds per century, as G. Thiercy of the University of Geneva Observatory has demonstrated. This result confirms in its own way the remark by E. Rosenstock-Huessy that we are "today laboring on a science of time" which, as he emphasizes, does not itself do justice to the true phenomenon of time.[2] And chronological time is but one aspect of a more encompassing phenomenon: it is the mental aspect of that constituent of the world which manifests itself, not as space, but as a basic phenomenon of space.

In our deliberations in the fifth chapter of Part I, "The Space-Time Constitution of the (consciousness) Structures," we have shown that at least three forms of time can be discerned: magic timelessness, with its emphasis on the vital sphere; mythical temporicity with its psychic accentuation; and mental, conceptual time with its spatial accent—a deficient agent of dividing.

The three-dimensional conceptual world of our fathers had no sensorium for the phenomenon of time. Living in a spatially frozen world, they considered the temporal world to be a disturbing factor which was repressed, either by being ignored, or by being falsified by measurement into a spatial component. That is to say, in the perspectival world-conception everything was measured in spatial terms, including the phenomenon of time and other phenomena devoid of spatial (though not spatializing!) properties, which were reshaped by measure into spatial components. For perspective-thinking man, time lacked all quality. This is the decisive factor: he employed time only in a materialized and quantitative sense. He lived by Galileo's maxim: "To measure everything measurable, and to make everything measurable that is not yet measurable."[3]

This maxim—an Aristotelian axiom driven to extremes—formed the leading motif of the perspectival age. But to measure is to spatialize; and rampant measurement leads to quantification. One of the best authorities on the theories and philosophies of the perspectival age, Werner Gent, stated that the age had declassed and degraded time to a mere numerical quantity (see p. 178). Stated in more precise terms: that era had perverted time by making it into an analytical measurable relationship and by materializing it. Because of the materialization the relationship gave rise in the course of the last few centuries to an extreme dualistic form of thinking which recognized only two antithetical and irreconcilable constituents of the world: measurable, demonstrable things, the rational components of science which were valid; and the non-measurable phenomena, the irrational non-components, which were invalid.

To the perspectival age time meant nothing but a system of measurements or relationships between two moments. *Time as a quality or an intensity* was simply not taken into account and was deemed to be only an accidental and inessential phenomenon. Time, however, is a much more complex phenomenon than the mere instrumentality or accidence of chronological time. The fact that we today still think in terms of the spatial, fixed, three-dimensional world of conceptuality is an obstacle to our realization of the more complex significance of the phenomenon. Anyone who dares to venture such a realization is accused of terminological obfuscation. But this should not prevent us from stating that time as a reality encompasses still other essential forms of appearance which are proper to it alone and not to space.

To the perception of the aperspectival world time appears to be the very fundamental function, and to be of a most complex nature. It manifests itself in accordance with a given consciousness structure and the appropriate possibility of manifestation in its various aspects as clock time, natural time, cosmic or sidereal time; as biological duration, rhythm, meter; as mutation, discontinuity, relativity; as vital dynamics, psychic energy (and thus in a certain sense in the form we call "soul" and the "unconscious"), and as mental dividing. It manifests itself as the unity of past, present, and future; as the creative principle, the power of imagination, as work, and even as "motoricity." And along with the vital, psychic, biological, cosmic, rational, creative, sociological, and technical aspects of time, we must include—last but not least—physical-geometrical time which is designated as the "fourth dimension."

This seemingly random enumeration of temporal aspects may be disconcerting to someone unable to disengage himself from his three-dimensional conception of the world. To a systematician these aspects will seem to be incongruent quantities. But they are not quantities: they are elements and functionals which cannot be conceived of or arrayed in spatial terms. The apparent lack of a system that seems to prevail in our enumeration in fact corresponds to the respective realities.

What is effected can be understood systematically, but the power to effect cannot, unless we wish to perpetuate the mistakes of perspectival man by erroneously converting intensities into spatial extensities. We should also avoid the error of placing the "effected" into a causal relationship with the "effecting." And we should avoid the additional error of considering them in a dualistic fashion as antitheses, since this would amount to yet a further systematization.

Nor can a purely categorical mode of consideration do justice to the temporal aspects enumerated. We are not dealing with incongruent phenomena but with varied aspects and manifestational modalities of a basic phenomenon devoid of any spatial character. In other words, a predominantly categorical evaluation is not appropriate here. Every categorical system is an idealized ordering schema by which actual phenomena are fixed and absolutized; as such it is a three-dimensional framework with a static and spatial character. Such categorical systems are able to deal with the world only within a three-dimensional and conceptual world-view.

We shall have to become accustomed to recognizing acategorical elements and the pre-eminent acategorical magnitude, "time," as an intensity. Its binding and integrating function is expressed in its acategorical efficacy. *Our previous and strictly categorical mode of thinking must be complemented by and integrated with the addition of the acategorical mode of realization.* We will have no success with mastering the tasks given to our epoch unless we have the courage to supersede the merely three-dimensional, spatially conceived systems.

This is not to say that we must reject them, only that they be reduced to their proper magnitudes and extensities. Intensities—hitherto spatialized and fixed—demand their own mode of arrangement, systasis.[4] Wherever we are able to perceive acategorical effectualities as such and not as categorical fixities, the world will become transparent. We are then no longer tied to the spatial structure of systems but will be able to see through them systatically (integratively). The transparently (diaphanously) emerging space will then no longer be a three-dimensional but already a four-dimensional reality.

With the terms "four-dimensional," and particularly "fourth dimension"—the form in which "time" is manifest in a physical sense—we have touched upon a key in a certain sense that can be of aid in clarifying our predicament. The fact that the vast complex "time," encompassing and co-constituting the world, has been ignored for centuries, even excluded from knowledge, or at best falsely spatialized, has left us unprepared to cope with the extraordinary implications of the phenomenon of time just when modern knowledge thrust it on our attention. As long as the epoch paid tribute to the three-dimensional world conception, time remained a suppressed force, and as such appeared with a vengeance when it was finally freed (or freed itself).

Like any suppressed or repressed force, when first released it overpowers, frightens, and confuses us in a destructive manner and seems to hold the upper hand. Because we were accustomed for generations to the old conception, we thought ourselves able to dominate it with our spatializing falsification. Imprisoned in our three-dimensional conceptual world, we believed time to be no more than an easily subdued and harmless accessory which could be employed with impunity merely as clock time. Since it turns out that time is much more, indeed is a *world constituent,* the degree of repercussions in the wake of this knowledge has been in proportion to the discrepancy between our previous estimation of time and its actual and enduring efficacy. But this discrepancy is so pronounced that we can only gradually realize that time means more than clock time.

Time first irrupted into our consciousness as a reality or world constituent with Einstein's formulation of the four-dimensional space-time continuum, that is to say, at the beginning of the present century. Consciously or unconsciously the time question has played a principle role in the natural sciences ever since. As a consequence of the new scientific theories, its interpretation and estimation have undergone an almost unnoticeable, but gradual year-by-year modification. Some references may shed light on this particularly noteworthy and fundamental state of affairs; these references will also provide a brief preliminary orientation on the subject that will be explored in detail in the course of the following chapters.

Prior to the exposition of the relativity theory, which is unthinkable without the time component, Planck advanced his quantum theory. The result was that linear continuity and the succession of temporal events were abandoned in favor of individual temporal impulses. This was followed by N. Bohr and the wave mechanics of de Broglie and Schrödinger, which gave validity to the principle of complementarity. According to the principle of complementarity, both matter and light are to be understood as being corpuscle as well as wave. They become visible in a sense both as a spatial magnitude, as it were, and as a temporal element.

In biology, the mutational theory of de Vries implicitly demonstrates time as an intensity; and mutation theory, together with quantum theory, wave mechanics, and the theory of relativity, form the four cornerstones of our present-day natural sciences. In addition, psychoanalysis makes it possible for us to speak today of a time phenomenon that could be called time-condensation, which occurs in psychic events and is manifest, for example, in dreams. And finally, technology outdoes itself from year to year in shrinking space by mastering time and temporally condensing great distances, either by supersonic aircraft or by narrowing them toward the temporal zero-point via radio and television.

We meet up with this same preoccupation in art: the introduction of time in painting destroys the pictorial content or—admittedly less frequently—shapes it according to different laws, as in the work of Juan Gris, Braque, and Picasso. And leaving aside other disciplines like philosophy, we can observe in poetry how the scenes and acts unfold in the plays of Thornton Wilder and Ferdinand Bruckner in utter disregard of clock time, creating expressive possibilities for truly "four-dimensional" time. In all of these examples time-freedom has already come into view.

The completely novel foundations of the new theories in science and of the means of expression in the arts rest on the inclusion of the time factor into the rigid, materialistic, and spatially conceived systems prevalent until 1900. Yet the incorporation of time into our reality is far from complete; even today there are far-reaching attempts being made toward understanding the phenomenon of time. We have designated these attempts as "temporic" attempts (see p. 26 f.). These endeavors—and again we are only giving an initial orientation—have shown extremely confusing results. It is not merely coincidental that we speak of an *irruption of time into our consciousness.*

We are confronted here with the irruption of the fourth dimension into the three-dimensional world which in its first outburst *shatters* this three-dimensional world. At first the unmastered time threatens to destroy space and its framework. In Dadaism, for example, it destroyed the structure of the sentence; in Expressionism and Surrealism it disrupted the spatial structural context, exploded the pictorial content, and mutilated the form; in psychoanalysis it is a constant threat to consciousness because of the psychic inflation and disruption of the fabric of rational thought. In biology the unmastered time initiated an unchecked increase of concern with the "life force" or *élan vital,* and for a long time biology was exposed to the danger of suffocating in an extreme vitalism. Even in physics the irruption of time has brought the threat of the ultimate destruction of matter and space, as demonstrated by the atomic bomb. Let us rest our case for the moment with these examples.

But in discussing this question we should not ignore the fact that there are intimations of the subsequent irruption of time into the three-dimensional world conception during the three generations preceding Einstein. It was Einstein's theory of relativity which invalidated the previous exclusive claim of the Copernican world system and replaced it with the space-time continuum. As a consequence we can no longer conceive of the world as being infinite and unbounded but rather "finite yet unbounded." We are obliged, in other words, to realize not only a totally new perception of reality that is diametrically opposed to the previous conception, but we are also compelled to become fully conscious of time—the new component—not just as a physical-geometric fourth dimension but in its full complexity.

We can of course concede that this necessity was at first restricted to physics. But what has occurred subsequently? More and more sciences began to wrestle with the time factor. Some have partially achieved an integral mode of observation, while others worked with four-dimensional factors which led to such tangible results as nuclear fission. At the same time the non-scientific world, notably heads of state and economic leaders, held onto their already obsolete three-dimensional dualistic-materialistic world conception, although they were already utilizing four-dimensional achievements. These they employed falsely, that is, in an inappropriate three-dimensional manner. And behold! the great amazement and consternation now that this entire world edifice began to fall apart.

"I have no time"—this million-fold remark by man today is symptomatic. "Time," even in this still negative form is his overriding preoccupation; but when speaking of time, man today still thinks of clock time. How shocked he would be if he were to realize that he is also saying "I have no soul" and "I have no life!" For perspectival man, time did not yet pose a problem. Only man today who is now awakening or mutating toward the aperspectival consciousness takes note of every hour of his apparent lack of time that drives him to the brink of despair.

Man today also lacks a secure base. Magic man was sheltered in mystery, as we today in sleep are still immersed in the nocturnal depths of the world. Like us in deep sleep, he was most profoundly sheltered. Mythical man was still secure, but his security—pervaded by the terrors as well as the bliss of dreams—held him suspended within the polar sway of events. And mental man, at least in his waking state, had already emerged from the shelter of the magic and the enclosure of the mythical worlds; his growing ego-consciousness freed him to a great extent from the earlier forms of being, and his previously sheltered existence gave way to his own efforts to gain security.

He achieved this security by means of his new faculty of directing thought which enabled him to create world-systems and to grasp realities that gave him stability in one respect in the form of philosophemes, and in another in the scientific understanding of matter. Whereas magic sheltering was still a genuine shelter, and the mythical, because it was already in motion, provided henceforth only enclosure, the security of the mental structure was—in accordance with its nature—purely fictive, that is, a design and projection of security by the ego onto the external world. The fiction of this security became obvious when the mental structure became deficient and degenerated into mere rationality.

Ever since the inadequacies of the rational came to light, man has suffered fears of exposure, abandonment, and "being thrown." He believes that he is standing at the brink, faced with the nothingness of the abyss where the "most courageous" assume their compulsory pose of grim heroism (Ernst Jünger and Jean-Paul Sartre) or attempt to escape it by a retreat into myth (as of late Martin Heidegger). The irruption of time must seem to everyone still convinced of the exclusive validity of the rational as the ultimate destroyer of the systems and conceptions that were deemed secure and afforded a sense of security. But the irruption of time is destructive only if we fail to realize what "time" actually is. If we are able to realize this, the irruption is not a further and ultimate loss of shelter and security, but rather a liberation.

There is yet another implication of this "I have no time"—the admission and declaration of impotence by European-American man: someone who has no time has no space. He is either at an end—or he is free. He is at an end if he does not realize the implications of "having no time," that is, that space has absorbed time, or that everything has become rigid and lifeless (the haste and harrassment—themselves a useless spinning of wheels—as well as busy managerism can be considered the counterpole of such rigidification); or if he does not realize that time, when employed as a mere divider, dissolves space. But if he realizes that "time" denotes and includes all previous time forms, he is free. Only the recognition of all temporal forms which co-constitute man can dissociate him from the exclusive validity of the mental time-form, establish a certain detachment, and enable him to integrate them.

The courage to accept along with the mental time concept the efficacy of pre-rational, magic timelessness and irrational, mythical temporicity makes possible the leap into arational time freedom. This is not a freedom *from* previous time forms, since they are co-constituents of every one of us; it is to begin with a freedom *for* all time forms. Only this form of freedom which proceeds from the concretion and integration of all time forms, and which can be achieved only by a consciousness which is free to stand "above" the previous time forms, can bring about a conscious advance or approximation to origin.

It is from origin, which is not bound to time, that all time forms constituting us have mutated. Origin lies "before" all timelessness, temporicity, and time. Wherever man becomes conscious of the pre-given, pre-conscious, originary pre-timelessness, he is in time-freedom, consciously recovering its presence. Where this is accomplished, origin and the present are integrated by the intensified consciousness. The irruption of time into our consciousness is the first indication, the initial motif of the consciousness mutation that is today acute. This mutation will bear its fruits of transforming the world if we succeed in superseding the irruption of time; but that is tantamount to what we have called the presentiation of origin, which can be achieved only by the successful fulfillment of the main task posed by the new mutation: the coming to consciousness of time-freedom, of the achronon.

2. The Awakening Consciousness of Integrity or the Whole.

The coming to awareness of "time" in its full complexity is a precondition for the awakening consciousness of time-freedom. The freedom from time in turn is the precondition for the realization of the integral consciousness structure that enables us to perceive the aperspectival world. The whole can be perceived only aperspectivally; when we view things in a perspectival way we see only segments. In conceptual terms, however, we can only approach the whole by way of "integrals" or "totalities."

But what are "integrals"? This frequently used concept must be defined in more specific terms because of its destructive effects, right down to the "totalitarian" conceptions where it was linked with the vitalist principle and represented only the vital aspect of time. An integral is not a fusion of discrete material parts; if it were, it would be only an amassment or sum. Nor is an integral the fusion of material parts with one of the possible temporal aspects as in totalitarianism. True integrals are constituted only where we assist spatial and temporal components in their own way to form a mutual, enduring efficacy. A true integral in this sense is "man as the integrality of his mutations" (see above p. 152 f., Part I, chapter 4, section 5). Integrals, therefore, are not summations of parts but occur where parts—which are always spatially bound—are consciously perceived with the powers which actualize them; "temporal" functionals together with spatial matter form integrals.

An integral mode of perception as represented today by several branches of knowledge has not yet been able to establish itself in the public consciousness because the man of today continues to think and act in accord with the three-dimensional conceptual world. Therefore he continues to regard only one aspect of the world as real: the spatial. Time for him has remained what it was: chronological time, or at best terms of delivery or expiration, and perhaps the span of life itself, although that too is mostly forgotten since it is a form of time which, because of its restricting effect, elicits feelings of anxiety.

What are the implications of such a partial and single-aspect view of reality? One implication is that we are not able to view the world integrally but instead segment the world. Yet it should be no surprise that anyone who realizes or recognizes only one aspect of the world, such as space, when the other (time) is already fully awakened to its efficacy and reality in man's consciousness, will one day find himself partitioned, or will seem to be only a fragment of a mass. That would mean that he is fragmented along with his world, or that he fragments and destroys himself, a prospect now imminent because of nuclear fission.

By unleashing two world wars our Europe has begun to a suicidal extent this self-destruction. Some might think this example ill-advised, believing that we can still blame one neighbor or the other for all our misfortunes. But there are still more indications of the possibly transient self-inflicted impotence of our continent. Let us not forget that the theories which have completely transformed the countenance of our time were born in Europe; and yet it would seem that we have for the time being been deaf to the serious consequences of these theories. We have created them but are unable to control them. To single out just one example of our impotence and paralysis, we could point to the fate of materialistic theories which were, like many others, conceived and worked out in Europe and have transformed the world. But they have been misused by others because we failed to muster the intensity of our consciousness so as to govern them responsibly. Instead of ourselves undertaking to reshape the obsolete, three-dimensional foundations of the new sociological theories, we have permitted the successor of European culture, Russia, to misuse them.

In Russia the Marxism of Hegel, Marx, and Engels has been presumptuously driven to extremes and perverted into Leninism and then Stalinism, because Europe adamantly retained a dualistic world conception long after its time. We of the European-Atlantic cultural community have as yet been unable to make the leap at the crucial moment from the three-dimensional world of our fathers into the four-dimensional reality of our day. And as long as we fail to make this leap, crises, uncertainty, and anxiety will continue to prevail; and they can destroy us in the short run unless we realize the new world reality. We must, in other words, attain a new attitude toward the actualities of the new reality which are crystallizing in a new perception of the world.

Our realization of this new attitude will be decisive in solving our pressing problems because the new frame of mind resulting from it corresponds to the new reality and is therefore sound. It is in any event sounder than the cold and dogmatic fanaticism of Eastern stamp, and for that reason is more certain, stronger, and superior. It is not might but strength that is victorious, for might or potency is always threatened by impotence. Anyone able to set aside power is liberated from impotence.

Since we already live in a four-dimensional reality, it is no longer legitimate for us to think and act mindlessly and unreflectively as though we were still in the three-dimensional world of our fathers and forefathers. Is there really any justification for us to feel insecure and depressed because of our present poor management of our affairs? It is by now only too obvious that something fundamental is out of kilter.

To illustrate our predicament we would cite a graphic example. We move about in our modern world in the same way a "wild man" from the primeval forest might have acted in the world of our fathers. Primitive man is anchored at best in the pre-rational or irrational world, and experiences it more or less vegetatively without the support of conceptual thought, and thus without any idea of space. How different from the three-dimensional, mental-rational-conceptual space-and-thought world of our fathers, who felt quite at home so long as the possiblity of an other-dimensioned world did not exist for their consciousness.

Or yet another comparison: we act and react like someone attempting to fly a supersonic aircraft in a room, that is, we attempt to employ a four-dimensional creation (the supersonic aircraft) within a three-dimensional world (the room). The airplane exceeds and transcends our erstwhile spatial perception.

A third example will suggest what can be gained if we include time in our mode of inquiry. The gains will be apparent if we successfully incorporate "time" into our reality as an integral complex, rather than as a conceptualized spatial part and partitioner. We refer to our continous enslavement to nationalism. Nationalism is prototypical of three-dimensional thinking. To consider man as an offspring of a nation is to perceive the nature and ways of one's own nation as being an enduring ideal. Such a static view is a three-dimensional, perspectival, and fixed conception. Yet on the basis of recent deliberations in studies on the philosophy of history and on sociology we should be regarding nations as being dynamic efflorescences of a larger cultural context.[5] Although such an awareness does not abolish nationalism, it at least transcends and integrates it into a more encompassing integral reality. It is not the nations—the parts—but the broader cultural context of the whole that holds the possibility of effectuality and of awakening consciousness.

This particular example seems fruitful and revealing since as it shows that a new and constructive perception of the world or of phenomena is not only possible but even embodies two essential components with which this perception can be realized. These components are the temporal and the integral. The temporal component appears in our understanding that nations are unique dynamic outgrowths of a larger culture and not merely static ideas. Moreover, as soon as we take this temporal component into account, the integral moment is also manifest since it integrates the aspects which heretofore have been seen in spatial terms as being inimical and antithetic into an "integral" or whole, achieving a new point of departure and a new perception in an essential area.

For this reason it is remarkable that all of the sciences today are manifesting a tendency toward an integral mode of inquiry, although positive results are obtained only when "time" is taken into account in the one or the other of its manifestations. This development has given rise to the recognition that the old antithesis between inorganic and organic does not exist, having been replaced by a closer relationship between physics and biology that is not restricted only to quantum biology. This also holds true of biology and psychology where the old dualism of body and soul has given way to a psychosomatic medicine that has evolved an integral conception of man, a perception of man as a whole (as in the work of G. R. Heyer and Arthur Jores; see below, p. 448). And the aspirations toward integrality in Karl Jaspers' existential philosophy form a bridge between psychology and philosophy. Philosophy itself has even established contact with its long-standing cultural antipode, literature, by its attempts to form a "metaphysics of literature."[6]

These integral achievements that together demonstrate a dissolution of erstwhile antagonisms and dualisms were possible only because their originators had consciously or unconsciously divorced themselves from an exclusively three-dimensional spatial framework. Wherever we encounter these integral endeavors which take into consideration the full efficacy and varied manifestations of the thematics of time we are conceptually approaching the whole. It is perceptible only through a mode of realization sufficiently bold to allow us to transcend mere conceptualization while preventing us from a regression to the imagistic world of the psyche or the magic vital sphere.

Since the realization of freedom from time is a precondition for the realization of the whole, we must observe that both require the additional capacity of consciousness crucial to the current mutation of consciousness whose elucidation forms the subject of our inquiry.

Mere mental wakefulness is not sufficient to realize the new reality. Diurnal wakefulness achieves only partition and division; it sheds light on the path, the "Tao,"[7] as long as mental consciousness dwells in the phenomena of diurnal brightness—itself, like conceptual time, a divider, dividing the night, dreams, sleep, and the world. As long as its dividing is not an end in itself it indirectly yields valid knowledge of the undivided. But if the world is regarded only through wakefulness, it loses its undivided dream-like and somnolent aspects and precipitates their separation. The dividing deed leads to death: the death of man and his entire culture. Wakefulness, then, is not adequate, least of all the attitude of all-or-nothing wakefulness. Clarity, however, is adequate, for it alone is free of brightness, twilight, and darkness, and is able to penetrate the whole where somnolent timelessness, somnial temporicity, and mental conceptuality all become diaphanous. Anyone who perceives in this manner is free from time and can see through the whole in which he partakes, not as a part, but integrally.

1*   The word "achronon" is formed by the prefix "a-," the *alpha privativum* expressing freedom, and the stem "chron" from Greek *chronos*, "time."

2   Eugen Rosenstock-Huessy, *Der Atem des Geistes* (Frankfurt/M.: Verlag der Frankfurter Hefte, 1951), p. 32.

3   See Jean Gebser, *Abendländische Wandlung* (Zürich: Oprecht, ²1945), p. 24 and Ullstein ed. No. 107, p. 20; *Gesamtausgabe*, I, p. 181.

4   *Systasis*, Greek for "put together," "connection"; it also has the connotation of "forming" and "origin." It expresses a process whereby partials merge or are merged with the whole.

5   Jean Gebser, "Notwendigkeit und Möglichkeit einer neuen Weltsicht," *Die Neue Welt-*

schau: Internationale Aussprache über den Anbruch eines neuen aperspektivischen Zeitalters, proceedings of the conference by the same title sponsored by the Handelshochschule, St. Gallen (Stuttgart: Deutsche Verlags-Anstalt, 1952), pp. 9-31; reprinted in Gebser, *In der Bewährung* (Bern: Francke, ²1969), pp. 23-37; *Gesamtausgabe,* V/I, pp. 177-188.

6   Max Bense, *Literaturmetaphysik* (Stuttgart: Deutsche Verlags-Anstalt, 1950).

7   The Chinese word *Tao,* commonly rendered as "path," can be traced to the same root *da:di* common to the words Zeus, day, Dais, time, and others (see our "Fifth Remark on Etymology, p. 558). See also Gustav Zollinger, *Das Yang- und Yin-Prinzip ausserhalb des Chinesischen: Tau, Tau-t-an - *Serm-an* (Bern: Francke, 1949), p. 43 ff., which substantiates the relationship of the Chinese Tao to the Egyptian god *Tot* and the Indian *Mani-Tou,* among others. See Matgioi, *La voie rationelle* (Paris: Bodin, 1907), p. xvi; the preface makes reference to remarks of M. Panthier in his *La Chine* (Paris: Didot). Matgioi with good reason points out that the word *Tao* is "substantially" identical with the Greek word *Theos,* from which Latin *deus* is derived. We would also mention that the concept of Tao was invested with its predominant significance by Lao-tzu's *Tao Teh Ching.* It came into being around 500 B.C. during the very epoch when the mutation from the mythical to the mental structure was also occurring in the West that made purposive, goal-oriented thinking possible. As Alexander Ular and Richard Wilhelm have pointed out, both Chinese characters making up "Tao-Teh-Ching" mean "right path" or "straightness," i.e., directedness, as well as "head" (from which thought, like Athena, springs forth); Alexander Ular, *Die Bahn und der rechte Weg des Laotse* (Leipzig: Insel, ⁵1920), p. 102 (postscript), and Laotse, *Taoteking: Das Buch des Alten vom Sinn und Leben,* translation and commentary by Richard Wilhelm (Jena: Diederichs, 1921), preface, p. xv ff. See also Gebser, preface to Laotse, *Tao Te King* (Bern: Huber, 1958), p. 7 ff.; *Gesamtausgabe,* V/II, p. 15 ff.

2

The New Mutation

1. The Climate of the New Mutation

Mutations have always appeared when the prevailing consciousness structure proved to be no longer adequate for mastering the world. This was the case in the last historically accessible mutation which occurred around 500 B.C. and led from the mythical to the mental structure. The psychistic, deficient mythical climate of that time presented a threat, and the sudden onset of the mental structure brought about a decisive transformation. In our day the rationalistic, deficient mental structure presents an equal threat, and the breakthrough into the integral will also bring about a new and decisive mutation.

The criteria which permit us to evaluate the individual phenomena of these processes both as an expression of the already realized consciousness structures and as manifestations of the new, are given by the designations we have assigned to the individual consciousness structures. The synoptic table at the end of the volume provides a survey of these designations. Let us once more note the major criteria:

1) "Origin" is not identical with the "beginning" since it is not spatially and temporally bound, whereas the "beginning" is always temporally determined.
2) The "Present" is not identical with the "moment" but is the undivided presence of yesterday, today, and tomorrow which in a consciously realized actualization can lead to that "presentiation" which encompasses origin as an ineradicable present.
3) The "aperspectival world" is a "world" whose structure is not only jointly based in the pre-perspectival, unperspectival, and perspectival worlds, but also mutates out of them in its essential properties and possibilities while integrating these worlds and liberating itself from their exclusive validity.

If we work out in detail the possibilities of realization in accord with the dimensions of the individual consciousness structures, and show how certain manifestations can be readily assigned to one of the previously effective degrees of consciousness, we have a touchstone for differentiating between the "new" and the "old" when dealing with the manifestations of today. With the help of our structurations of the various degrees or frequencies of consciousness it is possible in any event to determine whether, and to what extent, a particular manifestation originates in the magic, mythical, or mental sphere. If a manifestation cannot be assigned to any one of these spheres we may conclude that it is an expression or manifestation of the new consciousness structure whose possibility we have pointed out.

The large, indeed, immense number of "novelties" in all areas of our day-to-day lives, as well as in the sciences and the arts, which are today at the disposal of a truly "up-set" mankind would, by their very abundance, deluge anyone so bold as to regard these manifestations of a self-disintegrating world from a purely arbitrary standpoint. Even the wish to infer only their positive and constructive aspects is of little consequence despite good intentions, for such an attitude remains one-sided and fixed, and hence inadequate to the protracted demands of the restructuration of our reality.

In those rare moments of real, and that means effectual, mutation the criteria previously valid or in force become to a certain extent invalid, indeed they are to a considerable degree illusory and irrelevant. At the moment of mutation, a previously latent aspect of the world is not just set free: its release reveals for a few decades a more intense radiance of origin. And this circumstance releases our mutational period more or less from those criteria which are provided by the magic, mythical, and mental integumence or governance of the world (which present themselves to us as the basis of our mutation).

This ascertainment provides the point of departure for our inquiry. Because of its importance we repeat: Everything that is manifest as "new" in the spontaneity of a mutation, everything that becomes creative and actual by and in it, is distinguished by a basic and definitely change-effecting manner from all manifestations that were "previously" and exclusively actual and thus effectual.

If we hold to the criteria established in Part I for the previous consciousness structures and their forms of manifestation, it will be evident when we consider certain phenomena that they have nothing in common with the previous forms of manifestation. They are, in other words, not merely reactivations of the magical, mythical, and mental, but are truly proper to the new self-constituting integral domain, that is, to the manifestation of the new consciousness. As such they are the first visible indications of what we have defined as the "aperspectival world."

Mutational periods are times of disturbance and even destruction. The fact that a given vessel—in this case man—is compelled or enabled to realize an additional possibility, an additional possibility of the world, causes first of all a shake-up of the previously existing, habitual vital-psychic-mental order. The resultant disorder, if it is not mastered on the strength of insight into the occurring mutation brings on chaos rather than a restructuration and novel constellation of reality.

The tendency toward chaos, decay, decline, disruption; the loss and renunciation of once legitimate values; and the rise of the devalued and worthless, which are all prominent expressions of our epoch, present major obstacles to the interpretation of manifestations of the new consciousness. Everything is out of order; even so-called "positive" attempts undertaken here and there to "save" humanity or Europe should be viewed for the most part with no less skepticism than the equally undeniable attempts to destroy mankind.

When, in the course of the following pages, we are obliged to point repeatedly to phenomena of a predominantly negative character, it is not—and this must be emphasized—that we wish to be advocates of the ultra-modernist manifestations which pervade both everyday life and the arts and sciences. These manifestations we must accept for what they are: realities which we must consider as being not just meaningful but also sensible and sense-fulfilling. If we do not, we relinquish at the very outset all assurance of the continuation of the earth and of mankind.

Thus it is not a question of finding a positive side to the so-called negative manifestations—and this too must be emphasized. That would remain a "one-sided" achievement, whereas we are concerned with the whole. It would, however, be irresponsible of us if we did not concede that much of what is to be said is painful—painful in a completely unsentimental way. Responsibility implies pain for anyone cognizant of the danger brought on by merely blind courage.

One thing is certain: mankind is not defending a "lost position"; it is defending a position that it is unwilling or unable to give up even though the position itself is in the process of surrender, change, and mutation. Because the prototypical rational earth-dweller of today has lost his insight into the interdependency between human-terrestrial and cosmic—indeed "extracosmic"—events he is all too easily misled into believing himself to be unique and irrepeatable, and therefore already lost.

Man's severance from powers which cannot be proven restricts his ties to his past, which is then lost in uncertainty. At the same time he also forfeits his future, the mirroring of his past. This loss is even greater, since the present, as he understands it, necessarily also becomes irrelevant; a nothing, a nowhere, the impalpable point of severance and forlornness. And here we should re-emphasize that our concern is not with the conquest of a future, at least not that "temporal" future that is generally deemed to be the future. *Rather it is a question of what is future in us, that is, what is present to the same degree that all past in us is present.*

Such an attitude will enable us to escape one danger: that of assuming that everything we shall be considering in the following discussion could or should be understood as the design of a future world. Our sole concern must be with making manifest the future which is immanent in ourselves. It is not the concern of the present work to show the shaping of the future in "time" since this form of time is at an end. And because time as such is coming to an end and is being supplanted by time freedom, any temporal projection "forward" is illusory and illusionary.

By maintaining this attitude we escape yet another danger: that our discussion and deliberations on the manifestation of a new consciousness could in any way fix or determine the "future" or that we are irresponsibly and intentionally spoiling or tampering with—and thus limiting and fettering—an event which is occurring of itself. No man is so unique, as some think, that he is ever able to take on such responsibility alone.

There is yet a further aspect which is, so it seems, no longer present in the consciousness of most people today: the fact that during previous genuine mutational eras powers or energies took shape in human form which visibly embodied and effected the respective mutational principle throughout long periods. The appearance of such figures as Zarathustra, Confucius, Chuang-tsu, Lao-tzu, Buddha,

Mahavira, Socrates, Plato,[1] and particularly Jesus Christ precisely at the moment of a mutation is not merely fortuitous. All prognostication, not to mention prophecy, aside, it will seem plausible that at the moment of the mutation now occurring, the mutation will also have its incarnation. But it will be implicit from our subsequent discussion that this incarnation will differ in kind and essence since it must manifest itself not "in time" but in time freedom, and will be transparent.

This possibility of mutation appropriate to space-and-time-free diaphaneity should not be overlooked. Soon we will witness the rise of some potentate or dictator who will pass himself off as a "savior" or healer and allow himself to be worshipped as such. But anyone who does this in the days to come, and is thereby confined to time and is visible in it, has nothing to do with the true manifestation of the one who, in time-free transparency, will make the "future" present. The one who remains confined in time will thus be less than a mere adversary: he will be the ruinous expression of man's ultimate alienation from himself and the world.

Today there is still time to say this; but sooner perhaps than many suspect the end of time will come when it can no longer be said. We can only surmise in what form time-freedom will succeed time. In any event, the forms of this supersession already bear today the stamp of catastrophe and demise of the world. Just as the supersession of mythical temporicity by mental time was an end of the world—of the mythical world that had become deficient—it is today a question of the end of the mental world which has become deficient.

Any attempt to establish possible dates, even if they could be intimated by certain allusions confirmed by experience in ancient wisdom, would be irresponsible for it would determine the future which is not ours to establish. The future will ultimately establish itself, our role being at the very most that of participants. But one thing must be said: the coming decades will decide whether the fundamental transformation will occur during the next two generations, or not for the next two millenia. Since the decisive role in this event will be played by the spiritual, which is not earth-bound like the vital, destiny-bound like the psychic, nor causally linked like the mental; and since the spiritual may well precipitate the mutations, it is of signal importance whether or not the strength achieved by our consciousness will comprehend the originary presence of the spiritual.

Above and beyond this, it ought not to be forgotten that, in rational terms, what occurs "here" has its correspondence "there." The earth is not just a star among stars but a star *with* other stars. Any sweeping changes on earth are not only changes of the earth; they not only occur "here" (on earth) but also "there." Whether the changes taking place here initiate similar ones "yonder," or whether the changes in the "yonder" initiate the changes "here," is an idle question for anyone aware of the undeniable interconnection of materialized phenomena of which the earth, like every other star, is a part.

How mankind decides in the coming decades, or how it will devolve on mankind over the next few decades to be able to decide, and how it will be possible for mankind to endure and sustain the strength that is acute in the occurring mutation—on this will depend how the "law of the earth" will be fulfilled (see p. 79 f.). If mankind can endure the new tensions that are becoming acute as a result of the irruption of new heavens and the earth's migration through new regions of the universe—tensions which are becoming acute on the earth and thus in man as well—then the impending collapse will only mean the end of the exclusive validity of the hitherto dominant mental structure. But if man and the earth are unable to endure these tensions, they will be torn apart by them. Both, in other words, will perish in their present form, and after the great intervening breathing-spell a new earth and a new man will arise. The destiny of man and the earth will depend on the consciousness intensity which man is intended to attain, and which he would attain if he would succeed in living the new mutation.

In any event the temporal moment, that is to say the point of finality which is set for time, has a visibly prominent role. This is so because everything that occurs through and by us, everything that we do has its lasting effect; because what is done here can only be here undone; because we are in one way or another bound to the earth; and because misdeeds must be resolved here where they took place, whether in life or in death, where they engendered fruitfulness or barrenness in time and space. Therefore it cannot be a matter of indifference to someone who lives in clarity whether or not he will once again be given a time span, whether he will be permitted to turn this span here into time freedom, or whether he is appointed to sink unchanged below the limits of effectuality as an unsuccessful attempt of the wider context of nature rather than as the flower of its fulfillment.

In this connection it is necessary once again to mention our fundamental position: our deliberations on the manifestations of the new consciousness, which permit the inference of a concretion of the spiritual, do not refer to their visible "temporal" manifestation but to their time-free possibility in us and in the world. They refer to the original constellation of consciousness as it mutates to "Itself-consciousness," and its manifestation in man. The only "subject" of our inquiry, the subject which is to be clarified, is that which is today visible as the first manifestation of a time-free consciousness.

A second point to be pondered is what unavoidably proceeds from this first manifestation, to the extent that it has the opportunity to unfold and consolidate in man. When and where this unfolding will become reality is beyond any calculation. It is so inherently dependent on man's ability to complete the intensification of consciousness in himself that any prediction as to time and place would be merely speculation. It would be all the more speculative since the actualization of the new structure does not take place in time and space but in the freedom from space and time that it achieves itself by mutation.

On the basis of the initial manifestations of the new consciousness which will be discussed, we can undoubtedly take for granted that many today are in a position to achieve this mutation, particularly since there have been individuals in earlier times who have achieved this integral mutation.[2] For those individuals today on whom incidentally, everything most likely depends, it does not matter whether the full abundance or plenitude that unfolds as a new reality of the world via the achieved mutation is borne by mankind which has endured the demise of the rational world, or by a mankind (insofar as it can still be called mankind) which has had to endure the end of the earth as it has existed until now—that is, a complete mutational transformation of the earth.

It is important for us to take note of this, since if we do not understand this constellation our deliberations here will lose their inherent value for our lives. The forms and concomitant manifestations which the mutational breaking forth in earthly events will assume are predominantly, indeed, primarily dependent on us, the bearers of the mutation on the terrestrial plane.

Whether the mutation can take place to us and in us, and this means to our present mankind, or whether it will be fulfilled on a later mankind—this lies to a great extent in our hand, although our participation and responsibility must not be construed in anthropocentric terms. Stated in another way, the question of the "how and when" of the mutation is inseparable from the other question: will we be privileged, by our perseverance, to participate in the (co)formation of the emerging new mutation through our conscious completion of the necessary coming-to-awareness? Or stated yet a third way, what is of immediate importance is not the future in its temporal and external aspect, but its presence in us.

Part I of the present work has corroborated our first guiding principle (see p. 6 above): "Latency—what is concealed—is the demonstrable presence of the future." Its validity became evident according to the symmetry of structure (to cite but one example) whereby the "temporal component," as we might call it, was subject to a continuous transformation throughout the various mutations—a transformation that is necessarily a predisposition in us from origin as an actuality in order that it can manifest itself each time in a different form. And only our clear understanding of the fact that the concept of "time" no longer has exclusive significance in the incipient aperspectival "world" where "time freedom" (or being freed from time and thus free for the spiritual!) is characteristic can prevent us from mistaking the phenomena we are to consider.

It is principally to this truly transforming actuality that we must turn our attention if we are to be aware of the implications of the initial manifestations of the new consciousness. This actuality is of decisive importance because the "spiritual"—and it is the concretion of the spiritual which forms the principal subject of this second part of our work—can only become evident if we are successful in superseding the three-dimensional coordinate system in which only visible things are valid and relevant. We must attempt to perceive four-dimensional integrality which is space-and-time-free: only this space-time freedom, only "in" it, is the transparency of the spiritual—the diaphainon—perceptible, for it cannot be manifest in any visible form.

We would caution here that this does not imply some kind of attempt at spiritualizing the world apart from all reality. Every form of spiritualization is gained at the expense of renouncing or negating and suppressing the previous consciousness structures. But a truly integral perception cannot dispense with the foundation of the mental structure any more than the mental structure can dispense with the mythical, and the mythical with the magic, that is, if we are to be "whole" or integral human beings.

We must, in other words, *achieve the new integral structure without forfeiting the efficient forms of the previous structures.* If we are able to fully effect this integration, if our consciousness is successful in achieving the incrementation of dimensions in mutation—which in this instance "opens up" everything in its entirety—the second of our guiding principles will become evident (see p. 6 f. above): *Transparency (diaphaneity) is the form of manifestation (epiphany) of the spiritual.*

It is the understandable error of our present-day rationality to think that the uncontrollable frenzy of events could be contained by power, agreements, compromise, reform, or revitalization. In such instances it is always assumed that man is himself the shaper of the future. But anyone who indulges in this mistaken anthropocentric belief, this illusion proceeding from rational hubris, should be resigned to "the end with terror." He would be correct in only one respect: an end is approaching, namely, the end of his epoch. And since he is unable to free himself from the confines of his three-dimensional, conceptual world, this is tantamount to an "absolute end."

The dilemma of earth and mankind today will not be resolved by some sort of human machinations. If man is still capable, the dilemma will be resolved only by the full realization of the present consciousness mutation. This mutation will bring about the transformation for which magic imploring, mythical wish, or mental volition and goal-orientation are themselves insufficient. It is this mutation which effects the supervention of diaphaneity and the integration of our vitality, psychicity, and mentality.

While this is the basic position following from our deliberations in Part I, let it be recalled that we established three principal criteria for the mode of manifestation and expression of the aperspectival world. They are:

1) "Temporics," under which term are subsumed all endeavors to concretize time;
2) "Diaphaneity," that which is pellucid and transparent, which we can perceive as the form of spiritual manifestation. It is perceptible only in a "world" where the concretion of time transforms time into time freedom and thus makes possible the concretion of the spiritual;
3) "Verition," which as the integral "a-waring" or perception and impartation "of truth," is the realization form of the integral consciousness structure which lends to the aperspectival world a transparent reality.

The additional capacity of "verition," which becomes a reality with the new mutation, is the guarantee that someone who endures the effects and transformations that are manifest in him by four-dimensional integration effects in turn a transformation of events. This is not in the sense that he or she can exercise, say, a new kind of magic power, a new mythical equipoising or polarizing, or a new kind of mental superiority over persons, events, or processes. It is rather that his or her being present is in itself sufficient to effect new exfoliations and new crystallizations which could be nowhere manifest without his or her presence.

It is the coming-to-manifestation itself which is effectual. With the manifestation, with the presence, the effect is always indirectly evident. The magic-mythical attitude, in its deficient mode, collapses defenselessly in the face of the mental attitude, as shown by both the Mexican-Spanish and the Austrian-Swiss examples cited earlier (p. 5 and note 6, p. 8). The additional dimension of mental man's consciousness, which was inaccessible to mythical man, is the decisive factor that prevented mythical man from reaching him, although the reverse is not the case since it is the incremental strength of the newly achieved dimension in mental man that is effective.

The new consciousness structure has nothing to do with might, rule, and overpowering. Thus it cannot be striven for, only elicited or awakened. Anyone who strives for it, intending to attain it mentally, is condemned to failure at the outset. This is also true of those who think that mere desire and the power of imagination, that is, mythically-tinged volition, are sufficient to fully effect the new mutation. And it is equally true of those who believe that they can master the mutation by some machination, for they simply revert to magic compulsion and constraint.

What is needed is care; a great deal of patience; and the laying aside of many preconceived opinions, wishful dreams, and the blind sway of demands. There is a need for a certain detachment toward oneself and the world, a gradually maturing equilibrium of all the inherent components and consciousness structures predisposed in ourselves, in order that we may prepare the basis for the leap into the new mutation.

To what extent the factor of grace, the Christian conception, may have a role is for theologians to decide. It is not for us to be concerned whether the element of grace is an aid to liberating us from the anthropocentric mental attitude, nor should we attempt to invest it with an efficacy as if it elected the "chosen" and exalted them to a "higher" state. The new consciousness structure is not a "higher" structure. It cannot, in the first place, be determined or assessed in spatial terms, and in the second, it makes no claim to be an outgrowth of something "elevated." Lastly, it is an integral structure where such valuations as three-, two-, or one-dimensional are irrelevant.

Whereas the deliberations so far have dealt with the climate of the new mutation, we must now turn our attention to its dominant motif. This means that we must now venture an answer to the question of the why and whither of our critical juncture.

2. The Theme of the New Mutation

Today it no longer requires great effort to adduce the salient facts that mark our epoch as one of confusion and transition. But the major error is still made of regarding these facts, such as mechanization, collectivization, loss of religion, and specialization as the causes of our plight. This utterly fallacious reasoning is the source of the "new avenues" and useless reforms which have been proposed. These "facts" are merely symptoms—symptoms of the confusion which is the fundamental aspect of our situation.

Let us turn to a concrete example: the increasing technologization of our day. It is incorrect to regard the machine as being the initiator of all present-day horrors. We shall have to look more closely into the reasons which led to the invention of the machine, notably to the invention of the steam engine by James Watt in 1782. We should note that it preceded by just seven years the outbreak of the French Revolution which can be considered as a manifestation in the social sphere of the same forces heralded by technological discovery.

What led to the invention of the machine? The breaking forth of time. The machine, in the form of the steam engine, is the progenitrix of motoric forces that rent asunder the static, spatial construction that had been attained since 1500 A.D. We speak deliberately of the "breaking forth" of time inasmuch as we cannot yet speak of an "irruption of time into our consciousness." Precisely such an awareness of what was occurring was then lacking. Only today is this awareness available to us, and it is the concern of the present work to bring this irruption to awareness.

It is significant that the breaking forth of time lay outside man's mental or rational manipulation and retained its autonomy. That is, it remained free of man's waking conscious control, and consequently the motoricity of the machine arbitrarily began to dominate and compel man into its dependency. We have already indicated (p. 285 above) that motoricity is one aspect of the phenomenon of time, and we shall return to it in the next section. Here we must probe step by step deeper if we wish to discover the reason for our present situation.

We have brought out into the open the question as to the why of the most striking characteristic of our times, the machine. But the answer to why the machine originated (the initiator of motoricity) does not give us the ultimate reason we need to clarify our present transitional epoch. The previous answer, that the machine expresses the breaking forth of time, necessarily gives rise to the decisive question: How did time come to "break forth"?

It will be evident that we have been pursuing a line of questioning and inference from a logical-causal standpoint, while dealing with a complex phenomenon that in its complexity transcends the causal nexus. The practicable answer, therefore, will be satisfactory only in mental terms, while its integral validity necessarily remains hidden for the time being. Yet the possibility of a mental-logical account will, at least for the moment, have the advantage of being able to convince rationalists, and so let us follow this line of reasoning to its conclusion.

The decisive questions, then, are: Why did time break forth? and, Why is there today an irruption of time into our consciousness? The answer has been prepared in the first part of our discussion; moreover, a judicious application of the results of recent discoveries in anthropology will provide further documentation. Let us first consider the answer anticipated earlier.

From mutation to mutation man has accrued new dimensions of consciousness in addition to those already present in a given instance. The space-timeless, somnolent, magic consciousness was overlaid by the spaceless, temporic, dreamlike mythical consciousness, and this in turn was overlaid by the diurnal, spatial mental consciousness structure. The respective mutations came about whenever the previous awakening of consciousness was completed, and the conscious attitude was satisfied with what it had achieved. For example, at the moment when mythical consciousness realized the equivalence of soul with life in the form of temporicity, this consciousness was consolidated; the work of consciousness that the mutation had made possible was accomplished, and man had to turn to new tasks. He had to do this since mere persistence or inertia leads to decline and deterioration.

But it was commensurate with man's nature that he remained for a while in that state to enjoy, so to speak, his acquired possession and capacities. This is the beginning of deficiency and decline; to abide in a given state means to deteriorate. Thus myth began to deteriorate; the world of ordered temporicity turned into psychic chaos.

This chaos was not overcome until man accomplished the further step in the awakening of consciousness. This process unfolds from the eighth century B. C. onward, and is visible in two counterpoised developments: there is a positive increase in spatial awareness directly proportional to the negative and increasing deficiency of the mythical consciousness. The decline of the mythical consciousness visible in the quantification of myth described in Part I was countered by the growth of an awakening spatial consciousness. That is, the new consciousness activity begins in the mythical man who was still resting content with his former consciousness achievement. What follows is the irruption of space into his consciousness, the necessary mutation which is alone able to contain the inundation of the psyche by myth.

This is Plato's achievement; through him spatial thinking becomes characteristic of consciousness. The unbridled mythical-psychic inundation is contained and mastered by mental thought. The deficiency of myth is annulled by the efficiency of mental thinking; in this both are mutually dependent. Not until mythical man was able to rest in the fully consolidated mythical consciousness and surrender himself without additional effort to this consolidation did the deficiency of myth set in. This deficiency was manifest in the autonomous functioning of this consciousness which began in the moment that man himself no longer needed to work on its consolidation.

Mythical consciousness became autonomous, functioning spontaneously, and anyone who remained within it became its victim. He or she remained a victim until the alternative became unavoidable: either destruction in the acquired and no longer modifiable conscious attitude, or the accretion of a new consciousness structure. This new consciousness structure began to be evident when the consolidation of myth reached its height in the eighth century B. C.; the definite and full awareness of the new mutation expressed in the consciousness structure then new was fully effected with Plato. The two millenia which followed were devoted to consolidating the new consciousness, a process completed by 1480–1500 A. D. The ultimate consolidation and coming-to-awareness of space was Leonardo da Vinci's perfection of perspective.

Without necessarily defending in the following discussion an invariably suspect parallelism of the events which occur during various periods, we can, however, point to a probable similarity. This is based on the fact that man is the bearer as well as the objectified manifestation of these events—but not exclusively, and in each instance he is a changed man. This is the reason why everything on earth seems to repeat itself and why nothing actually new takes place. But this is merely a superficial judgement (see p. 36); new or at least novel events do occur. Man reacts in novel ways to the given reality in the various "epochs," that is, as a result of the specific consciousness structures, because his respective consciousness structure changes from mutation to mutation.

With this one reservation, or clarification if you will, we may observe the consequences in the wake of the consolidation of spatial awareness around 1480–1500 A. D., without being falsely accused of a biologizing intent. The course of consolidation is biological only to the extent that its bearer is a creature that is also amenable to biological inquiry. But since man is originally determined by origin, by the spiritual, our parallelism loses in part its possible causal character. It is therefore a question today of an analogous and not identical course of the mutational process. And this brings us back to the unambiguous question of why time broke forth—the subject we have indicated as being the central aspect of the current mutation.

When spatial consciousness was finally consolidated around 1480–1500 A. D. it was from that time onward liberated for new tasks. Waking, diurnal consciousness had been secured; man had come to an awareness of space; thinking had become feasible. After this achievement modern European man believed that he too, like mythical man once before, had accomplished all that could be accomplished and was content to remain in his state of achievement. But in this case, as before, a decline sets in because of this self-satisfaction, and, beginning with the Renaissance, mental consciousness increases in deficiency and deteriorates into rationalism. This marks the inception of quantification in the newly secured mental consciousness structure, a process we already noted in connection with the deficient epoch of the mythical structure. At the same time, however, the new mutation begins its course which becomes gradually but increasingly visible over the following centuries. This mutation will enter the general awareness at the moment when the deficient attitude reaches its maximum of rational chaos—a moment that we are approaching with finality during the present decades, as should be apparent to everyone.

Our present situation, then, can be related causally to the fact that, ever since the Renaissance, we have only gradually realized the new task arising from this circumstance that the previous major consolidation of consciousness had already been achieved, thus posing for us the urgent need to work on a new achievement of consciousness. A single generation, even ten generations are not sufficient to fulfill this demand of origin; but preparations could have been made during these generations, which is, in fact, what has happened.

This gives us the answer to our decisive question. The answer itself is decisive; it goes beyond the realm of symptoms and represents a valid diagnosis. Conclusiveness results from an understanding of the broader interconnections that, from origin, constellate terrestrial events.

But in what way does "time" play the leading role in this process? By now it should be clear how we wish "time" to be understood, and so let us for the moment continue with our previous definition: time represents an *aspect of the element of intensity which constitutes the world.* We are contrasting this in-tensive element dualistically with the ex-tensive spatial-material phenomena without any qualms since this will help rationalists to understand it. It will, of course, be evident that more is involved here than mere understanding, and also that the nexus of intensities and extensities is not a duality.

Even when we regard time in this reduced meaning it will be apparent that *time as an intensity must be the dominant theme* of the new mutation. It is the sole theme which we have not encountered in the previous mutations and, as we will clearly demonstrate, is the principal concern of our epoch.

Let us briefly reiterate the previous achievements of consciousness. Space and time do not exist for magic man. Even for mythical man, space is nonexistent, despite his awareness of time's natural and life-related aspect as manifest in self-contained, cycling seasonal time and its motion. This is the aspect of time which is spatialized and measured at the moment when mental man realizes space. Whereas mythical man lived from this inner movement, mental man thought by virtue of spatial, external actualities: everything for him became space, including time.

We have observed (pp. 173-4 and 178) to what extent space falsified time (particularly during the deficient rational period) by converting it from a divider into a fragmenter until it was utterly negated. Space, then, was realized while time has not been realized as a world component and world constituent, as an intensity and quality. Ultimately quality was ascribed solely to space; all things had to be spatial and be apprehended spatially. How could it have been otherwise, since even thinking could be exercised and could have stability only in spatial and systematic terms. It can come as no surprise that this theme of time made its presence known at the moment that spatiality had been realized. The time theme *had* to press toward emergence.

This reality and actuality of the world had to press toward mutation within man's consciousness in all its unsuspected abundance at that moment when this consciousness was no longer required to realize space. This new reality did indeed break forth unmistakably in a way which could not be overlooked at the very same time that space had been achieved by Leonardo's pupil Pontormo (see p. 100), and it has been continually in evidence ever since in the novel indications, manifestations, expressive forms and signals that culminate initially in the consequential double occurrence of the invention of the steam engine and the French Revolution.

There are good reasons for mentioning these two events together. The machine provides the means of existence for that "left" which awakens and discovers itself at the same time as the invention of the steam engine. From a sociological point of view, one is inconceivable without the other. These two events initiate a new chapter, a new age in the history of mankind.

Recent developments in anthropology have enabled us to discern two major successive cultural epochs. The first is that of agriculture and the domestication of animals. Further along in our discussion we will see that it is in turn divided into two fundamentally different epochs. The second is that of tool-making and crafts, which has decisively altered and co-determined the countenance and habits of human life over the past five to six thousand years.

Agricultural-domesticating cultures created the foundations for our life: domestic animals and agricultural production are their result. It is to these cultures that we owe the animals and plants which nourish and sustain us. And we should note that within the sequence of mutations which we have evinced, these animal breeders as well as the hunting and nomadic cultures are predominantly rooted in the magic structure. Strictly agricultural cultures on the other hand already take part in the mythical structure: they are matriarchal societies which are more consciously harnessed to the temporicity of growth and decay than those of the animal breeders and are more closely attuned to the maternal realm of the earth. Here arise the vegetative myths as well as a dawning awareness of the dark, subterranean realm that bears its fruits above ground.

While animal domestication was still a group achievement by the tribe, via the magic of animal totemism, agriculture was carried out under a different societal form, the matriarchal-mythical. This form of society underwent no further modifications until the rise of the tool-making cultures which culminated in craft culture.

In craftsmanship the individual plays the decisive role; it is no accident that the golden age of craft culture falls within the mental-patriarchal structure, where the emphasis has shifted from living events to matter and spatially palpable and comprehensible objects. As a domesticator man shaped living processes in animals and plants; as a craftsman he only shaped dead, material tools. Natural culture was displaced by artificial culture; nature is overlaid with art and artifice. Man begins a process of denaturation, turning away from the very nature from which he had wrested his necessary sustenance, and toward a new field of activity, arts and crafts, which provide him with additional means for making his life more endurable.

The last major cultural epoch of manual technology and craftsmanship ended approximately two hundred years ago with the invention of the steam engine and the abdication of the individual, who ever since the French revolution has been swallowed up by the mob. Just as the kings, the most visible representatives of the individual-patriarchal craft age, were abolished by the masses in the continuing revolutions since 1789, so has the craft tradition been gradually destroyed by the triumphal march of the machine.

The uncontrolled intensity of the "Left" (see p. 262 ff.) as well as the uncontrolled motoricity of the machine are, as negative manifestations of a "temporal" nature, visible indications of a new age, or more exactly, of a new mutation. The negative moment here is definitely symptomatic; it is conditioned by man's unawareness of events which affect him and results at the outset in confusion and in the destruction of previous and outlived forms and contents.

The machine is no longer an implement; it is an emancipated instrument. In a literal sense, it has e-man-cipated itself (ex *manu*) from the hand and thus from the control of man and become an autonomous and autocratic tool. Then there is the additional factor of the fatal effects of the dead movement and dynamism inherent in motorization which are perpetuated so long as man does not realize what fundamental powers he has given up by permitting the machine to become an autocrat and produce independent processes and courses of action. These processes, although guided for a long time by man, became ultimately uncontrollable in the machine, which is the *material-physical projection of man* (see p. 132).

While the man of craft and technology surrendered the naturalness of man the domesticator, man today is also surrendering his laboriously acquired second nature, culture, by losing his own artistic skills and workmanship. Thus his deculturation becomes evident in addition to his denaturation. The rootlessness and homelessness of today's salaried employees and factory workers, their remoteness from any sensitivity to art and their notorious "objectivity" are only too obvious proofs of the *loss of nature and art* which man has endured now for several generations.

Who today finds pleasure in nature or in a work of art such as a poem? Adults will at best recall a certain enjoyment of nature from their childhood (when they were still rooted in the magic realm), or that they had a certain pleasure in poems during their youth (when they lived in the mythical domain). But naturalness and beauty have in the meantime become illusory values to them; what counts now are the value-less facts, the material and the rational. All else is regarded with condescension as being of only sentimental value.

Because of this condescension, with its two-fold origin, man today is carrying out a self-imposed death sentence, negating and denying the greater share of his constituent being. If he cannot come to a new affirmation without straining to revitalize the nostalgic past, his self-inflicted execution will be unavoidable. Only by realizing the new mutation as an integral bearing or attitude and not as a quantifiable "enrichment" can man preserve himself from a complete loss of what is human.

Having recognized that "time" in an all-encompassing sense is the major theme of the new mutation, we must still inquire as to what means can be employed to describe or represent the new reality. The new mutation is a novel phenomenon; and we can do justice to new phenomena only partially by using old means. Let us attempt to delineate a form of statement which goes beyond that of mere mental conceptuality and is capable of opening up new domains of reality for us that will make the new mutation accessible to our consciousness.

3. The New Form of Statement

While the first part of this work was to a certain extent a setting or positing, the second part is an up-setting or dis-placement. The new perception of reality presupposes that the fixations, rigidifications, systems, and materializations which made up the deplorable state of the last century must first be upset. Much of what has been rationalistically posited, in other words, particularly the rationalistic and stereotyped thought forms and systems, must be de-rigidified and de-posed in order to open up an arena for the power and intensity that are pressing toward manifestation. So long as we think that we can master such intensities as time by forcing them into a system, the intensities will simply burst such systems apart.

Our new situation requires new means of description and statement. The new components which have irrupted into our reality demand new "concepts." But when we begin to sense the truly new, it is no longer new; it has already occurred.

We do not render its design, rather our consciousness must recover it. It is pointless to "master" this situation, at least intellectually, in a world of a disintegrating patriarchy. But we can face our situation in a humane way and supersede it by becoming conscious of our entire humanity as well as by clearing away all our self-constructed obstructions and conceptions which run counter to the new before they—and this also means us—are done away by the new.

This urgent necessity was perceived and described shortly after the French Revolution by two great figures, Novalis and Hufeland. The words of Novalis speak an unequivocal message:

> Wenn nicht mehr Zahlen und Figuren
> Sind Schlüssel aller Kreaturen,
> Wenn die, so singen oder küssen,
> Mehr als die Tiefgelehrten wissen,
> Wenn sich die Welt ins freie Leben
> Und in die Welt wird zurückbegeben,
> Wenn dann sich werden Licht und Schatten
> Zu echter Klarheit wieder gatten,
> Und man in Märchen und Gedichten
> Erkennt die wahren Weltgeschichten,
> Dann fliegt vor einem geheimen Wort
> Das ganze verkehrte Wesen fort.

> [When number and numeral cease to be
> a power o'er the creaturely;
> When lovers—and the poets—far
> more learned than the scholars are;
> When world to free life can return,
> and to itself again adjourn;
> where light and shade conjoin once more
> to the true clarity of yore;
> and tales and poetry provide
> to real world-history the guide;
> then can one cryptic word commence
> to drive the topsy-turvy hence.]

These verses express that "the world can return to (the) free life" of origin at any time (which is not to be understood as a retrogression but as a reinvigoration), so that it can place itself into the "true clarity" where all creatures are no longer under the sway of "number and numeral," the quantified and rationally systematized. This is nothing less than a description of what we have called the aperspectival world.

Only this clarity, this transparency—and not merely mental awakeness—are the "new strength of spirit" of which Hufeland speaks that could make possible the verition of the new reality: "Only a new strength of spirit kindled from a primordial divine source can create a new well-spring of life in the lifeless multitude which will surely engender a new life, purity, freshness, and strength in physical nature. *The half-born must come to full birth.*"[3]

"The half-born . . . "; although the concluding sentence of Hufeland's essay of 1812 refers to his own time whose presumable implications need not concern us here, the statement has a general validity which is inherent in every genuine utterance. The half-born is irrupting "time," the "new strength of spirit" which must be born completely, that is, come into full awareness and find its expressive possibilities. This is what is at stake.

Today we live in a world of up-set and dislocation; nothing has its former place. During the last two hundred years our world has slowly and irrevocably broken apart: religious ties, the old and secure social structure, the security of a craft tradition, the political structure of nations, even continents. The world, to be sure, cannot shatter, but space can—the perspectival, spatial world, the spatial construct of our thought which we imagined to be the real world and which began to distort the genuine world just when there was a new reality to be achieved.

But why did this world break apart? Why did the masses usurp the place of the individual? Why did man lose the last traces of dignity and become an object? Why did he lose his last vestige of security and become transformed from a self-sufficient and vouched-for citizen into an exposed, alienated, and disinherited being in a groundless vacuum, a being that has been "thrown" (Heidegger)? Because the spatial world which afforded him security and stability broke apart; and because he has not yet learned how to master the powers that initiated this break up; and also because these powers are still half-born inasmuch as they are already imparting themselves in truth but man is not yet "awaring" them. In other words, because man today is not yet conscious of the powers pressing toward realization.

The fundamental strength or intensity which is the theme of the new mutation must therefore come to awareness. It can enter awareness only on the one condition that we work out ourselves the mode of articulation which will give it the requisite clarity. Our attempt can only be inceptual or precursory inasmuch as we are today in a transitional period burdened by the proximity of deficient attitudes. To state this another way which will lead us directly into the problematics of the situation: a strength or intensity cannot be brought to consciousness by thinking alone since thinking knows only spatial sequentiality. The new strength of spirit with which we have to do here is *achronic;* it cannot be temporalized, for it is time-free. And this means it is also space-free.

None of the previous thought systems can make this strength of spirit perceptible. What means, then, are required to achieve its valid and clear perceptibility and to create a language appropriate to its essence? We have already remarked on the fact that phenomena of a "temporal" character cannot be encompassed in categorical systems. In categorical terms, the various manifestational forms of "time" are incompatible. No rational methodologist will concede that energy, dynamism, motion, intensity, motoricity, work, latency, etc., belong to the same system, particularly as each of these manifestational forms can be integrated vitally, psychically, or mentally according to its respective manifestational locus; and it would seem to run counter to any rational order to consider, say, psychic energy and motor energy as being inseparable.

If we do not decide to risk "upsetting" some persons and things, and indicate the inadequacy of systems with their categorical rigidities, we will not be able to approach the new world reality. Something with a temporal character cannot be spatially fixed. It cannot be fixed or prescribed in any form, and if we attempt to do so we change it by measurement into a spatial quantity and rob it of its true character. This is a clear indication that the qualities of time which are today pressing toward awareness cannot be expressed in mere categorical systems. And so long as they remain inexpressible they cannot effectively enter our awareness. We are compelled, in other words, to find a new form of statement.

This not inconsiderable task is further complicated because we must avoid attributing to the new form of statement characteristics which could appear to be "new" but would be in fact merely borrowings from consciousness attitudes already achieved. Even assuming that we were to discover an "ordering schema" for those "quantities" or "magnitudes" which are not amenable to categorization, this schema can be neither one of relationships or relativizing nor one in a dualistic opposition to the systems *which continue to retain their mental validity in the mental sphere.* An ordering schema based on a world of relationships would be a magic postulate; one which merely relativizes systematic points of view would be merely a mythical concept according to which the factor of movement and the "other" point of view would be mentalized. And if we considered the new form of statement to be a counterpart of the systems, we would be adopting a form of dualism—and would remain within the confines of three-dimensional spatial thought—because we would be placing a (dualistic) emphasis on the non-spatiality of the new form of statement in contrast to the spatiality of systems. And, finally, we must avoid any notion that systems have any kind of causal relationship to the new form of statement.

Such reservations imply merely that the new form of statement must not be one which could elicit a unification via relationships, a theory of correspondences or other relativization, or a dualistic or causal dependency. These three forms of realization are achieved, as before, by the magic, mythical, and mental attitudes. The new form of statement must be one of integration.

We are speaking advisedly of "forms of statement" here and not of forms of representation. Only our concept of "time" is a representational form, bound—like all forms of representation—to space. The search for a new form of representation would give rise to the error of establishing a new philosopheme at the very moment that philosophy is coming to an end. And this must be emphasized: the age of systematic philosophy of an individual stamp is over. What is necessary today to turn the tide of our situation are not new philosophemes like the phenomenological, ontological, or existential, but *eteologemes.*

Eteology must replace philosophy just as philosophy once replaced the myths. In the eteologemes the *eteon*[4] or being-in-truth comes to veracity or statement of truth, and this "wares" or guards verity and conveys the "verition" which arises from the a-waring and imparting of truth. Eteology, then, is neither a mere ontology, that is, theory of being, nor is it a theory of existence. The dualistic question of being versus non-being which is commensurate only with the mental structure is superseded by eteology, together with the secularized question as to being, whose content—or more exactly whose vacuity—is nothing more than existence.

Every eteologeme is a "verition," and as such is valid only when it allows origin to become transparent in the present. To do this it must be formulated in such a way as to be free of ego, and this means not just free of subject but also free of object; only then does it sustain the verity of the whole. This has nothing to do with representation; *only in philosophical thought can the world be represented; for the integral perception of truth, the world is pure statement, and thus "verition."*

The means for making this statement possible is systasis. We are using the term "systasis" to circumscribe the efficacy of all acategorical elements, that is, all types of manifestation and aspects of "time" which, because of their non-spatial character, cannot be the object of categorical systematization inasmuch as they are not "givens" or data but in a certain sense "givings" or impartations. Systasis is the conjoining or fitting together of parts into integrality. Its acategorical element is the integrating dimension by which the three-dimensional spatial world, which is always a world of parts, is integrated into a whole in such a way that it can be stated.

This already implies that it is not an ordering schema paralleling that of system. We must especially avoid the error of considering systasis—which is both process and effect—as that which is effected, for if we do we reduce it to a causal system. We must be aware that systasis has an effective character within every system. Systasis is not a mental concept, nor is it a mythical image (say) in the sense of Heraclitus' *panta rhei* ("all things are in flux"), nor is it a magic postulation of the interconnection of everything to and with everything else. And finally, it is not integral, but integrating.

Because systems are static abstractions of only passing or momentary validity, every system is lifted out of its isolation and concretized when we become aware that the principle of transformation renders illusory all so-called "ideal quantities" and destroys all fixities. By recognizing the effectuality of what we have defined as acategorical systasis within every system, we are able to replace mere mental synthesis by integral synairesis.[5]

Synairesis fulfills the aperspectival, integrative perception of systasis and system. This synairetic perception is a precondition for diaphany, which is able to be realized when, in addition to systasis and system, the symbol—with its mythical effectivity—and magic symbiosis are included, that is to say, present.

The task which the new mutation poses for us can be resolved only if we supersede the purely mental, spatial world of systematic thought. We achieve this by recognizing the validity of systasis in moving the efficacy of the non-categorical elements into the sphere of perceptibility. Systasis is the means whereby we are able to open up our consolidated spatial consciousness to the integrating consciousness of the whole. This integrating consciousness enables us to perceive and presentiate the integrity or integrality of the whole.

In the process of consolidating space-consciousness man has precariously placed himself at the outermost reaches of all manifestations. He brought about the isolation of the human, leaving it with only matter as its valid support. Today, the attachment to this consciousness structure and the desire to persist in it have led to those deficient results we have termed the rational deficiency of the mind. It is a process of rigidification which still continues. In this process, consciousness increasingly empties itself of the "time" it has negated, which, as a result of this attitude, itself becomes a lifeless spatial component. And the quantified motoricity of the machine and its lifelessness are in turn merely another expression of the spatialized concept of time.

This superannuated spatial world will break apart just as everything that becomes lifeless and rigidified breaks apart. The process of disintegration of which we are contemporary witnesses will take on various forms, *deformities which will engulf the entire earth and mankind with unprecedented degrees of terror before the turn of the next century. If the spiritual strength that is new to us has not been perceived until then, the suffering and anxieties of our day will have been in vain.* The longer we treat acategorical elements as if they were categorical quantities, the longer we delay the awakening of consciousness to the new mutation and imperil ourselves by courting falsified intensities.

Intensities, unless we mistake them for pressure and tension, are not measurable. When we measure them, we fragment them; and even such fragmented, re-sidual intensities like the concept of "time" are sufficiently virulent to disintegrate the spatial edifice whenever we incorporate them as a misunderstood fourth dimension into our three-dimensional world system. Such deeds are only a negative response to the task placed upon our consciousness. Rather than becoming ourselves aware of time, we allow "time" to overpower us; and instead of achieving temporal clarity—ultimately a form of time-freedom—we fall victim to the intoxication of time. For today it is the intoxication with time, the mirror of our time anxiety, which dominates us: mass production by the machine, the artificial acceleration of atomic decomposition on which the atom bomb is based, and the breath-taking pace of city life. (And we have apparently forgotten that breath is the essence of our earthly life.)

Now it should not be argued that the concept of systasis has anything in common with the so-called dynamic mathematics prefigured by Galileo's *Dialoghi della nuove scienze* (1638) and established by Newton in his *Philosophiae naturalis principia mathematica* of 1687. This form of mathematics permits calculation with infinitely small *variable* quantities. These quantities, which Newton called fluents, and their rates of change, which he defined as fluxions, are merely mathematical quantities. These quantities, known today as differentials and differential quotients, render causal processes measurable by mathematically fragmenting intensities. These spatialized "quantities" of intensity, because of their categorical manipulation of the spatial structure of Occidental or Western consciousness, will continue to exert a negative effect until we clearly recognize this rational falsification.

Also, we again emphasize that system and systasis are not to be considered, say, as antithetical ordering schemata, and that there is no exclusively causal connection between them. Systatic values or energies are contained in every systematic quantity. This fact was not present to consciousness as long as it was compelled to realize the reality of space and devote itself exclusively to space and its dimensions. From this arose, moreover, the momentous interlinking of space with matter whereby matter limits and "secures" space.

This will also make comprehensible the erroneous rational development which led to the materialism and mechanization to which latter generations have paid homage. As a result of its systematization, the three-dimensional consciousness rigidified in the material phenomena of space. Unless we are aware of this relation between space and matter we will misconstrue systasis in a perspectivistic, three-dimensional way as being a surrogate system.

We know ever since Einstein that energy and mass/matter are equivalent, indeed identical. Their difference is merely one of their transient form of manifestation. A categorical systasis therefore "comprehends" the ever-latent presence of the incalculable time-energy component in the measurable space-matter state; it is the expression of our recognition of the mutability of all phenomena to which no systematization can do justice. The synairesis which systasis makes possible integrates phenomena, freeing us in the diaphany of "a-waring" or perceiving truth from space and time.

Space and time are, after all, merely conditional realities and as such realities with a double relation. They are in the first place "objective" as the transitory structure of our universe, and in the second, "subjective" as the transitory structure and mirroring of our consciousness. This transitory character refers us to origin which, with respect to consciousness, becomes space-and-time-free when we fulfill and complete synairesis, the aperspectival imparting-of-truth. In this are consolidated the clarity and transparency of man and universe in which origin becomes present, inasmuch as origin, which "lies" before spacelessness and timelessness, manifests itself in consciousness as space-time-free present.

It is in other words our recognition of the acategorical systatic values (or elements) which first make possible the integral perception of the world. Without this perception the world remains an exclusively materially-spatially confined system devoid of diaphaneity.

This design for making possible the necessary integration with the aid of the unsystematic systasis, an integration which can be completed through synairesis, takes leave of the three-dimensional rational domain without leading us for that reason back to the two-dimensional world of polar movement or providing a possible escape into the unitary-relatedness of magic. Systasis is in no way irrational or prerational but rather arational.

The new form of statement based on systasis and synairesis, which retains the efficient co-validity of symbiosis,[6] symbol, and system, is a form of expression and realization that renders perceptible the content and principal motif of the new mutation while at the same time consciously fulfilling its impartation of truth.

1   See Jean Gebser, *Asienfibel* (Frankfurt/M.: Ullsteinbuch No. 650, 1962), p. 134 ff.; *Gesamtausgabe*, VI, p. 126 ff., and also Gebser, "Parallele Ansätze zur neuen Sicht," *Die Welt in neuer Sicht*, II (München-Planegg: Barth, 1959), p. 110 ff.

2   Within German culture, an integral mutation was most likely achieved by Meister Eckhart, who is still erroneously represented as a mystic. He attained universal integration by obtaining that "illumination," that supra-awareness realized every so often by Zen-Buddhism, not by a mystical submersion into the *unio mystica*. See Shizuteru Ueda, "Der Zen-Buddhismus als 'Nicht-Mystik' unter besonderer Berücksichtigung des Vergleichs zur Mystik Meister Eckharts," *Transparente Welt: Festschrift für Jean Gebser* (Bern: Huber, 1965), pp. 291–313. There is a laconic remark of Meister Eckhart extant that contains a restrained suggestion of that illumination which supersedes the mental state: "Whatever man is capable of thinking about God is not God. What God is in himself no one can discern, unless he be *moved into a light* that is itself God," in *Brevarium* (Leipzig: Insel, n.d.), p. 10, our italics.

3   C. W. Hufeland, *Geschichte der Gesundheit neben einer physischen Charakteristik des jetzigen Zeitalters: eine Vorlesung in der königl. Akademie der Wissenschaften zu Berlin* (Berlin: Realschul-Buchhandlung, 1812), p. 34.

4   The Greek word *eteos* means "true, real"; as an adverb, *eteon* means "in accord with truth, truly, really" and comes from the root *se:es*, meaning "to be"; see Menge-Güthling, *Griechisch-deutsches Wörterbuch* (Berlin: Langenscheidt, 281910), p. 239.

5   *Synairesis* comes from *synaireo*, meaning "to synthesize, collect," notably in the sense of "everything being seized or grasped on all sides, particularly by the mind or spirit"; Menge-Güthling (note 4), p. 542. Whereas synthesis is a logical-causal conclusion, a mental (trinitary) unification of thesis and antithesis (and falls apart because it becomes itself a thesis as a result of the dividing, perspectival perception), synairesis is an integral act of completion "encompassing all sides" and perceiving aperspectively.

6   The term *symbiosis* expresses here the magic form of realization, inasmuch as such realization is based on the *bios*, the "vital" and represents a "symbiotic" communally living unit.

3

The Nature
of Creativity

1. *Creativity as an Originary Phenomenon*

In creativity, origin is present. Creativity is not bound to space and time, and its truest effect can be found in mutation, the course of which is not continuous in time but rather spontaneous, acausal, and discontinuous. Creativity is a visibly emerging impulse of origin which "is" in turn timeless, or more accurately, before or "above" time and timelessness. And creativity is something that "happens" to us, that fully effects or fulfills itself in us.

All of this makes it suspect to any and all rationalists, for creativity reveals the limitations of understanding, and places every form of anthropocentrism into question. Creativity appears to be an irrational process, although it is actually arational. It cannot be adequately circumscribed by a strictly psychological interpretation, and the theological interpretation which comes to mind is a matter for theologians, whose controversies are best avoided by outsiders. This will necessarily exclude the question of the demiurge from our discussion. Our concern is with origin and its manifestation, creativity, which to the extent that it takes place in man is effected in the formation of consciousness. Through creativity preconscious origin becomes the conscious present; it is the most direct, although rarest, process of integration, and, even when realized for only the span of fractions of a second, can never be lost.

Every statement about creativity is open to doubt. Since creativity is a potency or energy it cannot be grasped systematically and can at best be perceived systatically. Since it is a potency which only rarely manifests itself in its full strength, the requisite empirical evidence for comparison is unusually limited. We must also take into account that its manifestations are mostly fragmentary and have a psychic emphasis, so that most statements about it have only limited validity. In any event, creativity is more than a creative, imaginary, intuitive, productive, or reproductive element. Its visible effectiveness is achieved where the strength of the inner constellation and the degree of intensity are equal to its potency, that is, where its demand is able to find a response. It is fulfilled in individuals to the same degree as in entire generations to the extent that they are ready for it.

Ever since the Renaissance and the resultant consolidation of spatial consciousness, the consciousness of Western man has been disposed toward a new creative achievement. This consciousness-reshaping of creativity is evident in the mutation now underway that is fully effecting itself today more than ever before. What is pre-given from origin is being effected: origin is luminescing in the present, disarraying, transforming, and liberating it.

Statements on creativity are uncommonly rare, although Socrates' *daimon* and Plato's *eros* may quite possibly be partial statements about it. The *daimon* is the force which ruptured the world of myth in the mutation that occurred during the last centuries before Christ and cleared the way for mutation to the mental, which is also expressed in the directed energy of the Platonic Eros. The so-called "libido" of present-day psychoanalysis has, by contrast, only a remote connection if any with the original phenomenon of creativity, and is at the very most—to the extent that it is regarded as an available amount of psychic energy or, more accurately, of psychic tension—a co-bearer or possibly participant in creativity, but not creativity as such.

Before turning to the effectuality of what can be called the creativity of the individual, to be examined in the next section, we should for the sake of clarification quote from the oldest known reference to this original phenomenon. It is of Chinese origin and is found in the *I Ching* or *Book of Changes*.[1] The statement on creativity, the Ch'ien, forms the first chapter of mankind's oldest book of wisdom.

The origin of the I Ching or *Book of Changes* demonstrably belongs to prehistoric times. Fu Hsi, who is held to be its first "author," is a "representative of the era of hunting and fishing and of the invention of cooking."[2] These ancient activities show that the origins of the book extend back into the magic structure. For many thousands of years it was a book of soothsayings and oracles, and was revised into a book of wisdom around 1000 B.C. by King Wên and his son, the Duke of Chou.

"They endowed the hitherto mute hexagrams and lines" which formed the original oracular signs "from which the future had to be divined as an individual matter in each case, with definite *counsels for correct conduct*. When it happened for the first time in China that someone, on being told the auguries for the future, did not let the matter rest there, but asked 'What am I to do?' the book of divination had become a book of wisdom. . . . Thus the individual came to share in shaping fate. For his actions intervened as determining factors in world events, the more decisively so, the earlier he was able with the aid of the Book of Changes to recognize situations in their germinal phases. The germinal phase is the crux. As long as things are in their beginnings they can be controlled, but once they have grown to their full consequences they acquire a power so overwhelming that man stands impotent before them."[3]

We have quoted these last lines since they can suggest to a thoughtful person how important it is to recognize the inceptual or germinal situations. It is a question of such a situation today, namely of the aperspectival world and its initial manifestations.

The revision of the former book of oracles into a book of wisdom mentioned in this connection indicates the decisive fact that around 1000 B.C. man began to awaken to a diurnal, wakeful consciousness. He no longer merely accepted the world but rather made decisions on "correct conduct"; he no longer merely endured fate but became its co-agent. And in the *Iliad*, some two centuries later, the identical process was completed, evident in the praise of Menis, directing and correct thinking (see p. 75 et passim), heralding the mutation from the mythical to the mental structure and leading to the triumph of cognizant, correct, and directed actions.

It is noteworthy that none other than Confucius himself, the founder of patriarchal thought in China (see above p. 79 f.) and purported author of the "Commentary on the Decision," was preoccupied in his old age with the Book of Changes. It is significant that the two earliest versions of the I Ching did not begin with the hexagram for creativity but with the maternal sign "Kên," the "keeping still, the mountain," and the "K'un," "the receptive":[4] a clear indication of the upsetting of the mythical-matriarchal principle in which the revising can be seen as a—considerably milder—step to the parallel deed, much more upsetting in both senses of the word, of Orestes' matricide (see p. 149 f. above).

These examples convey the significance of a climate already having a mental emphasis out of which the statement on creativity was revised and reformulated. We must also observe that the statement itself is older than the mental accentuation which Wên may have given it. It is undoubtedly in this sense that a remark of Richard Wilhelm's should be understood: "The Creative causes the beginning and begetting of all beings, and can therefore be designated as heaven, radiant energy, father, ruler. It is a question whether the Chinese personified the Creative, as the Greeks conceived it in Zeus. The answer is that this problem is not the main one for the Chinese. The divine-creative principle is suprapersonal and makes itself perceptible only through its all-powerful activity. It has, to be sure, an external aspect, which is heaven, and heaven, like all that lives, has a spiritual consciousness, God, the Supreme Ruler. But all this is summed up as the Creative."[5]

It is this qualification that lends the full import to the Chinese statement on creativity. This import is underscored by the circumstance that the name for creativity (and its character or image) like those of the remaining seven primordial characters "do not otherwise appear in the Chinese language," which further substantiates the great antiquity of this particular statement. This antiquity is in all likelihood further substantiated by the k-sound of the word "Ch'ien," whose magic proclivity for expression was discussed in Part I (above p. 172 f.).

In the light of these preliminary remarks we can assess the full significance of the Chinese statement in respect to its worth: creativity is the "primal power which is light-giving, active, strong, and of the spirit. [It] is consistently strong in character, and since it is without weakness, its essence is power or energy. Its image is heaven. Its energy is represented as unrestricted by any fixed conditions in space and is therefore conceived of as motion. Time is regarded as the basis of this motion. Thus the hexagram includes also the power of time and the power of persisting in time, that is, duration." For anyone who "draws this oracle, it means that success will come to him from the primal depths of the universe." And the image which represents creativity, the double trigram Ch'ien, "of which heaven is the image, . . . creates the idea of time. Since it is [by its repetition] the same heaven moving with untiring power, there is also created the idea of duration both in and beyond time, a movement that never stops or slackens, just as one day follows another in an unending course. [And not one night following another!] This duration in time is the image of the power inherent in the Creative."[6]

In his commentary which is based, incidentally, on primordial and subsequently lost versions of the I Ching, Confucius writes: "Great is the sublimity of the creative to which all beings owe their beginning and which permeates all heaven."[7] But whatever pervades the heaven also pervades the soul; and for this reason alone the pervasive, that is creativity, is of a spiritual nature.

2. The Nature and Transformation of Poetry

It was necessary to speak of the "primordial power" of creativity, which is for us a reminder of the "primal depths of the universe." During the consciousness mutations this originary potency becomes visibly manifest within the human domain. Although it is not origin, it renders origin perceptible. And as the potent "*duration in and beyond time*" it is the element which is today pressing to full conscious realization.

The statements in the earliest version of the *I Ching* express the sleep-like presence of this potency in consciousness. The statement quoted from the later version shows the beginnings of mentalization, but despite this, all of the statements are pervaded by the spiritual nature of primordial energy. Moreover, because the original potency imparts or reveals itself in the presently occurring mutation, it becomes perceptible to human awareness if and when this awareness becomes capable of subjectively "a-waring" the "objective phenomenon" given as a result of the new mutation.

It is the full effectualizing of creativity alone which enables man to realize or "recover" in consciousness the pre-given actualities. For this reason we must first inquire as to the mode in which this act of creative completion will manifest itself since it is only natural that this mode of effectualization will decisively affect the manifestations of the new consciousness that proceed from it. These manifestations of the aperspectival world are our primary concern in this discussion.

Creativity in man is an effectualization of the creative in the world. The creativity of the world or the "heaven" is genuine or primary, whereas that of man is secondary: a recovery in consciousness analogous to a tone which awakens to itself upon hearing its echo.

The creative capacity is not restricted to particular domains but is effective everywhere. Yet statements about it are to be found only in shaped or structured language, notably in poetry. The nature of poetry can furnish us today with an explanation of the process of creativity's full effectualization in man, and it is important that we know of this effectualization since it is the source of the new consciousness in man. It is also important for us to understand that the mode of effectualization or the "process" of poetry today necessarily differs from that valid and current heretofore: until recently it was mental whereas today it must be integral if it is to aid in the breakthrough of the integral consciousness.

When explaining the creative principle in man, it is not sufficient to use such problematic terms as intuition, imagination, emotion, or revelation, which are for the rationalist, moreover, highly suspect and unreliable working concepts. We shall therefore necessarily have to examine the subject of poetry in greater detail.

It is of fundamental importance to our inquiry and, accordingly, to our understanding of the manifestation of the aperspectival consciousness to answer two questions: What has the nature of poetry been until now? and, What is its nature today?[8]

It is by no means just a personal predilection which induces us once more to place poetic and linguistic concerns in the forefront of our inquiry. They are the most instructive means for disclosing the respective consciousness structure. The Bergsonian, Alfred North Whitehead, has expressed the same opinion: "It is in literature that the concrete outlook of humanity receives its expression. Accordingly it is to literature that we must look, particularly in its more concrete forms, namely in poetry and drama if we hope to discover the inward thoughts of a generation."[9]

When the first Occidental poet begins his song, its very opening words name its source: it is the Muse. In the *Iliad* these words are *Menin aeide thea* . . . , "Sing, Goddess, the wrath . . . ," and in the *Odyssey* they are *Andra moi ennepe Mousa* . . . , "Tell me, Muse, of the man. . . . " A considerable number of the Homeric hymns, such as those to Hermes, Aphrodite, Pan, Selene, the Dioskuroi, and to the mother of the gods, begin by summoning the Muse to sing.[10]

We find this summons even later, as in Hesiod's *Theogony* where the first one-hundred-fifty lines are devoted exclusively to the Muses, and in the beginning of the first and fourth Pythian Epincian Odes of Pindar. It is also found in Virgil and even Dante where the beginning of the "Purgatorio" reads, *O sante Muse, poi che vostro sono* . . . , "O sacred Muses to whom I, too, belong. . . . " As Ernst Robert Curtius has remarked, "Every page in the history of European literature speaks of them."[11]

What, then, does it mean that these poets bid the *Muse* to sing? What do the Muses mean? Homer spoke of them in the second book of the *Iliad:* "Everywhere were ye present and knowing, / Mortals hearken only to rumor."[12] It is apparent from other sources in antiquity that the Muses were called the "Mothers of the singers."[13]

The significance and etymology of the word "muse" are instructive. *Mousa* means "the ponderess," and this sense of the word is still alive today. Present-day English has such familiar expressions as "to muse" meaning "to ponder, to reflect upon, to be absorbed in thought," as well as "the muser," one who ponders or dreams. The ancients traced the etymology of the word for the Muses to *myein*, "to close," the reference being primarily to a closing of the eyes and mouth.[14] This unscientific derivation expresses, however, a significant relation of the Muse to the soul, to the psychic image-world of myth, for *myein* is closely akin to the word *Mythos* (see above, p. 64 f.). Recent scholarly etymology has traced the word *mousa* to *montja*, "the ponderess,"[15] which has the same root as *mens, menis*, and *maino* (see p. 74 and note 113, p. 112).

This suggests that the term "muse" has ultimately also a mental character expressing both the pondering element and the "wrathful" aspect of orienting thought which reflects on and directs the world of mythical imagery. Still united in the word "muse" are the antithetical elements which have separated in German into the two words *Müsse* and *Müssen* (see p. 126 f. and note 80, p. 110).[16] *Musse* is "to have leisure, to be contemplative"; *Müssen* is compulsion, compunction, "must," which is also the essence of *maino*.

This partly mental, partly mythical aspect of the word "muse" is reflected in two statements of Plato. At about the age of twenty, having burned his own poetic works and become a pupil of Socrates, he composed his youthful dialogue *Ion* in which he wrote: "Like the Bacchantes who could only draw up milk and honey from the streams in a state of rapture, so is the soul of the poet able to do the same only in the state of enthusiasm and ecstasy, as the poets themselves admit. . . . For a poet is not empowered to create until he has become enthusiastic and beside himself, and until clear reason no longer dwells in him. As long as he clearly retains his senses, no man is able to create poetry and prophecy. . . . But every poet can render beautifully into poetry what the *muse has impelled him to say:* the one in the form of mere dithyrambs, another as paeans of praise. . . . The one poet is devoted to one muse, a second poet to another; we say: 'he was seized by her,' but this still amounts to her holding him in her power. . . . But when someone has a song performed by this poet or that, [you are] immediately awake and your soul rejoices."[17] And in one of his late dialogues, *Philebos,* which some consider to be his last work, Plato calls the Socratic dialogues "Those orations where the philosopher's muse speaks her prophecies."[18]

From these considerations it follows that the signification of the word "muse" is extremely complex besides being closely related to the ability of the poet. It is not accidental that it is emphasized and occurs together with *menis* in the opening verses of the *Iliad* and the *Odyssey* at the moment that Western or Occidental poetry as we know it first took shape.

From all this it becomes evident what the Muse signifies, but who *is* she? In his article on the Muses, O. Bie has appropriately characterized the Muse whom Homer invokes as the "original muse."[19] This proto-Muse and mother of the Muses (who, as Plutarch records in his "Table Talk," bore in several instances the common name "Mneia"),[20] is Mnemosyne. She is the prototypical image that unfolds into three Muses: her daughters Melete, Mneme, and Aoide (contemplation, memory, and song), all of whom wear golden headbands, an obvious accentuation of the thinking forehead and head. Only later did the number of Muses increase to nine.[21]

What is the meaning of the name held by the proto-Muse? What is the meaning of both Mneia and Mnemosyne? Preller-Robert furnish a good definition: "Mnemosyne, i.e., memory or recollection, a goddess of the Titanic world, was well-known and celebrated as the mother of the muses. . . . [She] is essentially the memory of the great deed [i.e., the founding of a new world order via the struggle of the Titans], and the natural inspiration which emanates from the beauty and harmony of the world. Later on the name comes to designate a goddess of recollection, cognitive expression, and name-giving in general. Mnemosyne was customarily honored and depicted together with the muses."[22] Rudolf Otto has noted that the name "mnemosyne" contains the ancient Sanskrit word *manana* meaning "sacred musing, pondering, and meditation."[23] It is thus the same element expressed in the word "muse" which defines Mnemosyne.

Let us note, then, that Mnemosyne, the proto-Muse, is *recollection,* that is, the internalization of an event or a disposition of things, or the process or ability of becoming intimately aware of them. She is memory, the ability of thoughts and thinking, and ultimately, of thanksgiving, for "thinking" and "thanking" have the same root.[24] And thinking as well as thanking are the most subtle qualities of soul, *affairs à fleur d'eau,* or *à fleur d'âme,* as it were. But what is recalled, and why are thanks proffered? And we might add: What is dictated? since the word for creating poetry in German, *dichten,* is derived from *dictare.*

This question, too, can be best resolved on the basis of the ancient sources. In one of the "Orphic Hymns"[25] dedicated to the Muses, they are described as "polymorphic" and called "nourishers of the soul." This designation suggests that the Muses, as "nourishers of the soul," are associated in ancient mythology with water, the symbol of the life-pole, the creative aspect of the soul (see p. 215 f.) This is borne out by the numerous clues and verifiable instances brought to light by a careful scrutiny of the sources. Originally the Muses were water nymphs, or nymphs of the springs as Usener noted in his *Sintflutsagen* (Sagas of the Deluge)[26] and Friedrich Creuzer in his *Symbolik* as well as in his *Deutsche Schriften*,[27] both of whom cite Cicero's *De natura deorum* (III, 21). E. Jacobi[28] as well as Hastings' *Encyclopaedia of Religion and Ethics*[29] furnish additional examples which bear out the nymph-like nature of the Muses.

It is therefore not surprising that springs were particularly sacred to them in addition to certain mountains, notably the spring at Hippokrene and at Castalia near Delphi of which, in the words of E. Peterich, "the Roman writers say that one drink of her waters swept the poets into song."[30] Two more are mentioned by Karl Philipp Moritz: the source of Aganippe and that of Pimplea which *"flowed forth in perpetual abundance."*[31] In addition to these four E. Jacobi also mentions the source of Peirene in Corinth.[32]

There is also the river Olmeiso, whose source was on the Helicon which was sacred to the Muses, as we know from the sixth verse of Hesiod's *Theogony*. And according to Polemon, the muses were also revered in Athens where they shared in the cult of their mother and were offered *water* or milk and honey (without wine).[33] A further trace of the devotion paid to Mnemosyne can be found in the oracle of Trophonios in Lebadeia where, according to Pausanias (in Phillipson's account of the oracle in the context of its landscape)[34] the person consulting the oracle had first to drink of the waters of Lethe to forget all he had previously thought, and then of the waters of Mnemosyne to recall all that he had seen and heard within the cavern.[35]

In addition to these examples we can cite a further instance noted by R. von Scheliha. There Homer himself was said to be the son of a river god, Melas, and Aristotle, who honored this tradition, claimed that the poet's father was the spirit of a Muse (*daimon ton sygchoreuton tais Mousais*).[36] These instances round out the picture of the Muse which has survived in the mythical tradition.

The Muses are an image of the sustenance of the life-soul symbolized by water: a likeness of creativity in the world. At the very moment they are invoked by the poet they become a likeness of creativity in man. They are the poet's awakened recollection of all that has ever been brought about which channels his powers into the stream of the life-soul that he contemplates or that seizes him and compels him so that he *must* sing.

The Muse is the latent memory of the world, the remembrance of creativity, and of all that has been and is still to be effected in the world. It will be apparent that the Muse has a close connection to creativity and is able to elicit man's poetic capacities if we recall the qualities noted above: she is the source, perpetual abundance, and the sustainer of the soul. She is the mother of the bard and is thus herself receptive: the receptress and recollectress of creativity who awakens in the poet this recollection. She is thanksgiving and the compulsion to thought.

Just as there are on earth tranquil waters as well as springs, so too are some men like still ponds, mere mirrors of the heaven while others are like the springs. These we speak of as being *musisch*, "receptive or sensitive to arts and music." It is surely no coincidence that the German word for "creative" is *schöpferisch*, from *schöpfen*, "to draw up (water)," for the creative person "draws up" from the wellsprings of life, from the life-soul, bringing to the light of day and the thinking realm of consciousness what has been forgotten as well as what has not yet been realized. The creative person externalizes what has been recalled (see p. 192); recollection becomes memory. Because of the Muse the poet writes the invisible history of the world. *Poetry is the writing of history*—not the history of dates but *of the dateless*, particularly if we concede to the word "history" the complexity of meaning mentioned in Part I above (see p. 191 ff.). Poetry as history is the account of events, of events effected by creativity; it lends sense to the senseless and the non-directed, since the ever-present plenitude has no direction of itself.

In poetry mental man recalled and stated elements of creativity, placing them into the directing spatiality of his thinking. The Muse is an expression of the mental attempt to grasp the non-mental—and this means preeminently mythical truth. As long as the Muse dominates, man is moving within the mental sphere. It is a significant indication that today the Muses, after a nearly three-thousand year reign since Homer, are beginning to die, or are becoming the siren-like angels of death like those in Rilke's poetry.[37]

As a result of its time-anxiety and fear of recollection—the basis for all poetry—the present generation rejects poetry and lyricism, while the present-day poet strives to overcome the time-imparting remembrance by abjuring the Muses. This is an expression of his aperspectival endeavor: his concern is not primarily with the merely ponderable (or mental), nor with conceptualizing the non-mental (or mythical) but rather with the perceiving and imparting "in truth" of the "perpetual plenitude," the whole or integrity which is permeated by the spiritual energy of origin that is only obscured by the image-world of the psyche and restricted by thinking.

Before we consider the evidence in behalf of these assertions we should first examine the change which is evident in recent poetry because of the "demise of the Muses" mentioned above. From Homer to Dante poetry remained qualitatively unchanged. The image-world formed by the poet's "must" and the events and occurrences shaped by his thinking into a continuous record were a formative force on listener and reader. As Plato observed, they "awaken and their soul rejoices" because the ineffable, which as such oppresses thought, is stated in poetry, and its pervasive effect proceeds from the universal validity and authenticity that represents in imagery basic or primordial situations or even events, such as Odysseus' voyage to Hades, Achilles' wrath, Hector's farewell, and Dante's city of seven gates (planets), to mention only a few.

It would interrupt the train of thought of our discussion if we were to examine here Aristotle's theory of poetry as set forth in his *Poetics*, but we should mention his view of catharsis or moral clarification as stated in that work.[38] Aristotle himself wished it to be confined only to tragedy. As to its effect, it represents a powerful pedagogical moment as pervasive in early medieval Easter and Mystery plays as in such recent works as *The Tower (Der Turm)* by Hofmannsthal and *The Family Reunion* by T. S. Eliot, or in such novels as *The Bridge of San Luis Rey* by Thornton Wilder and *The Old Man and the Sea* by Hemingway.

Although to a lesser degree than in the mysteries of old, poetry itself has its own character of mystery, and it too can provide an initiation experience via catharsis even if only transiently and weakly. But as this is the effect of an effect, the result of a previous emotional experience, we shall not dwell on it further. The significance, and the reason we have mentioned it at all, lies in the fact that it may well have been in part responsible for eliciting an essential awakening of consciousness in the soul of Western man: the eliciting of ego-consciousness in poetry which we can discern for the first time in the poetry written at the turn of the thirteenth century.

We have already noted the inceptions of ego-consciousness in antiquity in the poetry of Sappho and particularly in the moving "Am Odysseus" (see p. 71 and 89 ff.). Anyone who has had occasion to peruse the poems of Cavalcanti following a reading of St. Francis of Assisi's "Song to the Sun," or the personal "Songs of the Virgin" by Berceo after reading the *Cid*, or the sonnets of Charles d'Orleans after the *Chanson de Roland*, cannot have remained unmoved by the personal intimacy achieved by these three poets. In a world still dominated by collective feeling and still imbedded in the gold ground of the Sienese masters, these poets have ventured to sing of their personal sorrows and joys and to use a word which has become more than self-evident to us: "I."

It is surely no accident that this occurs contemporaneously with Petrarch's discovery of landscape and space and with the anticipation of a perspectival style of painting by Giotto and the brothers Lorenzetti (see p. 15). Since then the content of a poem is no longer restricted to the evocation of collectively-held pre-conscious contents; it is henceforth accompanied by the partly conscious statement of moods and experiences that are echoed not only in feeling but in the rational understanding of the listener or reader, at least to the extent that such moods and experiences are common to all of humanity. This marks the beginning of the so-called lyric poem. And though its effect on the re-formation of primordial experiences is minimal, it continues to mould the turbulent gestations of the soul: pain, joy, sorrow, despair, lament, horror, and other psychic states.

This formative quality is the prime value of lyric poetry, although by comparison to the epic poem, it is a reduced value. Both the lyric and the epic poem afford life its support and space, which is evident from the fact that bereaved persons turn to poems of a sad or melancholy, rather than exuberant cast. There they find formed in the poems those things which threaten to overcome them; the poems set them aright and give their sorrow expression and form so that it can be mastered.

The existence of the lyric poem does not of course imply that the so-called "major" forms of poetry have not drawn their sustenance up to recent times from the same well-springs from which Homer drew. It is not really necessary to cite examples since none of the truly great poets, including those of recent generations, has completely abandoned a mythical subject matter: neither Goethe, nor the English Romantics, nor Hölderlin who attempted a reformulation of myth. From Racine to Cocteau the themes bear out this relationship to myth, although we must not overlook that Cocteau's work shows evidence of a maximum of mythical deficiency.

Even where we are at first glance unaware of any invocation of the Muses, they are still covertly invoked. We would cite merely the example of the touching introductory section of Hölderlin's youthful work *Hyperion:* "The beloved soil of my fatherland again affords me joy and sorrow. I spend every morning of late on the heights of the Corinthian isthmus where, like a bee among flowers, my soul often flies back and forth between the seas which cool the feet of my glowing mountains that lie to the right and the left."

Hölderlin has here drawn a primordial image. And the image calls to mind that even in antiquity the Muses were associated with the bees. As we know from Polemon, not only water but also honey were the sacrificial offerings made to the Muses in Athens. F. Nork has noted that "Varro calls the bees 'birds of the Muses' "[39] and in another passage cites a remark attributed to Pausanias that bees nourished Pindar with honey while he slept.[40] Rilke too knew or intuited these symbolic interconnections; in one of his most significant letters, the letter to Hulewicz on the *Elegies*, he writes: "We are the bees of the invisible. Nous butinons éperdument le miel du visible, pour l'accumuler dans la grande ruche d'or de l'Invisible" (Beside ourselves [i.e., as lost and mortal creatures], we collect the honey of the visible and store it up in the golden hive of the invisible).[41] We might note in passing that Rilke here harks back to an ancient symbolic tradition, as is evident from an ancient reference mentioned by Robert Eisler that bees build the invisible temple of God.[42]

With Rilke we come to our own times. He too has invoked the Muses at the beginning of his major work, the *Duino Elegies*. There he invokes the antipode of the Muses (which is itself symptomatic of our times), and this is, to the best of our knowledge, the only instance of such an invocation:

> Wer, wenn ich schriee, hörte mich denn aus der Engel
> Ordnungen? und gesetzt selbst, es nähme
> einer mich plötzlich ans Herz: ich verginge von seinem
> stärkeren Dasein. Denn das Schöne ist nichts
> als des Schrecklichen Anfang . . .

> [Who, if I cried, would hear me among the angelic
> orders? And even if one of them suddenly
> pressed me against his heart, I should fade in the strength
> of his stronger existence. For Beauty's nothing
> but the beginning of Terror . . .] (J. B. Leishman)

This angel is not an expression of the life soul, as were the Muses. It represents the death-soul or the power of death; it is the Egyptian soul-bird which developed through its various stages into Sirens and terrorizing Harpies, and into the avenging, plundering angel of death (see p. 207 f.). K. Kerényi has pointed out the extent to which the Sirens are expressions of a Hades-like schematic non-being.[43] Does this seem to be too far-fetched? These are merely the interrelationships hidden to consciousness whose discovery was a fitting task for a poet like Rilke. For although he anticipated many things, Rilke remained the ruler over a magical world of interconnections. This is the opening of the Second Elegy:

> Jeder Engel ist schrecklich. Und dennoch, weh mir,
> ansing ich euch, fast tödliche Vögel der Seele,
> wissend um euch . . .

> [Every angel is terrible. Still, though, alas!
> I invoke you, almost deadly birds of the soul,
> knowing of you . . .] (J. B. Leishman/Steven Spender)

This rejection of the living force of poetry symbolized by water, nymph, or Muse is singular, and its radicality is symptomatic of the extreme bondage of a poet caught up in negativity. Others were able to achieve a detachment by supersession. Precisely the estimation placed on water (which Rilke denies and thus denies the creative element by his invocation of the angel of death), and the change in this estimation, are important indications of the change in our structure of consciousness, and thus are also important for constituting this new consciousness. This consciousness is perhaps most clearly discerned where it is not only conceived of as "statement" but also with respect to the "source" invoked by the creative and speaking poet.

To St. Francis of Assisi water had taken on the aspect of chastity; he calls it "sor aqua . . . casta." The reason for this gradual fading of the ancient "inspirational" aspect can be found in the ascetic way of life which endeavored to mortify the natural side of man and purify it in accord with the Franciscan and Christian ideal. This mortification was not only reduced but overextended by Spinoza who insisted that "nature is a state to be departed from" (Exeundum est de statu naturae). Hölderlin, who in his letters always defended Spinoza (against Fichte), has given us a turn of speech which is "comprehensible" only from a spiritual vantage point.

Such a vantage point is one which admits the natural and soul-accentuated mythical structure that has been tamed by thinking, but is also one in which the intellectual-rational standpoint has been superseded. This structure is one where in contrast to emotive, mirror-like thinking we find the aperspectival structure of the spiritual that is perceptible only to "sober" insight. Hölderlin is the first to refer to water as being "soberly holy" (heilig nüchtern).[44] With this a leap has occurred; water is still "holy," that is numinous and permeated by mana, but the mana-ness is "sober" and thus no longer a "seizure." With a single stroke the "inspiring," mythical, and pathetic aspect has ceased to have the decisive or exclusive role. No longer are "spirits" invoked or dispelled; it is the spirit that speaks, the spirit of which Hölderlin sings in the metrical version of Hyperion:

Der leidensfreie Geist befasst
sich mit dem Stoffe nicht, ist aber auch
Sich keines Dings und seiner nichts bewusst,
Für ihn ist keine Welt, denn ausser ihm
Ist nichts.[45]

[The pure spirit, free of suffering, is
not concerned with substance, nor is it
aware of anything or of itself;
There is no world for it, since beyond itself
is nothing.]

Later we see Hölderlin, in his great hymn "Patmos," passing beyond the abysses of the soul, nature, and the confines of Ego:

Im Finstern wohnen
Die Adler, und furchtlos gehn
Die Söhne der Alpen über den Abgrund weg
Auf leichtegebaueten Brü(c)ken.
Drum, da gehäuft sind rings, um Klarheit,
Die Gipfel der Zeit,
Und die Liebsten nahe wohnen, ermattend auf
Getrenntesten Bergen,
So gieb unschuldig Wasser,
O Fittige gieb uns, treuesten Sinns
Hinüberzugehen und wiederzukehren.[46]

[In darkness dwell
The eagles; fearlessly these
Alpine sons surmount the abyss
Over fragile bridges.
Surrounding clarity, the summits of time
lie around in heaps;
And those beloved dwell near, languishing
On most inaccessible peaks.
O give, then, guiltless water,
Wings of devoted verity,
To cross over and yet to return.]

Here a new tone sounds. Despite the ambiguous image of the "summits of time," lying around "in heaps," we must not fail to notice that Hölderlin here associates time with water. Time (and thus recollection) has reached its maximum; it is piled up in mountains. Thus Hölderlin's cry, "give us guiltless water." This is not the water of inspiration or recollection, nor even Lethe's water of forgetfulness; it is nothing that charges or is charged with soul, for "the pure spirit is not concerned with substance." Rather, the pure spirit, not being "aware of anything or of itself" gains awareness of itself through man's poetic statement wherever such statement is dominated by innocence ("devoted verity") and sobriety, that is, spiritual clarity or the freedom from psychic and mental bonds.

It is surely a cause for reflection that Stefan George and R. M. Rilke in particular have adopted this wording from Hölderlin. Rilke for instance has written: "Quellen, sie münden herauf / heiter und heilig" (Well-springs surge forth, buoyant and holy); and George has directly appropriated Hölderlin's epithet of "holy sobriety."

The shift in poetry manifest by these examples should be apparent by now: there is a detachment from memory that is the initial step toward the supersession of time. Memory is always time-bound; and what is even worse, it temporizes the timeless without transforming it into temporal freedom. The turn away from memory, on the other hand, is a turn toward freedom; the poetic emphasis shifts from the recollected past to the present. This is the import of Hugo von Hofmannsthal's remark, "Poetry as present. The mystical element of poetry: the supersession of time."[47]

This change is not only expressed by Hölderlin (and in his wake, by Rilke and George). The turn toward time-freedom which encompasses and requires a new consciousness structure is not restricted to a particular nationality; it is a European phenomenon that has been underway since the French Revolution. It experienced some setbacks during the later Romantic period and in Naturalism, but since that time it has become unmistakably evident.

André Gide's estimation of Baudelaire is significant in this context: "The extraordinary novel achievement wrought by Baudelaire in poetry remained unnoticed when it first occurred. Only the novel manner of the way he treated the themes in his *Fleurs du Mal* was considered important (although this was not particularly significant). His truly revolutionary and unprecedented achievement was that the poet for the first time refused to abandon himself to the lyric ebb and flow and resisted facile 'inspiration.' He opposed the blandishments of rhetoric, of words and images and superannuated conventions, and treated the muse like someone obstinate who has to be subjugated, rather than one allowed to prevail over the poet's spirit and critical acumen. In short, he *prevailed upon art to master poetry.* In this he was in opposition to his contemporaries; and encouraged by Poe's example, Baude-laire subjected his art to science and conscientiousness, and charged himself as an artist with patience and resolve."[48] (In view of the original text, printed in note 48, the last sentence might be rendered perhaps more accurately: "In opposition to his contemporaries, Baudelaire—encouraged by Poe—applied knowledge and con-science [consciousness], patience and decisiveness to his art.")

Mallarmé too strives to achieve this *science et patience.* In the poem "Prose pour des Esseintes," of programmatic value for his own art, he speaks of a rejection of *mémoire* or memory, and continues:

Car j'installe, par la science,
L'hymne des cœurs spirituels
En l'œuvre de ma patience,
Atlas, herbiers et rituels.[49]

Before we attempt to translate these verses it should be noted that Mallarmé himself has defined the range of the final three words as signifying "la cristallisation d'une contrée (atlas), d'un vocabulaire (herbier), et d'un culte (rituel) nouveaux,"[50] a fact not previously recognized by German translators.[51] Turning now to a transla-tion, the verses may be rendered as follows in simple prose (we forego of course the emphasis inherent in the position of the rhyme words which include "spirituel"!): "For with the help of knowledge, I bestow in the work of my patience the hymn of spiritual hearts, the crystallization (transparency) of a new landscape, a new mode of expression, a new worship." And we reiterate that Mallarmé repudiates memory in the opening strophe which precedes this one: he "bestows from knowledge."

It is not fortuitous that it is the faun, the prisoner of nature, which implores the nymphs in the poem "Après-midi d'un Faune": "O nymphes, regonflons des Sou-venirs divers" (O nymphs, let us revive the diverse recollections). This satirical repu-diation of the Muses who awaken recollection is further emphasized by capitalizing the word "Souvenirs."[52]

This stanza of Mallarmé can also be translated in other ways, but one detail will always remain: that the poet is praising the work of consciousness, which is a turning away from the Muses and an effort to establish and crystallize three realms: *contrée* (space); *vocabulaire* (the word); and *culte,* that is, in a certain sense the mental, mythical and magic elements. This is the new obligation ("Ce nouveau devoir") of which Mallarmé speaks in the same poem and to which Gide alludes in the remark: "It cannot be denied that this 'new obligation' belongs to the order of spirit."[53]

Gide himself has unmistakably expressed this new state of affairs: "Cette *Muse* des romantiques, avec qui dialogue Musset dans ses *Nuits,* nous paraît aussi écaillée aujourd'hui que celle de Cherubini dans le portrait d'Ingres" (This "muse" of the Romantics with whom Musset converses in his *Nuits* seems to us today as shabby [literally: scaling] as the muse of Cherubini on the portrait by Ingres).[54]

The same endeavor can be found in the work of Paul Valéry; a stanza in his poem "Le Rameur" expresses it with all due clarity:

En vain toute la nymphe énorme et continue
Empêche de bras purs mes membres harassés;
Je romprai lentement mille liens glacés
Et les barbes d'argent de sa puissance nue.[55]

[In vain the entire, immense and continuous nymph
Strives to hinder my harassed limbs with her pure arms;
Piece by piece I shall break a thousand icy bonds,
And the silvery barbs of her naked potency.][56]

Elsewhere Valéry has underscored the meaning of this statement when he writes, "J'aimerais mieux écrire en toute conscience et dans une entière lucidité quelque chose de faible que d'enfanter à la faveur d'une transe et hors de moi-même un chef-d'œuvre d'entre les plus beaux" (If I am to write, I should infinitely prefer writing something feeble that was produced in full consciousness and utter lucidity, rather than being carried out of myself to give birth in a trance to one of the greatest masterpieces in literature). This should not be construed as an appeal to the validity of the mental structure; at the beginning of his L'Idée fixe, the ultimate judgement on perspectival thinking. Valéry has written: ". . . l'amertume et l'humiliation de me sentir vaincu par des choses mentales, c'est-à-dire, faites pour l'oubli" (. . . the bitterness and humiliation of being bested by things of the mind—things, after all, that are made for oblivion).[57]

T. S. Eliot has referred to Valéry's "extreme self-consciousness."[58] This encompasses a renunciation of the Muses. There is the remarkable observation which Valéry has made in his "Politics of Spirit" that man, by creating time, has created an abuse; he gained perspectives, but at the cost of living henceforth only to the slightest degree in the present.[59] In the same essay he has written several lines earlier in concrete terms of the word "spirit," with which he "does not intend in any way to denote a metaphysical entity" but simply a "*power of transformation*" whose efficacy is vastly different from that of natural forces. On the contrary, its efficacy lies in opposing or allying with one another the forces that are granted to us, from which among other results there is an "*increment of freedom.*"[60]

This is no longer a form of mental-systematic thinking, rather it is the actualization of systatic elements; and their association with one another is the initial step toward synairetic perception of truth. "Achille ne peut vaincre la tortue s'il songe à l'espace et au temps" (Achilles cannot vanquish the turtle so long as he ponders space and time).[61] Only someone who has overcome space and time is able to vanquish or overcome all that has become rigidified and unwound in space and time. This will aid in making comprehensible the following sentence of Valéry: "C'est l'execution du poème qui est le poème" (The composition or execution of the poem is the poem).[62] "L'œuvre est pour l'un le *terme;* pour l'autre, *l'origine* . . . " (For one the work is the *end,* for the other it is the *origin* . . .).[63]

This transcending of what we call the three-dimensional, perspectival world into an aperspectival world, this withdrawing from the mentality of the Muses into a diaphaneity of the most intense awareness is expressed in a remark of Valéry which T.S. Eliot found quite striking: "In my opinion, the most authentic philosophy is not in the objects of reflection, so much as in the very act of thought and its manipulation."[64] This is a clear renunciation of spatially-fixed systematization in favor of what we have defined as *systasis*. It is at the same time a negation of present-day philosophy in favor of *eteology* which does not merely perceive objects in relation to objects, but perceives thinking itself: a detachment from the mental world without irrationalizing it in contrast to Plato's praise of the "muses of philosophy."

The identical attitude shared by Mallarmé and Valéry is also evident in T. S. Eliot. "There is a great deal, in the writing of poetry, which must be conscious and deliberate. In fact, the bad poet is usually unconscious, where he ought to be conscious, and conscious, where he ought to be unconscious. Both errors tend to make him 'personal.' Poetry is not a turning loose of emotion, but an escape from emotion; it is not the expression of personality, but an escape from personality. But, of course, only those who have personality and emotions know what it means to want to escape from these things."[65] Here again we find, not a loss of ego and the poet as an instrument of the Muses, but a growing above and beyond the mental ego to freedom from the ego: to that freedom which is the guarantor of the spiritual.

In his poem of ten years later, "Little Gidding" (1942), T. S. Eliot composed verses which speak of the "detachment from self and from things and from persons." And here he has said, "This is the use of memory—for liberation."[66] In other words, he disassociates himself from the imprisonment by the Muses and temporalizing memory. And in the same poem are these verses:

> The moment of the rose and the moment of the yew-tree
> Are of equal duration. A people without history
> Is not redeemed from time, for history is a pattern
> Of timeless moments . . .
> History is now. . . .[67]

These verses hardly require comment, but we ought to point out something implicit which is noted by the commentator of the poem, Raymond Preston: the thousand years of the yew are *qualitatively* identical or equal to the hour of the rose; time is not to be understood as measurable time or duration but as "quality and intensity"[68]—a conception that will no longer seem strange to us.

Whereas poetry from antiquity until the Renaissance proceeded from the "musing" capabilities of the poet—the mental capacity of memory, the Platonic *metechein* or participating in the timeless memory of the world (see above p. 34, note 54) and the "perpetual abundance" which was temporalized by the poets from Homer via Hesiod and Plato to Virgil and Dante—we find a renunciation of this type of creativity after the French Revolution beginning with Novalis that becomes increasingly and pervasively conscious in its expression (cf. his poem, p. 307).

The "new obligation" gradually enters consciousness. It is no longer an obligation of ordering the soul and thinking (of the Muses); it is, as André Gide emphasizes, an obligation which belongs "to the order of the spirit." The source of creative power in man changes in proportion to the intensity of incursion of the new mutation; and this source shifts from the mental to the incipient integral structure of consciousness.

We shall have to concede that this renunciation is not a problem of generations, as though the attitude of Novalis or Hölderlin were mere swings of the pendulum from the attitudes of the preceding generation to their own. This is not so. In the course of the last several generations the renunciation or rejection has consolidated itself and gained in strength. As long as this fundamental change was not perceived, Novalis could be put aside as a magic poet, since his arationality could not be perceived as such, and Hölderlin could be branded as a mythical poet, although he had himself formulated the pre-eminent statement against myth (see p. 102); Mallarmé could be considered "obscure," despite his supra-luminescence, and Valéry accused of intellectualism despite his arational endeavors.

The constancy of the motif of the supplanting of the Muses by the spiritual and the supplanting of the temporalized by the time-free will now be apparent from the cited examples. It is perhaps not so much a question of mere constancy as one of the clarification and more conscious formulation of this motif, as in the case of the urbane yet convincing statement by Aldous Huxley in his book *Time Must Have a Stop* (a significant and not merely fortuitous title):

"For the nine Muses are the daughters of Mnemosyne; memory is of the very stuff and substance of poetry. And poetry, of course, is the best that human life can offer. But there is also the life of the spirit, and the life of spirit is the analogue, on a higher turn of the spiral, of the animal's life. The progression is from animal eternity into time, into the strictly human world of memory and anticipation; and from time, if one chooses to go on, into the world of spiritual eternity, into the divine Ground. The life of spirit is life exclusively in the present, never in the past or future; life here, now, not life looked forward to or recollected. There is absolutely no room in it for pathos, or remorse, or a voluptuous rumination of the delicious cuds of thirty years ago. Its Intelligible Light has nothing whatever to do either with the sunset radiance of those heart-rendingly good old days before the last war but three, or with the neon glow from those technological New Jerusalems beyond the horizons of the next revolution. No, the life of the spirit is life out of time, life in its essence and eternal principle. Which is why they all insist—all the people best qualified to know—that memory must be lived down and finally died to. When one has succeeded in mortifying the memory, says John of the Cross, one is in a state that is only a degree less perfect and profitable than the state of union with God. It is an assertion that, at a first reading, I found incomprehensible. But that was because, at that time, my first concern was with the life of poetry, not of the spirit. Now I know, by humiliating experience, all that memory can do to darken and obstruct the knowledge of the eternal Ground.[69]

The most recent generation—that following the generation of George, Rilke, and Valéry—has apparently overcome the uncertainties of this transformation to a degree that it is scarcely spoken of any longer. Here we would mention first Paul Eluard, and, from German poetry, Friedrich Hagen.

André Gide has said of Paul Eluard's poetry that "une telle poesie devient extraordinairement spirituelle" (poetry such as this lifts itself to utmost spirituality).[70] Eluard himself speaks of the "end of the imaginary" and states specifically that for him "perspective is no longer valid." And to his congenial German translator, Friedrich Hagen, he has remarked during his revision of the poems done into German, "Don't consider anything in terms of intellectual metaphor or in a figurative sense; consider it definitely as something concrete."[71]

In his poem "November 1936" there is the verse "que l'homme delivre de son passe absurde . . ." (may man be delivered from the absurd past).[72] In another context he has written this couplet, "Retraite":

Je sens l'espace s'abolir
Et le temps croître en tous sens

[I sense space abolishing itself
and time increasing in all directions][73]

This is the freedom from space and time, for space has dissolved here; and time—measuring and measured time—has become a force intensifying and achieving an aperspective range ("in *all* directions"): time becomes present.

This very same basic motif is expressed in the verse of Friedrich Hagen, whose only published volume of poetry is titled *Weinberg der Zeit*, "Time's Vineyard."[74] His poetry is original, clarified and purified, and free of all ballast from the past; it is pure statement, the imparting of truth, not evocation. Several of his poems are of a previously unachieved weightlessness and transparency and are raised to that "universal awareness" which Hagen has found characteristic of Eluard's poetry.[75] One of Hagen's poems containing these three essential components reads as follows:

Aber unter den schwarzen Steinen
die fahlen Gräser des Lachens der Freude

Kommt wir sammeln die Steine auf
Und decken die Schatten mit ihnen zu

und die Gräser richten sich auf und der Tag
erhebt sich zum Tanz auf ihren Spitzen

und das Licht vereinigt unsere Gesichter
zu einem einzigen Antlitz des Menschen.[76]

[Yet beneath the black stones
the sallow grasses of laughter of joy

Come we shall gather up the stones
and with them cover the shadows

and the grasses upright themselves and day
arises for its dance on their tips

and light unites our faces
into one single countenance of man.]

Paul Eluard's book of confessions bears the title *Donner à voir*, which we may translate as "imparting truth."[77] The work of both these poets expresses the eteological moment. This will be more evident in Hagen's work once all of his verse is published; in one volume of his poetry there is the verse, "Worte Sonnen seien, die morgen aufgehn werden" (words are suns that will arise tomorrow). The statement is true of his own words in any event which will be appreciated "tomorrow," for in them the "tomorrow" is already present. His poetry shows the same turn towards the new phenomena and actualities of consciousness which Mallarmé expressed in a verse written shorly before his death: " . . . l'astre muri des lendemains" (the star ripens from the morrow),[78] or in the translation of R. M. Rilke, "der reife Stern von bald" (the mature star of soon).[79]

What is here spoken of as being of tomorrow and of the future is already the present for all who are endeavoring to fulfill the "new obligation." On these pages there should be indications that there are not only new conceptions breaking forth but also that the realization process itself is something new: a fundamentally new "attitude" or "demeanor" which can be discerned in the change of estimation once accorded to the Muses.

There is today a change in man's creative relationship to the "primordial energy" which is pressing toward consciousness, a change with respect to creativity itself which corresponds to the changing and mutating consciousness, as we have described it in the first section of this chapter. It is only this state of affairs—the fact that the "source" of manifestations differs from that proper to the mental structure—which warrants our speaking of truly "new" manifestations for they do not by any means proceed solely from the old consciousness structure and its source.

With this we have completed an essential step in our investigations, and are approaching the manifestations which express or herald the aperspectival world.

1* *The I Ching or Book of Changes*, the Richard Wilhelm translation rendered into English by Cary F. Baynes (Princeton, N. J.: Princeton University Press, 1967), p. vii.

2* *I Ching* (note 1), p. lviii; see also Yüan-Kuang (Le Maître), *Méthode pratique de divination chinoise par le "Yi-King"* (Paris: Vega, 1950), pp. 19 and 20.

3* Richard Wilhelm in his introduction to the *I Ching* (note 1), p. liii; our italics.

4* *I Ching* (note 1), p. lviii.

5* *I Ching*, p. 6, note 7.

6* *I Ching*, pp. 3 and 6 f.; our italics.

7* *I Ching*, p. 370.

8   These remarks are based on our paper "Über das Wesen des Dichterischen," *Schweizerische Zeitschrift für Psychologie und ihre Anwendungen*, 3, 3 (Bern: Huber, 1944), pp. 216–231.

9* Quoted in Wyndham Lewis, *Time and Western Man* (London: Chatto and Windus, 1927), p. 1.

10 *Die homerischen Götterhymnen*, German version by Th. v. Scheffer (Jena: Diederichs, 1927), pp. 24, 78, 82, 101, and 102.

11* Ernst Robert Curtius, *European Literature and the Latin Middle Ages* (New York: Pantheon, 1953), p. 229. Curtius devotes a separate chapter to the importance of the Muses for literary history.

12 Homer, *Iliad*, II, 485–86. See also Preller-Robert, *Griechische Mythologie* (Berlin: Weidmann, ⁴1894), I, 2, p. 489 ff.

13 Eduard Jacobi, *Handwörterbuch der griechischen und römischen Mythologie* (Leipzig: Brauns, ²1847), p. 636 note.

14 Preller-Robert (note 12), I, 1, p. 107.

15 See Menge-Güthling, *Griechisch-deutsches Wörterbuch*, I (Berlin: Langenscheidt, ²⁸1910), pp. 355 and 379.

16 There is no definite etymological evidence that suggests a common root for "Muse," "musing," and "must"; see Kluge-Götze, *Etymologisches Wörterbuch der deutschen Sprache* (Berlin: de Gruyter, ¹¹1936), p. 405.

17 Quoted in the translation of Susemihl (Berlin: Lambert Schneider, 1939), I, 533D–534C and 535E–536D.

18 Plato, ed. Susemihl (note 17), III, p. 90 (*Philebos* 67B).

19   W. H. Roscher, *Ausführliches Lexikon der griechischen und römischen Mythologie* (Leipzig: Teubner, 1894–1897), II, 2, columns 3238–3295.

20   Plutarch, *Tischreden*, IX, 14,1; *Vermischite Schriften*, trans. Kaltwasser (Leipzig: G. Müller, 1911), I, p. 340 ff.

21   Friedrich Kurts, *Allgemeine Mythologie* (Leipzig: Weigel, ²1881), p. 367. See also Preller-Robert, p. 491.

22   Preller-Robert (note 12), p. 484 ff.

23   Rudolf Otto, *Das Gefühl des Übersinnlichen* (Munich: Beck, 1932), p. 140 note.

24   See Kluge-Götze (note 16), p. 95.

25   *Orpheus: Altgriechische Mysteriengesänge* (Jena: Diederichs, 1928), p. 99.

26   Hermann Usener, *Die Sintflutsagen* (Bonn: Cohen, 1899), p. 179.

27   Friedrich Creuzer, *Symbolik und Mythologie der alten Völker, besonders der Griechen* (Darmstadt: Leske, ²1819), III, p. 271. See also his *Deutsche Schriften* (Darmstadt: Leske, 1846), 2nd series, II, p. 83.

28   Eduard Jacobi (note 13).

29   A. C. Pearson, "Muses," in J. Hastings, *Encyclopedia of Religion and Ethics* (Edinburgh: Clark, 1917), IX, pp. 3–5.

30   Eckhart Peterich, *Kleine Mythologie* (Frankfurt/M.: Sozietät, 1937), p. 40.

31   Karl Philipp Moritz, *Götterlehre* (Berlin: Schade, ⁵1819), p. 233 ff., and also in Reclam's Universal-Bibliothek No. 1081/1084, p. 142 f.

32   Eduard Jacobi (note 13), p. 638.

33   W. H. Roscher (note 19), article "Musen."

34   Paula Philippson, "Der böotische Daimon Trophonios," *Griechische Gottheiten in ihren Landschaften*, Symbolae Osloenses, Fasc. Suppl. ix (Oslo: Broger, 1939).

35   Roscher (note 19).

36   Renata von Scheliha, *Patroklos* (Basel: Schwabe, 1942), p. 51.

37   We have already indicated that the Sirens, in accord with the mythical polarity of the event, are complementary manifestations of the Muses (see p. 207 f. as well as note 43, p. 240, and note 91, p. 244). Contemporaneously with us, Ernst Buschor has worked out this aspect in detail in his *Die Musen des Jenseits* (Munich: Bruckmann, 1944). The Sirens are powers of death and embody the "death pole of the soul," whereas the Muses, as E. R. Curtius has emphasized (note 11), p. 233, were "powers of life" embodying the "life pole of the soul" (see our discussion in Part I, chapter 6, sections 3 and 4, p. 205 ff.).

38   Aristotle, *Poetics*, VI, 1449 B 28; see also Aristotles, *Über die Dichtkunst*, trans. Alfred Gudeman, Philosophische Bibliothek 1, (Leipzig: Meiner, 1921), p. 9 f.

39   F. Nork, *Andeutungen eines Systems der Mythologie* (Leipzig: Dyk, 1850), p. 175 note.

40   F. Nork, *Mythologie der Volkssagen und Volksmärchen*, Sammlung "Das Kloster" 9 (Stuttgart: Scheible, 1848), p. 954.

41   Rainer Maria Rilke, *Briefe aus Muzot* (Leipzig: Insel, 1935), letter 106, p. 335.

42   This reference, as we have been informed by a knowledgeable friend, is in Robert Eisler's *Orpheus, the Fisher*. We have been unable to locate the quotation from antiquity in Eisler's *Orphisch-dionysische Mysteriengedanken in der christlichen Antike*, Vorträge der Bibliothek Warburg 1922/23 (Leipzig: Teubner, 1925), part 2.

43   C. G. Jung and Karl Kerényi, *Einführung in das Wesen der Mythologie* (Zürich: Rascher, 1941), p. 181.

44   Hölderlin, *Sämtliche Werke*, Grosse Stuttgarter Ausgabe, II (Stuttgart: Kohlhammer/Cotta, 1951), 1, p. 202, line 18.

45   Hölderlin, *Sämtliche Werke*, India paper edition (Leipzig: Insel, n.d.), p. 675.

46   Hölderlin (note 44), II, 1, p. 179, lines 5–15 (cited here in the presumably final version of the hymn).

47   Hugo von Hofmannsthal, *Andreas oder die Vereinigten* (Berlin: S. Fischer, 1932), p. 117.

48   "L'on ne s'aperçut pas aussitôt de l'extraordinaire nouveauté qu'apporta Baudelaire dans le champ de la poésie; on ne consentit longtemps à voir dans les *Fleurs du Mal* que la nouveauté des sujets traités (ce qui n'avait que peu d'importance); mais c'était une

révolution sans précédents que de ne plus s'abandonner au flux lyrique, de résister à la facilité de 'l'inspiration', au laisser-aller rhétorique, à l'entraînement des mots, des images et des conventions surannées; que de traiter la muse en rétive, qu'il faut soumettre au lieu de s'en remmetre à elle, esprit et sens critique liés, bref: que d'inviter l'art à maîtriser la poésie. Baudelaire, à l'encontre de ses contemporains, apporta dans son art, encouragé par Poe, science et conscience, patience et résolution" (André Gide, Anthologie de la Poésie française, avec une préface, Bibliothèque de la Pléiade (Paris: NRF, 1949), p. x. See also the German translation: "Vorrede zu einer Anthologie der französischen Dichtung," trans. Friedhelm Kemp, Merkur, 22 (December, 1949), p. 1167 f.

49   Stéphane Mallarmé, Oeuvres complètes, Bibliothèque de la Pléiade (Paris: NRF, 1945), p. 56.

50   See E. Noulet, L'Oeuvre poétique de Stéphane Mallarmé (Paris: Droz, 1940), pp. 256–258. Also in Textes Littéraires Français (Geneva: Girard, Lille & Droz, 1948), "Dix Poémes de Stéphane Mallarmé, Exégèses de E. Noulet," pp. 64–65.

51   See the respective translations:
        a) Stéphane Mallarmé, Dichtungen, trans. Kurt Reidemeister (Krefeld: Scherpe, 1948), p. 43;
        b) Stéphane Mallarmé, Gedichte, trans. Richard von Schaukal (Freiburg/Br.: Alber, 1948), p. 65;
        c) Stéphane Mallarmé, Gedichte und Der Nachmittag eines Fauns, trans. Remigius Netzer (Munich: Piper, 1946) (lacks this particular poem);
        d) Stéphane Mallarmé, Gedichte, trans. Fritz Usinger; bi-lingual edition (Jena: Rauch, 1948), p. 33 (perhaps the most felicitous translation).

52   Mallarmé (note 49), p. 51; see also the first version of the poem cited in E. Noulet (note 50), p. 241.

53   André Gide (note 48), p. li, and Merkur, p. 1179.

54   Gide (note 48), p. xxxi, and Merkur, p. 1172.

55   Paul Valéry, Poésies (Paris: NRF, 1933), p. 196.

56*   Paul Valéry, Poems, trans. David Paul, The Collected Works of Paul Valéry, edited by Jackson Mathews, Bollingen Series 45, I (Princeton, N. J.: Princeton University Press, 1971), p. 225. Compare also the German version by Rainer Maria Rilke:
        Vergebens sucht der Arm der riesig immerzu
        flutende Nymphe meine Kraft zu ändern;
        ich zerre langsam mich aus ihren kalten Bändern,
        und ihre nackte Macht bezwingt nicht, was ich tu.
        in: Rainer Maria Rilke, Gesammelte Werke (Leipzig: Insel, 1930), VI (Übertragungen), p. 330; Paul Valéry, Gedichte, trans. R. M. Rilke (Wiesbaden: Insel, 1949), p. 51.

57*   The first quotation is from Valéry's "Lettre sur Mallarmé" in Paul Valéry, Leonardo - Poe - Mallarmé, trans. Malcolm Cowley and James R. Lawler, Bollingen Series 45, VIII (Princeton, N. J.: Princeton University Press, 1972), p. 249; italics original. The second quotation, from Valéry's L'Idee fixe, is cited from Paul Valéry, L'Idée fixe (Paris: NRF, 1934), p. 13, and Idée fixe, trans. David Paul, Bollingen Series 45, V (New York: Pantheon, 1965), p. 7.

58*   T. S. Eliot, "From Poe to Valéry," a lecture delivered at the Library of Congress, November 19, 1948; in To Criticize the Critic (N. Y.: Farrar, Straus & Giroux, 1965), p. 39.

59*   Paul Valéry, "La Politique de l'esprit, notre souverain bien," Oeuvres I (Paris: Pléiade, 1957); cited here according to the German edition, Politik des Geistes (Vienna: Bermann-Fischer, 1937), p. 26. See also the English version by William A. Bradley in Paul Valéry, "Spiritual Polity," Variety, Second Series (New York: Harcourt, Brace, 1938).

60   Valéry, Politik des Geistes (note 59), p. 22.

61   Paul Valéry, Variété V (Paris: NRF, 1944), p. 301.

62   Valéry (note 61), p. 310.

63   Valéry (note 61), p. 305; italics original.

64*   T. S. Eliot, "From Poe to Valéry" (note 58), p. 40.

65 T. S. Eliot, *Selected Essays* (London: Faber & Faber, ²1932), p. 21; see also the translation by Hans Hennecke in T. S. Eliot, *Ausgewählte* Essays 1917–1947 (Frankfurt/M: Suhrkamp, 1950), p. 111.

66* T. S. Eliot, *Little Gidding* (London: Faber & Faber, 1942), p. 12, and *Four Quartets* (London: Faber & Faber, 1944), p. 40.

67* Eliot, *Little Gidding*, p. 15; *Four Quartets*, p. 43

68 Raymond Preston, *"Four Quartets" Rehearsed* (London: Sheed and Ward, 1946), p. 62. See also the commentary on these verses by B. Rajan, *T. S. Eliot, a Study of his Writings by Several Hands*, ed. B. Rajan (London: Dennis Dobson, 1947), p. 80.

69* Aldous Huxley, *Time Must Have a Stop* (N. Y.: Harper, 1944), p. 282.

70 André Gide (note 48), p. L, and *Merkur*, p. 1179.

71 Friedrich Hagen, *Paul Eluard* (Neuwied/Rhein: Lancelot, 1949), pp. 35, 36, and 53.

72 Paul Eluard, *Au rendez-vous allemand* (Geneva: Trois Collines, 1945), p. 76.

73 Paul Eluard, *Poésie et Vérité 1942* (Neuchâtel: La Baconnière, 1943), p. 89.

74 Friedrich Hagen, *Weinberg der Zeit* (Mainz: Internationaler Universum Verlag, 1949).

75 Friedrich Hagen, *Paul Eluard* (note 71), p. 35.

76 Friedrich Hagen (note 74), p. 40.

77 Paul Eluard, *Donner à voir* (Paris: NRF, 1939).

78 Stephane Mallarmé, *Oeuvres complètes* (note 49), p. 71.

79 Rainer Maria Rilke, *Ausgewählte Werke* (Leipzig: Insel, 1938), II, p. 360. Richard von Schaukal's translation (note 51b, p. 107) "den reifen Stern, der morgen walten wird," seems to fall short of expressing the essentials.

4

The New Concepts

1. Inceptions of the New Consciousness

Before we examine the manifestations of the new consciousness we must understand where they are to be found and in what forms they occur. We will not be able to lay hold of them systematically and will therefore have to devise schemata with which to organize them in a way that is commensurate with the principal motif of the new manifestations. Such an approach is provided by the concept of systasis.

One systatic concept is that of temporic concretion (see above p. 26 ff.). One of its forms of expression, the most pervasive in fact, is the fourth dimension. We shall have to consider both of these briefly if we are to have a basis for our verification, for it is no longer possible to rely exclusively on a methodology. By proceeding methodologically we could at the very most achieve a systematization of the new manifestations, but this would defeat our purpose inasmuch as a systematization spatializes whatever it encompasses; we would again find ourselves within the three-dimensional realm instead of having advanced into the four-dimensional sphere.

By introducing systasis into simple methodology, we are able to evince a new "method" which is no longer three-dimensional. This new method is four-dimensional diaphany; in this what is merely conceivable and comprehensible becomes transparent. Diaphany is based on synairesis, on the eteological completion of systasis and system to an integral whole, for integrality is only possible where "temporal" elements and spatial magnitudes are brought together synairetically. The concept which makes possible the "comprehension" or, more exactly, the perception of the "temporal elements" is that of systasis. If we also take into account the systatic concepts, the mere methodology of systems is intensified to synairetic diaphany; and this must be achieved unless we are to remain caught in the three-dimensional scheme of thought.

Before turning to the two motifs of the "fourth dimension" and "temporic concretion," we must first briefly examine the two inceptions of the new consciousness. The one is spiritual, the other, physical.

We have already touched on the spiritual inception: it is the altered relation of the creative individual to creativity itself since the decade of 1790–1800. The change, as we noted, is primarily the altered attitude toward one phenomenon of "time," recollection. This renunciation of recollection, it must be noted, is not an attempt to "repress" recollection but to supersede it. The supersession is at the same time a supersession of "time" and consequently a turn toward freedom from time. The submersion into timelessness and the drawing up into our measurable time, characteristic of earlier creativity, give way to the attempt to achieve the "new obligation" or the new task of *devoir* by clarity (*lucidité*), transparency (*cristallisation*), and intensified awareness.

This new spiritual inception is the new source to which the new manifestations owe their possibility of manifestation. We have verified this new source as it pertains to the realm of poetry, but it is only natural that the altered form of creative effectuation, in its altered form which taps new energies for its use, is not restricted merely to poetry. A similar achievement can be assumed for the originators of new conceptions in other fields, as is evident in physics from the account of de Broglie, the founder of "wave mechanics," in which he describes the realization of new concepts (of which we have given a detailed report elsewhere).[1]

The question now arises whether there is a new physical inception which corresponds to this new spiritual one, for there is always a tendency that those things which are constellated in the realm of the imperceptible become visible directly in the realm of the most tangible. We can thus surmise that the physical structure of man is changing and not just his spiritual structure, and that there is a similar mutation taking place.

It is surely somewhat risky to speak of changes in man's physiological structure today which can be verified as being mutational in origin; but it is permissible at least to indicate this possibility. We can, for example, discern a definite alteration in posture if we compare mythical with mental man. Two Tanagra figurines demonstrate this graphically (see figures 44 and 45). The one from the mythical attitude dates from the fourth century B.C., the one from the mental from the third century B.C.; both are representations of Persephone.

The differences in posture and bearing are quite apparent. The earlier figurine shows evidence of a distinctly nature-oriented rhythm, while the later one, recognizably upright in posture, shows a bearing with raised head and not the former stance of a head bowed in dreams of lunar configuration. We have here a structural differentiation illustrating the increased and consolidated consciousness of self, the Greek's greater sense of ego as a result of the mutation from the mythical to the mental structure.

The awakening to the mental consciousness which is repeated in Europe in the tenth and eleventh centuries A.D. is also evident in an obvious way in the pictorial arts of that period. The mutation which European man recapitulates during those centuries (see above p. 10 f.) has its visible manifestation as in the sixth to third centuries B.C. in Greece in the smile which the Romanesque madonnas are still lacking (see p. 78 above), which is already beginning to show in the countenance of the early Gothic madonnas and which reaches its full radiance in those of the thirteenth century. And whereas the child is still placed in the center of the depiction and thus

Figure 44: *Kore*; Greek, fourth century B.C., from Tanagra
(actual size: 19.5 cm).

forms an unquestioned and undisturbed unity with the madonnas of the early Romanesque era, the later depictions show that clearly discernible shift of position
towards the right and away from the center so that the child now emphasizes the
right side of the figure. This shift of emphasis breaks up the circular enclosure; the
mythical circle and the non-perspective world are torn apart, and mental directedness and the emphasis on the right come to the fore and are reflected by the smiling
countenance which is awakening to itself. (Early depictions of the madonna often

Figure 45: *Kore*; Greek, third century B.C., from Tanagra
(actual size 24.5 cm).

show the child being held—or still being held—on the *left* or heart (!) side, while
later depictions of the mental age almost invariably show it on the right.)

While in these two examples it is primarily the posture that evinces a mutational change of inner structure, specifically of the structure of consciousness, perhaps we can find a conspicuous symptom of a purely physical kind to verify this same
change. Such a symptom is given by the surprising formation of the Greek forehead.
We are referring to the definite outward formation of the cerebrum in the frontal

bone and the concurrent decrease in volume of the posterior cranium. The ancient Egyptian profile still shows a receding forehead, and it is significant that the Egyptian, bound to magic and myth, restricted the development of the protruding forehead—and consequently of the cerebrum—by bandaging and thus making it impossible.

This binding back of the frontal bone with bandages tied around the heads of children at an early age is still in evidence today among certain native tribes in Africa. The protruding frontal bone emerges only gradually among the Greeks of pre-Christian Mediterranean civilization, as can be seen from all depictions from the seventh down to the fourth century B.C. There is at first a short, steeply inclined forehead which is covered by the hair brushed forward; but *after* completion of the mutation in the fourth century, the forehead can be seen in works of Greek pictorial art in its clear, uncovered, and upright resplendence. A comparison of the profile of the head of the Egyptian queen Nefertiti with the steeper profile of any head from the third century B.C. in Greece will clearly reveal this contrast to anyone familiar with the respective works of art.

As for our own day, it will be obvious that such changes in structure, be they in posture and bearing, or in physiognomy, are not yet such that they allow us to draw conclusions about the completion of a mutation. There are as yet no demonstrable physiological inceptions that express the new structure of consciousness, which, however, does not exclude the possibility of changes in physiognomy which may be visible even though it would be premature to attempt to identify them. But the fact that a transfer of certain important processes from the cerebrum to the cerebral cortex seems to be taking place, and that there is a greater differentiation of humoral or hormonal functions means that we should not ignore them in a later consideration of these questions. We have already touched on them in cross-sections 10 and 15 (pp. 144 and 270) in Part I of the present work.

Above and beyond this, it would seem that the brain research of the last ten years (1950-1960) has indicated that the human brain harbors as yet unexplored possibilities for unfolding, possibilities which have been noted by Lecomte du Noüy and Hugo Spatz (see below p. 437 f.). On this subject little more can be said today, particularly as it is by no means certain that it is a question with regard to the present mutation, of a mutation for which the previous and traditional form of man is adequate for its manifestion and which therefore requires "only" additional and transformative capabilities of and in man to bring about its unfolding. For it may well be that some day the design might be more intensive, so intensive that the previous form of man would be inadequate for the realization of the mutation, and that the mutation would not merely bring on incremental capacities in man but would be by nature completely transforming. The fact that today the question as to the nature of man dominates the field of rational discussion almost exclusively in the form of anthropological or existential points of view is a clear indication that man today (at least the nothing-but-rational man) has not only become dubious but is in fact placing himself and his very existence in question.

For the moment, however, it would appear that the previous foundations—those which we have presented in Part I—are sufficiently strong to provide an adequate basis for a new mutation. It would be premature to speak of the necessity for a complete transformation of man (and thus of earth) before man gives evidence of his complete and utter failure.

It could even be suggested parenthetically that the present-day existentialist line of questioning is a positive indication of the acute state of the impending mutation. But this would be a false interpretation; this line of questioning has simply brought man as he has been until now into question, and has ultimately negated man. A negation of what has gone before does not, however, constitute an affirmation of what is now coming to fulfillment, which requires the efficient energies of what has been before for its manifestation. The anthropological and existential doubts about man are a declaration of the bankruptcy of philosophy.

Ever since philosophy announced the death of God, as postulated by Hegel and already anticipated in the Enlightenment (see note 33, p. 265 above), there was reason to believe that it would also have to announce the death of man. This is occurring today in the most degrading and loathsome forms imaginable—the *nausée* of Sartre—and accompanied by the formlessness of an instinct-driven psychologization of philosophy resulting from the unleashed psyche whose *religio* has been destroyed. This confession of suicide is the admission by the rationally rigidified representatives of our era that they in their torpidity are not equal to the "new task."

The time at which this announcement of the death of God was made is striking: it occurs in the decade following the French Revolution. Fichte's remark that "man is without predicates" underscores the reduction of God to human proportions and corresponds to the tendency expressed by the French Revolution we can define as the disengagement from patriarchy. The divine father or sovereign was deposed just like the earthly sovereign. It is a parallel to the matricide that did away with matriarchy (see above pp. 150 and 255).

This digression has been necessary to prevent the suspicion that the new mutation may in some way be deemed to be a process of divinization of man. The new energy irrupting in man is not might; it does not make him more mighty. But it should make him veritable; it intensifies the awakening consciousness, it lifts man out of his confinement in matter and the psyche, and changes him so that the spiritual becomes transparent to him. Wherever this increment of energy veers around into power or might, instead of becoming conscious as the "new task," it destroys man. Someone who is not equal to the mutation and misinterprets its demand will run aground on it, and the negative anthropocentricity of the recent philosophers is a clear demonstration of the truth of this statment.

Both new inceptions, then, the spiritual as well as the physiological, are to be considered in the sense of a task and not of presumption. Where courage does not go hand in hand with humility, man has thrown away his chance.

The wisdom of the church has fulfilled the new obligations of the mutation more wisely than was possible for the mere knowledge of that secularized theology, philosophy. The new dogma of Mary proclaimed on All Saints' Day, 1950, by Pope Pius XII[2] can be understood as a renunciation of the overly emphasized father-aspect of God that is itself a reduction of the divine. The reinstatement of the maternal principle to its rights, that is to its "lefts," and the reduction of the overemphasis on the paternal principle are a clear indication that the church is striving for recognition of the *whole* and integral man.

The accentuation of the assumption of the body shifts the religious emphasis to the sphere of *transfiguration*, which, being a transparent process, is one form of spiritual transparency or *diaphaneity*. The element of transfiguration or spiritual birth is henceforth in the foreground, rather than the crucifixion, the physical death. Will Christianity, in accord with the incipient mutation, change in keeping with the possibilities which are indicated for it? Will the church of the crucified become the church of the risen? Will Rome adopt the festival of the resurrection or *spiritual birth* as the more important festival, which has been prepared since patristic times in the Eastern church, rather than Christmas, the festival of *physical* birth?

However this may be, it is inescapable that the proclamation of this new dogma two generations ago would have met with the strongest resistance because of the credulity at that time with respect to matter. Today it is rejected only by the most strongly rational-oriented religious order and by the rational attitude of ultra-Protestantism. Here too we can discern an indication of the extent to which the three-dimensional consciousness is exhausted.

The dogma of Mary was the most productive and genial response to Existentialism, and for this reason we had to consider it. This dogma lends a positive support to the new spiritual inception which we have attempted to evince in our discussion, while it makes ever more apparent the exhaustion of philosophy in Existentialism. The dogma also articulates the supersession of space and time via its turn towards the spiritual; it is a noble message and an admonition to the "new task" or obligation, to which philosophy up to now has not been equal and on which it now threatens ultimately to founder.

It should now be apparent that both of the new inceptions do not justify any kind of claim or demand whatever; they are an obligation. It has been our task to underscore this in order to counter from the very outset every hybrid interpretation of these new inceptions. Having done this, we can turn to the new systatic concepts by virtue of which those manifestations that owe their possibility of manifestation to the realization of the new inceptions can be made perceptible.

2. *The Fourth Dimension*

The fourth dimension is freedom from time, i.e., *the Achronon*. The fourth dimension is not the concept of merely measurable time but the "form" of the temporal or temporistic principle which we have defined as time freedom. This is of decisive importance.

Since the fourth dimension has had a determining role in our epoch—indeed has become its hallmark, particularly since Einstein—we must examine it more closely. For the sake of clarity we should note at the outset that all definitions of the fourth dimension which utilize one of the previous forms of time are *temporic* endeavors; they are the expression of the new efforts to solve the problem of time which has been deliberately suppressed for centuries. We should also note that all previous attempts of a categorical nature were inadequate inasmuch as the "time" complex is acategorical. The problem was posed, but not resolved; and it cannot in fact be solved categorically.

The structuration of the process of consciousness emergence as it occurred in dimensioning, which we have carried out in the present discussion, is an additional reason for us to examine the essence of the new dimension.

And an additional circumstance must be mentioned: only time in the form of chronological time or as a geometricized magnitude is strictly speaking a dimension or mensuration. In the true sense of time freedom as an acategorical element the fourth dimension is an *amension*. When we nonetheless retain the term dimension our usage is justified by the dissolution and integration of the three spatial dimensions wrought by the fourth dimension; it resolves their measurability and in a certain sense "measures through" them. Only when understood in this way is it permissible to apply the traditional notion of dimension to the acategorical and integrative fourth component.

The notion that "time" is a "heterogenous dimension" of space, lying "transverse" as it were to the "vertical" spatial dimensions resting upon it, was formulated by no less a figure than the ontologist Nicolai Hartmann in his last work, published in 1950, "The Philosophy of Nature"(*Philosophie der Natur*).[3] The eighteen chapters of part one of his book are devoted to "dimensional categories" and provide an ontological-categorical analysis of three- and four-dimensionality. This analysis fails (and at the same time fulfills itself philosophically) by being unable to proceed beyond the definitions mentioned above: the compulsion to system and the categorical thinking inherent in it are philosophically a dead-end and prevent the perception of systatic elements. We have indicated this impasse in order to show that the terminological difficulty has already become apparent to categorical thinking although it is content to define the fourth dimension as "heterogenous," and, in so doing, merely avoids the issue by falling back into dualism.

In order to deal adequately with this "concept" which is central to the new perception of the world it is appropriate for us to reconstruct the genesis of the concept of the fourth dimension, and to observe the sphere of thought and the cognitive descipline from which it arose, as well as the disciplines that have subsequently modified and adopted it.

The point of departure for the notion of a space of more than three dimensions, be it of four, five, six, or *n* dimensions, was Euclid's parallel axiom. The undemonstrability of this axiom was first recognized by Friedrich W. Gauss (1777–1855), but since he feared the "outcry of the Boeotians" he did not publish anything about the geometry he had constructed without the parallel postulate which was to become the cornerstone of non-Euclidian geometry. Two Germans, Schweikart and his nephew Taurinus, were also occupied with such a possibility, and their demonstration occurred independently of Gauss in 1825.

Besides these attempts there were further demonstrations, again pursued independently, by the Russian N. J. Lobatchevsky in 1829 and the Hungarian J. Bolyai in 1832. Another advance came with B. Riemann's inaugural lecture of 1854 on the "Hypotheses on which Geometry is based," which further demonstrated the possibility of a non-Euclidian geometry. Riemann added his elliptical geometry, in which the sum of angles exceeds 180° and which is designated as the "second type of non-Euclidian geometry," to the geometry proposed by Lobatchevsky (hyperbolic), in which the sum of the angles is less than 180° and which is called the "first type of non-Euclidian geometry." These non-Euclidian geometries made it possible to represent spaces having more than three dimensions.

One particular form of these *n*-dimensioned conceptions of space was elaborated in 1905 by Einstein, who utilized and generalized Riemann's conception in his special theory of relativity. There he postulated the four-dimensional unity of space and time and demonstrated its validity for certain phenomena, whereby the constant that unifies time and space is the speed of light. To the spatial coordinates a, b, and c was added the new fourth coordinate t, time, where t equals $\sqrt{-1}$, which as the number i refers to the next greater coordinate system. This made possible the mathematical description of certain spatial phenomena, particularly those relative to one another as a result of having two different points of observation. The additional demonstration of the equivalence of energy and mass assured the purely physical importance of the four-dimensional coordinate system.

Let us pause and observe for the moment that by introducing time as a fourth dimension, Einstein made possible changes in our knowledge of certain phenomena and occurrences which altered the foundations of physics and mechanics. But when we speak today of a fourth dimension, a wider frame of reference than that of Einstein's theory of relativity forces itself upon the observer, one which links the fourth dimension not merely with time or even the measurable time of particular movements or velocities, as in the case of Einstein's theory, but rather with the assumption of an invisibly efficacious component.

As early as 1864/65 in a series of lectures on psycho-physics held during the winter of that year at the University of Graz, Ernst Mach had propounded the notion of a spatial conception augmented by an additional dimension, and suggested it as an explanation of previously inexplicable physical phenomena. Mach did this without knowledge of Riemann's concept which was not published until 1867.[4] Mach's suggestion of the possibility of such conceptions appeared in Fichte's Zeitschrift für Philosophie during the year 1865/66, and he elaborated on them in his book Die Geschichte und Wurzel des Satzes von der Erhaltung der Arbeit (The History and Root of the Principle of the Conservation of Work).[5] As the title indicates by its substitution of the concept of work for that of energy, Mach is concerned with a principle which, as we shall see, is related to "time." Whereas Einstein's conception of a fourth dimension is purely epistemological and physical-geometrical, Mach's conception has a distinctly psycho-physical coloration despite his positivist and phenomenological viewpoint (his so-called "Empiriocriticism").

At the hands of the materialistic "psychists," however, the fourth dimension took on a predominantly psychic character. They incorporated it into their cloudy field of inquiry as the "occult" component of nature, and attempted to clarify in a spiritistic manner the partially hidden, partially manifest substructure of nature. Among these psychists was the astrophysicist Friedrich Zöllner, who in 1886 published his Naturwissenschaft und christliche Offenbarung (The Natural Sciences and Christian Revelation).[6] In his ideological wake followed all of those circles who were prompted from a mediumistic and materialistic standpoint to describe the "supersensory" as the "fourth dimension" whenever it made an appearance at their spiritistic seances.

The disingenuous, latter-day mystics who are exemplified by Maurice Maeterlinck[7] also belong to this entourage. These mystics describe the effects of their mystical attitude, which is only a re-immersion into the pure polarity of the psyche and the manifestation of its resultant powers, as being "four-dimensional." But they fail to recognize that instead of superseding the three-dimensional world, they subsede it, as it were, in their reversion to a two-dimensional world.

Or, to mention yet another (and final) interpretation of the fourth dimension which should be included in this summary, we should note that of the contemporary French "traditionalists" in the circle of R. Guénon, as represented by Raoul Auclair[8] and Raymond Abellio.[9] These men are also among the proponents of the widespread and vigorous esoteric movement in France which follows in the footsteps of Saint-Martin, Fabre d'Olivet, St. de Guaita, Eliphas Levi, Saint Yves d'Alveydre, Matgioi, and Papus, among others. They consider the ether as a fourth dimension, which they understand not in the Greek sense as an element but as a "primordial" extra-spatial and extratemporal phenomenon.

Even this brief summary reveals two telling facts; one is the remarkable circumstance that non-Euclidian geometry was discovered simultaneously by several independent researchers; the other is the far-reaching adaptation of the concept of a fourth dimension by representatives of the most disparate disciplines and attitudes.

Let us first examine the question of the simultaneous discovery, which of course we are not the first to observe. Egmont Colerus too has noted this phenomenon[10] and observed that the concept of non-Euclidian geometries represents perhaps the most significant revolution in the history of science, and makes possible for the first time a conception of a fourth dimension.

Gauss, as we have seen, was occupied with the parallel axiom as early as 1799 and was the first to conceive of a non-Euclidian geometry. But he did not publish anything about it, a circumstance to which we will return shortly. Gauss first alluded to this discovery in a letter to the great astronomer Bessel in 1829.[11] And when the law student Schweikart informed him of his own essentially identical geometry, Gauss openly praised Schweikart. In 1825 Schweikart's nephew Taurinus published a discussion on this subject which was followed in 1829 by N. J. Lobatchevsky's exposition of his discovery of non-Euclidian geometry at the University of Kazan. And independently of the others, J. Bolyai published in 1832 his non-Euclidian geometry which was basically identical to that of Gauss. Including Gauss, there were then no fewer than five scholars—Gauss, Schweikart (and Taurinus) in Germany; Lobatchevsky in Russia; and Bolyai in Hungary—who, within one decade, realized independently of each other that form of geometry which allowed conclusions from which a four-dimensional world could proceed.

In any event, the quadruplicity of discovery of this particular concept which was to transform the world is a remarkable circumstance. And here we should mention the further and highly unusual fact that Gauss himself did not publish the results of his discovery but merely alluded to it once in his letter of 1829 to the renowned astronomer Bessel. Of this Colerus remarked that "such unusual behaviour by the greatest of mathematicians is today still in need of a psychological-historical explanation."[12]

Gauss' behavior is perhaps better understood if viewed as a parallel to Petrarch's reaction in a similar situation of discovery. When in 1336, some five hundred years before Gauss, Petrarch discovered landscape while climbing Mont Ventoux (see p. 13 f.), a discovery which opened up space and the realization of the third dimension, he was so shaken by this world-transforming discovery that he mentioned it to only one person in a letter. When Gauss discovered non-Euclidian geometry which, as a result of its n-dimensionality, made possible the realization of the four-dimensional continuum, he reported this world-transforming find to only one person—in a letter.

This coincidental and yet remarkable parallelism can even be extended, with the requisite reservations, to a parallel quadruplicity of the discovery of landscape that, so far as we can determine, also took place within the space of approximately one decade. This awakening consciousness of space broke forth independently four times during the years 1327–1337: in the frescos of Assisi by the Brothers Lorenzetti (1327–1328); in the last works of Giotto (1337); in the Arabic Sufi manuscripts of the same year; and in the aforementioned letter of Petrarch to Francesco Dionigi di Borgo San Sepolcro (1336).

No other possibilities of reality of the last six hundred years have had so great, indeed, so fundamental an impact on the forms of realization of European man. Our suggestion that there is a certain parallelism of discovery and the mode of communication of these two realities should not, however, be looked upon as an attempt to fit the events into a questionable theory of parallelism. The events cannot be generalized to the extent that all occurrences could be included in a strait-jacketed system of simultaneous occurrence—a kind of perpetually recurring cosmic-tellurian time table or cycle. On the other hand we cannot ignore the fact that all manifestations which occur within the terrestrial arena are at least in part necessarily subject to those laws and forms of manifestation that are naturally valid on earth and co-determine their unfolding.

Despite this reservation and admission, we would also point to a further circumstance deserving of our attention because it expresses a certain surprising structural regularity or symmetry. To be sure, we must proceed here with great caution and must also be prepared to temper the influence of categorical considerations imposed by our thinking on events which themselves have their own intrinsic, origin-given order. But it is permissible for us—and this is of considerable importance—to regard fundamental manifestations that become truly visible because of their own origin-given freedom, which are thus unimpeded by categories we have constructed, as being coincident or consistent. This is particularly true of the initial manifestation of two genuinely mutational phenomena which avail themselves of different areas or disciplines of human endeavor for their potential realization.

We have included this caution in order to counter possible objections that might be raised when we venture to relate to one another the respective first manifestation of a three- and then a four-dimensional reality. In the case of Petrarch, the upsurge of a new potential dimension occurred in the realm of the soul or spirit, whereas with Gauss and his contemporaries it took place in the purely mathematical, that is, essentially mental realm. In each instance the realm corresponds to the respective consciousness structure of the epoch in which their initiators lived. With this proviso drawn from the realm of the history of the mind rather than from a strictly scientific or exact interpretation of such living contexts and manifestations, we may now proceed to examine the question of regularity or symmetry.

As we have seen in Part I of our exposition, Petrarch's discovery of landscape was the potential discovery of space. Together with the Brothers Lorenzetti, Giotto, and the Sufi miniaturists he makes visible the possibility of "space." But the precise realization of the dimensions of space did not come about for another one hundred and fifty years until Leonardo achieved the realization of space-disclosing perspective toward the close of the fifteenth century.

We might, however, say that space—and this includes perspective and the third dimension—is already present in the manifestations by the four in an "imaginary" way, to use a common if not entirely apt expression. Those "loci" of which Petrarch speaks in his letter (p. 14) are already "space" whose manifold perspectivation is coalesced into precisely this "space." These "loci" are perhaps best described as "imaginary (three-dimensional) space"; or, in other words, Petrarch's landscape with its "loci" is the "imaginary space" that becomes an objectively real space only when Leonardo's theory of perspectivity and its application removed it from the realm of the imaginary.

While these dates and formulations are concerned with the gestation periods and phenomenologizations of three-dimensional space, very nearly identical periods of genesis can be adduced for the four-dimensional continuum that finds its expression as "spatial curvature" in the sphere and achieves genuine efficacy beyond its first "imaginary" form.

We do not know if Gauss spoke of the probable form of the continuum that bears and effects the "non-Euclidian" geometry which he discovered and named; nor do we know if he defined it as an "imaginary Sphere."[13] We do know that F. H. Lambert (1728–1777), extending the work of the Jesuit scholar G. Saccheri, spoke of an "imaginary sphere" which necessarily forms the basis of a geometry constructed without the unprovable parallel postulate.[14] Saccheri's work, *Euclides ab omni naevo vindicatus* (Euclid freed of all blemishes), was published in 1733.

We are here interested in the fact that the notion of an "imaginary sphere" is inextricably linked to the supersession of the Euclidian conception of space in the same way as the notion of Petrarch's "imaginary space" cited earlier was linked to the supersession of a merely two-dimensional world. As Petrarch's "imaginary space" became an objectively real space of three dimensions in the course of about five generations, so did the "imaginary sphere" become the objectively real known sphere of four dimensions—the "curved space" of physics—via Einstein's theory of relativity approximately five generations after Lambert.

It is also important that we not overlook that the intermediate links between Lambert or Gauss and Einstein are as significant as those between Petrarch and Leonardo da Vinci, which we noted in our discussion of the history of perspective (p. 15 ff.). That discussion might well have been entitled "The History of the Third Dimension." As to the "History of the Fourth Dimension," we would note that Riemann's discovery of the second type of non-Euclidian geometry laid the foundations for Einstein's application of the fourth dimension in physics, along with the work of Beltrami and F. Klein who were responsible for the ultimate and decisive demonstration of the "objective character of the negatively constant curved surface, i.e., the presumably imaginary sphere" during the years 1869–1871.[15] Here we can only allude to the decisive contributions made by Minkowski's geometry of numbers to Einstein's theory, to the special relativity theory as a geometry in four-dimensional space, and to Lorentz's "transformation" where various four-dimensional (spatial-temporal) coordinate systems relative to one another can be bilaterally converted, inasmuch as a discussion of these developments would lead us too far afield.

In the remarks above we have examined the first item pressing for consideration in our brief outline of a history of the fourth dimension, namely, the unusual simultaneity of discovery of non-Euclidean geometry which is the very foundation of a conception of *n*-dimensional and thus four-dimensional "spaces." With respect to this simultaneity it is of interest to note that it is an instance not of a double discovery, which is often met up with, but a quadruple discovery. Working simultaneously but independently in different countries, four men unearthed the basis for a new conception of the world and consequently of a new consciousness structure. It may not be amiss to suggest that there is a justification for the conclusion that the original consciousness has thereby sought to insure the *human* accomplishment of such a decisive step in the emergence of consciousness.

We are aware that such an interpretation will offend adherents of the anthropocentric attitude prevalent today. And yet it must be recognized that we are not by any means propounding a conviction that rests only on belief in some "divine" governance of affairs. Let us merely be content to consider this mutation of consciousness, like those preceding it, as being latent in our endowment, necessarily breaking forth at an organically determined moment and manifesting itself in accord with its intensity and transformative energy in a way that cannot be—and is not being—ignored or overlooked.

As to one fundamental conclusion resulting from these deliberations there can be no doubt: the discovery of landscape by Petrarch and his contemporaries can be placed in relation, indeed parallel, to the discovery of non-Euclidian geometry by Gauss and his contemporaries. The conception of landscape contains (at first imaginarily) the germ or prefiguration of three-dimensional, perspectivally fixed space which is only later realized. And the concept of a non-Euclidian geometry in turn is an anticipation, again imaginarily, of the later-realized sphere which is non-fixed, four-dimensional, and free of perspective (i.e., aperspectival) because it is a moving as well as transparent sphere.

In Part I of our discussion (p. 100 f.) we pointed out that the sphere is the "symbol" of the four-dimensional, integral consciousness structure. The concept of an "imaginary sphere," which emerged precisely when the realization of a non-Euclidian geometry proved inescapable, surely indicates the validity of this symbol for the aperspectival world. A further indication of its validity is given by the fact that once this "imaginary sphere" was freed from the imaginary it then assumed a four-dimensional character, at least to our geometric awareness.

It is of particular significance that we have also encountered the parallelism of the forms of expression and dimension of both structures (which are at first imaginary) in connection with their simultaneous discovery. This significance derives from the fact that the four-dimensional sphere, or, in geometric terms, space curved by time (!), is the only real basis for actualizing a four-dimensional system of coordinates. The simple sphere is merely three-dimensional; only the moving, transparent sphere is four-dimensional. And only the transparency guarantees the aperspectival perception.

This four-dimensionality of the transparent spherical surface will consequently be of decisive value to the four-dimensional character of, say, recent painting. Such painting will lose the abstruseness which it still has for many people today when certain of its examples are no longer viewed with the eyes of a three-dimensional consciousness. What must frequently seem to be distorted to the three-dimensional manner of viewing is resolved into a new form of harmony—we are speaking here of only the best works of recent painting—when the observer is able to perceive that this form of art is based neither on simple surface nor on the abstract space which this surface conjures up before us (in perspectivation), but rather on the moving and simultaneously transparent spherical surface.[16]

The conception of the "imaginary sphere," which is in no way merely fortuitous, is of constitutive import and value for the aperspectival world. As we shall see, it became "genuine" or "pivotal" not only in the geometry of Beltrami and Klein, and in the modified form of physics in Einstein's theory of relativity, but has also begun to alter fundamentally the basis of other areas of human expression and activity. The preconditions necessary for this are for the most part already completed, with one decisive exception. And this exception we shall have to consider as soon as we come to the second consideration which arose in our brief outline of the history of the fourth dimension—the adaptation of the concept of a fourth dimension by representatives of the most widely disparate disciplines.

One aspect remains to be clarified before we turn to this striking adaptation. Any adaptation, indeed, every realization of a fourth dimension can be a world constituent only if it is not considered as a merely incremental, but as an integrating dimension. If it is considered, in other words, merely as an incremental dimension and utilized as such, the result is merely a further expansion of "space" which can and would have a world-destructive effect. There are already initial and extremely tangible examples of the effects of an incompletely realized fourth dimension, as in the negative manifestation of atomic fission. For this reason we emphasize that the fourth dimension of the aperspectival world must serve consciousness as an integral function, as systasis; only then will it be a world–constituent. If it serves on the other hand as a merely incremental and expansive quantity it will destroy not just the mental-rational structure but also the genuine form of the incipient integral structure.

Having dealt with this basic reservation, we can now examine the various forms in which the concept of a "fourth dimension" has been adapted by representatives of the various disciplines. Here we shall not employ a chronological approach but rather a different schema of organization, that of the four structures of consciousness. Surprisingly, it will be seen that the individual representatives of the various disciplines adapt the fourth dimension in accord with the consciousness structure predominating in the particular discipline, a circumstance which could lead us to question in each given instance the integrative capacity of the concept.

There can be little doubt that the concept of the fourth dimension is the preeminent expression for heralding the new consciousness mutation. Nor should there be any doubt that this fourth dimension has in some form to do with "time," or, stated more felicitously, with the various forms of time which are effective in us according to the propensities of the respective structures. Which of these time forms, if any, is decisive? Can the underlying basis of a form of manifestation be treated or evaluated as a mere part of this form? In other words, can time or one of its forms constitute a part of three-dimensional space as the "foundation"—or more appropriately the systasis—of this space or spatial system? Can temporal or temporic phenomena—the heterogenous element of static space when judged from a mental standpoint—be incorporated into this spatial conception as a "fourth" element without bursting this space?

The concept of a fourth dimension unmistakably expresses the "new task" of overcoming the previous one-sided spatial fixity of consciousness. But such a supersession is accomplished only by integration, not by destruction. The introduction of time, the divider, as a fourth dimension destroys space *and* time, and the introduction of "temporicity" as a fourth dimension is tantamount to assigning an incongruent dimension to space inasmuch as temporicity can only function within the two-dimensional structure. And it is rationalistic nonsense to propose "timelessness" as the fourth dimension, since the timeless has its reality only in the one-dimensional structure. The obviousness of these conclusions, particularly in view of what we have noted in our discussion (Part I, chapter 5), should not blind us to the obviousness of the attempts by various disciplines to interpret the fourth dimension in magic, mythical, or mental terms.

The adaptation of the concept of the fourth dimension in certain circles to denote nothing more than manifestations of the "extrasensory" is a magic adaptation. Such manifestations are more appropriately characterized as those which such groups define as "extrasensory" and believe to be attainable via mediums. If we dismiss such pseudo-scientific trickery, it is not because we doubt the manifestations themselves; while materialists distrust them because they seem too lacking in matter, we reject them as being all-too-materialistic, indeed crypto-materialistic. The compulsion to materialize such vital and psychic splinters in various forms, to which are then ascribed "metaphysical" ("lying behind the physical") valuations—when at best these manifestations should be deemed "hypo-physical" (i.e., "lying under the physical")—merely demonstrates that all such "occultists" are in a certain sense *crypto-materialists*. The fact that this "fourth dimension" manifests itself only in the state of trance as the result of the subjects' reimmersion into the magic ego-less unconsciousness, indicates that this stimulation of a "lower" consciousness structure is irrelevant and has at best the status of a curiosity for the present-day consciousness.

The patent senselessness and worthlessness of the phenomena produced by such spiritistic and mediumistic means is clear evidence of their origin in the web of magic enmeshment, characterized by its fortuitousness and lack of directedness. There are other indications that manifestations produced in this manner from the inferior "supersensory" (which is actually "subsensory") should not be considered as manifest fourth-dimensional phenomena; these would include the evident interplay of unilaterally activated vital currents (magnetism) and the merging of the individual with the deficient, reestablished clan (as in the forming of a "unity" (!) of the participants in such "gatherings" where they sit in a circle and clasp hands). These things merely involve the reinvigoration of the forgotten power of "timelessness" which becomes deficient because the phenomena that become acute from its capabilities overpower those who have unnaturally invoked them. The procedure is unnatural because it contradicts the nature of the three-dimensional consciousness structure which is for the most part still proper to contemporary man.[17]

The fourth dimension as defined by Friedrich Zöllner in his work cited above (p. 342) is nothing more than the deficient timelessness which, when reinvigorated by mediumistic persons, is visible to rational man because the effectual modes of this state are manifest in an amply materialistic form in three-dimensional space. The purely spiritistic nature of Zöllner's attempts underscores the accuracy of our estimation. He may well serve as an example of the magic adaptation of the "fourth dimension" since he is apparently the first to apply this concept to magic phenomena, and the concept is still misused today by his numerous successors in spiritistic circles.

Jung-Stilling and Justinus Kerner, whose magical experiments preceded Zöllner's, were content to explain their results as Od-theories, life-magnetism, somnambulism, and the like.[18] Zöllner adapted a concept that was correct as such but applied it to an area inadequate to the concept. Even his clever "scientific" reference to Gauss, Riemann, and Fechner is not sufficient to disguise this. He defines the "fourth dimension" as a "complex spatial coordinate" of an imaginary character that leads to an "expanded view of space."

It is symptomatic that the misinterpretation and misdefinition of the fourth dimension immediately elicits the erroneous conclusion that it must be space-expanding. Zöllner already held to this definition in the preface to his *Prinzipien einer elektrodynamischen Theorie der Materie* (*Principles of an Electro-dynamic*

Theory of Matter, 1882). To bolster the plausibility of imaginary expressions evidenced by his definition of a fourth dimension, he claims the support of Gauss' exposition of the validity of algebraically "imaginary" quantities.[19] And finally he adduces the remarks of G. Th. Fechner, who, in his treatise *Die Tagansicht gegenüber der Nachtansicht* (*The Attitude of Day versus the Attitude of Night*, 1879), which spoke of the incontestability of Zöllner's spiritistic experiments. As a consequence of his interweaving of incongruent structures, Zöllner goes on to posit the phenomena evidenced by his spiritistic seances—the "spatial emergence" of the "extrasensory"—as the expression of the fourth dimension.[20]

It has, unfortunately, been necessary to explore this somewhat treacherous realm of the misinterpretations of fourth dimensionality since these misconstructions are still practiced today, and when employed irresponsibly, can lead to irresponsible conclusions and false teachings. The element of irresponsibility is inherent in these actions and interpretations because they are the result of practices in which the participants, particularly the medium, are in a condition where the responsible ego-consciousness is not only muted but essentially suppressed.[21]

The interpretation and adaptation, on the other hand, which is bestowed on the fourth dimension by modern mystics is mythical and as such is equally inadequate. Here we encounter the greatest possible variety: adherents of certain idealistic philosophies, psychophysicists, neo-mystics, and the majority of traditionalists. These representatives of a deficient mythical interpretation can all be considered as "psychists," a concept we have defined in Part I of this work (see p. 26). Their exclusive attachment to a mostly unconscious disporting in the psychic realm gives all of their statements a certain ill-defined and uncompelling quality which is inherent in the mythical structure. (Psychists are to the mythical realm what the spiritists are to the magic. The concept of "spiritism" derives, in fact, from "spirits" and has as little to do with "spirit"—not to mention the spiritual—as the mutilating psychism has ultimately to do with the "soul.")

It was Ernst Mach, as we have seen (p. 342 f.) who first applied the concept of the fourth dimension toward an explanation of certain processes of the psyche. Despite the integrity of his work and research, he represents the initial example of a psychistic interpretation of the fourth dimension. His epistemological reflections can still be discerned in Einstein's theory of relativity. Yet alongside his philosophical investigations, where he vigorously maintained a positivistic-phenomenological viewpoint, he was involved in acoustics, a purely magic realm. In particular, he propounded the view that knowledge was simply based on experience. In this he became a conqueror of mechanistic materialism and allowed, perhaps unconsciously, the primacy to pass from materialism to the energistic (and psychic) principle which dwells in both experience and work (to which he had devoted one of his first publications).

The norm of his conception is furnished by the autonomy of all energistic events whose fundamental pattern is given in psychic "temporicity." Strictly speaking, such energistics—conceived now as "experience," now as "work"—are his fourth dimension. It is that mythical cycle of occurrences which circles from pole to pole, from negative to positive and back again, that provides psychic and physical phenomena with their rhythmic regularity. Mach's emphasis on the value of work de-emphasizes the static, spatially-fixed concept of property. Since work is a movable asset while possessions are immobile assets, Mach transcends in his psychistic way the exclusive valuation placed on fixed, static three-dimensional spatiality. But these energistics of temporicity, which form in fact the basis of two-dimensionality, cannot be the fourth dimension; they are rather merely the reinvigorated potencies of the mythical structure.

It is of particular interest here that the conception of and emphasis on work was already instituted by Hegel in his *Phenomenology of the Spirit* (1807), since it links the fourth-dimensional concept with the evident emergence of a new mutation during the French Revolution. It was the "Awakening of the Left" which was responsible for instituting a dynamic and energetic concept of work and displacing the spatial-physical or bodily conception of possessions. This shift of emphasis of the sociological foundations reflects the "irruption" of time, whereas in Mach's interpretation it is evident that time is misconstrued to be a limited, psycho-physical form of time.

With the neo-mystics we are faced with a different situation. The flight from space that dominates their attitude causes them to seek and find a spaceless realm which is none the less not necessarily inanimate. In this they approach by retrogression the mythical consciousness structure whose character, as we have indicated, is spacelessness: the superficiality (i.e., surface-ness) sustained by the circle-closing polarity. The equally characteristic and extensive identification of soul and life in the mythological sphere all too easily misleads the mystics into the feeling that this life of correspondence to the stars and the tides, into whose flux they immerse themselves, is universal life in a corresponding universal soul. Their rejection of the mental, three-dimensional outer world for a two-dimensional one of contemplation and inner vision is a further temptation to view such "subscendence" of the three-dimensional as in fact a "transcendence." And whenever they describe the forgotten yet rediscovered and reinvigorated state of peaceful, submissive suspension in mental terms as a dimensional increment rather than a loss, they fancy this unrealized retrogression into the mythical structure to be the fourth dimension.

A prime representative of this attitude and misinterpretation of the fourth dimension is the highly respected Maurice Maeterlinck. His book *The Fourth Dimension*, which begins with a short critique of the main attempts by mathematics and physics to reach a solution, is devoted to an exhaustive consideration of attempts made by men outside the scientific sphere. As the fourth dimension Maeterlinck proposes eternity: "perpetual and all-encompassing simultaneity," and "infinity." Ultimately it is the great "unknown," "God."[22]

Maeterlinck also takes into account the ether, to the extent that this too is an unknown,[23] and thus comes close to conceptions held by certain traditionalists, such as Raoul Auclair mentioned earlier.[24] For Auclair ether is the basic substance of all matter, the original element of creation to which, as a "fourth element"—and simultaneously as a "first"—all manifestations return. For him time is the fourth *terminus* but not the fourth dimension of three-dimensional space. The cyclic interpretation employed here demonstrates the degree to which he is committed to "temporicity," to the point of ultimately confusing it with the fourth dimension.[25]

A particularly strange and somewhat perilous interpretation of the fourth dimension can be found in the writings of the pseudo-esoteric P. D. Ouspensky. His interpretation goes so far as to accommodate the temporal dimension to the three spatial dimensions by a form of trisection, in such a way as to create a six-dimensional construct wherein the three temporal divisions are then past, present, and future.[26] This quantification, subdivision, and blatant spatialization of "time"—already envisaged by Hegel[27]—is surely the most bizarre possible form of mythical-mental deficiency. It is further confused by its emphasis on "ecstacy," and the author's devotion to the magical attitude of his shaman-like teacher George Gurdjieff, "master" of the "School of Fontainebleau." Its Eastern lack of conformity to Western modes of thought endows it with a certain shimmering and psychic multifacetedness that is not without its attractions for disoriented "truthseekers."[28]

The conception of a fourth dimension which proceeds from Riemann's geometry on the other hand, which Einstein introduced in a generalized form into physics, is a mental conception. There it is defined as "time" and employed as a "continuum" for calculation as a fourth dimension of space, of "curved space." Since the mathematical formulation and unification of the heterogenous elements of time and space were successful only at the expense of time, time was subjected to a further spatialization (geometrization) for physical research.

The successful incorporation of time as a fourth dimension into three-dimensional space realized the union of space and time, or "space-time unity" which led to practical results, notably in nuclear physics. It is perhaps symptomatic that this inclusion of a dividing principle, one which is dynamic and energetic, transformed space into a "continuum." But there is yet a further symptom which underscores our definition of "time" as the pre-eminent divider in which destruction and sundering are inherent: the structuration of the atom, or rather its destruction by nuclear fission and the destruction of the spatial cohesion of matter that were made possible by Einstein's formulas. It is consistent and obvious that by establishing mental "time"—itself divisive and disjunctive—as the fourth component of a fourth-dimensional continuum the result would be the invention of the atom bomb and similar weapons of destruction. This "continuum" has here a strictly negative effect which leads to a no longer controllable dissolution.

Our mode of observation will undoubtedly cause annoyance and irritation in some quarters, and the tendency will be to deny its relevance to the "subject under consideration." We will deal with the irrelevance of such an objection shortly. But first we should like to make a further observation about the rationalistic conception of the fourth-dimensional continuum in order to underscore its complexity. The French scholar Paul Langevin has written the most fitting statement of this: "Physics had as its indispensable arena Euclidian space in which absolute time prevailed. The new conception [of relativity] is vastly different, a fusion of geometry and physics which renders the existence of absolute time and absolute space impossible."[29]

This summary remark as to the difference between the Euclidian and the non-Euclidian conception is intriguing for two reasons. First, it demonstrates that a rational description can be adequate for the most part; and second, it refers us to the magic component inherent in the concept of relativity. We have referred to this previously in our discussion of Einstein's space-time *unity*, as well as to its modification by the mythical complementarity principle (p. 209). Langevin's eminently rational formulation clearly shows that the concept of a four-dimensional space does not exclude a dualistic interpretation which must inevitably choose between only two alternatives whenever it is unable to achieve a synthesis.

The alternatives here are the concept of an unconditional absolute and the concept of the conditional relative. The unity postulate which has by nature a magic accentuation is coupled with the postulate of the relativity of events. The conception of a four-dimensional curved space, therefore, is not one of integrality and integration but one which effects a unity and a relativization. This relativization is the second magic component, for the decisive role is played by the *interrelationships* of individual spatial and temporal points (or space-time quantities) which, to the extent that they are measurable, represent a rational form of a magic point-like relationship.

This inquiry into the rationalistic concept of a fourth dimension, which uses the criterion of the consciousness structure on which the concept is based, permits the following conclusions. The introduction of the mental time-mode which partitions and measures "time" into the geometric-physical image of world as a fourth dimension has been successful. The previous three-dimensional space, that is, the hitherto valid mental conception of the world, has been superseded, and this supersession presents itself as an expansion of that conception of world since it has been achieved by the spatialization of "time." Thus it is only an apparent supersession, or more appropriately, an initial step toward a genuine supersession which would have to accommodate two heretofore unattainable demands: 1) that "four dimensionality" should have reality not only in the special fields of geometry and physics, but should be efficacious and concrete in all aspects and areas of life and thought; and 2) that for its integral effectuality the merely partitioning element "time" must be intensified by an all-encompassing temporal conception, even where "time" is manipulated as a relative and not an absolute "quantity" or dimension.

The introduction of mere "time" into the traditional concept of space will bring about only a partial supersession. And yet a supersession tantamount to a liberation must be achieved—not merely a spatial expansion which leads to spatial destruction. Three-dimensional space cannot be destroyed by a four-dimensional continuum any more than two-dimensional surface can be destroyed by three-dimensional space. The liberation from the world of one less dimension in any given instance is principally a liberation from the exclusive validity of the lesser-dimensioned structures. Viewed in these terms, the adaptation by rational science of the concept of a "fourth dimension" that employs a time concept which is no longer absolute but relative is an initial point of departure toward a fourth-dimensional consciousness of integrality and aperspectivity.

It remains for us to consider what form this intensified modality of "time" will necessarily take to guarantee the consolidation of this consciousness and to prevent it from running aground in a merely dynamicized and expanded spatial concept. Before we do so we would only point out that our interpretation of the physical-geometrical conception of Einstein's fourth dimension contains definite indications of a more general validity. It is distinguished by a lack of visuality (which is not to be confused with abstractness); it cannot be realized via mere mental conceptualization; and it therefore contains the seeds of a hitherto unknown mode of realization unconnected with the restrictions of three-dimensional conceptualization.

We have circumscribed this new mode of realization with the term "verition" or "a-waring." The removal of space and time from the mental conception of absoluteness affords the possibility of concretizing those now relativized quantities, particularly the quantity "time." We must be aware at the outset of the magic restriction of this relativization and consider that any necessary integration must be preceded by concretion. This concretion can never be fulfilled with respect to the absolute, but, in mental terms, only with respect to the relative. The concept of the "four-dimensional continuum" as "curved space" thus holds the incipient possibility of realizing the *integrum*, the "four-dimensional" transparent "sphere" in motion.

Because of the importance of these matters we do not hesitate to summarize in slightly different terms what we have just discussed. Einstein's theory of relativity constructed a unity of space and time that can be formulated, at least in mathematical terms. But it had to be conceived of in terms of constant decay and simultaneous renewal, paving the way for a process of expansion, as we might say, in consequence of the dividing capacity of the heterogenous quantity of "time." This process of expansion is a frenzied rush, pushing ever outward the boundaries of the microcosm as well as of the macrocosm, dissolving—indeed destroying—and exploding rather than overcoming the spatial structure.

The spectre of mere expansions and overstepped boundaries inflates our spatial world not only in a physical but also in a psychological sense; we are constantly hearing of the "expansion of consciousness." Even the conception of the expansion of the universe at this very moment, the notion that the universe is part of a process of expansion, can be traced to the same roots as the other examples cited.[30] The deceptive shrinkage of time and the equally deceptive "conquest" of space, exemplified by our transformed means of rapid transportation, are the negative caricatures of a misunderstood and misapplied "value." That value is, of course, rational time, ever divisive and destructive like Dais, the demonic (=divisive) principle (p. 174 ff.), a principle which because of its deficient-mental and unrecognized magic treatment has most likely increased today in virulence.

On the other hand we should not fail to observe that in this conception of a four-dimensional continuum the three structural and consciousness-forming components of the magic, mythical, and mental structures are present, even though in deficient form. The magic component is recognizable in the postulates of space-time unity and relativity. The mythical component is visible in the correlated complementarity principle which equates mass and energy, particle and wave as (polar) phenomena. The mental component is expressed by the spatialization of time and its fixed geometrical form as the fourth dimension.

Only the space-free, time-free component is lacking; and it will remain so until the error is perceived of mistakenly treating the fourth dimension as measurable rather than integrative and transparent time. A relation of space and time to and *inter* one another as provided by the theory of relativity is one where time curves space and space measures time. This makes of time a measuring-measured comparative component (as in Einstein's space-time model of the scale) that must be superseded. True time does not curve space; it is open and opens space through its capacity of rendering it transparent, and thereby supersedes nihilistic "emptiness," re-attaining openness in an intensified consciousness structure spoken of in Part I of our inquiry (p. 253).

Here it is appropriate to consider the possible objection which might be made to our mode of inquiry noted earlier (p. 351). If we are to counter this objection we must emphasize above all that our discussion was not intent on criticizing Einstein's theory of relativity, but rather on making its place visible within the sphere of vital-psychic-mental phenomena. Our categories and criteria are not those determined by humanistic or scientific methods but those of the mutationally-determined consciousness structures themselves. We are not presenting here specialized scientific contributions which examine phenomena from a partial sector in a sectarian or dissecting manner; we are attempting to encompass the phenomena as a whole from the inherent, living structural "laws" in their manifestations.

When we interpret the irrational number ($t=\sqrt{-1}$), for example, with emphasis on the "irrational"—on the mythical-magic aspect rather than the concept of number—as an approximation of a mathematically interpreted and applicable value, our "standpoint" is decisive: we are approaching the rational number from a consciousness structure, not from a specialized science. Herein lies the full relevance of our mode of observation.

The value of this mode of inquiry does not diminish the claim of mathematics, say, of being the exact and fundamental science among the sciences. We are not usurping the concepts it has formulated but are interpreting them with respect to their general validity. Since we do not apply them sectorally, the claim of mathematics is valid and relevant only to the extent that we acknowledge the basic significance and efficacy of the magic structure (to which mathematics, this fundamental branch of science, must be assigned) for the various other consciousness structures.

For it does not matter whether we are speaking of mathematics or of the magic structure—and we must remember that pure mathematics is pre-eminently a product of this consciousness structure—since the procedure of equating is fundamental to both. It is only the mental-rational procedure in mathematics that hypostasizes the point-like postulates, which constitute the system of relationships in the magic structure into absolutes, that deludes most mathematicians about the actual and workable roots of their discipline. Moreover it is this procedure which raises the "queen of the sciences" to the level of an absolute, a process of absolutizing which befell other "queens."

Incidentally, the well-known penchant of many mathematicians for music is a further indication of the magic coloration of this science. And the abundantly documented impatience that distinguishes many mathematicians (if this can be considered a distinction), otherwise common only among musicians, is symptomatic of the place of origin of their metier. Only magic knows fanaticism; it has its parallel in perspectival point-fixation which is, for the most part, not mental but deficiently magic as we have suggested earlier (See p. 153 f. and 262 above).

This digression was necessary because only a very few scholars and researchers are willing to admit the validity of a mode of observation that does not proceed from a sectorally restricted field of specialization. Yet it must also be observed that many people are beginning here and there to realize that such fragmentary examination of living and spiritual phenomena threatens to fragment the world itself, an end surely no one desires. Moreover, we are in no way condemning specialized science as such whose enormous results and achievements of knowledge are beyond cavil.

We would, however, object that it is no longer possible today for an individual to draw the sum of the specialized scientific endeavors and results in such a way as to be able to approach a relation to a realizable whole of things. Yet it is precisely this whole on which everything depends for us. We must not lose sight of the fact that the consciousness structures which constitute us are, in mental terms, an expression of integral wholeness. Accordingly, a mode of observation such as ours that proceeds from the presence of the consciousness structures that form a whole will, in fact, approach the integral comprehension of partial phenomena.

Summarizing, then, the results of our inquiry into the adaptations by the various disciplines of a concept of the fourth dimension, we might say that the attempt of the spiritists is inadequate since their adaptation results merely in a reinvigorated timelessness. The attempt of the psychists is equally inadequate for its is a reinvigoration of temporicity. The adaptation of the rationalists, on the other hand, is nearly adequate even though the fourth dimension is for them still conceptualized chronological "time" in an admittedly de-absolutized, relativized form.

Our examination has been restricted to a few representative examples of each adaptation; we will have occasion to refer to others in the further course of our exposition. Let us here note as a final result of our inquiry that none of the previous definitions or adaptations of the fourth dimension is sufficient to enable the mutation from which this concept has germinated to achieve the full realization of its efficacy. Until now the attempts with the fourth dimension have all been inadequate and are comparable to those made with the third dimension during the one–hundred–fifty years between Petrarch and Leonardo da Vinci. The inadequacy of these latter attempts is evident in their false, that is, reversed, inverted, and foreshortened perspectivation, and is equally recognizable in the cave frescos of Ajanta (India) from the fifth century A.D., which, interestingly, were not brought to full perspective but left in a form merely suggestive of perspective.[31]

Of what form, then, is the fourth dimension to be? This is the last question which remains to be answered. What form is it to take if it has to do with time but cannot be one of the previous "forms" of time: neither timelessness, nor temporicity, nor time itself? And what shall its form be if it is to be integrative? As an integrative form it would supersede space and time, since space is based on time just as surface is based on temporicity and the spaceless point on timelessness. The fourth dimension, therefore, must be free from these forms of time; freedom from space presupposes freedom from time. It is this *freedom from time that is the fourth dimension*. It is this freedom from time which must be realized.

Without freedom from time an effectual supersession of the spatial confinement of three-dimensionality is not possible. And we reiterate: the realization of this time-freedom must occur by the concretion, not merely by the relativization of time. Time must first become concrete and conscious in all its forms; something can be superseded and integrated only when concretized. The attempt at the concretion of time which leads to time-freedom is *temporics*. In the following chapters we shall examine these fourth-dimensional attempts and initial manifestations which are appearing in all areas of human inquiry. And while observing these aperspectival, four-dimensional manifestations, we will unavoidably have to recall their "location" and their "movement," their "where" and "how." We must not, in other words, lose sight of the capacity of man to be the agent of the mutational event. As we have seen, this capacity is creativity—the remarkable endowment of man with which he can manifest the consciousness-integrating and consciousness-constituting processes. We must, to use a metaphorical expression, become acquainted with the well-springs from which we draw our sustenance.

We have observed that one expression of the new consciousness is inseparable from the sudden four-fold and simultaneous discovery of non-Euclidian geometries inasmuch as it not only anticipates but also makes possible the concept of a fourth dimension. In turn, we have examined the various adaptations of this concept, and it was evident that none of them was an adequate and full guarantee for the effectuation of the new mutation. We have also seen that this new dimension must be time-freedom, and in view of the importance of this concept, we wish in conclusion to venture a definition of the nature of time-freedom or *achronicity*. However, since mere definition—in this case the conceptual delimitation of a term whose "basic characteristic" is freedom from temporal and spatial boundaries, that is, "open,"—would be incongruent, we shall be content to approach the essence of this "term" by posing and answering three questions. These three questions are: What is time-freedom? To what extent can it be realized? And in what sense is it the fourth dimension?

To these questions we give the following three answers:

1) Time-freedom is the conscious form of archaic, original pre-temporality.

2) Time-freedom can be realized by achieving each of the previous time-mutations from archaic pre-temporality. By granting to magic timelessness, mythical temporicity, and mental-conceptual temporality their integral efficacy, and by living them in accord with the strength of their degree of consciousness, we are able to bring about this realization. This concretion of the previous three exfoliations of original pre-temporality instantaneously opens for us pre-conscious timelessness.

As such, time-freedom is not only the quintessence of time, as we have stated earlier (p. 26), but also the conscious quintessence of all previous temporal forms. Their becoming conscious—in itself a process of concretion—is also a liberation from all of these time forms; everything becomes present, concrete, and thus integrable present. But this implies that preconscious origin becomes conscious present; that each and every time-form basic to the one-, two-, and three-dimensional world is integrated and thereby superseded.

This also means that we perceive the world in its foundations and are not exclusively bound to its vital, experiential, and conceptual forms. To adduce just one example: we no longer observe the world only from a fixed perspective, but perceive it as aperspectival and unfixed. Anyone conscious of the foundations cannot be perplexed or bewildered by the variety, transitoriness, or fixity inherent in the respective forms. *Anyone able to realize and thus concretize the three previously basic temporal forms already consciously stands in four-dimensionality.*

3) Time-freedom is the fourth dimension because it constitutes and unlocks the four-dimensionality outlined above. In—or rather through—time-freedom the foundations or bases become transparent right down to the original and pre-conscious pre-temporality. Time-freedom, its conscious form, is the fourth dimension; it is an *integrative dimension*, or, more exactly, it is the *amension* and not just an expanding or destructive spatial dimension. It is an acategorical element of systatic perception which makes possible the completion of synairesis, and thus it is the sustaining, indeed "a-waring" and transparent, spatially incomprehensible *amension*.

3. *Temporics*

Temporics is the concern with "time." Today this concern is omnipresent, indeed it forms the basic concern of our epoch. Everywhere we find attempts to introduce time into our understanding of the world now that it has been unilaterally spatialized and thus denatured or else completely disregarded. Such temporic attempts are an initial step toward a new, aperspectival world perception; they are an effort to extricate ourselves from "mentality" (from the exclusive validity of quantitative thought which has become deficient in rationality) and a running start toward achieving diaphaneity. Wherever this running start is successful, and man is able to escape from the compulsion of three-dimensional systematization, he supersedes the mental-rational structure and mere conceptual time, and transforms the mental-rational from a principal component into one which, along with the magic and the mythical, is integrated into diaphaneity.

It is possible to aid this process by the concept of acategorical elements which, as systases, surpass the mere concept of "time"; this renders perceptible all the aspects that are merely suggested and scarcely recognized in the mentally reduced concept of "time." It would show that time is an "ever-present abundance" or plenitude, spiritual and not psychic in nature. Where such temporic attempts fail, however, the conscious activation of "time" brings about a disruption in accord with its fragmenting nature. The result is then a negative supersession and thus a "subsession" of the mental consciousness structure.

Our temporic epoch is one of transition and reshaping. It is our task to extricate time from its rational distortion. Stated in this way, the problem may sound quite simple, yet the task is one of almost inconceivable difficulty. The solution to this problem has been "unconsciously" sought for generations, and during the last two generations the effort has taken on increasingly conscious forms. The necessity of solving this problem arises from the fact that since the French Revolution—indeed, since the Enlightenment—religious ties in the West have been severed. The pervasive modern problem facing us had been consigned by religion to the irrational sphere, thus removing it from the sphere of mental consciousness. Creative omnipotence, eternity, and infinity were unquestioned postulates of faith; and the security of the citizen in his human, social sphere relieved him of the need to seek new assurance.

It was only when this secure world collapsed in the wake of the revolution that the problems emerged, particularly when the inundation by the "left"—the "unconscious" collective powers which had been held back for thousands of years—not only threatened the demise of the mental structure but in fact accelerated this demise to such an extent that the collapse of rationality is today undeniable. And it is important that we have the courage to describe this demise, not as a demise, but for what it really is: the suicide of Western civilization.[32]

From a sociological standpoint, it began with the year 1789, although its preparation dates back to the Renaissance. From a religious point of view, it originated with the Enlightenment and became effective with the pronouncement of God's death, which means a destruction of man's innermost essence. From the standpoint of political power, this suicide began with World War I and was completed by the existential proclamation of man's death.[33] This was itself only the consequence of the destruction of man's inner being by the self-destruction of the divine in man, and by his rational denial of all the irrational and pre-rational aspects, by which he dispossessed himself of his own foundations.

With this, Europe's predominance has come to an end, completing at least in the area of power politics its abdication. Spiritually, the suicide which has been carried out—primarily the suicide of European Rationalism—opens the way for achieving a new point of departure. While one segment of the Europeans is preoccupied with self-surrender, i.e., self-negation, the other assumes the new task that lies beyond the reach of such negation. The ego has become insignificant; unable to offer the world any stability, it falls victim to the collective. The superiority previously held by the "ego" turns into impotence and leads to suicide, even if this suicide is manifest only in the ego's submersion into the mass; and the masses are merely an expression of an amorphous ego-lessness which arises from the loss of roots in the former "we" of clan or the community of believers.

We have discussed earlier the problems of the ego, the masses, isolation, and collectivism (p. 22 and 153 f.). These uncertainties are the present situation; and there is only one liberation possible from this cul-de-sac: it is not the re-submersion of the ego into the anonymity of the masses, but the supersession of the ego and the masses by achieving the supra-individual anonymity of the "Itself."[34]

To achieve this is to achieve ego-freedom and the actualization of a more intensive consciousness; at the same time it would uphold a detachment from one's own ego as well as the recognition of the temporal conditionality of all that is connected with the ego such as desires, feelings, and manifestations of will. The apparent alternative of our times with their schizoid character, either the individual or the mass-man, is a pseudo-alternative, valid only for rationalists and existentialists. Irrespective of one's choice, it leads to suicide: either to isolation or collectivization, either to exclusion of the world or to total absorption by the masses. Only the liberation from this alternative and its temporality is a guarantee of survival; and this cannot be achieved without the mutation into time-freedom.

The reader will have already noticed that the basic theme of the new mutation has been described in a variety of terms. This may give rise to a terminological confusion as a result of our habitual ways of thinking. We have described this basic theme as the "irruption of time," whereby time was understood as an "intensity and quality" and included all previous time forms: magic timelessness, mythical temporicity, and mental conceptual time. The theme was also defined as the "awakening or emergence of consciousness" of the "primordial energy" which it reflects and recapitulates. And finally it was identified as "time-freedom" and "open time."

In a purely rational sense, these concepts are in part mutually exclusive; this is the reason for the apparent confusion of expression. The insecurity evident today has led, particularly in the sciences, to a kind of hypersensitivity; never before has there been so much ado about the "methodological" and "terminological" exactness as in recent years. It is an alarming indication that more and more phenomena which are surfacing today for the first time are threatening to slip through the grasp of an inquiry devoted only to methodology and terminology. The dimension pressing toward mutation cannot be grasped conceptually, that is, three-dimensionally; it can be approached by thought, but never grasped or haptified.

For the rationalist this is a distressing situation; accordingly, because of his one-sided attitude, the situation is a sufficient reason to regard the phenomena being described as nonexistent. Yet anyone willing and able to make the leap from the crumbling spatial world will realize that all the "determinations" we have made are congruent. Perceived arationally rather than represented rationally (i.e., in dualistic terms), all of the expressions used here to describe the theme of the new mutation are an indication of the manifestational forms of pre-timelessness or the original energy that is appearing in our consciousness today as time-freedom.

The new world reality, which is at the same time also a world unreality, is to a great extent free of causality. Its reality is encompassed by the whole. In rational terms, it appears now as the cause, now as the effect. Although this hampers our understanding, it proportionally increases "verition." The separation of entities from becoming is a conceptual systematization; in the universe and on the earth the originary manifests itself as a transient effect, but also as an effectuator, albeit only in the universe and in man to the extent that he is bound by space-time.

It cannot be too strongly emphasized that the unique *plenitude and transparency (diaphaneity)* visible in the new mutation touches all phenomena and makes them perceptible. The confusion that could be elicited by the wealth and intensity of the terms we have used to describe the theme of the mutation is all the more comprehensible since it is not restricted to what is conceivable to the mental consciousness. We must not forget that in our era, which is now coming to a close, we are accustomed to considering the validity and necessity of everything from a mental standpoint. But the mental is not even adequate to "comprehend" the mythical, not to mention the magic.

We have conceded the status of reality to only an extremely limited world, one which is barely one-third of what constitutes us and the world as a whole. The new integral structure, on the other hand, requires us to recognize all "preceding" structures and the irrevocable efficient actualities which they integrate and make perceptible. This plenitude, which cannot be grasped systematically, is likely to elicit displeasure and annoyance. Displeasure already borders on anxiety: the systems are threatening to fall apart; it becomes apparent that they can encompass only a segment of reality as a result of their mental limitations. They can only encompass the palpable, spatially delimited part, whereas systases open up all of the structures.

For this reason systatic attempts are today indispensable, for without them even the systems would fall apart. Temporics is an expression of these systatic endeavors to bring to consciousness the abundance and freedom concealed "behind" the concept of time as they relate to all structures and all areas of our entire reality.

The most conspicuous temporic manifestation is without a doubt the *time-anxiety of our epoch*. It is the obvious indication that the time problem is demanding of us its resolution. It is always revealing to note the source of a person's or an epoch's anxiety; the object of anxiety is invariably the task or obligation placed on our consciousness. Paul Valéry stood the test of this time-anxiety at the moment when he was able to free himself from the overpowering effect of memory, from the nymphs (see p. 325 f.).

Every form of anxiety directed at an object is primarily a psychic problem. We spoke earlier of anxiety as such (see p. 133); here we must discuss further object-related anxiety, in this instance, time-related anxiety.

Whatever evokes anxiety in us does so because it overwhelms us. Anxiety may be evoked by new and unknown situations which we are not equal to, or by phenomena we are facing for the first time which suddenly come to the fore. The time-anxiety of our transitional era is evidence of the fact that we have been overwhelmed by the time problem and are not able to confront it, and that we have not realized it or become conscious of it. And until we recognize it, this new content of our awareness will continue to vex us and cause our anxiety.

There are various ways to react to a situation of anxiety. If we remain in a state of impotence brought on by the overpowering of the object or phenomenon causing our anxiety, we fall into resignation and surrender of self. This form of self-abnegation is quite frequent today. Another reaction to the overwhelming situation is to respond with a display of one's own might, that is, an attempt to gain power over the phenomenon which causes our anxiety. This is a magic response carried out with the aid of abstraction; the object of anxiety is seemingly divested of its power by being separated and isolated, and in a sense, placed out of the way into the vacuum of a bell jar.

Of course this is not a genuine solution, but merely the postponement of the problem—a rationalistic trick. Although isolated, the problem remains unsolved and virulent. This kind of response with respect to time has been in vogue ever since time became an abstract quantity, a mere rational concept of measurement. The person tortured and overwhelmed by anxiety uses abstraction to deal with an object or a phenomenon causing the anxiety in order to distance himself as far as possible from it. "Abstraction, as such, is a magic procedure, a way of ruling the world."[35] This statement by the Indologist Herbert Günther, which coincides with our own exposition of magic and its relationship to rationality, is further elaborated by a quotation which Günther takes from C. G. Jung: "The person who abstracts finds himself in a terrifyingly animated world which seeks to overpower and crush him. . . ."[36]

Thus abstraction too is just a form of capitulation and only seeming mastery of the problem. Above all the solution does not depend on control but on supersession. To achieve this, or, with specific reference to our problem, to surpass the anxiety of time—which is tantamount to a temporic attempt—we must realize that time-anxiety too is a projection. Ever since the Renaissance "time" has been pressing toward consciousness, toward time-freedom. It gradually emerges into the foreground as a central problem, although—as is always the case—man failed to notice the full extent of the "complex" which was pressing toward consciousness. Once he takes notice of it, the demand and task of the awakening of consciousness is achieved.

The plenitude of the constellation in us in each instance of consciousness emergence is the newness pressing toward awareness. The stronger and more protracted this process is, the greater are the overwhelming energies in us which become manifest when we extend them outward. In other words, the overwhelming power of "time" in us, our full preparatory predisposition toward time-freedom, is projected into the phenomenon which in our representational world corresponds to the inner complex. The energy of time-freedom flares up into consciousness as an overwhelming power of time. Consequently, as long as the awakening of consciousness is not achieved, the result is time-anxiety as well as time-abstraction. Both are transitory intermediate stages taking place within the intensification of consciousness and the confusing temporic manifestations of the new mutation.

In Part I (see p. 99 f.) we have already discussed the necessity for the concretion of time. This concretion can only be achieved if we retract our projection of time. Time-anxiety, in other words, turns into time-supersession and time-abstraction into time-concretion whenever we consciously realize the forces surging toward awareness and achieve time-freedom by our awareness of the differing forms of time. Therein lies to a great extent the "new task."

The endeavors devoted to this task are what we define as temporics. It is everywhere in evidence, particularly since Einstein's formulation of the theory of relativity. Temporic endeavors play a role in the most diverse forms in the most diverse areas in the most varied guises. Yet if we carefully observe them, remaining mindful of those things which derive from the individual consciousness structures that constitute us, it will be only too obvious that the new mutation is becoming manifest everywhere.

The striving toward integrality, indeed, toward the whole; the striving toward transparency, toward the supersession of systematics by the conscious perception-in-truth of the source and form of intensive, energic, motoric, dynamic, vital, psychic, and similar elements: all of these numerous strivings are indicators of the new mutation. The results they have effected are the initial manifestations of the aperspectival world.

What we have here called "temporics" reveals the basic concern of our transitional period: a coming-to-grips with all of the temporal forms so far achieved by consciousness. There is not a single area of contemporary life where this coming-to-terms is not occurring. The entire process is so complex that our time-anxiety is only too understandable. The intensity of consciousness is not yet adequate to the entire mutational process; yet the increasing demand also increases the intensity of consciousness.

It may seem presumptuous for an individual to dare to assume the task of revealing this mutation to perception "against" time (and thus against his own time), although protected by time-freedom (because he is not thinking personally or egocentrically, but in terms of the supra-personal innate in everyone, and in terms of the Itself, not of the self). The difficulties lie not only in coping with the language used to express this mutation,[37] although this is an extremely difficult and demanding task in itself; there is also the hardly surveyable abundance of the new manifestations to be dealt with, an almost impossible task for one individual in the face of the fragmentation of the contemporary sciences.

The requisite discipline and the necessary differentiations and nuancing, the struggle with a language inadequate for the new statement—such factors as these tend to discourage the individual when faced with such an undertaking. Since what is being presented, lived, experienced, and thought through on these pages is not a construction but a verition of all genuine modes of experience, this undertaking should and must be ventured. Anyone who strives to avoid the blandishments of the magic capacity for unification, endeavors to escape the delusions of the psychic sphere, and has recognized the dubious security provided by the rational systems, yet remains cognizant of the aid offered by all these areas, may be entitled to take the further decisive step. And someone who knows and accept the conditions, boundaries, and limits appropriate to the various consciousness structures may inquire as to liberation. After all, the anxiety of mankind is growing, and many are using this anxiety as a means toward dubious ends. The growth is a sign that the anxiety is hastening toward its culmination where it collapses, either initiating suicide or a liberation.

It is the task of this work to serve toward this liberation which can be completed only via the awakening consciousness of the spiritual. And, we might add, it is not a question of "being right," but of being true. This is a greater demand than the mentally-conditioned desire to be right which is, moreover, patriarchal and egocentric.

Before we begin the exposition of the manifestations of the new consciousness in the following chapters, we should note those characteristics that can be considered expressions of the new consciousness, since, as we have seen, they do not have a decisive role in any of the previous consciousness structures. It will be permissible for us to speak of the manifestations of the aperspectival world whenever we meet up with themes or motifs which can be described more or less in the following key terms:

the whole,
integrity,
transparency (diaphaneity),
the spiritual (the *diaphainon*),
the supersession of the ego,

the realization of timelessness,
the realization of temporicity,
the realization of the concept of time,
the realization of time-freedom (the achronon),
the disruption of the merely systematic,
the incursion of dynamics,
the recognition of energy,
the mastery of movement,
the fourth dimension,
the supersession of patriarchy,
the renunciation of dominance and power,
the acquisition of intensity,
clarity (instead of mere wakefulness),
and the transformation of the creative inceptual basis.

These key terms presuppose the overcoming, or at least an attempt at overcoming, certain "isms." Inceptions toward the supersession of the following "isms" are invariably the first manifestations of the aperspectival world: perspectivism; dualism; materialism; dialectics; positivism; nihilism; existentialism; pragmatism; psychism; vitalism; mechanism; rationalism; and spiritism, to name only a few. This of course assumes that the arational is not being mistaken for the irrational or possibly even for the pre-rational, and we would therefore make particular reference to our remarks in this regard in Part I (p. 147).

From the superabundant materials at our disposal assembled in the course of several decades we shall attempt to infer the indications and the evidence that are the most significant. It is difficult to make the selection, and our neglect of parallel aspects is necessary if we are to avoid turning the discussion into an encyclopedia or a catalogue.

Herewith we have laid the foundations for an understanding of the aperspectival phenomena; systasis and synairesis complete, pervade, and bring together what is not three-dimensionally comprehensible. Temporics as a systatic concept renders perceptible the contents and intensities which are here at stake. With this we can now turn to the manifestations of the aperspectival world.

1 Jean Gebser, *Abendländische Wandlung* (Zürich: Oprecht), 1943, p. 64 f.; ²1945, p. 67; ³1950, p. 58; Ulstein-Buch No. 107, p. 50; *Gesamtausgabe*, I, pp. 209–210. In his last published article, Einstein made a statement virtually identical in import to that of de Broglie: "Discovery is not a product of logical thought even though the end result in bound to a logical form" (Das Erfinden ist kein Produkt des logischen Denkens, wenn auch das Endprodukt an die logische Gestalt gebunden ist); see Jean Gebser, "Kulturphilosophie als Methode und Wagnis," *Zeitwende: Die neue Furche*, 27, 12 (December, 1956), p. 820; *Gesamtausgabe*, V/I, p. 129.
2 Hermann Volk, *Das neue Marien-Dogma* (Münster: Regensburg, 1951), p. 7 ff.
3 Nicolai Hartmann, *Philosophie der Natur* (Berlin: de Gruyter, 1950), p. 219.

4   Friedrich Zöllner, *Naturwissenschaft und christliche Offenbarung: populäre Beiträge zur Theorie und Geschichte der vierten Dimension* (Gera: Griesbach, 1886), p. 117.

5   Ernst Mach, *Die Geschichte und Wurzel des Satzes von der Erhaltung der Arbeit* (Prague: Calve, 1872).

6   Zöllner (note 4), p. 117.

7   Maurice Maeterlinck, *Die vierte Dimension* (Stuttgart: Deutsche Verlags-Anstalt, 1928).

8   Raoul Auclair, *Le Livre des Cycles* (Paris: Editions des Portes de France, 1947).

9   Raymond Abellio, *Vers un nouveau Prophétisme* (Brussels and Paris: A l'Enseigne du Cheval Ailé, Diffusion du Livre, 1947).

10   Egmont Colerus, *Vom Punkt zur vierten Dimension* (Vienna: Bischoff, 1943), p. 417 ff. In this book, as well as in his *Von Pythagoras bis Hilbert* (Vienna: Zsolnay, 1948), p. 318 ff., Colerus furnishes an account of non-Euclidian geometry to which we are indebted for our discussion.

11 See the *Briefwechsel zwischen Gauss und Bessel*, edited by the Royal Prussian Academy of Sciences (Leipzig: Engelmann, 1880), p. 479 ff. In the following we quote the most important passages from this exchange of letters on non-Euclidian geometry (all italics original).

On July 2, 1828, Gauss sent Bessel three papers, including the "Disquisitiones Generales circa Superficies Curvas," together with his letter (No. 160/62, p. 479 f.). Bessel replies on August 27, 1828 (no. 161/99, pp. 480–481): "I have familiarized myself with the greater part of your exposition on curved surfaces, but not sufficiently to have a clear and unimpeded synoptic view. This treatise has elicited my most profound admiration because of the novelty and elegance of method, as well as for the beauty of its results. . . ."

Gauss' reply (no. 163/63, pp. 487–490) closes as follows: "I have also given much thought to another subject that I have been pondering in my spare moments for nearly forty years. I refer to the first principle of geometry. I do not recall if I ever discussed with you my views on this subject. Here, too, I have further consolidated many aspects, and am now even more convinced that we cannot fully establish an a priori basis of geometry. In the meantime, it will be a while until I am able to prepare my *very extensive* investigations of this matter for publication. Perhaps it will not happen during my lifetime, since I cannot abide the clamoring of the Boeotians that will ensue if I *fully* articulate my views. — Yet it is remarkable that besides the well-known lacuna in Euclid's geometry that has remained, and likely will remain unbridged, his geometry has yet a further fault that no one has previously objected to, so far as I know—a problem whose solution, though possible, is not easily found. I refer to the definition of the *plane* as a surface in which the straight line connecting any two points is completely contained. This definition contains more than is necessary for determining a surface, and tacitly invokes a *theorem* that must first be proven."

On February 10, 1829, Bessel replies (no. 164/101, pp. 491–493): "I would very much regret if the 'clamour of the Boeotians' would prevent you from a discussion of your views on geometry. On the basis of Lambert's remarks, and of what Schweikart has told me, I perceive that our geometry is incomplete and ought to have a hypothetical correction, even if this means abandoning 180° as the sum of the angles of a plane triangle. This would be *true* geometry, while the Euclidian would be *practical*, at least for terrestrial figures. Your investigations, you say, are *very extensive*—and yet you persist in surveying and supervising! If I were the King of Hanover, I wouldn't allow you to survey, and would appoint someone else to do it, for better or worse. I assume you know that the interruption of your surveying was greeted by everyone, as we owed to it your treatise on planes, as well as the others that were published with it."

Gauss replies to Bessel's letter on April 9, 1830 (no. 166/64, pp. 495–497); the concluding passage of his reply is as follows (again the italics are original): "Your lack of inhibition in replying to my views on geometry has been a source of great joy, particularly as so few persons have an open mind for them. It is my sincerest conviction that the theory of space has a priori an utterly different place in our kowledge than the theory of magnitudes. Our knowledge of the former is utterly lacking *that* particular conviction of necessity inherent in the latter (i.e., of its absolute truth). We are obliged to admit that if the number is *merely* the product of our minds, space possesses a reality beyond our mind, a reality whose laws we are unable to fully prescribe a priori.—Incidentally, I have been unable to return to these matters since we spoke of them."

12 Egmont Colerus, *Vom Punkt zur vierten Dimension* (note 10), p. 148.

13 The correspondence from which the exchange of letters above has been taken makes no reference to the "imaginary sphere," and we have been unable to determine to what work of Gauss reference is made.

14 Colerus (note 10), pp. 416 and 418.

15 Colerus (note 10), p. 419.

16* Shortly after these lines were written, *Life* magazine published drawings by Picasso that demonstrate an entirely new kind of transparency and point toward the "sketches with light," as we call them, which Picasso has realized four-dimensionally, as it were, on a transparent spherical surface (see p. 482 below and figures 59-60 on that page); the drawings are in *Life*, 8, 4 (February 13, 1950), pp. 2-4. And Liliane Guerry's *Cézanne et l'Expression de l'Espace* (Paris: Flammarion), issued in December, 1950, documents for the first time in detail (from a perspectival-historical standpoint) that the surface in Cézanne's work is spherical! (We will examine in detail Picasso's "sketches in light" and Cézanne's curved space in chapter 9, section 3, p. 472 ff.).

17 We will return further on in our discussion to the devasating consequences, the inappropriateness and immoderation of the increasing application of "occultism" and spiritism. These practices are inappropriate and immoderate since they do not befit the mental structure; they are inadequate and "unheard of" or "out of place" (*ungehörig*) because they make accessible (*hörbar*) false and deficient phenomena of the magic structure, or permit the practitioners to become enslaved (*hörig*) to such phenomena. Wide ranges of such phenomena rooted in "timelessness," and much of what has sunk into the shades and slag thereof, are resuscitated by such practices: macabre sorcery mistaken for matters of the "beyond" because of its "super-sensory" aspect. This is a psychistic materialism of the most inferior sort which leads rational man ever farther away from genuinely spiritual phenomena. With the expected further spread of these practices under the name of spiritism, occultism, metabiology, and the like, a situation is created in which man—approaching his end—will be irrevocably severed from his original interrelationships and ties. And we are witnessing only the intimations of the full flowering or rather proliferation of these marsh-flowers that have sprung up in the stagnant and brackish waters stirred up by mediumism, which conjure a hoaxed semblance of a no longer vital authenticity. These occult and spiritistic teachings and practices generate denatured and deficient magic phenomena, and anyone coming under their spell is likewise denatured and becomes deficient. Our rejection of occult practices does not, obviously, apply to legitimate parapsychology, examined later in our discussion (chapter 8, p. 448 ff.).

18 See also Carl Gustav Carus, *Über Lebensmagnetismus und über die magischen Wirkungen überhaupt* (Basel: Schwabe, 1925).

19 Friedrich Zöllner (note 4), p. 93 f.

20 Zöllner (note 4), p. 131.

21 We must also include the misuse of hypnotism. The depressal of someone's consciousness in order to elicit the state of sleep (*hypnos* = sleep) or somnolent unconsciousness (the consciousness degree of the magic structure, see p. 121 f. in the text), is a violent act, a deprivation of freedom and an inadmissible disturbance of the private-personal development sphere. Any hypnotizing or hypnosis of contemporary man is an illicit, damaging, indeed destructive infringement on the bases of his vital-psychic-mental structure that should be avoided by anyone who values the integrity of his awakened ego.

Only when undamaged in its original substance can the ego make the necessary mutation into the "Itself."

22 Maurice Maeterlinck (note 7), pp. 80, 103, 118, and 162.
23 Maeterlinck (note 7), p. 91.
24 Raoul Auclair (note 8), p. 273 ff. and 297.
25 Since we have touched on the "ether" concept, we should mention that a few tradition-
    alists such as René Guénon (Les Principes du Calcul infinitésimal, [Paris: NRF, 1946, p. 12
    note) do not consider the ether as the fourth dimension but rather as a primordial ele-
    ment containing the other four to which these return upon dissolution. Inasmuch as this
    implies an integrative process, we felt that we should at least mention it.
26 P. D. Ouspensky, A New Model of the Universe (London: Kegan Paul, Trench, Trubner
    & Co., ²1934), pp. 425–432.
27 In his philosophy of nature, Hegel speaks of the three "dimensions" of time: present,
    future, and past. But he does make a restriction (and by so doing, anticipates later devel-
    opments): "There is, incidentally, no existing differentiation of these three time-
    dimensions in nature, where time is Now. They are necessarily only in subjective con-
    ceptualization, in recollection, and in fear or hope. Yet the past and future of time that
    exists in nature is space; it is negated time, just as suspended (aufgehoben) time, inver-
    sely, is the point at the outset, and develops time for itself"; Vorlesungen über die
    Naturphilosophie aus der Encyclopädie der philosophischen Wissenschaften im Grund-
    riss (Berlin: Duncker & Humblot, 1842), VII, 1 (of the complete edition), p. 57, paragraph
    259. A dimensioning of time, in any event will no more afford us a view of the whole than
    would a reduction. Let us, however, not lose sight of Hegel's sentence: "The true is the
    Whole," a postulate not amenable to dialectical and rational means; and yet it attains
    arational, valid expression through time-freedom since it affords us the possibility of
    consciously sustaining the whole in truth.
28 P. D. Ouspensky, Fragments d'un enseignement inconnu (Paris: Stock, 1949); German
    edition: Auf der Suche nach dem Wunderbaren (Innsbruck: Verlag der Palme, 1950).
    This last-named book brought to our attention one of Ouspenksy's further books: Ter-
    tium Organium: a Key to the Enigmas of the World (N.Y.: Knopf, ³1947). In this work,
    Ouspensky employs as his ordering schema the gradually increasing dimensionization
    of our reason ("sense"). It is indicative that to him, four-dimensional reason leads to a
    "spatial experiencing of time," to a "unified logic of the universe," to "magic," "idealis-
    tic philosophy," "unitary science," "mystical religion," and so on (see, for example, the
    chart at the end of his book). The aim of his four-dimensional "sense" has nothing in
    common with the consciousness structure based on four-dimensionality that we have
    demonstrated. His conceptions, for the most part, are no more than reinvigorations of
    the magic and mythical consciousness structures. They not only have little to do with
    time-freedom (achronicity) and the spiritual (diaphaneity), but lie completely outside
    the region where these may be validly conceived.
29 Paul Langevin, "Proces-verbal de la Societe de Philosophie, Paris, seance du 6 avril
    1922," quoted in Raoul Auclair (note 8), p. 273, note 1: "La physique avait essentielle-
    ment pour théâtre l'espace euclidien où régnait un temps absolu. La conception nou-
    velle [relativité] est tout autre: c'est une fusion de la géométrie et de la physique rendant
    impossible l'existence d'un temps et d'un espace absolus."
30 Jean Gebser (note 1), end of chapter 10; Gesamtausgabe, I, p. 210.
31 See Part I, chapter 2, p. 31, note 27.
32 See also Jean Gebser, "Notwendigkeit und Möglichkeit einer neuen Weltsicht," Die
    neue Weltschau: Internationale Aussprache über den Anbruch eines neuen aperspek-
    tivischen Zeitalters (Stuttgart: Deutsche Verlags-Anstalt, 1952); also in Gebser, In der
    Bewährung (Bern: Francke, 1962), p. 31, and Gesamtausgabe, V/I, p. 183.
33 See also Gebser, In der Bewährung (note 32), p. 102 f.; Gesamtausgabe, V/I, p. 250 f.
34 Gebser, In der Bewährung (note 32), p. 117; Gesamtausgabe, V/I, p. 265.

35   Herbert Günther, *Das Seelenproblem im ältesten Buddhismus* (Constance: Weller, 1949), p. 63.

36   C. G. Jung, *Psychologische Typen* (Zürich: Rascher, 1940), p. 412. See also Herbert Günther (note 35), p. 63.

37   Werner Heisenberg and Adolf Portmann have recently noted that the latest results of research lie, so to speak, beyond the present capacities of language. For their statements, as well as further discussion on this subject, see Gebser, *In der Bewährung* (note 32), p. 147; *Gesamtausgabe*, V/I, p. 294 f.

5

Manifestations of The Aperspectival World (I): The Natural Sciences

1. Mathematics and Physics

In the following chapters we shall venture to verify the basic undercurrent in the various sciences which is an expression of the occurring mutation. In this it will be apparent that certain new modes of observation and their results are all based on a conscious or unconscious predominance of the theme of time.

Within the sciences there is surely nothing so vexing, and nothing which encounters more objections than an investigation of specialized results by a writer "outside the field." Only too readily is he accused of the philosophical exploitation of results in whose discovery he has not participated.

Yet the attempt made on these pages is not the philosophical interpretation of specific scientific results. It is not even the attempt at a synthesis, nor does it result from a subjective opinion or predilection. Both its basis and its valuations differ since they have to do with consciousness. Our criterion is not philosophical but eteological; we are not attempting an interpretation but an imparting of truth: synairesis, not synthesis. This is to say that our criterion is based on the making evident of what is real, the verition of those things which reveal or impart their truth and become perceptible in truth because of an intensified consciousness. If we apply this to our investigation it means that we are making visible and examining the various new modes of observation as well as the results of the specialized sciences and the arts which parallel each other as parallel "symptoms," and thus as manifestations of the new consciousness. It also means that we are observing and making them evident as temporic attempts toward superseding three-dimensionality and its inherent compulsion to employ a systematic terminology.

Once again we mention deliberately that our interpretation of the specialized results of the sciences is not an attempt to capitalize on these results. It is rather an inventory which purports to evince the basic theme of our epoch, and is the signature, as it were, of the mutation of consciousness now occurring—the signature that is giving its stamp, negative or positive, to all significant manifestations of our epoch.

The fact that we have been able to make evident the various consciousness structures and to verify that there has been since the Renaissance a necessary restructuration, that is, mutation, and to demonstrate what its fundamental character is, indeed has to be—this exempts us from the charge that we are approaching our task in a subjective or philosophical-speculative manner (a task, moreover, which is not restricted to Europe alone).

It should also be taken into account that we have clarified the extent to which terms that in a categorical sense seem to be incongruent may—indeed must necessarily—be placed into relation with one another. Our verification of acategorical elements, as well as the emendation and complementation of the systems by systatic concepts, has made clear that our procedure cannot be argued away merely by an appeal to the specialized terminologies, at least with respect to those concepts which are only variations and aspects of the principal theme of the new mutation.

And finally it must be borne in mind that we have not merely striven to maintain a rational-mental rigor but an incorruptability vis-à-vis the psyche and a restraint of the vital aspects as well—possibilities of which even the most rigorous logicians are apparently still unaware. How successful we have been is another question; our responsible attempt is in any event an indication of an attempt at integral discipline and not just of a purely mental, that is, partial application of rigor.

This attempt will be construed as a philosophical misinterpretation only by those who are unable to extricate themselves from the strait-jacket of rationality or specialization. Only those persons who are not up to the challenge of the "new energy" as a result of their rational impoverishment will, in their attendant confusion and lack of insight into their atrophied irrational component, accuse us of mystification and irrationality where we are already at work in the realm of the arational. We must never forget that criticism in a given instance is primarily a criticism of ourselves, and not of others. By ignoring this simple fact, which frequently happens today precisely because of its simplicity, many people are led unintentionally to become traitors to themselves. Yet this same fact can be of inestimable worth to someone with an open mind.

Our criterion, then, is not philosophical. We are still in the process of interpreting. Our criterion is the evident fact of consciousness mutation, and our examination of the various specialized scientific and artistic results is made only with reference to this mutation, since these results are the visible manifestations of the emerging aperspectival and integral consciousness. This point of clarification should be constantly borne in mind during the course of our remaining presentation.

Let us now turn to these manifestations. As we might expect they are particularly evident in the fundamental discipline of all the exact sciences, mathematics. It is no accident that we have had to deal with it so often in both parts of our presentation and have already brought out the most important aspects. During the heyday of the Baroque era in the seventeenth century, an age which also attempted to get beyond the perspectival strictures of Renaissance space in the arts, there was a "downright frenzied forward thrust . . . in mathematics" of which Colerus speaks.[1] The traditional and predominantly static geometry of measurement set down by Euclid is displaced, after a nearly two-thousand-year exclusive reign, by Descartes' "analytic geometry" (1637), by Desargues' "projective geometry" based on perception and illustration rather than on measurement (!) (1639), and by the "dynamic mathematics"

(1638, 1687) of Galileo and Newton (see above p. 100). Projective geometry in partic- ular engendered to a greater degree than the others the modern "non-Euclidian" geometries[2] which brought into being the fourth dimension that Einstein intro- duced into physics in the form of "time." These new mathematical concepts, moreover, were the foundation on which for the first time modern technology could be developed.

Even by themselves—and there are other parallel phenomena which are famil- iar to every mathematician—these facts are a clear indication of the "irruption of time" into mathematical thinking. They elicit a wealth of phenomena of which the foremost, the technologizing and four-dimensionalizing of our world, speak an un- ambiguous language. For this reason it is unnecessary to examine at length the revo- lutionary and genial achievements of the "queen of sciences," apart from noting the "set theory" of Speiser; the "probability theory which today has undergone an unheard-of refinement and is progressing ever further into all of the sciences on its triumphal march, and is about to remodel the classic world-image dominated by 'laws' [!] into a 'statistic world-image' in which there is no certainty but only degrees of probability";[3] and the axiomatic system of David Hilbert whose axiomatics permit "all types of geometries to be clarified in their structure as well as in their limita- tions" and demonstrates "why geometries like the Euclidian, the non-Euclidian, and others are possible without being contradictory,"[4] a proof also of the validity of the various consciousness structures which are represented by the various geometries.

Yet already the perceptive Colerus noted the great dangers in the wake of set theory, as well as of the postulated "statistical world conception" and the "hyperlog- ization of mathematics" by Hilbert. All present-day attempts to realize the new per- ception of the world are exposed to the danger of a regression into reinvigorated consciousness structures, particularly during the process of realization before the new consciousness is consolidated. The reinvigorated structures are not imme- diately recognized for what they are because those who are realizing the new per- ception lack insight into the constancy and the continuing presence of the forgotten consciousness structures.

Thus there is nothing gratuitous about Colerus' warning that mathematics must not get mired in mere logistics and assume that it is "the ultimate recourse of a completed logistic-mathematical cosmos," since "this definitely magic view . . . contradicts the facts of history."[5] His warning is indeed necessary, for if not heeded the realizations already achieved would again be placed into question. The warning also points to the emerging struggle taking place among the most prominent repre- sentatives of this science and elsewhere who are attempting to grasp and consoli- date something which is apparently not yet evident in its full clarity.

With regard to physics we can and must be brief here so as not to be repeti- tious. We have already presented the recent developments of research in physics during this century in our book *Abendländische Wandlung* (The Transformation of the Occident)[6] in which we established the predominant role of the theme of time in physics. It would be a needless repetition here if we were to elaborate on the rise of the new theories in physics or attempt once more to describe them and make them comprehensible. It is sufficient for our purposes here to cite their most salient characteristics from which the general theme of our epoch will be evident. We have described this general theme in our earlier study as the "supersession of time" and the "supersession of the time concept."

Since no other science today enjoys the status or even credence accorded it by the general public as the exacting research in physics we would do well to give preference to its results. Nothing has had such a profound effect on the attitudes of the twentieth century and has altered them so markedly as certain new concepts elaborated by this science. The various theories of relativity by Einstein as well as the quantum theory of Planck have altered our perceptions and estimations of the world in a manner comparable only to the changes wrought in earlier, less mentalized ages by the great men of wisdom.

The statements and assertions of these men of wisdom, not verifiable by experiment or calculation, are no longer believed as they once were; our credibility today is directed at those men who, with their invisible mathematical formulae which are neither calculable nor verifiable by the vast majority, are leading the new perception of our world in its conquest of the public awareness. This already touches on an important characteristic of the new physics: its findings and their articulation are expressed in a non-visualizable form, although not as abstractions. This change in particular has enabled physics to supersede mere three-dimensionality.

This supersession of three-dimensionality is the decisive aspect. The incorporation of "time" into three-dimensional space altered this space, thereby altering the structure of our reality. This structural alteration in particular is an expression and visible manifestation of the change which our consciousness is undergoing by mutation.

The mechanistic world-image of classical physics valid until 1900 has been, in the words of C. F. von Weizsäcker, "more thoroughly destroyed than one would have expected. This is not a misfortune but rather a good lesson. An image of the world is more than a mere scientific theory; it must encompass, at least symbolically, the whole of reality. From the standpoint of individually verifiable phenomena, this whole is invariably a matter of faith, a belief which is a precondition for our lives. The old world-image of classical physics, too, attempted to represent the whole, but as its means were inadequate it necessarily failed to do so. Yet physics was the first of the natural sciences to possess a self-contained system, and therefore had the role of a showpiece, as it were, among the sciences independent of the image of world. Perhaps this role now devolves on physics in a new sense, for the new physics is the first self-contained system of knowledge about nature comprehensible in exact mathematical terms beyond the confines of the mechanistic world-view."[7]

What are the distinguishing characteristics of the new "physical world view"? We must first observe that we can no longer speak of a "view" of the world in physics but rather of a perception of the world. Moreover, even the so-called mechanistic world-view was not an image of the world but a conceptualization. It is an essential component of the new perception of the world in physics that it is no longer conceptualizable. But this is anticipating our discussion; let us first inquire carefully into the data or "givens" as a result of the most recent revolutionary discoveries and theories. In doing so we find that they evidence clear indications of what we have called the aperspectival world; we can discern in recent physical research in inceptual form the new components which we have demonstrated to be characteristic of the new mutation of consciousness.

We find for example that in physics:

1) "time" is taken into consideration for the first time, and the mere concept of time is superseded;
2) the same holds true of the overstrained rational dualism; and

3) "reality" is shown to be no longer adequately and exclusively realized by means of mental conceptualization and empirical visualization.

Let us restrict ourselves to these three points as they indicate consequences that will be immediately evident from the following discussion. Our task is, in the first place, to examine the data established by physics; and in the second, to determine their latent tendencies (although not in the sense of a philosophical interpretation). These tendencies are obvious because we have been able to show their basic import; they are in part seedlings and in part already exfoliating manifestations of the new structure of consciousness. The discovery of a relationship—which is significant or meaningful rather than sensible—between new and initially confusing concepts and a mutation occurring in human consciousness (whose theme we have worked out) sheds new light on these unsettling and contradictory results of scientific research.

Let us now examine the three points mentioned above, noting first the data and then determining in each instance the tendencies inherent in them. First, *the theme of "time,"* which we have shown to be very much in the forefront, is also predominant in physics. The primary role of the time concept in Einstein's theory of relativity has been noted on the preceding pages and examined in detail in our study of the *Transformation of the Occident.* As Raymond Jouve emphasizes, the consideration of "time," specifically of chronological time as the fourth dimension, is tantamount to a "découverte du temps" or a "discovery of time."[8] This "discovery" was prepared and precipitated by what we have called the "irruption of time."

We have seen that the genial deed of Einstein was his liberation of "time" from the state of a mere abstraction, and, to a certain extent, from its rationalization, since it now became a "relative" element (alongside the rational metric function) within a "world view" that no longer represented a merely static (three-dimensionally limited) world, but turned this world into a flux, transforming it into the recently conceived "space-time continuum." This change is manifestly evident: in place of the classical system of a spatial world there is now the space-time world as a continuum.

These are the given data; the tendencies or trends visible in them are by nature fundamental if we consider them as expressions of the incipient new consciousness. These given facts leave no doubt that the irruption of time into the most empirical of all the sciences is accompanied by the awakening consciousness (or discovery) not only of the concept of time, but also of time as a world constituent; and this discovery of necessity gradually gives rise to a completely new conception of the time factor—new at least with respect to our mental consciousness—in terms of nature, our image of the world, and our ways of thought.

The decisive step in this direction came as a result of Planck's quantum theory. His demonstration that nature does make leaps, as the saying goes, effectively demolished our prevailing view of time. Our world is not constructed continuously (or with respect to time, as a constant), as the mechanistic view of classical physics had held, but rather discontinuously and unpredictably. Planck also discovered the agent of this discontinuity: the new physical "constant," the h or Planck's constant, the so-called "quantum of action" which together with the "dimension of action" is a universal constant.

These are the given facts—where do they lead? First, there is the consequence that time is not a quantity—linear, constant, and causally determinate—but *sui generis* an "intensity." This implies that a perception from physics reveals the complexity of what had been hidden "behind" the mere concept of time. There can be no doubt that we are justified in relating the "quantum of action" to the "time" complex, although it runs counter to three-dimensional terminology. This justification is based on our distinction between systatic elements and systematic quantities or magnitudes.

As an indirect corroboration of our position we can cite a remark by Ernst Zimmer. Speaking of Planck's quantum of action or h, Zimmer observes that it "seems to be a quantity with a higher degree of reality than most of the other quantities employed in physics."[9] And this is not all, for Zimmer also maintains (in terms drawn from physics) that "in the quantum of action we have a quantity which is measured in space × time" (in which "time" is understood as physical-measurable time), and also that "the theory of relativity teaches us . . . that we can arrive at a generally valid insight only if we do not view events as divided into space and time but rather observe the four-dimensional world constructed of space and time. The 'action,' being a part of the four-dimensional world of thought is a universally valid property in contrast to energy [which Zimmer defines as a 'spatial magnitude']. It is not something visible like everything that can be divided up into space and time [which for Zimmer is a physical quantity of mass], *for it belongs instead to a deeper and more inclusive region* of truth. Therefore Planck's insight that it must be understood in atomistic terms is a perception which touches on the most profound previous knowledge in physics."

We must not forget that we are dealing here with the realm of physical research and must accordingly refrain from superimposing even to a slight degree its results and formulations onto other areas. As we shall see, such a transposition is in fact unnecessary inasmuch as other areas are themselves confronted with the same "tendencies" which we are here examining in our own way from the field of physics as they pertain to the awakening consciousness of four-dimensionality, tendencies whose perplexities each area is dealing with in its own terms.

Yet even if we remain strictly though not dogmatically within the framework of physics, Zimmer's definiton—which Planck himself recognized as relevant[10]—presents us with three statements which deserve closer attention: first, that the quantum of action is a *universal* magnitude with a *dimension* of action or effectuality; second, that it possesses a higher degree of reality and belongs to a deeper, more inclusive realm of *truth;* and third, that the "action" or effect has an atomic *structure,* a point made not only by Zimmer[11] but also by Heisenberg[12] who speaks of the "atomic structure of energy," a concept of structure which in both instances dispenses with any visible demonstrability and "grasps" the "material" phenomena only in mathematical terms.

It is not only symptomatic that we find here the terms dimension, truth, and structure; it is equally symptomatic that the discovery of the quantum of action, which includes its dimension of action or effect, opens up a more profound (or higher) region of truth and is ultimately universal and amaterial in structure. In principle it should be noted here that any new truth, reality, or structure, whether of a more profound or a higher form, is always accessible only via a new dimension. Each of these new forms is overdetermined with respect to the one which "underlies" it; in this sense both the *it* as well as the *h* overdetermine the strictly three-dimensional structure, *i* in each case being (in mathematical terms) the square root of -1, the "imaginary number" which reveals the next and higher-dimensioned coordinate system (see p. 341).

We will return in the next section to the concept of structure which is here stated in preliminary form in amaterial terms in physics. As for the definition of "action" or effect as a dimension we can consider it to be a systatic element. This is not to imply that we are postulating the quantum of action as a fourth dimension; but if we consider it as a systatic element since it is a potential effective factor which is manifest and "comprehensible" only spatio-temporally, that is, four-dimensionally, it has a systatic relationship to "time" as a fourth dimension. At least to the extent of being a physical-structural element of primordial efficacy, the Planck constant h is that "dimension" which requires for its self-manifestation the it-dimension of Einstein on the one hand, and intensifies and surpasses the four-dimensionality of the space-time continuum on the other.

The ultimate consequence here is the dawning of the universal—and therefore integral—possibility of the fourth dimension. To what extent physics will be able to comprehend the h as an intensity of the extensity it will depend largely on the mathematical possibilities which are beyond the ken of the author. It is definitely not possible to relate h to it as long as they are understood as categorical quantities, and as long as no means of expressing their acategoricality is found. Whether or not the course suggested here could be realized, and how the relationship itself could be effected in physics, are matters for basic research; our task as understood here has been restricted to furnishing the appropriate concept.

The discovery of such a relation could be facilitated by the not insignificant fact that even with respect to physics the possibility of the fourth dimension is revealed which we have described as its "essence": the fact that it is achronic, that is, time-free and therefore also space-free since, as we know, spatial-temporal phenomena cannot be dissected in a four-dimensional or synairetic perception into space and time. The fact to which we are alluding is this: in microphysics the quantum exchange of energy occurs in the realm of the so-called elemental particles. Among them are the electrons of which Planck has written: "According to Heisenberg's law . . . which forms one basis of wave mechanics, the location of an electron having a specific velocity is completely indeterminate. Not just in the sense that it is impossible to determine the location of such an electron but in the sense that the electron does not occupy a specific location at all. This is because a simple periodic material wave corresponds to an electron of a particular velocity, and such a wave has neither a spatial nor a temporal limit, otherwise it would not be periodic. The electron therefore has no specific location, or if you will, it is simultaneously found in all loci."[13]

The new physics also shows signs of a definitely new and novel conception of time, or, more correctly, a new valuation or estimation of time. This new estimation applies to the view held today that the world is finite. The principle that the world is finite (yet unbounded) is one of the axioms of Einstein's theory of relativity. This finitude applies to its spatial as well as its temporal components in conformity with the space-time continuum for which it was discovered. The most recent investigations, as reported by Pascual Jordan among others, show that the universe is barely ten billion years old.[14] Other physicists such as Arthur March estimate longer spans of time on the order of twenty to one hundred billion years,[15] while still others assume shorter time spans; Hoyle estimates five billion years,[16] C. F. von Weizsäcker two and one-half to three billion years,[17] Lecomte du Noüy a span of two billion just for our solar system and five billion for the universe as a whole.[18]

All of these represent the view that the world came into existence sometime; it came to be in space and time. Or better, space and time came into existence with it. Incidentally, the Christian notion of creation once again gains currency by this particular aspect of the new physics; and the *Samyutta Nikaya* contains a statement of Buddha that corresponds to a great extent with Einstein's formulation: "Ne pensez pas: le monde est éternel, il n'est pas éternel; il est infini, il est limité." The introductory use of the word "éternel" makes the definitions which follow somewhat confusing, but the sense of the statement is undoubtedly: "Do not think that the world is eternal, for it is not eternal. It is without an end (unbounded), it is finite (i.e., temporally limited and not eternal or infinite)."[19]

The age of the universe and of the earth belonging to it, which has been scientifically ascertained in various ways, is relevant to our discussion inasmuch as it proves that "state" which we have described as "pre-space-timelessness" to be real. C. F. von Weizsäcker has described this "state," noting that we can assume today that the world actually has an age: "Before this time, the world, if it existed at all, must have been in a totally different state from its present-day one. We cannot even try to depict that state, since the very use of a concept such as time does not arise."[20]

If we, however, realize this timeless state with our consciousness, then this state is transformed into space-time-freedom which is with respect to consciousness not only the most profound reality and truth, but also the amaterial and atemporal basic structure of the universe, which, to the extent that we can penetrate it with our consciousness, is free of matter as well as time. For that which we call space-time-freedom is nothing other than the "state" which lies before magic space-timelessness of which we have become conscious, as we have repeatedly stated on these pages.

There is a statement by Eddington which is utterly incomprehensible to three-dimensional thinking but which is fully transparent to four-dimensional "awaring" or perception of truth, if we regard it from the standpoint of the concept of space-time-freedom: "Events do not happen; they are just there, and we come across them. 'The formality of taking place' is merely the indication that the observer has on his voyage of exploration passed into the absolute future of the event in question; and it has no important significance."[21] (Here we cannot take into account that the concept of space-time-freedom sheds considerable light on the two basic concepts of Eastern thought, which in the form of "maya" and "nirvana" have hitherto been interpreted in mystic terms and which can become transparent to our consciousness[22] like everything else as soon as we are able to realize the fourth dimension as time-freedom.)

The data of the new physics as recounted above clearly show that the problem of time is of decisive importance to them, unlike the situation of classical or preclassical physics. The full significance inherent in the new estimation and judgement of "time" shelters tendencies which in all likelihood cannot be employed and evaluated in physics, although the tendencies toward space-time-freedom must be apparent to the physicist, even though he may not be able to "grasp" space-time-freedom because of the limitations imposed by the scientific forms of realization, such as measurement, to which he subscribes.

And yet a decisive step has been made in recent years precisely in this direction. In an address given in the second series of lectures on "The New Perception of World" entitled "Atomic Physics and the Law of Causality" at St. Gallen in February, 1952, Werner Heisenberg described a "state" of the microworld of elementary particles which distinctly evidences characteristics of what we have called time-freedom. In this lecture, based on his treatise "Paradoxes in the Time Concept in

Elemental Particle Theory" of 1951,[23] Heisenberg observes that "in very minute space-time regions, that is in those of the order of magnitude of elemental particles, space and time are remarkably obliterated in such a way that with respect to such minute times that we cannot even correctly define the terms 'earlier' or 'later.' Of course, in the world of macrophenomena nothing would be able to change the space-time structure, but we must reckon with the possibility that experiments with the events in extremely minute space-time realms will show that certain processes appear to take place in the reverse temporal sequence than that required by the laws of causality."[24] This takes into consideration for the basic structure of matter—the atomic process which for matter may well be its original process—the freedom from space and time which is proper to origin whenever we, as Heisenberg has done here, are able to bring this "state" to awareness.[25]

But it is not a question of physics demonstrating in "material" and "measurable" form one of the basic concepts of the new consciousness structure. Such verification may well be impossible or else can be achieved only after several decades of further research (for which Heisenberg's statement quoted above may well have been pathfinding). The real significance is that physics has worked out basic positions which not only potentially point beyond physics but also unequivocally point to components of the new consciousness, as is evident with respect to the theme of "time" in physics and its inherent tendency toward time-freedom.

This discovery of potential inceptions—a making visible of processes of the emergence of consciousness and thus itself a manifestation of the new consciousness mutation, and not a merely philosophical interpretation—could be dismissed as irrelevant only if it were to restrict itself to the (admittedly central) theme of time. But there are similar tendencies which can be shown for other important results of recent thought in physics, which brings us to our second point: *the supersession of dualism.*

The supersession of dualism is yet another result of the new physics. The way was prepared by Einstein who fused the oppositional categories of space and time into the unity of the space-time continuum. His verification that energy and mass/matter were not opposites but, as we have described above, merely differing manifestational forms of one and the same thing, points in the same direction. The most pointed statement of this new knowledge comes from Eddington, who calls "mass only another name for energy," thereby emphasizing the aspect of physical energy.[26] The consistent application of such discoveries in quantum theory as the "uncertainty principle" has led to such objective (and not merely philosophical) conclusions as that of Arthur March, who observed that "the world is inseparable from the observing subject and is accordingly not objectifiable."[27] Thus even the old antinomies of world versus man, object versus subject, became—like mental perspectivity—untenable from the standpoint of physics.

Further developments in quantum theory, such as those in "wave mechanics," have verified that light (and therefore matter itself) invariably occurs both as "corpuscle" and as "wave."[28] The rational inconsistency of this basic fact of physics was not explained in terms of, say, a principle of "duality," but rather by the establishment of the "complementarity principle" by Niels Bohr. What implications can be drawn from these data? We can infer in any event that the strictly rational scheme of thought can be described as no longer adequate. It is true that it still provides makeshift solutions, but its universal validity has been shaken. The great dualistic concepts which provided its tension and excitement have become tenuous.

The formal attempts to rescue the rational scheme are evident in such instances as the development of a "three-valued logic" which received its systematic form at the hands of H. Reichenbach,[29] an attempt, however, that may well be inconclusive because it does not go beyond mere systematization. This will be borne out by the publication of C. F. von Weizsäcker's "Quantum Logic," of which more will be said later (chapter 6, section 2) inasmuch as we do not need to concern ourselves for the moment with philosophical attempts. What is of interest here is that dualistic thinking with its three-dimensional structure is for the most part no longer adequate for the new knowledge and discoveries in physics.

Anyone who is compelled to recognize the irrelevance of the dualisms can no longer employ a form of realization based on the concept of oppositions represented by thesis-antithesis-synthesis. Here the new physics "oversteps" the bounds of the mental structure and is moving toward a mode of realization which, though not yet consciously, has begun to take shape in a four-dimensional and integral form. We can consider the concepts and insights, such as those we have adduced here from the new physics that have divorced themselves from the rigid conceptual framework of mechanistic physics, as initial manifestations of the new consciousness.

This second set of indications of aperspectivity can be augmented by further data which evidence the same tendency and have the identical close relationship to the problem of the supersession of dualism just dealt with as this has to the "discovery of time" discussed earlier. The third and last datum to be adduced here has to do with the visibility or conceivability of the new "image of the world" in physics that cannot be visualized; this brings us to our third point.

The *non-visualizable nature* of the present-day world "image" of physics is a fact which is repeatedly emphasized in physical research. All attempts to render the atomic structures and events in visual or graphic form and to force them into the realm of conceptuality, that is, the mental form of realization, may be considered today as failures. One such attempt among many was the Rutherford-Bohr model of the atom which was intended to show in visual form the processes in the atom. But as Arthur March has observed, "it had to be abandoned by quantum mechanics and be replaced by a totally non-visualizable and purely mathematical construct, since its visible-graphic form could not be reconciled with a fundamental law of nature, the principle of indeterminacy,"[30] and presented the actual processes not only in less precise but also falsified form.[31] As Heisenberg has remarked, "These atomic laws can be only imprecisely transposed into visual images of the atom, for Planck's quantum hypothesis on which these laws are based contains on principle a non-visualizable element."[32]

As a consequence of quantum theory, physics also was compelled to abandon its venerable principle of causality. On the basis of the universal "quantum of action" discovered by Planck we now know that the basic course of events is acausal, discontinuous, and indeterminate. Both the constancy and the sequential consistency which represent the basic laws of conceptual thought have become to a considerable degree illusory, at least in physics. "Today physics is no longer in a position to defend a strict determinism; it must of necessity reduce the earlier certainty of its predictions to mere probability. It is compelled to do so because the processes of nature do not cohere continuously as was previously believed but are interrupted by discontinuities through which we cannot trace the causality."[33]

These words of Arthur March are further accentuated with respect to the equivocal nature of conceptual thought by the further observations that present-day physics, for example, must concede that "our *intellect* [is] inadequate to understand nature and consequently we are unable to reproduce its mechanism by means of a *conceptual construct* . . . The inadequacies of our intellect prevent us from capturing reality in our *conceptual world*."[34] The mode of realization of the mental consciousness structure with its spatial confines is no longer sufficient to comprehend "reality"; only a new structure can achieve this. And how could nature be grasped by three-dimensional thought since its "building blocks," the "phenomena of the atomic nucleus" are, as C. F. von Weizsäcker has specifically noted, "beyond spatial dimensions."[35]

It is this "dematerialization"—which we might also define as a delimitation accompanied by a removal of temporal limits inasmuch as the "quantum of action" has no temporal limitation—which gives present-day physics its non-visualizable stamp. Again in the words of Arthur March: "This is the standpoint arrived at by physics today: the objective essence of things consists of a structure, and not something of substance. Let us take for example the electron; its appearance is that of something real, a substantial particle which belongs to the real and objective world and is not just something conjured up by our imagination. But let us not be deceived by this appearance. If we analyze in depth the experiences on which our faith in the existence of a substantive electron rests nothing remains except a system of constant relationships [which is termed a structure in mathematics] so that we are required to accept these relationships and not the substantive particles as the true reality. And the extent to which our doubts about the objective existence of a substantive electron are correct is proven by our experience with particles which shed their physical properties and behave not like a corpuscle but like a wave."[36]

It should be obvious that this perception of the world not only achieves a delimitation, thus tacitly admitting its escape from mental reflection and representation, but also establishes time-freedom and thus withdraws from the psychic realm; moreover, it achieves a de-substantivation and thus even a grasp of vital-magic components. All previous forms of realization fail in the face of new discoveries in physics which must accordingly employ invisible mathematical formulae to grasp "reality." Pascual Jordan has explained: "The marvelous discovery made by quantum- and wave mechanics is that the dubious realm of microphysical structures is amenable to *mathematical* description despite the impossibility of describing it in terms of the usual conception of reality; and such mathematical description, once we have become accustomed to it, turns out to be of surprising inner simplicity and transparent clarity."[37]

These remarks require no further comment; they speak most distinctly for themselves. In physical terms, the aperspectivity of this world-perception can still be structured mathematically. And it is symptomatic that a physicist chances upon the key words "transparent clarity" toward which aperspectivity tends as its realization form in place of the previous forms of representation and conceptualization. This is not to imply that aperspectivity is bound to mathematics; only in the area of physical research is it bound to numbers. But since a persistent rejection of the previous forms of realization has come about precisely in this area, it is undoubtedly an indication of the breakthrough into a new consciousness structure. The results of the new research in physics adduced here are thus in this sense at the very least inceptions and initial manifestations of an aperspectival kind.

Heisenberg once spoke of the mistaken "generalization of the rational [classical and mechanical] natural sciences, making [them] into a rationalistic world view," adding that "just as any generalization is immediately fruitful in opening new avenues of thought in many areas, so shall we today best serve the future by paving the way for the newly acquired forms of thought rather than by opposing them simply because they appear to be extremely difficult. Perhaps it is not too audacious to hope that the new spiritual energies will bring us closer to the unity of a scientific world view which has been so endangered in recent years."[38] These words contain an unspoken warning that the mathematized natural sciences in turn should not lead to an exclusively mathematical world view. And the expressed hope for the "new spiritual energies" is definitely aimed at the new consciousness mutation in our sense which Hufeland already intimated when he spoke of the necessity of a "new strength of spirit" (p. 307).

It will be necessary for us to give an account of the potential time-freedom, for it is in this space-time-freedom that the decisive atomic processes occur. If we do not, we will again falsify the world by reducing it to an expanded quantifiable framework, or become resigned to the inadequacy of such a framework. The fact that physics by its discoveries was forced to supersede the previously valid three-dimensional structure and concern itself with new forms of realization is as significant as the fact that these discoveries could have been made at all. The final discovery is invariably a realization of a predisposition, in this case of a predisposition toward a more intensive consciousness structure.

This predisposition is evident from a statement by Leopold Infeld: "The entirety of all possible events constitutes a four-dimensional world."[39] The remark indicates that we cannot represent the four-dimensional world since the "entirety of *all possible* events" can neither be realized by our understanding, nor grasped rationally. And apart from the non-visualizability identified here, Infeld's statement contains an additional significant indication, since "possibility" is a potency or a latent intensity, and therefore a quality. Four-dimensionality, therefore, also has a qualitative character in contrast to the spatial emphasis, measurability, and basically quantitative aspects of three-dimensionality. It is noteworthy that this qualitative aspect was implicitly underscored by this physicist and co-worker of Einstein. And we might add that the non-visualizability of the four-dimensional structure—which as four-dimensionality is an expression of the integrum, is always concerned with the whole, and is qualitative in nature—definitely has an arational stamp.[40]

Finally we would mention that the ultimate consequences of the nature of the electron—one of the elementary particles which are the building blocks of our world and of the universe—indicate that it is without substance. This means that it is a *transparent structure*. Arthur March has illuminated the non-substantiality and structural character of the electron,[41] drawing the consequences of W. Pauli's "exclusion principle."[42] This de-substantialization ultimately changes the non-visual nature of even the "material" realm into transparency or diaphaneity.

In April of 1958, Werner Heisenberg announced his "world formula": it is based on non-linear differential equations which exclude the principle of superposition of fields. The punctual (quantitative) summation is renounced in favor of (qualitative) involution; the product replaces the sum. The elementary particles lose their point-like character which we have given them by our previous habits of thought and can now be seen as structures. This has been a decisive step toward de-rigidifying thought. In April, 1964, George B. Cvijanovich and E. Jeannet in Switzerland successfully demonstrated, using K^+ Mesons in their experiments, that elementary particles of decreasing size below a certain point are not punctual but are, in fact, structures. Their demonstration—described as the "Bakunin effect"[43]—has unavoidably forced us to alter our understanding of reality from the predominantly conceptual nature of our thinking habits with their punctate character in favor of the mode of realization of the new, arational consciousness which we have endeavored to make evident on these pages.

The events which have taken place during the last sixty years are not an isolated process. Other areas of research manifest basic currents which we have indicated for physics. If this were not the case, then our insinuation that the new events in physics are tending toward aperspectivity and are initial manifestations of the aperspectival world would be nothing more than a willful reclassification. It is a question here of more than just the incorporation of physics into the aperspectival world-perception. Physics itself is tending toward aperspectivity; and, although within the limits of its own framework, it is beginning to evidence characteristics which, as we shall see in the following chapters, were sighted independently, and in some instances earlier, in other areas of knowledge.

We have intentionally refrained from any philosophical—not to mention religious—interpretation of the new physical knowledge and have assiduously avoided statements such as those of A. S. Eddington and James Jeans which would be most revealing in this respect. The facts which we have adduced speak for themselves, particularly when parallel facts in other areas speak the same language. It is not necessary to undertake transpositions with the ensuing problems from one field of study to another. Such attempts can invariably be challenged because of terminological rivalries, and the different points of departure in the various areas only lead to difficulties. It is useful by contrast to see the *interconnections* which the specialist, once he has become cognizant of them, cannot or dare not reject. In the realm of physics there is an emphasis on relationships, that is, on a partial aspect or secondary form of what we call the context or the synairetic completion. Yet time and again we catch a glimpse of a more encompassing context even in the statements and formulations of the physicists, as in the following remark of C. F. von Weizsäcker: "The spirit—which encounters the mystery of its own origin in objective nature—experiences how pure being becomes, as it were, transparent. . . . "[44]

2. *Biology*

It is of importance to observe that biology is still a young science. The need to investigate the *bios*, the vital realm and the processes of life, makes itself felt at the moment that "time" irrupts in the French Revolution—an occurrence which does not take place fortuitously. Biology owes its genesis primarily to Goethe, Johannes Müller, and Karl Ernst von Baer.[45]

The science of biology is an expression of the basic trend which dominates our transitional age since the turn of the nineteenth century. During this period biology has a significant role; we need only recall the significance of Darwin in the nineteenth, and the effects of Vitalism in the twentieth century (which we have examined in detail in our *Transformation of the Occident*). From a historical standpoint, a romantically-tinged biology was succeeded by a variety of counter movements of a materialistic, positivistic, and mechanistic bent. Like those in physics, these attempts were superseded at the outset of our century when, in the wake of the work of H. Driesch, J. von Üxküll, and de Vries, biology began to show revolutionary tendencies not unlike those which we observed in physics.

What are the distinguishing characteristics of the new biological perception of the world? In what respects has it undergone changes in recent decades, and to what extent are we justified in seeing its new concepts and formulations as initial indications manifesting the aperspectival perception of the world? If we again set forth the principal results of biological research and examine their inherent tendencies, it will be apparent that they parallel those in physics to a considerable degree. In our examination we will attempt to remain strictly within the framework of the science in question, even with respect to terminology. The superordinate concepts and categories, and most notably the systases, which interlace the various areas separated by their own terminologies, will thereby stand out all the more clearly.

The new biology, which has both influenced and in turn been influenced by other disciplines (notably psychology and medicine), is striving toward a new attitude of consciousness, toward a new kind of realization in which the incipient effectuality of the new mutation of consciousness is being manifested. In biology:

1) "time" is being taken into account as a quality;
2) dualism is being superseded, thus making it possible to postulate integrality; and,
3) the rational conception and the pre- and irrational onslaught of this discipline are being surmounted (or, as the case may be, deepened) by an emergent arational perception.

Let us confine our discussion to these three points, noting at the outset one important aspect which makes it especially difficult for biology as a science to find a new relationship to "time." Viewed from the systatic mode of observation where "time" is only one aspect of the acategorical world constituent which pervades, binds, as well as undoes the categorically and systematically graspable actualities, it is obvious that biology as a science of living processes, indeed of life itself, reaches deeper into the acategorical region than physics, with its facts that can be systematically and mathematically construed. There is, moreover, the vital moment with its magic accentuation which, as for example in anthropological biology, invariably tends to dominate. It is no accident that Goethe, a co-founder of biology, has his Faust—who gives rise to the pseudo-myth of the Faustian—restate the originary words of the Gospel of St. John into the aggressive-active form: "In the beginning was the deed."[46]

Those same energies which break forth in their societal form in the French Revolution emerge with equal vehemence in poetic and scientific form in the work of Goethe. These are the energies which had been suppressed by the denial of everything that comprised "time" in all its complexity. The warning of the Baroque age had gone unheeded and Europe had given free rein to an unchecked rationalism. In a sense biology as a science can be seen as a rebellion against rationalism, as the specifically biological form of the "irruption of time" which became more evident at the same time in the red flags, in the shrill, explosive whistle of the first steam engine, in the "Faustian" drive for deeds and death, in the awakening consciousness of the "unconscious," and in many other manifestations. For decades afterward, the line of questioning taken by biology is an inquiry into the forces of life and consequently into the validity of any and all systems—the system of mental-rational conceptualization as well as the equally outworn ruling system appropriate to the mental structure.

Having noted the historical development and the symptomatic and characteristic rise of biology, as well as its significance as a starting point of an inceptual aperspectivity, we can now turn to the three points enumerated above. It is possible to discern certain tendencies in the results of recent biological research that point toward the realization of the aperspectival consciousness structure.

There is first the *theme of time* in biology which comes to the fore at the beginning of our century. De Vries' discovery of natural mutations obliterates the old thought-cliche of a strictly rhythmic and evolutionary or even utilitarian and goal-oriented course of biological events. In our *Transformation of the Occident* we have already pointed out that there is an agreement in principle between the theory of mutation in biology and the quantum theory of physics: both sciences have overturned our conception of time as a continuous event. The fact of discontinuous, spontaneous, creative acts could no longer be denied; the quantity "time" took on for our consciousness a qualitative character and was transformed from an extensive, constant, and measurable magnitude into an intensive element with unpredictable actuality and effect.

The first to speak of *temps qualité* or "qualitative time" was E. Minkowski. His concept of *temps vécu* or "lived time"[47] not only proved fruitful for neurobiology, psychiatry, and for biology in general, but was also epoch-making not least because Minkowski himself never succumbed to vitalism. A. L. Vischer later brought together diverse investigations into the intensity-character of biological time, particularly as it affects old age. For an aging person the course of time is essentially different from that of a younger person; time differs with respect to both intensity and quality for youth and old age.[48]

The fact that biological research was later successful in engendering mutations in the laboratory, thus reestablishing the validity of a pseudo-causality, is of only secondary import. What is significant is that the mutations of inherited predispositions as observed earlier were mainly concerned with processes of increasing specialization. As an outgrowth of the histological work of Sauser (Innsbruck), W. Tritsch was able to observe that a species cannot arise via mutation; it can only be exhausted.[49] The discovery of spontaneous duplication of cell nuclei, and of "biological induction" by Sauser has on the other hand opened the way for the first time for an understanding of the emergence of species where each cell forms a "structured power field" "based upon" a structure. (The possibility of the minus-character of biological mutations, and of the plus or compensatory character of spiritual mutations in consciousness, has already been discussed above, p. 37 f.).

As to the theme of time, we must not overlook the *élan vital* of Bergson and its influence on vitalism. We have noted elsewhere the devastating effects of the false adaptation of his concept in German biology during the early decades of this century.[50] For Bergson, the *élan vital* is the "impetus of life," the "creative evolution," the tangible *durée* which is conceived of as the non-objective essence of being. In biology this concept of the *élan vital* is falsified into the "force of life" and becomes an uncontrollable, magical-vehement quantity: the nothing-but-vital which breaks through and negates all other structures. It required decades for this vitalism to be overcome and it lingers on today in the pseudo-vitalism of B. von Bertalanffy's "organismic" conception.

The erroneous integral or totality concepts, which later became slogans and degenerated into the deformities of totalitarianism after their usurpation by politics, can also be traced to vitalism. The results can be clearly recognized as those of a deficient integrality. Vitalism in Germany provided the scientific accompaniment synchronized to the hurrahs of the Wilhelminian era and later to the shouts of "Heil Hitler." This was primarily a German phenomenon and never really caught on in England, France, and Switzerland. It was opposed in France by Alexis Carrel[51] and later by his student Lecomte du Noüy who emphasized the religious aspect.[52] In England vitalism was opposed notably by J. S. Haldane,[53] and in Switzerland by Constantin von Monakow[54] and Adolf Portmann.[55] Opposition in Germany itself came principally from the circle around Viktor von Weizsäcker, although its opposition to the movement did not become visible until the war had begun and its full effect was felt only afterwards.[56]

It was necessary to return briefly to this context because one particular achievement—that of von Monakow—must be held in high esteem in the face of the vitalistic inundation in biology that followed the one-sided emphasis on the pre-rational and magic components. His achievement rests in the introduction of the notion of "chronogeneity" which takes into account the temporal structure of biological functions. This concept enabled the previously valid and purely spatially anchored localization of processes in the central nervous system to be intensified into a four-dimensional localization. It is important here to emphasize that for von Monakow the temporal emergence is not to be considered merely an outgrowth of an organic fixation which emerged throughout the millenia in the ever-increasing refinement of the organs; rather these temporal results are considered as something which is effectual even today in their *temporally-concretized quality*, inasmuch as primitive instincts and sublimated processes of thought are simultaneously manifest in the *temporal-spatial structure of the central nervous system.* [57]

Von Monakow's concept of chronogeneity has been advanced most notably toward a spatio-temporal understanding of biology in a lecture by A. Portmann. This lecture must be considered of programmatic value since it will have an enduring effect on the future scientific conception of fourth-dimensionality not only in biology but in the majority of the sciences.[58]

Portmann too recognizes the spatio-temporal structure of all biological forms of life: "The abundance of living forms presents itself to us as an enormous and impenetrable whole. It is a riddle in all of its forms: a riddle in its perfection, in its sensibility of adaptation to the varied requirements of the environment, and even more puzzling in those forms in which any conceivable purpose of life seems to be exceeded—forms which we are only able to describe in the language of our own purpose-free creativity, in the language of art. It is difficult to comprehend these forms of life with their long past of form transformations over millions of years which are still fully present today and in which future formations live among us in the plethora of structural potentialities preparing the next transformations."[59]

We find here in the words of a natural scientist—so far as we know for the first time—a consideration of that present which encompasses the past as well as the future, and thus also "the whole" and the potentialities or incomprehensible and latent intensities. Portmann defines "the whole" as the "actual unknown" yet to be investigated.[60] For him the "decisively new" in biological research is "the seriousness which is accorded the spontaneous activity of living forms which manifest the particular non-spatial reality of immanence."[61] This "non-spatial reality of immanence" as expressed in biological terms is without a doubt akin to our general concept of "time-intensity" or "time as a quality" on which time-freedom is "based," and which in turn is of a spiritual kind.

Our justification for attempting to evince this affinity above and beyond Portmann's discipline of biology and our own is given in Portmann's own words: "It is precisely the non-dimensional, the most obscure and incomprehensible things which are today the object of exact research."[62] This non-dimensional, however, is archaic pre-timelessness and therefore pre-spatiality, which are transformed into space-time-freedom if they are realized and integrated by us and thereby enter our consciousness from mere pre-consciousness. The inclusion of the "non-dimensional" into the mainstream of scientific inquiry is synonymous with the recognition of the fourth dimension in the sense (and the plenitude) of time-freedom, for time as a quality is non-dimensional; only the spatial has dimensions. We have for this reason called the fourth dimension an "a-mension." And if we comprehend non-dimensionality in the sense of what we have called "zero-dimensionality," it will be evident in another way that time-freedom in its pre-conscious state is the "immanence" of which Portmann speaks, the reminder of the "unique circumstance that all living beings are spontaneous active centers of action drawing on their own non-spatial depths."[63]

Portmann makes several additional consequential and audacious remarks: "It appears of particular significance and implication for the future that the new research into immanence brings once again the world of qualities into the center of our investigations after its estrangement from biological research and near oblivion [ever since Goethe and Müller]. The biologists themselves, like many even today, were of the opinion that the transformation of quality into quantitative relationships was the true object of work in the natural sciences!

"Today a new outlook is gradually gaining acceptance. It is true that wherever we are concerned with exactness we strive for measurement, the means for quantitative representation, and the greatest efforts continue to be applied toward the discovery of new means of measuring qualitative phenomena, specifically for events of immanence. The curve; the correlational schema as a precise formulation; measurements of extension as a manometer of what lies concealed: these are all everyday matters to the behavioral scientist.

"But those with greatest insight have long known that this transformation of quality into quantity does not touch the essence of the matter, and that it cannot be the aim of investigation but merely an aid to avoiding deceptions. The technique of measurement is ultimately not intended to convert immanence into quantity or to render it comprehensible as something quantitative as was earlier demanded. Rather, measurement is intended simply to assist us in achieving a more objective expression of our statements regarding this barely accessible reality of immanence."[64] "The new mode of observation—the regard for immanence—has not only opened anew the realm of qualities or brought about a new regard for organic formations; precisely this deeper incursion into the uniqueness of immanence has given rise to fundamental changes in our understanding of life."[65]

In the years since 1953 Portmann has decisively intensified his insights into the nature of life. He has worked out a completely new and fundamental point of departure for biology (though not for biology alone), as well as a basic attitude corresponding to the new consciousness, and formulated this in a particularly fortunate way. We will mention here only his demonstration of a purpose-free organogenesis and his concept of "undirected self-manifestation of life," discoveries of epochal significance that are supported by parallel discoveries in nuclear physics and psychoanalysis, by the juridical and historical sciences, and by our own phenomenology of consciousness and contemporary developments in the arts—to mention only a few—which in turn provide support to these discoveries and insights. We have examined this state of affairs in detail in various contexts elsewhere.[66]

Biology has been able to achieve something which physics has not. All the temporic attempts, that is, those endeavoring to incorporate "time" into the conceptions of thought and life, lead in physics merely to a qualitative understanding of the time concept, that is, if we are audacious enough to consider Planck's constant qualitatively. Then of course the "more profound wisdom," time-freedom, comes into evidence. But in biology, Portmann's introduction of non-dimensional, non-spatial, and qualitative immanence has achieved a closer approximation to the incipient conscious awareness of time-freedom. Owing to the work of Portmann and von Monakow, and to the mutational theory of de Vries and the "biological induction" of Sauser, we have today what might in conscience be described as a four-dimensional, aperspectival biology.

This new biology integrates the phenomenon of time; it considers "the whole" or integrality in an aperspectival manner rather than merely the quantifiable, divisible, and sectored spatial aspects in a perspectival, fixed form. "For what is decisive," in the words of Portmann once more, "is that the methods of the physical and chemical disciplines have not been rendered 'incorrect,' let us say, but that their 'correctness' simply bypasses the currently held goal. They are 'incorrect' in a new and very exact sense of the word."[67] These methods are no longer correct in a perspectival sense of being goal-directed (see above p. 79 f.), but "incorrect" and "undirected" or aperspectival in accord with the manifest fullness and plenitude of the whole. In a mental sense they remain "correct"; they are "incorrect" in an integral perception.

It is the major event of our epoch that the natural sciences have been able to make this leap from the mental to the integral, from perspectivity to aperspectivity. Their recognition of time as a quality is one of the effects of the numerous temporic attempts which lead to integration, attempts in which the efficacy and actuality of the new consciousness mutation is manifest. And commensurate with this integrality there is a new attitude toward rationalistic dualism which is tantamount to its supersession in biology. This brings us to our second point.

The *supersession of dualism in biology* begins to occur in this science at the moment when the "time" factor is taken into consideration. The traditional dichotomies of anorganic and organic, body and soul, become untenable since they are henceforth seen as unities rather than opposites. The Indian scholar Sir Jagadis Chandra Bose has demonstrated the unity of the anorganic with the organic realm;[68] and the notion of a "unity of body and soul" which was inherent although not explicitly postulated in the work of Goethe and Carus achieved its breakthrough in the work of H. Driesch. This concept was accepted and further refined by J. von Üxküll, H. Prinzhorn, and many others and has resulted in the "psycho-physical" and later "psychosomatic" medicine of the last four decades.[69]

It would not be amiss if we were to posit the parallelism between the postulate of the "unity of body and soul" in biology and the "unity of space and time" in Einsteinian four-dimensional physics. In both instances it is a question of systatic acts of completion which differ, however, because of the marked differences in the data of the two sciences. The demonstration of psychic energy by C. G. Jung does not isolate the energetic principle from the temporicity which is inherent in the psyche. Physics, on the other hand, still separates "time" from "energy" because it considers "time" only as a magnitude and is of course compelled to treat it as such in its measurements.

From an entirely different quarter Arnold Gehlen also arrives at a supersession of dualism, one which is, however, not consistently worked out. Gehlen appropriates on the one hand Scheler's concept of man's "world openness"—in a restrictive sense since he is speaking of the intellect and thus excluding the "spirit"—a notion that later reappears in a modified form as the "open world" of Heidegger (see below p. 411). On the other hand, Gehlen draws on Novalis' conception of the "inner outer world," whereby "world openness"[70] is the "structure of our motivations" that is to a great extent determined by our "soul." For Gehlen the soul is not just an "inner world" but because he defines man primarily as an "active being," the soul is the "inner outer world." This term is "to denote that certain processes in man occur under the influence of the outer world and are 'occupied' by impressions of the outer world. They are thus to be understood as phases of the encounter with the world which a being active and open to the world can be expected to achieve."[71]

Here we should note that the supersession of dualism, to the extent that it is achieved, should never be equated with its elimination. *It cannot and must not be a question of wishing to abolish this conceptual basis of the mental structure but merely of superseding its claim to exclusivity.* The mind retains its validity, but it does not retain its predominant position. This is the decisive point. It is also not a question of "sub-seding" the mental structure by replacing it, for example, with the polarity principle. The mental structure is superseded when it is replaced by the principle of integration—and this is time-freedom or the achronon.

It is, of course, true that the restatement of these new and novel actualities using only language as a means of expression still presents difficulties today. As Portmann has accurately observed, "the language of science is not as advanced in this respect as the research."[72] It is not fortuitous that this reservation is made precisely at the juncture in his discussion where he appears to oppose the qualitative and the quantitative. But he is not dealing with an opposition: "immanence" as a quality in relation to the world of measurable quantities is not dualistic principle any more than time is with respect to space or the soul with respect to the body. From an epistemic standpoint this state of affairs can be comprehended only if immanence and time (as an intensity), as well as the soul, are considered as systatically perceptible elements on the one hand, while the quantitative and the body, as well as space, are considered as systematically fathomable magnitudes on the other. They do not constitute a systasis or unification or a totality from a synairetic standpoint, but are a continuously effective completion or actualization of origin in the present which permit us to perceive synairetically the transparency of the whole.

A significant and decisive transformation, like the change affecting the oppositional concepts dealt with above, has begun with respect to the validity of the division of the world into subject and object. We have seen in the previous section that this dualism can no longer be maintained in physics; the same attitude is gradually gaining currency in biology as well. This change was inaugurated by the "environmental theory" of J. von Üxküll, a theory of the "interconnections"[73] of the world and not of the oppositionalities of the world previously held to be valid. Today there is no longer a predominance of certain perspectively fixed relationships to an opposite, but even in the natural sciences there is an insistence on the diaphanous and aperspectival manifestation of interrelationships and not merely on the relativistic establishment of relations.

The supersession of the subject-object dichotomy is not the same as their loss. As we pointed out in Part One (p. 7 above), it no longer threatens man with the loss of subjectivity or with identification with an object. On the contrary, there is now the decisive supersession of the personal Ego and the impersonal world (or the masses) by the "supra-personal" or, more accurately, by the "apersonal" Itself which is not blindly subjugated to the relationships, dependencies, conditionalities, and temporal strictures—and consequently to the under-determining structures and forms of realization—and is therefore capable of perceiving the interconnections.

This leap from the mental into the integral, on the basis of which the supersession of dualism in biology is taking place, is an event of historical significance for mankind. It constitutes one of the manifestations of the aperspectival world. This leads us to our third and final point:

The rational comprehension of life is overdetermined into an arational perception of life. Once again we expressly remind the reader that arational is not to be confused with irrational; the irrational belongs to the mythical realm, the arational to the integral. The mathematical structures of physics, for example, which are no longer rationally comprehensible and elude a conceptual and three-dimensional realization are in this sense preformations of arational perception. These new structures of physics are the expression of a four-dimensional consciousness. This is all the more true since consciousness with its propensity for transparent perception, as we have called it, which replaces the conceptualization or representation of the world, has begun to manifest itself in the new concepts of biology. (Together with others, the noted biopsychologist Armin Müller has concurred with our view that "a new structure of consciousness is pressing towards completing and complementary expression" whereby the magic, the mythical, and the mental are to be "refined toward a new acquisition on a higher plane of consciousness.")[74]

Goethe's idea of the *Urphänomene* or originary phenomena, as for example the *Urpflanze* or original plant, is in its romantic-idealistic form a first expression of the perception that for each phenomenon there is a basis in an original or primordial conception, an originary (and thus pregnant and potential) original design. This factor of potentiality, incidentally, brings his concept into proximity with Plato's conception; and in this they both point to something beyond the realm of the rational. And since the middle of the last century, the theory of evolution, with its materialistic emphasis, has prevailed, ultimately giving rise to a mechanistic conception. This was followed in turn by vitalism with its emphasis on the organism.

The idea of a basic design or *Urpflanze* was replaced therefore by a conception which we might call a mechanistic schema and succeeded by one of organic totality which was nourished by the irrational "life force." The original design or pattern, laden with energy; the mechanistic schema, rife with the possibility of development; and the organic principle, hyper-laden with dynamism: they were all displaced during the second and third decades of our century by the Gestalt-principle. This was a further leap of the conceptions since the qualitative accentuation replaced a merely energy-laden evolutionistic or functional-vital emphasis, and also endeavored to encompass integrality or the whole rather than the reductive manifestational form of a totality.

Advocates of the Gestalt-principle were Woodger, von Bertalanffy, Katz,

Friedmann, and even Viktor von Weizsäcker with his "Gestalt-circle" theory.[75] The Gestalt principle was advantageous because of its vividness and because it gave a qualitative form to the otherwise blind energies. But it soon turned out to be inadequate. The Gestalt-principle in biology is definitely analogous to the concept of models in physics; yet, like the models, the Gestalt as a perceptible form was not only inadequate to the "actual unknown," but in fact falsified it. It was at this point that Sauser's conception of "structured energy fields" enabled biology too to "think" in terms of "structures." This is not to imply that these biologically-conceived structures are identical to those of physics. They are identical in principle: they result from the same processes of realization, but they differ in kind because the physical structures are atomic and become diaphanous in mathematical form, whereas the biological are bound to living cells.

It should be mentioned here in passing that J. von Üxküll conceived of structures as musical, that is, magically-emphasized structures laden with energy and movement which formed the "basis" of the biological and which he in consequence defined as "scores,"[76] although his conception of structure was not as profound as that held later by others. The magic attunement of von Üxküll, a kind of counterpoint to the nearly mythical conception of biology in Viktor von Weizsäcker's "Gestalt-circle," becomes overprominent in his last book. It emphasizes the aspect of the overpowering might of life and bears the appropriate title "The Omnipotent Life" (Das allmächtige Leben); not surprisingly it deals with musicality and the might of life, two characteristics whose magic conditionality we pointed out in Part I of the present work. This magic conception was as natural for von Üxküll, who came from the vitalist tradition in biology, as the mythical with its accentuation of the psychic component was for Viktor von Weizsäcker, the founder of psychosomatic medicine. Previously, as in the case of Darwin and Haeckel, the emphasis had been on the strictly mental-rational component which had proved to be inadequate.

Essential to the concept of structure, as W. Tritsch has expressed it, is that structure is "neither energy nor relation, neither time nor space but is essentially both," and that we do not see reality "as a magic but as a controllable reality" if we perceive it as "energy and relation, appearance and limit or contour," that is, not singly or fragmented but "as a context, as structure."[77]

As an ultimate consequence, or more exactly, as an ultimate transparency we can discern luminescences of that "non-dimensionality" even in the concept of structure in biology behind the unity of space and time where it first became effective—a non-dimensionality on which this very space-time unity is based and whose conscious form is nothing other than space-time–freedom.

Both physics and biology have by their new concepts taken leave of the strictly mental approach. Both sciences have integrated magic as well as mythical conceptions as recognizable in their unitary and totality postulates. It is this triad of the vital, the psychic, and the mental which first made possible the leap into the "fourth dimension" and facilitated the demonstration of the integral, or, more correctly, the integrating component and ability of our new structure of consciousness which is overdetermined by one dimension over the previous structures, by the dimension of space-time–freedom.

This space-time–freedom, however, is not magic-vital, mythical-psychic, nor mental-rational. It is spiritual; and in this sense the fourth dimension in all its plenitude is the initial expression of a concretion of the spiritual. This fourth dimension is as incomprehensible in systematic terms as the spiritual itself, but its efficacy and actuality are perceptible systatically. The perceptibility is, however, of a diaphanous kind and in this the expression of a faculty or capacity of man which has been only rarely achieved.

All of the scientific concepts we have adduced point to characteristics which we have presented as being necessary for the integral structure: four-dimensionality; transparency (diaphaneity); integration; arationality. All of these not only render the whole complex of "time" amenable to our perception but also effective, and at the same time go beyond mere totality to make the whole or integrity diaphanous. They point to a "non-dimensional" structure "behind" the physical and biological data and phenomena of the different structures, a structure which is pre-magic, pre-temporal, and pre-conscious, and which, because of the new consciousness, is transformed into space-time–freedom. What we have discerned here reflects the first manifestations of the aperspectival world in the natural sciences.

It is self-evident that the natural sciences cannot do without the intellectual-quantitative approach; Portmann has already spoken to this question (p. 383 above). We have ourselves repeatedly emphasized—even in Part I of our discussion—that the acquisition of a new possibility of consciousness, the arational-integral, does not invalidate earlier realization forms of consciousness such as the mental-rational. On the contrary, the mental-rational consciousness that forms the basis of scientific inquiry retains its worth. What it loses is its claim of exclusivity on which it still insists.

What we have discerned from the above discussion is thus also an indication of the renunciation today which is the abandonment of the exclusive validity of the previous structure of consciousness, inasmuch as the natural sciences too have now begun to perceive the spiritual whole—that quality whose evident and conscious perception is made possible for us by the new consciousness. W. Heitler has recently (1961) also pointed out this necessity: "Only when we clearly perceive even now from our scientific standpoint the existence of such realities (which permit us to assume scarcely known spiritual actualities and effectualities that have little to do with the clock-work mechanisms we are presently concerned with in the sciences) can we successfully escape the desolation of an extreme materialistic and mechanistic 'world-view.' "[78]

1   Egmont Colerus, *Von Pythagoras bis Hilbert* (Vienna: Zsolnay, 1948), p. 201.
2   Hans Kayser, *Lehrbuch der Harmonik* (Zürich: Occident, 1950), p. 81.
3   Egmont Colerus (note 1), p. 349.
4   Colerus (note 1), p. 351.
5   Colerus (note 1), p. 361 f.
6   See Jean Gebser, *Abendländische Wandlung* (Zürich: Oprecht, 1943 ff.); *Gesamtausgabe*, I, pp. 171–320.
7   Carl Friedrich von Weizsäcker, *Zum Weltbild der Physik* (Leipzig: Hirzel, ³1945), p. 33.
8   Raymond Jouve, "Presences du Temps," *Construire: Temps du Monde et Temps de l'Homme*, Etudes et chroniques par Raymond Jouve et al. (Paris: Dumoulin, 1943), p. 13.
9   Ernst Zimmer, *Umsturz im Weltbild der Physik* (Munich: Knorr & Hirth, ⁴1938), p. 94 f.; our italics.
10   Max Planck in his preface to Zimmer (note 9), p. 5.
11   Zimmer (note 9), p. 94.

12 Werner Heisenberg, *Wandlungen in den Grundlagen der Naturwissenschaft* (Zürich: Hirzel, ⁸1949), p. 100.

13 See also Gebser (note 6), ²1945, p. 197; ³1950, p. 175; Ullstein ed. No. 107, p. 147; *Gesamtausgabe*, I, p. 298 f.

14 Pascual Jordan, *Die Physik des 20. Jahrhunderts* (Braunschweig: Vieweg, ⁷1949), pp. 144–153, particularly p. 148.

15 Arthur March, *Der Weg des Universums* (Bern: Francke, 1948), p. 57.

16 Fred Hoyle, *The Nature of the Universe*; cited from the German edition, *Die Natur des Universums* (Zürich: Atrium, 1951), p. 80 ff.

17 Carl Friedrich von Weizsäcker, "Das neue Bild vom Weltall," *Die Neue Weltschau: Internationale Aussprache über den Anbruch eines aperspektischen Zeitalters* (Stuttgart: Deutsche Verlags-Anstalt, 1952), p. 66.

18* Lecomte du Noüy, *Human Destiny* (New York: Longmans, Green, 1947), p. 55.

19 Alexandra David-Neel, *Le Bouddhisme* (Monaco: Editions du Rocher, 1949), p. 127.

20 Carl Friedrich von Weizsäcker (note 17), p. 69; see also Gebser, "Die vierte Dimension als Zeichen der neuen Weltsicht," in *Die Neue Weltschau* (note 17), p. 266, and Gebser, *In der Bewährung* (Bern: Francke, 1962), p. 51 ff.; *Gesamtausgabe*, V/I, p. 201 ff.

21* A. S. Eddington, *Space, Time and Gravitation* (Cambridge: University Press, 1935), p. 51; see also Gebser (note 6), ¹1943, p. 42; ²1945, p. 43; ³1950, p. 37; Ullstein ed. No. 107, p. 33; *Gesamtausgabe*, I, p. 194 f. See also especially Gebser, *In der Bewährung* (note 20), p. 76 ff.; *Gesamtausgabe*, V/I, p. 225 ff.

22 Gebser, *In der Bewährung* (note 20), p. 131 f.; *Gesamtausgabe*, V/I, p. 279.

23 Werner Heisenberg, "Paradoxien des Zeitbegriffs in der Theorie der Elementarteilchen," *Festschrift zur Feier des zweihundertjährigen Bestehens der Akademie der Wissenschaften in Göttingen* (Berlin and Göttingen: Springer, 1951), I, Mathematisch-physikalische Klasse, pp. 50–64.

24 Werner Heisenberg, "Atomphysik und Kausalgesetz," *Die Neue Weltschau II* (Stuttgart: Deutsche Verlags-Anstalt, 1953), p. 132. A preliminary version was published in *Merkur*, no. 54 (August, 1952); the quotation is on p. 710.

25 It would lead too far afield here if we were to examine the time theory of E. A. Milne, particularly as it is in all likelihood superseded by Heisenberg's theory noted above. We would note only that Milne distinguishes between a static, quantitative τ-time of the stable Newtonian system, and a logarithmic qualitative T-time of the unstable system by Einstein, Lorentz and de Sitter. The essence of this conception is its attempt to give at least to one time form a qualitative aspect, which is tantamount to a concretition of time, itself a preliminary step toward attaining aperspectival time-freedom. Since Milne's discussion touches upon the Gestalt-mathematics of Hermann Friedmann, we refer the reader to Friedmann's debate with Milne in his *Wissenschaft und Symbol* (Munich: Biederstein/Beck, 1949), p. 63 et passim. See also our discussion of Friedmann's Gestalt-mathematics in *Abendländische Wandlung*, (note 6), ¹1943, chapters 21 and 23 and particularly chapters 21 and 24 in the third and subsequent editions. Literature on E. A. Milne is listed in Friedmann, *op. cit.*, p. 63.

26 Jean Gebser (note 6), ¹1943, p. 68; ²1945, p. 75; ³1950, p. 68; Ullstein ed. No. 107, p. 58; and *Gesamtausgabe*, I, p. 217.

27 See the *Schweizer Lexikon* (Zürich: Encyclios, 1948), VII, col. 1224.

28 Gebser (note 6), chapter 7.

29 Hans Reichenbach, *Philosophische Grundlagen der Quantenmechanik* (Basel: Birkhäuser, 1949), p. 159 ff.

30 The uncertainty principle, or indeterminacy relation, as it is sometimes called, is a consequence of the quantum theory which Werner Heisenberg noted as being inherent in Planck's constant h that precludes the simultaneous measurement of the location and velocity of an elemental particle. If, say, the precise measurement of the electron's location is attempted, the illumination uncontrollably alters the velocity of the particle, caus-

ing its indeterminacy. The precise location, on the other hand, is lost if the velocity is being measured. This imprecision of measurement can be expressed mathematically as a relation whereby each measurement is connected with a change in the system, thus altering its state. This alteration occurs in a way we are unable to analyze which, however, does not prevent us from anticipating or determining its effects. The indeterminacy principle is one of the pillars of modern quantum mechanics (see the *Schweizer Lexikon* (note 27), VII, col. 670).

31   Arthur March (note 15), p. 21.

32   Werner Heisenberg (note 12), p. 47.

33   Arthur March, "Die Neuorientierung der Physik," *Die Neue Weltschau* (note 17), p. 47.

34   Arthur March (note 33), p. 43; our italics.

35   Carl Friedrich von Weizsäcker, *Die Geschichte der Natur* (Zürich: Hirzel, 1948), p. 114.

36   Arthur March (note 33), p. 50.

37   Pascual Jordan, *Das Bild der modernen Physik* (Hamburg-Bergedorf: Stromverlag, 1947), p. 37.

38   Werner Heisenberg (note 12), p. 21.

39   Leopold Infeld, "Einsteins neue Theorie," *Merkur*, no. 40 (June, 1951), p. 528.

40   See also Jean Gebser, "Die vierte Dimension als Zeichen der neuen Weltsicht," *Die Neue Weltschau* (note 20), p. 261 ff.; also in Gebser, *In der Bewährung*, (note 20), p. 58 ff., and *Gesamtausgabe*, V/I, p. 208 ff.

41   Arthur March, "Die Denkweise der heutigen Naturwissenschaften," *Die Neue Rundschau*, 63, 2 (1952), pp. 244–259.

42   Wolfgang Pauli, *Exclusion Principle and Quantum Mechanics*, Editions "Les Prix Nobel en 1946" (Stockholm: Nordstedt, 1948).

43   G. B. Cvijanovich and E. Jeannet, "Anisotropie dans la désintégration π-μ des mésons π^+ créés dans la désintégration $K^+ \rightarrow 2\pi^+ + \pi^-$," *Helvetica Physica Acta 37 (1964), fasc. 3, as well as "The evidence for asymmetry in π-μ decay observed with π^- mesons produced in τ—$2\pi^+ + \pi^-$ mode," Internal Report, Institute of Physics, University of Bern.

44   Carl Friedrich von Weizsäcker (note 7), p. 163.

45   Ernesto Grassi and Thure von Üxküll, *Von Ursprung und Grenzen der Geisteswissenschaften und Naturwissenschaften* (Bern: Francke, 1950), p. 138.

46   It is, moreover, about time that this pseudo-myth is recognized as such, as it obscures the real processes of general consciousness development by the Germanicizing, nationalistic tendency. The utter falsification which results from this is evident in the assumption that the Gothic style is the first "Faustian" and heaven-storming expressive style. Today we know that Gothic sprang forth from the wealth of forms in the Islamic heritage that penetrated Europe via Spain; see for example *Ars Hispaniae* (Madrid: Ediciones Plus Ultra), the first volumes of which were published in 1950 and 1951.

47   E. Minkowski, *Le Temps vécu*, Collection de l'Evolution psychiatrique (Paris, 1933), particularly chapter 1.

48   A. L. Vischer, *Das Alter als Schicksal und Erfüllung* (Basel: Schwabe, 1942).

49   Walter Tritsch, "Die Wandlungen der menschlichen Beziehungen," *Die Neue Weltschau* (note 17), p. 157.

50   See Jean Gebser, (note 6), chapter 19 ("A View of Vitalistic Biology") and chapter 20 ("Unfortunate consequences of Biology"); *Gesamtausgabe*, I, pp. 246 ff. and 249 ff.

51*   Alexis Carrell, *Man, the Unknown* (New York and London: Harper, 1935); French edition: *L'Homme, cet inconnu* (Paris: Plon, 1935). Regarding Carrell see Gebser (note 6), in particular the third edition (1950), chapter 15 ("Carrell: peripheral areas of telepathy"); Ullstein ed. No. 107 p. 73 ff.; *Gesamtausgabe*, I, p. 230 ff.

52   Lecomte du Noüy (note 18).

53   J. S. Haldane, *The Philosophy of a Biologist* (London, 1935); German edition: *Die Philosophie eines Biologen* (Jena: Fisher, 1936). See Gebser (note 6), particularly the third and

later editions: chapter 22 ("Haldane and the supersession of vitalism"); *Gesamtausgabe*, I, p. 257 ff.

54 Constantin von Monakow and R. Mourgue, *Biologische Einführung in das Studium der Neurologie und Psychopathologie*, authorized trans. from the French by Erich Katzenstein (Stuttgart: Hippokrates, 1930).

55 The reader should consult in particular the two works of Adolf Portmann, *Die Biologie und das neue Menschenbild* (Bern: Lang, 1942), and *Biologische Fragmente zu einer Lehre vom Menschen* (Basel: Schwabe, 1944).

56 Viktor von Weizsäcker, *Der Gestaltkreis* (Stuttgart: Thieme, ³1947). See also his *Wahrheit und Wahrnehmung* (Leipzig: Koehler & Ameland, 1942), and his *Gestalt und Zeit*, "Die Gestalt" no. 7 (Halle: Niemeyer, 1942), and *Anonyma* (Bern: Francke, 1948).

57 In view of the importance of Monakow's conception we have here made an exception to our rule and have included an abbreviated discussion of his idea from our book *Abendländische Wandlung* (note 6), ²1945, p. 135 f.; ³1950, p. 123 f.; Ullstein ed. No. 107, p. 104 ff.; and *Gesamtausgabe*, I, p. 258 ff.

58 Adolf Portmann, "Die Wandlungen im biologischen Denken," *Die Neue Weltschau* (note 17), pp. 73–93. See also Portmann's *Neue Wege der Biologie* (Munich: Piper, 1960), p. 102 ff.

59 Portmann, "Wandlungen" (note 58), p. 90 f.

60 Ibid., p. 77.

61 Ibid., p. 78.

62 Ibid., p. 79.

63 Ibid., p. 78

64 Ibid., p. 79 f. Portmann has often spoken of the question as to quality, as for example in his *Das Tier als soziales Wesen* (Zürich: Rhein, 1953), p. 364, as well as in his later writings where he incorporates the qualitative element into scientifically-based evaluation as a constitutive and concrete factor. For more on this question see Portmann's "Neue Fronten der biologischen Arbeit," *Transparente Welt: Festschrift für Jean Gebser* (Bern: Huber, 1965).

65 Portmann, "Wandlungen" (note 58), p. 86.

66 See Jean Gebser, (note 20), p. 20, note 6; pp. 48, 56 ff., 62, 64 f., 136, 139, 146 f; *Gesamtausgabe*, V/I, p. 171, note 6; pp. 198, 206 ff., 211–212, 213–214, 284, 286–287; 294 f. By identifying "non-purposive" processes as well as "undirected, autonomous development," Portmann has definitely superseded Darwin's one-sided theory of evolution. By his new concept, Portmann has made visible the limits of the validity of evolution, as well as expanded its former essentially pragmatic, purposive intent.

67 Portmann, "Wandlungen" (note 58), p. 80 f.

68 Gebser, *The Transformation of the Occident* (note 6), chapter 21, *Gesamtausgabe*, I, p. 254.

69 For further bibliographical details see the literature cited under "Biology" in our *Transformation of the Occident* (note 6), and also Hans Prinzhorn, *Leib-Seele-Einheit* (Potsdam: Müller & Kiepenheuer; Zürich: Füssli, 1927), which deals with the problem from its psychological aspect.

70 Gehlen's conception of "world openness" has one significant limitation, inasmuch as it accedes to a suggestion of Josef Pieper that it be integrated with Aquinas's notion of the "universal." See Arnold Gehlen, *Der Mensch* (Bonn: Athenäum, ⁴1960), p. 36. Aquinas clearly refers to the closed cosmos with his notion and is thus in complete opposition to the arational concept of true openness, as befits the spatially and temporally unlimited nature of aperspectivity.

71 Arnold Gehlen, *Der Mensch* (note 70), p. 279; see also pp. 22 f., 33, 37 f., 175, 209, 278, and 366 ff.

72 Portmann (note 58), p. 78.

73 Ernesto Grassi and Thure von Üxküll (note 45), p. 140.

74   See Armin Müller, *Bios und Christentum* (Stuttgart: Klett, 1958), p. 258.

75   In this regard see Gebser (note 6), part 2: "Biologie."

76   Jakob von Üxküll, *Das allmächtige Leben* (Hamburg: Wegner, 1950), p. 90 ff.

77   Walther Tritsch (note 49), p. 149.

78   See Walter Heitler, *Der Mensch und die wissenschaftliche Erkenntnis* (Braunschweig: Vieweg, ²1962), p. 75. We strongly recommend this incisive, clear, and extremely significant work of the well-known physicist.

6

Manifestations of the Aperspectival World (II): The Sciences of the Mind

1. Psychology

What happens following the announcement of God's death at the outset of the last century? What do the heralds of God's demise seek thereafter? Man? And what do they find? They find the shadow of God, just as Faust finds Mephisto, his dark side, and—turning away from the Father-God and the diurnal visibility of space—finds the domain of the mothers that is "neither place nor time."[1] The unknown God was lost, and now man searches after the unknown, the unconscious.

At the precise moment when the patriarchal world collapses, when the *Roi Soleil* is washed away by the rising tide of the "awakening left," the image of the heavenly father pales. With the age of the machine and the mass, man begins to change from a subject to an object and is transformed from a creative craftsman to a servant: a slave to the machine. During such time of loss, man is threatened by the loss of himself, and consequently begins a new search. Since he is no longer an individual and a person, he searches for the impersonal, the factual "here" and not the "beyond." He no longer seeks what he believes but can never know (or so he thought), but only the not-yet-known, the "unconscious."

Research into the unconscious becomes a general topic. It forms the beginning of biology as a science and the pursuit of the unconscious foundations of life. At the same time it is the beginning of five other sciences in search of the same foundations: archaeology, geology, mythology, occultism, and psychology. After the heights of the heavens have been lost, the sciences pose themselves the task of "exploring the depths."[2] It is the beginning of that journey into the "emptiness" whither Mephisto sends Faust, in whose nothingness he "hopes to find the sum of the universe."[3] The layers of the earth are discovered—the fascination they engender is well described by Stifter in his novel *Der Nachsommer*—along with the layers of the soul, and finally the mythological layers of earlier times revealed. The Unknown—the once "accursed" phenomena—are now investigated.

With all this, time suddenly becomes visible; man becomes aware of time. The past, the forgotten and spatially invisible, that is, latencies and intensities, take on the shape of their past or intangible reality. Goethe's friend Winckelmann becomes the founder of archaeology, discovering the past as a past reality. To Goethe's contemporaries the earth, notably mountains and their layerings, reveals the presence of time. Mythology opens the way for an understanding of past times. Psychology occupies itself with the non-spatial processes of the soul. Occultism hunts out the invisible causes and powers of previously suspect phenomena which form the subject of investigations by Carus, Jung-Stilling, Justinus Kerner and Brentano.

The phenomenon of the "unconscious" anticipated in late scholasticism and particularly by Leibniz, now became the principal object of investigation of psychology in the wake of Kant, the Romantic poets, Goethe, and his friend Carus; and the basic outlines of both psychology and biology were drawn by J. O. de Lamettrie. Although his work *Histoire naturelle de l'âme* (1745) was publicly burned, his two works of 1748, *L'homme machine*, presenting a mechanistic conception of the world, and *L'homme plante*, which began comparative biology, anticipated later events, and, together with Diderot and the Encyclopedists, laid the groundwork for the announcement that God is dead.

Since the super-terrestrial no longer affects man, the subterranean surges upwards. Dupuis assembles the first compendium of myth during the first years of the French Revolution;[4] at about the same time, as Goethe reported from Rome, Karl Philipp Moritz begins to "compose his mythology of the ancient gods in a purely human sense," that is, as an anthropocentric mythology.[5] It came out in 1791 just a year before the book of Dupuis; and they were followed in 1800 by Noël's attempt to systematize the rationally unfathomable myths in his *Dictionnaire de la Fable*.[6] His work was continued in Germany by Creuzer and Herder.

Archaeology begins with Winckelmann and leads directly to the discovery by Schliemann of the historical levels of Troy (see above p. 101 f.). Goethe describes the scene of Faust's descent into the domain of the mothers and Helen (the Helen for whose sake the Hellenes destroyed Troy, thereby becoming historical) as the "dark gallery," and this "dark gallery" is an apt image of the subterranean excavations of archaeology and psychology. Geological and psychological levels dominate the conceptual world of investigations, henceforth oriented only toward the earth and man. These levels open up time to our view—time that is lost in the unknown and shines forth in origin, in Goethe's concepts of "primal phenomena," "primal words," "primal stone," "primal plant," and even in the "archetypes" of C. G. Jung. All such concepts vividly show the efforts undertaken to grasp the non-spatial. The unknown is no longer sought in theological, but rather researched in anthropological terms, and the search culminates in the discovery of "time" in its various modes of manifestation, whose common characteristic is their non-spatiality.

These suggestions should suffice to indicate the extent to which the "irruption of time" has transformed consciousness since the French Revolution. It was then that technology, as thought out by Leonardo da Vinci, began to become a reality, as did the interest in antiquity prefigured during the Renaissance; and the same holds true of archaeology, also toyed with in the Renaissance. The Unconscious, preformed as a term and concept by late scholasticism and by Leibniz, becomes the password of the scientific psychology then emerging. The constellations formed around 1500 become obvious by 1800 and irrupt in all areas of European applied knowledge. By 1900, the consciousness structure of the European has been transformed to the extent that he is able to express the consequences of this occurring mutation via new concepts, and to form them consciously on the basis of the newly emerging modes of realization.

The year 1900 is not only significant because of Planck's establishment of the quantum theory; it is the year Sigmund Freud published his *Interpretation of Dreams*. In 1902 de Vries successfully formulated his theory of mutations; in 1905 Einstein published his first theory of relativity and Freud his *Introductory Lectures on Psychoanalysis*. In 1910 Rilke's *Aufzeichnungen des Malte Laurids Brigge* is published, an "inner novel" stressing psychic events; and the novel, like Goethe's *Werther*, K. Ph. Moritz's psychological novel *Anton Reiser*,[7] the psychologically-tinged novels of Stendhal, the occultistic works of Maeterlinck, and even the four-dimensional space-time continuum of Einstein, is unthinkable without the discovery of *n*-dimensional, non-Euclidian geometry by Gauss, Goethe's contemporary, and by Riemann.

With Freud's *Interpretation of Dreams*, the formulation of the "unconscious" acquires common currency, pervading and altering the general consciousness. In terms of physics, "clock time" is an aspect of the fourth dimension, and likewise the "unconscious" represents in psychological terms another aspect of the fourth dimension. Research during recent decades into the unconscious, particularly by Freud and Jung, lead to results indicative of the essential root of the authentic fourth dimension, the achronon, or time-freedom, if we are only willing to regard these results and the terminology of this research into the psyche as a reflection of the basic aperspectival trend of our epoch.

The discovery of this basic trend is abetted by attitudes and positions in contemporary psychoanalysis which emphasize:

1) time as an intensifiable factor and as energy, and
2) the supersession of dualism; moreover, it provides evidence of
3) the initial manifestation and awareness of the pre-temporal, the time-free which can neither be conceptualized rationally nor experienced irrationally but can only be perceived arationally.

Let us turn our attention to the evidence in support of these three points, bearing in mind that we are deliberately restricting our discussion to psychoanalysis, thereby giving priority to the empirical rather than the experimental psychology. This is all the more permissible in that the pragmatic direction is ultimately an off-shoot of the experimental with an overly materialistic emphasis. Among examples of this (materialistic) direction we would mention the behaviorism of John B. Watson;[8] the psychology of biological inheritance or so-called "destiny analysis" of L. Szondi;[9] the physiological, engrammatic and mnemetic theories of R. Semon;[10] the theoretical as well as Gestalt psychology of D. Katz[11] and M. Wertheimer;[12] and the existential psychology of L. Binswanger[13] (who surpassed the lack-of-other relationship and the estrangement-from-the-other inherent in Heidegger's *Dasein* by introducing the theme of love). All these psychologies are, to a certain extent, intermediaries and valuable complements to the mainstream of psychology, although they manifest only fragmentarily the inception of the new consciousness. We can pass over them with a certain justification inasmuch as we have touched upon the significant, though hardly known, neurobiological research of von Monakow in the preceding chapter.[14]

In the results and concepts elaborated during the last three to four decades in psychoanalysis there are initial indications of characteristics of the new aperspectival consciousness structure, despite the problematic constellation imprinted on each psychology by its own subject matter. This constellation results from the ambivalence and polarity immanent in the psyche itself which colors all psychological assessments and expressions pertaining to it. By taking this into account we shall be able to understand the indications in accord with psychological research and theory. Such indications confirm that in this branch of knowledge too, there are aperspectival inceptions irrupting.

Now, with respect to 1): The new psychoanalysis is expressive of both the theme of time in general as well as of time in respect to its various aspects; in general inasmuch as the psyche or the unconscious is not comprehensible spatially; in terms of aspect inasmuch as the phenomenon of time is divested of its conceptual character and becomes recognizable as a new aspectuation and mode of manifestation. It was Sigmund Freud's courage, his willingness to take dreams seriously, that has opened both of these vistas; the effects of the "unconscious" were brought to awareness, and with these effects, an aspect of time that disclosed the multi-leveled nature of the phenomenon of time. As Einstein's fourth dimension and Planck's quantum theory resulted in the "discovery of time" for physics (see above p. 371), so psychoanalysis and the "interpretation of dreams" accomplished this for psychology.

In dreams the course of events is "more intense" and more rapid than in waking consciousness. By determining this, Freud shows that in dreams the succession of events is temporally compressed and condensed: dream time is distinct from clock or conceptual time.[15] Furthermore, the preoccupation with dreams has opened our understanding of creativity, which expresses itself at the moment of manifestation as a time-free act with clearly qualitative emphasis.[16]

Finally, because of its psychic spacelessness, the unconscious is definitely temporal as well as effectual, since for Jung "the structure of the psyche is not static, but dynamic."[17] In this sense Jung speaks of "psychic energy." This utterly contradicts earlier attempts by previous generations to localize the psyche in the static, spatial world of conceptuality. We must be careful not to misconstrue Jung's concept of psychic energy in an Aristotelian sense;[18] it is not a "forming principle," or presupposition, but a result of experience; it is not metaphysical but empirical. This psychic energy is "nothing other than the intensity of the psychic process."[19]

A later definition by G. R. Heyer speaks of the energy of the psyche as a "power field," thereby giving a particularly apt expression to the particular structure of psychic energy.[20] Although the concept "power field" of the psyche may remind us of the terminology of physics, it is nevertheless obvious that the non-spatiality of the psychic configuration is underscored by the field notion. Since the "field" is a two-dimensional surface, it corresponds to the two-dimensional nature of the psyche.[21]

If we are sufficiently bold as to consider the "unconscious" as an acategorical element, which is suggested by the spacelessness of the psyche, then the emergent awareness of the unconscious is nothing other than the psychic form of time's irruption into our consciousness. The unconscious also acquaints us with yet another mode of "time's" manifestation that could not have become fully valid until dreams were accepted as an expression of the unconscious. In its own way, this mode of manifestation reveals to us the relativity of time as well as its attendant intensity. The pursuit of the unconscious is the psychological expression of temporics.

Our questioning of the validity of the concept (or element) of the unconscious in no way invalidates it; rather our questioning must be understood as a concretion and differentiation of a general phenomenon that only gradually reveals all of its aspects. As we have already indicated in Part I, we can no longer speak today with impunity of the "unconscious," but only of degrees of intensity of consciousness (see p. 204), a terminological advance beyond the dualistic thought-cliché "unconscious:conscious" that extricates the highly differentiated structures of the various degrees of consciousness from this simplistic antithesis. (Incidentally, G. R. Heyer has reformulated our concept of "degrees of consciousness," using the more fortunate term "frequencies of consciousness," thus eliminating the last vestiges of its spatial and rational stasis.)[22]

We come to our second point, 2): the supersession of dualism in psychology. As our example of the terms unconscious:conscious demonstrates, terms still current today in the language of psychoanalysis, there do not seem to be grounds, at least in the area of psychoanalysis proper, for overcoming dualism. Moreover, we find in the present-day writings of the most prominent representatives of this branch of science recurrent reference to the psyche in terms of "opposition" although the psyche is actually polar (see our discussion in Part I, chapter 4, sections 3 and 4). It is of course understandable that a science dealing in an empirical manner with the irrational should choose to retain pre-eminently rationalistic concepts and modes of expression. Yet it must not be overlooked that the introduction of the concept of "ambivalence" by Bleuler (see above p. 206) signifies a fundamentally anti-dualistic shift in psychology. [23]

In the analytical psychology of C. G. Jung we can discern a manifest attempt to overcome dualism in terms of his two basic theses: the "theory of individuation" and the "quaternity theory." The theory of individuation strives toward achievement of a psychic wholeness of the "Self." This "Self" has nothing in common with that of Indian metaphysics popularized in the works of Paul Brunton;[24] it is only a "psychological factor"[25] wherein consciousness and the subconscious can achieve a "psychic totality." The Self is "a superordinate quantum above the conscious ego. It encompasses not only the conscious but the unconscious part of the psyche as well, and is, so to speak, a personality which *we* are too."[26]

Jolande Jacobi, who together with Toni Wolff is the authorized interpreter of Jung's analytic psychology, explains this statement as follows: "We know that unconscious processes have a compensatory and not a 'contrasting' relationship to consciousness; unconscious and conscious are not necessarily opposites. They complete each other, constituting a Self."[27] To a certain extent this Self is between the conscious and the unconscious, but "it is not only a middle point but also the circumference, as it were, encompassing the conscious as well as the unconscious. It forms the center of the psychic totality just as the ego is the center of consciousness."[28]

Seen in this way, Jung's theory of individuation, with its demand for a Self, shows itself to be an attempt at overcoming the psychic dualism that is the terminological heritage of Freud's materialistic psychoanalysis. That such an attempt bears the seeds of extremely dangerous complications has been duly noted by V. E. von Gebsattel,[29] inasmuch as the "Self" becomes an "inner God," or merely an anthropologized and psychologized form of the dethronement of God. We have indicated in another context the human dangers attendant upon the process of individuation;[30] similar dangers are evident in Jung's quaternity postulate. Yet it is significant that he tries to surpass the rational without necessarily falling into irrationality. Jung's sense of the inadequacy of the "trinity" is the reason for his emphasis on the emergent consciousness of the "fourfold," and he is at least partially successful in his attempt to displace the trinity by quaternity. This, too, is tantamount to the annulment, or at least the abolition, of God. In one of the quaternity constellations which Jung adduces, "Satan" appears as the fourth aspect;[31] and in his tetralogically-constituted theory of functions, the fourth function is always "inferior."

The danger is that this may all seem obligatory and deterministic, yet this need not be the case; regarded rationally, everything psychic (including the constellation mentioned above and its psychological interpretation) is not, for the most part, compelling. This is apparent from another passage where Jung posits the feminine element as a fourth aspect in place of "Satan" and the inferior function,[32] thereby extending the trinity by the feminine element as such. This extrication from the trinity is doubtless a symptom of the need to surpass three-dimensional rationality and the consequent dualism of good and evil. As a psychologist, Jung rightly restricts himself to a psychological interpretation, but by so doing, he psychologizes in an extremely one-sided manner the general impulse felt today to outgrow three-dimensionality.

And yet we find in this psychological attempt an attempt at integration in an undogmatic manner befitting the symbolic form of representation of the psyche. It is of interest here to note the interpretation given this question by one of Jung's best-known students, J. Jacobi. On this incorporation of the feminine aspect into the trinity and the resultant transformation into quaternity, and also on the psychological attempt at four-dimensionality, she writes: "Along with the number three, an archetype and age-old symbol of the 'purely abstract spirit,' particularly in the Christian religion, Jung has posited the number four as a most significant archetype for the psyche. With this fourth member, the 'pure spirit' receives its 'corporeity,' and thus an adequate form of manifestation for physical creation. Together with the masculine spirit—which represents merely one-half of the world—the four contains the feminine, corporeal aspect as its counterpole, rounding out the first into a whole."[33]

It is true that Jung inadequately differentiates between trias (triadicity) and trinity (see above p. 86 f.). It is also true that he equates "Satan" or the "shadow"—the "inferior function" in the Faustian sense—with "woman" (also in the Faustian sense as Helen or the "eternal feminine" leading us onward) via his tetralogical formulation or symbolization as supraordinate elements, thereby making a psychological attempt at a "totality" beyond dualism. Nonetheless, Jung's psychological attempt is an attempt to overcome the three-dimensional paternal world,[34] even though the overcoming is couched in the ambivalent expression befitting the psyche. He does reach out "beyond dualism" via a conscious regression into polarity, while his rational interpretation of the psyche is an effort to break out of the dualism; not backwards but forward, not into a mythical two-dimensionality but into an integral four-dimensionality. Such an endeavor stands in the twilight of maximum ambivalence peculiar to the psyche; and the fact that Jung as a psychologist remains particularly attached to the psychic shows up the particular inherent weakness of his discipline—namely, the lack of any spiritual moment; it is here psychologized, leaving us with only the psychological configuration spoken of earlier.[35] A totality is achieved here only by acceptance of the other pole; man is degraded to a mere vehicle and functionary of the psyche. The totality achieved via the "Self" supposedly places man beyond good and evil—a rational deduction—but can only be achieved with the ambivalence of the psyche, and consequently with no binding or obligatory quality.

Thus, from the standpoint of aperspectivity, nothing has been surpassed or superseded; it is a psychological attempt—which is impossible to carry out—at the concretion of the spiritual and as such is symptomatic of our age. But here in a psychologized image of the world, the diaphainon, "translucence"—itself not bound to polarity any more than to dualism since it renders darkness as well as brightness transparent or diaphanous—cannot be an effectual spiritual element. Notwithstanding this, Jung's attempt, within the given limits and boundaries of psychology, remains an admirable conception, and "viewed psychologically," it must be deemed a decisive and courageous step toward aperspectival four-dimensionality.

It is to this psychologized four-dimensionality that J. Jacobi alludes when she observes that "in a transitional age, whose signature is a transition from 'three' to 'four-dimensional' thinking as a result of discoveries in the sciences, notably in modern physics, it is perhaps more than fortuitous that the modern orientation of analytical psychology, C. G. Jung's psychology of complexes, has chosen the archetype four as a central structural concept for its theory. Just as in modern physics it was necessary to incorporate time as the fourth dimension (and regard it as essentially distinct from the three well-known dimensions) in order to acquire an encompassing view of the totality, so too the 'inferior,' the fourth function, the 'totally other' in psychology—despite its distinctness—had to be differentiated and incorporated into psychology for an integral understanding of the psyche, just as time was incorporated into physics. If only because of this fundamental novelty and its consequences in the conception and treatment of the psyche, the psychology of Jung may take its place alongside those sciences that are fundamentally transforming the previous image of the world and shaping a new one along common guiding principles."[36]

More revealing than the general soundness of these remarks is the endeavor that they bespeak, since their full comprehension is difficult because of the psychological factors involved. We can in any event observe that analytical psychology not only strives to master dualism by a re-awakening of symbolic thinking, but also endeavors to go beyond the two-dimensional psychic and three-dimensional rational data. These attempts could be possible without ambivalence or ambiguity if analytical psychology were to consider spiritual indications that directly or indirectly touch it, as for example has been done in the area of psycho-religion by V. E. von Gebsattel[37] and Josef Goldbrunner,[38] in psychosomatic medicine in the work of A. Mitscherlich,[39] in psycho-biology as demonstrated by the research of G. R. Heyer,[40] and in biology along the lines set down by A. Portmann.[41]

Although Jung's later research is definitely not directed toward the perception of the spiritual, one of his earlier basic concepts, that of "archetypes," is definitely arational in nature. To preclude misunderstandings let us first examine the subject of his last works, since their terminology could give rise to confusion as to basic concepts. We refer to the phenomena which underlie "synchronicity," which Jung investigated during his last decade. By synchronicity he understands "a perceptually experienced parallelism or simultaneous occurrence of external or internal processes which cannot be causally related."[42]

The collection of examples that Jung cites for these processes of a parapsychological nature (psycho-physical coincidences) clearly shows that they belong to the magic structure and are, consequently, spaceless and timeless;[43] their "explanation" is to be found in the natural "relationality" of the magic structure. The non-causal coincidence of processes is based on what we have called the "vital nexus" (p. 48) and should not be mistaken for acausality. Events not comprehensible causally belong to the magic realm and are pre-rational phenomena. Acausal events, by contrast, being free of causation, are arational by nature and as such cannot be experienced vitally (only the magical is experienceable vitally (p. 250)); they are perceived if at all only aperspectivally. Viewed in this light, Jung's concept of synchronicity has nothing in common with acausality and arationality, although it brings to our awareness the reality of pre-rational and pre-causal phenomena; and therein lies its merit. (We shall return to this concept in chapter 8 since it deals primarily with parapsychological phenomena.)

But we have a different situation with respect to the other of Jung's concepts which anticipates an arational world perception from the standpoint of analytical psychology. This brings us to our third point:

3) the emergence of arational time-freedom in the concept of "archetypes" developed in analytical psychology. What are the "archetypes," the primal images inherent in the psyche and verifiable in dreams, fantasies, myths, stories, poetry, and other psychically-conditioned manifestations? Let us limit our discussion to the various definitions of this important concept of Jung, as well as to some individual comments by von Gebsattel, J. Jacobi, and A. Portmann.

Jung speaks of these phenomena as follows: "They represent or personify certain instinctual factors of the dark, primitive psyche, that is, of the actual if invisible roots of consciousness."[44] They are an "eternal presence, and it is merely a question of whether or not consciousness perceives this presence."[45] "Their form is comparable to the axial system of a crystal which is preformed, as it were, in the bittern, without itself possessing a material existence. This existence first appears as the ions, and later the molecules, are attracted and arranged. In itself, the archetype is an empty, formal element; a *facultas praeformandi,* or an a priori given possibility of representational form. . . . As to the determination of the form, a comparison with the formation of crystals is again illuminating: the axial system determines merely the steriometric structure, but not the concrete form of the individual crystal. The latter may be small or large, or endlessly varied; only the axial system is constant in its principally invariable geometric relations. The same is true of an archetype; its nature can be defined in principle, and it possesses an invariable core of meaning, but this determines its mode of appearance only in principle, never concretely."[46]

The multiplicity of appearances of the archetypes in imagistic form Jung explains in another context: "What an archetypical content primarily expresses is first of all expressed as a simile or metaphor. If it speaks of the sun and identifies it with the lion, the king, the hoard of gold guarded by a dragon, and of the power of man's life and health, it expresses neither the one nor the other, but rather an unknown third which to a greater or lesser degree is expressed by all the metaphors—although, to the perpetual chagrin of the intellect, it remains unknown and inexpressible. For this reason the scientific intellect repeatedly falls prey to the temptation of trying to explain it."[47]

The concept of the archetype Jung has borrowed from St. Augustine, without, however, incorporating Augustine's religious-philosophical definition, as Paul

Schmitt for example has done.[48] The concept is, it is true, akin to the Platonic "idea"; but in contrast to it, the archetypes are not expressions of highest perfection residing in an eternity remote from mundane concerns. Rather, they have a bi-polar structure and are, in a way, the "organs of the soul," or, in the words of Bergson, *les éternels incréés*.[49]

Von Gebsattel has shown that the archetypes can be understood numinously, while Jung, in contrast, emphasizes their biological-neurological anchorage and designates them from the outset as genetically or engrammically determined factors (the term is Semon's). The materialistic assurance doubtless results from the stamp of the era of declining materialism on Jung's mode of thought, from which he finally was able to extricate himself during his last decades. Elsewhere we have demonstrated this materialistic tie of some of his essential concepts, and noted the necessity that they be superseded.[50] A. Portmann has underscored this same necessity, and speaks significantly in this connection of the "initially [i.e., in early childhood] wide-open structural capacities" and their "imprint" by life itself, so "that in the field of psychology one should be extremely cautious about assuming the inheritance of the psychic structures discovered."[51]

Jung himself abetted the liberation of the archetypes from biological determinism (in a secondary, not primary sense) by later referring to them as "archetypical structures";[52] they are to be understood as "power centers and power fields of the unconscious."[53] Portmann points to the primacy of man's "open capacities" in the formation of these psychic structures. His justifiable demand for a purely descriptive rather than genetic formulation of the "archetypes" surely represents a decisive step toward their proper understanding, since the open capacities which Portmann shows to be primary place the genetic inheritance of these capacities into a determined rather than determining position.

To what, then, do these archetypical structures point? Although analytical psychology speaks of structures, this does not necessarily make them conform to those of physics or biology. The justification for considering atomic, biological, and archetypical-psychological structures as a common aperspectival manifestation is not based on the use of the same terminology, but on what we might say lies "behind" or (temporally) "before" whatever they circumscribe. It is based on the pretemporal and pre-spatial "state" which is not rationally comprehensible or imaginable, but which they make evident. The becoming-evident of this state on the basis of these formulations is the same as their coming to consciousness, which transforms this state into aperspectival time-freedom, whence it becomes perceptible.

We must consider it fundamental here that none of the structural concepts named would be conceivable without the merging effectivity of four-dimensionality. In other words, in each instance the rational dualism must be surpassed and "time," in its appropriate form of manifestation, must be included in the deliberations: for physics, as clock time and the energy quantum; for biology, as an inductive element as well as a variable intensity; for psychology, as the effectivity of the unconscious and as psychic energy. These formulations denote acategorical elements, and not categorical quantities; the acategorical elements over-determine and transform the three-dimensional system into four-dimensionality and make possible the arational perception of what is no longer rationally representable.

The concept of the archetype may be regarded as an incipient manifestation of the aperspectival world, for despite its psychological determination, it is ultimately apsychic. Only the forms of appearance of the archetypes are psychic phenomena, which in their allegory and imagery evidence an irrational character. The archetypes themselves and the "archetypical structures" are "eternally present"; this means that they are time-free. They are such that although "lacking a material existence" they preform the psyche. This means that they are not only immaterial, as the psychic is in and of itself, but amaterial; they underlie and preform the psyche achronically and amaterially. Moreover, to the "intellect they are unknown and inexpressible," that is, they are not merely irrational but arational insofar as their incomprehensibility and inconceivability do not prevent us from raising them into perceptibility.

To the same extent that it is true of atomic and biological structures, the "archetypical structures" are not representable and inconceivable. They point to a rationally unrealizable "state" before time and space, and indeed before space-timelessness. That is the case when the archetypical structures are regarded as symbolic manifestations of what "lies" before space-timelessness; when they are so perceived, then the achronon appears in them, clearly revealing that like all symbolic expressions, the archetypes too are of pretellurian origin (see p. 221). This state was discovered in psychology via the concept of "archetypical structures"; it was discovered in physics by C. F. von Weizsäcker (see p. 374 f.), and in biology by A. Portmann in his notion of "immanence" (see above p. 382 f.). Thus, mere rationality and irrationality have been overdetermined toward arationality; and in psychological research too, the achronon, time-freedom, is becoming perceptible.

2. Philosophy

Our view that the perspectival-rational age is coming to a close is also reinforced by philosophy in such a way as to leave nothing to be desired in the way of clarity.

In Martin Heidegger's book *Holzwege*[54] there is a chapter written in 1946 entitled "The Saying of Anaximander." This saying deals with the presumably earliest expression of Western thought. And because we in the West feel such an affinity for what is contained in this philosopheme, Heidegger describes us as "the latest late arrivals of philosophy."

Philosophy, which began with the Greek thinkers at the moment of mutation from the mythical to the mental consciousness, is coming to a close. This is indicated by Heidegger's eschatological (end-of-time) statements that follow the remark cited above: "Are we on the brink of the most enormous transformation of the entire earth and of the time of historical space wherein it is suspended? Are we on the eve of a night leading toward a new dawn? Are we about to depart on the trek into the historical landscape of earth's evening? [Tr. note: Heidegger is here playing on the ambiguities of the word for the West or Occident in German, *Abendland*, "land of the evening."] Is this land of evening just now coming into being? . . . Are we today "occidental" in the sense that the night of the world comes on only via our transition? What do we care for all the historically calculated philosophies of history that dazzle us with the superficialities of the historically assembled material, attempting to explain history without ever considering the bases of their explanations from the essence of history, and this from Being itself? *Are* we the late-comers? Or are we at the same time the early arrivals of the dawn of an entirely new age which has already left behind our present conceptions of history?"[55]

There is a certain irony in the fact that Heidegger, in his secularized "Theology without God" (as Egon Vietta has designated French Existentialism which derives from Heidegger),[56] is led to eschatological attitudes, whereas Alois Dempf has given us a "Self-critique of Philosophy"[57] with which he reduces the anthropological-existential point of view to a reasonable dimension via a grand survey of philosophy (though without belaboring a Thomistic viewpoint as so often happens with other Catholic philosophers).

The weighty objections that can be mounted against all existentialist efforts, be they the existence-illumination of Jaspers, the existential-analytic fundamental ontology of Heidegger, or the psychoanalysis-infected existentialism of Sartre, must not deter us from an appraisal of existentialism. Aside from the spiritual impoverishment and the anthropocentric reductionism evident from the treatment of human existence by prominent thinkers today as their exclusive concern, there is also a certain ambiguity best illustrated by Heidegger, an ambiguity even conceded to Heidegger by one of his best friends.[58] By this very ambivalence Heidegger's thought demonstrates the Janus-faced aspect of our epoch, most acutely manifest in the German world. The Anglo-Saxon regions by contrast have largely ignored the European anxiety about existence which underlies all existentialism. Yet even there, as Heinrich Straumann has recently demonstrated,[59] existential seeds can be seen germinating particularly in the pragmatism formulated at the turn of the century by William James and John Dewey.

We have a very different situation with the phenomenology founded by Husserl. To the extent that it is known at all outside the German-speaking world, it is mostly rejected (as for example by Guido de Ruggiero).[60] Phenomenology is preeminently a qualitative theory of essence and, as Hedwig Conrad-Martius emphasizes,[61] forms a counterpole particularly to radical existentialism. As its earliest interpreter, Adolf Reinach, points out, it is concerned "not with existence but with essence: with all possible modes of consciousness as such, irrespective of where, if, and when they occur."[62] We will have more to say about phenomenology later in our discussion.

In *Being and Time* (1927) Heidegger has exhausted and driven to its limits the assertions of speculative, private philosophy and, by hyperformulation and hyperdifferentiation, has placed its very value into question. Heidegger no longer basks in the light of previous philosophies but stands in the twilight of transition. The question as to the "meaning of being," and the previous reply that it is a "being toward death," a psychic mood transposed into an ontic position, has been succeeded by a new ambiguity. The circuitous route to this ambiguity led through the mythical realm, which is tantamount to an implicit recognition of the psyche: "the paths through the woods" (*Holzwege*).

In a patently ambiguous manner, Heidegger's *Holzwege* does, however, contain an uncompelling and distorted inception of an arational nature. These "paths through the woods" exhibit neither the lack of relationships nor the extreme existential isolation of contemporary man, although according to Grimm's dictionary a wood path is a path into the "woods for practical and economic reasons, not for connecting two places."[63] The pragmatic emphasis in this definition is as significant as the human unrelatedness which is further underscored by the suggested "contrast between the wood path and the straight and 'correct' street."[64] It is symptomatic that although the straight and directed has formed the bases of Western thought since at least 500 B.C., Heidegger recognizes them as being inadequate. It is only regrettable that while rejecting the mental-rational, Heidegger regresses to the irrational and is only able to intimate the illumination of the arational via occasional opalescent "luminescences" (see p. 410 below).

The basic change in philosophy that aims at its own supersession is not only evident in Heidegger. If we pursue the general trend of contemporary philosophical schools, it is apparent that spatially limited, conceptually bound thinking of a rational character is beginning to give way to new modes of realization that are truly aperspectival in nature. The inceptual supersession of the three-dimensional mentality in philosophy (and therefore its own supersession) is manifest in:

1) the incorporation of "time" as a proper element in philosophical thought;
2) the admission of the inadequacy of rationality; and
3) the turn toward the Whole and toward diaphaneity.

As regards 1), the problem of time has been moving into the philosophical forefront since the turn from the eighteenth to the nineteenth century. We have repeatedly remarked on the general falsification of time and the neglect of the time question (also in connection with the work of Werner Gent). Georges Poulet has subsequently made an important contribution to this subject in his *Études sur le Temps Humain*; in his foreword he specifically emphasizes that the time question, in our sense, did not yet pose a problem for the Christian Middle Ages.[65]

It was most likely Pascal who paved the way for the "irruption of time" which came about indirectly and is visible today only after it has become clear what of time's immanent essence was obscured by the false employment of the "concept" of time.

At the very moment when Descartes introduces his analytic method—a method which is invariably quantitative—Pascal is drafting his philosophy of the heart, preeminently valuative and qualitative in character. Let us ask, then, in Romano Guardini's words, "What is the heart in Pascal's sense? We find that it is above all not an expression of emotion in contrast to logic; it is not a feeling in contrast to the intellect; it is not a soul as opposed to spirit. *Coeur* is itself spirit and a mode of spiritual manifestation. The act of the heart is an act 'giving' knowledge. Certain objects come to be present only by the act of heart . . . We are face to face here with a basic structure of man . . . The phenomenon is inseparable from the relationship of essence to value; 'value' is the preciousness of things."[66] For Pascal the heart "is the organ of the value-properties of Being and all beings."[67]

This interpretation, based on Pascal's texts, is significant because it excludes the merely rational as well as the purely irrational. Moreover, Pascal himself emphasizes the notion of *netteté*, "neatness," a concept that contains "the aspect of clarity and purity."[68] In this connection Pascal says: "There are two kinds of spirits: one is geometric [in Guardini's words, "abstract, logical"] and the other could be called 'de finesse.' The way of perceiving that befits the first is slow, tenacious, and inflexible; the second has a certain flexibility of thought and is capable of orienting itself toward the various lovable aspects of whatever it loves."[69] Although indirectly, this expresses what we have called perspectival ("inflexible") thinking, as well as the encompassing clarity and transparency of our reciprocal perception and impartation of truth in aperspectivity.

Pascal also introduces two definitely time-bound concepts: that of *ennui*, "boredom," and that of *divertissement*, temporal "diversion." Though at first negatively, he grasps the efficacy of the dammed-up and spatialized energies; it is precisely the time aspects that are suggested in these utterly new notions which Guardini interprets theologically,[70] while Herbert Plügge evaluates them in terms of psychology and anthropology.[71] G. Poulet, on the other hand, does not touch on these important concepts at all.[72]

Ennui and *Divertissement* are expressions of man's search for genuine time. As Pascal writes, man should in fact be able to "sit in his room at peace,"[73] in other words, to have time. The conscious quest for time begins notably with Hegel who, in his *Phenomenology of the Spirit* (1807), was the first to deliberately treat the subject of "work." But work relates to property as time relates to space!

In the wake of Hegel follow the vast analyses of time. Kierkegaard introduces the concept of temporality in his *Concept of Anxiety* (1844) by relating the individual moment to eternity, thus opening an aspect of time "of which the Greeks lacked knowledge." Similarly, the "culmination of Greek art in sculpture lacked the momentary glance (of the eye). . . . Christianity, utterly in contrast, presents the image of God as an eye."[74]

Following Kierkegaard is Bergson, who takes up the analysis of time in his first work, *Time and Freedom* (1889). And yet time and freedom are incompatible with determinism; their conjunction explodes the "systems." As to freedom, Jaspers has remarked that according to Kant, "reason cannot grasp how freedom is possible."[75] Here, following the incorporation of time, begins the definite escape from the hold of three-dimensional habits of thought. In *Time and Freedom* Bergson demonstrates that "each debate between the determinists and their adversaries includes a prior blending of duration with extension, succession with contemporaneity, and quality with quantity."[76] Consequently he devotes the first two chapters to the concepts of intensity and duration, which serve as a foundation for the subject of freedom in the third chapter.

This first work of Bergson (as well as his entire *oeuvre*) has pioneered the illumination of time's essence, and remains even today a fundamental influence on the formation of the new thinking for which his *chef d'oeuvre, Creative Evolution* (1907), has been decisive. In that work Bergson not only presents the distinction between *durée* and *temps*, "duration" and "time" (see p. 178), but also elucidates time's creative aspect: "Time is invention or it is nothing at all."[77]

With this, time is unfettered from space; it becomes space-free and acquires an independence which cannot be imputed to it merely by logical inference.[78] Nevertheless, a certain passing parallelism (if not in fact a dualism) is established between vital and physical forms of time. Bergson's "life-philosophy" (and his philosophical influence) is so well-known that it needs no exposition here; abetted by Nietzsche and Dilthey,[79] it went on to influence German vitalistic philosophy, notably that of L. Klages and Hermann Graf Keyserling (both of whom, regrettably, introduced serious misunderstandings). And later, in his confrontation with Hegel recorded in *Being and Time*, Heidegger somewhat willfully resolved the time question, the Hegelian conception that time is only a "perceived concept"[80] and that "the spirit, in accord with its essence, appears by necessity in time," via his own formulation of "temporalization," "primordial time," and "inner-temporality."[81] For Heidegger, "the spirit does not descend into time, but exists as an original temporalization of temporality."[82]

This is not the place to examine Heidegger's questionable interpretation of Bergson's definition of time;[83] but it should be noted that contemporaneously with *Being and Time* studies by Nicolai Hartmann, Gabriel Marcel and Alfred North

Whitehead were published which examine the problem of time from ontological, existential, and metaphysical viewpoints respectively. Husserl's decisive phenomenological contribution to this question (in his *Erfahrung und Urteil*) was not published until 1948.[84] Basing it on his work in transcendental logic (1929), Husserl furnished the incisive formulation that "space-thing constitution presupposes a time constitution" (p. 187, note 43).

This is in rough outline, indeed, very rough outline, a sketch of the temporic endeavors in philosophy since the "irruption of time" was manifested during the French Revolution. This crucial process has been described in a philosophical-historical recapitulation and summary by Werner Gent in his three books on time (1930-1934), which we have already mentioned (p. 178 and note 43, p. 187). We will return in the next chapter to the more sociologically oriented philosophies, notably to the Leninist interpretation of dialectical materialism, and to English realism whose extreme form is represented by North American pragmatism.

By now it ought to be evident to what extent the incorporation of and pervasive encounter with the question of time has brought about a fundamental change in philosophy. All aspects of time previously hidden by the "concept" of time are now visible, and its multi-leveled nature has become clear. At the same time, the recognition of time as intensity and quality, as an independent value and an inherent element, has exploded the formal-logical systems of previous philosophies. Philosophy is mutating from the spatially-bound representational and three-dimensional world into the four-dimensional perceptual world of aperspectival space-time–freedom. This means that philosophy is superseding itself. As a consequence of conscious over-determination by the achronon, the philosophemes—always tied to three-dimensional systems—are changing into four-dimensional eteologemes, that is, into pure utterances and impartation of truth via the increasing transparency of what is true.

With these assertions we are already in the complex of questions surrounding our second point. This we would like to consider not just from the stance of existential and vitalist philosophy, but also from that of philosophies with a psychological, as well as a logicistic and mathematical basis, whose impulses stem primarily from their encounter with the new physics. Although surprising with respect to logicism, these philosophies have in their own way ventured, or will have to venture, the leap out of their compulsion to purely rational systems and conceptualism.

As to 2), the admission of the inadequacy of rational thought is expressed in various ways even in the philosophical movement bearing the imprint of the eidetic sciences.[85] F. Gonseth, like Whitehead a mathematician and philosopher,[86] has designated this movement as a new "open philosophy." Its foundations lie in those sciences based on closed eidetic thinking. E. R. Jaensch has decisively contributed to the natural sciences, [87] and the Gonseth circle, with its publication *Dialectica*, edited by Gonseth, P. Bernays, and G. Bachelard, is representative of this new scientific philosophy.[88]

It was at the first meeting of the circle in Zürich (1938), where Jan Lukasiewicz developed his multi-valued propositional logic, which was further developed and refined by H. Reichenbach as "three-valued logic" (in his *Philosophische Grundlagen der Quantenmechanik*).[89] It has successfully opened up logic and extended the systemization in philosophy along lines necessitated by the new physics, notably by the indeterminacy of Planck's energy quantum. As an "open philosophy," it too attempts to grasp the arational consequences of the new physics without sacrificing rationality. Yet this attempt breaks up the previous foundations of philosophy, and it will be interesting to follow its further development, which seems secure as long as it takes into account merely physical time. How long that will be possible is another question.

Reichenbach's three-valued logic is based on the indeterminacy principle of the energy quantum discovered and formulated by Niels Bohr and Werner Heisenberg. Reichenbach defines the new logic as follows: "The usual logic is two-valued; it is constructed with the aid of the truth values 'true' and 'false.' Yet it is possible to introduce an intermediary truth value that could be designated as 'indeterminacy,' and to apply this truth value to the group of propositions which in the Bohr-Heisenberg interpretation are called 'meaningless.' . . . If we have a third truth value called 'indeterminacy,' then the *tertium non datur* is no longer the definitive formula; there is the tertium, an intermediary value represented by the logical condition 'indeterminate.' "[90]

As we have suggested (p. 376), C. F. von Weizsäcker's work on quantum logic may well become the philosophically decisive event of our epoch. Werner Heisenberg,[91] its true author or at least inspirer, remarks that this "non-Aristotelian" logic is more encompassing than previous endeavors of three-valued logic, and in its results can be compared to "non-Euclidian" geometry. It opens possibilities for thought which we urgently need to warrant the new reality, a reality whose coming to awareness was utlimately revealed by the discoveries of nuclear physics.

These instances of liberation from the hitherto closed system are highly significant, and we should observe that they were initiated by what we have called the arational "energy quantum," characterized by a temporal intensity value and potential time-freedom. Whether incorporation of the "third truth value" will turn out to be something other than a Trojan horse for philosophy remains to be seen. The danger is at least immanent in the case of Hans Reichenbach, although C. F. von Weizsäcker will most likely be able to avoid it. In any event, the previous compulsion to systematization has been undone; this in itself is an aperspectival inception within logicistic and mathematical philosophy.

The extent of this break-up is evident from a lecture of M. Bense on the results of the third meeting of the "Dialectica" group (1951)[92]. In his words, "Open philosophy" is a philosophy "without ideological tendencies or the ghost of an absolute." It works "with open concepts, is distrustful of an unalterable position, and shuns the prison of fixed concepts." This is quite evidently a rejection of what we have called the perspectival fixity of space-bound conceptuality. "Open thinking," as this group calls its mode of realization, is an aperspectival endeavor, and at the same time an admission of the inadequacy of the previous rational mode of realization (although, via expansion, differentiation, and derigidification rationality is adapted to new elements and events).

All of this has been accomplished without reference to psychology, although Karl Jaspers (in his *Psychology of World-Views*)[93] and later C. G. Jung have discovered the determining influence of specific psychic attitudes that give each philosophy its decisive stamp. This has demonstrated the subjective aspect of each philosopheme, which has only a limited and sectored objective correctness: a most disquieting finding, which understandably generally evokes emotional reactions. This finding has not only revealed the limits of philosophy—limits are always spatially determined—but has also weakened the claim by philosophy of universal validity and objectivity.

Consequently, the very structure of philosophy itself, its claim to exclusive validity, has been placed into question from the existentialist position of Jaspers and Sartre, who both introduce psychological factors (as opposed to Heidegger). And since philosophy is the preponderant expression of the mental structure, this has upset the exclusive validity and dominance of the mental structure itself. Just as the mental consciousness is here placed into question, or at least an attempt made to relativize it, so did Aristotle bring his irony to bear on the mythical consciousness of his day while himself consolidating the new mental consciousness. (Irony always reveals the attempt to achieve detachment.) In his *Metaphysics* he speaks of the "mythical embellishments" used by the ancients to "convince the masses to believe in certain entities" (the gods).[94]

The weakening of the exclusive validity and predominance of the mental structure is clearly expressed in the existentialist relationship to subject and object: "All existentialists reject the differentiation between subject and object and thereby devalue intellectual knowledge in philosophy. According to them, true knowledge is not gained by the intellect, but by the living experience with reality."[95] (Yet it is precisely this emphasis on "lived experience" that exposes existentialism's false start toward superseding the subject-object dualism!) Or, in Heidegger's words: "Thinking begins when we have experienced that reason, glorified through the centuries, is the most obstinate adversary of thinking."[96]

Existentialism is not alone in discarding the purely rational (and thus dualistic) mode of thought. The same is true of the "transcendental logic" advanced primarily by W. Szilasi in his work *Macht und Ohnmacht des Geistes;*[97] it too contains an aperspectival inception, possibly a decisive one. Szilasi proceeds from the radical change of stance achieved by Georg Simmel, who wrote that "transcendence is immanent in life."[98] This signal insight was further heightened by Szilasi's differentiation between the concepts of "transcendent" and "transcendental"; transcendental logic demonstrates that postulation of transcendence is no longer tenable or necessary. This consideration alone already manifests a supersession of dualism, since the immanent world, our so-called reality, is no longer opposed to an ultimately unattainable transcendent world.

In philosophy, this transcendent world was the limit, or what we have called the perspectival point; all thought only came as far as the limiting point where immanence turned into transcendence. Thus the supersession of immanence was possible only through a metabolic attitude, a regression into the unperspectival, irrational world. As a result of Simmel's formulation and Szilasi's demonstration, which indicate that the transcendent is not a separate region of the world but a transcendentality, an immanent power or possibility of being—that is, indeed the basic possibility of our being as such—the perspectivally-fixed understanding of the world *opens up*, since now the irrelevant perspectival point is no longer there and hence need not be superseded or transcended.

The about-face or change into the opposite is thus no longer necessary. Man no longer needs to recoil from a limit of thought and revert to psychism, into the "captivity of the soul," nor is he required to remain in the cul-de-sac of perspectival fixity; rather in him and in the world an aperspectival vista or perception opens. Surely it is not fortuitous that Szilasi's notable demonstration includes the formulations of a "more original time," of the relationship of transcendence to time, as well as fundamental assertions about "spiritual being" and "Being-spirit."[99] In addition, his statements accomplished an important further step: the supersession of the extreme secularity and anthropological barrenness, indeed, wretchedness of the exclusively existential position and quest.

There could hardly be a clearer expression stating the rejection of the validity of rationalism, with its inherent dualism, and of the denunciation of rationalism as such than in the above examples. It is only natural that precisely in existentialism the relationship of this not-yet-secured arational position initially led to mostly "negative" results: to a kind of distress and anxious helplessness. This arational position is a threat only if we fail to surmount the emptiness, abyss, and nothingness that are transiently attendant upon the rejection of every old position. *Being and Time* expresses this precarious and ambiguous situation which Sartre later intensified; yet it is surmountable, and there are indications that it is being superseded.

This brings us to 3): the turn toward the whole and diaphaneity in recent philosophy. It is expressed in the renunciation of the demand for conceptualization, an act which permits the mutation from the three-dimensional mentality into four-dimensional integrality of the whole. The traditional philosopheme consequently becomes an eteologeme.

Where are we to find such aperspectival indications in philosophy? First, in Heidegger's changed position, and second in certain results of E. Husserl's phenomenology. Besides Bergson, Husserl is undoubtedly the most decisive thinker of the preceding generation.

The phenomenological philosophy founded by Husserl does not proceed from the eidetic sciences, nor does it investigate contingent facts. It proceeds descriptively, and its essential object consists of the essential interconnections which are gradually envisaged via intuition.[100] The emphasis is no longer on the categorical systems but, without denying them, on the emergence of concerns characteristic of the essence of aperspectivity: to see not only through interconnections, but through the essential interconnections. Moreover, Husserl's term "pure consciousness" elevates Dilthey's vitalistic and magically underscored theory of lived-experience to a certain transparency. Husserl's formulation rests to a great extent on the notion of intentionality which he adopted from Brentano. In the second chapter of his *Ideas of Pure Phenomenology and Phenomenological Philosophy,* Husserl has laid out the "General Structures of Pure Consciousness."[101] It would seem that behind the dividing wall of phenomenological terminology the same basic trend in philosophy becomes evident that we have discerned as being inherent in other disciplines. Our concept of systasis, which together with system make synairesis possible, may be seen as a terminological transfer of the phenomenological notion of the illumination of essential interconnections.

Heidegger, too, takes up the concept of "pure consciousness" introduced by his teacher Husserl.[102] And it is significant to note that Heidegger, who himself points to the limitations of mere "representation" or "conceptualization," frequently speaks of the "transparency" of certain states of affairs and thoughts.[103] To be sure, transparency for Heidegger is always related to ontology; but regardless of its intent, it is symptomatic that in his attempt to clarify Being as a mode of realization, he speaks of emerging transparency and not of living, experiencing, and representing.

Szilasi also employs this new figure of speech when he notes that the limitation of man to only one possibility of being imperils that very being, a peril we can counter by "making transparent the harmonious interconnection of forces of being as effectively lived power."[104] Here, in transcendental-philosophical terms, is an expression of our own attempts to clarify consciousness structurations: man is always placed into question if he sees only one possibility of being as his mode of realization and ascribes exclusiveness to only the magical, the mythical, or the mental structure. Only the diaphanous "verition" of all consciousness structures and the efficacious modes of being that they make possible allow that "presentation" of which Szilasi speaks in which "the 'was' and the 'will be' " vanish. "The whole is at once. The 'was' and the 'will be' disssolve absolute presentiality, that is, they dissolve time."(!)[105] This diaphaneity is further expressed in other statements of Heidegger: in what he defines as the "dimension of truth" and the "luminescence of being"; or when he speaks of the "deconfined whole of openness" as being "beyond numerical calculation"; or when he clarifies Rilke's statement regarding the "sphere of Being" as "Being as a whole" and points out that "This sphere of Being and its sphericality we must never objectively conceptualize."[106]

To determine whether these formulations derived from ontology are related to our concepts, which originate in consciousness structures and their mutations, we must examine them briefly. It should be noted that we do not intend to interpret them aperspectivally, but only to investigate whether there is an inherent affinity or common tendency among the rather similar designations that derive from various sources. Merely an "accidental" coincidence of terminology carries no weight of proof; the correspondences acquire import only when the basic trend emerges from or can be divined in the variously acquired and diversely conditioned terminologies.

What emerges through the translucence of Heidegger's "dimension of truth" is, in philosophical terms, what we have called in terms of physics the fourth dimension or in our circumlocution the integral (and integrating) dimension. His definition of truth as "unhiddenness,"[107] expressed by the Greek word alétheia, is a first indication of this constellation.[108] It is expressed even more clearly through his dissociation from the current mental-rational interpretation of truth: "The so-called critical concepts of truth, which since Descartes base truth on certainty, are mere variations on the assumed notion of truth as correctness. This familiar essence of truth, the correctness of representation, stands and falls on the basis of truth as unhiddenness of essents."[109] Aside from the fact that the expression "correctness of representation" parallels our discussion of mentality, Heidegger further remarks that "beyond the essent, yet not away from it, but proceeding from it, something else happens: an open region is present among the essents as a whole; it is a clearing, a luminescence."[110]

Does his "luminescence of Being" tend toward what we have called the achronon, space-time–freedom? There are indications of such possible kinship. For the luminescence is "thought from the side of the essent, more Being than essent. This open middle is not encompassed by the essents; rather the illumined midst itself, like the dimly-known nothingness, encompasses all essents."[111] This ontological definition of the "illumining midst" as nothingness suggests our description of pretemporal and prespatial efficacy (luminescence). "Luminescence" can be terminologically transposed to describe the emergent consciousness of the space-time–free middle, the "clearing" which is perceptible only as space-time–freedom (and not conceivable in Cartesian or scientific terms).

Despite the formidable difficulties in relating the various ontological aspects with aperspectivally realizable etiological veracities, it appears that the "luminescence of Being" is already "more" than, or different from mere philosophical definition of ontological aspects; it would seem to be etiological veracity. All the more so, inasmuch as such veracity makes illusory the implicit antithesis between transcendence and immanence, for "the luminescence into which the essent is situated is in itself at the same time concealment."[112] Transcendence and immanence are only differing forms of the presence of "clearing" or the achronon. Here the irrational and the rational are superseded by the inherent arationality of the achronon: they become perceptible in transparency (diaphaneity) as a "dimension of truth."

Heidegger also speaks of the luminescence or clearing as "openness."[113] He proceeds from Parmenides' construction of Being ($\H{o}\nu$) "as a well-rounded sphere" (in Heidegger's phrase, "the presence of the present"), from Rilke's notion of "the real, holy and full sphere and roundness of Being" as well as from Rilke's "world-immanent-space" and Pascal's "logic of the heart." Heidegger has written: "In his invisible, innermost heart, man is first inclined toward the loved: the ancestors, the dead, childhood, and those to come.[114] This places it into its widest compass which reveals itself as the sphere of presence of the whole, intact relationship. This presence, to be sure, like utilitarian consciousness and calculating activity, is one of immanence. Yet the immanence of non-utilitarian consciousness remains in the inner space, which for all of us is beyond quantitative calculation and can freely overflow the limits into the whole, the open."[115]

These considerations lend to the "sphere of Being" a transparency not attained by either Parmenides or Rilke. The imagistic-mythical relation of Parmenides, and the expressly magic confinement of Rilke, both of which have only potential transparency, are here surpassed. In his own way, Heidegger points to what we would call Rilke's magical attunement and interwovenness: "The sphere of Being named here, i.e., of essent as a whole, is the openness as well as the closure of the limitless interflux and hence reciprocally effectual pure energies."[116]

Despite the complex and multi-leveled relationships of the entire "state of affairs," the emergence of such "concepts" as "non-utilitarian consciousness" to complement the calculating, spatializing "utilitarian consciousness" is revealing, particularly as their emergence into consciousness "opens the entire sphere of presence of whole, intact relationship"; time changes into the originary present due to the recognition of the "deconfined whole of openness." Thus the de-spatialization of the three-dimensional spatial world, characteristic of the utilitarian consciousness, is over-determined by the "non-utilitarian" consciousness. While discussing Rilke's notion of "completeness" as it pertains to the "sphere of Being," Heidegger points out that it may be interpreted only "with respect to Being as completeness of all of its aspects." This "concept," perceiving the whole as a "sphere of Being," is definitely aperspectival. Perspectively we can see only one side; the completeness of all aspects of Being is perceptible only aperspectivally. With the sphere, the whole becomes transparent.

Thus through Heidegger it may have become evident that certain characteristics of the integral consciousness structure, the aperspectival world, are also manifest in the most recent philosophy.[117] Instead of conceptualization it speaks of emergent transparency; instead of a system it speaks of the whole; instead of mental "pyramidic" triplicity it speaks of the sphere as the sphere of the present of relationships to wholeness. And the extended and despatialized "three-valued" logic of Reichenbach is yet a further indication that the purely rationally-conceived world must accept the indeterminate and the previously non-usable. It must also accept that by setting out to surpass itself via this very acceptance, it is destined to surpass itself in the belief that its salvation lies in an expanded rationalism, a danger which may be countered by Weizsäcker via his "quantum logic" (pp. 407 and 417, note 117). Viewed as a whole, such inceptions of arationality are found also in the philosophical endeavors: existential, ontological, logical, and particularly in non-Aristotelian quantum logic.

The sphere is the expression of the aperspectival world. Aperspectivity is the "verition," the "awaring in truth" of the whole and consequently of its spiritual manifestation, the diaphainon, inasmuch as the whole is perceptible only as transparency wherein origin, also containing the entire future, is time-free present. To attain this consciously, without abandoning the "earlier" consciousness structures, is to overcome rationality in favor of arationality, and to break forth from mentality into diaphaneity.

1   Goethe, *Faust*, II, 1: "Finstere Galerie" scene.
2   Ibid.
3   Ibid.
4   C.-F. Dupuis, *Origine de tous les cultes ou religion universelle* (Paris: Agasse, 1792), x. For additional information see note 83 on p. 110 above. A German version of the one-volume edition of 1820 was published under the title *Ursprung der Gottesverehrung* (Leipzig: Eckhardt, 1910).
5   Karl Philipp Moritz was not only one of the early modern mythologists but also the initiator of the first "experimental psychology"; see his *Götterlehre* (Berlin: Schade, ⁵1819), also in Reclam's *Universalbibliothek*, no. 1081/1084. This circumstance is of import because it demonstrates the amalgamation of mythology and psychology at the inception of both sciences that still prevails today in the collaboration between K. Kerényi and C. G. Jung, as in their *Einführung in das Wesen der Mythologie* (Zürich: Rascher, 1941). As to the importance of K. Ph. Moritz' psychology, of which Goethe spoke in the fourteenth book of his *Poetry and Truth*, see the essay on Moritz by Fritz Ernst in *Iphigeneia und andere Essays*, Schriften der Corona VI (Munich: Oldenburg, 1933), pp. 106–117, reprinted in his *Essais* (Zürich: Fretz & Wasmuth, 1943), II, p. 62–77. It should be noted here that the Spanish consider humanist Luis Vives of Valencia, the friend of Erasmus, as the "father of the new empirical psychology," a view shared among others by Ortega y Gasset, Eugenio d'Ors, Gregorio Marañón and Juan Zaragueta. See Juan Luis Vives, *Dialogos* and *Instrucción de la mujer cristiana*, Collectión Austral nos. 128 and 134 (Buenos Aires: Espasa-Calpe, 1940). Among the many commentaries see especially G. Marañón, *Luis Vives* (Madrid: Espasa-Calpe, 1942), and also *Vivès, humaniste espagnol* by Eugenio d'Ors, Gregorio Marañón, Juan Zaragueta et al., Collection Occident, Etudes Hispaniques (Paris: Plon, 1941). The same can be said for Petrus Hispanus (see the text, p. 12), but this is only conditionally true of both men inasmuch as the purely anthropological and scientific study of psychology does not begin until the French Revolution. There the basic notion of the mind, already given an anthropological emphasis by Protagoras, becomes exaggerated to a kind of exclusive anthropocentrism. Protagoras had understood man as the measure of all *things* (see the text, p. 77), but after the French Revolution man is considered to be the measure of *everything*. It is of note that this exaggeration was prefigured not long after the Renaissance by the orator Pierre Charron (1541–1603) in the preface to the first volume of his *Traité de la Sagesse* (Bordeaux, 1601): "La vraie science et le vrai étude de l'homme c'est l'homme." Alexander Pope incorporated this maxim into his didactic poem "An Essay on Man": "The proper

study of mankind is man," which in turn reappears in G. E. Lessing's *Nathan der Weise* of 1779, i.e., shortly before the French Revolution; there the Templar, speaking to Daja (act 1, scene 6): ". . . aber das eigentliche Studium der Menschheit ist der Mensch." Since then the co-emphasis on the human that is present in the incarnation of God has been overaccentuated and reduced to the purely human. This completes the falling away from God and begins mankind's descent to hell, the (necessary) plunge into the depths of the earth and the soul or psyche. The words of Jean Paul are only too apt: "It is true, mankind has awakened—but I don't know whether from the bed or from the grave. It still lies like an awakened corpse, face down, looking into the earth" (Jean Paul, *Augenblick und Ewigkeit: Gedanken aus seinem Werk* [Munich: Piper, 1947], p. 67).

6   Fr. Noël, *Dictionnaire de la Fable, ou Mythologie Grecque, Latine, Egyptienne, Celtique, Persane, Syriaque, Indienne, Chinoise, Mahométane, Rabbinique, Slavonne, Scandinave, Africaine, Américaine, Iconologique etc.* (Paris: Normant, 1800, ²1803), II.

7   Karl Philipp Moritz, *Anton Reiser: ein psychologischer Roman* (Berlin: Maurer, 1785), v.

8   John B. Watson, *Der Behaviorismus* (Stuttgart: Deutsche Verlags-Anstalt, 1930).

9   L. Szondi, *Schicksalsanalyse* (Basel: Schwabe, 1944); see also his *Triebpathologie* (Bern: Huber, 1952), I.

10   Richard Semon, *Die Mneme als erhaltendes Prinzip im Wechsel des organischen Geschehens* (Leipzig: Engelmann, 1904), and also his *Bewusstseinsvorgang und Gehirnprozess*, ed. Otto Lubarsch (Wiesbaden: Bergmann, 1920).

11   David Katz, *Gestaltpsychologie* (Basel: Schwabe, 1944).

12   Max Wertheimer, *Drei Abhandlungen zur Gestalttheorie* (Erlangen: Verlag der Philosophischen Akademie, 1925).

13   Ludwig Binswanger, *Grundformen und Erkenntnis menschlichen Daseins* (Zürich: Niehans, 1942).

14   See also Jean Gebser, *Abendländische Wandlung* (Zürich: Oprecht, 1943 seq.), the chapters devoted to psychology; *Gesamtausgabe*, I, pp. 277–320.

15   Sigmund Freud, *Gesammelte Werke chronologisch geordnet* (London: Imago, 1942, rpt. 1948), II: *Die Traumdeutung*, p. 500 ff.; III: *Über den Traum*, p. 581 ff.

16   Ernst von Aster, *Die Psychoanalyse* (Bern: Francke, 1949), p. 69.

17   Jolande Jacobi, *Die Psychologie von C. G. Jung* (Zürich: Rascher, 1945), p. 88.

18   We will forego here any attempt to use in support of our thesis the effect of what Freud has defined as the "libido," i.e., the impulse or drive aspect of the psyche. The concept has been enlarged by C. G. Jung to include the religious, and he has variously defined it at different times, notably as "psychic energy."

19   C. G. Jung, *Über die Energetik der Seele* (Zürich: Rascher, 1928); 2nd ed. rev. and exp., *Über psychische Energetik und das Wesen der Träume* (Rascher, 1948). With reference to the quotation see also J. Jacobi (note 17), p. 86 f.

20   G. R. Heyer, *Vom Kraftfeld der Seele* (Stuttgart: Klett, 1949); a second edition of this important work was published in the Kindler paperback series as no. 2009 (Munich: Kindler: 1964).

21   For more about this concept of Heyer's which has significantly contributed to a non-rationalistic understanding of psychic events see Jean Gebser, "Über die Polarität," *Jahrbuch für Psychologie, Psychotherapie und medizinische Anthropologie*, 11, 2 (Freiburg/Munich, 1963), p. 96 f.; reprinted in the *Gesamtausgabe*, V/II, p. 31 ff.

22   See G. R. Heyer, *Seelenkunde im Umbruch der Zeit* (Bern: Huber, 1964), as well as the commentary along the lines of the present discussion in Gebser (note 21).

23   The term "ambivalence" has by now surely shown itself to be inadequate inasmuch as it mentalistically restricts the psychic constellation of "polarity." And we have frequently alluded to the unsuitability of the terminology employed by psychoanalysis which inevitably uses rationally fixed conceptual antitheses instead of psychically irrational polarities to circumscribe an irrational psychic phenomenon. We have also noted the consequences of the undifferentiated usage of "antithesis" and "polarity," as well as the "either-or" nature of the first contrasted with the "as well as" aspect of the second; see Jean Gebser, *Über die Polarität*" (note 21).

24   Paul Brunton, *Das Überselbst* (Zürich: Rascher, 1940); see also his *Die Weisheit des Überselbst* (Zürich: Rascher, 1949).

25   V. E. von Gebsattel, *Christentum und Humanismus* (Stuttgart: Klett, 1947), p. 184.

26   C. G. Jung, *Die Beziehungen zwischen dem Ich und dem Unbewussten* (Zürich: Rascher, 1935), p. 98. See also the commentary on this quotation by J. Jacobi (note 17), p. 200 f.

27   Ibid.

28   C. G. Jung, *Psychologie und Alchemie* (Zürich: Rascher, 1944), p. 69.

29   V. E. von Gebsattel (note 25), p. 45 ff.

30   Jean Gebser (note 14), chapter 29; *Gesamtausgabe*, I, p. 291.

31   C. J. Jung, *Symbolik des Geistes* (Zürich: Rascher, 1948), p. 410 ff.

32   C. G. Jung (note 28), p. 575.

33   J. Jacobi (note 17), p. 82 note.

34   With all due reservation we would point out that the Jungian school has considered the proclamation of the Papal Bull of Nov. 1, 1950, "Munificentissimus Deus," on the Assumption of the Virgin Mary, as a confirmation of the quaternity concept, although it clearly bears a neo-gnostic stamp.

35   The notion that "a therapy must be found from the side of the spiritual" (J. Goldbrunner, *Individuation: die Tiefenpsychologie von C. G. Jung* [Krailing vor München: Wevel, 1949]; and Victor E. Frankl, *Ärztliche Seelsorge* [Vienna: Deuticke, ⁴1947]) and is to be accomplished by "existence analysis" is a reference to the idea of Logos as spirit. It has taken shape in Frankl's "logotherapy" which is not to be confused with arational diaphany—the supra-determined efficacy of the spiritual, the diaphainon, in aperspectivity.

36   J. Jacobi (note 17), p. 83 note.

37   V. E. von Gebsattel (note 25).

38   Josef Goldbrunner (note 35).

39   Alexander Mitscherlich, *Freiheit und Unfreiheit in der Krankheit: Das Bild des Menschen in der Psychiatrie* (Hamburg: Classen & Goverts, 1946).

40   G. R. Heyer, "Psychobiologie," *Krankheit und Kranksein* (Bremen: Schünemann, 1952), pp. 219–242.

41   Adolf Portmann, "Das Problem der Urbilder in biologischer Sicht," *Eranos Jahrbuch, Sonderband*, 18 (Zürich: Rhein, 1950), pp. 413–432.

42   Kurt von Sury, *Wörterbuch der Psychologie und ihrer Grenzgebiete* (Basel: Schwabe, 1950), col. 199. The definition of "synchronicity" given here can be regarded as being accepted by Jung and his school. The second edition of the dictionary (1958) contained the following emendation: "The phenomenon [of synchronicity] co-exists with causality and seems to be rooted in archetype" (col. 389).

43   C. G. Jung, *Über Synchronizität*," *Eranos-Jahrbuch*, 20 (Zürich: Rhein, 1952), p. 271–284. See also Jung's chapter "Naturerklärung und Psyche," in C. G. Jung, *Synchronizität als ein Prinzip akausaler Zusammenhänge* / Wolfgang Pauli, *Der Einfluss archetypischer Vorstellungen auf die Bildung naturwissenschaftlicher Theorien bei Kepler* (Zürich: Rascher, 1952). This joint publication by Jung and Pauli came out only after the present book was in press.

44   C. G. Jung and Karl Kerényi (note 5), p. 117 f.

45   C. G. Jung (note 28), p. 303.

46   C. G. Jung, "Die psychologischen Aspekte des Mutterarchetypus," *Eranos-Jahrbuch*, 6 (1938; Zürich: Rhein, 1939), p. 410. See also the commentary on this quotation by J. Jacobi (note 17), p. 75.

47   C. G. Jung and Karl Kerényi, *Das göttliche Kind* (Amsterdam: Pantheon, 1940), p. 92. See also Gebsattel's comment (note 25), p. 28.

48   Paul Schmitt, "Archetypisches bei Augustin und Goethe," *Eranos Jahrbuch*, 12 (1944; Zürich: Rhein, 1945), p. 95–155. See also Paul Schmitt, *Religion, Idee und Staat* (Bern: Francke, 1959), p. 441 f.

49   J. Jacobi (note 17), p. 75.

50   Jean Gebser, *The Transformation of the Occident* (note 14), chapter 29; *Gesamtausgabe*, I, pp. 290 and 295 f.

51   Adolf Portmann (note 41), p. 427.

52   C. G. Jung and Karl Kerényi (note 47), p. 91.

53   J. Jacobi (note 17), p. 74.

54   Martin Heidegger, *Holzwege* (Frankfurt/M.: Klostermann, 1950).

55   Heidegger, p. 300 f.

56   Egon Vietta, *Theologie ohne Gott* (Zürich: Artemis, 1946).

57   Alois Dempf, *Selbstkritik der Philosophie* (Vienna: Herder, 1947).

58   We refer to the point made by Wilhelm Szilasi: "In *Sein und Zeit*, as well as in *Das Wesen des Grundes*, an ambiguity, even though productive, has not been surmounted . . . " (*Macht und Ohnmacht des Geistes* [Bern: Francke, 1946], p. 262). The emphasis here is on the adjective "productive"; and we wish to note the fact that Szilasi refers merely to the ambiguity of Heidegger's concept of transcendence.

59   Heinrich Straumann, "Gibt es einen amerikanischen Existentialismus?" *Neue Zürcher Zeitung*, no. 809 (April 14, 1951), p. 14.

60   Guido de Ruggiero, *Philosophische Strömungen des zwanzigsten Jahrhunderts* (Köln: Schaffstein, 1949), p. 228.

61   Adolf Reinach, *Was ist Phänomenologie?*, preface by Hedwig Conrad-Martius (Munich: Kösel, 1951), p. 6.

62   Reinach, p. 26.

63   J. and W. Grimm, *Deutsches Wörterbuch*, IV, 2, col. 1784.

64   Ibid.

65   Georges Poulet, *Études sur le Temps Humain* (Paris: Plon, 1950), p. 1.

66   Romano Guardini, *Christliches Bewusstsein: Versuche über Pascal* (Leipzig: Hegner, 1935), p. 176 f.

67   Ibid., p. 178 f.

68   Ibid., p. 177.

69   Ibid., pp. 35 and 179.

70   Ibid., p. 86.

71   Herbert Plügge, "Pascals Begriff des 'Ennui' und seine Bedeutung für eine medizinische Anthropologie," *Tymbos für Wilhelm Ahlmann* (Berlin: de Gruyter, 1951), p. 229 ff. See also Wilhelm Josef Revers, *Die Psychologie der Langeweile* (Meisenheim am Glan: Westkulturverlag Anton Hain, 1949), p. 24, and Dora Brauchlin, *Das Motiv des "ennui" bei Stendhal* (Strassburg: Heitz, 1930).

72   Georges Poulet (note 65), p. 48 f.

73   Romano Guardini (note 66), p. 86, which also quotes Pascal's fragment 139.

74   Søren Kirkegaard, *Der Begriff der Angst* (Jena: Diederich, n.d.), p. 84.

75   Quoted in Magdalena Aebi, *Kants Begründung der "deutschen Philosophie"* (Basel: Verlag Recht und Gesellschaft, 1947), p. 21. See also Karl Jaspers, *Philosophie* (Berlin, 1923), III: *Metaphysik*, p. 229.

76   Henri Bergson, *Zeit und Freiheit: Eine Abhandlung über die unmittelbaren Bewusstseinstatsachen* (Jena: Diederichs, 1920), p. 1.

77*   Henri Bergson, *Creative Evolution*, tr. Arthur Mitchell (New York: Modern Library, 1944), p. 371.

78   Werner Gent, *Das Problem der Zeit* (Frankfurt/M.: Schulte-Bulmke, 1934), p. 32.

79   See in particular Wilhelm Dilthey, *Das Erlebnis und die Dichtung* (Leipzig: Teubner, 1905, ⁴1913).

80   Martin Heidegger, *Sein und Zeit* (Halle/S.: Niemeyer, ⁵1941), p. 434.

81   Ibid., p. 333.

82   Ibid., p. 436.

83   Ibid., p. 433

84   Edmund Husserl, *Erfahrung und Urteil*, ed. Ludwig Landgrebe (Hamburg: Claassen & Goverts, 1948), paragraph 64, p. 303 ff.

85   We are speaking here about the rational as a deficient form of the mental structure. It need not be emphasized that any philosophy can lead to *Grenzsituationen* that cannot be solved mentally, not to say rationally. Such solutions were actively possible only where the concept as such was not employed rationally as an *abstractum*, as for example in Gracián. He defines the concept (el concepto) as an act of reason expressing a relation between things (un acto del entendimiento que exprime la correspondencia que se halla entre los objetos); Baltasar Gracián, *Agudeza y arte de ingenio*, Colección Austral, vol. 258 (Buenos Aires: Espasa-Calpe, 1942), p. 19. It should be obvious that Gracián is here anticipating the modern notion of a concept in contemporary philosophy, and is deserving of greater recognition.

86   Max Bense's outline of the history of philosophy, an exposition of philosophical currents between the two world wars in the European–Anglo-Saxon realm, must be regarded in the same light; see Max Bense, *Die Philosophie*, Series: Zwischen den beiden Kriegen I (Frankfurt/M.: Suhrkamp, 1951). In a similar book written at about the same time, F. J. von Rintelen has unmasked existential philosophy in a felicitous phrase as a "philosophy of finiteness" while attempting to transcend this finiteness—actually an end—by an "answer from the spirit"; see Rintelen, *Philosophie der Endlichkeit als Spiegel der Gegenwart* (Meisenheim/Glan: Westkulturverlag Anton Hain, 1951), p. 472 ff. We would also mention in this context the vademecum through the history of modern thought by Robert Heiss, *Der Gang des Geistes* (Bern: Francke, 1948). The supersession of the mental by the rational, and the attempts to transcend the rational are given cogent expression in this book.

87   E. R. Jaensch, *Über den Aufbau der Wahrnehmungswelt und die Grundlagen der menschlichen Erkenntnis* (Leipzig: Barth, ²1927).

88   *Dialectica: Internationale Zeitschrift für Philosophie der Erkenntnis*, ed. Ferdinand Gonseth, Gaston Bachelard, Paul Bernays (Paris: Presses Universitaires de France; Neuchâtel: Editions du Griffon), 1947 seq.

89   Hans Reichenbach, *Philosophische Grundlagen der Quantenmechanik* (Basel: Birkhäuser, 1949).

90   Ibid., p. 159.

91   See Werner Heisenberg, *Physik und Philosophie* (Stuttgart: Hirzel, 1959), p. 167 ff.; also Ullstein ed. No. 249, p. 152 ff.

92   Max Bense, "Philosophie ouverte: ein Kongress der Exakten in Zürich," *St. Galler Tagblatt*, 192 (April 25, 1951). See also the report on these "Third conversations of Zürich; in the *Neue Zürcher Zeitung*, 1031 (May 11, 1951).

93   Karl Jaspers, *Psychologie der Weltanschauungen* (Berlin: Springer, 1919).

94   Aristotle, *Metaphysics*, XII, c. 9, 1074b. In the translation of Eugen Rolfes, vol. 3 of Meiner's Philosophische Bibliothek (Leipzig, 1904), p. 101; in the edition of Adolf Lasson (Jena: Diederichs, 1924), p. 177.

95   I. M. Bochenski, *Europäische Philosophie der Gegenwart* (Bern: Francke, 1947), p. 113.

96   Martin Heidegger (note 54), p. 247.

97   Wilhelm Szilasi (note 58).

98   See Hans Barth, "Hinweis auf Georg Simmel," *Neue Zürcher Zeitung*, 3324, 70, (November 17, 1957). Szilasi does not make reference to this insight of Simmel's.

99   Wilhelm Szilasi (note 58), p. 246 ff., 284 ff., et passim.

100   See I. M. Bochenski (note 95), p. 142.

101   Edmund Husserl, *Ideen zu einer reinen Phänomenologie und phänomenologischen Philosophie; Erstes Buch: Allgemeine Einführung in die reine Phänomenologie*, special issue of the *Jahrbuch für Philosophie und phänomenologische Forschung*, I (Halle/S.: Niemeyer, 1913).

102   Martin Heidegger (note 80), p. 47 note.

103   Ibid., pp. 51, 303, 333.

104   Wilhelm Szilasi (note 58), p. 196.

105   Ibid., p. 243.

106   Martin Heidegger (note 54), p. 278.

107   Ibid., p. 39 f.
108   Heidegger also translates *aletheia* as *Entdecktheit*, "discoveredness"; see Heidegger (note 80), paragraph 44, p. 212 ff.
109   Martin Heidegger (note 54), p. 40.
110   Ibid., p. 41.
111   Ibid., p. 41.
112   Ibid., p. 42.
113   Ibid., p. 42 ff.
114   Here we encounter the corrective influence of psychiatrist R. Binswanger on Heidegger, in Binswanger's reproof that the necessity of "being in the world in a state of sorrow and anxiety" (*In-der-Welt-Sein-als-Sorge*) must be emended and extended to include acceptance of "being at home in the state of love" (*Beheimatetsein-als-Liebe*); see Binswanger (note 13).
115   Martin Heidegger (note 54), pp. 278 and 282.
116   Ibid., p. 278.
117   It will be apparent that we have restricted our discussion principally to the two extreme forms of contemporary philosophy, the "latter day" form (especially Heidegger's) and the "antiphilosophical" type of Reichenbach, as Alfred Stern has cogently termed it in his article "Antiphilosophische Philosophie," *Neue Zürcher Zeitung*, 469 (March 3, 1952). Stern is primarily referring to the last work of Hans Reichenbach, *The Rise of Scientific Philosophy* (Berkeley: University of California Press, 1951). At the present moment (1964) we would also add a reference to the new "quantum logic" of Werner Heisenberg and Carl-Friedrich von Weizsäcker (see text, p. 407). A student of Weizsäcker's has called this the "logic of complementarity"; see Eckart Heimendahl, "Gegensatz und Komplementarität," *Transparente Welt: Festschrift für Jean Gebser* (Bern: Huber, 1965), p. 6 ff. This "quantum" or "complementarity" logic promises to be the most fruitful concept of a new, pure philosophy tending towards what we have described as "eteology" (see the text, pp. 326 and 424). We have avoided a discussion of religious philosophy as represented by such men as Solowiev, Mereschkowski, Mounier, Unamuno, Berdiaiev, Dempf and others, even though it does not merely insist upon a return to the Christian faith, but in fact contains the first steps toward a view of Christianity adequate to the new consciousness structure. This, however, can only be successfully accomplished if posited on a basis other than that of the conceptual antitheses of Faith (religion) and Knowledge (philosophy). The extent to which the Logos is being displaced by the Spiritual, the abstract by the concrete, the dualistic by the integral, in religious philosophy is also evident in the latest book of N. Berdiaiev: *Existentielle Dialektik des Göttlichen und Menschlichen* (Munich: Beck, 1951), pp. vi, 125 and 178 ff. In his concluding chapter, Berdiaiev takes note of the presently arising "new era of the spirit wherein spirituality will attain its highest realization." This realization "presupposes an alteration of human consciousness, a re-orientation and revolutionary change of the consciousness previously perceived to be static." Commensurate with the degrees of consciousness, the previous consciousness will be superseded. See also Nicolas Berdiaiev, *Cinq Méditations sur l'Existence* (Paris: Aubier, 1936), particularly the fourth meditation on the time problem, p. 133.

7

Manifestations of the Aperspectival World (III): The Social Sciences

1. Jurisprudence

Law and the administration of justice are sociological formations and presuppose the mental structure. The judge is always the director, and the law—the right—clearly emphasizes the "right side" (the patriarchal, manly, light). The very meaning of the word "law" (*Gesetz* = setting, positioning) assumes space and hence is spatially determined and bound. The structural interconnections of right, law, and patriarchy to the right—the wakeful consciousness and its directed right thinking—have been presented in detail in the first part above (p. 79).

To make clear the extent to which each verdict is a mental act requiring mental foundations, we would point to less mentally emphasized cultures that lack laws. The mythical affinity still evident in modern China, for example, recognizes law at best in the limited Confucian-patriarchal form of regulations. For the rest, precept and tabu prevail; but they are not laws. Their place is filled by "custom" as given in the old books of wisdom,[1] our knowledge of which we owe to Richard Wilhelm. The basic distinction between a law and a custom has been noted by a distinguished observer of China: "Those men to whom a generous destiny had entrusted with the task of establishing a constitution for the societies to which they belonged had the duty of finding norms for a communal life. In Europe, the choice in such cases was almost always made of promulgating laws whose validity depended upon the power of the state which was able to enforce such laws.

"The Chinese chose another way. They created customs for common life. The difference between a custom and a law lies in the recognition that the validity of a custom is found in a deeper or earlier level of the human soul. Its acceptance or standing resides at the pre- or subconscious level, whereas laws are obeyed or disobeyed consciously.

"Now I do not wish to maintain that there are no laws in China, or no customs in Europe. Yet we Europeans surely base our common life primarily on rights and laws while the Chinese, by contrast, base theirs on custom."[2]

Customs, however, must not be confused with morals, since "morality is always a conscious idea."[3] But custom is undoubtedly akin to what we Europeans call tact. The word "tact" clearly indictes an affinity to the heart, the organ of the mythical consciousness. The foundation of tact is the heart just as customs are appropriate mainly to the mythical consciousness. Even today, "to be tactful" means to act according to custom, that is, well-mannered. Understood in this way tact is a fulfillment of a law which is not stipulated mentally; where tact prevails, no law is needed.

Since jurisprudence and law, or "rights," are manifestations of the mind or mental structure, as well as being the sociological safeguards par excellence, it is understandable that they are always invested with conservative and traditionalistic properties. All fixed positings are static (and thus spatial and expressly mental). For our investigation the decisive question is whether there is a basic change in jurisprudence. If there is actually emerging today a form of realization which is no longer perspectively fixed, then despite its conservative character this fundamentally important field must furnish indications of decisive and transforming events or irruptions in its foundations, its organization, and its operations.

This is in fact the case. Jurisprudence is in the process of establishing new foundations. This is less evident with respect to the philosophy or the history of law than with respect to the concrete evidence of recent practice in legislation and legal decisions. Initial and decisive inceptions indicative of this change are evident from the turn of the century onward in the works of Eugen Huber, Hans Fehr, A. Egger, and Radbruch, for example. During the last decade, besides several works of W. F. Bürgi, the publications of Hans Marti are particularly revealing of the new foundations, new valuations, and the structural changes in jurisprudence since the French Revolution. We shall base our discussion primarily on the work of these men.[4]

The evidence indicative of change in jurisprudence, as well as of a perspectival beginnings, may be summarized under three headings:

1) The consideration of time;
2) The supersession of dualism;
3) A tendency toward arationality.

We will limit ourselves to the most recent research and will forego a discussion of Montesquieu's unique work, the *Cahiers* (1716–1755), in which he has strikingly anticipated the new attitude toward jurisprudence only now coming to realization. Montesquieu's grand maxim is an imposing expression and guiding light: "If I knew of something useful to me and injurious to my family I would banish it from my mind. If I knew of something useful to my family but not to my country, I would seek to forget it. If I knew something useful to my country and harmful for Europe, or useful to Europe and harmful for humanity, I would regard it as a crime."[5] Nor shall we go back to Grotius, Rousseau, and Gierke, or include the contributions of Helmut Coing, Erik Wolf, and Georg Stadtmüller,[6] since they have only intuitively explored new ground without having circumscribed it with the clarity possible today.

In terms of our investigation, the theme of time is doubtless the most important, and we shall begin with it.

1) The consideration of time has been expressed in jurisprudence in a variety of ways since the French Revolution. The law in force until then was "static law." In

the center of this still predominantly Roman juridical system was the "fundamental inviolability of private property . . . which on the other hand despised labor and thus legislated only peripherally."[7] The famous statement *Qui iure suo utitur neminem laedit* (Whoever uses his right injures no one) is an expression of this rigid, absolute attitude. Because of the emphasis on the absoluteness of subjective legality, possession and property, law was spatially fixed and hence totally mental. The temporal factor or the factor of changed and differentiated relationships were hardly considered. By contrast, contemporary legislation demands an increasing attention to juridical effects and allows, for example, the application of the *clausula rebus sic stantibus* which permits a subsequent change of fixed contracts, recognizing changed circumstances. This is tantamount to recognition of the temporal factor. And today's increasing practice of shortening statutes of limitations expresses a dissolution of the previous fixity and stability of law.

While former laws were mainly individualistic, the emerging new ones are primarily social. The basic concern is no longer the guarantee of property, but the security of work. While possessions and property are static and spatially fixed, work and accomplishment are temporal and "dynamic." Duguit and his school have founded an (admittedly one-sided) "dynamic law" and stress exclusively the "judicial function" even at the expense of the individual, considering only the effectiveness of justice in and for society. It is becoming increasingly evident that justice in the old mental sense is suffering losses which are not so much aimed at eliminating law as such but rather at impairing its exclusive validity, as befits the mutation of consciousness. The left element, the transfiguring factor of law since the French Revolution, introduced the left, the "non-rights" into law. Ultimately this results in a materialistic and decadent notion that "right is what is useful."

The "irruption of time" in law has upset mental man's base, revealing its inadequacy. The recognition of work as value, required and achieved by the awakened left, is a recognition of time insofar as activity is a temporal value realizable in time and temporal process. The overthrow of the king, the "rex" as the "right," by the powers suppressed through the centuries (powers assuming not so much form as virulence from the unconscious effects of the awakening left), parallels the shift of emphasis from property to work. This process shows the exhaustion of the mental structure. If work is time, then the process of socialization, becoming more evident since the turn of this century, is an exact parallel to the revolutionary recognition of time in physics as well as in other natural sciences.

In both cases there is the danger that time might be judged as a numerical quantity rather than as a qualitative element. Physical-geometrical time and the calculation of labor are devaluations of genuine, primordial time, the achronon. The after-effects of deficient mental, that is, rational quantitative thought still threaten the consolidation of the new, integral consciousness structure. The great aftershocks have not yet passed. The effort to abolish the entire mental structure is not yet recognized as a major error; and the irrational component has in the main not yet been mastered.

Yet with respect to its being mastered, we should note that a decisive step has been taken in recent years by Hans Marti (since 1958). He has made evident the magical and mythical components of jurisprudence that until now have not been acknowledged because of a one-sided rationalistic attitude. It is his major achievement that he has brought to perception, from a high arational observation point via lucid language and diction, the prerational and irrational components so as to avoid an unconscious reimmersion in them, and has in this way shown them able to be mastered.[8]

The influence of the "left element" is well described by W. F. Bürgi: "Today the right to private property is increasingly questioned from outside by the communistic demands for expropriation, and undermined from inside by the growing demands of the new legislative limitations and taxes favoring the interests of the community. . . . Explicitly opposed to the various threats to ownership ["own," as in "my own" is always ego-bound!] is the immense development of legal areas concerned with the requirements of work and the protection of the employee. Modern legislation not only protects the personal interests of the employee, but deliberately advances employment as such, since its significance for the state and the economy is fully recognized.

"For these reasons labor and its representatives enjoy today an almost unlimited prestige in utter contradistinction to the conceptions of not only ancient Rome but of pre-revolutionary Europe. Whereas work was then considered to be almost dishonorable, the conviction became ever more widespread during the last century that only those whose activity is useful to the community have a justifiable existence. In Eastern Europe the recognition of the 'right to work' is inseparable from the 'work requirement' in the interest of the community, and lapses are punishable as sabotage.

"Today property is put on the defensive almost everywhere and endures the socio-political attacks and growing impositions by the state with difficulty and in a materially weakened form. Labor, on the other hand, enjoys maximal recognition, and its security has become the central task of modern legislation."[9]

The weight of evidence from these remarks documenting the shift of emphasis from property to labor in several important new laws has never before been marshalled with such clarity.[10] We will necessarily have to restrict ourselves to a few examples: crucial erosions of rights of ownership can be seen in price ceilings and limitations of commerce, while the new land rights and agrarian reform (at the immediate expense of private property), revised social rights, clearing rights, cartel legislation, insurance, new stockholder's rights, etc., all serve to protect the rights of labor.

The change of emphasis from property to labor is clearly indicated by the frequent allusions to the managerial revolution among business leaders and directors in the American and European economies. Juridically this new managerial class demonstrates that the power of the highest employees is increasingly prevailing at the expense of the boards of directors, who represent property interests.[11]

The dissolution of former rights, the reduction of the individual's pre-eminence because of restrictions are manifest in the ever more prevalent manner in which new legislation is formulated. Skeleton descriptions and broad provisions replace particular provisions and precisely formulated rights. The rigid, perspectival fixity and the strict directives give way to a more flexible attitude permitting the judge a latitude of free interpretation in accordance with the temporally changing requirements. The old judicial form to which Goethe objected, "Laws and rights are inherited / like an eternal sickness / . . . reason becomes non-sense, blessing disaster: / woe unto you, that you are a grandson!"[12] has hardly any claim to validity in dynamic modern justice.

W. F. Bürgi points out that this new state of affairs contains positive aspects although such aspects cannot be expressed as long as the emphasis remains on the materialistically calculatable utility of work, that is to say, as long as it is valued only quantitatively. For example, the work of the mind or spirit—whose value cannot be established quantitatively in terms of remuneration—is doomed to hunger unless it surrenders the freedom that enables its creative process. But this would engender a loss of its genuine, spiritual quality.

This example demonstrates that a recovery in the form of a strengthening of the aperspectival bearing may emerge when work is valued as a quality and no longer mistakenly valued as a quantitative expenditure of time and material utility. As long as "time" in the form of work is dealt with quantitatively by sociology and jurisprudence, there is a danger of sociological and jurisprudential atomization. This is an exact parallel of the erroneous manipulation of "time" as a geometric-physical quantity of mass in physics, which also subjects it to the danger of atomization. It parallels in addition the frequently mistaken treatment of the unconscious by depth psychology, where the overextended amplification of the psychic-temporal element holds the threat of inflating and indeed atomizing the "soul."

Perhaps the abandonment of perspectivally fixed and codified laws in favor of a delimiting framework is an initial and a positive indication of aperspectival manifestation within law, which is otherwise merely an expression of the mental-rational, perspectival consciousness structure. In this connection Bürgi observes that "Precisely the deepened knowledge of our times concerning the relativity of each phenomenon is most likely the reason for the intensified appeal for dynamic or functional rights during recent decades for a justice that responds to the constant change of life's processes and thus attempts to integrate the element of time or the law of continuous transformation into the juridical order. Since the relaxation of rigid rules tends to respect individual differences, it institutes increased potency of the qualitative aspects. Modern laws such as ours have to a great extent met many needs by incorporating delimited frameworks and broad provisions, without of course questioning the static principle of a given juridical order."[13]

Were we again permitted a parallelism, we could say that the delimited frameworks and broad provisions in the area of jurisprudence are similar to the energy quantum, and the indeterminacy principle resulting from it, in physics. It is common to both that they explode the spatially, causally, and perspectivally-fixed, rigidified conceptual systems and open up an arena for freedom. Both are pervaded by valuations leading to the questions of intensity and quality of events. Such a comparison, if permissible, is most instructive, although it can be achieved only systatically and not systematically. The same primordiality manifest in the quantum of action appears in principle in the employment of indeterminate broad provisions. Thus jurisprudence becomes something other than a mere law: it becomes verition, the perception and imparting of truth.

Once we understand that "work" is not just a measurement of earnings, and successfully disassociate it from quantification, then the dangers inherent in this form of time-irruption in law and its assumption of specifically mental consciousness will be surpassed. The consideration of time manifest in the application of the *Clausula rebus sic stantibus* in practice, as well as in the reduction of statutes of limitations and in a more liberal interpretation of laws pertaining to the evaluation of work, can doubtless lead to an integration of jurisprudence through an aperspectival fulfillment of significance. ("Fulfillment of significance" is aperspectivally over-determined with respect to mental rational sensibleness, which expresses only a sense, a directedness; see p. 79.) The appropriate application and the qualitative nature of the broad provisions, with their inherent openness and recognition of "temporal" factors, indicate that such integration is possible.

As in all areas, the sterile, rational dualism in jurisprudence is surpassed when "time" is recognized as a "qualitative" potent element in the spatial three-dimensional world. This brings us to:

2) The supersession of dualism in jurisprudence. It is recognizable in two salient facts; the one, pointed out by W. F. Bürgi, shows that the subjective laws have lost their absolute character. Yet the loss of absoluteness is equivalent to the abandonment of dualism, since it is conceivable only on the basis of absolute principles. The other fact is that the previous separation of public and private laws can no longer be strictly maintained within the new legislation. This is symptomatic expressly when we are dealing with the problem of labor, as in the right to work and the related rights to security. Thus the old subject-object antithesis has to a great extent been rendered obsolete in the conduct of law.[14]

It is most significant that man today more than ever begins to speak not merely of law but also of "justice and fairness," as well as "rights and responsibilities."[15] This too expresses the inceptual supersession of rational thinking-in-alternatives that admits only the opposites of justice and injustice, evident also in the legal adjustment for damages in accord with the actual indebtedness. Adolf Arndt has clearly demonstrated (1955) the untenability of the dualistic "division of just and unjust, public-objective and subjective rights." He emphatically states that "the dualistic structure of analytic and causal thinking, extending from antiquity to the modern epoch of a rational world, operates axiomatically with the alternatives of either-or. Has not the time come for overcoming this fragmented thinking . . . ?"[16]

Another assessment leading to our third point is the "predominant division today of economic interests into individualistic, superindividualistic, and communal, or so-called 'trans-personal' interests" (Radbruch's term)[17] Owing to this division, "the dominant socio-juridical relationships are regarded from an ultimate viewpoint of economics, which corresponds to the transition from purely individual to a more collective attitude toward life. Essential to this tripartition of interests is the inclusion of the median, the mediating super-individualistic category which contains elements of the other two, which can vary in emphasis from case to case."[18]

This third example also suggests the supersession of mere dualistic thinking and its rationalism; the move toward the more-than-rational "conception" of realities is obvious. This leads to the last point:

3) The tendency toward arationality in the new jurisprudence. Here it should be noted that arationality does not imply a total exclusion of causality. With respect to causally founded rationality, arationality is over-determined by the possibility and recognition of indeterminate and open elements. This is well expressed in modern definitions of law which are quite frequently approximate and exemplified by a singular case, that is, they are exemplary rather than directed, fixed, and absolutely binding, and are consciously left non-definitive. The same basic tendency is evident in contemporary legal suits where quite frequently the judge's verdict corresponds to the expressed desires and goals agreed upon by both parties. Thus the law is applied only as an external formality, or where the so-called economic and functional interpretation has taken on increasing significance, or in other cases where the judgement is reached on the basis of individual and superindividual interests. This is an "open justice."

In other words, jurisprudence gives evidence of the same process of liberation from compulsive systematization and spatially-bound conceptual incarceration that philosophy has set out to do. This dissociation from an exclusive rationality is occurring without losing control of reality or reverting to irrationality by our mastery of both modes of realization, as demonstrated by Hans Marti (p. 420). Thus law is overdetermined to the same extent as philosophy; both overdeterminations are possible because of the incorporation of what we call systasis. Just as philosophy is no longer philosophy in a mental sense but is becoming eteology (p. 326 and "eteologeme" in the index), mentally-conditioned justice in its new, overdetermined form is becoming what we have tentatively called "verition" or "a-waring." As custom became law and mythologeme became philosopheme, law, in the mutation occurring today, is becoming an expression of verition and the philosopheme is becoming an eteologeme or veracity. To the same degree that "open thinking" in the new "philosophy" contains characteristics of aperspectivity, "open justice" at least potentially expresses these same characteristics. It should be emphasized that the equation of "open thinking" with "open justice" does not rest on the fortuitous coincidence of terms. In both cases this "openness" relates to the same process of de-systematization and deperspectivation of thinking, as well as of justice, by the inclusion of the time element.[19] So once again temporic efficacy makes the decisive transition possible.

Since the paramount significance of justice for the mental consciousness is now evident, it will be understandable that the indications of radical change in the conception of justice express and manifest the mutation toward the integral consciousness structure and the aperspectival world which is occurring. The liberation from space and perspectival rigidity is already accomplished. If we can grasp work as a qualitative value and not as a quantity, we will have achieved the possibility for the requisite liberation from time. Then the achronon and the diaphainon will take on equal validity for jurisprudence.

2. Sociology and Economics[20]

Since the announcement of God's death, theology has been replaced and mis-placed by anthropology, which could be viewed as a pseudo-theology. Whereas man's main mode of relationship to God was a fixed, constant quantum with a paternal emphasis in accordance with his mental consciousness, the decline of the paternal attitude has rendered such a relationship obsolete. Its place has been assumed by man thrown back upon himself. The predominant question is no longer the theological man versus God, but the anthropological man versus man. This reduction and leveling, man's questioning of his relationship to himself and his surroundings, is the basis of all sociology.

Although the announcement of God's death has darkened the heavens, the earth has not become brighter. The earth contains dead levels that are excavated just as the earth-bound and deficient magically–stressed levels of the soul are excavated and revived; and the minus-side of nature, the atomic world of "minutest quanta" and its virulence, is dis-covered. All this knowledge leads to the threshold of a darkness of life and spirit. Man has become a gravedigger. But is humanity intent on digging its own grave?

This is the one salient and obvious aspect. Is there another? Can a blind world exclude God (who cannot be excluded) just because it had projected its own outmoded patriarchal aspect of the mental consciousness structure into God? Can such a world continue to exist after the destruction of heaven and the fall into the grave-like abyss of the earth? Can such a humanity—for this does not concern only its

Western part—renew itself and reverse its "descent into hell"? Although we cannot be certain, we can presume so, since the first signs of a fundamental restructuration are becoming visible. We were not entrusted to the earth to lose ourselves for its sake; whoever does so perishes with it. But will those who do not succumb be able to surmount the gaping abyss? The insignificance and helplessness of the massive sociological efforts seem to speak against such success. The same dread and horror which once overshadowed the mutation from the mythical to the mental, as manifest in the matricide of the *Oresteia*, are amassing throughout the world during our present transitional epoch. It has accomplished patricide and thus sealed the ultimate fate of mental predominance.

But it was not God who was murdered; it was the father. In particular, the predominance of patriarchy within ourselves has been superseded, and thus we too have transcended the conceptualized God. Like the Old Testament demand—the co-founder of the mental consciousness—that man should not fashion an image of God, the corresponding requirement today is that we should not conceptualize God; the undistorted divine must be perceptible in its transparency. As the command to renounce God's image meant the supersession of the deficient mythical consciousness, the demand to avoid conceptualizing God is a supersession of the deficient mental-rational consciousness.[21] As already noted, this is a marker pointing across the abyss into which many are plunging and will continue to plunge as long as they regard the task only from its negative aspect as a renunciation, and not from its other aspect as work yet to be done.

It is not the task of today to replace what has been superseded by something "new." One such attempt to contrive a substitute was the Fichtean Ego which Goethe ridiculed. Fichte maintained that an "ego," "*das* Ich," should be replaced by a masculine ego, "*der* Ich." But a mere "placing in (another's) place," that is, re-placement, is tantamount to an enthronement which always has patriarchal, three-dimensional properties. The examples of such recurrent attempts are so numerous as to be redundant if we were to repeat them.

We are thus confronted by something fundamentally different: with a "task" in a two-fold sense. The renunciation of the paternal principle is a liberation; for the moment it is the last and most decisive liberation that will permit mankind to achieve an undistorted rather than one-sided understanding of the divine.

Every sociology, every aspiration that does not reach the truly divine aspect via relationships among persons, is merely renunciation, grave-digging without resurrection, although a resurrection is immanent even in the dawning of every new day.

A basic error of all contemporary sociology is its assumption as self-evident that there are reliable human interrelationships, be they social, emotional, or whatever. But in mental terms, the genuine bond between persons goes always through God. To express it mentally once again, the valid point of relationship resides in Him. All other inter-human bonds that neglect this fundamental aspect are merely deliria, transient feelings, and shifting projections of the transitory ego. While searching for the traces of aperspectival reality, we may despair at finding any in contemporary sociology, and yet they are present.

But where shall we seek them? In what branch of sociology? In the theoretical, the political, the cultural, the philosophical, or the religious? Or in political economy, anthropology, prehistory, ethnology, or education? Or in the patho-sociology, the form in which the psychotherapy known as applied psychoanalysis and depth-psychology present themselves, since they resolve neurotic disturbances which stem primarily from the loss or dis-placement of the individual's relationship to himself and his surroundings?

Since we have already dealt with psychology, we can put it aside. Although it may appear inappropriate to someone who represents any of the many specialized scientific branches of sociology, we shall nevertheless attempt to survey the entire field in order to discover indications in sociology of the new consciousness structure.

We are not interested in the efforts to achieve some ideal based on a lost ethos and forgotten morality. Neither are we defending ideological class interests nor investigating the theoretical relationships of economics. They merely reveal—and this is their sole merit—the dead-end streets.

For what is the point of preaching an ethos or regaining a religion when both have died? What has been done cannot be undone. What is the good of directing competition and the distribution of goods and engaging in market analysis in order to "justly" apportion the products acquired by common labor, if all relevant theories fail to exclude special interests? Or what is the use of philosophical and religious edifices of thought, recognized only by an ineffectual minority, when they originate from the personal attitude of an individual thinker and are ultimately unconvincing? All of these decade-long attempts to manage the material, the ideal, the political and other relationships among men have as yet only created more confusion. The misunderstandings increase; moreover, counter to all sincere efforts of sociology, certain political and social circles are intent on increasing these misunderstandings.

The prospect is a darkened heaven and an earth that is becoming a grave. This dual diminishment breeds the ghost of forbidden enrichment which under these conditions can be manifest only materially. Greed for power and profit grow, and those who have succumbed to them do not see that the grave they are digging is also their own. To overlook these palpable realities is to have a total lack of common sense. It is impossible to change them; such a mentality is bent on death, and at best it will collapse of itself.

But if this mentality could be displaced or overdetermined by integrality, then the leap into the arational would succeed. There are indications in the various branches of sociology that are decidedly inceptual aperspectival formulations. They point beyond the merely mental and its deficient rational form of rationality, yet in no way fall back upon the psychic and vital spheres.

We are dealing then with the evidence of ideal, material, or other points of departure, or with general concepts which must be extricated from the confusing tapestry of opinions, theories, resentments, postulates, teachings, ideologies, etc. These points of departure will be visible in a limited number of various concepts. They are distinguished from all others in that they are realizable only by a consciousness structure which is overdetermined in relation to the mental. Consequently, they contain the virulence and strength utterly lacking in mentally-bound reform concepts. This immanent power guarantees that we are not dealing with arbitrarily selected concepts but with concepts which sooner or later will acquire validity in the restructuration of the general consciousness.

The time-bound political aspect, as well as the outmoded consciousness of Marxian materialism and its emendation by Asiatic despotism, its heritage born of resentment and its resentment-laden ideology and one-sided pseudo-religiosity, would suggest that it be given only the most cursory investigation. Its fanaticism precludes any possibility of de-perspectivation, although its demand for the recognition of labor is a most decisive and significant step, and has aided in the breakthrough of the main theme of our transitional epoch. It has, nevertheless, paradoxically remained mired in hypertrophied materialism of a dialectical kind, and regards work, the predominant temporal element, merely as a quantity, thus degrading it to a mere measurable material quantum. Although its mission was to supersede rationalistic materialism, its reversion to it is explicable in terms of its source: it stems from the irrational left with its inherent psychic determinism for which the rational is the new element. This contrasts with mental-rational man, for whom the arational is the new.

The new manifests itself in sociology in the following indications:

1) in the consideration of time;
2) in the supersession of dualism; and,
3) in a tendency toward arationality.

A consideration of Marxism leads immediately to:

1) The consideration of time. Seen not only from the standpoint of jurisprudence, but also of sociology, the new evaluation of labor is the sociological form of the irruption of time. This trend was prepared by the peasant wars and was already visible in them; it was stabilized by Puritanism, particularly in the United States of America where, as Max Weber has shown,[22] work was elevated to an almost religious maxim. It permeated the French Revolution and was later formalized by Marx and Engels. It gained world-wide significance via the three Russian revolutions, of which the first occurred during the crucial year 1905, the year of Einstein. The acceptance of this new aspect of time has transfigured human life after thousands of years at its very roots.

Not only the left's struggle for equality, but also its claim to supremacy—indeed, its claim to exclusivity—although counter to the elements of the merging future, as well as its retention of a quantitative estimation of work time, has left it caught up in rationality. This despite its temporic inception and the fact that Marx and Lenin regarded labor as a qualitative value. Even Kruschev advocated labor as a quality at the party congress in October of 1961, as has been demonstrated with all objectivity and requisite restraint by Ludwig Preller.[23] The postulate of freedom, which is fully and validly realizable only arationally and assumes indeterminacy and at least partial acausality, has been turned into its opposite by oriental-tyrannical Bolshevism, into slavery. The other postulate, that of brotherhood, is present only in the Russian man, but not in the party member. The third postulate, that of equality, has—despite the recognition of "personhood in the community" (to use the indicative phrase of Ludwig Preller)[24], sunk to a mere leveling and inhuman collectivization of man, manifesting only a deficient form of society or community.[25]

Despite the temporic inception and decisive achievement, the initial movement assuming form in Marxism is in reality today, at least in Marxistic-Leninistic Bolshevism, on a side track. Is there an open way, a new start to surpass this situation, so that the accomplished leap and the achieved new attitude can be effective in restructuring, changing, and liberating the world? The insights of those sociologists from diverse backgrounds who are evaluating work not just quantitatively seem to provide a new point of departure.

We are indebted to the socio-political work of Ludwig Preller (1962) for a decisive advance. In his evaluation of work and leisure(!), he distinguishes with previously unachieved clarity clock-time and time quantity from qualitative time and the requisite qualities of time. Since he proceeds from structures as "spatio-temporal interconnections," he successfully surpasses static systematics and unmasks the false and oblique alternatives (and dualisms), resulting in a new constellation of the social order and sociopolitics, which for him flow into a "social polity."[26]

The qualitative dimension of time in political economics is discussed by Arthur Lisowsky: "Just as the quantitative valuation of currency is not actually a 'valuation'— in which the non-measurable qualitative moment always plays a role—but rather a quantifying 'weighing,' so the division of time in the sense of clock-time is also a quantification."[27] And further elaborating this remark, he points to the views in Kosiol's Theory of Wage Structure and establishes that "time as the sole criterion of wage measure transcends the purely quantitative measurement of time-spans."[28] Both works of Lisowsky considered here endeavor to "incorporate qualitative time" into economic thought.[29] He proceeds from the concept of "Gestalt," widely used during the 1930s, to come to grips with the qualitative elements.

Yet he also defines gestalt-thinking as structural-thinking and distinguishes it from quantitative, numerical thinking:[30] "The proverb 'Time is money' is a typical product of the abstract, numerical thinking in economics. . . . The contrary notion that 'time works for us' is a recognition of concrete economic thinking."[31] After all, "the qualitative time experience is the essential aspect for the scholar in humanities. For him, life and events are not a quality-less unrolling of a temporal course as if it were a dead framework that can be sliced and chopped, i.e., destroyed by metrical beats into equal time-quanta (segments); rather it is a meaningful [!] unfolding and completion. It is not ruled by meter, but by rhythm. The characteristic of rhythm, however, is that its 'back and forth' in fulfilling the specifically valid laws of meaning is uneven when measured against the uniform marks of the stopwatch. And yet it acquires in itself an equal significative value even though it is qualitatively not comparable."[32]

Lisowsky himself comments on these statements: "Since our concepts and forms of thought are ultimately quantitative, it is possible to reach the 'deeper foundation of things' only suggestively by 'life-preserver words.' "[33] His insight into the necessity of "time related thinking" (thinking of time as quality)[34] is relevant to the total formation of political economics, above all to work hours, wage evaluation, marketing and distribution time, and valuation. And he comes to the conclusion that "in industrial economy we must understand time and its course in a dual manner: as a uniform, exact, qualityless temporal interval (as for example the term of interest)[35] and as a value-infused and value-setting succession of historical (formative) processes (for example in the evaluation of necessities), where the division into equal quantities has only the secondary import as an aid to order."[36]

In a number of his writings, W. A. Jöhr shows that quantitative thinking in its mechanistic form is being surpassed in political economics. Although in an uncompelling terminology, his discussion of the Keynesian system contains a symptomatic statement: "The inadequacy of the concepts borrowed from mechanistic thought requires to a certain extent the introduction of a new dimension," which would develop as a qualitative element on the basis of Keynes' theory or policy of occupation.[37]

Fritz Marbach, in one of his basic writings, has also underscored the necessity of the qualitative dimension; in political economics not only "mere numbers" matter, but that they "become values."[38] As Christian Gasser reemphasizes, the "working man" must not become "an expense factor, a quantitative element."[39] He too opposes "quantitative thinking"[40] and points to similar attitudes toward this problem among American political economists such as Elton Mayo, F. J. Roethlisberger, and other associates at the Industrial Research Department of Harvard University.[41] Basing his work on their conclusions, French economist Georges Friedmann demands a "three-fold valuation of work."[42] And even Norbert Wiener, creator of cybernetics, who has called the "mechanical brains" a two-edged sword, emphasizes that "any use of a human being in which less is demanded of him and less is attributed to him than his full status, is a degradation and a waste."[43]

The stance against the supremacy of quantitative thinking, and the recognition of the necessity of "qualitative thinking" is also found in the socio-philosophical writings of Romano Guardini.[44] It also appears in the new emphasis on structure already considered by Lisowsky, who avoided the mere vitalistic-holistic interpretation fashionable in the 1930s. Even Karl Mannheim speaks of the necessity of "structural renovation" whereby a "spiritual-mindful integration" could extricate us from the contemporary "value crisis" to the extent that previous values are given an "inherently qualitative estimation."[45]

This new structural thinking is also well elaborated by Walther Tritsch, who specifically points out that there is no genuine structure without the incorporation of a time-value. "Time can be experienced only as a structure"[46] and not conceptualized or apprehended. The term "experience" here ought not be understood vitalistically, as is apparent from Tritsch's most recent work, where for the first time in sociology "structure" is understood as an expression of the potential, the possible. As Tritsch points out, "Structures determine not merely the singular realization, as do formations, but various possibilities of any realization. Today we are interested precisely in the possible, the virtually [and potentially] present, and not merely in the temporally-bound, singular event. Herein lies the difference between our way of seeing and that of the morphologists and cultural mystics, the believers in Gestalt and the intuitionists of destiny prevalent in the first half of this century. This difference manifests the breakdown of all previous world-views determined by time and a spatial point of perspectivity."[47]

This statement by a sociologist corresponds to that of the physicist Leopold Infeld (and since they were developed independently of each other, the correspondence is significant): "The totality of possible events constitutes a four-dimensional world" (see p. 378). The concept of structure thus also receives at the hands of this author the qualitative emphasis for sociology which allows space-time-free origin to shine through the qualitative potentiality. "The hidden or the possible of the future" is valued as present in the supersession of the "mere now," the quantitative moment. It is an aperspectival mode of realization capable of surpassing the temporally quantitative and rigid perspectival thinking, striving to reach "wholeness" also in sociology, whose conscious realization presupposes the dequantification of time.

It is significant that sociology—in its political-economic branch particularly tied to concepts of quantity and number—considers the qualitative aspect not only as a value of labor or goods, but also as genuine quality. This is particularly evident in its recognition of "leap-like" processes in political economics. This most significant recognition is found in the work of Fritz Marbach, who points out that "the factual transition from a free to a controlled currency economy occurred in a leap-like manner. Even pure currency policy tends more toward 'mutation' than toward evolution."[48] Thus time is decisively surpassed as a quantitative succession and a determined quantum in political-economic thought as well, and time is recognized as an indeterminate element in its fullest possible potential, quality, and intensity.

This recognition of acausal, indeterminate processes leads directly to:

2) The supersession of dualism in sociology. It is most evident in the recognition of the mutational principle for political economic events that determine human social life. The admission of this principle means that events are not only partially detached from the quantitative and measurable course of time, but also acquire the character of qualitative intensity. Moreover, by surrendering deterministic thinking in favor in indeterminate processes or possibilities, we destroy the principle inherent in antithetic, dualistic, rational, linear, and causal thinking. In his sociological philosophy, Max Brod recognizes that today there are "rare and isolated cases of emerging disruption of the causal structure in man," which he designates with the "abbreviation DSC (*disruptio structurae causarum*)."[49] It is an indication that in social thought the old rational, dualistic mode of thought is being superseded.

The same acausal inceptions can be found in Romano Guardini,[50] who expressly states that "quality cannot be deduced at all; not from a quantity since they are essentially different; and different aspects cannot be derived from such differences. Quality can only be based on itself. The basis for qualitative effect lies in the quality of the cause. Must then the quality of the effects be derived from the quality of the cause? No. Indeed the effects are 'grounded' in the cause, yet they cannot be derived from it. There is no derivation for quality. Quality emerges ('educitur,' is 'educed' as medieval philosophy says)."[51] Expressed in our terms, it presents its own truth.

The anthropological-sociological writings of Lecomte du Noüy point toward the same spiritual climate. He stresses the necessity of "considering the laws of chance"[52] and warns against the "mechanisms of logical thinking."[53] He maintains that "Rationalism must not be a philosophy; it is a method of work. Its prestige is borrowed from science. It does not exist without science."[54] Based on the "law of chance" and the "necessity of freedom," insofar as man is not closed but remains open to the development of his possibilities,[55] and based on his valuation of rationalism as a mode of operation, Lecomte du Noüy arrives at his qualitative, indeterministic position: "The human being ceases to obey the rigorous physico-chemical determinism."[56]

It is of fundamental importance that political economics (Marbach), sociological philosophy (Guardini and Brod), and a biologically-anchored anthropology (du Noüy) have accepted indeterminism, for this enables an effective supersession of the rationally limited dualism which previously was opposed only by an anti-dualistic position. This symptomatic anti-dualism has thereby acquired a previously lacking justification. The necessity of escaping from the ultimate alternative of individual versus collective has become unavoidably evident to the most diverse sociologists. This is even indicated by Wilhelm Röpke's theory of the "third way,"[57] which provides a compromise between capitalistic and communistic economies (between a free and a planned economy), supported as a neo-liberalism by certain powerful political interests. Yet his model-thinking (see p. 387) excludes him from any extra-systematic thought and prevents his breakthrough to the new consciousness structure.

It is quite a different story with the socialist position. There Fritz Marbach's openness toward indeterminism allows him to establish "that neither an individualistic nor a purely collectivistic economy adequately corresponds to the social climate of the modern world-view."[58] This same view is maintained by Ludwig Preller, who stresses the integrative principle and succeeds in dissolving the false alternatives (and dualisms) between individual and mass (a mass which exists only rarely, if at all). His integrative principle (in accord with Husserl) is the "complete interconnections of parts which determine each other" and manifest perceptually the whole, which he designates as the space-time potency of the "web of interrelationships."[59]

The rejection of the dualism of the individual versus the mass is also found in social philosophy. The same effort to overcome dualism, as with Röpke, can be found in Martin Buber. But Buber's insight into this necessity is limited by postulations emerging, as with Röpke, from a realistic understanding of the untenability and the danger of the momentary situation. Yet their postulations cannot effectively clarify it because of their predominantly mental attitude. "Beyond the subjective and this side of the objective, on the narrow ledge where I and Thou encounter each other, is the realm of the in-between. This reality [the realm of the in-between], whose discovery has begun in our day, points the way for coming generations, leading beyond both individualism and collectivism."[60] Despite the promise of this point of departure, Buber's mentalistic conclusion is disappointing: "Here the genuine third is announced; once recognized, it will help us to recapture the genuine person in the human species and to establish a genuine community. For philosophical anthropology, this reality presents a point of departure capable of progressing toward a transformed understanding of the person on the one hand, and the community on the other. Its central object is neither the individual nor the collective but the human with the human."[61] In the face of the contemporary sociological situation this is only a pious wish, since it fails to surpass the mental limitations; it is only relevant insofar as it has recognized the untenability of dualism.

In contrast, Romano Guardini is not only more courageous but also stands closer to reality. With requisite severity for today, he maintains that "the feeling for the intrinsic being and a proper sphere of man, the previous basis for all social conduct, is rapidly disappearing. With increasing frequency, humans are treated like objects as a matter of course—from the innumerable modes of statistical 'inventory' by the authorities, to the inconceivable violations of the individual, the group, and indeed of entire peoples. This happens not just out of necessity and paroxysms of war but as a normal procedure of government administration.

"Yet it appears that we shall not be adequate to this phenomenon if we continue to regard it only from such viewpoints as the loss of respect or unscrupulousness in the application of power. This is surely the case, yet such ethical defects would not be so pervasive and accepted by the victims if the entire process were not supported by structural changes in the experience of the relationship to the self and to other.

"All this may have a two-fold significance. Either the individual is absorbed into the whole [the collectives], becoming a mere vehicle of functions—a terrible peril threatening in all events—or man merges into the vast framework of life and work and relinquishes the no longer possible freedom of individual movement and formation: he withdraws into his core to save his being."[62]

This stern admission—whose realization will be unavoidable if we fail to master mechanization, the irruption of quantitative, rigid, and autonomous empty time—is not pessimism, but a conscious renunciation of freedom, an overdetermined freedom. It parallels our suggestion (p. 151 et passim) that the alternative individual versus collective, personal encapsulation versus impersonal ag-glomeration, can be resolved only by the supersession of both: by the achievement of an apersonal, supra-individual and supra-collective "Itself" constituting the "core" as well as the "essential" in man (see p. 134 f.). In accordance with our previous practice, we shall not designate the "Itself" by the term "the Self" so as to prevent its being identified with the notions of India, the merely psychological definition by C. G. Jung, or its mental-rational misinterpretation by Buber.[63] Max Brod must have meant the "Itself" and not the ambiguous "self" when he spoke of the "Depth-Ego."[64]

Only when Buber does not advance his own postulates but falls back upon Hasidism (we are indebted to Buber for our knowledge of it) do we find a hint of the attitude sketched above. It should be noted that Hasidism is an extensive, esoteric movement which emerged in the middle of the eighteenth century in eastern European Judaism.[65] It united the wisdom of tradition with the insights into the inevitable requirements of the future. An indication of this is contained in a saying of one of the greatest Hasidic rabbis, spoken to his community: "What do I demand of you? Only three things: not to look askance from within yourself, not to look askance at another, and not to think of yourself."[66]

In an entirely different way, Arnold J. Toynbee has expressed a tendency to renounce or surpass dualism. His *Study of History*,[67] as he himself admitted,[68] is not so much a work of history as a vast design for sociology. His two main theses are thoroughly anti-dualistic: a) cultures emerge through superimposition, and b) their effectiveness and existence correspond to the optimal demands placed upon them by the given world situation and survive as long as they are capable of responding in accordance with such demands. Both theses contain a partial rejection of causal dependence and biological determinism (still prevalent in Spengler in the form of linear succession) and place structural elements and interdependencies in the foreground.

Toynbee's implicit emphasis on structures and interdependencies is explicit in the broadly conceived *World History of the Most Recent Times* by J. R. von Salis, who introduces a well-founded yet entirely new kind of historical writing.[69] From von Salis' mode of exposition it follows that for him history is not, as previously conceived, a temporal stream and course of events, but a manifestation of interrelated and combined events whose effective interrelationships form history. In this approach the structural elements of nations and cultural regions are considered to the same extent as the sociological and spiritual structures. This work initiates a universal-integral writing of history. It is world-open, and to a great extent rejects the mere linear presentation in favor of a many-faceted description of the whole event. Thus it assists the irruption of the new consciousness structure in one of the most difficult and crucial areas. Since historical events are conditioned by sociological factors, this work could not have been left unmentioned here.[70]

From a sociological view, the same holds true for modern ethnology, above all Frobenius' theory of cultural spheres. This has had a most enduring influence, and from it Frobenius developed his morphology of cultures. It would seem that its elaboration in recent years at the hands of his students has changed it from mere gestalt theory into a theory of structure. It has been epoch-making for our estimation of alien, so-called "primitive" cultures. It removed the mental-rational presuppositions and enabled the continuously deeper penetration into the alien forms of reality and realization, and justifiably placed into doubt the sole validity of our form of reality.[71]

The cultural morphology of Frobenius has added decisively to our recent ability to perceive the uniquely human, as well as the reality of mankind as multifariously structured and not dualistically divided. (The schizoid, if not schizophrenic, character of our epoch is at least a clear indication of the devastating consequences of the mental, rational, and dualistic position driven to extremes.) Frobenius' theory (as well as its salutary distancing from us and our consciousness structure) was no doubt partially responsible for the leap into the arational attitude. In any case, the dualistic attitude which has contrasted the "cultivated" (the European) with the "primitive" (of lesser value) was surpassed by Frobenius' theory of cultural spheres. The consequences of this deed can hardly be overestimated, since it freed the path to an attitude encompassing all of mankind.

All of these partially attempted and partially achieved rejections of rational dualism bring us to:

3) The tendency toward arationality in the new sociology. Basically it should be noted that the demonstration of the various consciousness structures carried out in the first part of this book is in itself an arational realization. The human being as a whole is multifariously structured. Since we are today in a position to survey the entire mental-rational structure without confusing it with the irrational or the pre-rational, it ought to be evident that at least potentially we have achieved an over-determined structure we have called "arational," whose essence is to consciously integrate all other structures.

The multifarious structure of reality is also the point of departure of Walther Tritsch,[72] who further emphasizes the qualitative aspect and also stresses the "structure of the possible."[73] Together with A. Marrou, A. Varagnac, and A. J. Toynbee, Tritsch proposed a unanimously accepted resolution that was declared mandatory by the *Commission de Coordination des Sciences Historiques* of the *Centre Européen de la Culture* in Geneva (December, 1951). It demands that every historian, pedagogue, and sociologist respect "the distinction of three mainstreams in the events of humanity: a) the material; b) the social; and c) the spiritual. Although they superimpose and mutually influence one another, not one of them is a singular determinant of the other. This objective method of making mutually acceptable distinctions can bring an end to false alternatives in research and instruction, and to redundant conflicts prevalent among those historians who are exclusively materialistic, sociologistic, or idealistic in their assumptions" (we refer the reader to the full text in note 74, p. 442).

This recognition signals at least a partial elimination of the exclusively rational interpretation, and thus it shows evidence of an arational character. It makes possible not only a systematic view of "phenomena" but also a systatic, structural, indeterminate, and hence aperspectival perception wherein a systatic element, that of interdependency, is in the forefront (as opposed to mere systematics).

Incidentally, Martin Buber may have aimed at something similar in 1923, yet as a consequence of his (temporally-bound) mental-rational limitations, it was expressed only fragmentarily in his definition of the "unified ego":[75] "In the lived reality there is unification with the soul, the gathering of powers in the core, the decisive moment of man. . . . [This] gathering does not regard the instincts as too impure, the senses as too peripheral, the disposition as too evanescent—everything must be incorporated and mastered."[76]

Our consciousness structuration has shown a parallel form of realization between the multifariously structured consciousness and its anchorage in man as a whole. Inherent in the structuration is the impossibility for individual consciousness structures to determine one another; in their superimposition they overdetermine each other. Hence the psychic overdetermines the vital, the mental overdetermines the psychic, while the overdetermination occurs integratively in the integral consciousness structure, and thus the potential element inherent in each individual structure becomes visible. We have already stressed that this structuration is not a system or a schema; rather, it makes visible the interconnections.

The perception of interconnections presupposes the presence of the temporal aspect just as each structure is realizable spatio-temporally, that is, four-dimensionally. And inasmuch as Husserl has already emphasized the perception of interconnections, thus arationally superseding rational fixity and rigidity (p. 409), it is significant that we can ascertain an emphasis on the "grasping" of interconnections in philosophical sociology. In connection with a discussion of acausal, creative aspects, Max Brod underscores man's freedom to perceive the "all-encompassing interconnections of being."[77] And proceeding from his deliberations on the acausal nature of the qualitative, Guardini stresses the "essential interconnections"[78] and conceives of them, not in Husserl's sense, but as a unification of causally non-determinable "phenomena." Even political economics in its own reduced field speaks of the necessity to recall the "total interconnections"[79] when dealing with organizational systems, and to consider the entire person inclusive of his (vital) instincts and psychic components.[80]

In any case, this increasing attention to interconnections is arational, making possible an integrating mode of realization and a liberation from mere systemization, as well as lending perceptibility to an "open" world.

The integrating effectuality of the arational mode of realization manifests itself in the fact that today universal concepts are emerging ever more frequently in sociology. Thus Lecomte du Noüy speaks of the self-constitution of a "universal consciousness."[81] Hans Zbinden has shown the "awakening of a new conscience," a "new sense of world," meaning the supersession of sectoral nationalism;[82] and Alois Dempf has circumscribed an "integral humanism,"[83] furthering a theory of the whole man.[84] In addition we should consider Pestalozzi's insistence on a child's being treated as a human and not as a possession, with its far-reaching results, as well as the contemporary demand that woman be treated as a human being and not just as a woman, a further step toward the "whole person" and "integral humanism."

The work of Hans von Eckardt, *Die Macht der Frau* (Woman's Power), bears witness to this socio-culturally important process.[85] The medieval church denied woman her soul. In modern times she is seen as a possession of man, giving rise to the problematics of marriage; and the reconstruction of marriage from the depths of human relationships has been a prime concern of Max Picard.[86] The foundations of the sociological change manifest in and occasioned by Western estimations of love, particularly with regard to the Latin countries of Europe, have been described by Denis de Rougemont.[87] Even Buber aims at an understanding of the "whole man."[88] And in political economics, W. Röpke in his book *Civitas Humana*[89] has become an admonisher in economics for a secularized *civitas dei* (Augustine).

Various sociologists furnish indications of that other concomitant of the integral mode of realization, the emergent opening world. Among the indications we can discern two kinds: those pointing to a structural change in specific areas, and those of a more encompassing nature. Ludwig Preller must be credited as being the first sociologist (1962) to ascribe a crucial role to the principle of integration (p. 431). He has succeeded in creating a hitherto unachieved design for a new social order as a correlative to the contemporary changing consciousness.

André Siegfried has pointed to a specific characteristic of Western man: his capacity to administer. It is a result not only of a distancing from oneself and the means employed—most effective in economy and industry—but also from the underlying knowledge of the concept and value of time.[90] It is this dual knowledge of the value of space and time that forms the primary basis for an open perception of the world. It is not accidental that in recent years André Siegfried became the advocate of "open government" and strove to establish the value of "meritorial" rather than "formalistic" procedures. This "meritorial procedure" is "open" inasmuch as it is not oriented toward laws and formulas but toward the "preamble," or intent. This is of extraordinary importance for governance, as it is then bound to decide flexibly, openly, and with justice to the general sense of the directives, rather than rigidly, arbitrarily, and literally. (In addition we would note that the initial inceptions of the "meritorial procedure" were enacted in 1493 in the Hapsburg monarchy!)[91]

A different aspect of the emergent openness has been indicated by J. A. Schumpeter, who observes that during the course of the last generation the public has gradually assumed the place of the patron in support of intellectuals.[92] This means that those engaged in mental work are no longer dependent on patriarchy but face an open world, indeed are for the first time a part of the general public.

This double-edged problem of the public leads to two general ascertainments which Romano Guardini has formulated lapidarily: "In any event, man today does not experience the world as a protective enclosure."[93] This is the contemporary situation in all its severity; man is no longer protected and secure. (Guardini's assessment parallels our own, presented in the first part of this book.) This situation elicits two reactions: the most prevalent is that we feel pushed out, helpless, unprotected and "thrown"; the second is that we recognize the open world and sustain it through openness.

To what extent Western man tends toward this openness, at first justifiably felt to be a loss, is obvious from J. A. Schumpeter's remarks. He notes the "loss of domesticity" recognizable in the flight toward the public: flight from the home into restaurants, clubs, apartment houses, and hotel apartments. Schumpeter subjects this phenomenon to an instructive sociological analysis.[94] The flight, more obvious in the United States than in Europe, is not only a rejection of intimacy, but a deeper sociological restructuration, a lessening of rigidity. This is revealed by a parallel phenomenon.[95] Architecture may be considered as the artistic expression of sociology. With this in mind, it is not irrelevant to note that for the last thirty years architecture has demonstrated a tendency toward greater openness (we will discuss this later in chapter 9).

These sociological assertions, all of which are inceptions of an open perception of the world, may be evaluated in our view as indications of a de-rigidification and hence of the emergent arationality of man. Alfred Weber, who has demonstrated the end of the currently attained intellectual-rationalistic level of consciousness,[96] points implicitly to the irruption of arationality. Lecomte du Noüy describes it explicitly by underscoring the inadequacies of the previous rational mode of realization and showing the need for a new mode of realization.

Alfred Weber expressly states: "Neither the Euclidean spatial conception nor the concomitant quantitative conception of time that man has developed can actually encompass the world in its being and becoming. Both are merely means of orientation whose limits are immediately clear. Both fundamental categories—the three-dimensional conception of space, as well as the quantitative conception of time—are merely human categories inadequate to encompass the spiritual world.

"Moreover, the basic principle of intellectualistic causality . . . appears to fail . . . The newest claims of physics, even where still content with mathematical formulations of quantity, motion, and change in inanimate space and time, show that, observed more closely, such an approach within the previous intellectual, formal language of Euclidian space, time, and causality is inadequate. It is necessary to construct an appropriate formal language and specific concepts which exclude causality and the old space-time conceptions in order to reach a more exact description of the world processes by an artificial, mathematical, four-dimensional construction unifying space and time. This means in truth the end of an all-encompassing inventory of the world via every-day intellectualistic categories . . . , the end of codification of inanimate nature. With respect to animate nature, vitalism has long since shown that its secrets are not amenable to explanation and opinions based on the notion of external cause and effect. Rather, we must assume intellectually inaccessible, immanent and transcendent powers of volition and formation in order to gain some comprehension of what has come here into being and is capable of building and rebuilding itself anew.

"Today no one assumes that the intellectual-formal categories [i.e., rational conceptions, formulations, and representations], which are inadequate for explaining being and becoming, could say anything about *imperatives*, about the essence and emergence of values as rules for our actions, or about the meaning of the world. All this is beyond the ken of an intellect developed for practical, human purposes. . . .

"The intellect therefore, as the ultimate authority, has been banished not only from the religious but also from the philosophical-metaphysical sphere. Once again a revolutionary end. While the Eastern world conception and meaning remained magical, as in China, or attained a magical-mythical-metaphysical form of comprehension as in India, it has in the West come to rest in a plane of intellectualism through the influence of the intellectualistic mental-rational philosophy of the Greeks. This plane is today crumbling. . . . This collapse has clearly circumscribed the limits of intellectualism and has revealed the possibility of a meta-causal and extra spatio-temporal world comprehension."[97]

The last statement in Alfred Weber's confirmation of the collapse of the mental-rational "plane" contains the only intimation of the possibility of a new constellation of consciousness. It is only an indication; the mode of realization is only intimated and not described. But being formulated by a sociologist, it is extremely valuable and very definitely contains a basis for departure. The necessary leap is effected only when we consciously realize that the "possibility of extra spatio-temporal world comprehension" is achievable in a space-time–free world perception. Viewed in terms of consciousness, the "extra-spatio-temporal" is the primordial pre-space-timelessness which lies "before" consciousness. In emerging consciousness, it transforms space-timelessness into space-time–freedom, permitting the mutation from an unconscious openness to a conscious openness, whose essence is not "being in" or "being in opposition to" but diaphaneity, that is, spiritual transparency.[98]

Lecomte du Noüy too points implicitly to space-time–freedom: "Man will at last be able to think 'universally.' His mechanical intelligence has come to the rescue of his moral intuition. He has gained centuries by eliminating space and time which separated him from the suffering of his brother and erected isolating barriers around him."[99] Elimination (removing limits, de-limiting, de-restricting) or the supersession of space-time by this conscious process is synonymous with the possible acquisition of the achronon, space-time–freedom.[100]

Since space-time–freedom is neither a being-in nor being-in-oppostion-to, but an openness, a diaphaneity, then it is evident that the new mode of realization is neither an identification nor control of objects. It is not achievable by some perspectival conception and can only be effected in aperspectival truth sustaining. Perhaps José Ortega y Gasset had this mode of realization in mind in his address, "Truth as man's accord with himself."[101] In any case, Lecomte du Noüy has established it on the basis of his research in sociology and neurobiology: "Man with his present brain does not represent the end of evolution, but only an intermediary stage between the past, heavily weighted down with memories of the beast, and the future, rich in higher promise. Such is human destiny."[102]

This conception has been shared recently by Hugo Spatz (see p. 338) who, on the basis of his brain research, regards the developmental possibility of one part of the cortex, the basal neocortex, as certain.[103] These assertions, relating to the already established unfolding in the brain that, as he points out, might have occurred mutationally, afford proof for our structurally discovered mutations of consciousness.

This coincidence of findings originating in sociological research, further supported by neurobiological, ethnological, and prehistorical evidence, with our clearly demonstrated "unfoldings" of consciousness structures via mutations, is not just significant in itself. It is also important in regard to the mode of realization of the "universal consciousness," as Lecomte du Noüy calls it, which we have designated as the integral, mankind-open consciousness. This realization form is direct perception: "It is necessarily the brain, made up of cells, which evolves. But this organ has reached a stage where its physico-chemical and biological activity manifests itself on a different plane through psychological phenomena which are perceived directly. Their existence coincides with our perception of them, without intermediary mechanism."[104]

The inceptions presented from sociology toward an "open world," unlimited by three-dimensional space, as well as the indications of a qualitative mode of realization of perception—no longer merely rational conceptualization—indeed, the suggested possibility of space-time–freedom occurring through the emergent consciousness and supersession of space-time, should make evident that sociology, too, is manifesting tendencies toward arationality, tendencies that may be evaluated as initial manifestations of aperspectivity.

1   *Li Gi: Das Buch der Sitte des älteren und jüngeren Dai*, trans. Richard Wilhelm (Jena: Diederichs, 1930).
2   Peter Bamm, *Feuilletons* (Stuttgart: Deutsche Verlags-Anstalt, 1949), p. 141.
3   Ibid. p. 142.
4   See *inter alia* the following works by Wolfhart Friedrich Bürgi:
        a) *Recht und Macht: Schriftenreihe der Freisinnig-demokratischen Partei des Kantons St. Gallen*, No. 2 (1942).
        b) "Individualistische und kollektivistische Strömungen im geltenden Privatrecht, insbesondere im Hinblick auf Eigentum und Arbeitsleistung," *Individuum*

und Gemeinschaft: Festschrift zum fünfzigjährigen Jubiläum der Handels-Hochschule St. Gallen (1949), pp. 307–327.

c) *Freiheit und Sicherheit im Recht*, Rektoratsrede, St. Galler Hochschulverein (St. Gallen, 1951).

d) "Die Wandlungen des Rechts," *Kommt der vierte Mensch?* (Zürich, Vienna, and Stuttgart: Europa, 1952), pp. 33–45.

e) "Das Recht in der veränderten Welt," *Die Welt in neuer Sicht*, I (München-Planegg: Barth, 1957), pp. 88–107.

f) "Probleme des Rechts im Zeitalter der Integrationen," *Zukunftsaufgaben in Wirtschaft und Gesellschaft: Festschrift zur Einweihung der neuen Gebäude der Hochschule St. Gallen für Wirtschafts- und Sozialwissenschaften* (Zürich, 1963), pp. 287–296.

g) "Bedeutung und Grenzen der Interessenabwägung bei der Beurteilung gesellschaftsrechtlicher Probleme," *Études de droit commercial en l'honneur de Paul Carry, Mémoires publiés par la Faculté de droit de Genève*, 18 (Geneva, 1964).

h) "Die Polarität als soziologisches Grundphänomen für das Recht," *Transparente Welt: Festschrift für Jean Gebser* (Bern: Huber, 1965), p. 69 ff.

See also the following publications by Hans Marti:

i) *Urbild und Verfassung: Eine Studie zum hintergründigen Gehalt einer Verfassung* (Bern: Huber, 1959).

j) "Naturrecht und Verfassungsrecht," *Rechtsquellenprobleme im schweizerischen Recht: Festgabe für den Schweizer Juristenverein, Zeitschrift des Berner Juristenvereins*, 91, 2 (1955), p. 74 ff.

k) "Recht in neuer Sicht," *Wege zur neuen Wirklichkeit* (Bern: Hallwag, 1960), pp. 105–140.

l) "Verfassung," *Transparente Welt: Festschrift für Jean Gebser* (Bern: Huber, 1965), pp. 77 ff.

5   "Si je savois quelque chose qui me fût utile, et qui fût préjudiciable à ma famille, je la rejetterois de mon esprit. Si je savois quelque chose utile à ma famille, et qui ne le fût pas à ma patrie, je chercherois à l'oublier. Si je savois quelque chose utile à ma patrie, et qui fût préjudiciable a l'Europe, ou bien qui fût utile à l'Europe et préjudiciable au Genre humain, je la regarderois comme un crime" (Montesquieu, *Cahiers 1716-1755*, [Paris: Grasset, 1941], p. 9 f.).

6   See *inter alia* Helmut Coing, *Grundzüge der Rechtsphilosophie* (Berlin: de Gruyter, 1950), and Georg Stadtmüller, *Das abendländische Rechtsbewusstsein* (Nürnberg: Glock und Lutz, 1951).

7   W. F. Bürgi, note 4, item b), p. 311.

8   Hans Marti, note 4, particularly items i), k), and l).

9   W. F. Bürgi, note 4, item b), pp. 313–317.

10   Ibid., pp. 318–325.

11   Elsewhere we have indicated the perils inherent in management in situations where, in the West, the manager can function in a sociological role analogous to the party-political role invariably filled in the Eastern bloc by the commisar; see Jean Gebser, "Auflösung oder Überwindung der Persönlichkeit," *Kommt der vierte Mensch?* (Zürich, Vienna, and Stuttgart: Europa, 1952), p. 49 f.; J. Gebser, *In der Bewährung* (Bern and Munich: Francke, 1962), p. 113; *Gesamtausgabe*, V/I p. 261.

12   Goethe, *Faust I*, 1972–1976.

13   W. F. Bürgi, note 4, item c), p. 12; Bürgi's italics.

14   Ibid., p. 13 f.

15   W. F. Bürgi, note 4, item b), p. 315.

16   Adolf Arndt, *Rechtsdenken in unserer Zeit: Positivismus und Naturrecht* (Tübingen: Mohr, 1955), p. 17. Arndt points to the "symptoms of change in our thought structure" as well as to the negative consequences of "Aristotelian dualism," noting that "this

dualism . . . is by no means self-evident but rather can be shown to be highly proble-matic." He also makes the important observation (p. 19; his italics): "Is it not worth noting whether a new concept of time, having altered our image of the world funda-mentally via the natural sciences, is not also making itself felt in the humanistic field of jurisprudence, and paving the way for a *polar* understanding of law and rights, and also ethics as a whole, rather than a dualistic dissociation of these continua? . . . A new concept of time in jurisprudence, as well as a fresh understanding of temporality and all that rightly befits time, will be able to make visible a hitherto unknown classification of moral law and legality, of justice and injustice." As to the limitations of validity inherent in the dualism of legal thought, see the inceptive suggestions by Marti (note 4, item k), p. 109 et passim. The question of "polarity as a basic phenomenon of law" has received a revealing examination, with particular regard to its fluctuating estimation in jurispru-dence, in W. F. Bürgi's discussion (note 4, item h).

17   W. F. Bürgi, note 4, item b), p. 316.
18   Ibid., p. 316.
19   The importance of the time factor and its effect on justice has also been explored by Erich Genzmer, "Zum Verhältnis von Rechtsgeschichte und Rechtsvergleichung," *Ar-chiv für Rechts- und Sozialphilosophie,* 3 (Meisenheim/Glan, 1955), p. 341 ff.
20   Since this section was written (1951–1952), the divisions within the various branches of sociology, including several new ones, have become more rigid as well as more differen-tiated. Despite this we have refrained from rewriting the text, and consequently this section will seem somewhat lacking in method when viewed from the present vantage point of the discipline. Nevertheless, this section still contains some valid suggestions, abetted by further insights from the scholarship of the intervening decade in support of the original conception. Because of these emendations we have felt compelled to change the title of this section on "sociology" to "Sociology and Economics."
21   It should be apparent that man was able to attain mental conceptualization as a form of realization only by forsaking mythical imagery. This is evident in the transposition of the mythical trias into the mental-dogmatic tri-unity or trinity idea; the latter belongs, as an idea, to the conceptual world with which we dealt earlier (see text, p. 87 ff.).
22   Max Weber, "Die protestantische Ethik und der Geist des Kapitalismus," *Archiv für Sozialwissenschaft und Sozialpolitik* (1903–1904); reprinted in his *Gesammelte Aufsätze zur Religionssoziologie* (Tübingen: Mohr, ³1934, ⁴1947), I.
23   Ludwig Preller, *Sozialpolitik: Theoretische Ortung* (Tübingen: Mohr, 1962), pp. 48 ff., 54 f., 299 note 27.
24   Ibid., p. 298 et passim.
25   Whether or not a basic correction of communism will take place via esoteric elements, supposedly represented even in the Komintern according to reliable sources, will ap-pear, if at all, only indirectly. (Zen and Hesychasm seem to be the leading contenders in this reform.) In any event, the high degree of discipline required for those making up the highest cadre of the Komintern (such as the conscious renunciation of the ego for the sake of an idea) is not to be underestimated with respect to its effects; it is on the same plane in a secularized form as the religious orders and their demand for absolute obedience and self-denial. It is a hypertrophied form of discipline to which we in the West have nothing equivalent to oppose, particularly as military obedience, partly de-generated to the form of "corpse loyalty," is of itself no real comparison to the true-to-line attitude of the communist (with respect to the cadre, not to the despots).
26   Preller (note 23), pp. 9 ff., 73 f., and 126 f.
27   Arthur Lisowsky, "Absatzdenken als historisches Denken II," *Die Betriebswirtschaft: Zeitschrift für Handelswissenschaft und Handelspraxis,* 31, 12 (Stuttgart, December 1938), 276, column 2.
28   Ibid., p. 277, col. 1, note 20. See also Kosiol, *Theorie der Lohnstruktur* (Stuttgart, 1928), particularly p. 8 (cited in Lisowsky).

29 Arthur Lisowsky, "Absatzdenken als historisches Denken I," *Die Betriebswirtschaft: Zeitschrift für Handelswissenschaft und Handelspraxis*, 31, 2 (November, 1938), 241, col. 1–2.

30 Arthur Lisowsky, "Absatzdenken als Gestaltdenken," *Die Betriebswirtschaft: Zeitschrift für Handelswissenschaft und Handelspraxis*, 30, 8 (August, 1937), 178–185.

31 Lisowsky (note 29), p. 243, note 7.

32 Ibid., p. 242, col. 2.

33 Ibid., p. 242, note 5.

34 Ibid., p. 245, col. 2.

35 To which we must add that this is so only as long as the currency retains the identical purchasing power, as was presupposed in the nineteenth century. The constant fluctuations in buying power today during the term of interest introduces qualitative changes into the quantitative passage of time!

36 Arthur Lisowsky (note 27), p. 279, col. 2.

37 Walter Adolf Jöhr, "Die Leistungen des Konkurrenzsystems und seine Bedeutung für die Wirtschaft unserer Zeit," *Schweizerische Zeitschrift für Volkswirtschaft und Statistick*, 86, 5 (1950), pp. 398–415.

38 Fritz Marbach, *Zur Frage der wirtschaftlichen Staatsintervention* (Bern: Francke, 1951), p. 59.

39 Christian Gasser, "Die menschlichen Beziehungen im Betrieb," *Mensch und Betrieb* (Frankfurt/M.: Breitenbach; St. Gallen: Zollikofer, 1949), p. 22.

40 Ibid., p. 23.

41 Ibid., p. 39.

42 Georges Friedmann, *Der Mensch in der mechanisierten Produktion* (Köln: Bund, 1952), p. 395 ff.

43 Norbert Wiener, *The Human Use of Human Beings: Cybernetics and Society* (Boston: Houghton Mifflin, 1950), pp. 16 and 189. As to the qualitative elements, Günter Schmölders' emphasis on human behavior in the economic sphere seems to be a fortunate starting point, inasmuch as it limits the purely deterministic point of view to its appropriate role; see Günter Schmölders, "Ökonomische Verhaltensforschung," *Ordo*, 5 (Düsseldorf: Küpper, 1953), p. 203.

44 Romano Guardini, *Lebendiger Geist* (Zürich: Arche, 1950).

45 Karl Mannheim, *Diagnose unserer Zeit* (Zürich: Europa, 1951), pp. 144, 222, 224, and 226.

46 Walther Tritsch, "Die Wandlungen der menschlichen Beziehungen," *Die Neue Weltschau* (Stuttgart: Deutsche Verlagsanstalt, 1952), p. 155.

47 Basic observations on this potential structural concept can be found in Walther Tritsch's article cited in note 46, as well as in his *Die Erben in der bürgerlichen Welt* (Bern: Francke, 1954).

48 Fritz Marbach (note 38), p. 61.

49 Max Brod, *Diesseits und Jenseits* (Winterthur: Mondial, 1947), I, p. 22 et passim.

50 Romano Guardini (note 44), pp. 74 f. and 157 note 5.

51 Guardini, p. 158, notes 7 and 8, and Guardini, *Unterscheidung des Christlichen* (Mainz: Grünewald, 1935), p. 138. It should be emphasized that Guardini speaks in this connection of "quantitative thinking," as well as of the "qualitative leap" that forms the subject of his book *Der Ausgangspunkt der Denkbewegung Sören Kirkegaards*. Here we will only indicate his principal argument: "Merely quantitative thinking, as prevalent even today to a great extent in the natural sciences (though not only there), basically desires to dominate; it is despotic. Theroretical problems have here become ethical decisions" (Guardini, *Unterscheidungen des Christlichen*, p. 140, note 1, and 466 ff.).

52* Lecomte du Noüy, *Human Destiny* (New York: Longmans, Green, 1947), p. 247.

53* Ibid., chapter 1, passim, and p. 12.

54* Ibid., pp. 229–230.

55* Ibid., pp. 176–177.

56* Ibid., p. 178.

57   Wilhelm Röpke, *Die Gesellschaftskrisis der Gegenwart* (Erlenbach bei Zürich: Rentsch, 1942).

58   Fritz Marbach (note 38), p. 60.

59   Ludwig Preller (note 23), pp. 4 f., 6 f., 19 f., and 299.

60   Martin Buber, *Dialogisches Leben* (Zürich: Gregor Müller, 1947), p. 457.

61   Ibid., p. 457 ff.

62   Romano Guardini, *Das Ende der Neuzeit* (Basel: Hess, 1950), p. 75 f.

63   Martin Buber (note 60), p. 87.

64   Max Brod (note 49), I, pp. 111 f., 114, and 120.

65   Martin Buber, *Der Weg des Menschen nach der chassidischen Lehre* (Pulvis-Viarum-Druck, Amsterdam: de Lange; Köln: Kiepenheuer, ²1950), p. 44, note 1.

66   Ibid., p. 35.

67*   Arnold Toynbee, *A Study of History* (London: Oxford University Press, 1934–1954), x.

68   During the plenary session of the conference of the *Comité International des Sciences Historiques* on September 1, 1950, in Paris; we would note in this context that particularly in Germany there has occurred a partly fruitful but nonetheless misleading historization of sociology to which Carlo Antoni, with his true Latin eye for realities, has devoted a refreshing and revealing study: Carlo Antoni, *Vom Historismus zur Soziologie* (Stuttgart: Koehler, 1951).

69   J. R. von Salis, *Weltgeschichte der neuesten Zeit* (Zürich: Füssli, 1951–1960), III.

70   Salis himself has begun to speak of this fundamental point of view; see his "Geschichte als Form und Kraft," *Die Welt in Neuer Sicht*, I (München-Planegg: Barth, 1957), pp. 66–87.

71   It was unfortunately unable to prevent the rise of ur-monotheism, a doctrine symptomatic of the rational incapacity of its founders and proponents to discern structures different from ours with respect to consciousness and to recognize their legitimacy. The doctrine of an ur-monotheos confuses monotheism, which is only mentally conceivable, with a still potent idolatry that can be experienced only magically. The projection of rational conceptions into "world images" held by an earlier mankind has given rise to such erroneous interpretations as those that define purposive behavior that stems from the vital nexus of "primitives" and early cultures as "rational" or "rationalistic." J. A. Schumpeter, for example, speaks of the "rationalistic behavior" of an orangutan or a primitive in his *Kapitalismus, Sozialismus und Demokratie* (Bern: Francke, ²1950), p. 200. But since the "primitive" has a pre-rational consciousness structure, rationality has at best to do with behavior to the extent that pre-rationality bears within itself the potential of a later possibility for rationality.

72   Walther Tritsch (note 46).

73   In principle Thomas More should also be considered as a precursor of this mode of realization which takes into account what is potentially qualitative. His *Utopia*, published in 1516, is definitely a "temporic" first step taken during a mentally-oriented age. "Utopia," which means "without place," points toward a regard for a potentiality existing within "temporality" but not fixed spatially. This perhaps explains the pejorative connotation attached to the word "utopia" by an age that recognizes only quantitative spatial thinking. Furthermore, it has been recently discovered that the woodcuts illustrating the first edition are faithful reproductions representing the monasteries of Mt. Athos. We owe this insight to Mr. Baldwin, who was one of the last members of the "secret Society of Mt. Athos." This secret society was founded by the Byzantine emperors at the height of their splendor and supported by them for centuries. The society in turn was to accord the emperors, in a kind of openly political leadership, the opportunity to rule according to direct instructions of the "uncreated light," the ultimate divine recourse of the Mt. Athos divines. The *Utopia* is a recreation of the statutes of the "Secret Society of Mt. Athos." Apparently the monks of Mt. Athos, who were repeatedly forced to flee iconoclastic attacks, had instructed Thomas More, thereby initiating him into the public governance as well.

74   The complete text of the resolution reads as follows:
      La Commission de coordination des sciences historiques du Centre Européen de la
      Culture, réunie à Genève les 10 et 11 décembre 1950, a adopté en principe et prend à
      son compte une définition de méthode historique proposée, après exposé de M.
      Tritsch, par M. André Varagnac au Comité International des sciences historiques, et
      approuvée à l'unanimité par ce Comité a sa seance du 1er septembre 1950 tenue à
      Paris sous la présidence de M. Arnold J. Toynbee.
          M. Varagnac a insisté sur la nécessité d'une vue de l'évolution historique très différ-
      ente de celle qui régnait au siècle dernier. Il a estimé qu'il est impossible aujourd'hui
      de soutenir que l'évolution d'une culture aristocratique ou "supérieure" soit l'in-
      dice visible d'une évolution parallèle de toute la société considérée, et qu'il faut, au
      contraire, dissocier le processus évolutif en plusiers courants superposes:
          1. A la base, une progression par paliers successifs, bien plus lente qu'on ne le
      pensait: celle des "statuts techniques" auxquels il est fort possible que correspon-
      dent des types d'orientation psychologique profondément différents.
          2. Un second substrat est constitué par les organisations sociales de la production
      et de l'échange, par les types de relations entre divers secteurs de sociétés divisées—
      ainsi les rapports entre maître et esclave, seigneur et serf, employeur et employé.
          3. Enfin la superstructure se manifestera dans les cultures "supérieures," telles
      qu'on les enseigne et telles qu'on en étudie classiquement la succession.
          On pourra donc distinguer dans l'évolution humaine trois éléments distincts, su-
      perposés, et trop souvent confondus:
          1. un lent processus matériel et technique, irréversible et universel;
          2. des évolutions sociales distinctes, localisées et réversibles;
          3. une superstructure au moins partiellement irréversible et universelle, comme le
      serait une objectivation croissante de l'esprit humain.
          Il ne peut donc plus s'agir de voir partout une évolution dans le sens du matéria-
      lisme dialectique, en attribuant aux relations toujours multiples de la matière ce qui,
      en réalité, est toujours le résultat d'un ordre imposé par un choix. Car un choix ne
      peut se faire qu'à partir d'idées préconçues qui presque toujours sont nées dans des
      conditions matérielles antérieures.
          Il peut encore moins s'agir, certes, d'attribuer toute l'évolution historique à la
      seule influence des évolutions d'idées, ou des initiatives personnelles d'hommes
      indépendants, en négligeant l'analyse préalable des conditons matérielles. Car
      celles-ci, bien que ne dictant pas telle ou telle orientation idéologique de l'évolution
      historique, interviennent néanmoins en rendant tel chemin impraticable ou telle
      nouvelle solution souhaitable.
          En distinguant trois courants différents de l'évolution humaine—i) matériel, ii)
      social, iii) spirituel—qui se superposent et qui s'influencent mutuellement sans pou-
      voir se déterminer complètement les uns les autres, cette méthode objective peut,
      dans la recherche et dans l'enseignement, mettre fin aux fausses alternatives et aux
      querelles oiseuses entre historiens exlusivement matérialistes, ou sociologues, ou
      idéalistes.
          Elle assignerait à chacune de ces contingences partielles son rôle réel et son do-
      maine scientifique particulier.
          En conséquence, les historiens membres de la Commission se proposent de pro-
      pager et d'encourager chez leurs élèves une application de ces principes de
      méthode.
75   Martin Buber, "Ich und Du," in Dialogisches Leben (note 60), p. 97.
76   So too, Dante's insistence that all texts be read in four senses ("si posso intendere e
      debbonsi sponere massimamente per quatro sensi," Convito, t. 1, cap. 1), may indeed
      point to the anticipation of an integral arationality in tradition.
77   Max Brod (note 49), I, p. 120.
78   Romano Guardini (note 44), p. 76.

79   Christian Gasser (note 39), pp. 23, 28 and 30.

80   This "whole man," to be sure, would seem to be considered as such in industry and
      commerce in America and the Soviet Union only to the extent that his one hundred
      percent output is desired; and this in the last analysis is a purely quantitative matter with
      pseudo-qualitative overtones. The same can be said of the stimulation of worker pro-
      ductivity by music that is done in some firms, further evidence for our contention that
      music belongs to the vital realm. This practice is symptomatic of the pseudo-holistic
      conception of man applied for the sake of increasing profits, and not for man's sake; it is
      also an expression of the devaluation of the life-sustaining powers of the auditory sense.

81*   Lecomte du Noüy (note 52), pp. 258 and 261.

82   Hans Zbinden, Die Moralkrise des Abendlandes (Bern: Lang, 1940). See also his Welt im
      Zwielicht (Zürich: Artemis, 1951).

83   Alois Dempf, Theoretische Anthropologie (Bern: Francke, 1950), p. 238.

84   Ibid., p. 247.

85   Hans von Eckardt, Die Macht der Frau (Stuttgart: Schuler, 1949).

86   Max Picard, Die unerschütterliche Ehe (Zürich: Rentsch, 1942).

87   Denis de Rougemont, L'Amour et l'Occident (Paris: Plon, 1939).

88   Martin Buber (note 60), p. 18 f.

89   Wilhelm Röpke, Civitas humana (Zürich: Rentsch, 1944).

90   André Siegfried, L'Ame des Peuples (Paris: Hachette, 1950).

91   Walther Tritsch, "La réforme de l'Etat: Procédé formaliste ou procédé méritore?" Revue
      de l'Intendance Militaire, new ed. no. 15 (3e trimestre 1950), pp. 55–74.

92   Joseph A. Schumpeter (note 71), p. 235 ff.

93   Romano Guardini (note 62), p. 70.

94   Joseph A. Schumpeter (note 71), p. 256 f.

95   Rainer Maria Rilke, too, views this de-sheltering coming from America as a loss of inti-
      mate touch with our surroundings and objects of culture in our possession; cf. his letter
      of November 13, 1925, Briefe aus Muzot (Leipzig: Insel, 1925), p. 335 f. And yet his maxim
      "Il faut toujours travailler," adopted from Cézanne, testifies to an attitude not based on
      possessions. His definition of "openness" reveals this ambivalent attitude, inasmuch as it
      emphasizes the magical: "You must understand the concept of 'openness' . . . as be-
      ing the degree of the animal's consciousness which places it into the world without
      being in oppostion to it at every moment as we are. The animal is in the world; we stand
      before it as a consequence of the unique turns and intensification taken by our con-
      sciousness" (Letter of June 25, 1926); see Maurice Betz, Rilke in Frankreich (Vienna: Tal,
      1938), p. 291.

96   Alfred Weber, Kulturgeschichte als Kultursoziologie (Leiden: Sijtthoff, 1935), p. 397.

97   Ibid., p. 394 ff.

98   In the new edition of his book (note 96), Alfred Weber has designated future man as the
      "fourth man" (see his additional chapter 8: 'Zur Gegenwartsfrage: Kommt der vierte
      Mensch?' [Munich: Piper, ²1950]). We have already mentioned his rather pessimistic
      conception and his account of the symptoms of dissolution evident in the rational con-
      sciousness structure which overlooks inceptions of integrality; see in this context our
      discussion in the article "Auflösung ober Überwindung" (note 11), pp. 47–57. There we
      noted (p. 54): "In contrast to our view, Alfred Weber does not discern the great human
      epochs as the archaic, the magic, the mythical, the mental, and the emergent integral.
      Rather, he places his 'first man' into a zoological early stage along Darwinistic lines, his
      'second man' into a magic-mythical early history (not distinguishing between the magi-
      cal and the mythical), his 'third man' into our era of Western civilization, and the 'fourth
      man' into the future." The passage and its full context are reprinted in Jean Gebser (note
      11: In der Bewährung, p. 111 f., and Gesamtausgabe, V/I, p. 259 f.).

99*   Lecomte du Noüy (note 52), p. 261.

100   Emphasis here is on the conscious act of completion. We mention this to preclude any
      confusion between the "universal consciousness" mentioned here and in our earlier

discussion, and that postulated by E. Osty, director of the French Institute of Parapsy-chology, which can be manifested only via a medium. With reference to this "spiritistic" approach, see Hans Driesch, "Magische und okkulte Bestrebungen in der zeitgenössi-schen Philosophie," *Mensch und Kosmos: Jahrbuch der Keyserling Gesellschaft für freie Philosophie 1949* (Düsseldorf: Droste, 1949), p. 187.

101 José Ortega y Gasset, *Das Wesen geschichtlicher Krisen* (Stuttgart: Deutsche Verlags-Anstalt, ²1951), pp. 43–50.

102* Lecomte du Noüy (note 52), p. 225.

103 Hugo Spatz, "Gedanken über die Zukunft des Menschenhirns und die Idee vom Über-menschen," in Ernst Benz, *Der Übermensch: eine Diskussion* (Zürich and Stuttgart: Rhein, 1961), p. 366 ff.

104* Lecomte du Noüy (note 52), p. 231; italics original. We should mention that the French do not invest psychological phenomena with a psychic overemphasis as do the Ger-mans. The phrase "psychological phenomena" obviously refers to the spiritual realities (with a religious emphasis) envisaged by du Noüy in the concluding chapter of his book.

8

Manifestations of the Aperspectival World (IV): The Dual Sciences

Having dealt with the basic sciences we would now turn to the dual sciences. Here we are less concerned with their results which evidence, as it were, a double quantity of aperspectival inceptions and manifestations in comparison to the individual sciences whose fusion brought them about. We wish rather to consider these double sciences in themselves, as they are already as such expressions of an aperspectival mode of realization.

This is more or less clearly expressed by the two prototypes of the dual sciences, quantum biology, also called biophysics, and psychosomatic medicine, also called psychobiology. Quantum biology unifies two hitherto mutually exclusive and antithetical disciplines: physics, concerned with "inert" matter, and biology, concerned exclusively with the life processes. Psychosomatic medicine also unites two formerly exclusive disciplines: psychology, with its concern with the impalpable realities of the psyche, and medical biology or physiology, concerned with purely somatic processes.

What makes the dual sciences potentially aperspectival disciplines in a certain sense is the fact that their very emergence is already an expression of the "supersession of dualism," a prerequisite and indicator of an arational mode of understanding. Pascual Jordan and Viktor von Weizsäcker were the first to show the novel impulses that could radiate from these new disciplines.

Together with Erwin Schrödinger and Ernst Dessauer, Pascual Jordan is the most prominent representative of quantum biology, a field he co-founded with his work *Die Physik und das Geheimnis des Organischen Lebens* ("Physics and the Mystery of Organic Life").[1] In his book on "Creativity in Nature" (*Das Schöpferische in der Natur*, 1949), Pascual Jordan indicated the inherent moment of free decision in the acausality of molecular physics, where the "element of creativity is central"[2] to the definition of organic life processes. This is tantamount to a recognition of "time" as a quality. This physicist's courageous comments on questions of organic life are particularly revealing:

"Could it not be that the ultimate and most decisive directing processes in organic life are so refined as to be no longer located in the area of causal-mechanical constraints, but in the realm of free events required to make decisions? This is a possibility for thought, even if at first glance a fantastic possibility. It is no wonder that when this possibility was first mentioned, most biologists summarily rejected it. Yet the experiences and experiments of the past ten or twenty years have uncovered a plethora of facts that no longer permit us to view this question as hypothetical but as a decisive, indeed patently and reliably decisive question. What I have suggested is not only a logical possibility, not just a conceivable possibility for discussion, but simply a fact. Organic life is really so. We must accept it as a fact that in its essential and crucial acts, life is directed by processes immanent in the area of nucleo-physical and molecular-physical acausality, where mechanically calculated predictability does not prevail, and where there is no unwinding of a clock-work protected against unpredictable, incalculable events. The ultimate directing acts in organic life occur in the zone of those natural processes where unforeseeable decisions have surprising effects."[3]

What just a few years ago was rejected as a "fanciful possibility" is today a demonstrated fact. No longer do we need to respect causal mechanical constraints for critical processes; we are no longer imprisoned in the rational mode of thought but are in a position to assume an acausal, free process. And the very thought of it liberates us from the "cage" of mechanical-causal thinking;[4] such a free process is thus not perspectively fixed but is simply aperspectival.

Similarly, psychosomatic medicine (see p. 384 above) is implicitly outlining an arational mode of realization. This is evident from Alexander Mitscherlich's remarks which indicate that the new basic attitude in psychosomatics is not based on "the scientific theory of psycho-physical dualism," an attitude for which Viktor von Weizsäcker's design of a gestalt theory[6] furnished the first possibility. Weizsäcker has stated this as follows: "The basic factor in the relationship between body and soul is that they are not two things juxtaposed and influencing each other, but that they mutually interpret one another. Via the psyche we acquire awareness of the body's unconscious reason and passion, and through the body we are informed of the natural needs of the psyche. This mutual explanation may occur in diverse ways: explanation, fantasy, foreboding, insight. Descriptive science on the one hand, and poetry on the other are the two ends of a series which need not be intentionally interrupted.

"Nevertheless, mistakes and errors occur, which are troublesome in medicine, particularly if the work of explanation is isolated and dominant. Psychophysical causality is an example. Within a limited context one could easily say that an illness comes about due to physical processes, such as poison, or due to a psychic process, such as dread. Yet with a more complete consideration we must correct these statements and say that not the illness, but only symptoms arise in this way. In an illness it is impossible to observe whether the psychic or the physical appearance is the cause or the earlier occurrence; they occur simultaneously."[7]

But let us return to von Weizsäcker's student, Alexander Mitscherlich. After further ascertaining that "new knowledge can suddenly, as in mutations," chance upon man,[8] Mitscherlich indicates the inadequacy of purely rational methods for the investigation of invisible, minute structures in nuclear physics, as well as in psychoanalysis (no longer a rationalistic psychology in the sense of a mere psychology of consciousness).[9] Psychoanalysis has "given anthropology the certainty that man's existence is rooted in various basic regions of being, and that the methods for an understanding of man must be appropriate to such regions. Thus there also cannot be a heuristic principle which sets aside this knowledge by grasping man only partially from a particular mode of thinking."[10]

This important suggestion is a renunciation of the previous claim to exclusivity by the rational element. The recognition that various "basic regions" or "modes of existence" are valid runs parallel to our exposition of the total-constitutional effectivity of the various consciousness structures. This parallelism between Mitscherlich's "modes of existence" and our "consciousness structures" is not an artificial approximation, as will be obvious from Mitscherlich's following remarks: "Man's differing modes of existence demand differing modes of knowledge which must remain incommensurate with each other as an expression of the basic incommensurability of human existence with each of its forms of knowledge. The obligation proceeding from such knowledge requires us at the very least to view synoptically those forms of knowledge that cannot truly be synthesized."[11]

Our own attempt at a synoptic view of the various consciousness structures, the various modes of existence and realization, has resulted in our construction of a "synoptic table," precisely because these modes of existence and realization cannot be perceived systematically. Thus, commensurate with the inadequacy of rational systematization, we have educed the synairetic element that pervades all modes of existence in manifold aspectuations. This element, beyond the synoptic vividness, thus permits the integration of systematically incommensurable, yet systatically commensurable regions of reality in synairesis. Mitscherlich's statements show evidence of the same attitude toward the limitations of the nothing-but-rational mode of thought; they are significant since the recognition of such limitations includes an attitude that goes beyond the irrational and the rational. In its ultimate consequence it is arational and consequently is not exposed to the danger of regression to the irrational. The same symptomatic distance to both attitudes, a distance which reveals a "position above" and thus manifests a new structure, is present both in our attempt to make vivid the different consciousness structures and in the following remarks of Mitscherlich:

"The concept of 'overdetermination' pioneered in psychoanalysis and previously applied only to dream interpretation, is eminently suited to the analysis of human existence. It enables us to dispense with the old expedient of visualizing the various levels of being that man pervades, and which all too easily present themselves to the observer in antithetical or dualistic terms, as in the conceptual pairs body-soul, rational-irrational. In the existence of man, these modes of being presenting themselves to man's knowledge as levels [structures], are realized as overdetermined, that is, more than simply determined: organic processes become transformed unconsciously into psychic, psychic into rational processes.

"With respect to history, it is impossible to regard man from a generalized aspect of one historical segment. It is singularly important to recognize this, since the claim to exclusivity of a rational monism as developed by the scientific era is not generally considered erroneous. For where exclusive validity is accorded to the causal mode of operation, the other modes of existence are not only denied validity but also their effectivity within the encompassing fabric of the phenomenon of man is drastically curtailed."[12]

This attitude that we must perceive "the encompassing fabric of the phenomenon of man," and consider it as something other than a circular process binding the vital-physical to the mythological-psychic dimension, leads to the observation that "in order to grasp freedom, other forms of thinking beside the scientific are mandatory."[13] Failure to consider them can lead to overlooking the existence of "conceivably powerful energies."[14] "For man, freedom and nature can no more be deemed separable than body, soul or spirit can be detached from the more encompassing unity of a person and rendered into an unequivocal [rigidified, perspectival] description of the person in terms of one of his components."[15] "There are in man independent spheres completely intertwined . . . : the world of spirit and matter, of life and soul . . . . The spherical pervasion of the spirit by matter, of the body by spirit, is for all aspects of human life a proto-element. Regarded in this light, such aspects may be said to constitute life as quality. How they are perceived shows the level of an individual's creative freedom."[16] "The decisive factor in human existence is not definable psychically and not somatically."[17] "The possession of spirit as a primordial element"[18] (as a consequence of man's non-specificity) is crucial, and this decisive recognition leads Mitscherlich beyond the merely psychological interpretation of C. G. Jung and the pronounced polarization of Weizsäcker. While Mitscherlich has recently (since 1953) returned in part to a psychoanalytic stance, Arnold Gehlen has contributed the significant notion of "drive-quanta"[19] to psychosomatic medicine.

Going beyond this, G. R. Heyer has, in his writings, established a psychobiology,[20] thus freeing psychoanalysis from its reputation of being rationalistic and rigidified. Heyer granted each individual phenomenon its own sphere of reality and its appropriate frequency of consciousness, and thus did not so much explain these phenomena as illuminate the interpenetration of the various areas. And Arthur Jores, coming from clinical medicine, has stimulated medical thought to new reflection by showing that medicine can no longer avoid psychosomatics if it wishes to liberate itself from its rationalistic-mechanistic cul-de-sac. Without exaggeration, and in a style acceptable to present-day thought, as well as in a form amenable to clear reason, he has made evident the genuine values and roots of being human.[21]

The remarks quoted above reveal the extent of aperspectival inceptions particularly in the dual sciences. Our supposition of several years ago that the dual sciences would have a crucial and generally transforming and restructuring role in the future, and will thus contribute decisively to the awareness of the newly emergent consciousness structure, has thus been unmistakably corroborated.

To what extent this holds true for a third dual science, parapsychology—which we must discuss briefly—is another question. At first glance one is inclined to classify it as a border science or as an area of specialization. Yet inasmuch as it was founded on Gustav Theodor Fechner's "psycho-physics"[22] (not to be mistaken for "psychophysical" or later, psychosomatic medicine), it is a dual science. The concept "parapsychic" was coined in 1889 by Max Dessoir. Parapsychology is a theory about phenomena which occur alongside ("para") the normal course of psychic life without necessarily implying an illness. It can also be termed scientific occultism. It is concerned with an experimental explanation of those phenomena which escape material-causal interpretation, and is largely bound up with the observations of mediums in a state of trance. What C. G. Jung has attempted to subsume under the psychological concept of "synchronicity" (p. 399 f.) are predominantly parapsychic phenomena. Structurally they are pre-causal and not acausal, and, as telepathy shows, do not manifest a causal nexus but flow from the spaceless-timeless effectuality of the vital nexus. Parapsychology investigates on the one hand parapsychic phenomena, on the other paraphysical and parabiological phenomena. It has proven the fraudulence of many mediums and advanced experimental proofs of the existence of clairvoyance in space and time. Owing primarily to the works of J. B. Rhine,[23] the occurrence of telepathic capacities (thought transmission) is today no longer deniable, even by science.[24]

Such phenomena have made a remarkable impression on the public. This can be explained on the basis of the nothing-but-rational attitude for which these phenomena are an annoyance. They disrupt the causal connection of mechanistic thinking and are thus highly irritating. Yet this disruption of the causal nexus does not demonstrate that these phenomena are arational. As is evident from our description of the magical consciousness structure, they are primarily based on the pre-rational and occur in the unilluminable, egoless, dormant darkness of the magical. Their foundations lie in the "vital nexus" (pp. 48, 50, 251), the "communion" relationship characteristic of spaceless-timeless magic (see p. 163). Strictly speaking, parapsychology is a dual science researching the effectiveness of the magical region and its emergent manifestation in the mythical and mental zones, and endeavoring to unite the vital with the psychic-mental. Yet even today it is still guilty of insufficiently recognizing the basic structure of its investigative field. Its previous conceptions in no way explain the basic phenomenon; we can only glimpse its emanations in the form of psycho-energetic manifestations. As long as parapsychology approaches its field with a predominantly rational attitude, it is working inappropriately. The rational interpretation, the mental illumination of the pre-rational darkness merely destroy this darkness and thus its reality escapes our rational grasp. The essence of the arcane, the occult, is its spaceless-timeless concealment; it can never be made visible.[25] Yet it could become transparent if we would perceive such phenomena arationally, and not approach them rationally or permit them to mislead us irrationally, or allow them to overpower us prerationally.

The attitude we have described here as inappropriate, indeed as improper, results for example from a remark, probably derived from Schopenhauer, "acting at a distance," which was supposed to explain magical processes. This attitude, however, neglects the fact that the magical region is determined by spacelessness and timelessness, so that any terminology operating with space-time concepts is faulty. Categorical, calculative thought destroys the acategorical elements and clearly proves to be a kind of "principle of indeterminacy" (see note *30*, p. 389), even if the disruptive factor here is not the physical intrusion altering the course of events via the experiment. The disruptive factor is the rational, dualistic thinking itself; by measuring and dividing, it intrudes into space-timelessness, and this in turn is disrupted by the spatio-temporal measuring intervention of rational thinking.

A further example of the traditional and inappropriately dualistic character of the parapsychological method stems from the distinction between "animism" and "spiritism." From time to time, paraphenomena such as "ghosts" were interpreted either as this-worldly (psychically, animistically), or as other-worldly (spiritistically). As a parapsychologist, Peter Ringger warns against such a dualistic mode of interpretation.[26] But it was primarily Gebhard Frei who brought about a much-needed clarification; by not proceeding dualistically, he did justice to the origin of differing phenomena by ascribing various phenomena now to the vital sphere, now to the psychic regions.[27] This was a significant step toward a fitting and aperspectival perception of phenomena that ultimately elude mere conceptuality.

As soon as parapsychology is able to surrender the rational method in favor of diaphany, even if only partially, the results of its research will lead to an astounding incrementation of aperspectival knowledge. And it is to be emphasized once more that it is not the phenomena produced by parapsychology which are arational; rather, its efforts to assimilate other structures of reality and consciousness besides the predominant mental structure form the basis for an inception of an arational mode of realization. This mode will be completed when this dual science has dissociated itself from the mental-rational consciousness structure; when it grasps that something which cannot be illuminated ought not to be illuminated, that illumination would destroy it, and that it can be made transparent. Then, instead of the inferior fascination with the deficient magical phenomena to which many serious parties are succumbing today, a perception of space-timelessness and its pre-causal structure will emerge—archaic, primordial pre-spaceless-timelessness as the consciously emergent space-time–freedom.

1 See Erwin Schrödinger, *Was ist Leben?* (Bern: Francke, 1946; rev. ed., 1951), as well as Pascual Jordan, *Die Physik und das Geheimnis des organischen Lebens* (Braunschweig: Vieweg, ⁶1948).

2 Pascual Jordan, "Das Schöpferische in der Natur," *Mensch und Kosmos: Jahrbuch der Keyserling Gesellschaft für freie Philosophie, 1949* (Düsseldorf:Droste, 1949), p. 81.

3 Ibid., p. 80; italics original.

4 Ibid., p. 77.

5 Alexander Mitscherlich, *Freiheit und Unfreiheit in der Krankheit: Das Bild des Menschen in der Psychiatrie* (Hamburg: Claassen & Goverts, 1946), p. 14.

6 Viktor von Weizsäcker, *Der Gestaltkreis* (Stuttgart: Theime, ³1947), and *Wahrheit und Wahrnehmung* (Leipzig: Koehler & Amelang, 1942), as well as his *Gestalt und Zeit,* Sammlung "Die Gestalt," no. 7 (Halle/S.: Niemeyer, 1942).

7 Viktor von Weizsäcker, *Anonyma* (Bern: Francke, 1946), p. 23 f.; italics original.

8 Alexander Mitscherlich (note 5), p. 14.

9 Ibid., p. 50.

10 Ibid., p. 51.

11 Ibid., p. 51 f.

12 Ibid., p. 52.

13 Ibid., p. 69.

14 Ibid., p. 70.

15 Ibid., p. 70.

16 Ibid., p. 86 f.; our italics.

17 Ibid., p. 88 f.

18 Ibid., p. 65 f.

19 Arnold Gehlen understands these "drive quanta" as repressed instinctual and aggressive impulses variously able to be released at any time. They can be understood not only as quantities, but more importantly, as quanta, i.e., intensities whose effect cannot be temporally predicted, thus accounting for a certain indeterminacy or acausality for this area. First suggestions and intimations toward a definition of the drive quanta can be found in Arnold Gehlen's "Das Bild des Menschen im Lichte der modernen Anthropologie," *Die Neue Weltschau,* II (Stuttgart: Deutsche Verlags-Anstalt, 1953), pp. 81–99.

20 With respect to G. R. Heyer's "psychobiology" it can be said that it more accurately corroborates the new data of aperspectivity than does psychosomatic medicine, inasmuch as it goes beyond the latter's determinability and thus attains a broader basis with

particular respect to the decisive spiritual inceptions and an estimation of wholeness than were previously available to A. Mitscherlich. Heyer, through his works, marshalled impressive and persuasive evidence; we refer specifically to the works cited above (notes 20, 21, 22, and 40 on pages 413 and 414), and also in G. R. Heyer, *Der Organismus der Seele* (Munich: Lehmann, ⁴1959).

21   With reference to the works of Arthur Jores and their importance for a new vantage point in medicine, we would mention his *Der Mensch und seine Krankheit* (Stuttgart: Klett, 1956), *Vom kranken Menschen* (Stuttgart: Thieme, 1960), *Die Medizin in der Krise unserer Zeit* (Bern and Stuttgart: Huber, 1961), and *Menschsein als Auftrag* (Bern and Stuttgart: Huber, 1964).

22   Gustav Theodor Fechner, *Elemente der Psychophysik* (Leipzig: Breitkopf & Härtel, ³1907), II.

23*   See the two works of J. B. Rhine: *New Frontiers of the Mind* (N. Y.: Farrar & Rinehart, 1937) and *The Reach of the Mind* (N. Y., 1950).

24   See also Jean Gebser, *Abendländische Wandlung* (Zürich: 1943 ff.), chapters 14 and 15; *Gesamtausgabe*, I, pp. 225–234.

25*   See also Jean Gebser, "The conscious and the unconscious: a misleading dilemma," *Proceedings of the First International Conference of Parapsychological Studies* (N. Y.: Parapsychology Foundation, 1955), pp. 58–59. Together with Karl Jaspers and Adolf Portmann in a broadcast over Radio Basel on January 8th, 1954, as a part of a lecture series by Gebhard Frei on the subject of "Problems of Parapsychology" the author had the following to say:

"Having been asked to discuss my position on parapsychology, I would emphasize above all the necessity of understanding that it is a recent as well as necessary field of scientific inquiry. Let us first inquire as to the consequences of its being a recent science and return at the conclusion to the question of its necessity.

What are the manifestations of its youth and consequent lack of experience? There are two. One is that it appears not fully cognizant of the reality structuration of the phenomena it seeks to investigate, and consequently works with the wrong means and begins in the wrong places. Secondly that it has an inappropriate name with respect to the areas of its inquiry. Regarding the first point, that it is not fully cognizant of the reality structure of the phenomena under investigation and approaches them at the wrong place with the wrong means, the following must be said. The telepathic and pre-cognitive or prophetic phenomena, for example, occur in a structure of man's reality that does not have a rational nature. Consequently its structure differs as to time and space from the rational structure which is itself spatially and temporally bound.

While investigating the phenomena mentioned, however, most researchers attempt to illuminate facts and circumstances of only tenuous spatial-temporal nature with the spatial-temporal means and approaches at their disposal. This is comparable to a scientist's attempt to investigate the structure of snow or ice with the aid of a quartz lamp, which would have the effect of melting away the very object under investigation because of the lamp's heat, rather than of rendering the object visible.

What one must do, therefore, is to elaborate a methodology appropriate to the structure of the phenomena, no simple task despite some useful steps in that direction. Nor should one make the mistake of attempting to apply a strictly physical or psychological method. Moreover, one would have to be content further to begin with the critical investigation of the so-called lesser phenomena, in themselves still sufficiently inexplicable. The approach would then be such as those used at Duke University and the Universities of Utrecht and Freiburg im Breisgau. In other situations people have previously been concerned with exaggeratedly non-materialistic phenomena, motivated perhaps by an unconscious protest against materialism.

But in so doing, it is easy to become involved inadvertently in the dangers of investigating abnormal or even pathological and deficient atavistic phenomena like possession, since they are the most exciting and spectacular. And this is not to mention those unappetizing—to my mind at least—practices of the Spiritists who conjure, or believe that they conjure, so-called 'spirits' or ghosts when in a state of lowered consciousness and consequently lowered sense of responsibility. And even if these were spirits, it is still my contention that it is inadmissible and objectionable to disturb the dead in such an irresponsible manner by repeatedly importuning those who have departed and calling them back against their will. No man has the right to summon those who have departed their visible, earthly form; if at all, only God has this claim, it may be said in passing.

More important, we would emphasize that telepathy, prophecy, telekinesis, and levitation are not only parapsychic phenomena, but also—let us retain for the time being the prefix 'para'—parabiological, paraphysical, and even pararational. This is to say that these phenomena spring from the elemental, fundamental regions of man, and brings us to the second point, which is that 'parapsychology' is an incorrect appellation with respect to the phenomena under investigation. Parapsychology deals neither with paraphenomena (or secondary phenomena, as it were) nor with those of an exclusively psychic nature, but rather with fundamental phenomena.

For this reason I have suggested on another occasion that we speak of parapsychology as a 'fundamental phenomenology,' and the noted French philosopher and sociologist Gabriel Marcel has proposed, in the wake of this suggestion, the name of 'basic psychology.' Neither the one nor the other is completely satisfactory, and they are intended to serve as a stimulus to other suggestions.

On one subject we cannot avoid an honest accounting: there is not a single one of us alive able to live without that previously unobserved and unadmitted measure of inner knowledge and prescience. We might define this inner cognizance as telepathic ability, or inner prescience, in more imposing terms, as prophecy. There are many seemingly insignificant daily occurrences which we call 'chance,' that is, if we become aware of them at all. But why? and why do these things in fact happen to us? The world, and our own lives as well, are considerably richer than we ourselves know, and they are more certain than most of us believe them to be.

This brings me to my last point. It would indeed be fortunate if we had a branch of critical inquiry, responsibly open to both human and divine things, that would concern itself for the time being exclusively with the phenomena we call 'chance.' At a time when a biologist such as Lecomte du Noüy speaks of the 'laws of chance' and physics recognizes indeterminate processes, why should not parapsychology—or however we wish to name it—continue with the preliminary work done by Wilhelm von Scholz in his book on fate and chance? [Wilhelm von Scholz, Der Zufall:eine Vorform des Schicksals; Die Anziehungskraft des Bezüglichen, Stuttgart: Walter Hädecke Verlag, 1924].

Such accidental occurrences make visible a previously obscured fundamental pattern and a mysterious wealth of interrelationships present in events which are truly fortunate, and doubtless also permeate various telepathic and vital relationships, and basic abilities, of man. Proceeding from these matters, the so-called science of parapsychology could create such knowledge of events so as to demonstrate that the individual can place more trust in his own life and in himself than he now does. In this it could decisively contribute to allaying the prevailing mood of anxiety from which so many of our contemporaries suffer and which obscures the face of our epoch (a face itself composed of our own many faces). If this new science were able to demonstrate to those unable to believe, who thus fall prey to superstition [Aberglaube, "substitute faith"], the extent to which certain inexplicable happenings in their lives have a meaning, then much would already have been accomplished. This would also pose anew the question of fate and freedom in a new light.

Although I am not a parapsychologist, it is my opinion that it is to these things and phenomena to which one must turn, for they are amenable to inquiry, and enhance the visibility of the meaningful richness of life. On the other hand we should avoid those things and phenomena which are mysterious or secret. The arcana, too, belong to the plenitude of life's meaning, and if we uncover them we destroy them. Let us not forget that the invisible is but another form of the visible, and take comfort in the brave yet humble remark of Romano Guardini: 'It is the nature of mystery to be mysterious.' "

26   See particularly the articles of Peter Ringger: "Die Parapsychologie am Wendepunkt," *Neue Wissenschaft: Zeitschrift für Parapsychologie* (Baden/Switzerland) 2, 1 (October, 1951), 7 f., and "Rufer in der Wüste," 2, 6 (March, 1952), 179 f.

27   This clarification was made by Gebhard Frei in his lecture on "Animismus—Spiritismus" over Radio Basel as part of a series on problems of parapsychology, broadcast in January and February of 1954.

9

Manifestations of the Aperspectival World (V): The Arts

1. Music

The essence of each and every art is, in the main, the expression of the pre-rational and irrational, while the mind has the role of an ordering power. Consequently art resides for the most part within the magical and the mythical consciousness structures. Its roots probably lie much deeper since it is the form of human expression closest to origin.

Since art is predominantly at home in the non-rational regions, then, strictly speaking, any mental interpretation is inappropriate. Any interpretation of a work of art is inevitably hazardous since what is expressed in tones, or assumes shape in buildings, or in outline or color, cannot be duplicated in language. How then can the medium of language elucidate works of music, painting, and architecture if they create non-linguistic expressions? Whatever is a speechless, genuine, and immediate expression cannot be translated into words. The sympathetic, analytic, or comparatistic "speaking about" art offers us little indication, least of all about aperspectivity, although it is most clearly (or most strongly) mirrored—and consequently most discernible—in the arts, the seismographic expressions of man. Since the aperspectival is not only something new but new to the structure of consciousness, and has concerns different from the previous consciousness structures, we need only to make these new concerns visible.

Is the new music structurally new music or merely novel?

In our previous chapters we have journeyed through the sciences, and on the basis of predominantly binding statements have established certain predominant new states of affairs. They are primarily the new valuations of the time problem: the attempt to overcome rationalistic dualism, as well as the effort to perceive the world freely, universally, and to a certain extent from all sides, that is, arationally and aperspectivally. It is only natural that we must find these same preoccupations, these incipient manifestations of the aperspectival, in the arts, and above all in the new music. Of·course, the emergence of these aperspectival manifestations cannot be merely incidental but rather must be clearly a major concern for music itself as part of the shift in the structure of its values. It is in accord with the structural conditions of the new music that the aforementioned preoccupations are actually emphasized. Recent music attempts:

1) to resolve in its own way the time problem temporically;
2) to escape dualism; and
3) to attain an arational mode of expression.

Our undertaking is restricted to making visible the concerns of the new music. This has nothing to do with critique, evaluation, rejection, or defense of atonal, polytonal, extended, or electronic music. We are intent on reading the facts and therefore promote no school or faction. In contrast, we hope that the following remarks can clarify, even for those who "can't make any sense" out of recent music, what problems it is attempting to solve and what new forms of expression, as in all other arts, it attempts to formulate—consciously or as yet unknowingly. Since here too the time problem is predominant, we shall begin our discussion with it.

1) The temporic efforts—those concerned with the problem of time—are to be heard in all the works of the new music. And where major contemporary composers and interpreters have occasion to discuss their own musical concerns, we find a hitherto unnoticed agreement in their preoccupation with the temporic.

For Igor Stravinsky, musical creation is "based primarily upon an exclusively musical experiencing of time—*chronos*, of which the musical work merely gives us the functional realization."[1] Another of his statements again underscores the extraordinary significance that he accorded to the time phenomenon: "Music establishes an order between man and time."[2] Moreover, in connection with his discussion of some of Stravinsky's works, Ernest Ansermet remarks that "in music Stravinsky sees the self-concretion of time."[3]

But what kind of time is he speaking about? Although this question forces us into a terminological labyrinth, we must raise it. Stravinsky furnishes us with an answer: "Everyone knows that time passes at a rate which varies according to the inner dispositions of the subject and to the events that come to affect his consciousness. Expectation, boredom, anguish, pleasure and pain, contemplation—all of these thus come to appear as different categories in the midst of which our life unfolds, and each of these determines a special psychological process, a particular tempo. These variations in psychological time are perceptible only as they are related to the primary sensation—whether conscious or unconscious—of real time, ontological time. . . . What gives the concept of musical time its special stamp is that this concept is born and develops as well outside of the categories of psychological time as it does simultaneously with them."[4]

From his subsequent discussion, but particularly from his music, it is apparent that he favors "ontological time" (or ontological time as he understands it). Ansermet's designation of the phrase "ontological time" as a *plaisanterie*[5] when "speaking about music" is just as permissible as Adorno's reproach that Stravinsky "conjures away" time, "playing the *temps espace* against the *temps durée*," and that he introduces the "waning of subjective time," thus leading us to "forget lived time and surrender ourselves to spatialization."[6]

Applied to music, Adorno's estimation of time is as inadequate as Ansermet's; both remain confined in Bergsonian dualism. Adorno opposes lived time to clock time, yet music is concerned with more than these two temporal forms, and Ansermet remains entrapped by them: "We have only two possibilities of mastering time: in ourselves as psychic and qualitative time—this is musical time or tempo; and outside of ourselves, in the universe where time becomes automatic, measured by a clock or a metronome[7]—this is the time of Stravinsky. Its character of necessity [since ontological time is factual necessity but not freedom] explains Stravinsky's claims regarding tempo; yet we must make clear that his understanding of time differs from our own."[8]

It is obvious that the time-forms defined by Stravinsky, as well as by Adorno and Ansermet, are contradictory. We should like to contrast them with a definition advanced by Hermann Scherchen, since his temporal forms correspond to a great extent with our mythical and mental. Scherchen contrasts the "metrum—the capacity of order that can resist time—with the rhythm—a life process lost in time."[9] In addition to the time-forms of the rhythmic-natural-universal (and also psychic) and the measured-metric (automatic), there is also magic time: timelessness. It is found in the primordial music that significantly was discovered only during the last decade. Examples are the "songs" from the Canary Islands,[10] as well as several from the Andes that have become known through the Indian songstress Yma Sumac.[11] They are distinguishable in their pure form in that they are manifestations without beginning and end, a chance intrusion of the voice and a chance ending: a sleep that has, as it were, become sound.[12]

The new music—and everything points to this—is in a position to abolish previous time-forms. In its mode of expression it seems to approach timeless music, although it overdetermines toward time-freedom. Thus, "time-freedom" again in this instance means consciously surpassed timelessness. An indicaton of this new structuration of music can be found as early as Ferrucio Busoni's *Entwurf einer neuen Ästhetik der Tonkunst*, published in 1906. Busoni maintains that it is the destination of music to become free since its "matter is transparent" and it itself is "free."[13] H. H. Stuckenschmidt has devoted an important chapter to this postulate, "The Musical Style of Freedom" in his book *Neue Musik*, noting that Schoenberg's *Six Pieces for Piano*, Op. 19, composed in 1911, approach "an absolute freedom in harmony, melody, rhythm, and form."[14]

Regardless of the terminology with which one attempts to express musical facts of temporic character, one consideration is decisive: it is not the terminological superstructure above the new musical events, not a mere superimposition that is important, but the musical event itself and the new mode of expression sounding in it. In other words, the fact that Stravinsky, Ansermet, Adorno, and Scherchen use different terminologies, for example, to discuss the concept of time is less important than the fact that they, and others, all investigate the problem of time. It must not be forgotten that already in his early theoretical writings Schoenberg discusses this problem with reference to Einstein's theory of relativity, declaring its urgency.[15]

The same is true of Ernst Křenek, who indicates in his Vienna lectures of 1937 various parallels between the new physics and the new music.[16] These parallels are related to instability, non-visuality, and four-dimensionality (to which the new quadruplicity of twelve-tone music corresponds), as well as to the understanding of time as such. In addition, Křenek not only speaks repeatedly of the particular importance and value that must be attributed to "the relationship of music to time," but also shows that the "essential trait of the new music is the reassessment of the problem of form, that is, how the relationships of the piece of music to time are realized in the orderings which regulate the course of its elements."[17]

Křenek, moreover, deals with the form of appearance of time within the new music, comparing the "course" of time in the new compositions with the movement of a parabola. The "parabola turns at a definite place, and a point [or a musically formulated thought] that moves along it retraces from that place on all previous movement. Yet it never gets back to where it began [as is the case, say, with the circular forms of Bach fugues] . . . This form . . . is to a certain extent *without beginning and conclusion;* it is possible to think of yet another piece, another serial form, which could have preceded the beginning, and whose retrogradation could have come after the end. Because of this, the formal shaping of the new music, despite its perfection of construction, appears rather fragmentary, and consequently gives the impression of affliction and dissatisfaction as a consequence of its fragmentariness. Therein lies its lofty truthfulness, that it does not hide the instability of its condition, but affirms and emphasizes it."[18] And here lies the difference between primordial and new music: in the Canary Island and Indian songs we find a primordial sadness and resignation far from waking consciousness, which corresponds to the formed insight into the fragmentarity and thus permits the fullness of the whole to be transparent.[19] Therein is reflected not only theoretically but audibly the structural change which has irrupted through the new valuation of time in music.

Paul Hindemith has also given an account of this in his introductory lecture at the University of Zürich (November 1951). He developed "new theoretical and psychological views in music concerning space and time," which he entitled "Musical Inspiration," thus broaching the question of creativity.[20] That such an acutely conscious confrontation with time is taking place via such diverse proponents of the new music as Hindemith, Křenek, Schoenberg, and Stravinsky, shows that this question must play a significant part in their music.[21]

We do not wish to lose our way in an interpretation of musicological terminology. We would only offer one conclusion of Ernest Ansermet in order to show the results of all these temporic attempts, citing the instance of Stravinsky. In connection with Ansermet's statements cited above as to the specific time-character of Stravinsky's music, as well as the divergence between his own and Stravinsky's time conception, Ansermet remarks that "it is precisely these peculiarities of his art that lead Stravinsky to two discoveries which are of general significance and may be considered the most significant in contemporary music."[22] These two discoveries, according to E. Ansermet, are polymetrics and polytonality,[23] which lead us directly to our second point, namely, the supersession of dualism in the new music.

2) Our deliberations have repeatedly made it possible to observe that wherever time irrupts in a previous system or realm of expression, the systems or realms were disrupted. The same process can be consistently demonstrated in music. Wilhelm Furtwängler identifies this fact as follows: "*Since the turn of the century* there has been a genuine and deeply intruding transformation in the tone material underlying music. It was Arnold Schoenberg who gave the decisive impulse to the movement within music to overcome the previously unlimited sovereignty of the major-minor tonal system. The group associated with Schoenberg—whose following includes an increasing number of modern musicians throughout the world—proclaims that this system, having served as a foundation for the great European

457

evolution of music since the Renaissance and Baroque, has become superannuated. Atonal music, as it has been called since then, came into being. . . . "[24]

We wish to cite here a few additional remarks of Furtwängler, although he employs a Spenglerian terminology symptomatic of Spengler's failure in the face of new tasks. (Spengler understood the third dimension—which applied to painting yielded the possibility of perspective—as a "temporal depth-dimension."[25] This was the decisive failure of his theory of history, as a result of his predominantly Faustian, biologically stressed "predecision."[26]) Furtwängler's prejudgement is pathos-ridden and emotional, deriving from the influence exerted over him by Spengler's and Klages' biologism and vitalism; it culminates in his rejection of the new music as "biologically inferior, intellectualistic, antiptolemaic, and antagonistic to the Ego."[27]

If we make careful allowances for Spengler's false terminology, Furtwängler's statements are none the less valid: "Music experiences its realization in the dimension of time. The tonal cadence lends to the musical event—which until the Renaissance proceeded from one tone to another on one level, on one plane [unperspectival!]—the possibility of superordinate, recapitulate interconnections, and hence a depth articulation [spatial articulation!] previously unknown. It is not inappropriate to speak here in Spengler's terms [i.e., the third dimension as revealing time and not merely space] and posit a parallelism between tonality and the discovery of perspective. Tonality relates to the dimension of time, wherein music has its realization, as space to the pictorial arts as the third dimension, the dimension of depth. Both tonality and perspective owe their discovery to the same life-impulse. . . . "[28]

The parallelism between tonality and perspective, as shown by Furtwängler (and not, as it may seem from the text, by Spengler), is valid despite Spengler's false definition of the third dimension. The fallaciousness is already evident in Furtwängler's first statement in which the "dimension of time" is seen as an abstraction; but abstraction cannot contain lived experience. Primordial music is lived experience realized in timelessness and not in a temporal dimension. In contrast, the new music reveals itself in the "a-mension of time," that is, achronically. Or, more accurately, as a consequence of its temporic attempts it is on the way toward the discovery of achronic (time-free) expression.

Stravinsky is not the only one to compose polymetrically and thus temporically, that is to say, by the simultaneous use of several meters or tempi. Other examples are the *Choros* of Villa-Lobos[29] where both vocal and instrumental music display a similar metrical character, and Maurice Ravel's *Bolero*. Hermann Scherchen once remarked that in the *Bolero* "stasis in time" dominates,[30] in contrast to "Stravinsky's time anxiety." The whole of recent music is replete with various attempts to solve the problem of time through composition; scarcely any metric and rhythmic means have been left untried. The motoric, the exotic, the folkloristic are evident as early as Liszt, as well as more recently in the works of Bartók, de Falla, Milhaud, and Halffter, to mention only a few. And in the music of Francis Poulenc, for example in the second movement of his *Aubade*,[31] a richness and relaxation of rhythm are evident which are utterly new in their magic and perfection.[32] The theoretical formulations of Furtwängler, on the other hand, are the result of flawed thinking, since they rest on his biologizing preconceptions and document his consequent misunderstanding of the new music.

The "tonality" which we, then, understand to be the characteristic of perspectival music from the Renaissance until 1900, consists of the opposition and contrast between major and minor, consonance and dissonance, with the predominance of one fundamental tone. It must occur within the contours of the "tonal space of the octave" and each musically self-contained utterance is related to it. Its fulfillment is found in triadic harmony.

"Atonality" (we retain this designation as a blanket designation despite the theoretical controversies surrounding it) is the supersession of tonality. This supersession in music is identical with the supersession of perspectivity by aperspectivity, an estimation in which Werner Kass also concurs.[33]

Karl H. Wörner has defined atonality with notable precision: "Music is atonal when the tones of the octave are no longer centrally coordinate to the keys of the major-minor system or the modes of the church scales."[34] "Polytonality,"[35] in turn, according to Wörner, is distinguished by "the simultaneous juxtaposition of several keys."[36]

Atonality as well as polytonality represent the supersession of tonality, of perspectival music. It is not by chance that Boris de Schloezer speaks of *musique atonale* as music "freed from the burdensome compulsion of an a priori ordered tonal space."[37] This assessment is the fulfillment, as it were, of a demand made by Liszt's pupil Busoni in 1906 that the next step in musical creation must lead to "tonal dislimitation." For "previously all of music was founded on the two series of seven, the major scale and the minor scale," thus constituting a "limitation and 'fencing in' of musical expression."[38] Hermann Pfrogner was then able to assert that the "Major and Minor world, based on the law of seven" is surpassed by the "emergence of the harmonic law of twelve"[39] (twelve tone music). H. H. Stuckenschmidt speaks of the doubly accomplished supersession achieved by "the avoidance of the octave" among the composers of free atonality, as well as by the "avoidance of the major-minor triad which is accepted with a hundred associations and welcomed by the habituated instinct of the ear whenever it appears. The major-minor triad is still an all-too-typical phenomenon and can only promote functional misinterpretations of all sounds of its own milieu."

"If one attempts," Stuckenschmidt continues, "to substitute a chord with a major triad at some arbitrary point in a work of free tonality, for example in a piano piece from Schoenberg's opus 19, it immediately juts with aggressive power from the structure of this music and unsettles the ear more emphatically—in the sense of being a mistake, of being in the wrong place—than would the original chord."[40] We find here the same conception as in René Leibowitz' remarks about the "false octave relationship."[41] As Herman Erpf suggests, the same process occurred in music that occurred in other areas, namely, "the rejection of fixed points of reference."[42] The prophetic words of Liszt that "any chord can follow any other chord"[43] have been realized in the new music where "triads have the effect of disturbing the order."[44]

What follows from all this? Primarily two facts: that classical music, reaching its brilliant apogee in Bach, was perspectival music in accordance with its epoch; and that this tonal music is being superseded by atonal music. No longer is music dominated by a spatial system; it is being structured spatio-temporally. In the words of Léon Ollegini: classical music was a *musique fermée* and the new music is *musique ouverte*.[45] Ernest Ansermet makes the same assessment: "Ever since Liszt, the classical tonal order has opened itself to chromaticism. . . . The classicists have conceived only closed forms. . . ."[46] He adduces an example from Bartók that has an "open melodic form."[47] Werner Danckert, who justly equated "spatial construction and 'perspective' in painting" with the "basic law of contrary motion" and "consonance and dissonance in music," notes the musical correspondence between the achieved "abolition of haptic spatial perspective" and the "abolition of the predominant contrapuntal voice progression, the pull and shove in symphonic space" already accomplished by Debussy.[48]

The same attitude is expressed for his own music by Stravinsky: "In view of the fact that our poles of attraction are no longer within the closed system which was the diatonic system, we can bring the poles together without being compelled to conform to the exigencies of tonality. For we no longer believe in the absolute value of the major-minor system. . . . "[49] Ernst Křenek had already noted that the "fetish character" of the dualism dissonance versus consonance was an invention of constructional thought.[50] In addition, he maintained that "the enduring strangeness of the new music. . . . [results from] the annihilation of the closed form."[51] This closed form, namely, the tonal "space" of the octave, the septenary system, is disrupted; the opposites major:minor and consonance:dissonance are surpassed; the form of the characteristic triadic cadence is abandoned; and the perspectival relationship to one fundamental tone has become invalid.

In the new music there is a manifest "drive toward the original" directed at the "banishment of abstract thought," of the mental-rational, already evident—as W. Danckert has shown—in Debussy, in the "avoidance of the intellectually underpinned sound world, the music of ideas, as a break with the rational direction compulsion of tonic-dominant harmony."[52] A "reflection on the rhythmic powers of music" has begun, in the words of H. Strobel, to which we have already alluded (p. 458 ff.).[53]

In music, then, the same fundamental process is occurring that we have so frequently documented above. It is an attempt to surpass the mental-rational world of representations, neither regressing into the irrational or the prerational, nor denying the limited validity of the mental.

The supersession of the major:minor dualism reflects, to name only one parallel, the supersession of the energy:matter dualism achieved in physics. The major tonality as the active, energetic element is no longer opposed to the minor, the passive and material element, thus ending the dominance of the major tonalities in classical music.[54] In an unexpected, indeed, surprising way, the supersession of the previously predominant major tonality with its persistent masculine character mirrors a fundamental sociological fact frequently mentioned on these pages: the overcoming of patriarchy. So too, the symptomatic rejection of the triad, which in a metaphorical sense is an expression or an equivalent in music for the trinity. The trinity itself is of decisive significance for the mental consciousness structure and emphasized its patriarchal character.[55] The same holds true of the continual fixity and perspectival direction in music towards one fundamental tone, a rigidity displaced in a wholly aperspectival way by the primordial power of the entire expressive capacity of music.

All this occurs because music is rejecting the septenary system. And this is not insignificant, since another septenary system valid for millennia in astronomy also had to be abandoned in the course of the past one hundred and fifty years.[56]

The surpassing of the expressly mental-rational dualism is achieved by music itself, and not by the theory of music. Hence music is in the process of a leap toward a new structure. This leads us to:

3) The attempt of music to realize arationality. Some of the appropriate keywords, such as "open music," indicate the aperspectival and consequently arational character of the new music. Terminologically this expression seems to parallel those

of "open justice" and "open thinking." Since all areas of endeavor today are in a state of transition or mutation, it would be difficult to establish without a more exacting examination to what extent this is an actual and not merely a terminological coincidence. In such a state of non-consolidation, all other terminological concepts are in flux; the Janus-aspect of all contemporary expressions tends to promote theoretical quarrels inasmuch as all concepts and designations, depending on the consciousness attitude of the discussants, can be interpreted rational-perspectivally, or yet again already aperspectivally.

Our task, however, is not to provide an occasion for mere interpretation. According to his attitude, each individual will perceive the aperspectival relationship among the "opennesses" in philosophy, justice, and music, since they all originate in temporic inceptions and are all based on what we called the irruption of time. Or, because of a rigid rational stance, he will try to force these manifestations and formulations into a system and adapt them to his conceptual capacity instead of permitting their more congruent realization through a synairetic perceptual process. For this realization the no longer spatially positioned eteological "systasis" and "structure" are more appropriate than the habitual systematization in terms of an exclusive all-or-nothing conceptuality, and its belief that it can remain convincing in the new region (if it recognizes it at all).

Viewed purely terminologically, it is striking that in the new literature on music the word "system" is hardly ever mentioned, whereas there is everywhere talk of "structure." Yet, notwithstanding this discovery, it must be borne in mind that the concept of structure is nowhere explicitly established. Only the manner of its application permits the occasional appearance of systatic components appropriate to our "concept" of structure, which is that each structure must always be perceived spatio-temporally to prevent its degeneration into an abstract system. The temporal component must be considered in an achronic sense as a timeless primordial phenomenon and not as the one or the other expressive form of "time" as a conception.

An indication of the affinity between the new musical structure and aperspectivity is expressed (as H. Erpf and, with reference to him, H. Pfrogner point out)[57] where certain significant interval relationships can no longer be derived from the major-minor system, but rather from what they call the "structure of interconnections." This structure is arational. It also explains the terminological choice of H. Pfrogner who describes atonal music (the twelve-tone series) as "four-dimensional in nature."[58] But the arationality inherent in each genuine four-dimensionality is expressed by E. Křenek who speaks of "structure" expressly in our sense. For him atonal music is not a style (i.e., something oriented) but a structure. Atonality effected a "structural transformation of the materials" of music expressly parallel (with respect to matter or material, as Křenek points out) to the new physics where the once "dense, heavy, weighty, stable," the "self-contained," was changed into a "free-floating, self-moving formation."[59] It thus lost its one-sided rigidity and attachment to spatiality or system, expressions of the perspectival and the rational.

Křenek's suggestion also describes the effect of the new music on us, music based on the new kind of structure. Its instability and impalpability are manifest in the lack of melody, of major-minor systemization, and of fixed point of reference in a basic tonality that make this music unendurable to all who still view the rational as the non plus ultra of all modes of realization. This is understandable; whoever lacks the assurance of his life and thought within himself, and must project it into a rationally conceived representation with which he constructs a system of security, must necessarily despair when faced with this music. For nothing in it affords him support, and consequently he falls into the error of labeling it as unstable. Like the other arts, music is today nothing else than the attempt of mankind—awakening to aperspectivity—to find an expressive form that allows its spiritual security to manifest freely, knowing or feeling secure in its own "Itself."

After all, anyone having stability and security does not need to project them into a representational form, does not need to represent them outside of himself, so that they comfort him "retroactively." He is free of this compulsion; and there can be no doubt that the new music is striving toward such liberation. This does not mean that one must regard it as "beautiful"; the criterion of "beauty," which dualistically includes the "ugly," is to a great extent irrelevant for the valuation of aperspectival manifestations, as already indicated above (p. 24 f.). This assessment is not a rejection of the beautiful as such, as long as the so-called "beautiful" is not a temporal convention or an aesthetic escape or an emotionally charged interpretation of elements which can be described only inadequately by such terms as "harmonious" or "natural."

This disavowal of the possibility of emotive evaluation has leveled against the new music the accusation of being "intellectual." Yet it is utterly paradoxical to reproach the most accomplished masters of the new music for their purely theoretical and thoughtful endeavors while they devoted themselves to music "intellectually" in their striving for mental neatness. The reproach comes usually from those who demand of art a lulling and an irrational-emotional satisfaction, the reveling and bathing in feelings whereby art, a purely spiritual and primordial utterance, is degraded to a purpose. It is a rational attempt to measure the immeasurable, an utterly non-sensical procedure of perspectival nature no longer valid since the "irruption of time" has dissolved our representational world. (We need not emphasize that this assessment in no way advances an isolating position of "art for art's sake.")

Whatever one may say, the new music is neither beautiful nor ugly in the traditional sense; therein is manifested its arationality. If it were reducible to dualistic criteria, it would not be arational.[60] Since it is arational, at least in its most successful attempts, then it is not intellectualistic for then it would merely be rational in a different manner. But it is spiritual. Whoever sees rationally, sees fragmentarily; it is important to recall this basic definition of the rational. Whoever "sees" arationally, perceives the whole, and if at all possible, perceives it as a "structure of interrelationships."[61] And it is neither a vital, a psychic, nor a mental mode of realization but an integral-spiritual. Toward this are striving the new art and the new music, along with the other disciplines of our epoch.

Thus it is not accidental that both criteria—integrality and spirituality or diaphaneity—are of clearly fundamental concern to the new music.

E. Křenek already speaks of the "spiritualization of music," distinguishing between rationalism-intellectualism on the one hand, and spirituality on the other; it is the latter that he attributes to the new music.[62] H. Scherchen underscores this discovery of Křenek in his discussion of atonality and twelve-tone music, noting that "in it the place of the old, mechanical-natural connections are taken by purely spiritual regularities."[63] And H. H. Stuckenschmidt observes that the creations of the new music aim toward "a purely spiritual art."[64] Willi Schuh stresses that for Alban Berg tone is "nothing a priori, no container into which the music is poured, but the ultimate radiation of the whole musical event," and that the sound manifests not only sense but also "spiritual qualities."[65]

We should like to add that for us, speaking purely subjectively, Alban Berg's sound is, as it were, round and spherical; the musical matter of the tones is, in our estimation, remolded from a mere spatial sound into an encompassing "tonicity" radiating fullness. In its weightlessness it brings to perception the first novel shimmer of diaphaneity in music. Incidentally, W. Danckert has made the same claim for Debussy: "Debussy's harmony is not without adherence to tonality. Yet it is based less on the goal-orientation of the individual members of the harmonic sequence than on the encompassing, enshrouding, enclosing power of 'tonicity.' . . . Debussy's chordality . . . is a harmony of distance-relationships," whereby Debussy abandons the old "box image": "Nearness and distance coalesce into an inseparable unity."[66] Debussy's tonality is no longer linearly oriented, whether vertically (harmony) or horizontally (melody). Danckert expressly notes that "[Debussy's] tonality is spherical" (Danckert's italics).[67]

The music of Erwin Grosse (Karlsruhe) has this spherical, diaphanous character (without sounding like Debussy), and the same expressive power and transparency is evident in some compositions of Luigi Nono. The same is true, although only in a very few cases, for the productions of electronic music, where for the sake of novelty a further falling off into mechanistically intellectualistic music often occurs to a degree that sometimes an empty course of disintegration results. These creations are examples of our age in which some paths are being pursued toward an abyss and self-destruction, while at the same time in a less spectacular but compensating manner the realization of the constructive and life-sustaining consciousness mutation is being accomplished.[68]

Whereas the diaphanous character of Debussy's music, which demonstrates an inceptual liberation from all spatial "box images," can be considered to be beyond doubt, it is nevertheless noteworthy that the "sign" of the aperspectival world, the transparent sphere interconnecting nearness and distance, has in music become a reality. The diaphanous character of this music is an indication of its spiritual nature, its sphericity an indication of its integral nature.

Hence the arationality of the new music is evident, for the integral cannot be made perceptible with the perspectival rational modes of realization. To a certain extent this music presupposes the "new," the aperspectival and integral man. This intention is expressed in Stravinsky's statement: "For myself, I cannot begin to take an interest in the phenomenon of music except insofar as it emanates from the integral man. I mean from a man armed with the resources of his senses, his psychological faculties, and his intellectual equipment. Only the integral man is capable of the effort of a higher speculation that must now occupy our attention."[69] The speculation Stravinsky envisages here concerns the discussion of his own music; his remarks are indicative of his point of departure: the unification of the senses (the vital), the psychic capacities (the mythical), and the intellect (the mental).

Nonetheless, this summation does not yield a whole but only a summated man; Stravinsky's music is a convincing witness for this. The whole man of the integral consciousness structure is not simply a sum of earlier structurations but is new in that he overdetermines these structures by the verition of "time" through which the past that co-constitutes us gains *conscious* efficacy. Such an integral man is evident in the case of Stravinsky from his intent. In his own way H. H. Stuckenschmidt also evokes this integral man when he remarks that the new music introduces the "supersession of subjectivism."[70] Yet the most forceful definition of the realization of the new via music comes from H. Scherchen. In connection with an analysis of a measure of Beethoven's "Eroica" Symphony showing six voices with differing meters, Scherchen notes: "The polyrhythm of the following example [reproduced below] occurs in the 'Eroica.' No ear can analyze the plenitude of contrasts although it can experience it audially. In our enjoyment of music we employ levels of capacity far in advance of our organic development. The musical work of art [since Beethoven] permits us to establish capacities in practice enabling us to intuit subsequent man and his reality. It points once again to the absurdity of the old adage 'nothing is new under the sun' invoked to discredit the limitless drive of creativity."[71]

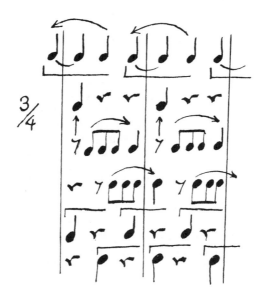

2. Architecture

Architecture today is the pre-eminently sociological art even to a much greater extent than music. Music builds and sustains the community mostly through emotion;[72] contemporary architecture, on the other hand, structurally determines the mode of social life. To what extent this holds true is evident from the writings of Frank Lloyd Wright[73] and Le Corbusier.[74] One of their basic concerns is solving the problem of the individual versus the collective in such a way as to remove the individual from the destructive dualism.

Immanent in the sociological endeavors of architecture is an aperspectival inception. Yet despite the importance of this aspect, we prefer to begin with the new structure of architecture. First of all, it is most important to inquire whether time does or does not have a role. If it does and is expressed architecturally without signifying mere social purpose, then certainly the problem of opposites must also have been unmistakably resolved in architecture. At the same time, it would demonstrate the attempt to attain arationality in architecture.

Let us proceed to deal with architecture in the same way we have dealt with other areas. The methodical inquiry into the same problems appearing in the various areas of contemporary expressive forms will, in addition, appeal to all who rank methodology above the still too infrequently practiced diaphany. Thus for the investigation of the new architecture it is essential that the three following concerns have a decisive significance:

1) The question of time, transmuting the previously valid architectural understanding of space;
2) The question of dualism, solved architecturally in some salient form; and
3) Arationality, transparently permeating recent architectural endeavors.

Let us turn to the first question, 1) The problem of time. We shall disregard here theoretical writings, particularly as we find few theoretical suggestions on this subject in the limited literature at our disposal. The work by S. Giedion, *Space, Time and Architecture*,[75] however, would seem to set a new standard in this respect. How much this work of architectural history is indebted to the thought of recent physics is obvious from the title, which can be considered a deliberate parallel to A. S. Eddington's book on relativity, *Space, Time and Gravitation*.[76] Giedion's evaluation of perspective in the space conception of the Renaissance, and the fundamental role it has had, is in full agreement with our own.[77] He speaks of the "dissolution of perspective"[78] and the transformation of space into space-time[79] evident in Cubism. (We shall return to this question in the section on painting.) This is true not only of painters but inceptually also of Walter Gropius, specifically with regard to his *Bauhaus* in Dessau.

Frank Lloyd Wright points out that in the new architecture space is measured in a new way, namely by time. "The new standard of space" consists in the "space measurement in time."[80] With reference to the effects of mechanization and the automobile on the new urban settlement and planning, he notes: "It is significant that not only have *space* values entirely changed to time values, forming a new standard of measurement, but a new sense of spacing is here."[81] How is this manifest architecturally? By the widespread validation and application of the maxim "form follows function." (The maxim does not originate, as is generally assumed, with Louis Sullivan but rather, as Wright has pointed out,[82] with Sullivan's teacher Dankmar Adler, although recently Sherman Paul seems to prove the opposite).[83] Incidentally, the functionality expressed in the formulation "f-f-f" is frequently misunderstood because of a non-dynamic, pragmatic, and goal-oriented interpretation.[84]

Since the temporal aspect in architecture can manifest itself only as dynamics and movement, it is revealing that a specific type of construction was to be of lasting influence even in America: it broke away from the static and spatially-bound mode of construction. We refer to the German Pavilion at the International Exposition in Barcelona (1929), designed by Mies van der Rohe (see figure 46). Elizabeth Mock of New York's Museum of Modern Art observes about this edifice: "He [Mies van der Rohe] proceeded in a brilliant and original manner of his own which . . . was received with special enthusiasm in the U.S. Roof and walls freely placed in relationship to the regular pattern of the supporting columns, become independent planes intersecting to define a continuous flow of space. Here was something of Wright's emphatic shelter and lively interpenetration of space, but also a lightness, an orderliness, and a differentiation between structure and wall planes which was closely related to Le Corbusier."[85]

This characterization is not a theoretical interpretation of an architectural

Figure 46: Mies van der Rohe, German Pavilion at the Barcelona World's Fair, 1929.

structure but an inference of its essence. And it is quite striking that this inference names elements symptomatic of the aperspectival mode of realization. Fixed relationships yield to more flexible ones; the inclusion of the dynamic time-element dissolves and loosens the rigid space and makes it fluid. In place of space boxed in by walls there emerges a world of transitions and interconnections. Separations (in a totally rational sense) are replaced by a fusion and the abstract space becomes a concrete space-time continuum emanating with unhindered lightness; separating and dividing wall planes are clearly distinguishable from the structure; the emphasis is on the structure and not on the walls.

The dissolution of space, effected by the irruption of time, is nowhere as striking as in the new creations of architecture; in this sense it is definitely four-dimensional and aperspectival. Certainly at a first glance our perception, accustomed over centuries to frozen "harmonious" proportions, will not take kindly to the new "functional" (Sullivan/Adler) as well as "organic" architecture (Wright). It is no more harmonious (in the old sense of the term) than the music of Schoenberg, who demonstrated that harmony (in the old sense) is of secondary import;[86] it is aharmonious and not inharmonious. Or better, expressed in architectural terms, the new architecture is aproportional. Discussing the superannuated "systems" of proportion, Wright stresses that "proportion is nothing in itself. It is a matter or relation to environment modified always by every feature, exterior as well as interior."[87]

This architecture is free of style to the same extent that the new music is free of measure (see note *61*, p. 510), since a style—as Wright points out—is nothing other than "some form of spiritual constipation."[88] "In any true concept of organic architecture, style is the expression of character. There is no longer any question of 'styles.' "[89] Yet "a truer style can always be found in the structure for the purposes of the building. . . . Thus style is achieved because the character (the secret of style) is an expression of a principle that builds from within outward—a principle that is valid for all architects who love reality more than any 'classical' prescription."[90] Thus a style is not a pattern or a superior norm imposed from outside but is a quality of an inner certainty of character. The emergence of this qualitative element is symptomatic; it is unmistakably reminiscent of the qualitative character of "time" as an original phenomenon.

The new conception of space based on the new valuation of time has led to what is today called a "free plan." Le Corbusier took the initiative and was the first to apply the diagonal, and in particular the free and non-geometric curve in his buildings.[91] A beautiful example of the application of the free curve is the Brazilian pavilion at the New York World's Fair, 1939, by Lucio Costa and Oscar Niemeyer Soares (figure 47). It "was remarkable for its open, freely curving plan."[92] The Finnish architect Alvar Aalto also "developed his own form of the free curve."[93] Rigid and spatially fixed ground plans give way to those which are open, free, and moving. Elizabeth Mock writes: "The old convention of the symmetrical, rectangular plan, divided into immutable compartments, has finally been broken down, and the newer convention of the 'open plan,' sometimes accomplished at considerable sacrifice of quiet and privacy, is being more thoughtfully approached."[94]

With his own buildings, as in his multi-family houses in the Doldertal, Zürich (see figure 49), Alfred Roth has achieved a "transition from rigid and closed to loose and open construction."[95] He maintains that "the new structures awaken the understanding for the intrinsic value and interconnections of things in general."[96] Thus he calls our attention to the qualitative time incorporated by contemporary architecture, and the consequent replacement of systematic divisions by an open world of interconnections. "The new architecture in its contemporary form is an immediate expression of the recently consolidated and intensified time-consciousness."[97]

In purely physical terms, the new architecture no longer builds rigid, circumscribed spaces but spatio-temporal continua. In other words, time, to the extent that it is expressible architectonically, has transformed closed, three-dimensional architectural space into dynamic, open space-time. And the key word "open space" leads us directly to:

2) The supersession of dualism in architecture. To what extent is there a dualistic principle in architecture? Heretofore each building constituted an essential op-

Figure 47: Lucio Costa, Oscar Niemeyer Soares, and Paul Lester Wiener, Brazilian Pavilion at the New York World's Fair, 1939.

position between interior and exterior. The primordial image of the house—the cave—was the sheltering darkness. Early medieval castles still shy away from light (not only on the side of possible enemy attack but also toward the courtyard). Not until the Renaissance, notably in the "Palazzo Duccale" of Urbino, with its giant exterior windows, is the living space brightened in keeping with the advent of mental illumination. And what of today? The walls separating the interior from the exterior are beginning to fall, and their place is being taken by glass. "The house opens outward where 'indoors' and 'outdoors' become a unity," as Wright says.[98] This is true not only of public buildings like the "Bauhaus," Dessau (see figure 48), the Illinois Institute of Technology in Chicago,[99] the Museum of Modern Art in New York,[100] the "Ciudad Universitaria" in Madrid, or the schoolhouse in Holland built by J. Duiker, in which a heated ceiling permits open air instruction in winter.[101] It also holds true of private houses, for which one built by Edward D. Stone in Old Westbury, Long Island, N.Y., can serve as a representative example (see figures 50 and 51).[102] It is exactly as Elizabeth Mock describes it: "Living space extends into the garden and walls of glass bring the view into the house. The boundary between inside and outside becomes negligible."[103]

A more striking form of the supersession of the previous dualism between interior and exterior is hardly conceivable since it is achieved in man's most private domain, his domicile. Seclusion and isolation are relinquished; man not only begins to think and play music in the open but also to live and dwell. Wright's expression "spacious openness"[104] is not just an Americanism; it accords with the new and necessary aperspectival structure of reality. This "opening up" in city planning as a consequence of the supersession of a perspectively fixed form of life was recently demonstrated in an arresting manner by Jürgen Pahl, student of Hans Scharoun.[105] Scharoun himself must be mentioned in this context: in his "New Philharmonic Hall," Berlin, for instance, he has masterfully and boldly surpassed the rigidity of fixed perspective and initiated new formations deeply indebted to the new consciousness.

Once again the key term "openness" leads us further to:

3) The arationality of the new architecture. The new and frequent utilization of glass illuminates an additional characteristic of the aperspectival world: transparency (already clearly exemplified in the Bauhaus, Dessau). As S. Giedion remarks, "in this case it is the interior and the exterior of a building which are presented simultaneously. The extensive transparent areas, by dematerializing the corners, permit the hovering relations of planes and the kind of 'overlapping' which appears in contemporary painting."[106] This diaphaneity or transparency evidences an arational character. How remote from the mirror-world of once regal salons, where as if by magic the perspectives pretended to achieve a deceptive infinity!

In the realm of the rational everything is oriented toward a center. The individual grasps this center only partially, sectorially, and perspectively. "Centralization was the ideal of Monarchy. Integration is the ideal of democracy," says Wright, adding, "Monarchy has fallen."[107] The focal point once sought externally is found by the "new man" within himself. This is the integration and supersession of rational fragmentation. Every integration has an arational character. As the inhabitant of his future city "Usonia" Wright envisions the "democratic citizen responsible in himself. He is the only unendangered man since he is the man disciplined from within."[108] It is not only a prophetic but a truly prognostic statement in full accord with what we have called a man of the integral consciousness structure.

Figure 48: Walter Gropius, *Bauhaus*, Dessau, 1925-26 (section).

Figure 49: A. and E. Roth, Marcel Breuer, two multi-family dwellings in the Doldertal, Zürich (Switzerland), 1935-36.

It is not accidental that Le Corbusier strives toward *clarté* and designs a *Cité lumière* and a *Ville radieuse*, and Wright's vertebrate and voluted constructions, as in his "Keith" and "McCord" houses, manifest "with increasing decisiveness the joining of partial forms." "Spirals and vertebrae become a sphere[!]. Such shell forms (e.g., the Hollywood Hills Clubhouse) float in space more or less like leaves of water lilies float on water."[109] Quite apart from this, the transparent sphere is the quintessence of arational integration.

Figures 50 and 51: Edward D. Stone, A. Conger Goodyear House, Old
Westbury, Long Island, N.Y.; 1940. (Above: view from the outside;
below: view from the inside looking out.)

3. Painting

During a discussion in the *Kunsthalle*, Bern, Fernand Léger recounted his
many years of association and collaboration with such architects as Le Corbusier,
Alvar Aalto, and others.[110] As a modern architect, he repeatedly felt the need to
break through the walls, as it were, by applying to the white and separating surfaces a
form of painting commonly called decorative, figurative, or abstract that would be

more aptly characterized as structural. This need is already aperspectival in nature, and its solution by Fernand Léger is an aperspectival realization. This was expressed most convincingly by his "Peinture decorative," created for the French Pavilion at the Trienniale in Milan, 1951. At the request of the French architects, he covered a wall surface (13.30 × 6.45 m) in order to open up the limited space, and, as Léger says, to make the dead wall vanish (see figure 52).[111] The colorful elements of this painting—black, blue, red, yellow, and green on a white base—restructure the wall by extending and making elastic the otherwise divisive, dead, confining surface and strikingly abolishing the feeling of spatial three-dimensionality without a regression to a two-dimensional surface effect. This at least was the impression which the mural evoked in the observers in Milan and later in Bern: a decidedly fourth-dimensional impression, achieved above all by the new treatment of the time-element, which color, in a systatic sense, may be considered to be. It is not fortuitous that Léger speaks of *couleur-lumière*, "color as light."[112]

This brief indication of the irruption of time in painting, lending it the temporic character which is the common stamp of all 'Isms" since Cézanne, suggests that we investigate this aperspectival manifestation further. Let us again proceed methodically and inquire in what way our three salient characteristics are also manifest in recent painting:

1) To what extent is the irruption of time found in painting?
2) To what extent is there an emergent supersession of dualism? and,
3) To what extent does it have an arational and hence aperspectival character?

Figure 52: Fernand Léger, "Peinture décorative" for the French Pavillion at the Trienniale, Milan, 1951; (Original size: 13.20 × 6.45m).

471

The example of Fernand Léger is an inceptual step for answering the first question.

1) Does time as a systatic element constitute the power which, compared with three-dimensional, spatially bound and perspectival time, lends contemporary painting its aperspectivity? And if so, to what extent?[113]

It may well be no accident that in the year 1828—the year non-Euclidean geometry was discovered—Delacroix in Paris saw his own views confirmed by the lectures of the scholar Michel Eugène Chevreul on color complementarity, which at the time had caused considerable stir, and for the first time observed this law in his painting.[114] What is the significance of this emphasis on color? Théodor Géricault, born during the years of revolution (1791–1824), had transgressed against all of the classicistic rules in his painting "The Float of Medusa" (1819). He had been preceded in England by the pioneering Swiss, Johann Heinrich Füssli (1741–1825).[115] Both burst the rigid form, dynamize the pictorial event, and unabashedly embrace an ecstatic use of color: the imaginative, the psychically temporal, comes to an emotional irruption. And Delacroix is the first to master this time aspect in painting.

The use of complementary colors, later developed by Van Gogh, is the recognition of the psychic reality whose basic structure is temporal polarity and complementarity. The ultimate arbiter in painting is no longer the limiting and spatializing line; rather, the psychic configuration of polarity is here recognized for the first time. Consequently, Delacroix also rejects the line; he calls the straight lines "monstrous" since they do not appear in nature and exist only in man's brain. Where humans apply them, they disrupt the elements.[116] This statement clearly reveals an anti-mental attitude. His revolt against the mental-rational attitude is also pronounced in his drawing technique: he does not form the drawing in linear contours but unfolds them from oval shapes.[117] For the first time a premonition irrupts that the three-dimensional conception of the world will yield to "curved space" which, as we know, is the basic form of the four-dimensional space-time world.

While this sense for spherical space—in contrast to the horizontal-vertical perspectival fixity of three dimensions—is still embryonic with Delacroix, it comes to full expression in Cézanne (1838–1906). Previous judgements of his paintings emphasized those structural elements that Cézanne himself selected as most relevant to his painting, namely that underlying his paintings were the primordial forms of "cone, ball, and cylinder." These elements, notably their effect on the observer, indicate Cézanne's disassociation from mere three-dimensionality. But not until the end of 1950 was it recognized that Cézanne's paintings, created two generations earlier, were totally new; they are not only based on a conception of spherical space but also explicitly depict this spherical space. We are indebted to Liliane Guerry for this extremely important insight.[118] On the basis of exhaustive analyses of Cézanne's most important works, she has demonstrated that Cézanne established a space which "integrates the work of art into the breath of time."[119] Cézanne's "visual field is spherical . . . and his composition issues from curvature."[120] "For him the universe is a spheroid."[121] As Liliane Guerry expressly points out, this occurred several decades before Einstein.[122]

In contrast to the Renaissance painters, space for Cézanne is a "continuum."[123] "It arises from the curve and not from the straight line, as the theoreticians of the Renaissance still maintained."[124] The various sketches reproduced in L. Guerry's book make this clear, as in the picture "Pastorale"[125] reproduced here along with its diagram. At the same time we are contrasting it with a Renaissance masterpiece by Sandro Botticelli, "Christ's Interment in the Tomb," from the first decade of the sixteenth century, which evidences a strictly geometric, perspectival composition particularly visible in the accompanying diagram (see figures 53-56). The demonstration of the spherical pictorial surface is also significant, since it shows in which preformed and predisposed areas the necessity of a new perception of the world emerges from latency to efficacy.

This new perception takes shape spontaneously in the artist, and this creative achievement is merely recapitulated by the scientific theory, in this instance by Einstein's. This circumstance is a guarantee of the authenticity and the life- and consciousness-befitting necessity of this restructuring of our perception brought on by the irruption of time. Such a new perception appears spontaneously in consciousness and has the nature of a mutation. The new capacity of sight, breaking with the old and enabling perception of new interconnections and transparent vistas, appears suddenly like a leap, as it were: a mutation from the three-into the four-dimensional world. Viewed in this context, Liliane Guerry's remarks take on a specific contour: "Instead of ossifying into rigidity, a contrived dodge rather than stability; instead of refusing to merge with the pulse of time, the work of art accepts agitation, and this agitation forms the basis of its spatial harmony." The work of art "integrates itself with the universal rhythm; it is no longer a closed world outside of natural time and space, frozen in autonomy. . . . Henceforth it is an integrating component of the universe in motion."[126]

To what extent Cézanne brought about the supersession of three dimensionality—ever inseparable from geometric perspective—has been demonstrated by Fritz Novotny in his study of "Cézanne and the End of Scientific Perspective" (1938). He has noted that "within [Cézanne's] painting, scientific spatial perspective—linear and aerial perspective—has decreased significantly in value. . . . The life of perspective has vanished, perspective in the old sense is dead."[127] The process initiated by Cézanne is completed toward the end of the 1880s by Van Gogh, Gauguin, Ensor, and Hodler.[128] The supersession of perspective is visible in yet another innovation; as Novotny points out, Cézanne presents within the same painting "multiple viewpoints" and "various visual axes." In a still life, for example, when "contrasted with the view of the table surface from above . . . the objects on the tables—jugs, plates, baskets—often appear in a much slighter vertical angle and indeed often appear in profile."[129]

Thomas Herzog refers to this same circumstance: "In his painting, Cézanne lays out a still life for example to appear as if it were viewed almost from above. Because of this, the opening of a cup becomes circular. Yet where the color rhythm demands it, the profile line of the cup is accorded full justice, as if he were looking at the cup from the front. Even in his landscapes, for instance in buildings, one can find the 'offenses' against the shortening of perspective. The observer only slowly realizes this, because the rhythm of color and contour compel the eye to perceive the entirety of the picture [i.e., the whole, and not just the perspectivally accented central arrangement] and to experience a self-sufficient pictorial world. This is why Cézanne espouses the 'cubistic manipulation' of observing the object from two angles. He wants the surface to become animated through the simultaneous frontal and top view, forcing upon the observer a kind of agitated vision as if he were moving in a space inhabited by the things depicted."[130]

Both of these references are by no means concerned with a mere detail. They touch upon the restructuration into aperspectivity of our previously valid mode of

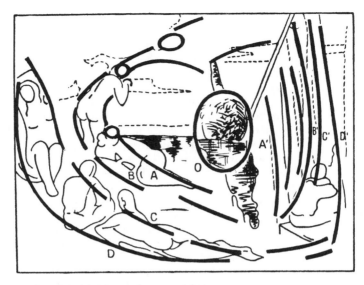

Figures 53 and 54: Paul Cézanne, "Don Quichotte sur les rives de Barbarie" (Don Quixote on the Barbary Coast, or "Pastorale" as it is sometimes titled); diagram (above, after L. Guerry) and (below) reproduction of the original.

seeing. Moreover, they underscore Liliane Guerry's fundamental recognition that the pictorial plane in Cézanne is spherical. At the same time, it should be noted that since Cézanne this spherical picture "surface" should be evident to anyone observing the creative work of the masters of the past two generations from this "viewpoint." It must also be noted that this is not intended to generalize Liliane Guerry's finding; rather we have here an aperspectival manifestation that is, self-constituting,

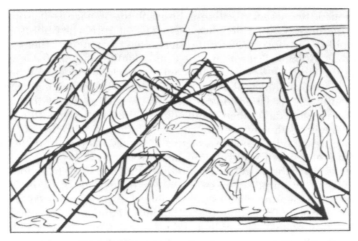

Figures 55 and 56: Sandro Botticelli, "Christ's Entombment" (1605); diagram and reproduction of original.

inherent in the new perception of the world. We must not forget that the perspectival effect has not been lost in modern painting, even if it is no longer achieved in an emphatically linear manner. Cézanne himself is an outstanding example of this. Even so, modern painting is not simply unperspectival; it does not negate perspective, particularly the effect of depth that is attainable. Rather, it surpasses perspective, freeing itself of the dominance of merely sectorial linear perspective. Thus it is a-perspectival, and the former depth-effect restructures itself into transparency.

After Cézanne the most powerful expression of this is by the Cubists. To confirm this with requisite objectivity, we would refer not to our own statements on the subject (p. 24 ff.) but to those of Th. Herzog which, symptomatically, were written at the same time as ours during the winter of 1947-48. [131]

In connection with the passage cited above on the uniqueness of Cézanne's rendering of an object from two viewpoints, Herzog has observed that "Cubism goes one step further: it seeks to present the infinitude of space itself, from which all forms are cut out, and with which they are filled, as it were. The Cubists seek to see things not only from above or in profile but also seek to penetrate them. Hence the unusually rapid change of viewpoint. The Cubist continually grasps a new fragment with each shift and experiences via this continuous visual movement the relationship between form and space as a dynamic, continuously changing process—as the fourth dimension. [This dimension curves space, rendering it spherical, and makes transparency possible rather than depth effects.] This fourth dimension is the main concern of Cubism's equally intuitive and comprehensible production. It is in this sense that we are to understand the remark by Georges Braque, one of the fathers of Cubism: 'The senses destroy form; only the spirit forms.' "[132]

If we disregard the art-historical interpretation that Cubism's concern is rendering visible the "infinitude of space"—whereas in fact and not merely interpretatively the fourth dimension manifests the spherical shape of the space-time continuum (and its transparency) rather than the infinity of the universe, reflected in the "two observation points" of the depicted spherical plane, on which alone these observation points are visible—if we bear these reservations in mind,[133] Herzog's further elaborations on this subject in connection with Picasso's cubism are valid: "The real riddle of Picasso, which was to preoccupy not only Paris but the entire world, began when Picasso joined Georges Braque in the Cubist experiment. During this initial period of Cubism, Picasso transformed the forms of objects back to their corresponding cubistic forms, modified the hues of their surfaces in varying degrees of brightness, yet allowed the object to remain recognizable. The intent is clear: captured in its basic surface form, the body must be grasped as something inhabiting space. In the second period the natural image was completely dissolved. The cubistic forms, corners, surfaces, and lines, glimpsed in ever-new constellations by the shifting viewpoints, are conjoined in such a way that an illusion of a dynamic process occurring in endless space is created. Here too, the intent is recognizable: anyone wishing to portray the infinitude of space must also paint time as the fourth dimension. He must show how each act of seeing superimposes a spatial figure, glimpsed now in this way, now in that, over the respective previous spatial figure. The aim is to make palpable a kind of spatio-temporal process out of the wealth of intersecting and complementary spatial components."[134]

A hitherto overlooked detail of Cubist painting exemplifies the effectuality and influence of the—probably still unconscious—concept of "curved space," of the spherical universe. It is found in the fact that Juan Gris, Georges Braque, and Pablo Picasso in particular did not paint many of these pictures, as the Cubistic fashion would suggest, on a rectangular surface, but rather on oval surfaces. Examples of these oval paintings are so numerous and well known that enumeration is unnecessary. On the other hand, let us once again touch upon the previously adduced problem of the poly-aspectual depiction of things. This mode of depiction was first attempted by Moritz von Schwind and Goya, who showed a profile and a frontal view in the same drawing,[135] followed by Cézanne's unified rendition of profile and top view. Cubism and Futurism went still further by attempting to present not just a dual view but multifarious views in the same painting. Cubism was first in attaining a transparency of the spatio-temporal impression of the whole. Since then, even without the use of cubistic elements, this aperspectival mode of seeing has not been lost in modern art, as we have already pointed out (p. 24 f.); it can be found in the creations of Georges Braque and Pablo Picasso from the 1940s—to mention just two examples reproduced in Part I (figure 1, p. 25, as well as figures 2 and 3 on pp. 27-28).

An additional example of a painting in which things are rendered aperspectivally from various viewpoints in the same picture is Picasso's "Woman of Arles" (figure 57). Alfred H. Barr, Jr., says of this painting: "In the head may be seen the cubist device of simultaneity—showing two aspects as a single object at the same time, in this case the profile and the full face. The transparency of overlapping planes is also characteristic."[136] It is noteworthy that the key word "transparency" (diaphaneity) occurs in this context. Since aperspectivity is always concerned with the whole, it cannot disregard this characteristic. Wherever the spatio-temporal mode of depiction or expression goes beyond the purely temporalistic technique (one which considers "time"), this diaphaneity must be manifest, for the aspired-for whole eludes perception as long as we see only one of its sides.

It is questionable whether we can view these attempts merely as expressions of "simultaneity"; at the moment when diaphaneity becomes manifest, whatever is presented appears as a whole, exempt from space-time limitations. What is designated as mere "simultaneity"—in which there are always inherent magical residua since simultaneity expresses a dissolution of temporal succession and time—is restructured into time-freedom by the transparency achieved by depiction. To be terminologically precise, it is not a question in such instances of the realization of simultaneity, but of the achronon. Simultaneity is magical resolution of time, a re-

Figure 57:   Pablo Picasso, "The Woman of Arles," 1913.

gression into the condition of timelessness. Time-freedom is a supersession of this timelessness, verified in the verition of the whole.[137]

In all this it must not be forgotten that the Cubist experiment is one of the numerous variations of temporic style preparatory to aperspectivity. On the one hand it seems to destroy the forms, which is quite understandable since it dissolves three-dimensional space; on the other, it reverts to certain primordial forms and thereby "presentiates" them at the very moment it excludes the harmony of the human body from depiction (the nude had been one of the prime subjects of perspectival painting). In this regard, it is noteworthy that particularly in and following Cubism paintings frequently depict guitars, mandolins, and lutes. We know today, on the basis of new research in symbolism, that these instruments symbolize the primordial form of the female body; they are to a certain extent its primordial image.[138] The substitution of the primordial form of the human body, the nude, now taking place in modern art—this emphatic "presencing" of a primordial image—can be considered a further explanation of the hitherto latent temporic concern of modern painting.

From time to time these temporic concerns have been clearly and distinctly articulated by individual artists; Theo van Doesburg (1883–1931), for example, called some of his "abstract" paintings "Space-time constructions."[139] Other examples can be found among the Futurists some years earlier;[140] we would mention only Gino Severini's "Restless Dancer" (figure 58). Severini himself insisted that it deals with

Figure 58: Gino Severini, "The Restless Dancer," ca. 1912–1913.

the "total impression of the dancer, past and present, near and far, small and large, as they appear to the artist who has observed the dancer during various periods of her life."[141]

The consideration of time in painting, as elsewhere, initiated the attempts to overcome rational dualism. For this too, there are numerous examples, some of which we wish to consider in relation to:

2) The supersession of dualism. The application of color complementarity by Delacroix is a secession from opposites, from dualism, and a movement toward correspondence, toward polar complementarity. These are not merely contrastive effects of colors played off against each other; rather the painting obtains its vigor from a polar nexus, from the interrelationships of the colors. The structure has undergone a fundamental change or transformation. And ever since Delacroix, the question of color complementarity has been unavoidable in painting. Not only Van Gogh, but most of the later masters sought out and worked with pure colors. At the very moment when Einstein resolved the opposition of matter versus energy, the Fauvists made a demand ultimately traceable to Cézanne that the painting should be "form (and/or line) and color."[142] In this there is a notable parallelism between physics and art, and in both it is rooted in the need to realize the new perception of world.

The preoccupation with overcoming dualism is reflected in painting in yet another way. Insofar as we can judge, it became acute for the first time with Cézanne. We must not forget that a painting is constantly experienced as an opposite; it was an object for its creator as well as for the observer. Liliane Guerry logically concludes that on the basis of Cézanne's inclusion of time "the boundaries between the space of the observer and the space of the work of art are eliminated. One identifies and harmonizes with the other. . . . "[143] The concluding deduction which Liliane Guerry draws from her investigations points to this same phenomenon, underscored, moreover, by a statement of Cézanne's: "Just as the artist has surpassed time by integrating himself into its rhythm, so is he from now on the master of space. And only now can he say in summary: 'I feel colored by all the nuances of the infinite. Henceforth I am one with my painting.' "[144]

It would definitely be counter to the attained frequency of consciousness if we were to interpret Cézanne's statement in mythical or psychological terms. We are dealing here—for those who have ears to hear—with a supersession of time and space, object and subject, with a liberation from them and a conscious participation in the whole. It has nothing to do with some mythical, magical immersion in a mere space-timelessness, or with a mere psychologically explicable identification.[145] To be sure, those who in their mental limitation and spatial captivity reiterate the cliche of "loss of the middle,"[146] will be unable to recognize the new consciousness structure manifest in the adduced examples. Since the whole is space-time-free, it knows no middle. Only in space and spatial thought is there a middle. Whoever applies three-dimensional criteria to the aperspectival, four-dimensional art of our day and speaks of the (spatializing) middle (whereas the whole, in its freedom from spatio-temporal concepts, is transparent) ill-advisedly stirs up controversy at the wrong time and place. The loss of the middle is not a loss, but a gain of the whole.[147]

What is true of Cézanne is to a great extent true of the contemporary masters. Paul Westheim has expressed this with regard to Paul Klee: "The tragic conflict between external image and represented image, Being and Sense, has been overcome by Paul Klee. Or, more accurately, the conflict no longer exists."[148] The same solution is noted by Henry-Daniel Kahnweiler with regard to the painting of Juan Gris and its correspondence to modern music: "The masters of twelve-tone music have undertaken the suppression of dualism and are being led by convictions akin to those of Juan Gris."[149] Let these examples suffice. They signify a liberation from the rational mode of seeing and thinking, without a regression to irrationality; on the contrary, they overdetermine the rational toward the arational. Thus some remarks may be in order about:

3) The arationality of the new painting, and indications more clearly demonstrating the aperspectival manifestations of this art. Picasso's well-known remark, "I do not seek, I find," expresses at the very least his arational attitude. This attitude does not presume any intentionality, since intentionality is perspectival and oriented. To clarify this remark of Picasso, Werner Haftmann quotes Hermann Hesse: "In his *Weg nach Innen*, Hesse says: 'If search means that one has a goal, then finding means to be free, to stand open, to have no aim.' "[150] In this context belongs the theory of *figures ouvertes* developed for landscape painting by André Lhote with reference to Cézanne; it enables "the false totally intellectual delineation or outline" of things to be replaced by connecting transitions.[151] Here too we no longer find a purposive search but an open understanding: the finder carries his goal within and need not seek it externally.

In general, however, arationality in painting just as in the other areas we have considered is only a consequence, or rather, an encompassing circumscription of an attitude which becomes efficient when the "irruption of time" becomes efficacious. This efficacy brings about the supersession of dualism and perspectival rigidity; it transforms the three-dimensional space world into a spherical, four-dimensional, space-time world. In painting it opens the closed space in the same way as it opened closed thinking and closed justice, or as mere systems were overdetermined into structures. In painting the terms aperspectival and arational coincide in the same way that atonal and arational do in music.

On the previous pages we have already encountered indications of aperspectivity expressed in painting by a commensurate aperspectivity. It appears through the most frequent characteristics of the spherical ground of the picture, the emphasis on structure and open space, as well as diaphaneity or transparency.

Whichever of the numerous new styles since Impressionism we may consider, even where they stand in curious opposition to each other, as emotion-ridden Expressionism opposed disciplined Cubism, it is nonetheless clear that they are all attempts to discover a new and valid form of expression. This is their one common concern, particularly as they endeavor to solve the same problem. This is true even if they cannot yet account for the depth of their concern and consequently introduce a contradictory terminology. This shows to what extent they were preoccupied by the creative process of transformation and consequently lacked a clear distance with which to judge themselves and their work. Only because of this is it understandable that some call a particular form of art abstract while others call it concrete; yet both sides fail to notice that perspectival art is the most abstract since the three-dimensional contrived space afforded by perspectivity is an abstraction.

All artistic styles since Impressionism are spontaneous forms of temporic, attempts to surpass the perspectival three-dimensionality by the inclusion of time. Yet it becomes ever more evident from decade to decade that art is no longer concerned with things as such, abstract or concrete forms, imitative, prototypal or archetypal art, but rather with the visible manifestations of structures lying "behind" and constituting things and thoughts. As Picasso has formulated this fact, "it is not the facade of things, but their hidden structure"[152] that occupies contemporary artists. It is the identical concern with disclosing the interconnection of the whole through the spatio-temporal structure which we have repeatedly encountered.

The emphasis on structure is today for many of the best artists [153] the most prominent feature linking the various "styles." This is also preparatory to attaining an open "world without opposite." With this phrase[154] we do not mean a thou-less, relationless perception of world but an unrestricted, de-limited world that reveals to our perception the fullness and wealth of connections of the unobstructed whole. The "loss" of the opposite appears a loss only to those who lack assurance in the "Itself" and cannot dispense with the supposedly protective walls of their systems and the possessiveness of their rigidified ego. To surrender the opposite is to gain together-ness: genuine inter-human participation. In this togetherness the thou, be it a partner, world, or the divine, is no longer thought, understood, or grasped as an opposite. Subject and object lose their previous dualistic and antagonistic character of opposition, and the antagonism engendered by preserving a misunderstood ego-valuation transforms itself into a creative tension emerging from the togetherness of life-sustaining and complementary poles. The spatio-temporal structures appearing in contemporary painting dissolve the merely spatially fixed systems. The systems retain their hold only where they make circumscribed areas of reality (the world of opposites!) manipulable, as in science, technology, and necessarily discursive conceptual thought.

We must therefore not become confused by the innumerable names of styles, nor by their apparent contrarity. Impressionism dissolves form; Pointilism discloses the vibrations of space. The Primitivists (Henri Rousseau, le Douanier, and his followers) radically denounce perspective and attempt to break new ground from an infantilistic attitude; Fauvism masters a new relationship between line and color, that is, between space and time; or, with reference to Paul Klee's definition of line and color, the artist masters the relationship between the quantitative (measurable line) and the qualitative (color).[155] Expressionism attempts an emotionally laden onslaught against the residua of a conception and depiction of the naturalistic, three-dimensional world; Futurism, particularly Cubism, forms inceptually the new, spherically transparent structure of the world. Surrealism succumbs to psychic temporicity by approaching the time problem—not without impunity—from the puberty zone, embellished by the churnings of psychoanalysis; the so-called Abstractionists—whose paintings could be more appropriately called structural—completely detach themselves from any form of palpable three-dimensional objectivity.[156]

What intense effort has been expended by the past two generations in their search for ways to express the new world perception! How many creative lives and their works have opened further avenues, or more exactly, have discovered new bases for departure, even with their mistaken attempts. How many failures to overcome perspectivity, which corresponds to the approximate number of false starts before the discovery of perspective during the generations preceding Leonardo da Vinci (p. 15 f.)! How often a mistakenly chosen basis of departure has at least shown how the new consciousness structure cannot be realized, whether as the magical emphasis of the "Sunday painters," the psychic emphasis of the Surrealists who merely sub-realistically flung from themselves their dream world and the psychic crises of the epoch,[157] or the emotion-ridden and thus equally psychically-dominant false starts of Expressionism. In contrast, the later works of the major artists, notably those of Braque, Léger, Matisse, and Picasso, reunify all the elements shaped by the various attempts: Cézanne's spherical space; the "abstraction," that is, the structuration of the Futurists, Cubists, and "Abstractionists," as well as some Tachists; the pure color values that consolidated from Delacroix via Van Gogh to the "Fauvists"; and the "disjunction" pioneered by Cubism and Expressionism. With these masters begins the realization of what Franz Marc articulated: "More and more I begin to see behind, or better, see through things."[158] This transparency gradually becomes perceptible.

Although they may appear playful, Picasso's "light drawings" are here symptomatic examples (see figures 59 and 60 below).[159] A. Calder's "Mobiles" are also worthy of mention in this context (figure 61 on p. 483)[160] as well as certain "spherical photographs" (see figures 62 and 63 on p. 484), all of which are merely an indication that there is a drive toward an aperspectival perception in the general

Figure 59:   Pablo Picasso, Classic Head,"
flashlight sketch, ca. 1949.

Figure 60:   Pablo Picasso, "Flowers in a
Vase," flashlight sketch, ca. 1949.

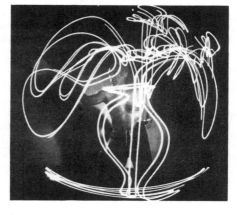

(Both "sketches" were done by Picasso with a penlight in a darkened room during the course of a few seconds, and were photographed by Gjon Mili.)

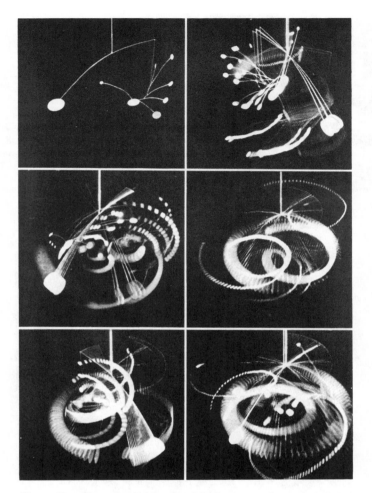

Figure 61:   Alexander Calder, "Mobile," 1936; steel wire and aluminum; at rest (above left) and in motion.

consciousness.[161] All these attempts make vivid the desire to step out of the previous framework. This desire is brought out with unusual force in one of the most important transparent pictures of Georges Braque, a picture of sunflowers (painted in 1946). Apparent to any observer is the predominance of curved lines clearly showing a spheroid pictorial surface. This pictorial surface, for which the rectangular frame is naturally inadequate, reaches into the frame which is exploded and dissolved by the pictorial structure (see figure 66 on p. 485).

Each genuine structure shelters the possibility for the emergent transparency in Franz Marc's sense. While incorporating the spatio-temporal elements, it ultimately emerges from space-timelessness which is surpassed in conscious process and thus changes into space-time–freedom, the achronon. Paul Klee has expressed this: "There, where the central organ of all spatio-temporal motility, whether as the brain or the heart of creation, incites all the functions, who, as an artist, would not

Figure 62: Arrangement of camera, which is affixed on cables strung from two buildings and aimed at the silvered sphere suspended above it in such a way as to be able to photograph the image on the sphere.

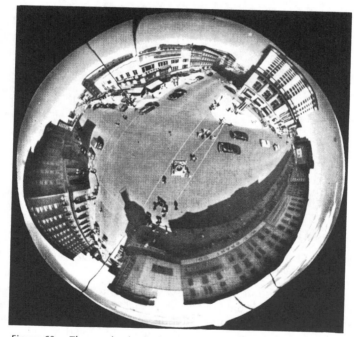

Figure 63: The result: the "spherical photograph" of Dale Rooks and John Malloy, Grand Rapids, Michigan, U.S.A.; ca. 1949.

wish to live there . . . in the origin of creation?"[162]—in the origin emerging to presence through the artist. As Hans-Friedrich Geist says, Paul Klee's work mirrors "a presentiment of the spiritual origin" of things.[163]

Klee himself states that the task of the artist is "to lend duration to Genesis [origin]."[164] Kurt Leonhard in turn comments on this remark: "The distanciating

 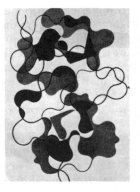

Figure 64:   Grains of
starch embedded in
lacquer.

Figure 65:   Sophie Taeu-
ber-Arp, "Lignes d'été,"
1949.

Figure 66:   Georges Braque, "Sunflowers"; oil; 1946.

tectonics of Picasso and the sensitive, delicate structures of Paul Klee contain perhaps the most powerful promise for the future bequeathed to us by the most recent
past. Both have demolished the walls of appearance behind which stretch the unlimited and only apparently contradictory possibilities of the modern soul."[165] In an
almost lyric manner, Paul Klee's work elicits a transparency of the once dual regions
of night and day, dream and wakefulness, life and death; as he notes in his diary, "I

am not at all comprehensible in this world. I dwell with the dead as well as with the unborn, and somewhat closer to the heart of creation than is usual. And not nearly close enough."[166] This is the same consciousness attitude evident in Cézanne's words: "Nature is not at the surface but in the depths, and colors are an expression of this depth at the surface; they surge up from the roots of the world."[167]

These "roots of the world," invisible to the mere eye, the "secret structure of things"—they have been brought to perception by Picasso and other artists of our epoch. We would mention particularly the paintings of Ernst Wilhelm Nay (since 1955) whose agglomerations, spheroid and disc forms evoke sub-atomic events. Even Klee himself has revealed botanic micro-structures.[168] Among others, Sophie Taeuber-Arp and Hans Haffenrichter followed his example. The painting by Sophie Taeuber-Arp, "Lignes d'éte," evinces a remarkable structural affinity to a micro-photograph of starch granules imbedded in lacquer (see figures 64 and 65 on p. 485). Hans Haffenrichter's painting "Energie" on the other hand, recalls a macro-structure equally invisible to the naked eye. It is a macro-structure of a spiral nebula in the constellation *canes venatici* ("The Hounds"), photographed by the Mount Palomar and Mount Wilson observatories (see figures 67 and 68). It is hardly plausible to call such affinities accidental coincidences since a great number of such structural affinities have been demonstrated.[169]

Although in Klee's work a psychical and at times magical emphasis prevails, he nevertheless successfully evokes the poly-valence and transparency of the whole.[170] Of course Picasso's pictures, such as his still life paintings in Antibes (Musée Grimaldo), are more transparent, as are the contemporaneous works of Matisse (after 1943) and Léger (from 1948 to 1951).[171] They all exhibit a common stylistic trait: the whiteness of the ground that integrates what is "depicted," rendering it transparent. This is evident in Picasso's still life "Vase with Foliage and Sea Urchins" (1946), despite our black and white reproduction (see figure 69 on p. 488).

All of these aperspectival inceptions clearly show the arationality of modern

Figure 67:   Hans Haffenrichter, "Energy"; Egg-tempera; 1954 (original size: 48.5 × 38 cm).

Figure 68: Extragalactic nebula in the constellation "The Hounds" (canes venatici); photograph by the Mount Wilson and Mount Palomar observatories).

painting. Even partial regressions, such as those of the first "Abstractionists," Expressionists, and Surrealists who strove to overcome three-dimensionality primarily from the psychic, lead beyond the irrational and the rational, as is apparent in the late work of Klee and even of Kandinsky.

Today, at the mid-point of the century, the words noted by Franz Marc in 1915 are coming to fulfillment: "In the twentieth century we shall live among strange faces, new paintings, and unheard of sounds. Many, lacking an inner glow, will freeze and feel nothing but coolness, and will flee into the ruins of their recollection."

4. *Literature*

With this section devoted to literature, works of art in language, we approach the conclusion of our exposition of aperspectival manifestations. Here we will seek proof for the contention that man's basic form of expression, his language, reflects those structural and mutational changes taking place that we have attempted to demonstrate in various areas. If the change cannot be demonstrated in language since the French Revolution, that is, in its structure and subject matter, then the indirect manifestations of aperspectivity pressing toward expression in the sciences, although not called into question, would remain ultimately unfounded. If it is possible, however, to discern such manifestations in poetry, grounded as it is in language, then to a certain extent it would represent the crowning confirmation of our undertaking.

Such verification is fundamental and definitive in yet another respect: poetry, as we have already discussed elsewhere,[172] is more than mere epic, drama, or verse; poetry is, and perhaps primarily, historiography (p. 192). Yet it is not a history of dates, manifest events, and occurrences. Poetry is a writing of history of the date-

Figure 69: Pablo Picasso, "Vase with Foliage and Sea Urchins"; oil; 1946 (original size: 45 × 38 cm).

less; it is the record and declaration about the invisible events and happenings that are effective from origin, and become present in the poetic word, attaining their tangible manifestation in social, political, and scientific actualities. The great poets are a visible example that poetry is the writing of history of the dateless—of events which would remain intangible if there were no poets. In the works of such poets as Homer, Sappho, Virgil, the Troubadours, Dante, Shakespeare, Goethe, Hölderlin, and Mallarmé, the ever-new realities assume a form whose effectiveness does not wane, since the decisive and intangible events become visible in them.[173]

This aspect of poetry deserves to be emphasized since a fundamental change in the conception and manner of writing history constitutes a temporic effort. History, after all, is pre-eminently a "time" problem. It is not accidental that the great encounter with this problem occurred in Hegel's philosophy of history. It led to the situation, as Karl Löwith again emphasized, that "Hegel's students, not the least of whom was Marx, inquired in all seriousness how history could continue after Hegel. It was Schelling who first brought about the emancipation from Hegel's closed system."[174] As noted by Rosenkranz, the matter-of-fact Hegelian, Schelling had stated in his inaugural lecture in Berlin (1841) that mankind must be "moved beyond its previous consciousness."[175] He articulates as a conscious demand what had already been achieved by the great historians of the dateless: by the poets, notably since Hölderlin. In their works, in the structure of their language, and the subject matter of their writings, the movement of human consciousness beyond its previous stance is already a reality. In other words, in poetry we can discern the mutation, the movement, the shift of consciousness which has overdetermined the previous three-dimensional toward the four-dimensional mode of realization. For it to happen, the time problem had to emerge into the forefront in some visible and demonstrable form; and this was the case in both linguistic structure and thematic expression.

During the course of the last twenty-five years we have addressed ourselves to this subject in various ways. Consequently we shall avoid, as far as possible, reiterating the numerous examples of this aperspectival manifestation we have furnished in our previous publications.[176] Moreover, just as it has not been feasible to discuss all of the available evidence for the areas previously considered, so will we be unable here to include the greater part of the extensive available documentation, primarily for lack of space—a condition perhaps favorable to the clarity of presentation.

Once again we shall employ our familiar schema, posing for poetry three questions, and attempting to answer them:

1) To what extent is the time-theme acute in poetry as a systatic element?
2) To what extent is dualism surpassed without a regression to the irrational or to a persistent adherence to mythical irrationality?
3) To what extent does poetry manifest arational inceptions and consequently realize diaphaneity?

One of Hölderlin's aphorisms contains an answer to all three questions: "We are familiar with the inversion of words in the period. But the inversion of the period itself must be even greater and more effective. The logical placement of the periods, where development follows reason, goal follows development, and purpose follows the goal, where the subordinate clauses are always placed at the end of the main clauses to which they relate: all this is seldom, if ever, of use to the poet."[177]

Hölderlin has applied this consideration in his own poetry. Thus the logically and perspectivally oriented description is replaced by the alogical and aperspectival utterance. In Hölderlin's poetry mere mythologemes and philosophemes change to eteologemes. His annulment of the sovereignty of the period, with its continuous time and course of events (reason-development-aim-purpose), by inversion overdetermines rational determinism into arational indeterminism, or better, causality by acausality. It can be said in all justice that this treatment of inversion is more than a philological concern with syntax. It is structural, changing the structure from spatial systematics to spatio-temporal synairetics. This gain attained via the inversion of the period, anticipates at one stroke all the temporic achievements following Hölderlin: the liberation from the oriented course of time, from the restraints of measured time and rhythmic temporicity.

In other words, with Hölderlin the achronon comes to light. The main concern is no longer with sequence, with the succession of parts after each other. Hölderlin's concern and utterance bear on the true and undivided whole, without sequence, presentiated in each genuine word. "In the beginning," or rather, "In origin" (since the Greek text reads *arche*) "was the word." In Hölderlin's later poetry, origin becomes present. His statement, his pure utterance (and eteological word), "Time is long, but the True comes to pass,"[178] applies not only in general but specifically to his own work. In his history-writing of the dateless—the true, the diaphainon, is dateless—what once appeared as timeless is elevated to time-freedom; it comes about (*ereignet sich*), it "owns up to itself" (*wird sich seiner selbst eigen*): even the timeless comes to consciousness as the achronon. Whatever is the most distant past and most remote future, whatever appears temporally bound, becomes time-free present. That this is not just our own arbitrary interpretation is evident from Hölderlin's own words, which deserve to be quoted in full: "I have seen it once, the one thing that my soul sought, and the fulfillment which we pose beyond the stars and push to the end of time—I have felt its presence. The most exalted was there—in this circle of human nature and things, it was there."[179]

Hölderlin's aphorism on inversion admits the transparency of time-freedom as well as the acausality that represents the supersession of dualism and the arationality that surpasses and overdetermines the mental-logical; not via a reversion to irrationalism but through the verition or awaring of the whole.

And we must also consider, as Hannes Maeder points out, that Hölderlin cultivated the "profound word"; in other words, he restored to language what is proper to it. Language that was once description becomes through him pure utterance. This Hölderlin achieves by the "fracturing of construction" and a specific kind of caesura in his verse: "The prosaic word order, where the subject (determined) precedes the predicate (determinant), is for Hölderlin unsuitable since the conceptual predicate reduces the subject to a mere object of expression [in the sense of something to be described], destroying its independence as a profound word. Consequently Hölderlin inverts the logical sequence and places the predicate first in order that the subject—now at the conclusion—appears in its full intensity and significance because of the tension created. This can be seen in the following verses from the 'Patmos' hymn:

> Doch furchtbar ist, wie da und dort
> Unendlich hin zerstreut das Lebende Gott.

> (But it is terrible how here and there
> unendingly God disperses the living.)

The subject *Gott* (God) appearing at the conclusion has a terrifying effect. Hölderlin has applied this inversion consciously . . ."[180] (as evidenced by the relevant aphorism quoted above which Maeder goes on to cite).

If one wished to systematize, one could well say that this aphorism preformed everything of decisive importance achieved by the generations of poets since Hölderlin. It is a declaration of supra-wakefulness, of sovereign clarity and heightened awareness. It compactly answers our three questions, to which we should now address ourselves, considering the most important poets since Hölderlin.

1) It should be observed that for the last one-hundred-fifty years the theme of time has a four-fold structure-modifying role in poetry. Since it is complex, it is not surprising that this theme manifests itself in various ways, and that the complexity

can be perceived most readily when we distinguish clearly among its various forms of manifestation. Such discrimination is inherent in any exposition, and is thus equally indispensable for our attempt. In this sense we can say that the time theme is articulated in poetry as follows:

a) essentially, to the extent that language itself (in word and sentence) is treated as a primordial phenomenon by recognizing its originating-creative nature;

b) psychically, insofar as extrinsic plot yields to what is called "stream of consciousness" (*monologue intérieur*);

c) thematically, insofar as poetry begins to deal explicitly with the time problem; and,

d) structurally, insofar as a new estimation of grammatical aspects, and a novel use of syntactical freedom are evident.

Essentially, the time problem comes to the fore when the word acquires its own worth through Hölderlin, who dissociates it from its purposive subservience to description. Since the word, along with color and tone, belongs to the three primordial, non-spatial phenomena, the emergent independence of the word is a recognition of time's potency, which we have described in a complex sense as intensity and a world constituent. Moreover, it is revealing that in painting color as such, and in music tone as such (we are thinking here primarily of Alban Berg), have taken on an entirely new value. Just as genuine poetry since Hölderlin no longer employs the word to describe the world, so art, beginning with Hölderlin's contemporary, Delacroix, and particularly since the "Fauvists," no longer employs color to depict objects.

Tone, color, and word are no longer means or an end for something; they themselves are treated as qualities. Since they are not spatial elements, their three-dimensional utilization has ended. They must be recognized themselves as the expression and valuation of what ultimately is verified to us in the achronon. As timeless-temporal elements they are no longer used perspectivally or purposively to measure "reality"; they are themselves the realities and agencies. Today there is no longer any doubt that the word was of principal concern for Hölderlin; this is evident not only in the most recent research. It is equally evident to the open-minded reader of Hölderlin's poetry as it is so well disclosed in the faithful and exemplary work of Norbert von Hellingrath and Friedrich Beissner.[181]

Yet—and this is decisive—the recognition of the word as such can be found in an ever increasing measure throughout European poetry since Hölderlin. Francesco Flora points out the original use of the word by Giacomo Leopardi (1798–1837), also a contemporary of Hölderlin: "If I had to say wherein the greatest power of Leopardi's poetic word lies, I would have to admit that it consists in a kind of withdrawal: he divests the word of all taste, color, and scent of practical communication, and employs it as a completely circumscribed parable which has lost all terrestrial sense, and is thus purer in its fully intact form."[182] And in another passage Flora notes that "the uniqueness of Leopardi's poetry consists of its syntactical, melodic, and visible proportion; the individual words and the traditional word groups are placed into a new balance."[183]

In French poetry the unique valuation of the word begins with the great triumvirate Baudelaire, Verlaine, and Rimbaud, whereby the French language underwent an obvious and enduring derigidification, achieving its pinnacle in the crystallization of words by Stéphane Mallarmé later aspired to by Paul Valéry.[184]

In Spain these tendencies are weaker; they are not really discernible in the work of José Espronceda, but are present in the poetry of Gustavo Adolfo Bécquer, attaining their most valid expression until now in the works of Jorge Guillén.

The fundamental transformation in England begins with the "sober intoxication" (see p. 323) of William Blake and with the unpretentious temporicity of William Wordsworth. It is ultimately achieved by the Jesuit Gerard Manley Hopkins (1844–1899), who reveals in every respect—via syntax, meter, rhythm and vocabulary—the new fundamental tone, the new consciousness structure. This it acquires to such a degree that his poems were not even published until twenty years after his death (1918).[185] Hölderlin's late poetry had become accessible only a few years before (!), and even then there were difficulties of understanding it until finally in England the "new tone" became established via the work of the American, T. S. Eliot.

In the first half of our century T. S. Eliot, Paul Valéry, Jorge Guillén and R. M. Rilke[186] are the most prominent poetic representatives of the new consciousness structure.[187] This group was preceded by another, the *art nouveau* Europeans, who also sought to heighten the value of the word. Yet from their pseudo-priestly stance, they were more intent upon venerating and celebrating the word than expressing it: Stefan George in Germany, Gabriele d'Annunzio in Italy, Rubén Darío in South America, Ramón del Valle-Inclan, followed by Juan Ramón Jimenez in Spain, all of whom not incidentally resembled each other even to their very appearance and bearing.

Common to all of these recognized representatives of European poetry since Hölderlin and Leopardi is their regard for the word as an expressive power. As a pure word it no longer describes, recounts, represents, discusses,* or is utilized perspectivally; rather it raises origin into the present, rendering it transparent in its aperspectival and multivalent plenitude. From the accounts of Homer to the descriptive poetry of classicism, the word was predominantly a tool: it represented, recounted, and described the world. In other words, a temporally qualitative, primordial element was placed in the service of measuring, mental thought. Yet ever since Classicism, the structural transformation is fundamental; the word becomes word, expressive power with independent value.[188] One could responsibly and unashamedly say that this is a unique achievement; it transmutes the image of the world and is effected in the most human and most important expressive medium—language. As it occurs at the very foundation, it is consequently of fundamental significance and effect. The word is freed from its spatio-temporal bounds, rendering space-time diaphanous and giving birth to aperspectival language capable of expressing the new consciousness structure.

Psychically the time-theme irrupts with Goethe's descent to the Realm of the Mothers in *Faust* (p. 393). The spatially intangible, subterranean powers and energies of the psyche, once negated by rationalism, become the content of the novel—"novel" only in name—for Goethe (*Werther*), Moritz (*Anton Reiser*), Constant (*Adolphe*), Hölderlin (*Hyperion*), and Stendhal. Later E. T. A. Hoffmann, Edgar Allan Poe, Gérard de Nerval, and Lautréamont exhume this shadowy world while revealing the dangers and destructive possibilities of the psychic temporicity. This leads

---

*Translator's note: The words used, "erzählt, darstellt, erörtert," with the author's italics, emphasize the quantifying and spatializing aspects incumbent on these "traditional" words for narrative; see also p. 258 f. above.

later to the new kind of prose which Edouard Dujardin designates as *monologue intérieur* ("stream of consciousness")[189] exemplified by Rilke's "Notebooks of Malte Laurids Brigge," and by Marcel Proust and James Joyce. Yet this psychologization of literature reaches a nadir several more times, furnishing a vivid contrast to the clear path charted for us by such poets as Rilke, Valéry,[190] Eliot, and Guillén. These nadirs are embodied by the "Destructivists," the Expressionists, Futurists, Dadaists, and Surrealists, and by the magic-artiste nihilists, the circle of Infantilists, and the pseudo-mythmakers.

The German Expressionists such as R. J. Sorge, Carl Sternheim, and Fritz von Unruh, as well as the Italian Futurists led by F. T. Marinetti, broke out of rationality with such aggressiveness and emotionality that for a few years they excited the feelings of the public—but only the feelings. In so doing, they destroyed some dilapidated and outlived forms but were themselves buried by the collapse.

The Dadaists attempted to reach behind the words and produce sounds they believed to be primordial sounds; the Surrealists uncontrollably hurl out their associations, thinking them to be "super-real;" both groups destroy any and all forms and structure of language with consummate thoroughness. It is sufficient to mention Hugo Ball, Tristan Tzara, Richard Hülsenbeck, Kurt Schwitters, André Breton, René Crevel and L. Aragon.[191]

The Dadaist attempt to revive the word as a magical sound may be considered as an effort to reawaken the mostly lost acoustic symbolism. (Hans Kayser's "Harmonics" is a salutary effort to bring back such sound symbolism to consciousness.[192]) Since this is a rationally imposed attempt to revitalize a consciousness structure whose magical validity has been doubly and triply overdetermined at least by the mythical and mental capacities, it merely represents deficient mental man's submersion into magic. As a consequence of this deficiency, he is no longer in control of the conjured-up magic and is overpowered by it. In other words, the revived acoustic symbolism of dadaistic formlessness no longer possesses efficient potency, but is by nature deficient. It is a kind of magical reduction where only the demonic and atomizing aspect of the acoustic magic is at work.

A similar deficiency was made current by Surrealism; the submersion into the psyche and its unobstructed evocation institutes an irrealization which could be called a psychic phantasmagoria. The pseudo-esoteric veneer of André Breton's later writings, for example, his *Arcane 17*, indulging in the disruptive Saturnian aspect of the number seventeen[193] (about which he wisely remains silent), exemplifies the chasms and shallows into which any attempts lead that undertake to surpass rational three-dimensionality by under- rather than overdetermination. The Surrealists are overpowered by the conjured-up temporicity of the psyche. Rather than transforming time into time-freedom, they "gain" an overdimensioned time in the form of inflated temporicity. They never attain the unaffected spontaneity of prerational poetry, as in the poetry of the Far East, which does not know time in our Western sense of measuring and ordering. This is exemplified by the "Story of Prince Genji, written around the year One Thousand by our time reckoning by Murasaki, called Shikibu, lady in waiting to the Empress of Japan,"[194] where the chronological succession of events is not maintained by the sequence of individual chapters; rather, in terms of our sense of time, what occurred later is related "too soon," and what occurred earlier is narrated "too late."

The Nihilists too fall prey to the magical fascination. Franz Kafka, and especially Jean Cocteau, Gottfried Benn, Ernst Jünger, and Federico García Lorca construct the magically and psychically ambivalent nihilism with crafty skill: the frivolous, irresponsible, verbally magical, and irresolute (which Cocteau exaggerated to the point of narcissism). Cocteau, Benn, and Jünger embellish emptiness and chaos by deceit and shadow-boxing. Cocteau may be considered the exponent of this kind of literature which can be called "tinsel" literature owing to its flashy pseudo-problematics. By contrast, Kafka's genuine greatness and tragedy, his rebellion against patriarchy, remain unresolved, as Max Brod has noted in a humanly moving account.[195] Kafka's generation initiates the psychological effort at liberation from the paternal dominance that had been determining and formative for the mental consciousness structure (Hasenclever's *Parricide* and Freud's theory of the Oedipus complex are manifestations of the same problem). And the many present-day child-father conflicts, as any clergyman or psychotherapist can attest, are acute individual attempts to overcome the mental-paternal world that has outlived its previous form, and—since an aperspectival, universal humanity-consciousness has emerged—can no longer claim exclusivity.

The Infantilists, as we would call them, attempt to escape three-dimensionality by resubmerging into a childish mode of expression to regain "lost time" (*temps perdu*), in this instance their lost childhood. But instead of subduing it, it subdues them. The work of Gertrude Stein is the most famous instance of such infantilism. In his book *Time and the Western World*, Wyndham Lewis has given an excellent account of the Infantilists.[196]

Among the pseudo-mythmakers are J.-Cowper Powys, Teixera Pascoais, as well as Thomas Mann of the great Joseph tetralogy. Since they overemphasize a no longer potent consciousness structure, they are akin to the Infantilists. Yet they are distinguished from the Infantilists, especially Thomas Mann, by their evocative attempt to construct this mythical consciousness structure by rational means. In the case of Italo Svevo this attempt disintegrates into psychoanalysis. The mythical power of Herman Melville, effected in *Moby Dick*, is later attained only in Ernest Hemingway's *The Old Man and the Sea*.

The psychic form of the "irruption of time" into our consciousness, manifesting itself since the French Revolution in the psychists mentioned earlier, contains all of the characteristics of a virulently emerging psychic energy. What it effects is as ambivalent as the psyche itself. It destroys and builds; it seduces and leads. The appearance of this aspect of "time," of this psychic energy, expresses clearly the multiformity of the time-theme in poetry pressing toward manifestation in the attempts to surpass conceptual, perspectival language.[197]

Thematically, time is expressed relatively late in the new poetry. Marcel Proust's *Remembrance of Things Past* (*À la recherche du temps perdu*) is one of the important milestones for recent Western poetry. This is not a new assertion; but it is substantiated less by the previous insistence on the importance of style, technique, social setting, and thematics, in Proust than by recognition of the principal theme stated in the title. Let us note the interpretation of Paul C. Berger: "The true content of Proust's book is time, while the involuntary or spontaneous recollection, as Bergson called it, plays the principal role. As there is a plane geometry and a solid geometry, so are there two kinds of novels since Proust: one, common to all writers, is based on a two-dimensional psychology, and one, discovered by Proust, is founded on psychology in time.

"This new procedure of inner stethoscopy, studying the constant change of entities and things, never determines the character of an individual, as the character is in constant change, and reconstructs the total person by observing him under diverse, external circumstances at various times and through different eyes [i.e., completely aperspectivally]. While the forms of all other writers are predetermined [perspectivally fixed] and frozen into firm and arbitrary traits of character, Proust portrays his heroes as changeable and sometimes contradictory. . . . Proust's method of describing a figure does not separate the present from the past, which the figure more or less consciously lugs along behind.

"Thus he practices a four-dimensional psychology where time or the past represents the fourth, the inner dimension, which no one undertook to investigate before him. . . . Proust [was able] to grasp the concrete duration and project the reverse flow of past into the present—to rediscover the past by integrating it into the lived moment. In this moment of fusion, time is conquered, the inexorable flight of months and years is subdued by the spirit."[198]

Proust's work concludes with the volume entitled Le temps retrouvé (Time Regained). Despite the fact that Bergson is the godfather of the overall conception of this work, Proust nonetheless surpasses him. The search for lost time, which is first presented as the past, and the discovery and manifestation of psychic time, coupled with the devaluation and disillusionment with clock time, lead him in this concluding volume to time-freedom. There Proust writes: "When a sound or a scent once sensed and long inhaled—at once present and past, real and not just factual, ideal yet not abstract—come to life again, the enduring and usually hidden essence of things is soon liberated, and our true, seemingly long-expired Self awakens, reanimated by the heavenly nourishment that infuses it. A minute, free from the order of time, has, so that we may feel it, recreated the human in us free from the order of time."[199]

As far as the novel is concerned, James Joyce and Robert Musil stand beside Proust as the greatest novelists of the new style in our epoch. Common to all is their spatio-temporal thinking and depiction. Each poses and resolves the time problem in his own way. With regard to Joyce, Max Rychner, one of the most attentive observers of our era's literary tendencies, has shown this implicitly by referring to the time and place of Ulysses (June 16, 1904, in Dublin): "Let us think of Dublin on a map as related by lines to thousands of points over the entire world. Corresponding to this spatial system of relations we can consider that there is a temporal system whose lines stretch from June 16, 1904, to thousands of temporal points in the past, constituting an immense network of significances. Joyce has constructed his Ulysses in accordance with this technique. Every act, every word of his characters, has the brief everyday meaning, related to the mere moment of the day; yet each points to the great regularities according to which life orders itself in perpetual renewal. In the same way every moment is pregnant with many future possibilities. The 'simple fact' in an insignificant man's routine, of itself ridiculous, becomes transparent to the penetrating glance, revealing the great figurations of the spirit. It does not thereby become great but significant. Released from its mere individual meaning, it becomes a participant in the whole significance of the world, just as a colorful thread woven into a carpet has a significant function in a greater network of interconnections."[200]

In a note prefaced to the third volume of his immense novel, The Man without Qualities (Der Mann ohne Eigenschaften), Robert Musil has indicated with the precision that is his hallmark his aperspectival concerns, which we know to be attainable only by incorporating the temporal element: "Some will ask: what is the standpoint of the author, and what are its results? I cannot vindicate myself. I treat the object neither from all sides—which is impossible in a novel—nor from one side, but rather from various sides which belong together."[201]

In discussing Proust, Joyce, and Musil, we must not forget Virginia Woolf who, with her sovereign control of time, leads the main character in *Orlando* through the centuries. In *Mrs. Dalloway* she shapes the "inner monologue" with inimitable sensitivity to psychic processes; and in *The Years* she summons that inexorable natural time, which, if one solely submits to it, forebodes the fatal danger to which she tragically succumbed.

Also, we must not overlook Thomas Mann's major undertaking in the *Magic Mountain* to explicitly deal with and resolve the time problem. We should also mention Hermann Hesse's significant attempt at spatio-temporal synthesis in his *Glass Bead Game* (much indebted to Kayser's "Harmonics"), an attempt to make transparent the interplay of spiritual currents of the various consciousness structures of the Orient and the Occident. It is significant despite the drowning of the hero at the conclusion (an indication that the leader of the transparent game in the water succumbs for the present to the sea, the element of the soul). In this context we should not overlook the dynamic preoccupation with time in recent American literature, manifest in the work of Ernest Hemingway, Thomas Wolfe, William Faulkner, and others.

Finally we must mention the last novel of Hermann Broch, *Die Schuldlosen* (The Innocent). In it, Hermann Broch endeavors to present the "new consciousness" in full agreement with our own exposition (as he indicated to us after having read some of our writings). He detaches himself from three-dimensionality and becomes aware that "man has burst his limits [limits are always spatial] and has entered the multiplicity of dimensions"[202] which remains "unsurveyable" as long as he has not found genuine four-dimensionality.[203]

For all the authors mentioned, with the possible exception of Hermann Hesse, the novel has ceased to be the "novel of development," which is to say, the expression of an oriented process, a process to which time even in the new physics is no longer subject. This lack of fixity is expressed in the very title of Musil's work: *The Man without Qualities.*

During the last decade (since ca. 1955) the new generation has consistently followed the path opened by the structural inceptions described on these pages. It is irrelevant whether or not the new generation of writers knew Musil's stated principle "to narrate nothing in temporal sequence" (first published toward the end of December, 1952).[204] This new generation, in accord with the aperspectival concern of our epoch and the comprehension of reality via the arational consciousness, has decisively altered the fundamental structure of what was once, but is no longer, "re-counting," as in narrative or the traditional novel. We would mention only Lawrence Durrell, Uwe Johnson, Siegfried Lenz, Hans Ernst Nossack, Alain Robbe-Grillet, and Claude Simon. Literary criticism has also realized the implications of the new consciousness-based tenor which we have elucidated in terms of the changed valuation of the phenomenon of time; we have already explored the merits of one of its representatives, Kurt Leonhard.[205] Besides Leonhard, there is also Werner Weber who has formulated a lucid and convincing description of the new time problem over the past decade.[206]

It is not only the novel but the drama as well that has altered its structure. In the new drama the development or dramatic climax, the mentally oriented plot and its course toward a fixed and predetermining goal, is replaced by the "relational system of realities" of which Max Rychner has spoken in connection with *Ulysses*.[207] The first to deal with time thematically and to represent past, present, and future symbolically in the drama was Guillaume Apollinaire in his *Couleur du Temps*.[208] Ferdinand Bruckner came closer to a solution and he was the first who ventured to realize on stage the temporal complexity of various interrelated plots instead of a temporal course of events. If our memory is accurate, it was his *Die Verbrecher* ("The Criminals") that was staged with not one, but seven locales (seven rooms) where the intertwining plots unfolded.[209]

The most decisive step toward a spatio-temporal drama, aperspectival in character, was taken by Thornton Wilder. Inceptions for this are already present in *Our Town*, and time is clearly and unmistakably incorporated and evaluated in *The Skin of our Teeth*.[210] The Antrobus family, in every phase of the play, is a family of our age as well as a representative of the whole of historical mankind. In Wilder's plays, the everyday life of the present merges at any moment into millennia and the millennia intertwine with daily life. The events are released from the temporally-bound individual sphere and transposed into universality: all times—including the sea itself, psychic time symbolic of the universal soul into which the second act transfigures the auditorium and the audience—are visible all at once, aperspectivally and not in perspectival succession.[211]

In verse, T. S. Eliot and Gottfried Benn are the first poets instrumental in expressing the theme of time, since the occasional indications manifest in Hopkins,[212] in Walt Whitman, and later in Ezra Pound and others, can be considered merely inceptual.

Time is a theme in the poetry of Eliot and Benn in that *The Waste Land*[213] and Benn's early poems[214] evoke manifold times. Yet while Benn did not proceed beyond the evocative technique—his poems of the 1940s show the perfection of this artistic means and nihilistically seek in this their justification—Eliot in his *Four Quartets*[215] incorporates the theme of time and guides it toward clarification. We have already discussed a notable example above (p. 327).

Structurally, the new valuation of time in poetry emerges purely in the diction, and is thus primarily amenable to an examination of grammar and syntax. We have spoken above of Hölderlin's inversion of the period, and it is evident again in the poetry of R. M. Rilke, among others.[216] The magnificent poem by Mallarmé, "Un coup de dès jamais n'abolira le hasard," which Stanislaus Fumet declared the first cubist poem,[217] contains "ruptures of construction" and syntactical liberties that have been annotated in detail by Claude Roulet.[218] Hopkins indulged in an unequalled freedom of diction and style, and is the first to employ an expressly "colon style": where one might expect a "because" or a "since" Hopkins places a colon, thus interrupting the oriented course of events and superseding perspectivity, which is displaced by the acausal relationship and the pure utterance.

Marcel Proust has constructed periods of a length previously alien to French, a language distinguished from all others by its clarity of construction. The purely rational construction, the syntactically clearly articulated sentence, is extended, indeed exploded, by page-long periodic sentences. Each of these sentences is a world, expressed by the spinning-out of every subordinate clause and by the multifarious relation of every word, every event, and every evocation to all the others. His is an almost oceanic style, floating the utterances on waves until the breathless wave of the sentence breaks, its foamy crests, airy spray, and ground swell taken over by the next unfolding wave. This style reflects the psychic dimension: Proust's language traverses the sea of the soul, rediscovering the temporal duration of the psychic which permits him to reach the shore of the achronon following his experience of the sea. Like us, Proust is a survivor of the shipwreck of timelessness, in which he experiences temporicity and comprehends time without perishing (as did the Surrealists), and in which the awareness of being free from the ordinances of time is revealed to him.[219]

James Joyce partially dissolves grammatical construction and gives free rein to the powers of association. Thomas Mann exaggerates the constructions to the point of mannerism, seeking to illuminate the multi-facetedness of the phenomena described by the aid of stylistic excess. Since it is of merely passing import, we need not elaborate on the total destruction of all grammatical coherence practiced by the Dadaists and even the Surrealists, among others.[220] All of this signifies an attempt to reject the purely discursive rationalistic mode of thought. Now and then it succeeds, granting us the realization of an aperspectival inception. Frequently it merely shatters old, proven values without attaining the new, space-time–free realization. Yet it can no longer be ignored today that, attendant upon this rejection, a number of grammatical categories have undergone a fundamental functional alteration as they are used or avoided in modern poetry.

Despite the attraction that an exposition of this particular state of affairs has for the present writer, we shall forego here a repetition of our detailed description of the new structure of grammar in the interest of proportion and admissibility and shall restrict ourselves to a few general remarks summarizing our earlier detailed exposition and documentation. We are concerned here with the novel employment of certain grammatical categories which fundamentally reveal the new consciousness structure. These include:

a) the adjective and the adverb,
b) the substantivation of the infinitive,
c) the rejection of "because" or "since,"
d) the rejection of "as" or "like" (simile),
e) modification of the comparative degree,
f) beginnings with "and," as well as
g) the new rhyme.

The most noticeable change has occurred since Romanticism in the usage of adjectives. Until classicism, the adjective was used to modify the substantive, and often lent things an anthropomorphic character, depriving them of their independence and subordinating them to a perspectival anthropocentrism. The "furious" or "courageous" sword and similar formulations of that epoch are familiar to everyone. Or it was used as an "adorning attribute," as in classical antiquity, although it has been overlooked until now that the *epitheton ornans*, for example, "the owl-eyed Athena," is a numinous ascription and not at all an adornment. Since Romanticism the adjective has been losing its meaning as a mere descriptive term and has become a relational word. This is most saliently expressed where adverbs are changed into adjectives, as for example in Kafka's phrase, "and while greeting, [he] stepped into the lateral grass."[221] Ever since Hölderlin and Heinrich Heine, examples of the new, aperspectival use of adjectives can be found, as in the works of Franz Kafka, Georg Trakl, Paul Valéry, Rainer Maria Rilke, Salvatore Quasimodo, and Jorge Guillén, among others.[222]

In all these instances the one-sided rigidity is superseded. Instead of the previous reference of the adjective to *one* substantive, the attribute now emphasizes the relationships among things and is effective in all directions. An action is no longer observed from the standpoint of the subject, but also from the object. Kafka no longer says, "and while greeting, stepped laterally into the grass," but "and while greeting, stepped into the lateral grass." The temporal "stepped" moves into close relationship with the spatial "lateral grass"; space and time are joined. The relationship is no longer determined adverbially from one side with reference only to the object, but also adjectivally with reference to the world, for in this instance the "lateral grass" is the world.

The new usage of the adjective–Reto R. Bezzola has defined it as "adjectival ambivalence" and the "attribute-dissolving element"[223]—points to the changed valuation of the subject. This altered valuation is also visible in the increasing substantivation of the verb in its infinitival form. Since the substantive can be considered to be the static and the verb the actuating element of a sentence, the new use of the substantive indicates an activation of the substantive and a resolution of the opposites and relates the fixed, the static, to the temporal in the closest way possible.[224]

While the new employment of the adjective and the substantivation of the infinitive structurally resolve perspectival rigidity, rejection of "because" expresses the extrication from the exclusive claim of causal thinking. By "rejection of 'because' " we mean the stylistic peculiarity in the new poetry tending to avoid "because" or "since," conjunctions that have always established reasons in terms of the causal nexus. Their avoidance reflects a recognition of acausality and an insight into the ever-present manifold aspectuality of possible relations and interdependencies. Replacement of the "because"by a colon, for example, is a frequent stylistic device in modern literature found in Hopkins, and used subsequently not only by T. S. Eliot[225] but by other poets, and occurs with increasing frequency even in prose.[226]

What we some years ago called the "rejection of simile" is also symptomatic for the new consciousness structure.[227] In one of his letters from the time of the First World War, Rilke rejected the usage of "like" and "as"; this same rejection later occurs in the work of Paul Eluard.[228] The simile, being always a systematization, is experienced as a lie; the perpetual one-sided, rigidifying determination inherent in the use of "as/like" can no longer be endured by an understanding that has transcended exclusive systematization. Every postulation of likeness, or similarity, insofar as it is a postulation, is experienced as a violation. The rejection of simile in the new poetry expresses the systatic element and the awareness that the concern can only be with interrelationships and not with likenesses.

The "rejection of simile" is expressed in an intensified form in the new use of the comparative degree. This usage underscores the validity of rejecting the measuring, mental comparison in favor of the living and almost acausally present wealth of relationships. Recently the comparative has been used solely for its own sake without the "than" previously deemed necessary. Thus Rilke's statement, "The more envisaged world wants to flourish in love."[229] When considered in relation to the rejection of simile, this example, among countless others, is neither a mere comparison as an afterthought, as Werner Günther has suggested,[230] nor a heightening or introspection of the sense, as Hans Egon Holthusen has understood it.[231] Particularly evident here is rejection of any one-sided relationships: the traditional relation to an object of comparison via the now eliminated "than" becomes redundant. The relationship is now open and no longer perspectively fixed: it signifies all possible relations. This form of the comparative is overdetermined. In other words, the spatial position of co-ordination and superordination of two proximate things is replaced by an attempt to establish the spatio-temporal interrelationship. Or expressed still another way, the comparison of parts is replaced by a relationship to the whole which is always overdetermined with respect to the parts.

A similar emphasis on context is expressed in the new stylistic peculiarity of beginnings with "and" that is akin to the recurrent use of "and" endings by James Joyce, for example. Hugo von Hofmannsthal's "Ballade des äusseren Lebens" (Ballad of External Life) begins with the line, "And children grow up with deep eyes."[232] Federico García Lorca's romantic ballad "La casada infiel" (The Unfaithful Wife) starts with an "and": "Y que yo me la llevé al río"[233] (And I carried her to the river). Sentences beginning with "and" in the new prose have become commonplace; there the "and" is not required to enumerate or sum up or even to intimate such functions. This new "and" and its novel usage emphasizes interconnections which are not exhausted in enumerative and narrative-sequential thought and its summation of parts.

A poem, for instance, is not placed in space as a self-contained and thus spatially limited construction, but rather participates in the whole; its "and" beginning joins with the invisible, to which it communicates visibility and audibility throughout the poem. The "everlasting plenitude" of an event is not sectored, or perspectively fixed; rather, this artistic and stylistic device expresses the open structure of being. A parallel can be found in the new music, for example in Manuel de Falla's ballet *The Three-Cornered Hat*, which begins right in the very middle of its principal theme.[234] Let us also recall that the "and" beginnings and endings in James Joyce, for example, correspond to a characteristic of modern music, as Křenek points out: the new music is music "without beginning or end" (p. 457). The "and" acquires a new value, and by so doing, alters the structure of language. Instead of being a knot splicing the thread of a story, it becomes a word of plenitude.

The earliest example of this may well be Hölderlin's "Hälfte des Lebens" (Half of Life):[235]

Mit gelben Birnen hänget
Und voll mit wilden Rosen
Das Land in den See,
Ihr holden Schwäne,
Und trunken von Küssen
Tunkt ihr das Haupt
Ins heilignüchterne Wasser.

(Hanging with yellow pears
And full of wild roses
The land into the lake,
Ye lovely swans,
And drunken with kisses
You dip your heads
Into the holy-sober water.)

This sort of "and" is clearer still at the beginning of Hölderlin's poem "An einem Baum" (By a Tree): "Und die ewigen Bahnen / lächelnd über uns / hin zögen die Herrscher der Welt" (And the eternal paths / smiling above us / attract the rulers of the world). This is no longer a summary "and," but rather opens as it were the "mundane region" to a more encompassing one, achieving with this a decisive structural change in language.[236]

The same re-evaluation of once insignificant words is reflected in the new rhyme. Not only the copula "and," but, in marked contrast to the usage of classicism, the articles, relative pronouns, pronouns, prepositions, conjunctions, adjectives, adverbs, etc., are used as rhyme words. Rilke rhymes "und" (and) with "Mund" (mouth); Mallarmé rhymes "maints" (few) with "demains" (tomorrow) and "au" (at the) with "numero" (number); Edith Sitwell rhymes "these" with "trees," and Verlaine rhymes "delà" with "à la," to cite a few among scores of examples.[237] Just as each color is of equal value in modern painting—the maxim of the new painting since the turn of the century—so is each word of the poem in the new poetry of equal importance: there are no more filler or make-shift words, just as in painting transitional expedient colors are excluded. The fact that no one part is over or undervalued (as was true in perspectival poetry and painting), and that the constant validity of the whole excludes emphasis of any part, lends this mode of rhyming its aperspectival imprint. Thus it must not be confused with the rhyme-mannerism of the Baroque, in which Góngora excelled. Its mode of rhyming is an ecstatic and playful emergence from the strictness of the Renaissance.

Today it expresses a responsibly shaped and non-Alexandrian consciousness structure. Similar things or processes are related only when they occur within the same consciousness-frequency. Although Baroque poetry is a precursor of the new consciousness structure, it is still confined within the mental structure, whereas the new poetry expresses the integral, aperspectival consciousness. A rhyme of the dative "dem Tode" (death) with "Kommode" (chest of drawers) by the young Rilke must seem sacrilegious to the mental-rational, as well as Baroque world.[238] The clash between spatially incongruent quanta is distressing to the three-dimensional spatial world. It is quite different in the non-Euclidean, four-dimensional world of Einstein's space-time continuum whose space-time configuration finds its linguistic equivalence in this pair of rhyme words. In this world temporal events such as death can freely associate with things of space, such as a chest of drawers, and join in rhyme.[239]

This last structural instance, the new mode of rhyme, shows the depth of time's irruption into poetry. Above all, it shows that it has been mastered in language.

Now, having attempted to answer the question of "time's" effectuality in poetry, the other two questions dealing with the supersession of dualism and with arationality have been implicitly answered by the preceding discussion. So too, it may be argued that the attentive reader of this section will have noticed before now that the answer to the question of time will have more or less included an answer to the other questions. It shows the urgency and the key position attributed to time; moreover, it shows that the acceptance of the fourth dimension—even in its preform of multifarious systases and temporic attempts—logically and naturally incorporates the supersession of dualism and the achievement of arationality.

It is particularly instructive that this also occurs in poetry, since poetry emphatically resides in the mythical consciousness structure for which mental meter and rational sentence construction constitute a disciplining superstructure. It is of signal importance that the intensification of poetry and of the poetic word, as well as of poetic language, have led to the re-psychologization of poetry only in the negative temporic attempts, whereas the successful attempts point beyond the mythical and mental. And this is all the more important, as should be obvious, since the structure of language itself has begun to change. Furthermore, it is of fundamental significance that the changes in language are not limited to one language, but have been emerging and assuming form in all European languages for the last one hundred and fifty years, languages that once lent the most pregnant expression to the exclusive validity of the mental-rational consciousness structure.

In the most successful attempts so far, the restructuration has led to a most clarifying result, visible in the answer to our second question.

2) The supersession of dualism in the new poetry is reflected by the structurally changed usage of certain sentence elements as noted above. Through the transvaluation of the subject, evident in the new usage of the adjective and in the substantivation of the infinitive, its position to the object and the world is freed from the previous dualism. The novel use of the comparative renounces an antithetic relationship, while the rejection of the "because" frees thought from rational causality without regressing into irrationality. Since causality includes in its structure dualism, it too is surpassed by the rejection of simile.

We shall not attempt to proceed thematically here with our demonstration by adducing individual utterances of the above–mentioned poets. We can say in general, however, that the technique of portraying everything in black and white, of an imprisonment in pathos, of a purposive and merely descriptive rendering, can be found ever less frequently in their work.

Magic and myth, on the other hand, are flourishing with astonishing purity among those poets who have authentically surpassed the mental-rational structure. As an example to illuminate this supersession, we would cite only the new attitude toward death; it can be said that it begins with one of the latest utterances of Hölderlin: "Life is death and death is also a life."[240] It is also intimated in Hugo von Hofmannsthal's *Andreas*, probably the most consummate work in German prose in several generations. In this context we should not overlook an entry from Hofmannsthal's diary of 1906: "For life and death one can gird one's loins. But what is incomprehensible is how both are present at the same time."[241] A similar attitude is frequently expressed by Paul Valéry, as in this statement of 1913: "Death in the . . . biological sense forms an *indispensable part of life*."[242]

By contrast, J. Anker-Larsen formulates this attitude even much more clearly in the sense of Hölderlin and Hofmannsthal: "Life and death entered being together with me. They are two continuously present sides of this my being in time. Sometimes the one and sometimes the other predominates within me yet they always work together; and with my being in time they both vanish with me. Whoever has experienced the eternal now [the present] does not see a bottomless abyss between 'life' and 'death.' Here words are again lacking. I can haltingly say: The eternal now is Being, and time is existence. Whoever transforms existence into Being has nothing more to do with 'life' and 'death.' "[243]

While Anker-Larsen stresses Being, years before the publication of Heidegger's *Being and Time*, Jacques Chardonne, in his statement concerning the problem of life—death—stresses love and not Being: "With the writing of *Claire* I have attempted to depict perfect love barely troubled by the image of death, or by the insignificant influence of life and persons. Presently I am inclined to say that not even such shadows are present in perfect love. For them nothing changes, and the one loved is immutable, outside time, and freed from death."[244] Yet the most valid expression to date of this attitude toward death is offered by Rainer Maria Rilke. His ultimate interpretation is completely mythical-polar, yet it transcends the mythical: "Death is the inverse, the undescribed side of life: we must attempt to achieve the greatest awareness of our existence which resides in both unlimited regions and nourished by both . . . This true form of life penetrates both regions, the blood of the greatest circulation courses through both: there is neither a here nor a thereafter, but rather the great unity,"[245] and: "Like the moon, life too surely has another side turned away from us; yet is is not its opposite but its complement to perfection, to completeness, to the real, intact and complete sphere of Being."[246]

Here mythical configuration comes into play in its purity, overdetermined moreover by the integral consciousness. Rilke's image of life and death is in accord with the fundamentally mythical view of the East and contains characteristics which, as we have seen, belong to the mythical structure as such: death is a constantly present shaded side of life complementing the sun side, and forming with it a circular and unlimited course. Richard Wilhelm has brought this to attention by suggesting that both of the Chinese primal principles, Yin and Yang, the sun-illuminated side and the side away from the sun, the shaded side, are to be understood as sides of one and the same mound.[247]

What is new and definitely aperspectival in Rilke follows on his evocation of the mythical configuration and his clear rejection of the rational, which is invalid for this basic phenomenon. Life and death constitute a unity of polar complementarity and are no more mentally conceivable opposites than the here-and-now and the hereafter. The new aperspectival aspect comes forth in Rilke's text where the image of the mythical circling is overdetermined by the integral "verition" of the "real, intact and full sphere of Being." We would note that the mythical configuration is structurally more akin to poetry than the mental; yet it is rarely expressed with the pure vividness achieved by Rilke, although it underlies his genuine poeticism even where the mental element is employed in the poetic meter.[248] Both the mythical and the mental structures are integrated into the integral-arational structure via the fundamental utterances quoted above. It is significant that both are surpassed, that is, also "preserved," in the double connotation of the word (aufheben-to supersede; to preserve).

The consequences of the structural changes in language indicated, as well as the utterances of Rilke quoted above, lead us in conclusion to the question:

3) To what extent is arationality manifest in the new poetry? The rational mutates toward the arational wherever the irruption of time no longer leads to psychic atomization but rounds out the systatic completion of systematizations, and wherever "time" and its complexity no longer serve as dynamizing means of disruption, but are an effectual, overdetermining element. The description of temporic endeavors in poetry which avoid relapses into the magical and mythical have revealed the sudden move, the inceptual mutation toward the arational.

Wherever the linguistic structure is freed from the perspectival fixity without reverting to linguistic chaos, initial aperspectival, no-longer-rational but arational manifestations are visible. The description of the linguistic-structural changes has implicitly shown the new arational character of language. Where the stylistic inversion of rational syntax transforms the sentence, as has happened since Hölderlin, notably in Mallarmé, Rilke, and Eliot, without reverting to irrationalism, the merely rational sequence of tense is surpassed without negating time. The achronon shines forth and its sustaining-in-truth presupposes that the rational is not just negated, but overdetermined, whereby it necessarily foregoes its claim to exclusivity. But wherever the conceptual, the mental-rational world is surpassed, the magical is again audible, the mythical again intuitable. The mental is reduced to its proper sphere of the conceptual, visible, palpable, and demonstrable, and can no longer function obtrusively, but must open the path, the leap toward verition. The audibility, the intuitability, and the conceptuality of the world are overdetermined by the time-free transparency.[249]

Since the world is no longer distorted by spatial-perspectival visibility and mental conceptuality, this diaphaneity becomes evident as we have seen in the new poetry. Stephane Mallarmé excels in such transparency, which Rilke attains now and then.[250] It is prevailingly characteristic of the poetry of Jorge Guillén; it constitutes the essence of the later and greatest poems of T. S. Eliot, and is inherent in the intense *clarté* in the verses of Valéry[251] whose "Faust," as Haftmann notes, describes "the secret of the whole."[252] In the whole, the spiritual, the diaphainon, becomes perceptible. We have already given evidence that the spiritual transcends psychologization and intellectualization in the new poetry in our remarks on the nature and transformation of poetry, pp. 316–330 above. Arational diaphaneity is a precondition for the sustaining-in-truth of the spiritual. The new poetry and language contain the initial realizations of this new consciousness-capacity. With diaphaneity the achronon becomes perceptible since diaphaneity itself is achronic.

Proust's statement about "freedom from the order of time" is not a solitary remark. Rilke has said that "wishes are recollections coming from the future." And Lou Albert-Lasard, who is the source for this quotation, comments that Rilke intended this to mean "that to a certain extent the future is already contained in the present and although veiled, it is efficacious. What we call future is just as potent as our so-called past. United in us they constitute the eternal present," which is not so much eternal as time-free.[253] The same achronic attitude speaks to us in Mallarmé's verse: "The star ripens from tomorrow" (see p. 329); T. S. Eliot expresses it as " . . . the things that are to happen / have already happened."[254]

Such statements are not really "comprehensible." They are, nonetheless, true: they are eteologemes, impartations of truth. They are not comprehensible because they supersede the mental-rational; they are arational statements perceptible and impartable only to those for whom the diaphaneity and the achronic structure of the world have become evident.

But there is an aid to evidencing the veracity of the four statements of Proust, Rilke, Mallarmé, and Eliot. There are two statements, or better, two arational deductions based on the empirical research of two of the most eminent physicists of our century (see p. 374). Eddington writes: "Events do not happen; they are just there and we come across them. The 'formality of taking place' is merely the indication that the observer has on his voyage of exploration passed into the absolute future of the event in question; and it has no important significance."[255] And Heisenberg explains that "in very minute space-time regions, that is in those on the order of magnitude of elemental particles, space and time are remarkably obliterated in such a way that with respect to such minute times we cannot even correctly define the terms 'earlier' or 'later.' Of course, in the world of macrophenomena nothing would be able to change the space-time structure, but we must reckon with the possibility that experiments with events in extremely minute space-time realms will show that certain processes appear to take place in the reverse temporal sequence than that required by the laws of causality."[256]

Although they belong to differing regions of reality from our standpoint, the four statements of the poets and the two of the physicists evidence a striking concurrence. All six utterances, profoundly "knowledgeable" about origin also know of its presence, its present. All six statements may be described in our sense as arational and achronic. Their aperspectivity is further expressed in the fact that they bind together the beginning and the end of our exposition of the manifestations of the aperspectival world by tying together the two regions of thought farthest away from one another: physics and poetry. This fact or circumstance reveals the aperspectival mode of "awaring" the truth of the world, of the whole.

1*   Igor Stravinsky, *Poetics of Music* (Cambridge, Mass.: Harvard Univ. Press, 1947), p. 30.
2   "La musique met un order entre l'homme et le temps," in Ernest Ansermet, "L'expérience musicale et le monde d'aujourd'hui," *Recontres Internationales de Genève 1948* (Paris: La Presse Française et Etrangère O. Zeluk, 1949), p. 28.
3   "Ceque Strawinsky voit dans la musique, c'est le temps qui se concrétise," Ernest Ansermet (note 2), p. 45.
4   Igor Stravinsky (note 1), p. 30.
5   Ernest Ansermet (note 2), p. 46.
6   Theodor W. Adorno, *Philosophie der neuen Musik* (Tübingen: Mohr, 1949), pp. 123, 126 and 128.
7   It should be evident that the time of the universe—natural, rhythmic time—is by no means to be identified with chronological time as happens here. The temporic confusion besetting both Stravinsky's and Ansermet's definitions comes about because they do not recognize that psychic temporicity corresponds to a considerable extent to the organic time of the universe, to which we contrast the automatic time of the clock and metronome as spatializing and measuring time. Yet this is of less importance than the fact that both Stravinsky and Ansermet get involved with the question of time at all and wrestle with it with such insistence and regard for the principles involved.
8   "Nous n'avons que deux possibilités d'appréhender le temps: en nous, comme temps psychique ou qualifié, c'est le temps de la musique ou *tempo*; hors de nous, sur l'universe où il devient le temps automatique que bat l'horloge ou le métronom, c'est le temps de Strawinsky. Son caractère de nécessité explique les exigences de Strawinsky à l'égard du mouvement, mais il faut qu'il soit clair que lorsqu'il parle du temps, il n'entend pas la même chose que nous"; Ernest Ansermet (note 2), p. 46 ff.
9   Hermann Scherchen, *Vom Wesen der Musik* (Zürich: Mondial, n.d. [1946]), p. 149.
10   "Isa Canaria" on Columbia recording no. V 525 (WK 1942); "Para mi que ando perido"; "Es tanto lo que te quiero." Guitarrista: Antonio Ossorio; cantor: Manuel Hernandez (78 rpm).
11* Yma Sumac, *Voice of the Xtabay; Inca Taqui*, Capitol W 684 (33-1/3 rpm); Telefunken-Capitol CL 15647–CL 15650 (78 rpm).
12   The recordings mentioned in notes 10 and 11 above of songs from the Canary Islands and from Peru are strikingly different. Those of the Canary Islands, marred by an anachronistic, Hispanicizing guitar accompaniment, are likely of more ancient origin. In several of the Peruvian songs we find evidence of rhythmic and even melodic elements, and, understandably, it is not to these but to the basic nature of the music to which we refer: its "unawareness," the unquestioning, unintentional mode of utterance, and the naturalness of its expression of sadness and melancholy which we find moving. It is of

505

secondary importance whether we relate this forlornness to ourselves—we who have lost magical unity as the exclusive and thus universally valid response to life—or whether we merely attribute to this magic response our feeling of being abandoned, a feeling that could be explained just as well as being a nameless, egoless yet seemingly inescapable state of sheltered suspension.

13   Ferruccio Busoni, *Entwurf einer neuen Ästhetik der Tonkunst,* Insel-Bücherei 202 (Leipzig: Insel, ²1916), p. 8. The book was first published in 1906.

14   H. H. Stuckenschmidt, *Neue Musik*, volume 2 of the series *Zwischen den beiden Kriegen* (Frankfurt/M.: Suhrkamp, 1951), pp. 39–54.

15   We have not had access to the relevant writings of Arnold Schoenberg. Our reference is made on the basis of the literature on his work, including the study *Arnold Schönberg*, edited by Alban Berg, W. Kandinsky, Anton von Webern et al. (Munich: Piper, 1912).

16   Ernst Křenek, *Über neue Musik* (Vienna: Ringbuchhandlung, 1937), p. 87 ff.

17   Ibid., pp. 15 ff. and 33 ff.

18   Ibid., p. 89; our italics.

19   For purposes of clarification: Křenek's admission that modern music is fragmentary, as well as our suggestion that wholeness could be transparently visible through this fragmentariness, is marked by a sense of sorrow directly parallel to the Christian conception of the partial and incomplete nature of human endeavor. This notion of completed yet fragmentary formations has nothing in common with the recent vogue in art and literature of fragmentary expressive forms. Nothing is shaped or formed by this fashionable pulverization which merely mangles and ultimately atomizes what remains of unformed substance, casually and often irresponsibly jotting down, daubing on or sounding off. "Artists" of this bent, who are merely atomizers, surrender themselves by distorting and disjointing form, instead of rendering into form what has been placed as a task into their care. (On this subject, see the text of chapter eleven in the second part, "The Two-fold Task," p. 535 ff., and Jean Gebser, *In der Bewährung* (Bern and Munich: Francke, 1969), p. 125 ff.; and *Gesamtausgabe*, V/I, p. 273 ff.

20   Paul Hindemith, "Musikalische Inspiration," *Neue Zürcher Zeitung*, no. 2632 (November 28, 1951); see also the editorial note to this partial reprint of Hindemith's inaugural address at the University of Zürich.

21   Not only musicians, but also music historians have begun to sense the need for reconsidering in a new way the question of time. As J. Handschin expresses it: "The anthropology of music in turn will to an ever increasing degree include the concept of time," whereby an ever greater "need for a leading idea will occur, which necessarily can only be a transcendent idea"; Jacques Handschin, *Musikgeschichte im Überblick* (Lucerne: Raber, 1948), p. 85.

22   "Pourtant, ces particularités mêmes de son art devaient conduire Strawinsky à deux découvertes qui sont d'une portée générale et que l'on peut considérer comme les plus importantes de la musique d'aujourd'hui," Ernest Ansermet (note 2), p. 47.

23   Ibid., p. 47 ff.

24   Wilhelm Furtwängler, *Gespräche über Musik* (Zürich: Atlantis, 1948), p. 116; our italics. We have deliberately allowed an opponent of modern music to have first say.

25   Oswald Spengler, *Der Untergang des Abendlandes*, rev. ed. (Munich: Beck, 1923) I, pp. 220 and 313.

26   The concept of "predecision" comes from Adolf Portmann ("Die Wandlungen im biologischen Denken," *Die neue Weltschau*, [Stuttgart: Deutsche Verlags Anstalt, 1952], p. 88). It encompasses the influence of one's own vital-psychic-mental constitution on one's thought, deductive processes, and formulations. These influences, unknown to most authors, are imprinted on them during their formative years by the prevailing *Zeitgeist*; and there are also those infected by the immediately preceding or already surpassed *Zeitgeist*. Inevitably, it is this constitution of uniquely varied but purely subjective predilections, with its particular inclinations and reactions that for the most part

determines in advance the individual's results in the scholarship and research he considers to be objective. Moreover, we tend to believe that hardly anyone escapes "predecision," for each of us is a child of our times. Predecision is inherent in human disposition; and yet its influence can be restricted if the individual concerned can achieve a certain distance from himself, although even this remains variable. With respect to the author himself, he surmises that his personal predecision—and not that resulting from the times—is based in his basic disposition of both natural and spiritual constituents which brings him to view events as sense-full, i.e., meaningful and not just sensory events. This is, ultimately, a Christian predecision that encompasses responsibility—courage and humility—on the one hand and carries a sense of obligation to the supra-personal—in a spiritual, not a materialistic or even idealistic sense—on the other.

27   Wilhelm Furtwängler (note 24), p. 130.

28   Ibid., p. 124; the emphasis is Furtwängler's.

29   Villa-Lobos, Choros, HMV W 941 (78 rpm); see also his new and unusual songs, "Serestas," HMV P 760–761 (78 rpm).

30   A remark of Hermann Scherchen in a conversation with the author; we here append a comment since the phrase "stasis in time" can be variously understood. Stravinsky's preoccupation with time, together with his attempt to master it metrically rather than rhythmically, can be considered symptoms of "time anxiety." Stasis in time tantamount to a flight from it is reflected, for instance, in the recurrent melodic and rhythmic theme in Ravel's Bolero that is tenaciously held under the spell of the metrical drum figure. (Recordings of this work by Scherchen and even Ravel are preferable to Mengelberg's avowedly pathos-ridden interpretation because they are for the most part antipathetic.) The pathos, or feeling of sorrow, is conveyed in this work by the strict hold of the nearly overpowering metric element on the melody, and not by an acceleration or "heightening" of the effect of movement toward the close as in Mengelberg's interpretation where the drum figure is speeded up but nonetheless retains its hold. The static element here is evident in the nearly automatic repetition of the metrical drum figuration, to which the melody is subordinated throughout the entire Bolero.

31   François Poulenc, Aubade: Concerto choréographique pour piano et 18 instruments, Piano: François Poulenc; Orchestra of the Concerts Staram directed by Walther Staram (recorded in the Théâtre des Champs-Elysées), Columbia LF 33/35 (78 rpm). This recording of the five-movement work was made in the late 1920s and had unfortunately only limited distribution.

32   It is noteworthy that this movement of Poulenc's work exhibits similarities to the third movement (Allegro assai) of Bach's Second Brandenburg Concerto. The similarities are as surprising as Poulenc's "loosening" of the tonal material in striking contrast to the late classical form.

33   Werner Kass (pseud.: Werner Karsten), "Die Stellung der modernen Musik innerhalb der 'neuen Weltschau,' " St. Galler Tagblatt, no. 452 (September 27, 1951), pp. 2, 3, and 9. This article represents the contribution of musicology to the "International Conference in St. Gallen" on the "New World Perception." The following is an excerpt from this article: "In earlier times the music we wished to hear had to be created in the very room where we were; today it penetrates the walls of our dwellings, which we thought impenetrable, in the form of electromagnetic waves, rendering three-dimensionality an illusion as a spatial boundary from an acoustic standpoint. And since the three-dimensional principle was receding, or if you prefer, was developing toward four-dimensionality, the musical symbol of three-dimensionality, the triad, could no longer be retained. This did not come about either as a recognition of a logical or as a physical necessity; it was intuitively rejected by the artistic sensibility as being no longer useful. Just as painting distanced itself from perspective and sought an aperspective orientation, so did music abandon the norms of tonality and sought a new ordering in atonality. How this step was

accomplished in each case, and how the destruction of the tonal framework had already begun during the Romantic era and the era of Impressionism in music belong to the realm of the history of modern music."

34   Karl H. Wörner, *Musik der Gegenwart: Geschichte der neuen Musik* (Mainz: Schott, 1949), p. 128. See also Eric Blom, "Twentieth-Century Music," *This Changing World* (London, 1944), chapter 18, pp. 220–221.

35   Karl H. Wörner (note 34), p. 130. See also Ernst Kurth, *Musikpsychologie* (Berlin: Hesse, 1931), p. 174 f. and note.

36   The initial steps toward a music going beyond the confines of the octave were made by Mozart in works composed after 1781; we have already alluded to the novelty of Mozart's music in the first part of our text (see p. 101 above). Luigi Dallapiccola has recently done the same in his article, "Die moderne Musik und ihre Beziehung zu den übrigen Künsten," *Die neue Weltschau*, (Stuttgart: Deutsche Verlags-Anstalt, 1953), II, p. 51 f. He notes in support of his thesis the first thirty-two measures of the overture to the *Abduction from the Seraglio* (1781), the Symphony No. 40 in G minor, and in particular *Don Giovanni*; the ultimate characterization of these elements as atonal or polytonal we gladly entrust to the musicologists. It is noteworthy that the inception of polymetrics is to be found in the First Symphony of Beethoven, written in 1800, to which Hermann Scherchen has called attention (note 9), p. 149.

37   "Liberée des sujétions d'un espace sonore a priori structuré"; Boris de Schloezer in the second discussion of the *Recontres Internationales de Genève 1948*, (note 2), p. 247.

38   Ferruccio Busoni (note 13), pp. 35 and 38 f.

39   Hermann Pfrogner, *Von Wesen und Wertung neuer Harmonik* (Bayreuth: Steeger, 1949), p. 25.

40   H. H. Stuckenschmidt (note 14), p. 59.

41   René Leibowitz, *Schoenberg et son école* (Paris: Janin, 1947), p. 280.

42   Hermann Erpf, *Vom Wesen der neuen Musik* (Stuttgart: Schwab, 1949), p. 120.

43   Cited in Stuckenschmidt (note 14), p. 40.

44   Ibid., p. 59.

45   Léon Oleggini, *Au Coeur de Claude Debussy* (Paris: Julliard, 1947), p. 180.

46   "L'ordre tonal classique s'est ouvert au chromatisme, il s'est ouvert depuis Liszt. . . . Les classiques n'ont conçu que des formes fermées sur elles-mêmes . . . "; Ernst Ansermet (note 2), p. 58. It would be appropriate to mention here that René Leibowitz has noted in Liszt's "Nuages gris," one of his last compositions, essential characteristics of the basic change in music. Leibowitz also furnishes evidence for the signal influence of this genial artist, notably on Richard Wagner, but on other contemporary and subsequent composers; René Leibowitz, *L'Évolution de la Musique de Bach à Schoenberg* (Paris: Correa, 1951), pp. 144–153.

47   Ernest Ansermet (note 2), p. 58.

48   Werner Danckert, *Claude Debussy* (Berlin: de Gruyter, 1950), pp. 155 and 162.

49*   Igor Stravinsky (note 1), p. 37.

50   Ernst Křenek (note 16), p. 31.

51   Ibid., p. 16.

52   Werner Danckert (note 48), p. 144 f.; our italics.

53   Heinrich Strobel, *Paul Hindemith* (Mainz: Schott, ³1948), p. 5.

54   In the first chapter of his study, Werner Kass demonstrates that music of the classical period is dominated by the major (masculine) tonality with its definitely orienting character; Werner Kass, "Die tonsystematischen Grundlagen der akkordharmonischen Musik," (working title; in manuscript).

55   Apparently only the major triad can be related to the trinity, whereas the minor triad reflects the ancient trias (see the text, p. 86 ff., for a discussion of trinity and trias).

56   The reader is asked to permit an allusion here, which will be seen later to be binding. There can be no question that the musical system based on seven fundamental tonalities, as in the classical age, was related to the system of sevens in astronomy and cosmog-

ony that was valid until 1781 and consisted of the seven heavenly bodies Mercury, Venus, Earth, Mars, Jupiter, Saturn, and the sun.

The term "harmony of the spheres" is only one expression of this relation between the world of tones and that of the stars, known to Fray Luis de Léon among others; see his "Oda a Francisco Salinas," *Oxford Book of Spanish Verse* ed. by James Fitzmaurice-Kelly (Oxford: Clarendon, ²1940), pp. 108–109, particularly stanzas two, three, and five. (German translation by Walther Meier in the *Neue Schweizer Rundschau* XII, 1/2 [May-June 1944], p. 84 f.)

There are numerous references in literature and science (e.g., J. Kepler) to this relationship between the octave and our planetary system, as well as to the harmony of the spheres based on the teachings of Pythagoras (cf. the works of Hans Kayser on harmony). This system of correspondences was shattered in 1781, i.e., shortly before the French Revolution, when Herschel discovered the first of the planets beyond Saturn, Uranus. It is not accidental that this discovery coincided with the French Revolution; the old restraints (the Roi Soleil, the monarchy) were broken, "old ruler Saturn," as he had been called by the alchemists, was overridden, and the heliocentric system circling around a fundamental tone came to be, over the past five generations, what we might call the cosmocentrically-structured system. And on the basis of the most recent astronomical research we know that our system as a whole is revolving around a stronger center than the sun.

Nor is it accidental that the discovery of Uranus coincides with the age of Mozart, in whose music we can discern evidence of utterly "new" tones (see the text, p. 101 f.). The overture to *The Abduction from the Seraglio*, which in its thirty-two measure introduction, explored by Luigi Dallapiccola (note 36), came into being precisely in 1781. And it is not just fortuitous that the discovery of Neptune, the second trans-saturnian planet (1846) coincides with the creative period in the life of Richard Wagner, whose music, notably after *Tristan und Isolde*, is generally considered the beginning of formal dissolution of the classical style in music. And what about 1930, the year of discovery of the third planet after Saturn, Pluto? The temporal distance is too short to allow a judgement as to which contemporary composers of transitional music in our day have most decisively fulfilled the task of superseding the old harmonic structure and thereby fostered the emergence of a more definitive new music.

In this it must not be forgotten that every discovery corresponds to a particular state of consciousness. Nothing is discovered "outside" that the consciousness has not first awakened to. Only those things clearly discernible to consciousness are actively effectual; as long as certain inner relationships remain unknown they are only latently present. The effects of latent phenomena on human expressions and formative opportunities are, however, unquestionably of lesser import than those of acute potency. The three planets beyond Saturn existed before we caught sight of them, just as the structure of the atom was present before atomic physics discovered it. Yet the effects of this discovery of the physics of the atom on our daily life (atom bomb, atomic energy, radioactive isotopes for combatting disease, and many others) first became possible and thus effectual when nuclear research in physics perceived that the atom itself was not the ultimate unit of energy and matter, but was in turn composed of other subatomic particles previously thought to be inconceivable.

In like manner, it was only after the discovery of planets beyond Saturn that shattered the previous system did the system elicit responses in our consciousness and become actively potent when our consciousness "discovered" the existing phenomenon. Here again is an indication worthy of greater consideration with respect to the consequences of the French Revolution. In any event, the octave and the septiform system, and its characteristic dualism, emphasis on the major tonality, and spatial-acoustic demarcation and limitation has become a *fausse relation*, a false system of relationships. The celestial language is a distinct language, and genuine art is its undistorted echo and untarnished mirror.

57 Hermann Pfrogner (note 39), pp. 13 and 23 f.
58 Ibid., p. 16. It should be mentioned in this context that H. Scherchen, in his discussion of Beethoven's Ninth Symphony where for "the first time a linear harmony is developed" (in the finale), has observed that "here the ear is confronted with the task of recognizing in the two-dimensional *horizontal* course of the recitative, the *vertical* basis of its three-dimensional chordal thrust" (Hermann Scherchen, note 9 above, p. 210; italics original).

Our emphasis on H. Pfrogner's definition of dodecaphonic music as a music of four dimensions also implies our agreement with him that the irruption of the fourth dimension into music manifest here opens two avenues to the future of music: 1) an atonal route with the extirpation of the three-dimensional world by the four-dimensional, and the sole domination of the twelve-tone row or scale; or 2) a post-tonal path: the interpenetration of the three-and four-dimensional worlds where the seven-step major and minor scales (three-dimensional) and the twelve-tone scale (four-dimensional) permeate each other. Pfrogner's defense of a "post-tonal chromaticism" (note 39, pp. 19 and 23) leaves no doubt that he considers 2) to be the necessary and organic, a viewpoint in full agreement with our own, since the first alternative would lead to an abandonment of the very foundations of music, and thus to self-surrender and destruction.

We must never forget that attainment of four-dimensionality does not imply or demand that it be exclusive. On the contrary, only when it is posited and put into effect as inclusivity, integrating and not fragmenting, will it assist in the valid manifestation of the new consciousness. An exclusive four-dimensionality, rejecting all other consciousness structures and all modes of realization of other dimensions, is nothing but empty modernism, dissolution, and destruction; and this is as true of music as it is for other areas, a fact that we cannot too strongly emphasize.

59 Ernst Křenek (note 16), pp. 49, 51 and 86.
60 We would, however, note here that this does not imply, say, our rejection of "older" music. The music of Bach, the shining apex of mental music in the best sense of the word, does not become dubious because of our assertion (and his music is not just by chance avowedly "music meant to be read").
61 Again this sheds light on the fact that arationality as the "perceiving and imparting of truth" of the whole is an aperspectival mode of manifestation, predicated on an aperspectival consciousness structure. The arational nature of the new music is also evident from an "accidental trifle," as we might say in rationalistic terms: the new music is frequently notated without the traditional use of bar lines or measures. Thus, although it is not "unmeasured," it is music liberated from the (artificial) divisions or divisors able to reveal transparently the whole.
62 Ernst Křenek (note 16), pp. 29–32 and 106.
63 Hermann Scherchen, *Musik für Jedermann* (Winterthur: Mondial, 1950), p. 153 f.
64 H. H. Stuckenschmidt (note 14), p. 57.
65 Willi Schuh, *Zeitgenössische Musik* (Zürich: Atlantis, 1947), p. 67.
66 Werner Danckert (note 48), p. 99.
67 Ibid. p. 99. When we assess linear music (melody, recitative) as two-dimensional, and chordal music as three-dimensional—as does Hermann Scherchen—it is apparent that spherical music will be four-dimensional. This music of spherical tonality corresponds to the "curved space" of the universe of modern physics, as well as to the spherical background demonstrated in the pictures of Cézanne (see note 16, p. 364 above). Danckert—the first to consider these essential characteristics—has drawn parallels between the music of Debussy and the painting of Cézanne, although without knowledge of the spherical pictorial ground in Cézanne's work established by Liliane Guerry in her book (published the same year as Danckert's), *Cézanne et l'Expression de l'Espace* (Paris: Flammarion, 1950).
68 In essential agreement with our position are Wolfgang Hammer, "Musik als Sprache der Hoffnung," *Theologische Existenz* no. 99 (Munich, 1962), p. 25 ff.; Kurt von Fischer, "Moderne Musik," *Moderne Literatur, Malerei und Musik* (Zürich and Stuttgart: Flam-

berg, 1963), pp. 331–400; Friedrich Blume, *Was ist Musik?* Musikalische Zeitfragen 5 (Kassel: Bärenreiter, 1960); Will Hofmann, "Die expressionistische Reduktion im Dienste der Synairese," *Transparente Welt: Fesschrift für Jean Gebser* (Bern: Huber, 1965). Regarding the new estimation see also Leopold Conrad, *Musica panhumana* (Berlin: de Gruyter, 1958).

69   Igor Stravinsky (note 1), p. 27.

70   H. H. Stuckenschmidt (note 14), p. 175.

71   Hermann Scherchen (note 9), p. 81; italics original.

72   Observe, for instance, adults who join with other old friends in songs of their university days or sentimental songs of their youth, and it will be seen to what unexpected degree the onetime emotional bond is reawakened by the group singing. Equally strong is the revival of the entire ideological atmosphere of that period, which has made an essential and for the most part indelible imprint on those persons involved. Every new generation should be permitted to have its own songs; young Europeans, for example, should be allowed to forget the sentimental, nationalistic songs of the past. But this remains a formidable task; only a very few are able to shake off such emotional poisonings as they grow older.

73   Frank Lloyd Wright, *When Democracy Builds* (Chicago: University of Chicago Press, ²1945); a bilingual German edition was published under the title *Usonien* (Berlin: Mann, 1950).

74   Le Corbusier, *Quand les Cathédrales étaient blanches* (Paris: Plon, 1937). For more on a four-dimensional "feeling for space" see Le Corbusier, *New World of Space* (New York.: Reynal and Hitchcock; Boston: Institute of Contemporary Art, 1948).

75   S. Giedion, *Space, Time and Architecture* (1941; Cambridge, Mass.: Harvard University Press, ⁶1946).

76   A. S. Eddington, *Space, Time and Gravitation: An Outline of the General Relativity Theory* (Cambridge: University Press, 1935).

77   S. Giedion (note 75), chapter 2.

78   Ibid., pp. 356–358.

79   Ibid., p. 401.

80*   Frank Lloyd Wright, *When Democracy Builds* (note 73), p. 77.

81*   Ibid., pp. 44–45; italics original.

82   Frank Lloyd Wright, *On Architecture: Selected Writings* (New York: Duell, Sloan and Pearce, ³1941), pp. 200–201.

83   Sherman Paul, *Louis H. Sullivan: Ein amerikanischer Architekt und Denker,* Ullstein Bauwelt Fundamente 5 (Frankfurt/M.: Ullstein, 1963), p. 28.

84   Adolf Portmann, "Die Gestalt: Das Geheimnis des Lebendigen," *Jahresring 1961/1962* (Stuttgart: Deutsche Verlags-Anstalt, 1961), p. 13 f. Portmann discusses the misapplication and misconstruction of the "f-f-f" formula as, for example, by Henry van de Velde. The formula, as understood by later architects as well as by us, connotes function both as the expression of release from stasis, as well as dynamism inherent in the lines, and not in the sense of Galilei's functionalism or purpose. By mentioning this caution, we hope to prevent any misunderstanding of the meaning of the term "function." As to the validity of the "functional" and its structuring quality for the aperspectival world see Jean Gebser, *In der Bewährung* (note 19), p. 122: *Gesamtausgabe,* V/I, p. 270.

85   Elizabeth Mock, *Built in USA since 1932* (New York: Museum of Modern Art, distributed by Simon & Schuster, 1945), p. 22; German edition with identical pagination: *In USA erbaut 1932–1944* (Wiesbaden: Metopen-Verlag, 1948).

86   See the relevant discussion in Werner Kass (note 54).

87   Frank Lloyd Wright (note 82), p. 161.

88   Ibid., p. 211.

89*   Frank Lloyd Wright, *When Democracy Builds* (note 82), p. 53.

90   This statement of Frank Lloyd Wright is quoted in the exhibition catalogue of his works at the Kunsthaus, Zürich, 1952, p. 14.

91   Elizabeth Mock (note 85), p. 18. A particularly good example of the application of free curvature is Le Corbusier's church at Ronchamp built in the 1950s.

92   Ibid., p. 20.

93   Ibid., p. 18.

94   Ibid., p. 20.

95   Alfred Roth, *Die Neue Architektur/The New Architecture/La Nouvelle Architecture* (Zürich: Girsberger, ⁵1951), p. 6, column 3.

96   Ibid, p. 6, col. 1

97   Ibid., p. 5, col. 3. The word "time consciousness" that occurs in Roth's discussion, interestingly, can only mean within his context the concretion of time, and not one's "awareness of his epoch."

98   See the review of the Frank Lloyd Wright exhibition in Zürich in the *Neue Zürcher Zeitung* 260 (February 5, 1952).

99   See the illustrations in Elizabeth Mock (note 85), p. 96 f.

100   Illustrations in Elizabeth Mock (note 85), p. 88.

101   See the illustrations in Alfred Roth (note 95), p. 5.

102   The use of glass as a building material dates back to the "Crystal Palace" of the London International Exhibition of 1851; Giedion provides interesting details (note 75, pp. 184–189). A more recent example of this use of glass is the Lever House on Park Avenue in New York designed by Skidmore, Owings, and Merill, built in 1951–1952; illustrations in *Life*, International Edition (July 28, 1952), pp. 52–54. Evidence that the characteristics of a new architecture became increasingly prominent in the architecture of the 1940s is contained in Giedion's profusely illustrated book, edited at the behest of the International Congress for Modern Architecture (CIAM): *A Decade of New Architecture / Ein Jahrzehnt moderner Architektur / Dix Ans d'Architecture Contemporaine 1937–1947* (Zürich: Girsberger, 1951).

103   Elizabeth Mock (note 85), p. 22.

104   Frank Lloyd Wright, *When Democracy Builds* (note 73), p. 132.

105   Jürgen Pahl, *Die Stadt im Aufbruch der perspektivischen Welt*, Ullstein Bauwelt Fundamente 9 (Frankfurt/M.: Ullstein, 1963). Perceptive and clarifying arguments on the new method of construction, including that used by Hans Scharoun, creatively augmenting those characteristics of recent architecture as we have defined them can be found in Jürgen Pahl, "Wege zu aperspektivischem Bauen," *Transparente Welt: Festschrift für Jean Gebser* (Bern: Huber, 1965). In this regard see also the similar heuristic arguments of Tino Walz, "Architektur aus neuer Sicht," *Die Welt in neuer Sicht* (München—Planegg: Barth, 1959), II, pp. 21–40.

106   Giedion (note 75), p. 403.

107   Frank Lloyd Wright (note 82), p. 161.

108   Ibid., p. 159; we would particularly note here that the italics are Frank Lloyd Wright's.

109   Adolf Vogt, "Frank Lloyd Wright und Le Corbusier," *Neue Zürcher Zeitung* 383 (February 21, 1952).

110   Fernand Léger delivered the address mentioned at the opening of a major exhibition of his works at the Kunsthalle, Bern, April 10, 1952.

111   In his extensive monograph *Fernand Léger et le nouvel espace*, Douglas Cooper furnishes further evidence for Léger's "muralistic painting," and notes that "Léger evoked a new sensation of space by the forward or backward movement of one color placed against another." Léger himself has said of these color effects, "The apartment, which I will call the 'inhabited' rectangle, is to be transformed into the 'elastic' rectangle. A pale blue wall retreats; a black wall advances; a yellow wall disappears (destruction of the wall)." Douglas Cooper, *Fernand Léger et le nouvel espace* tr. François Lachenal (London: Lund Humphries & Co.; Geneva: Éditions des Trois Collines, 1949), p. xi.

112   Ibid., p. 92.

113   In order to prevent any misunderstandings as to subject and terminology we would mention that time, viewed thematically within the categories of art history—specifically

time as temporicity and later as measured time—first appears symbolically and then allegorically in the art of antiquity, the Middle Ages, and the Renaissance. Erwin Panofsky's study of "Father Time," in his *Studies in Iconology* (New York: Oxford University Press, 1939; Harper Torchbook TB 1077, 1962), pp. 69–93, discusses the transformation of symbolic representations of Chronos into the allegorical depiction of Saturn. Dagobert Frey has dealt with expressions of the sense of time in the religious art and architecture of both the Orient and the Occident in his *Grundlegung zu einer vergleichenden Kunstwissenschaft: Raum und Zeit in der Kunst der afrikanisch-eurasischen Hochkulturen* (Innsbruck and Vienna: Rohrer, 1949).

In contrast to these two works, both exceedingly informative because of their choice of subject, our own concern is with time in an integral sense, and not only with the mythical or mental ramifications of the time problem. Our investigation examines time, not as a subject represented in two or three dimensions, but as the integrating element of four-dimensional works of art. We perceive, in other words, not only temporicity and conceptualized time, but time-freedom; not the mythical subject Chronos, nor chronological measure, but achronicity.

114   Thomas Herzog, *Einführung in die moderne Kunst* (Zürich: Classen, 1948), p. 18.

115   Ibid., p. 15 f.

116   Quoted in Kurt Badt, *Eugène Delacroix: Zeichnungen* (Baden-Baden: Klein, 1951), p. 24. See also Herzog (note 114), p. 17.

117   Kurt Badt, p. 27 ff.

118   Liliane Guerry (note 67).

119   "Espace . . . qui intègre l'oeuvre d'art au souffle du temps," Liliane Guerry (note 67), p. 11.

120   "Le champ visuel [est] sphéroïde . . . [et] l'espace [est] engendré par la courbe," Liliane Guerry (note 67), p. 13 f.

121   "A lui aussi l'univers apparaît telle une sphéroïde," Liliane Guerry (note 67), p. 18.

122   Beginning her study from a purely art-historical basis, M. Guerry suggestively proposes that the lack of "geometric perspective"—three-dimensional perspective—in the early paintings of Cézanne can be traced to his "intuitive, natural manner of seeing." She defines his kind of perspective further as a "perspectiva naturalis," and finds a plausible relation between it and the practice of the Greeks in their vase painting.

123   Liliane Guerry (note 67), p. 90.

124   "C'est un espace engendré par la courbe, et non par la droite comme l'ont cru les théoriciens de la Renaissance," Liliane Guerry (note 67), p. 15.

125   This painting of Cézanne (1870) has received various titles from the art historians. L. Venturi entitles it "Pastorale," with the remark, "This picture has been called 'Don Quixote on the Barbary Coast,' but there is no compelling reason for the title" (On a donné à ce tableau le titre: 'Don Quichotte sur les rives de Barbarie', mais on ne voit pas de raison suffisante à ce titre), Lionello Venturi, *Cézanne* (Paris: Rosenberg, 1936), I, no. 104, and II, 89. F. Novotny has given it the title "Idyll" and "Outdoor Scene" in his *Paul Cézanne* (London: Phaidon, 1948), plate 14. G. Jedlicka calls it "Outdoor scene (Pastorale)"; Gotthard Jedlicka, *Cézanne* (Bern: Scherz, 1948), plate 8. Liliane Guerry (note 67, p. 20) names it "Don Quixote on the Barbary Coast" (Don Quichotte sur les rives de Barbarie).

126   "Au lieu de se raidir en une fixité qui n'était pas une stabilité, mais un artifice constructif, au lieu de refuser de s'adapter à la pulsation du temps, l'oeuvre d'art accepte la mobilité et c'est cette mobilité qui devient la condition de son harmonie spatiale. Elle (l'oeuvre d'art) s'intègre au rythme universel, elle n'est plus un monde clos, situé hors du temps et hors de l'espace naturel, durci dans son autonomie, . . . elle est désormais [depuis Cézanne] partie intégrante de cet univers en mouvement," Liliane Guerry (note 67), p. 180. These remarks, moreover, can be considered applicable to sculpture since about the time of Rodin. It is perhaps symptomatic that Mme. Guerry refers to a "closed world," a notion that Cézanne rendered outmoded. He has made possible the new

openness of structure, the new mode of perceiving and thinking that we have encountered in the other areas we have already examined.

127 Fritz Novotny, *Cézanne und das Ende der wissenschaftlichen Perspektive* (Vienna: Schroll, 1938), p. 102.

128 Ibid., p. 137.

129 Ibid., p. 36, note 53.

130 Thomas Herzog (note 114), p. 148.

131 We also refer the reader to the studies by Guillaume Apollinaire (*Les Peintres Cubistes* [Geneva: Cailler, 1950]) on the cubist painters, in which Cubism is interpreted through the eyes of a contemporary friend of the artists.

132 Thomas Herzog (note 114), p. 148 f.

133 This reservation is perhaps all the more justified inasmuch as we do not wish to interpret modern painting in terms of art history, but rather decipher the salient manifestations as we have done in the areas already examined. Since the fourth dimension, as we have shown, is not just a temporal concept or just some kind of time without definition, but is in fact achronicity or freedom of and from time, there should be no possibility of terminological misunderstanding when we refer to the discussion by Theodor Herzog which is accurate from the standpoint of art history.

134 Thomas Herzog (note 114), p. 152.

135 In his introduction to an exhibition of Picasso's graphic art, Erwin Gradmann says of this simultaneous profile-and-full-face effect: "This is an equilibristic acrobat's trick with lines, known significantly ever since the Romantic artists introduced it as the artists spoof of the five dots. It is evident in Moritz von Schwind's 'Akrobatischen Spielen' (1858), and is present in somewhat less pungent form in the Munich lithographs (*Bilderbogen*). It was practiced in France by Bertall, the caricaturist and Daumier-follower, and was even done in Spain as a kind of studio joke by Goya"; Erwin Gradmann, "Picasso," introduction to the exhibition of water colors, drawings and graphic art (1903–1949) from private Swiss collections. Cf. *Graphische Sammlung der Eidgenössischen Technischen Hochschule* (Zürich, winter 1950), p. 10. The significance of this remark lies less in the historical judgement of the "line equilibristics," "artist's spoof" or "studio joke" than on the fact that this wholly aperspectival manner of perception and rendering had already begun in the Romantic period.

136 Alfred H. Barr, Jr., *Picasso: Forty Years of his Art* (New York: Museum of Modern Art, ²1939), p. 77, no. 100.

137 Daniel-Henry Kahnweiler too has noted the "simultaneous" grasp of an object that Juan Gris depicts "from above, from below, from the front, from the side, from within," etc. S. Giedion has also employed the term "simultaneous" when speaking of the "Woman of Arles" and a picture of the *Bauhaus*, Dessau, which are reproduced on the same page, and which both exhibit, as he notes, an "overlapping of surfaces" expressing transparency; see Daniel-Henry Kahnweiler, *Juan Gris* (Paris: NRF/Gallimard, ⁵1946), p. 162, and S. Giedion (note 75), p. 401–402.

138 The Eranos Archive (Moscia/Ascona, Tessin, Switzerland) has pictorial material documenting the fact that the form of such instruments, particularly of our modern guitar, violoncello, and violin, can be traced to the primal form of the female figure as it was formed in prehistoric times.

139 Illustration in Henry-Russel Hitchcock, *Painting toward Architecture* (New York: Duell, Sloane and Pearce, 1948), p. 29.

140 In his instructive article in the *Neue Weltschau*, G. F. Hartlaub also speaks of the incorporation of the time factor by artists of Futurism and Cubism, and notes the "acausal" inceptions, in our sense, which they illustrate; G. F. Hartlaub, "Abstraktion und Invention oder der Umbruch in den bildenden Künsten seit hundert Jahren," *Die Neue Weltschau* (Stuttgart: Deutsche Verlags-Anstalt, 1952), pp. 181–214.

141 Quoted in Thomas Herzog (note 114), p. 152.

142 On this famous maxim as it pertains to Cézanne see Liliane Guerry (note 67), p. 72.

143   "Ainsi s'abolissent les limites entre l'espace du spectateur et celui de l'oeuvre d'art. L'un et l'autre s'identifient, s'harmonisent . . . ," Liliane Guerry (note 67), p. 11.

144   "De même qu'il a transcendé le temps, parce qu'il s'est intégré à son rythme, le peintre est désormais maître de l'espace. Et c'est alors seulement qu'il peut conclure: 'Je me sens coloré par toutes les nuances de l'Infini. Je ne fais plus qu'un avec mon tableau,' " Liliane Guerry (note 67), p. 180.

145   It is noteworthy that Cézanne discovered time, centuries later, in the Provence where Petrarch earlier had discovered space. Sainte-Victoire, which Cézanne so frequently depicted, is besides Mont Ventoux the most characteristic peak of the western Provence whose cities, notably Avignon, Les Baux, and Aix-en-Provence have played such important roles in the development of the European spirit. Together with Van Gogh's Arles, they are spiritual centers whose effect has been mostly recondite and mysterious. The birthplace of Nostradamus, Salon, also lies within the quarter formed by those cities, whose field of tension is heightened by the complementary principles recognizable on the one hand in the city of the anti-popes (Avignon) and the city of the occult tradition (Aix-en-Provence) on the other.

146   Hans Sedlmayr, Verlust der Mitte (Salzburg: Müller, 1948).

147   In 1931, i.e., two years before the attempt to "purify" "degenerate" German art, Hans Sedlmayr, author of the polemical Verlust der Mitte, published a programmatic article in which he discussed the necessity of a new "attitude" towards art, an attitude diametrically opposed to his present position. Basing his observations on works of psychology, phenomenology, and structuralism by Max Wertheimer, Kurt Kaffka, Heinz Werner, Kurt Lewin, and others, he noted that "such an attitude toward the work of art is neither a purely 'visual' perception, nor a spiritual-intellectual process disjunct from the physical. Rather, it touches all layers—psychological and intellectual-spiritual—of the whole subject, as Heinz Werner's experiments have shown"; Hans Sedlmayr, "Zu einer strengen Kunstwissenschaft," Kunstwissenschaftliche Forschungen, 1 (1931), pp. 7–32, particularly p. 14.

148   "El concepto trágico: apariencia y representación, ser y sentido, queda superado en Paul Klee. O más bien: no existe ya;" Paul Westheim, El Pensamiento artístico moderno (Mexico: Ars, 1945), p. 22.

149   "Les musiciens dodécaphonistes se sont attaqués à la suppression du dualisme, mus par des considérations qui s'apparentent à celles de Juan Gris;" Daniel Henry Kahnweiler (note 137), p. 162.

150   Werner Haftmann, Paul Klee (Munich: Prestel, 1950). This maxim of Picasso's, moreover, is purely Taoistic and coincides with the unintentionality taught by Chuang-Tzu in his parable of the pearl: "The yellow emperor journeyed to the North from the Red Lake, ascended Mount Kun-lun and looked toward the South. On the homeward journey, he lost his magic pearl. He dispatched knowledge to look for it, but knowledge was unsuccessful. He then sent out clear vision but clear vision was not successful either. He then sent out eloquence, but it too was unsuccessful. Finally, he sent out unintentionality, and it succeeded in finding the pearl. 'It is indeed strange,' the emperor remarked, 'that unintentionality was able to find it' "; Reden und Gleichnisse des Tschuang Tse, ed. Martin Buber (Leipzig: Insel, 1922), p. 47. See also Dschuang Dsi, Das wahre Buch vom südlichen Blütenland, translated and annotated by Richard Wilhelm (Jena: Diederichs, 1940), p. 86. Wilhelm's translation of the four traits differs from Buber's; he calls them "knowledge, acuity, cognition, and self-forgetfulness" respectively. But this is not a contradiction of Buber's version if we consider the wide latitude possible in Chinese where the words are more contentual than conceptual.

151   André Lhote, Traité du Paysage (Paris: Floury, ⁴1948), p. 47. In the original he speaks of a "délinéation mensongère et toute intellectuelle."

152   "No la cachada de las cosas, sino su estructura secreta," quoted in Paul Westheim (note 148), p. 22.

153   Among others not named here we would mention Max Ackermann, Willi Baumeister,

Julius Bissier, Hans Erni, Hans Hartung, Ernst Wilhelm Nay, Ben Nicholson, Jackson Pollock, Nicholas de Staël, Otto Tschumi, Maria Elena Vieira da Silva, Fritz Winter.

154　In this regard, see our ninth "Indication of the new consciousness" in Jean Gebser, "Die Welt ohne Gegenüber," *In der Bewährung* (note 19), pp. 119–134, and *Gesamtausgabe*, V/I, pp. 267–281, where these questions and quotations are considered at greater length.

155　Paul Klee, *Über die moderne Kunst* (Bern-Bümplitz: Benteli, 1945), p. 19.

156　The structural aspect, as well as a definite sense of transparency, is more clearly and convincingly evident in the work of the "younger abstractists" than in the work of Wassily Kandinsky, for example, one of the founders of abstract art. We are also thinking of the works of Fritz Levedag and several artists mentioned in note 153 above.

As to Kandinsky, we are obliged to note that his book, *Über das Geistige in der Kunst, insbesondere in der Malerei* (Munich: Piper, ²1912; illus. reprint, Bern-Bümplitz: Benteli, 1952), is not merely a spiritual rejection of Naturalism, but in fact a psychic revolt. This embarrassing error is manifest on virtually every page, where the "psychic" and "vital experience" is placed in the foreground. The basic psychic emphasis of his work is also visible in pictures from his later period, which can be considered more or less as Mandala-reminiscences.

157　Salvador Dali is an example demonstrating that surrealist art could revert not only to psychic deficiency but even to the exclusively magical. It is sufficient to recall that he illustrated Maurice Sandoz' story "The Windowless House," a description of a lemuric cavern world already suggested by the title; see Maurice Sandoz, *Das Haus ohne Fenster*, illus. Salvador Dali (Zürich: Morgarten-Verlag Conzett & Huber, 1948).

158　Quoted in Ottomar Dominick, *Die schöpferischen Kräfte in der abstrakten Malerei* (Bergen: Müller & Kiepenheuer, 1947), p. 14.

159　We refer to those drawings by Picasso we have designated as "sketches in light" (see note 16, p. 364 above). Picasso drew them in the air by means of a small flashlight in a darkened room while they were photographed by Gjon Mili. It is noteworthy that Picasso intended to make additional drawings of this kind, executing the figures in motion while he turned around in a circle. The photographic plate would have then shown a picture drawn, as it were, on a transparent sphere.

160　We might also see in the wire sculptures or "mobiles" of A. Calder an experiment in time and space perception tending toward a diaphanization of matter. Suspended in mid-air in constant motion, these mobiles aid the viewer in overcoming his habitual sense of time and space, since the spatial "corporeity" has here entered a surprising symbiosis with the weightless temporal element of movement.

161　A "sphere experiment," as we might call it, was carried out by two American photographers, Dale Rooks and John Malloy. They were successful in capturing ingeniously on one photograph the peripheral and posterior aspects along with those customarily in front of the objective. The results of this experiment are "spherical" photographs, as it were, encompassing a location as a whole in the reflection presented to the objective by a silvered sphere.

162　Paul Klee (note 155), p. 47.

163　Hans-Friedrich Geist, *Paul Klee* (Hamburg: Hauswedell, 1948), p. 24.

164　Paul Klee (note 155), p. 43.

165　Kurt Leonhard, *Die heilige Fläche: Gespräche über moderne Kunst* (Stuttgart: Deutsche Verlags-Anstalt, 1947), p. 77.

166　Quoted in Georg Schmidt, "Paul Klee," *National Zeitung* (Basel), 89 (February 23, 1941).

167　Quoted in Werner Haftmann (note 150), p. 87.

168　We came across this fact in 1940 when a volume of colored illustrations crossed our desk: *Microcosmo* (Milan: Ulrico Hoepli). The colors and lines of the micro-vegetal structures were tangible reminders of pictures by Paul Klee.

169　Further illustrations of such coincidences or correspondences can be found in Georg Schmidt, Robert Schenk, and Adolf Portmann, *Kunst und Naturform / Form in Art and Nature / Art et Nature* (Basel: Basilius-Presse, 1960). See also *Der grosse Brockhaus*

(Wiesbaden: F. A. Brockhaus, 1958), XIII (Supplement), part 2, the two plates "geistige Welt: Weltbild ii/iii" following p. 32. Our figures 64-65 on p. 485 are reproduced with the kind permission of J. R. Geigy, A. G., Basel.

170   With regard to Klee, we refer particularly to the most important monographs on his work by Werner Haftmann and Will Grohmann, respectively. The attitude of both authors is in agreement with that of the present writer. (Will Grohmann also edited the volume of Paul Klee's *Handzeichnungen* in the Insel-Bücherei.) The same can be said of the succinct but suggestive introduction to Klee's *oeuvre* by Hans-Friedrich Geist, who together with D.-H. Kahnweiler is one of the courageous proponents of the point of view expressed in our text (p. 26 and note 64, p. 35).

This attitude apparently lies outside of the conceptual capabilities of a causality-ridden rationalism, inasmuch as it emphasizes that the various "primitivisms" of Picasso, for example, such as the incorrectly named "Periode Nègre" (1907-1909), were not imitations of Negro art, but in fact just the opposite: a genuine resuscitation of earlier forms of expression in Picasso's own art that led him to discover early types of art, in this instance, Negro art. The remarks of H.-F. Geist are particularly appropriate for countering the irresponsible tendency of some interpreters to equate certain pictures of Klee, Picasso, and other contemporaries with the art of children. In such an estimation we find the same short-circuited reasoning evident among some archaeologists such as G.-H. Luquet, who superimpose impressionistic, expressionistic, and even perspectival elements onto prehistoric painting because their interpretations are made merely on the basis of external similarities between prehistoric and contemporary painting, without any reference to or knowledge of the various consciousness structures. D.-H. Kahnweiler has also registered and substantiated his objections from his own vantage point. For if we overlook these considerations, we are in danger of falsifying reality. Not only the visible aspects and possible similarities are decisive, but rather the various consciousness structures on which they are based, and which, because of their impalpable nature, elude the simplifications of rational understanding by the archaeologists. They commit the same error as those historians of religion who speak of a "primordial monotheism" or the sociologists who find "rationalistic behavior" among "primitives" (to which we have referred above, p. 441, note 71). The sources to which we have made reference in this context are: Hans-Friedrich Geist (note 163 above); also his "Die Aufgaben einer bildnerischen Erziehung und die Kunst," *Die Neue Weltschau* (Stuttgart: Deutsche Verlags-Anstalt, 1953), II, pp. 197-228; as well as his "Die Aufgaben einer bildnerischen Erziehung und die Kunst; von der Kinderzeichnung zum Studium der Formelemente," *Werk: Schweizerische Monatsschrift für Architektur, Kunst und künstlerisches Gewerbe* (Winterthur: Verlag Buchdruckerei Winterthur AG.) 39 (April, 1952), no. 4, pp. 129-136; Daniel-Henry Kahnweiler (note 137), pp. 154-158; G.-H. Luquet, *L'Art Primitif* (Paris: Doin, 1939).

171   For example such pictures of Fernand Léger as the "Composition au Roi de Coeur" (1948), "La Guitarre jaune et le Vase bleu," and "Nature morte au Tapis bleu" (both 1950); cf. the nos. 85, 87, and 92 in the catalogue of the Léger exhibition at the Kunsthalle, Bern, Spring 1952. See also the reproductions of the two 1950 paintings, "The Colored Tents" and "Balloons" in the special issue, "Abstract Art" of the journal *Das Kunstwerk* (Kunstwerk-Schriften 19/20, Baden-Baden: Klein, n.d. [1952]), pp. 16-17.

172   Jean Gebser, "Rainer Maria Rilke und unsere Zeit," *Das Schweizerische Rilke-Archiv* (Zürich: Niehans, 1952), pp. 31-39; *Gesamtausgabe*, VI, pp. 220-225.

173   We have elsewhere suggested that Rainer Maria Rilke belongs among the poets mentioned here (cf. the author's address at the dedication of the Swiss Rilke Archive in the Swiss Landesbibliothek, Bern, note 172 above).

174   Karl Löwith, "Martin Heidegger: Denker in dürftiger Zeit," *Die Neue Rundschau* (Frankfurt/M.: S. Fischer) 63 (1952), 1, p. 15.

175   Ibid., p. 15.

176   We refer to our discussions—and only the most important in this connection are cited

here—in our previous publications: 1) *Rilke und Spanien* (written in 1936 but not published until 1939), (Zürich: Oprecht, ²1946); *Gesamtausgabe,* I; 2) *Der grammatische Spiegel: neue Denkformen im sprachlichen Ausdruck* (written in 1941, first published in 1944) (Zürich: Oprecht, ²1963); *Gesamtausgabe* I; 3) "Die drei Sphären; Bemerkungen zu T. S. Eliots 'Die Familienfeier,' " *Almanach für die Bücherfreunde* (Zürich: Oprecht, 1945); *Gesamtausgabe* VI, pp. 210–214.

177 Quoted in Hannes Maeder, "Hölderlin und das Wort," *Trivium* (Zürich: Atlantis) 2 (1944), 1, p. 47.

178 Friedrich Hölderlin, *Sämtliche Werke,* Grosse Stuttgarter Ausgabe (Stuttgart: Kohlhammer & Cotta, 1951), II, 1, p. 195.

179 Quoted in Max Brod, "Auf der Suche nach einem neuen Sinn unseres Daseins," *Die Neue Weltschau* (Stuttgart: Deutsche Verlags-Anstalt, 1952), I, p. 221 f.

180 Hannes Maeder (note 177), p. 46 f.

181 Recent Hölderlin research has emphasized the several levels of his *oeuvre;* various studies have uncovered his mythical, his philosophical, and his Christian components. Taken in their entirety, they reveal to what extent Hölderlin, by unifying these structures in an anticipatory way, already manifests the aperspectival perception that overdetermines these structures. We would single out the following studies from the Hölderlin literature:

a) Literary-historical interpretations by:

Romano Guardini, *Hölderlin und die Landschaft* (Stuttgart and Tübingen: Wunderlich, 1946);

Norbert von Hellingrath, *Hölderlin: zwei Vorträge* (Munich: Bruckmann, ²1922);

Norbert von Hellingrath, *Hölderlin-Vermächtnis* (Munich: Bruckmann, 1936);

Wilhelm Michel, *Friedrich Hölderlin* (Weimar: Lichtenstein, 1925);

Wilhelm Michel, *Hölderlins Wiederkunft* (Zürich-Gallus and Vienna: Scientia, 1943);

Wilhelm Michel, *Hölderlin und der deutsche Geist* (Stuttgart: Klett, 1947).

b) philosophical interpretations by:

Martin Heidegger, *Erläuterungen zu Hölderlins Dichtung* (Frankfurt/M.: Klostermann, 1951);

Kurt Hildebrandt, *Hölderlin: Philosophie und Dichtung* (Stuttgart and Berlin: Kohlhammer, 1939);

Johannes Hoffmeister, *Hölderlin und die Philosophie* (Leipzig: Meiner, 1944).

c) mythological interpretations by:

Hans Gottschalk, *Das Mythische in der Dichtung Hölderlins* (Stuttgart: Cotta, 1943);

Arthur Häny, *Hölderlins Titanenmythos,* Zürcher Beiträge zur deutschen Literatur- und Geistesgeschichte 2 (Zürich: Atlantis, 1948);

Lothar Kempter, *Hölderlin und die Mythologie,* Wege zur Dichtung: Zürcher Schriften zur Literaturwissenschaft 6 (Horgen/Zürich: Münster-Presse, 1939);

Louis Wiesmann, *Das Dionysische bei Hölderlin und in der deutschen Romantik,* Basler Studien zur deutschen Sprache und Literatur 6 (Basel: Schwabe, 1948).

d) Christian interpretations by:

Romano Guardini, *Hölderlin: Weltbild und Frömmigkeit* (Leipzig: Hegner, 1939);

Eduard Lachmann, *Hölderlins Christus-Hymnen* (Vienna: Herold, 1951);

Marianne Schultes, *Hölderlin - Christus - Welt* (Krailling vor München: Wevel, 1950);

Robert Thomas Stoll, *Hölderlins Christushymnen: Grundlagen und Deutung,* Basler Studien zur deutschen Sprache und Literatur 12 (Basel: Schwabe, 1952);

Helmut Wocke, *Hölderlins christliches Erbe* (Munich: Leibnitz Verlag, 1949).

e) Indispensable for Hölderlin research are the investigations published in the *Hölderlin Jahrbücher,* ed. Friedrich Beissner and Paul Kluckhohn (Tübingen: Mohr, 1948 ff.).

182 "Se io dovessi dire in che consista la maggior forza del tono poetico leopardiano direi che è una specie di privazione: egli toglie alla parola ogni sapore e colore e odore di communicazione poratica, e la pronunzia come una metafora interamente trascritta, la quale ha perduto il senso terrestre ed è più pura conservandone interamente la forma";

Francesco Flora, "Giacomo Leopardi," in Giacomo Leopardi, *Tutte le opere; Le Poesie e le prose* (Milan: Mondadori, 1940), I, p. xliii. We have translated "tono" as "word" since Francesco Flora specifically defines it as "storia della parola vuol dire tono."

183   "L'originalità della poesia leopardiana è in una proporzione sintattica e melodica e visiva che adopera parole e gruppi di parole tradizionali in un nuovo equilibrio"; Francesco Flora (and L. Nicastro), *Storia della Lettera italiana*, III.: F. Flora, *L'Ottocento*; L. Nicastro, *Il Novecento* (Milan: Mondadori, 1940), p. 137.

184   This "service done to the word" is evident not only in Mallarmé's poetry but also in the vast literature attendant upon it. We would particularly note the following:

    a) Pierre Beausire, *Essai sur la poésie et la poétique de Mallarmé*, Bibliotheque des Trois Collines (Lausanne: Roth, 1942);

    b) Henri Mondor, *Vie de Mallarmé* (Paris: Gallimard, NRF, 1941);

    c) Henri Mondor, *Histoire d'un Faune* (Paris: Gallimard, NRF, 1948);

    d) Henri Mondor, *Mallarmé plus intime* (Paris: Gallimard, NRF, 1944);

    e) Henri Mondor, *L'Amitié de Verlaine et Mallarmé* (Paris: Gallimard, NRF, 1930);

    f) Henri Mondor, *L'heureuse Rencontre de Valéry et Mallarmé* (Paris/Lausanne: Editions de Clairefontaine, 1947);

    g) Henri Mondor and François Ruchon, *L'Amitié de Stéphane Mallarmé et de Georges Rodenbach: Lettres et textes inédits 1887 à 1898* (Geneva: Cailler, 1949);

    h) Francis de Miomandre, *Mallarmé* (Paris, Mulhouse and Lausanne: Bader-Dufour, 1948);

    i) E. Noulet, *L'Oeuvre poétique de Stéphane Mallarmé* (Paris: Droz, 1940);

    k) E. Noulet, *Exégèse de Dix Poèmes de Stéphane Mallarmé*, Textes Litteraires Français (Lille: Girard; Geneva: Droz, 1948);

    l) Jean-Pierre Richard, *L'Univers imaginaire de Mallarmé* (Paris: Seuil, 1962);

    m) Claude Roulet, *Elucidation du Poème de Stéphane Mallarmé, "Un Coup de Dés jamais n'abolira le Hasard"* (Neuchâtel: Ides et Calendes, 1943);

    n) Claude Roulet, *Eléments de Poétique Mallarméenne d'apres le Poème "Un Coup de Dés jamais n'abolira le Hasard"* (Neuchâtel: Editions du Griffon, 1947);

    o) Jean Royère, *La Poésie de Mallarmé* (Paris: Emile-Paul, 1919);

    p) Jacques Scherer, *L'expression littéraire dans l'oeuvre de Mallarmé* (Paris: Droz, 1947);

    q) Camille Soula, *La poésie et la pensée de Stéphane Mallarmé; essai sur le symbole de la chevelure* (Paris: Champion, 1926);

    r) Albert Thibaudet, *La Poésie de Stéphane Mallarmé* (Paris: NRF, n.d.);

    s) Kurt Wais, *Mallarmé* (Munich: Beck, [2]1952);

    t) Special issue: "Stéphane Mallarmé (1842–1898)" of *Les Lettres*, 3 (Paris, 1948).

185   Gerard Manley Hopkins, *Poems* (Oxford: University Press, 1918; [2]1933); see also the bilingual German edition translated by Irene Behn: G. M. Hopkins, *Gedichte* (Hamburg: Claassen & Goverts, 1948).

186   Regarding the word, and its valuation by Rilke, Mallarmé and Leopardi, see Werner Günther, *Weltinnenraum: Die Dichtung Rainer Maria Rilkes* (Bern: Haupt, 1943), p. 312, note 10; and p. 225, note 2 of the second edition (Berlin/Bielefeld: Schmidt, 1952). With respect to Jorge Guillén, we would refer to our translations of eight of his poems in Winstone/Gebser, *Neue spanische Dichtung* (Berlin: Rabenpresse, 1936), p. 25 ff.; reprinted in Jean Gebser, *Gedichte* (Schaffhausen: Novalis, 1974), p. 177 ff.; see also Gebser, *Rilke und Spanien* (note 176), p. 39 and notes 42 and 43; *Gesamtausgabe*, I, p. 40 and pp. 84–85; Gebser, *Der grammatische Spiegel* (note 176), (1944), p. 17 f., and ([2]1963), p. 21; *Gesamtausgabe*, I, p. 154.

187   For reasons of space we can only allude here to the representatives of the more recent generation of poets succeeding the four major poets of our day: Wystan Hugh Auden, Christopher Isherwood, and Stephen Spender in England, who are indebted to both Eliot and Rilke.

188   This new consciously achieved value of the word must not be mistaken for the magical

force present in, say, the "Merseburg Charms." It is characteristic of today's valuation that the word is employed integrally in its plenitude and wealth of associations, notably in the works of Mallarmé and Rilke. Today the word is nowhere merely a primordial root, a magical sound, a mythical image or a mental concept—never merely evocative, descriptive or narrative—but rather articulates all of these together. This integrality and strength of utterance of the poetic word also distinguish the poems of Giuseppi Ungaretti, Salvatore Quasimodo, Kurt Marti, Wolfgang Schwarz and Richard Haldenwang, to name only a few of the younger poets. See also the excellent studies by Kurt Leonhard, who from his own insight has evolved an interpretation of the structural transformation in poetry, and evinced its salient phenomena, characteristics, and stylistic aspects. Particularly with respect to its inception and formation, it is an interpretation congruent for the most part with our own. His studies treat the work of Ingeborg Bachmann, Paul Celan, Hans Magnus Enzensberger, Helmut Heissenbüttel, Karl Krolow and others of the post-war generation. Cf. Kurt Leonhard, Silbe, Bild und Wirklichkeit (Esslingen: Bechtle, 1957), as well as his Moderne Lyrik: Monolog und Manifest; ein Leitfaden (Bremen: Schünemann, 1963).

The new poetry has also been called "absolute poetry," a misnomer inasmuch as it is not mental-rational and does not treat the word as a rational absolute; rather the word is integral, that is, an utterance. As long as one speaks of "absolute" poetry there is the danger of associating it with Alexandrinism, as has already happened, and ignoring the fact that this rests in a different consciousness structure than contemporary poetry.

189 Edouard Dujardin, Le Monologue Intérieur (Paris: Messein, 1931).
190 For German-speaking readers we would note two works on Paul Valéry; one is by the congenial translator of Valéry's Monsieur Teste, Max Rychner, the other by Ernst Wilhelm Eschmann, who has incontrovertibly proven himself to be a poet of the "new tone" by his interlinking of the everyday with a universal scope through the various time-structures, notably in his Tessiner Episteln; see Max Rychner, Zur europäischen Literatur zwischen zwei Weltkriegen (Zürich: Atlantis, 1943); the four essays on Valéry are on pp. 145–164; Paul Valéry, Herr Teste, trans. Max Rychner (Leipzig: Insel, 1927); Ernst Wilhelm Eschmann, Tessiner Episteln (Hamburg: Ellermann, 1949).
191 The anthology of Dadaist poetry by C. Giedion-Welcker and some of the sentence-fragments contained therein furnish convincing evidence that even the rubble poetry of Dadaism shows occasional flashes of pure poetic content; see C [arola] Giedion-Welcker, ed., Poètes à l'Ecart / Anthologie der Abseitigen (Bern-Bümplitz: Benteli, 1946).

Also, the admirable later path chosen by Hugo Ball, one of the founders of Dada, indicates that not everyone from this world of bits and pieces was himself similarly fragmented; see Hugo Ball, Byzantinisches Christentum (Munich: Kösel & Pustet, 1931), and also his Flucht aus der Zeit (Munich: Kösel & Pustet, 1931).

In connection with Surrealist poetry we would note the anthology by Maurice Nadeau, Histoire du Surréalisme (Paris: Editions du Seuil, 1945/1948), II, as well as the book by Anna Balakian, Literary Origins of Surrealism (New York: King's Crown Press, 1947).

A clarification is here in order concerning the often quoted remark of André Breton from the "Surrealist Manifesto" that has occasioned much confusion: "Everything indicates a belief that a point of spirit exists from which life and death, the real and the imagined, past and future, the communicable and the incommunicable, high and low cease to be regarded as contradictions. One would search in vain for another motive force in Surrealist activity than the hope of determining this point." By the use of magic-psychistic means (inasmuch as it considers mandatory the rendering of outpourings of the unleashed "subconscious" and automatism, i.e., the spiritually-uncommittal), Surrealism here is striving to satisfy the secularized need for a unio mystica, as is evident from this quotation where the magic point is mentioned and not the whole, and where the psyche is mistaken for the spirit.

192 Hans Kayser, Lehrbuch der Harmonik (Zürich: Occident, 1950); see also our Abendlän-

dische Wandlung (Zürich: Oprecht, 1943 ff.) and *Gesamtausgabe,* I) for further references to the extensive area of "world harmonics."

193 André Breton, *Arcane 17* (Paris: Sagittaire, 1947).

194 Shikibu Murasaki, *Die Geschichte vom Prinzen Genji* (Leipzig: Insel, n.d.), II. For a discussion of the magic-mythical sense of time still prevalent in India, Indo-China, Japan and China, see the examples in Jean Gebser, *Asienfibel* (Frankfurt/M.: Ullstein Buch No. 650), and *Gesamtausgabe,* VI, chapter 2 et passim.

195 Max Brod, "Ein Brief an den Vater," *Der Monat* 1 (June, 1949), nos. 8/9; Kafka's text of the "Brief an den Vater" is in *Die Neue Rundschau* 63 (1952), 2, pp. 191–231.

196 Wyndham Lewis, *Time and Western Man* (London: Chatto and Windus, 1927).

197 Literary historians have also noted the connection between time and psychic energy in its manifestation as fantasy or imagination. Emil Staiger, for example, has written a book with reference to the time question in Heidegger's *Sein und Zeit* entitled *Die Zeit als Einbildungskraft des Dichters* (Zürich: Niehans, 1939). It is concerned with the role of time in the works of Brentano, Goethe, and Gottfried Keller. Fritz Strich, in turn, has shed light on many aspects of the time question in his *Der Dichter und die Zeit* (Bern: Francke, 1947). Theophil Spoerri, indebted to Kassner's theory of the imagination, has contributed much on this subject in various articles published in *Trivium* (Zürich: Atlantis, 1943-1951). Much earlier than Staiger, Strich, and Spoerri was Wilhelm Dilthey, whose *Das Erlebnis und die Dichtung* touched on this question and attempted to resolve it from a stance closely akin to Vitalism. We have noted above the book by Georges Poulet (text p. 404): *Etudes sur le Temps Humain* (Paris: Plon, 1950).

198 Paul C. Berger, "Marcel Proust," *Das Buch* 3, 2 (Mainz, 1951), p. 20 f.

199 Quoted from Berger's translation (note 198), p. 19.

200 Max Rychner, *Zur europäischen Literatur* (note 190), p. 122; our emphasis. A good introduction to the work of James Joyce can be found in the selection edited by T. S. Eliot (Zürich: Die Arche, 1951). The distinguished translation by C. Giedion-Welcker presents German readers for the first time with fragments of Joyce's late major work, *Finnegan's Wake*. The translation is particularly deserving of note because of its remarkable transposition into German of what is essentially untranslatable. We would also mention that James Joyce has recorded several sections of *Finnegan's Wake* that are of great aid in the understanding of the work. These recordings convincingly convey the magic intensity, the mythical wealth of image, and the mentally ordered composition of his poetry. Specifically the linguistic intentions, which elicit in the hearer a wealth of interrelationships via the novel use of words, are unmistakably revealed. The recording in question was made for the Orthological Institute, 10, King's Parade, Cambridge, by the Grammophone Co., Hayes, Middlesex, and is labeled "James Joyce reading Anna Livia Plurabella."

201 Robert Musil, *Der Mann ohne Eigenschaften,* III (Lausanne: Imprimerie Centrale, 1943), 11; (vols. 1 and 2 were published by Rowohlt, Berlin, in 1930–1933).

202 Hermann Broch, *Die Schuldlosen* (Zürich: Rhein, 1950); in particular, the ninth story.

203 The semi-annual international conference "Rencontres Universitaires de St-Christophe" at the University of Paris devoted its Easter, 1951, session to the theme "The Nature and Technique of the Novel." In his report, Claas Pach noted the results and conclusions of the conference from which we quote the following representative excerpts: "1) The modern novel strives toward a far-reaching identification between the reader and the characters of the novel. . . . This is achieved by the technique of 'monologue intérieur.' 2) The modern author recognizes the primacy of language, of the word itself as the poetic medium, and no longer the plot. 3) The significant role of the concept of time in conjunction with the world view of the twentieth century and the abolition of the historical aspect of the novel in favor of a present inseparable from an immanent past. 4) The complete dissolution of the 'subject'. . . . The new formation of the novel as a mysterious formation of our being, and consequently the end of the novel as a historical form." See Claas Pach, "Die 'Recontres Universitaires de St-Christophe' be-

handeln Wesen und Technik des Romans," *Schweizer Rundschau* 51, 2 (Einsiedeln, May 1951), p. 113 f.

204 Robert Musil, *Der Mann ohne Eigenschaften* (Hamburg: Rowohlt, 1952), p. 1632.

205 With regard to Kurt Leonhard see note 188 above.

206 See the two publications by Werner Weber, *Figuren und Fahrten* (Zürich: Manesse, 1956), and particularly *Zeit ohne Zeit* (Zürich: Manesse, 1959). See also his lecture of the latter title in *Die Welt in Neuer Sicht* (München-Planegg: Barth, 1959), II, pp. 41–61.

207 Max Rychner, *Zur europäischen Literatur* (note 190), p. 123.

208 Guillaume Apollinaire, *Coleur du Temps* (Paris: Editions du Bélier, 1949), p. 17.

209 The difference in structure precludes identification of this staging with the multiple Shakespearian staging of the Globe Theatre, since Shakespeare's plot has a uniformly progressing action accented or complemented by the sub-plots. In the case of Bruckner, however, several interconnected plots unfold polymetrically, as it were.

210 Thornton Wilder, *Wir sind noch einmal davongekommen* (*The Skin of our Teeth*), German version by Gentiane (and Jean) Gebser (Zürich: Oprecht, 1944).

211 After Wilder Tennessee Williams (*The Glass Menagerie*) and Arthur Miller (*The Death of a Salesman*) express the new sense of space and time, as Arnold H. Schwengeler has persuasively argued in his reviews of these two plays (*Der Bund*, Zürich, February 9 and May 10, 1951). A different embodiment of the valuation of time can be found in the so-called "Theatre of the Absurd" (Sartre, Beckett, Ionesco and others). This is rather a "Theatre of Despair" or "Theatre of the Desperate": those who perceive only the losses and cannot draw upon the attendant gains which such losses make possible.

212 Gerard Manley Hopkins (note 185), German edition, p. 39.

213 T. S. Eliot, *Collected Poems 1909–1935* (New York: Harcourt, Brace & Co., 1936), pp. 69–98, or *The Waste Land and other Poems* (London: Faber & Faber, 1942); there is a German translation of the poem by Ernst Robert Curtius in T. S. Eliot, *Ausgewählte Gedichte, Englisch und Deutsch* (Frankfurt/M.:Suhrkamp, 1951), pp. 21–61.

214 Gottfried Benn, *Gesammelte Gedichte* (Berlin: Verlag Die Schmiede, 1927).

215 T. S. Eliot, *Four Quartets* (London: Faber & Faber, 1944).

216 Werner Günther has listed examples of various inversions in the appendix of his book on Rilke (note 186), 1943 edition, p. 267 ff.

217 Stanislas Fumet, "Correspondances," *Les problèmes de la peinture; sous la direction de Gaston Diehl* (Paris: Confluences, 1945), p. 299.

218 Claude Roulet (note 184, m).

219* In connection with Proust's "oceanic" style we would mention the style of Jean Paul [Friedrich Richter] which in certain respects may be considered as a prototype of Proust's. We must not overlook the fact, however, that German lends itself to periodic sentence structure to a greater degree than French. And having mentioned a German "Romantic" author, we should also recall Adalbert Stifter to whom, as we noted in the text (p. 393), time is revealed in his description of the geological strata of a mountain range in his novel, *Der Nachsommer*. Stifter, moreover, is the originator of a question and an answer as to time that anticipates much of what is known today and goes far beyond Kant's definitions: "How would it be if time and space were in fact not real at all? If they were only the *framework* imprisoning our *conceptions*, the *law binding* our *conceptions* from which we cannot escape? Then God, and perhaps other spirits would reside in *timelessness* or rather eternity" (our emphasis).

220 The author is aware that many important names have not been included on the preceding pages. Scandinavian and Russian authors, among others, have not been mentioned, despite the widespread influence of Leo N. Tolstoy and Jens Peter Jacobsen for example (notably on R. M. Rilke), to say nothing of the pervasive influence of Dostoevsky.

221 Franz Kafka, *Betrachtungen* (Leipzig: Rowohlt, 1912), p. 3.

222 The following is a compilation of passages similar to the quotation from Kafka, and is intended to suggest that our conclusions on the basis of the example cited have not merely been read into the text. The passages quoted below should demonstrate this;

they have, incidentally, been further developed in the discussions in our other books, *Rilke in Spanien* (note 176), p. 39 ff. and notes 41–43 and 45 (*Gesamtausgabe*, I, pp. 40 ff. and 76), and *Der grammatische Spiegel* (note 176), 1944 edition, p. 13 ff and notes 3 and 7, 1963 edition, p. 16 ff. (*Gesamtausgabe*, I, p. 151 ff.

From Hölderlin:

"langsame Stege" (slow bridges), "wohleingerichtete Eichen" (well-furnished oaks), "feige(s) Grab" (cowardly grave), "dunkles Licht" (dark light);

from Heinrich Heine:

"ein Meer blauer Gedanken" (a sea of blue thoughts) and "der Wirt trug einen hastig grünen Leibrock" (the innkeeper was wearing a hastily green dresscoat) (for source references see below, under A);

from Georg Trakl:

"das blaue Lachen des Quells und die schwarze Kühle der Nacht" (the azure laughter of the spring and the black coolness of night), "unserer Hände elfenbeinerne Traurigkeit" (the ivory despondency of our hands), "grüne Stille des Teiches" (verdant quiet of the pool) (see below, B);

from Paul Valéry:

"la nuit verte des prairies" (the green night of the meadows) (C); elsewhere we have countered the argument that these examples are merely instances of synaesthesia (D);

from R. M. Rilke:

"stand an gestern begonnenem Fenster" (. . . stand at the window started the day before" [Leishman, 1938]) (E); further examples of a similar kind cited in Werner Günther (F);

from S. Quasimodo:

"Salgo vertici aerei precipizi" where the adjective "aerei" (airy) refers not to a noun in perspectival sense, but aperspectivally to both "vertici" (summits) and "precipizi" (abysses) (G);

from Jorge Guillén:

"con folaje incesante busca a su dios el árbol" (the tree with unceasing foliage seeks its God) (H); and "Por sus aguas aún verdes / Llega el campo de antes" (with its waters still green / Comes the earlier field) (I).

A) If our recollection is correct, the examples quoted are from Heine's *Harzreise*.

B) Georg Trakl, *Die Dichtungen* (Leipzig: Kurt Wolff, n.d.); Manuldruck (Munich, 1921?); the quotations from the poems "Offenbarung und Untergang," p. 195; "Rosenkranzlieder; Amen," p. 78; "Abendländisches Lied," p. 137.

C) Paul Valéry, *Poésies* (Paris: Gallimard, NRF, 1942), p. 29 (in the poem "Le bois amical").

D) See J. Gebser, *Der grammatische Spiegel*, especially p. 46, note 3, of the 1944 edition, and p. 18 f. of the 1963 edition; *Gesamtausgabe*, I, p. 152 f.

E) Rainer Maria Rilke, *Späte Gedichte* (Leipzig: Insel, 1935), p. 44 (beginning of the poem "Die grosse Nacht"); the poem is also found in Rilke's *Ausgewählte Werke* (Leipzig: Insel, 1938), I, p. 340.

F) Werner Günther (note 186, 1943), p. 259 ff.

G) Salvatore Quasimodo in his poem "Vento a Tindari" from the collection *Acque e terre*, quoted in Reto R. Bezzola, "Die Dichtung des absoluten Wortes," *Trivium* 3 (1945), no. 2, p. 130 ff., particularly p. 137, where Bezzola indicates the frequency of this novel use of the adjective in modern Italian letters since Leopardi.

H) Jorge Guillén *Cántico* (Madrid: Cruz y Raya, Editiones del Arbol, 1936); see the poem "Arbol del Oroño," p. 210, as well as his *Cántico*, Primera Edición completa (Bueños Aires: Editorial Sudamericano, 1950), p. 296.

I) Jorge Guillén, *op. cit.* cf. his poem "Mecánica celeste; El Campo, la Ciudad, el Cielo," pp. 128 and 406 respectively. We published a translation of both poems into German in 1936 (see note 186) which we reprint here, with slight modifications, as the original publication is long out of print:

Herbstlicher Baum

Schon reift
das Blatt seinem genauen, ruhigen Falle entgegen,
fällt. Fällt
in den ewig grünen Himmel des Teiches.
Gelassen
in sich hinein sinnt der Herbst im letzten Verfall.
Sehr zart
gibt sich das Blatt der Reinheit der Kälte nach.
Stromabwärts
sucht mit unaufhörlichem Laub seinen Gott der Baum.

Das Feld, die Stadt, der Himmel

Fluss in der Stadt. Wie gross!
Mit seinen noch grünen Wassern
kommt das frühere Feld.

Strassenplatanen
ahnen verlangend
einen ruhigen Wind.

Erobern die unermüdlichen
Statuen endlich
den Himmel über den Plätzen?

Wieder der Fluss. Er entfliesst
mit dem Felde. Er nimmt
die Gier der Strassen nicht auf.

Doch ist es gleich. Danket,
danket den Statuen! Schon
Geht der Himmel zwischen den Häusern.

223 Reto R. Bezzola in *Trivium* (see note 222, G), p. 137.
224 See Jean Gebser, *Der grammatische Spiegel* (note 176), 1944, p. 23 ff., ^{2}1963, p. 28 f.; *Gesamtausgabe*, I, p. 159 f.; and also Werner Günther (note 186, 1943 ed.), p. 259 f.
225 See in this connection Jean Gebser, "Die drei Sphären" (note 276) and *Gesamtausgabe*, VI, p. 210 ff.
226 See Jean Gebser, *Der grammatische Spiegel* (note 176), 1944, p. 27 ff.; ^{2}1963, p. 32 f.; *Gesamtausgabe*, I, p. 161 f.
227 Later on Gottfried Benn too rejected the use of "like" and considered it an empty formalism; see his *Probleme der Lyrik* (Wiesbaden: Limes, 1951), p. 16.
228 See Jean Gebser, *Der grammatische Spiegel* (note 176), 1944, p. 26 f., ^{2}1963, p. 31 f., *Gesamtausgabe*, I, p. 161.
229 Rainer Maria Rilke (note 222, E), in the poem "Wendung," pp. 24 ff. and 309 ff. respectively.
230 Werner Günther (note 186, 1943 ed.), p. 264.
231 Hans Egon Holthusen, *Rilkes Sonette an Orpheus* (Munich: Filser, 1937), p. 158.
232 Hugo von Hofmannsthal, *Die Gedichte und kleinen Dramen* (Leipzig: Insel, 1923), p. 12; see also *Gesammelte Werke, Gedichte und lyrische Dramen* (Stockholm: Bermann-Fischer, 1946), p. 17.
233 Federico García Lorca, "Romancero gitano," *Revista de Occidente* (Madrid, 1926), p. 45; see also his *Obras completas* (Buenos Aires: Losada, 1938), IV, p. 26. Our translation of

this "romancero" was published in *Lorca oder das Reich der Mütter* (Stuttgart: Deutsche Verlags-Anstalt, 1949), p. 45; *Gesamtausgabe*, I, p. 119 f., based on our earlier version of 1936 in *Neue spanische Dichtung* (note 186), p. 31 ff.

234   Manuel de Falla, *The Three Cornered Hat (El sombrero de tres picos)*, The Philharmonia Orchestra cond. Alceo Galliera, Columbia CAX 9551/9554, DX 1258/1259 (78 rpm). In this connection see also Jean Gebser, *Lorca oder das Reich der Mütter* (note 233), p. 49; *Gesamtausgabe*, I, p. 120 ff.

235   Hölderlin, *Sämtliche Werke*, Grosse Stuttgarter Ausgabe (Stuttgart: Kohlhammer & Cotta, 1951), II, 1, p. 217.

236   We have indicated in another context the use of "und" (and) beginnings in poetry, notably in medieval folksong and in the sacred lyric poetry of the Baroque era; but this was an outgrowth of different circumstances and occurs only rarely; see our *Der grammatische Spiegel* (note 176), ²1963, p. 7 and 30; *Gesamtausgabe*, I, pp. 147 and 160. See also our "Probleme der Kunst," in *Die Struktur der europäischen Wirklichkeit* (Stuttgart: Kohlhammer, 1960), p. 37 f.; *Gesamtausgabe*, V/I, p. 139 f. We have encountered the following six examples from medieval and Baroque poetry:

From Uhland, *Volkslieder* (fourteenth century):

Und als man singet und als man spricht:
die herren streiten dapferlich
zu Hönnauf auf der heiden;

and from the same collection (twelfth century):

Und unser lieben Frauen
der traumet ihr ein traum:
wie unter irem herzen
gewachsen wär ein baum,
  Kyrie eleison!
Und wie der baum ein schatten gab . . . ;

From a manuscript dated 1603 the lines:

Und welche frau ein götzen hat
die schläft wol one sorgen . . . ;

In Stieler's *Geharnischte Venus* (1660) are the lines:

Und, wo ich dirs, Zelinde, schenke
so heiss ich Peilkarastres nicht . . . ;

Thümmel (1776) writes,

Und wer des Lebens Unverstand
mit Wehmut will geniessen . . . ;

And finally, there is this passage in *Texte des Mittelalters*:

Und weshalb wir in sunden gedeyen. . . .

The use of "and" beginnings from a different basis of consciousness evidently does not begin until Goethe, Hölderlin, and Heine, with occasional instances found in the poetry of Scheffel, Chamisso, E. M. Arndt and Prutz, and continues down to the present in the examples previously mentioned of Hugo von Hofmannsthal, Federico García Lorca and others.

237   Further examples of this new use of rhyme are cited in our *Der grammatische Spiegel* (note 176), 1944, pp. 29–36, ²1963, pp. 34–44; *Gesamtausgabe*, I, pp. 162–169.

238   Rainer Maria Rilke, *Mir zur Feier* (Berlin: G. H. Meyer, 1899), p. 53, in one of the poems from the cycle "Mädchengestalten." It is reprinted in his *Gesammelte Werke* (Leipzig:

Insel, 1930), I, p. 302, following its republication in the new edition of *Mir zur Feier* of 1909 under the title *Die frühen Gedichte* (Leipzig: Insel, 1909).

239 See also Jean Gebser, "Rainer Maria Rilke und unsere Zeit" (note 172), p. 35 f.; *Gesamtausgabe*, VI, p. 222 f.

240 Hölderlin (note 235), II, 1, p. 374.

241* Hugo von Hofmannsthal, "Tagebuch," *Corona* 6 (Munich: Oldenburg, 1936), no. 5, p. 578 (entry for June 8, 1906); *Gesammelte Werke in Einzelausgaben: Aufzeichnungen* (Frankfurt/M.: S. Fischer, 1959), p. 143.

242* Paul Valéry, *Leonardo - Poe - Mallarmé*, The Collected Works of Paul Valéry, ed. Jackson Mathews, Bollingen Series 45 (Princeton: Princeton Univ. Press, 1972), VIII, p. 9. The original text reads: "Car la mort, au sens biologique, fait *partie inséparable* de la vie . . . " (Valéry's italics); Paul Valéry, *Les Divers Essais sur Léonard de Vinci; Oeuvres* (Paris: NRF, 1938), p. 40.

243 J. Anker–Larsen, *Bei offener Tür* (Leipzig: Grethlein, 1926), p. 64 f.

244 "J'ai tenté en écrivant 'Claire' de peindre l'amour parfait, à peine troublé par l'idée de la mort, et les contre-coups légers de la vie et des caractères. A présent je dirais que même ces ombres n'existent pas dans l'amour parfait. Rien ne change pour lui, l'être aimé est immutable, hors du temps, affranchi de la mort"; Jacques Chardonne, *Chronique privée* (Paris: Stock, 1940), p. 41.

245 Rainer Maria Rilke, *Briefe aus Muzot* (Leipzig: Insel, 1935), p. 372. The italics in this and the folowing quotation are Rilke's.

246 Rainer Maria Rilke, "Zwei Briefe an Gräfin Margot Sizzo," *Insel Almanach auf das Jahr 1937*, p. 109. The letter from which this quotation is taken (Epiphany 1923) is also reprinted in R. M. Rilke, *Briefe* (Wiesbaden: Insel, 1950), II, p. 381 (letter 373).

247* *The I Ching or Book of Changes*, the Richard Wilhelm translation rendered into English by Cary F. Baynes (Princeton: Princeton University Press, 1967), p. 297 (book ii, ch. v, para. 1). See also Jean Gebser, "Rainer Maria Rilke und unsere Zeit" (note 172), p. 37 and p. 224 respectively. The identical attitude can also be discerned in recent psychosomatic medicine. Viktor von Weizsäcker has written that "death is not the opposite of life, but the counterpart of procreation and birth. Birth and death behave toward one another like the obverse and reverse sides of life, and not like the mutually exclusive opposites of logic. Life is birth *and* death"; see Viktor von Weizsäcker, *Der Gestaltkreis* (Stuttgart: Thieme, ³1947), p. 1.

In order to avoid any misunderstandings, we would mention here that the contemporary attitude toward the problem of life versus death overdetermines earlier attitudes. The famous line in the hymn of Notker Balbulus (840–911), "Media vita in morte sumus," which Martin Luther rendered as "Though in midst of life we be / snares of death surround us" (1540), shows evidence of a resignation and sadness in the face of death unknown to present-day poets. The earlier attitude embodied in the hymn will continue as long as life and death are considered to be opposites—and this attitude is gradually being supplanted. The same holds true with respect to the Occidental understanding of the words of Buddha: "Life and death are one." Here the unitary thought of the magical-mythical structure predominates, transferring to death the irrelevance attributed to life (Maya). (This quotation of Buddha was communicated in writing to the present author by the late Oskar Schloss, the well-known publisher of Buddhist literature; unfortunately he did not furnish a source reference.)

248 By celebrating the imagination, Rudolf Kassner, himself confined to the mythical structure, has brought about perhaps his major accomplishment: he has brought his predominantly spatial-thinking, generation, to an awareness of the mythical time-form. Kassner has noted that Rilke did not hold the antithesis inherent in classicism; see Kassner's book *Buch der Erinnerung* (Leipzig: Insel, 1938), p. 306. See also Werner Günther (note 186, 1943 ed.), p. 270, note 6. It is only natural that Rilke as a true poet is opposed to antitheses inherent in the conceptual world that can only destroy the imagistic world of poetry. What is significant here is that Rilke did not remain in a state of "opposition";

instead, he not only accords primacy to mythical correspondence and complementarity wherever the subject—or more correctly, the image or *Anschauung* requires it—but surmounts both by the "full sphere of being."

249 Of course it does not need to be emphasized that the various poets aspire to this arationality in a variety of ways according to their various basic disposition. Rilke, having a greater magical affinity, and Valéry, a more obvious mental affinity, strive in the direction of Guillén's genuine perception and evincing of the diaphanous. The same constellation can be discerned in the other arts; Rilke is more closely akin to Klee than is Valéry, for instance, who stands in turn closer to the geometric-abstract painters, as well as to Le Corbusier and Stravinsky; Guillén, on the other hand, has a closer affinity to Frank Lloyd Wright and Alban Berg.

250 Werner Günther also emphasizes that Rilke "in his creative intuition became aware of the miracle of metamorphosis, of the sudden emergence of transparency of the intensely visualized object," (note 186, 1943 ed.), p. 65.

251 Hans Egon Holthusen noted this transparency in the works of Valéry and Eliot: "In Valéry's poems the world attains the utmost luminescence and spirituality. Everything is rendered crystalline and transparent"; in *Der unbehauste Mensch* (Munich: Piper, 1951), p. 16. Holthusen has also pointed out that Eliot's *Four Quartets* are written in a "language that combines crystalline clarity and transparent depth of thought progression with the power to realize the most intense sentience" (loc. cit., p. 92).

252 Werner Haftmann (note 150), p. 97.

253 Lou Albert-Lasard, *Wege mit Rilke* (Frankfurt/M.: S. Fischer, 1952), p. 162.

254 T. S. Eliot, *The Family Reunion* (New York: Harcourt, Brace & Co., 1939), p. 98; see also Jean Gebser, "Die drei Sphären" (note 176, 3). The thought that the future is the co-agent in the creation of our given present is first found, to the best of our knowledge, in the writings of Friedrich Nietzsche, and is later of utmost importance to C. G. Jung's analytic psychology. That dreams can also foresee or previse is merely a psychic complement of the integral importance and qualitativeness of this insight.

A certain kind of temporal freedom, albeit implicit, is a prevailing characteristic of the poetry of St.-John Perse, particularly in his *Anabase*. Poets of the stature of Rilke, Hofmannsthal, Eliot, and Larbaud used their influence on behalf of his recognition. In her interpretation of the *Anabase*, Gerda Zeltner-Neukomm implicitly points to his timefreedom when she writes that: "here the spirit has yesterday and tomorrow, the negation and affirmation of things at its disposal, and yet is able to withdraw from both since it never associates with them"; Gerda Zeltner-Neukomm, "St-J. Perse als Dichter der Fremdheit," *Überlieferung und Gestaltung; Festgabe für Theophil Spoerri zum 60. Geburtstag* (Zürich: Speer, 1950), p. 205.

255* A. S. Eddington, *Space, Time and Gravitation* (Cambridge: University Press, 1920), p. 51.

256 Werner Heisenberg, "Atomphysik und Kausalgesetz," *Die neue Weltschau* (Stuttgart: Deutsche Verlags-Anstalt, 1953), II, p. 132. See also note 24 on p. 389.

10

Manifestations of the Aperspectival World (VI): Summary

1. The Aperspectival Theme

The theme of our epoch is aperspectivity. The irruption of time into perspectival, spatial thought is manifest in all areas of our lives. The emerging consciousness of time as an immeasurable and mentally inconceivable world constituent—this is the basic, aperspectival manifestation. The same preoccupation was discernible in the most diverse areas, as the fourth dimension became visible as time-freedom. And it was possible to discern this preoccupation, despite the categories and terminologies which traditionally would have impeded the revelation of common concerns, via the concept of acategorical systasis which has not only simplified our task but has in fact made it possible.

Just as the conquest of space was accompanied by a disclosure, an "opening up," as it were, of the planes and surfaces of the unperspectival world, so too is today's emergent perception accompanied by an opening of space. The irruption of time gradually leads to the conquest of time through our consciousness. This conquest includes the supersession of time in its entire complexity.

Many of the aperspectival inceptions appearing around us are for the time being experiments. Just as perspectivity was not discovered in one stroke, so aperspectivity cannot be discovered in one moment. Yet on the basis of the original manifestations, we can and must clearly understand the theme of our mutational epoch. Without such an awareness, no new and responsible constitution of reality can be realized.

The numerous indications we have been able to demonstrate as being similar are trustworthy. Those phenomena that are not amenable to spatial-conceptual thought we have been able to perceive by our insight into acategorical efficacy, which is not demonstrable by categorical concepts or systems and becomes evident in our unprejudiced perception of structural interconnections and our recognition of systasis.

Someone able to renounce the exclusive claim of the mental structure, as mental man once renounced the mythical, does not by any means renounce the mental-rational; like the magical and mythical, it too is required for certain areas of reality. But as the mythical is an overdetermination of the magical, the mental an overdetermination of the mythical, the integral consciousness structure is an over-determination of the mental. Its mode of realization is not exhausted in quantitative or conceptual thought, in the mythical intuition of the symbolic images of the world, or in the experience of magical unity and power. The new mode of realization ir-rupts in verition—the perception and impartation of truth which signifies the whole and renders it transparent wherever we succeed in liberating ourselves from spatially-bound conceptuality without reverting to irrationality.

This need, this necessity, is obvious everywhere. The key-words reflecting this situation reappear as the basic concern in all manifestations of the areas we have investigated: the openness that is transfigured into plenitude whenever we realize that the disruption of space by time does not lead to emptiness, to *nihil*, to nothing-ness or *nada*, but to transparency. By unifying the systems into spatio-temporal syn-aireses with the aid of systatic structures, instead of spatially-bound syntheses, we perceive interconnections and thus overdetermine the space-time world by space-time–freedom or the achronon. Moreover, by surpassing dualism we resolve the division of the world in favor of the whole.

The whole, which we dimly experience in magic, which becomes visible to us in the polarity of the world of descriptive imagery, and which we attempt to concep-tualize in a mental-rational summation of parts: the whole becomes perceptible throughout all domains; origin becomes present. Our recognition of the trans-figuration, the transclarification of the world—sustained by religion, *religio*, the bond with the past, though increasingly disrupted by reason—is becoming a bond, an obligation to the present, *praeligio*. The profound Christian truth with regard to transparency, the diaphaneity of the world, becomes perceptible. The genuine irruption of the other side into this side, the presence of the beyond in the here and now, of death in life, of the transcendent in the immanent, of the divine in the human, becomes transparent. God's incarnation was not in vain. Religion inten-sified to *praeligio*—and this is intended to circumscribe the profound Christianity of the integral consciousness structure without any theological claim[1]—is presenta-tion of origin, the recognition of creation and creativity, and the integration of our lives as one of the numerous and meaningful forms revealing integrity or the whole.

This new, self-constituting consciousness structure discovers and surpasses the ultimate and most profound antithesis of rationalism between faith and knowl-edge, religion and science. Not only because it becomes gradually apparent to what an unsettling degree scientific theses themselves often emerge from presupposi-tions based on belief—even the world of numbers and their laws has a limited valid-ity applicable only to the materialized aspects of our space-time world—but also because antitheses of this kind are not reconcilable with the new consciousness structure. It is in the transparency of faith and knowledge, and not with their aid, that the sphere of Being becomes perceptible in its entire diaphaneity. (We would again refer to the "synoptic table" at the end of the book in connection with this summary.)

We have found inceptions of the new perception of world in manifestations in both the sciences and the arts. The one group was until recently predominantly ra-tional and indebted to knowledge, while the other was predominantly irrational and hence indebted to the acceptance of faith. It has become evident that both manifest signs of what we have called arationality. This, too, is a guarantee that the aperspecti-val theme is becoming an aperspectival reality.

2. *Daily Life*

The new consciousness which was anticipated and first took shape in the creations of artists, thinkers, and scientists, will not be fully valid so long as it is not lived in daily life. What form can it take? It will take its own necessary course. Yet the confusion of the present situation requires a certain readiness, open-mindedness, and co-operation of each individual.

It will happen of its own accord since the structure of the new mode of real-ization has begun to manifest itself with an undeniable intensity in the most diverse areas of our lives. But each individual's attitude and mode of behavior can ensure that the process consolidating the new consciousness can occur without a detour through a possible catastrophe. There have been enough teachers: we have en-countered them in the course of the foregoing pages as the precursors of the new consciousness. So also are the latent teachers at work, the trustees of the reflected radiance of primordial wisdom.

It is equally evident that in time the new structure must infuse the public con-sciousness with its strength. The foundations of our thinking are already changed and restructured by events, and no one can escape the restructuration for too long. Imperceptibly the new structure will acquire validity for all as a matter of course. Those who do not accept it and persist in the old will be left aside in the course of the next generations. The final efforts toward survival by the various forms of syncretism were surpassed by the efficient mental consciousness-potency of Christianity. Ow-ing to an increased technologization and a false application of time to technology, the deficient mental structure—rational consciousness—will dig its own grave. It will be surpassed by a more intensified Christianity, by the integral consciousness. This is not a prophecy but a presentation of a natural unfolding vividly manifest in the Spanish-Mexican, and Swiss-Austrian examples cited earlier (pp. 5 f., 8, and 273).

The immense processes of transformation like those taking place today, and the far- and deep-reaching mutations that have been occurring for generations and extend into the present, are neither accidental, nor explicable in ontological, exis-tential or sociological terms. They are latent in origin; they are always back-leaps, so to speak, into the *already (ever-)present future.* This is the way in which origin, bud-ding and unfolding in space and time, emerges on earth and in our daily lives. The divine spiritual source and future of that which appears to us as an event ought never be forgotten when attempts are made at mere explanation. And origin, from which every moment of our lives draws its sustenance, is by nature divine and spiritual. Anyone who denies this denies himself, and there is today a considerable number who do.

Those who do not deny but rather affirm it in their open-mindedness and simplicity are already the co-creators of aperspectivity, of the integral consciousness structure. This is founded on the emergent consciousness and on the transparency of the whole. Once only did the disciples of Christ perceive his transfiguration. This singular diaphaneity of the world on earth, this unique manifestation of spiritual power, is not a past event. The annual celebration of Pentecost, among other events, evidences this. Regarded historically, humanity is perhaps living in the three-day period of descent into hell. Have we passed through this descent in the events of the first half of our century? However this may be, in those days only Christ's followers could see his transfiguration, but one day it will be the larger community. It is not accidental that the sense for transparency is irrupting everywhere.

What does all of this have to do with daily life? Something decisive, since what is emerging in the greater context must be concurrently co-prepared in the lesser. This does not mean that it is the number of those who realize and live the new that is decisive; decisive is the intensity with which the individuals live the new.

Anyone with a sense of detachment from himself also gains a detachment from the world, including a sense of tolerance. Today everyone is in a position to achieve this within the scope of his possibilities. Everyone has the means today to achieve self-transparency, and to give an account of the conditions, temporal limits, and the limitations of his feelings, thought, and actions. Everyone today can become aware of the various temporal forms which all point to origin, and everyone can experience timelessness in the union of conjugal love, the timelessness of nightly deep-sleep, the experience of rhythmic complementarity of natural temporicity which unites him in every heart-beat and rhythmic breath with the courses of the universe; and everyone can employ measured time. The magic, mythical, and mental structures may, in other words, become transparent, particularly in their ever-valid effectualities as our co-constituents. This is a beginning if only because the individual learns to see himself as a whole as the interrelationship and interplay of magic unity, mythical complementarity, and mental conceptuality and purposefulness. Only as a whole man is man in a position to perceive the whole.

But does not our life in the factory and the office, the senselessness of our labors today, automation, mechanization, and technologization stand in the way? On the contrary: all the more clearly will the false form of time's irruption be evident as expressed in motoricity and the scramble for worthless "goods" and the like which must be overcome. Our environment, the factories and offices, is our own creation, and we have allowed the formlessness of this void to be imposed on us by the empty mechanisms. Such an environment will change to the extent that we are able to realize our task, and for this everyone has the requisite leisure and sense of obligation. Between the hours of earning a living and bedtime there are many hours to be used wisely, though not for the superficial gain of becoming "cultured" or "learned." The hours and days are to be spent not only purposively but also meaningfully. What is today called "free time" must not be squandered leisurely but employed to acquire "time-freedom."

Epochs of great confusion and general uncertainty in a given world contain the slumbering, not-yet-manifest seeds of clarity and certainty. The manifestations of the aperspectival world evinced above show that these seeds are already pressing toward realization. This means that we are approaching the "zenith" of confusion and are thus nearing the necessary breakthrough. (The past decade alone—since 1954—has demonstrated the accuracy of this claim. On the one hand there is a further entrenchment of rationalism, materialism, frenzy for progress, and senseless activity, all effected by time-anxiety. On the other, although less dramatic, is the increase of aperspectival manifestations, as we have seen.) The confusion in the individual's everyday life, his lack of fulfillment in his work, his isolation in the masses, his powerlessness over against the idle running of anonymity, whether of mechanisms or of bureaucracies—this insecurity and enslavement are only reflections of the general malaise.

The untenability of this situation is as obvious as the fact that it must be overcome. What is valid in general is also valid in particular, in the individual. The restructuration of the entire reality has begun; it is up to us whether its final irruption, its final consolidation, will occur with our help, or despite our lack of insight. If it occurs with our assistance, then we shall avoid a universal catastrophe; if it occurs without our aid, then the valid completion of the present mutation will cost greater pain and torment than we have suffered during the past sixty years. All work, the genuine work which we must achieve, is that which is most difficult and painful: the work on ourselves. If we do not freely take upon ourselves this pre-acceptance of the pain and torment, they will be visited upon us in an otherwise necessary individual and universal collapse. Anyone disassociated from his origin and his spiritually sensed task acts against origin. Anyone who acts against it has neither a today nor a tomorrow.

Each attempted and successful clarification of the confusion in our daily lives and actions, each interception of anxiety, each achieved grain of certainty, each distanciation from oneself—regardless of how slight—each discarded prejudice and resentment: these are necessary achievements in order to establish the new reality and to obtain for each and all a sense of meaningfulness. Everyone is free to achieve this. Whoever gambles away this freedom has gambled and lost his life and death.

What of the millions who remain deaf? Their joys—power and possession—will dwindle over the coming years, either owing to their false and destructive use, whereby these "goods" destroy each other, or to the restructuring of consciousness which unmasks the unimportance of these false values. Such unmasking will rob many of their material pseudo-security and place on them social demands to which they cannot adequately respond.

The new attitude will be consolidated only when the individual can gradually begin to disregard his ego. As long as our thinking is exclusively self-centered the world will remain fragmented. At best the "Thou" will become visible to the "I"; but never the whole. The danger today of ego-isolation and ego-loss, indeed ego-cide, has been discussed above (p. 153 f.). Self-isolation is a withdrawal in the face of the masses, the deficient mode of community. In time it will lead to the loss of the ego and to ego-cide, since the flight back to the masses brings about the destruction and annulment of the "I." What is necessary is neither egotism nor egolessness. Egolessness is a deficient regression into magic while a mere egotism is a deficient continuation in the mental-rational structure. Only the overcoming of the "I," the concomitant overcoming of egolessness and egotism, places us in the sphere of ego-freedom, of the achronon and transparency. Ego-freedom means freedom from the self; it is not a loss or a denial of the "I", not an ego-cide but an overcoming of ego.[2] Consciousness of self was the characteristic of the mental consciousness structure; freedom from the "I" is the characteristic of the integral consciousness structure.

For someone able to place the whole ahead of his ego in his daily affairs (although this does not mean a loss of ego), for someone able to act out of ego-freedom, the world and even his daily life will become transparent. And when this happens, the events and phenomena of his surroundings will set themselves right. Both the social and the technological systems (which result from an over-emphasized rationality whose deficient emphasis has made them possible) will restructure themselves since they are incongruous with the new mode of realization and its restructuration of the world.

Since this mode of realization excludes a simplistic goal-orientation which permits it to function in only a limited area of reality, the surrounding world will be altered in all its aspects as we alter them to correspond to the requirements of our respective consciousness structure. Then will the nightmare of our times come to an end: the false employment of machines whose empty motion and mere motoricity threaten to become autonomous. Then it will become apparent that both they and the most recent technology are our physical projections (see p. 132) which we can retrieve and master, particularly since there are occasional four-dimensional inceptions present in technology.

Fedor Stepun says that the film corresponds to our wish to be released from the three-dimensional gravitational pull;[3] yet today it is still a machine that force-feeds images.[4] Radio's capacity to nearly nullify space and time; the temporal telescoping of spatial distances by the airplane; accelerators such as the cyclotron which are able to release atomic events and reactions—all of these technological achievements can become liberators if their underlying time-components become transparent for us.

Since it institutes an empty movement, present-day technology is an unmastered time; it is the most impressive example of rational man's failure when faced with his task of resolving the problem of time. Instead of intensifying time, man has quantified it by rational thinking into a cascading motion. This failure, which encroaches on our daily lives with increasing force, will be successfully corrected when the awareness of the foundations and the true demands of a genuine technology are pioneered. This awareness will restructure technology to the same degree that it is now about to reshape our entire reality. Then, in the most successful realizations, the "every-day" will be an "all (i.e., universal)-day.".

1   See in this connection our paper "Die vierte Dimension als Zeichen der neuen Welt-sicht," *Die neue Weltschau* (Stuttgart: Deutsche Verlags-Anstalt, 1952), p. 270; also in *In der Bewährung* (Bern: Francke, ^{2}1969), p. 65 f., and *Gesamtausgabe*, v/ı, p. 215, where we stated: "The new (aperspectival) age has overcome the rational era just passed—an era marked by strong anti-religious feeling—and is at the same time the counter current to the unchristian nihilism of our time. This also implies that the aperspectival age can no longer, and will not be anti-religious. Only rational thought is anti-religious; arational thought, by reason of its transparency, will enter into a new and intensified relationship to religion. We must not forget that the Christian notion of transfiguration is of a transparent and time-free nature. The new age, brought on by the new consciousness structure, will be distinguished by a profoundly Christian religious intensification; but its religiosity will be less emotional. It will be a religiosity of insight and presentation." We will return to the question of transfiguration in the next section.

2   We would add that in addition to Max Brod (see text, p. 432), René Le Senne has striven for a transcendence or surpassal of ego in his characterological psychology via a realization of *soi*, of the "Itself." This process is to enable the individual to acquire new *valeurs* (values), to be open vis-à-vis the universal, and acknowledge the predominance of the spiritual; see René Le Senne, *La destinée personelle* (Paris: Flammarion, 1951).

3   Fedor Stepun, "Das Wesen des Films: ein soziologischer Versuch," *Soziologische For-*

schung in unserer Zeit; Leopold von Wiese zum 75. Geburtstag dargebracht (Köln: Westdeutscher Verlag, 1951), p. 246.

4   Our space here is insufficient for an extended treatment of the film. What is symptomatic of the film—dissolution of static images into movement—demonstrates to what extent it is a temporic attempt. The possibilities of film even today have not been sufficiently recognized, even where it has been utilized to invert or suspend the sequence or course of events by means of montage. All such manipulations of time are still merely experimental. In this regard several remarks by Sergei M. Eisenstein are revealing; one is that montage ought not to be of the kind employed by Griffith and the American film, i.e., merely "tempo" and a means for sequencing or stringing together, but as potential montage able to burst the confines of the "four-sided cage" of the frame (the spatial construct), and, via montage impulses between individual montage sequences, explode the conflict of action or plot. Thus the time element is here still misused; time is an "explosion." As so frequently happens, the negative, destructive aspect comes to the fore at the outset, even in the case of experiments with film, a phenomenon we have repeatedly encountered. We should recall the initial negative effects of atomic physics, of the psychic inflation threatening psychoanalysis, of the shattering of space in painting, and of the dadaistic dissolution of language in poetry. This phenomenon might well be described as a "process of creative destruction," as J. A. Schumpeter has called it. See S. M. Eisenstein's last book, *Film Form* (1948), from which excerpts were published serially in *Sight and Sound* 19 (new series), 7 (November, 1950), pp. 294–297; and Joseph A. Schumpeter, *Kapitalismus, Sozialismus und Demokratie* (Bern: Francke, ²1950), p. 134.

11

The Two-Fold Task

"What is done today in the name of art is impotence and untruth; this includes music after Wagner as well as painting after Manet, Cézanne, Leibl, and Menzel. Where do we find the great personagés who could justify the claim that there is an art of inescapable, fated necessity? Let us seek the self-evident and requisite task awaiting such art."

These sentences were written in 1917 by Oswald Spengler and remained unchanged in the second edition of 1922;[1] as his remarks in other contexts show, they do not pertain only to the arts.

Today, a generation later, we no longer need to seek the great "personages" (how dated this term sounds!). Those who, each in his own area, have begun to change our world-conception into a new world perception have been allowed to speak in the preceding chapters. Nor do we need to seek any longer new tasks. The "self-evident and requisite task" awaiting us is now clear; it is unmistakable, the obvious consequence of all the temporic efforts and inceptions of the last five generations. It is a necessary task since without it we would give ourselves up, rather than achieving what has been given us to do.

Since Spengler did not discern a task either for the arts or for the other areas of our lives, he wrote off the West. Nevertheless, although we are in a similar if not more catastrophic post-war situation than Spengler (who had a precursor in the Wagner of the "Twilight of the Gods" and a successor in the Alfred Weber of the "Fourth Man"),[2] it has befallen our generation to perceive and resolve the task entrusted to us.

Then as now, our situation is fraught with danger since we are confronted by a two-fold task. To the extent that the task is compelling, the danger is also increased: if we fail to fulfill the task, we abandon ourselves.

Throughout the preceding discussion, we have constantly indicated the possibility of this surrender. The aperspectival world is not yet consolidated and everything is still in flux; above all, the modern addiction to novelty, ultra-modernism, the rejection of heritage, of tradition in the best sense of the word, do not belong to it. On the contrary, the first part of our study should have demonstrated that the insightful recognition of our foundations—which modernists wish to discard absolutely—are of decisive importance. It will depend on us whether the problem of aperspectival time is resolved successfully, or whether it is misunderstood in terms of the deficient, rationalistic mentality. A further rationalization of time would lead to a general atomization, whereas the achronization of time would transcend the contemporary situation toward constitution and consolidation of the efficient new consciousness structure.

If we surrender to the destructive deficient powers, if we ascribe to rationality a character of exclusive validity, if we continue to measure time with inappropriate measure, then we shall have indulged in mis-measurement, a hubris (*Ver-messen* = "mismeasure," *Vermessenheit* = hubris, presumption) which is not only inadequate but runs counter to the task. If we are able to assist in the breakthrough of originary power which is irrupting to manifestation, instead of assisting the powers of unbounded machination, we can escape destruction. Since the dangers of self-destruction are great, let us briefly summarize them. (These summary remarks are merely simplified restatements of those reservations discussed *in extenso* in their respective sections of the main text. To evaluate them in any other way would be a misunderstanding.)

In mathematics there is a danger of atomization and deficient quantification unless it can be kept from collapse into mere logistics and statistics (see p. 369).

The geometric-physical treatment of time in physics has led to an atomization that can be restrained only if the qualitative elements of Planck's conception can be brought to awareness, and if the achronic structure of "matter," implicitly formulated by Heisenberg, is taken to heart.

The exclusion of the spiritual dimension from the inquiry into life processes will lead biology to the atomization of humanity—the robot-like propagation of artificial insemination as a mechanical exaggeration of vitalism is a good example of this—unless insights such as those of Adolf Portmann are respected. If the efforts of "molecular biology" are successful, and applicable to "controlled" genetic processes (almost a certain possibility for the 1970s), humanity will be endangered in such a way that the inconceivable and catastrophic consequences of unleashed nuclear power—and it is horrible just to mention this—would appear almost harmless by comparison.

In psychology the dangers lie in psychic inflation and its deformation into psychism; in the psychic obsession that threatens to atomize the soul and drown man in the artificially stimulated whirlpool of hyperamplified "archetypes" and "complexes," especially when psychology forgets or even psychologizes the spiritual dimension; and in its application to the office or factory for the purpose of greater "output."

In philosophy the danger lies in non-commitment; mere concepts, categories, exegeses, analyses, and systems no longer lead to an intensified search for truth but rather to a complete dissolution and, ultimately, atomization of thought.

In jurisprudence the prevalence of "use value" and the privileges of anonymous sectors (trusts as well as governments), together with a refusal to recognize the basis and relationhips between property and work, may lead to a decline of a qualitative justification for life, thereby destroying the structure of human interrelationships.

Sociology, whether political, economic, or cultural, is threatened by an ultimate loss of quality in that the individual is threatened by a resubmersion into the anonymous mass, and consequent atomization.

Among the dual sciences, parapsychology is exposed to spiritualistic occultism (a kind of psychic materialism), an occultism hoping to find a spirituality of the "beyond," although it usually finds only traces of materialistic spiritualism, that is, products of psychic decomposition.

The progressive accentuation of the metric-motoric elements of music (as in the case of Stravinsky) would eventually lead to a complete divesting of meaning and an atomization of tones (and it remains to be seen whether electronic music can escape this danger).

As Frank Lloyd Wright has pointed out, the continuous construction of skyscrapers and prefabricated houses will lead to a catastrophe in architecture. The frenzied quantification is tantamount to a barricading of man, a reduction of life to the ant-hill and social atomization instead of freedom.

The atomization has partially come about in painting. The misplaced use of the psychic aspects of time, the unrestrained hurling of mostly pathological and inflated psychic contents onto canvas (in Surrealism), the disruption and explosion of spatio-corporeal forms without the requisite experience of spatial restructuration, are exemplary of this, even in some works of Picasso.

In poetry and indeed in language in all forms, including everyday usage, the threat of dissolution is imminent. The misunderstood virulence of the temporal component, the "rush and race" against time, results in the "hounding to death" of language. The mania for acronyms, the random use of words, the mass of daily publications are all indications of the threat of atomization to language.

In everyday life, few are aware that the motorization, mechanization, and technologization impose quantitative conditions on man that lead to an immeasurable loss of freedom. Machines, film, press, radio lead not only to mediocrity and a dependency relationship, but also to an increasing de-individuation and atomization of the individual. The extent of these dangers is exemplified by present-day sports. What was once play has become a frenzy of record-setting. The attendant devotion of the individual—submerging himself in the mass of spectators—to a worthless phenomenon is a symptom of the contemporary transitional era. The addiction to speed reveals the deep anxiety in the face of time; each new record is a further step toward the "killing of time" (and thus of life). The preoccupation with records is a clear sign of the predominant role of time. Even the mass psyche is enslaved by time; it attempts to surpass and free itself from time in a negative way without realizing that each new record brings us closer to the death of time instead of leading to freedom from it. The addiction to overcoming time negatively is everywhere evident. The previous thresholds of time are surpassed everywhere; not only via the radio but through supersonic aircraft, or (another extreme example) by medical attempts to extend human longevity. Precisely these exertions, fleeing into quantification, are a temporal flight born of the time-anxiety which dominates our daily lives.

These are a few of the obvious dangers resulting from the mistaken solutions and applications of time. If they are not stopped by fulfillment of the task assigned to us, they will lead to relinquishment of ourselves, and the final loss of mankind through atomization and dissolution. Since the pronouncement of God's death there has been a danger of man's death. From the day when the materialized powers began their struggle with the newly emerging potency, from the day when such powers began to hunt time to death (and are in turn being hunted to death), the Mephistophelian of *Faust* has assumed dominance. The divine is no longer perceived by man; at best, man reluctantly rationalizes it and obstructs the perception of origin as it endeavors to transform itself into time-freedom. The head of Zeus which once gave birth to Athena (the well-aimed thought), fell to the guillotine when thought began to usurp the spirit; the gods and the conceptualized paternal god were beheaded. On this place of judgement and scaffold the opposing principle is celebrating its heinous surfacing: where the symbol of luminous life-powers, the sun-king, is dethroned and decapitated, where the *Roi Soleil*, the sun, has set, emerge the shadowless "Schlemiels."

The light of that greater invisible sun—perhaps it is "the whole" of whose light our sun is a mere reflection—was not perceived. The break with the mental did not render the whole transparent—this capability is only now beginning to gain ground; instead, the counterprinciple of the decapitated and dethroned came to the forefront of power. Mankind's journey to hell began. Faust does not solve the Mephistophelian problem; Mephisto disappears, a "diabolus ex machina." And the result is James Hogg's defense of the Satanic; (it is significant that his defense recently became known on the continent via André Gide).[3] In his great poem, Mallarmé himself wrestles with the satanic-demonic principle and includes it as the fourth principle in his major poem.[4] Like the Gnostics and alchemists, he anticipates the quaternity theory, which was also postulated by C. G. Jung in his psychology with the inclusion of Satan. (When will we notice how limited such correspondences and contrasts are, for instance "God versus Satan"? When will we cease to express the whole in a psychic-mythical framework or in mental systems as a "pole" or as a "magnitude" respectively?)

It is the same demonic principle once known as the "diabolus in musica," the forbidden harmony of the tritone now audible in the new music.[5] The first movement (among others) of Bela Bartók's Quartet No. 5 (1934) is similar to a medieval witch dance and deliberately exploits the tritone.[6] Is Paul Valéry's *Mon Faust*,[7] by contrast, a supersession of this principle? His Faust chides Mephisto that whatever he had wished and willed for man has been achieved since Goethe's time by man himself, leaving Mephisto no power over him. Did Valéry foresee the end of man's descent into hell? Does the insight into Mephisto's powerlessness restore to mankind the strength it needs today more than ever?

The exhaustion of a consciousness structure has always manifested itself in an emptying of all values, with a consistent change of efficient qualitative to deficient quantitative values. It is as if life and spirit withdrew from those who are not co-participants in the particular new mutation. As myth overdetermined and replaced magic, the effective strength of the magic spell changed into mere bewitchment, and finally into empty quantitative rituals. The Tibetan prayer wheels furnish a good example. When mind overdetermined and replaced myth, the psychic chaos became evident in the innumerable monsters and demons of not only Indian but other far-eastern temples, as well as in the fragmentation of Greek myth described by Karl Kerényi.[8]

Today, while the integral is overdetermining and dissolving the mental-rational consciousness, the mental capacity of thought is being mechanized by the robots of calculation—computers—and this is being emptied and quantified.[9] Prayer wheels, the fragmentation of myth, and computers are expressions of man who remains confined in his familiar consciousness frequency while the necessary "tide-turning" new consciousness mutation begins to superimpose itself over the exhausted consciousness structure. Each excess of quantification leads to power-lessness, vacuity and helplessness. Wherever this is evident it is an indication that the inadequate consciousness structure is already surpassed. In this light, the computers are a negative omen of the new consciousness structure and its strength.

In the computers, the deficient mental world is surrendering itself and manifesting success in our task. And there can be no question that our task will be resolved, since it originates in necessity. The only open question is whether it will be resolved soon; if not, the solution would demand unthinkable sacrifices of those who are surrendering themselves. The number of those who will experience the solution depends on the temporal intensity of the emergent consciousness structure. If the task is not accomplished in time, it will lead to an almost complete self-surrender of mankind. This is the decisive two-fold sense of our task.

1   Oswald Spengler, Der Untergang des Abendlandes (Munich: Beck, ²1923), I, p. 379; the italics are Spengler's.

2   See in this regard our paper "Auflösung oder Überwindung der Persönlichkeit" in the series "Kommt der vierte Mensch?" (Radio Beromünster, Winter 1952), published the same year under the same title (Zürich, Vienna, and Stuttgart-Europa: Verlag), and reprinted in In der Bewährung (Bern: Francke, ²1962), p. 111 f.; Gesamtausgabe, V/I, p. 259 ff.

3   James Hogg, Vertrauliche Aufzeichnungen und Bekenntnisse eines gerechtfertigten Sünders, introd. André Gide (Stuttgart: Deutsche Verlags-Anstalt, 1951).

4   Claude Roulet, Elucidation du Poème de Stéphane Mallarmé "Un Coup de Dés jamais n'abolira le Hasard" (Neuchâtel: Ides et Calendes, 1943), p. 23.

5   On this subject see Hanns Hasting, "Zur Frage der modernen Musik," Stimmen der Zeit 142 (73, 10; July 1948), 304.

6   A remark made by Bartók to his friend Karl Kerényi, the Hungarian mythologist, who in turn shared it with the author. As Pierre Bourgeois has pointed out to me, J. S. Bach has also used the tritone, albeit in a manner differing from Bartók's. It occurs three times in the St. Matthew Passion: in the alto recitative "Ach Golgotha, unselges Golgotha" (in the syllables "-ges Gol-"); it is again used in the phrase "ans Kreuz" ("Der Segen und das Heil der Welt wird als ein Fluch ans Kreuz gestellt") in the same aria. The tritone also occurs in the chorus "Lasst ihn kreuzigen" (Let him be crucified) in the syllable "kreuz."

The degree to which the basic current of the "new" is sensed even by those who attempt to bring it to the fore with means inappropriate to the times is illustrated by a remark of Jean-Paul Sartre: "What I am after is the ever-present expression of complexity"—which, however, cannot be attained by playing off God against Satan in a dualistic manner as Sartre does. The case of T. S. Eliot is quite different. In an essay cited earlier, "Die drei Sphären," we noted the presentation and simultaneity, the interplay of several spheres of reality in Eliot's Family Reunion. Eliot later told the author that he had not consciously striven for this while writing the play. This mode of presentation—no longer merely "complex" but integral—Eliot later underscored in an address given in Germany in 1949: "It is in fact the prerogative of poetic verse drama to be able to show us simultaneously several levels of reality" (T. S. Eliot, "The Aims of Poetic Drama"). See

Jean Gebser, "Die drei Sphären; Bemerkungen zu T. S. Eliots 'Die Familienfeier,' " *Almanach für die Bücherfreunde* (Zürich: Europa-Verlag/Oprecht, 1945); *Gesamtausgabe*, VI, p. 210–214. T. S. Eliot, "Die Aufgaben des Versdramas," *Die Neue Rundschau* 61, 2 (1950), p. 201 f.; and T. S. Eliot, "Die Familienfeier," German translation by Gentiane (and Jean) Gebser for the premier in the German-speaking countries, Festival Week, Zürich, 1945; manuscript in the archive of the *Schauspielhaus*, Zürich.

7   Paul Valéry, *Mon Faust* (Paris: NRF/Gallimard, 1946).

8   Karl Kerényi, *Die Mythologie der Griechen* (Zürich: Rhein, 1951).

9   More on this subject in our paper in the collection *Kommt der vierte Mensch?* (note 2), pp. 259–266.

12

The Concretion
of the Spiritual

Whatever happens on the earth—man must share the responsibility. But the earth itself is not just something here and now; it is no more the center of the universe than is the sun. Both the heliocentric and the geocentric world-views have become obsolete in favor of the whole which, since it is not spatially localizable, has no center.[1] What happens to the earth—and the earth is nothing but an event which in materialization has become progressively slower—originates in more encompassing and spatio-temporally non-localizable interconnections.

It is also a star among stars, just as humans are only human among other human beings. On its great journey across the millennia it hastens through the changing landscapes of "heaven," transforming its own countenance and man's. In man, who is the consciousness of the earth and its interconnections with distances and proximities, the influences which affect our entire solar system as one system among many have their enduring effect. All efforts to conceive of these factors in spatial and temporal terms are futile, and yet it is certain that they can be realized by us in a space-time-free manner.

Of course, nothing that exists exists for its own sake; it exists for the sake of the whole. In origin, the whole is pregiven for man; it takes on for man its conscious character in the time-free present, for consciousness is not restricted to time and space. It cannot be concretized in conceptuality since conceptuality deals only with abstractions and absolutes. It can be fathomed only dimly in vital, magic life, and is realizable through imagination and experience, as in myth and mysticism, only in a twilight of consciousness. It is approached in thought, but thought immediately closes itself off since in its process of deduction discursive thought always excludes any openness in its compulsion to system.

The new mutation of consciousness, on the other hand, as a consequence of arationality, receives its decisive stamp from the manifest perceptual emergence of the spiritual. (The poets' rejection of the psychic and mental aspects as a "source" of poetic creation, as discussed in chapter 3, section 2 of Part II above, and their turn toward the spiritual are only one indication among many of this circumstance.)

Two apocryphal statements of Christian doctrine clarify in their way what is meant here: "This world is a bridge, cross it but do not make of it your dwelling place,"[2] and "I have chosen you before the earth began."[3] They point to the spiritual origin prior to all spatio-temporal materialization. We may regard such materialization as a bridge that makes possible the merging or coalescence, the *concrescere* of origin and the present. The great church father Irenaeus presumably had these sayings in mind when he stated: "Blessed is he who was before the coming of man."[4] We have seen him; he revealed himself in space and time. In his departure he was beheld by his disciples in his transparency, a transparency appropriate only to the spiritual origin (if anything can be appropriated to it), the transparency which a time-free and ego-free person can presentiate in the most fortunate certainty of life. The grand and painful path of consciousness emergence, or, more appropriately, the unfolding and intensification of consciousness, manifests itself as an increasingly intense luminescence of the spiritual in man.

Throughout the millennia the traditionalists, the "initiates," have seen man's previous journey as a decline, a departure from the affinity to and a distanciation from origin. Painful as this distanciation may be, it has served the requisite intensification of consciousness. Only distanciation contains the possibility for the awakening of consciousness.

The phenomenon releasing origin is spiritual, and with each consciousness mutation it becomes more realizable by man. With respect to the presently emerging mutation we may speak of a concretion of the spiritual. The word "concretion" here is not to be considered as the antithesis of "abstraction." Quality and quantity, or efficiency and deficiency as we have posited them, are an expression and modes of effectuality of various degrees of *intensity.* And with this in mind, we specifically speak of the spiritual and not simply of spirit. Our deliberations in the first part (p. 229 ff.) have shown that the concept of "spirit" is replete with such a multitude of aspects inherent in the previous consciousness structures, be they vital, experiential or imagistic-conceptual, that this aspectuation is necessarily unable to impart-in-truth a clear description of the concerns of heaven and earth, God and man. Concretion, then, does not mean a transformation of the intangible into something tangible or substantial, but rather the completion of *con-crescere,*[5] that is, the coalescence of the spiritual with our consciousness.

Since the spiritual is not bound to the vital, to the psychic, or to the mental, but rather shines through to us in their efficacy—be it vital, experiential, conceptual, or reflective—a new possibility for perceptual consciousness of the spiritual for the whole of mankind one day had to shine forth. Previously the spiritual was realizable only approximately in the emotional darkness of the magical, in the twilight of imagination in the mythical, and in the brightness of abstraction in the mental. The mode of realization now manifesting itself assures that in accordance with its particular nature, the spiritual is not only given emotionally, imaginatively, abstractly, or conceptually. It also ensures that in accordance with our new capacity it is also perceptible concretely as it begins to coalesce with our consciousness. This will have presumably shed some light on our second principle (p. 6 f.): the shining through (diaphaneity or transparency) is the form of appearance (epiphany) of the spiritual.

This diaphaneity is all-encompassing: it is a transparency of space and time as well as of light, of matter and soul as well as of life and death. An utterance of Max Picard that "Everything that stems from spirit is transparent"[6] understates, for the transparency of the spiritual pervades the whole and the whole is transparency. Thus the perception and imparting of truth, the "verition" of diaphaneity, supersede the mere mental-rational validity of antitheses and is the realization of the achronon shining forth in it. This time-free present (the achronon) is just as real and efficacious a time-form as those that have preceded it in consciousness, and failure to recognize them would impede its realization. We should note that this synairetic process, which makes the integral consciousness structure accessible, is a new capacity, and not a mere sum of the old. Anyone who understands this synairetic process to be a summation is thinking mentally and synthetically; consequently he fails to perceive arationally and does not attain the basis for the meaningful solution to our task.

It is in this arational sense also that the designation "integral consciousness structure"—of which today's man, in mutation, is the bearer—should be understood. This designation refers to man as a whole to the extent that he can constitute himself as a consequence of the new mutation. It does not contain even the shadow of hubris, and because of its Christian stamp, is protected from all misinterpretations such as those of Nietzsche and the Gnostics, whose superiority doctrines include claims of power and similarity to the divine. This must be clearly understood.

The extrication from the mental-rational, which man is today accomplishing; his increasing capability, not just of viewing the world as a representation but also of perceiving it as transparency; the supersession of the once necessary duality which enabled the detachment requisite for consciousness-intensification: all these processes of restructuration point to a fundamentally new mode of realization, overdetermining and mutating from the previous realization.

Once man sought truth; this was achieved over the millennia by philosophy; once man believed truth, and this bond was made possible over the millennia by *relegio* and later through religion. And wherever we think and believe, those attainments endure. But for those capable of "a-waring" the whole, the true, this "verition" is no longer a philosophical search nor a faith beset by doubts but a discovery without that search which throughout the ages was, as it were, merely the preparation.

The undivided, ego-free person who no longer sees parts but realizes the "Itself," the spiritual form of being of man and the world, perceives the whole, the diaphaneity present "before" all origin which suffuses everything. For him there is no longer heaven or hell, this world or the other, ego or world, immanence or transcendence; rather, beyond the magic unity, the mythical complementarity, the mental division and synthesis is the perceptible whole. To this he does not need the retrospective bond (religion). It is pre-ligious; its presence is achronic, time-free, and corresponds to man's freedom from ego. Magic *pro-ligio,* mythical *relegio,* mental religion become co-supports for praeligio(n) which is the intensified and overdetermined expression of all the others. What is "before" space and time, what has become ever more intensely realizable via the time-lessness, temporicity, time and space (owing to the various consciousness structures), becomes perceptible in conscious achronicity. The pre-temporal becomes time-free, vacuity becomes plenitude, and in transparency the spiritual comes to perception: origin is present. In truth we ware the whole, and the whole wares us.

1   Seen in this way, one could say today: the *center is everywhere*. But this does not in-
        clude the previously unthinkable demand on the inner security of the individual with
        respect to himself and the whole; see Jean Gebser, "Zu den Bildern von Hans Haffen-
        richter," *Baukunst und Werkform* 10, 1 (Nürnberg, 1957), pp. 10–11. Our statement that
        ultimately even the heliocentric world view no longer has duration and stability—and it
        has a limited validity only to the extent that we consider it in relation to our small solar
        system—is justified by the discovery of extragalactic star systems. This discovery, too, has
        brought about an opening up: an opening of the sky, a removal of barriers, whose
        implications for our lives, our thought and perceptions, only very few persons have
        hitherto realized in consciousness; see Jean Gebser, *In der Bewährung* (Bern: Francke,
        ²1969), p. 114; *Gesamtausgabe*, V/I, p. 291 f.
2   See Benedikt Godeschalk, ed., *Die versprengten Worte Jesu* (Munich: Hyperion, 1922),
        p. 88.
3   Ibid., p. 104.
4   Ibid., p. 129.
5*   For evidence that the word "concrete" is derived from *concrescere*, see Hermann
        Menge, *Lateinisch-deutsches Schulwörterbuch mit besonderer Berücksichtigung der
        Etymologie* (Berlin: Langenscheidt, 1908), p. 151; Walde/Hofmann, *Lateinisches Etymo-
        logisches Wörterbuch* (Heidelberg: Winter, ³1938), I, p. 288; *Shorter Oxford English Dic-
        tionary* (Oxford: Clarendon, ³1959), I, p. 363.
6   Max Picard, *Die unerschütterliche Ehe* (Zürich: Rentsch, 1942), p. 105.

Postscript

At a time when mankind is suffering (in the West) from scepticism and suspicion or (in the Soviet bloc)[1] from ideological anxiety, anyone audacious enough to recall some basic values that run counter to the superficial course of events and seem to lack any immediate "efficiency" in a world given over to quantification is all too readily dismissed as being, in the familiar clichés, "unrealistic" and "idealistic." These are perhaps the most innocuous of the terms used by those who confuse realism with material utility and thus fall prey to a dualistic fallacy even where it has nothing to do with idealism.[2] As a type, they lack perception of those powers of which realism and idealism are only conceptual and classifying aspects. In addition there is the obstinacy resisting change which emerges even where it is obvious that it is unable to resolve an intractable problem. A person for whom the present, even during his or her finest hours, is no more than a time-bound moment, will not participate in the emerging transformation. Only those will succeed for whom the present becomes a time-free origin, a perpetual plenitude and source of life and spirit from which all decisive constellations and formations are completed.

It is quite understandable that without this awareness of the ever-present origin much of what has been presented on the previous pages may sound unacceptable, for it is not amenable to discursive, measuring thinking. In particular it will be nearly unacceptable to those who in their technological overconfidence fail to recognize the seriousness of our situation and insistently reiterate that we have "advanced majestically" with our "progress." Yet any dispassionate observer of our contemporary events who endeavors to go beyond the confines of his own life as a member and a participant of humanity, will have to concede that remarks as presented on these pages must be ventured. The era of irresponsible play with the "Twilight of men and the gods" should by now be over. The fact that our epoch is one of suffering should not mislead anyone into continuing to treat this suffering lightly or smugly, or bemoaning the uncertainty of the future. Each of us, after all, whether as individuals or as a species, suffers in accord with its measure. Our freedom is not to evade this measure, but to not let it overwhelm us. If we fulfill its demands, the future each of us carries within himself will be decided. A cheerful seriousness, able to "ware" in truth the primordial spiritual element, befits our generation. Like all ages, our generation too has its task. The author has endeavored to make this task as evident as is possible and seemly for one individual.

It is perhaps permissible in this connection to recall that it is not unimportant for someone who has something to put forward to know from what situation, from what stage, and from what structure of life he states what he has to say. Permit me to note that I am aware of the extent to which the problems take on various aspects depending on the circumstances, age, and the structure of one's own personal life. How an unresolved situation in one's own life, for example, when projected onto the world and its phenomena, can make the world's state of affairs seem to be an unresolved problem. Or how a profusion (or lack) of vital, or psychic, or mental discipline can tempt one to undisciplined utterances. Or how the ebb and flow of one's inner tides can alter the fundamental import of every statement.

The self-evident precondition of any statement with claims to universal validity is the awareness of such conditionalities and limitations so that one can fend them off. Without such awareness, without the true wakefulness inherent in such awareness, a responsible utterance is impossible. The fact that exactly twenty-one years have passed since the basic conception of this work was formed, and that its preparation and execution extended accordingly over various phases of life, can conceivably be considered a guarantee that the "new," for example, is not merely to be interpreted in a psychological sense as a generalization of the increase in anima-and-shadow awareness of the author's own personality. Nor is the naming of the new to be regarded as an outgrowth of that attitude familiar from its aggressive anti-traditionalism and intent on world betterment—the sign of those who dozed through their middle years or just let them slip past without ever learning the divine gift of balanced thinking. On the contrary, the manner in which we have here attempted to regard and describe things is today binding and efficient (in our sense) perhaps because it is obligated to the spiritual and not to some idols, ideals, or pseudo-realities.

What then could be of consequence if not the spiritual? Every tear, if we are permitted a metaphor here, can be said to express the sadness and suffering of the universe: the mute anguish of all the oceans, compressed into a single consuming droplet—just as it is equally less than any droplet, merely lachrymose and transitory like the rainfall or the oceans which too could pass away one day if the threatened visitation by fire becomes a reality. For who is to think of the rarer tears of joy? Who would be that audacious, knowing how painful and consuming they too can be?

We have not presented here a thesis. Theses are parts of rigidifying, perspectival thought. It has been our endeavor to open up the perception of the new reality and its corresponding mode of realization, "verition" or "a-waring," which is made possible by the new consciousness structure. The aperspectival manifestations were presented along with the tasks which they articulate, the dangers they conceal, the liberation to which they lead. It is incumbent on each individual, on his structure, detachment, and responsibility, to perceive their validity.

We have not attempted a synthesis but rather the discovery of the basic concern of our epoch. In this I have not limited myself to specialized areas since "the meaning is obscured if one sees only tiny, finished segments of being."[3] This saying of Chuang Tzu can perhaps justify my audacious attempt to furnish a more encompassing survey while remaining cognizant of the existing omissions. For someone concerned with the perception and imparting-in-truth, with the "verition" of the whole, however, what is absent is merely another form of what is present.

We have attempted to point toward clarification of a complex situation whose resolution will occur tomorrow, if not today. The manner in which this resolution will occur, its time and extent, its effectuality for us or for non-European mankind or even for a mankind that has undergone and survived peril-averting destruction, will depend on the extent of our conscious participation in the construction of a new reality. Anyone who resides in origin and the present is protected and sustained by life and the spirit.

In conclusion, my gratitude to all without whose friendship and trust this book most likely would not have been completed: to my friends of many years, and to the scientists of various disciplines, who have shown interest in the concern of this work on the basis of their broad understanding and have contributed many valuable suggestions.

Burgdorf (Canton of Berne), Switzerland, June 1952

Jean Gebser

Addendum: The deliberations in this postscript seem to me to have a validity today perhaps more than ever, and consequently I may be justified in leaving them unchanged.

Berne, June 1965

J. G.

1   The very fact that in the West ideologies are highly suspect today is a further indication that a deperspectivation and derigidification of our "attitude" to the world and its problems has already begun to enter the general awareness. On this subject see Jean Gebser, *In der Bewährung* (Bern and Munich: Francke, 1962), p. 150, and *Gesamtausgabe*, V/I, p. 297.

2   L. L. Whyte has stated this in a sense very close to ours: "the materialist and the idealist will become anachronistic reminders of the age before the unitary process was recognised"; see Lancelot Law Whyte, *The Next Development in Man* (London: The Cresset Press, 1944), p. 162. A German edition of the book, entitled *Die nächste Stufe der Menschheit*, was published by the Pan-Verlag, Zürich (presumably in 1948). It is basic to an understanding of Whyte's book that many of his courageous steps forward are illusory because he postulates a "unitary process," which invariably has a magic accentuation. And it should also be noted that he does not proceed beyond the Darwinian concept of evolution.

3   Dschuang Dsi, *Das wahre Buch vom südlicheñ Blütenland / Nan Hua Dscheng Ging*, trans. and commentary by Richard Wilhelm (Jena: Diederichs, 1940), p. 13.

Remarks on Etymology

Prefatory Note

In these remarks we are attempting to examine the word roots and the individual root-sounds in particular from an elemental standpoint, that is, as constituent elements whose inceptual unitary-magic configuration and auditory content we must leave intact if we are to discover their essential nature.

We are aware that our interpretation, like any other, is open to criticism. Such criticism is likely, first, if the magic component or content of the root sounds is rejected from a rationalistic standpoint. It is also possible because the requisite source material for such an undertaking is limited inasmuch as there are no "root dictionaries" (see note 8 on p. 157) available; we have been forced to feel our way along the root interconnections in a slow and painstaking way, guided only by our intuition. For a majority of our examples, their correctness has been corroborated by the references quoted, but a very few of our attributions should be considered for the time being as conjectures whose correctness will have to be decided by the etymologists with reference to our method of interpretation.

The remarks which follow are based primarily on the sources listed below (further sources will be noted in special cases where necessary), cited according to the following abbreviations:

B = Emile Boisacq, *Dictionnaire étymologique de la langue grecque* (Paris: Klincksieck, ²1923).

EM = A. Ernout & A. Meillet, *Dictionnaire étymologique de la langue latine* (Paris: Klincksieck, 1932).

KG = Friedrich Kluge, *Etymologisches Wörterbuch der deutschen Sprache*, edited by Alfred Götze (Berlin: de Gruyter, ¹¹1934).

M = Hermann Menge, *Lateinisch-deutsches Schulwörterbuch mit besonderer Berücksichtigung der Etymologie* (Berlin: Langenscheidt, 1908).

MG = Menge-Güthling, *Griechisch-deutsches und deutsch-griechisches Wörterbuch mit besonderer Berücksichtigung der Etymologie, I: Griechisch-deutsch*, by H. Menge (Berlin: Langenscheidt, 1910).

W =   Alois Walde, *Lateinisches etymologisches Wörterbuch* (Heidelberg: Winter, 1906)
WH =   Alois Walde, *Lateinisches etymologisches Wörterbuch*, edited by J. B. Hofmann; vol. I (A-L) (Heidelberg: Winter, ³1938); vol. II (M-Z) (Heidelberg: Winter, ³1940-1956).

First Remark on Etymology

The Root kĕl

The meaning of $\sqrt{}$ kel ($\sqrt{}$ = root) is "to hold, shelter, conceal (in the earth)"; see MG 296 and WH 195. The words listed below, in addition to those cited in the text (note 7, p. 156), all derive from this root:

kalypto (Greek) = to cloak, cover, cover up, veil: B 400, W xix, EM 167, MG 296;
Kalypso = Greek nymph: B 400, MG 296;
kalia (Greek) = nest: Mg 296, W 111, EM 167;
kalybe (Greek) = shelter, lodging, arbor: MG 296;
kalymma (Greek) = shroud, cover, veil: MG 296;
kalyx (Greek) = hull, husk, pod, calyx, cup, chalice: MG 296; Latin WH 400
      ($\sqrt{}$qel);
kylix (Greek) = cup: MG 296; Latin WH 400 ($\sqrt{}$qel);
kelyphos (Greek) = rind, bark: EM 167;
chroma (Greek) = color: WH 247;
chros (Greek) = skin: WH 247;
varna (Old Indian) = envelope, color: WH 247;
krypto (Greek) = conceal, hide: B 522 f., WH 297;
krypte (Greek) = crypt: B 522 f., WH 297;
kali, kalika (Sanskrit) = bud: MG 296, Latin WH 400 ($\sqrt{}$qel);
calix (Latin) = sources as for kalyx above;
Kelch (German) = chalice (as for kalyx);
celare (Latin) = to shelter, conceal: EM 166 f., MG 296, WH 196;
cc-culare (Latin) = to shelter, conceal (as for celare);
oc-cultum (Latin) = secret (as for celare);
clam (Latin) = secret(ly): EM 486, WH 196 f.;
caligo (Latin) = darkness, night: M 101, MG 296;
cella (Latin) = chamber, cell: EM 167, KG 295, 305, MG 296, WH 196 f.;
Keller (German) = cellar (as for cella);
Klause (German) = cell, closet (as for cella);
Zelle (German) = cell (as for cella);
hell (German) = bright, light: KG 239, 244;
Höhle (German) = cave(rn): MG 296, KG 294, 295, 309, 707 (see text above, p. 126
      and note 7, p. 156);
Hölle (German) = hell (as for Höhle);
Halle (German) = hall (as above);
Helm (German) = helmet (as above);
hohl (German) = hollow (as above);
(Frau) Holle (German) = ["Character in Germanic mythology, leader of the wild

Horde, of the host of the dead and the monsters. In fairy tales mostly a kind spirit." *Herders Volkslexikon* (Freiburg: Herder, [11]1952), p. 709];

hehlen (German) = to conceal (as for Höhle);

hüllen (German) = to envelop, shroud (as above);

Hülse (German) = hull, husk (as above);

Hülle (German) = covering, shell (as above);

color (Latin) = (nocturnal!) color: MG 166 f., M 139, WH 247;

coloro (Latin) = to dye or color dark or brown (as for color);

Kali: the Indian goddess; in Bengal the "dark" or "black" woman: MG 296;

heil, heilig (German) = whole, hale, holy: in all probability from √kel, but not fully clarified; see the respective conjectures cited in the text above (note *10*, p. 237);

hören (German) = to hear: B, entry *kleo*√ kleu, KG 255: pre-Germanic √klu, MG 322, entry *kleo*: √klew, klu. We would recall here our discussion of hearing as the pre-eminently magic sense.

Helen(a): in his book (see note 107, p. 111 above), II, 561, F. W. Müller assumes for this name the Sanskrit (?) root *var, svar,* or *sar (car?)* because of its original initial digamma. This would suggest the root kel, given the familiar sound shift of the *centum* and *kentum* groups of initial consonants in Indo-European (for more on this shift, see, among others, A. Meillet, *Introduction à l'etude comparative des langues indo-europëennes* [Paris: Hachette, 1937], p. 157 f.). It should be recalled in this connection that Helena, originally identical to Selene, was a lunar deity and the sister of the Dioscuri (see our "Fifth Remark on Etymology," below, as well as Wilh. Bousset, *Hauptprobleme der Gnosis,* Forschungen zur Literatur des Alten und Neuen Testaments, x (Göttingen, 1907), p. 78 ff.; Roscher, note 76, p. 109 above, I, 2, column 1971; Gruppe, note 17, p. 183 above, pp. 163 and 1569, et passim). This kinship to the *D*-element of the Dioscuri would place them into the transition between the mythical and mental structures mentioned earlier, to which the name of their sister, Clytemnestra, also points.

Clytemnestra: sister of Helen and the Dioscuri, wife of Agamemnon, whom she slays, and mother of Orestes, who by murdering her becomes guilty of matricide. The parallel between the destruction of Clytemnestra by Orestes, and the destruction of the city of Helen (Troy) by the Hellenes, and the fate of Helen, is obvious; it is underscored by the fact that the root of the name Clytemnestra—if it is indeed related to *klyo/kleo* and derived from the root *klew,* as MG maintains (p. 324 f.)—is an augmented form of *kel,* the probable root for "Helen." In any event, Helen and Clytemnestra are not merely kin; they share a root-kinship, and thus also a fate-kinship. More on the basic configuration expressed by these names will be found below in our "Fifth Remark on Etymology."

Second Remark on Etymology

The Root-group qer:ger (gher):ker

The meaning of the root qer [q(w)er, (s)qre] is "to revolve, bend, curve, drive": B 458, MG 336, WH 221, 179; "to cut, sever": WH 170; "to separate, sever": W 143, WH 205; "to form, shape": W 143, 149;

the meaning of the root ger(gher) is "to desire, strive": MG 617; "to desire, like": WH 657 f.; it denotes an "intense agitation of the emotions": WH 658;

the meaning of the root ker is "to grow": MG 328, W 149, Wh 204; "to make grow, rise, nourish": MG 328, WH 204; and "to injure, strike": MG 319. In this the tension which comes about from the meaning of "nourish" on the one hand, and "injure" on the other, makes evident the unity inherent in the primordial root; see also below under Ker = the goddess of death, and ker = the heart or agent of life.

These roots—or this root-group—express a certain movement or animation in contrast to those of the "basic" root kĕl, an animation characteristic of the soul or psyche that is circular ("revolve") and related to "libido" ("like, desire, strive"). These roots clearly show the activation of the soul, which, in coming to consciousness, gives the mythical consciousness structure its distinctive stamp.

Derived from these roots are, among many others, all synonymous, the following words, which are to a great extent attuned to the context of the Kronos mythologeme:

chronos (Greek) = age, time: B 1072 $\sqrt{}$gher;

Kronos: see our discussion in the text which begins on p. 170; see also note *17*, p. 183;

Chiron: name of one of Kronos' sons; it represents one aspect of this Titan brought to its unfolding. Chiron, a Centaur, was a renowned physician, musician, seer, and the teacher of Asclepius, Jason, Achilles, and others (MG 621 f. $\sqrt{}$gher). In this is represented the birth of directed thought from circular movement, which in turn had mutated from the magic enmeshment of the sheltered cavern world. This process is reflected in the evolution of the *R* from the *L*: the energy of the soul or psyche is manifest in the formation of the *R* and is conscious by virtue of its polarity with the *L* (see the text, p. 172 f., and notes *20* and *21*, p. 183);

Kore/Kora: the daughter of Demeter (whose other name is Persephone): B 496 f., MG 328 $\sqrt{}$ker. Kore is carried off by Hades (Pluto), one of Kronos' sons, and becomes his consort in the nether world and ruler over the realm of the shades. Not incidentally, one of the surnames of Hades, Klytopolos, is reminiscent of the cavern aspect, inasmuch as it is based on the root *klew* (MG 324 and 322, entry *kleo*). The most detailed monograph on the mythologeme of Kore is Richard Foerster's *Der Raub und die Rückkehr der Persephone* (Stuttgart: Heitz, 1874). Foerster still distinguishes the two aspects of the figure of Kore-Persephone which have been traditionally opposed as being mutually exclusive: the "lunar" viewpoint recognized the lunar or moon aspect, the "tellurian" or "agrarian" view recognized the grain or corn aspect. Both interpretations, like Foerster's (op. cit., p. 25 f.), have failed to see that in a world of temporicity, as we have described it, the moon is a determinant of the growth of the grain crops. Seen from the mythical view, the grain can only ripen according to the progression of moons; not until the mental mode of observation is maturation tied to daylight and the sun. Hence the traditional and irreconcilable antithesis—either moon goddess or grain goddess—is antithetical only from a mental standpoint; from the mythical, the moon and the grain are correspondences. We can see this correspondence with respect to Kronos: the crescent, or lunar aspect, corresponds to the sickle, or harvest aspect. We would also recall here the popular belief that the moon and fertility are interrelated. Examples of what is to be done, or not to be done, with the waxing of the moon are well-known.

Demeter: daughter of Kronos, mother of Kore. Although the derivation of the name from Ge-meter (ge = earth, meter = mother, or earth-mother) is possible (see Kern, "Demeter," Pauly-Wissowa [note 12, p. 182 above], part volume 8 [1901], column 2713 f.; also Welcker [note 17, p. 183 above], I, p. 385 and Preller-Robert, *Griechische Mythologie* [note 12, p. 182 above], I, p. 747), the conjecture of W. Mannhardt, who provides the best summary and examination of the numerous ancient and modern explanations of the name, cannot be disregarded; see his *Mythologische Forschungen* (Strassburg: Trübner, 1884), p. 202-350. Mannhardt derives the name from the Cretan word *deai* = *crithai, krithe,* meaning "barley," whose root is gher (MG 332 and 622, entry *chersos*). The possibility that this root is contained in the name Demeter is not merely because ears of grain are an attribute of Demeter in the Eleusinian rites, but also particularly because this root, as noted, is valid for the progeny of Kronos, which truly has the same "roots": Kronos, Chiron, Demeter, Kore, and:

Ceres, the Latin name for Demeter: EM 172, W 115, WH $\sqrt{204}$ ker; also Wissowa's article "Cetes," Pauly-Wissowa (note 12, p. 182 above), part volume 6 (1899), column 1970, and the article by Th. Birt in Roscher (note 12, p. 182 above), I, column 860; the name is related to *creare* and *crescere:*

creare (Latin) = to beget, bring forth: EM 221, W 148 f., WH 288 f. $\sqrt{}$ker;

crescere (Latin) = to grow: EM 225, W 148, WH 290 $\sqrt{}$ker;

Garbe (German) = sheaf: KG 185 $\sqrt{}$gher. The sheaf relates to the harvest aspect of Kronos;

Gerste (German) = barley: MG 332 $\sqrt{}$gher;

krithe (Greek) = barley: MG 332 $\sqrt{}$gher;

Hirse (German) = millet: W 115 $\sqrt{}$kel (entry "Ceres");

koros (Greek) = satiation, satiety: W 115, WH 204 $\sqrt{}$ ker;

korennymi (Greek) = to satiate, satisfy (hunger): W 115, WH 204 $\sqrt{}$ker;

korthys (Greek) = sheaf of ears, shock of sheaves: B 496 f. $\sqrt{}$ker;

korthyo (Greek) = to rise: MG 328 $\sqrt{}$ker;

kore (Greek) = a (growing, maturing) girl: B 496 f., MG 328 $\sqrt{}$ker;

curvus (Latin)= curved, arched: B 458, 473 f., WH 279 $\sqrt{}$qer;

circus (Latin) = circle: B 473, WH 220 f., 132, 458 $\sqrt{}$qer;

Kirce (Greek) = Circe (as for circus);

korone (Greek) = ring: B 473 f., WH 277;

kirkos (Greek) = ring: B 458 $\sqrt{}$qer, WH 220 f. $\sqrt{}$qer-q?;

corona (Latin) = ring, corona: B 473, WH 238 $\sqrt{}$qer-q?;

Krone (German) = crown (as for corona);

crena (Latin) = cleft, cut, crenature: KG 296 $\sqrt{}$qer; WH 288$\sqrt{}$ (s)qre, an extension of$\sqrt{}$ qer;

Kerbe (German) = kerf (as for crena);

caro (Latin) = originally, "slice, section, piece (of flesh or meat)," later, "meat": W 97 ff., WH 198 $\sqrt{}$sqer?, extension of $\sqrt{}$qer;

cena (Latin) = meal-time: WH 198 $\sqrt{}$qer. Cena was current in Latin for "meal-time" along with the word *daps; daps,* in turn, is derived from the root *di* = to separate, clearly evidencing the close relation that exists between the two roots. See in this connection our "Fifth Remark on Etymology," below.

cur (Latin) = why? for what reason?: WH 313 √qer. We would recall that this
question was elicited in Greek by *ti men* (*ma:me;* see text, p. 77 above). A
similar relationship exists between the roots *qer* and *ma* as between *qer* and
di. (Here one might well ask: are the roots *ker (qer)* and *ma:me* the basis of
the name of the god Hermes, whose etymology according to B 282, note 3, is
still unexplained? Proper to his status as the guide of souls is circular motion:
taking and giving, the escorting of souls out of life as well as into life—
motives conveyed by the root *qer.* Measurement and direction, as well as
judgement, are Hermes, and are expressed by the root *ma:me* in the Latin
form of Hermes, Mercurius, both proper to roots seem to be present,
although in reverse order: *mer-cur!*);

carmen (Latin) = song, poem: W 99 √ker; according to WH 196 f., the root is perhaps *qar,* and according to EM 150 f., √*gen* (?); see the text, p. 145 above,
and note 36, p. 159. We would note that song and poem are a self-
completing, self-contained sequence of sounds—a sounding circle.

kerdan (Old Prussian) = time: KG 246 √ker-dha (here again the two roots mentioned under *cena-daps* occur together);

choros (Greek) = dance, round (also of the stars), chorus: B 1067 √gher; see also
the text, p. 81 f., above, and note *121,* p. 112;

chortos (Greek) = fenced courtyard: B 1066 √gher;

hortus (Latin) = garden: B 1067, WH 660 √gher;

Garten (German) = garden: WH 660 √gher;

chairo (Greek) = to rejoice: MG 617 √gher;

begehren (German) = to desire, wish, covet: MG 617 √gher;

gern (German) = to like; gladly: MG 617 √gher:

gratus (Latin) = desirable: EM 414, WH 617 √gher;

chre (Greek) = necessary, destined: MG 626 √gher;

horior (Latin) = to drive: WH 675 f. √gher;

gurges (Latin) = whirlpool: M 331, W 278 √qer; WH 627 f. √ger (The devouring
vortex, the devouring Kronos!);

Grund (German) = ground, basis: KG 2221 √gher (the mythical image—which
takes place in the two-dimensional sphere—has a "ground"; the cavern—√
kel—does not);

krater (Greek) = mixing vessel: MG 316 f. √ker;

kerannymi (Greek) = to mix: MG 316 f. √ker;

hehr (German) = august, exalted: KG 239 f. √ker;

Herr (German) = lord, sir; its original meaning was "venerable, honorable" (and
Kronos is depicted as a hoary old man!): KG 247 √ker;

Greis (German) = man hoary with age [hoary, from hoar, "old," hence "venerable, august"] : KG 216 √gher;

grau (German) = gray: KG 216, W 517 √gher (√kĕl forms *color,* the darkest color
of darkness, √gher the color of the twilight or half-light proper to night and
the mythical realm);

ravus (Latin) = gray, grayish-yellow: W 517 √gher;

chreos (Greek) = guilt, transgression, sin, atonement, expiation: MG 626 √gher;
(guilt and expiation united in the same word, just as devouring and disgorging are united in Kronos);

chreios (Greek) = necessity, desire, wish: MG 626 √gher;

chraomai (Greek) = to need, yearn for: MG 626 √gher; see there also chreo,
chrao, chreia, chema, chrezo, chresimos, chrestos.

In all likelihood, the following also belong to this group, despite roots that are merely similar:

krino (Greek) = to separate, sort, select: MG 333, WH 205 √kri;

cerno (Latin) = to sort, sift, separate, sever: WH 205 √(s)qeret;

krites (Greek) = judge: MG 333, WH 205 √kri; B 392 f. √ker;

kairos (Greek) = right measure, right moment, time, hour: MG 292 √kri; B 392 f. √ker;

krisis (Greek) = separation, severing: MG 333 √kri;

crimen (Latin) = crime: WH 151 √ker + qer + suffix –men (i.e., with √ma:me?); in other words, the "righting" measurement (√ma:me) of the soul's animation—myth—is from a mythical standpoint a "crime," a destructive deed;

cor (Latin) = heart: EM 210 f., WH 271 f. √kerd (√ker and D-root! See the "Fifth Remark on Etymology," below); it may be permissible to consider this D-element as an expression of the severing heart-beat that makes possible the circulation of the blood.

kēr (Greek) = heart: B 450 √kerd;

Herz (German) = heart: KG 247 √kerd;

Ker (Greek) = death-bringer, goddess of death: B 393 rejects a kinship with kēr = heart; see our discussion in the text, p. 196 f.;

credo (Latin) = believe: B 412 √ + √ker + √dhe (belief or faith always contains disbelief as a negative component: dis-belief, that is, the partitive, di-secting principle expressing the root dhe; see the "Fifth Remark on Etymology");

curro (Latin) = run: M 191, W 162 √qer-s;

cursus (Latin) = course (as for curro above);

currus, carrus = wagon: M 191, 109, W 162, 101 √qer-s;

Karren (German) = cart, wagon (as for curro);

cardo (Latin) = pivot, center, hinge: WH 166 f. √(s)qer;

kordax (Greek) = merry dance (of ancient comedy): WH 166 √(s)qer; MG 328 and 518 (skairo) √sker;

crux (Latin) = (martyr's) wood, cross, torture, torment: WH 296 f. √(s)qreu-; related to curvus = curved, arched: WH 317 √(s)qer. Since the S-element may be considered to have the same expressive value as the dental D- and T-element, whereas qer is expressive of the circle and rotation, the nature of the cross is most clearly evident in its root: the divider of the circle and thus the disrupter of destiny.

kruzi (Old High German) = cross (as for crux);

Kreuz (German) = cross: WH 296 (as for crux);

cross: KG 329 (as for crux)

christos (Greek) = the annointed, the Messiah: MG 627 √ghri: augmentation from √gher with the I-element, the "I" or ego-element of our culture; there is in any event, an interconnection between the name "Jesus" and the words "I," ich (German), je (French), yo (Spanish), and io (Italian); we have already noted in the text (P. 89 f.) that Jesus is the bearer of the "I" or ego. It may also be of significance that the surname christos was chosen from among many other possible names; it was possibly prefigured by the Hebrew name "Messiah," which undoubtedly derives from a ma:me root and contains, in addition, the partitive-directing-judging S-element. The significance of the derivation of Kronos and Christos from the same root may be seen in the soul- or psyche-awakening power that we were able to evince for Kronos; and the fact that in "Christos" this same power can also be felt would seem to corroborate the discovery that in medieval literature Christ is equated with Saturn (the Latin form of Kronos). The esoteric-alchemistic treatise of the year 1400, entitled "The Book of the Holy Trinity" (*Das Buch der heyligen Dreyvaldekeit*, i.e., three-fold and not triune!), with an unfortunately somewhat perilous Christian tone, contains miniatures of the "Saturnalian Passion of Christ." The miniatures are more suggestive of a "satanic" passion (Saturn = Satan!), although the emphasis is on the particularly qualitative and positive aspect of Saturn, a fact which we may consider a mitigating circumstance, for "in the higher esoteric sense, Saturn was deemed the lord of purification from all things of a burdensome, weighty nature [as in the cavern- and Hades-worlds]; the misfortune which Saturn brings immediately has the effect of a purification" [which the alchemists expressed by giving him the lily as his attribute, as it is also a symbol for Christ]; Gustav Friedrich Hartlaub, "Signa Hermetis," *Zeitschrift des deutschen Vereines für Kunstwissenschaft*, 4 (Berlin: De Gruyter, 1937), pp. 99 and 110 ff.; on p. 111, figure 9, is a reproduction of one of the miniatures noted above. It is unnecessary to point out that these elemental etymological references are in no way intended to call into question the salutory nature or the numinosity of Jesus; on the contrary, we would hope that our references would rather be a warning against an over-emphasis on the Christ-principle, that is, on the surname or later name subsequently conferred on him (inasmuch as he awakened the souls to the "I"). What might be dangerous is the constant reference in the treatise to the "Christ impulse" that tends to steer in the direction of the anti-Christian. In any event, the relationships between Kronos and Christos are undoubtedly more closely knit and more fundamental—and also less speculative—than is assumed by the alchemistic or neo-gnostic interpretations. The "Lord" (the appellation, we would recall, derives from the root *ker*) was concerned in His own way—which cannot be explained in anthropocentric, anthropological, or anthroposophic terms—with these basic phenomena.

This compilation, like the others in these "Remarks on Etymology," makes no claim to completeness in any form whatever. We have not included many words whose sense or root would make them appropiate here, so as not to unduly extend the compass of our remarks, nor have we cited the parallel words in other languages, such as *jardin, créer, coeur*, etc.

Third Remark on Etymology

The Root-group kel:gel:qel

An additional root-group must be mentioned here which encompasses the same domain of life (or, more accurately, domain of the soul) as the one preceding. This is, surprisingly, the group to which the roots *kel* (not *kĕl*), *gel*, and *qel* belong. Because of the final *L*, it might be initially assumed that the words deriving from these roots belong to the *kĕl*-domain, but a careful consideration of their sounds will show that we are dealing with an intermediate stage between the expressions of the √kĕl on the one hand, and of the root-group *qer:ker:gher:ger* on the other. The initial *G* is no longer a pure guttural (in the sense of *K*), and the *Q* is even less so. Both are sounds which have moved forward from the depth and darkness of the throat—a *K* which is approaching the dental region—and sounds which thereby have taken on the aggressive nature already evidenced by final *R*.

The meaning of √*kel* (whose vowel is of lesser moment when compared to that of *kĕl*) is "to incline, bow, bend";

that of √ gel is "to clench, form into a ball, devour" (WH 227);

that of √ qel is "to move, excite, drive, turn" (M 134, WH 250) and, emphasizing this character, it expresses (according to WH 194) not just "urging, instigating," but also "keeping, holding, sustaining."

From these roots are derived:

kyklos (Greek), cyclus (Latin) = circle, cycle, wheel, disk: B 531 √q(u)el; MG336 √qel;

wheel: KG 465, WH 247 √q(u)el;

Rad (German) = wheel: KG 465 √q(u)el;

kylindo (Greek) = to roll: MG 337 √qel;

Kundala (Sanskrit) = ring: MG 337 √qel;

kaláyati (Old Indian) = drives, holds, carries: WH 194 √qel;

dolphin: MG 131 (entry *delphys*) √gelbh (meaning: maternal lap, womb); √gelbh, an augmentation of √gel + √b(o) = being, nascence? See also note *71*, p. 242 above;

Delphi (as for dolphin);

Quelle (German) = source, well-spring: KG 462 √q(u)el (see the text, p. 249, and note *2*, p. 263 above);

Qual (German) = torment, agony: KG 461 √g(u)el (see the text, p. 249, and note *2*, p. 263 above);

celer (Latin) = fast, swift [celerity]: WH 194 √qel;

columen, culmen (Latin) = acme, zenith, culmination: W 400 √qel;

calix (Latin) = chalice, cup: WH 400 √qel; MG 296, on the other hand, gives √kel;

Kelch (German) = chalice: WH 400 √qel;

çakra (Sanskrit) = circle: B 531 √q(u)el;

globus (Latin) = globe, sphere, ball: EM 406 f., WH 609√gel;

glomus (Latin) = dumpling, clew, ball: EM 408, WH 609√gel;

gula (Latin) = throat: M 331, W 277, WH 625 f.√gel;

Kehle (German) = throat: KG 293, W 277√gel;

columna (Latin) = column: WH 250√qel;

colo (colui, cultum) (Latin) = cultivate, build, revere, attend to: M 138, WH 24 ff.√qel;

klao (Greek) = break, smash: MG 149√kel;

klino (Greek) = incline, lean against: B 470 f., WH 235√kel;

kline (Greek) = bed, bier: B 470, WH 225√kel;

clino (Latin) = incline, lean against: WH 235√kel;

kelomai (Greek) = to drive, animate: B 1072, MG 316, WH 235√kel;

Kult (German), from Latin cultus = cult:√as for colo; in the cult (colo = attend to) *relegere* is still effectual: the careful ritual which overlooks nothing and establishes the *relegio*.

boule (Greek) = will, wish, volition: MG 113√g(w)el; see also our remarks in the text, p. 196.

Fourth Remark on Etymology

The Mirror-roots regh and leg

The meaning of the mirror-root **regh** is "movement in a straight line" (see note
  22, p. 184, reference is to EM);
the meaning of the mirror-root *leg* is "light" (and this means directed light) in
  contrast to and in reversal of the "undirected darkness" inherent in the *kĕl*
  domain; see also the text, p. 127.
From the root *regh(reg)* are derived:
regere (Latin) = to make straight, to steer or guide: EM 417 f., W 520;
rex (Latin) = king, regent: EM 417 f., W 524;
rectus (Latin) = straight, right: EM 816, W 519;
erigere (Latin) = to erect, set upright: W 196;
regula (Latin) = rule(r), straight edge, plumb-(guide-)line, splint: EM 417 f., W 520,
  524;
rekha (Old Indian) = stroke, line: KG 476;
Reihe (German) = row (straight line): KG 476;
oregein (Greek) = to stretch, strive, aim: EM 417 f., MG 410;
orktos (Greek) = upright, stretched: MG 410;
recken (German) = to stretch, rack: KG 474;
rechnen (German) = to reckon, calculate: KG 473;
recht (German) = correct, right: KG 473;
rechts (German) = (on the) right: KG 473;
richten (German) = to direct, right, judge: KG 473;
Reich (German) = realm: KG 476;
reich (German) = rich: KG 476;
arche (Greek) = beginning, origin: MG 90;
archo (Greek) = to begin: MG 90;

In the Italian word *diritto*, the Spanish *derecha*, and the French *droite*, all of
which can be traced to Latin *di-rigere*, the root *di:da* = to divide, is also evident;
more on this will be found in the "Fifth Remark on Etymology" below. Since we
are dealing here with another mirror-root and its signification, we would mention
in connection with the mirror-root and its inversion, *kĕl:leg* (see the text, p. 127),
that from it are derived not only *logos* = speech (see note *9*, p. 157 above), but
also:
lux (Latin) = light, lustre, daylight, eyesight (!): WH 841 √le(u)k, akin to √le(u)g;
lucere (Latin) = to luminesce, light, be bright: WH 823 f. le(u)k, akin to √le(u)g;
  MG 346 √le(u)g;
leuchten (German) = to luminesce, light, be bright (as for lucere);
Licht (German) = light: KG 357 traces the word to the Indo-European double stem
  le(u)k(o)t √le(u)k; observed from our elemental etymological standpoint,
  the dental element of this dual stem points to its power of separating the
  dark and darkness; WH 824 √le(u)k, akin to √le(u)g; MG 346 √le(u)k (see
  the text, p. 127 and note *9*, p. 157);
leukoo (Greek) = to whiten, make white: MG 346 √le(u)k;
leukos (Greek) = bright, light, luminescent, white: MG 346 √le(u)k; WH 824
  le(u)k, akin to √le(u)g. Since √kĕl describes "what is concealed, hidden,"

and thus the dark, the true value of the mirror-root *leg:lek* is evident here since the root also expresses daylight as "opposed" to the nocturnal and cavern darkness. It also sheds new light on the *leukosis* mentioned in note *88*, p. 110 above.

lex (Latin) = law, legality: WH 334;

lectus (Latin) = couch, bed: W 330 √legh;

lēgo (Latin) = send: WH 779 f.;

lĕgo (Latin) = collect: WH 780;

lego (Greek) = collect, read, gather, count: MG 340, W 330;

lexis (Greek) = speech: M 340, W 330;

logizomai (Greek) = calculate, consider ("logic" also belongs here): W 330;

religion (from Latin re-lego): M 497 f., WH 351 f.;

relegio (Latin) = careful, conscientious observance (W 520): √as for religion and lego.

Fifth Remark on Etymology

The Root da:di

The meaning of the root da:(da:di, dai, dhe, dheu) is "to give, divide, sever, cut apart."

Having discussed *K, L,* and *R,* we would observe that the sound *D* in general that it is the divisive, dividing sound. It is a dental, formed, as the term indicates, at the incisors; and it is not just fortuitous that the definite article of the Germanic languages begins with *d* or *th* (English: "the," German "der, die, das"). Nor is it merely fortuitous that the words "eat," and "tooth" (*dens,* Latin, *odous,* Greek, and *Zahn,* German) derive from a voiced D-root (MG 395, KG 702, W 171√de).

The following words can be traced to √ da or its variants:

dais (Latin) = meal, portion, share, sacrificial meal: MG 126√dai:da;

daps (Latin) = meal, mealtime: MG 126√dai:da, WH 323√da(i):di:da. The parallel occurrence in Latin of *daps* and *cena*—which also means "mealtime," but is derived from the root *ker*—is significant with respect to the two types of mealtime. Even today, in Italian the evening meal is called *cena!*

daio, daiomai, daizo (Greek) = to divide, separate, tear asunder: MG 126√dai:da; see the text p. 94, and notes *134*, p. 113, *148*, p. 115, and *13*, p. 157;

datu (Sanskrit) = part: MG 126√dai:da;

datram (Sanskrit) = something apportioned; as for datu;

dáyate, dati (Sanskrit) = he divides, cuts off: MG 126√dai:da, KG 706√di:dai, WH 323 f.√da(i):di:de;

Zeit (German) = time: KG 706√di:dai; WH 349 f., does not list a root, only the stem *di-no*;

time, tide: KG 706√di:dai; WH 323 f., entry "daps," interprets the second syllable as a formative *men,* "as in the case of *daimon*" (see note *134*, p. 113, and note *148*, p. 115);

tid (Danish, Swedish, Anglo-Saxon) = time; according to KG, the same as "time" above. See also Walter W. Skeat, *An Etymological Dictionary of the English Language* (Oxford: Clarendon, 1935), p. 646, column 2;

dai-mo (Indo-European) = section: KG 706√di:dai;

daimon (Greek) = daemon, inferior divinity, soul, attendant spirit, genius: MG 126 (as for daio above). With regard to the second syllable, -*mon*, see MG 382, entry "monos" = god of censure, blame (Monism!)√mu, on which the word "myth" is of course based, and which formed the point of departure for our presentation of the mythical structure (although we adduced the roots given for Kronos in order to clarify the nature of mythical time);

Teil (German) = part, portion, sector: KG 616 f.√dhai, MG 126√dai:da;

didomi (Greek) = I give: MG 146√do; F. M. Müller, *Die Wissenschaft der Sprache* (note 107, p. 111), I, p. 469√dá;

do (Latin) = I give (French: *je donne*; Spanish: *doy*): as for didomi;

dátram, danam (Sanskrit) = gift: √as for didomi;

donum (Latin) = gift: √as for didomi;

tithene (Greek) = nurse, wet nurse: B 970√dhe(i):dhi; MG 267 (entry "thao") √dhei, dhe, dhi;

thesthai (Greek) = to suckle, nourish:√as for ththene;

dhatri (Sanskrit) = wet nurse: √as for tithene;

dháyati (Sanskrit) = he suckles (nourishes himself): √as for tithene;

titheme (Greek) = to place, lay, put, calculate, count: MG 569√dhē, dhō, dhe;

Tat (German) = deed: KG 613√dhe:dho (see also the text, p. 128);

tun (German) = to do: √as for Tat;

Tod (German) = death: KG 620√dhe(u): dho(u);

dad (Anglo-Saxon) = deed: KG 613√dhe:dho;

dad (Old Frisian) = dead: KG 623, 620√dhe(u):dho(u);

Tag (German) = day: KG 608√deg(u)h:dog(u)h; MG 567 (entry *tephra*)√dhegh (the *D*-principle, separation or severing, preceding the guttural principle of nocturnal darkness!);

dáhati (Sanskrit) = he burns: √as for Tag);

dies (Latin) = day, (appointed) time, term, limit: WH 349 f. adduces a stem, di-(no), rather than a root, and considers Old High German *zit*, as well as modern German *Zeit* as belonging to the same stem;

Zeus: MG 255√dei, di, dje (Greek Zeus = Latin *dies*);

deatai (Greek) = he shines: MG 128√as for Zeus;

dideti (Sanskrit) = he lights, illuminates: as for Zeus;

Jupiter (from *dies* = Zeu + pater = father); √as for Zeus;

dévas, devá (Sanskrit) = deus: √as for Zeus;

deus (Latin) = god: √as for Zeus;

Zeichen (German) = sign; token: √as for Zeus;

Teufel (German) = devil; Abel (see text, p. 128, and note 14, p. 157) derives it (as well as "devil" and French *dieu*) from devá;

totus (Latin) = whole, total: according to W 632 f. and M 760, this word belongs to the family of *tumeo*, for which (W 770) √te(u) and (M 770) √tew, tu are conjectured;

thymos (Greek) = will, drive, wrath, sense: MG 275 f. √ dhew:dhu; see also our remarks in the text, p. 196

Athene (Greek) = Athena; according to Pauly-Wissowa (note 12, p. 182), fourth part-volume (1896), column 2007, Rückert's conjecture—that Athene is akin to tithene (above)—is the most acceptable, in which case the *A*- is to be understood as an alpha intensivum (preceding√dhi!). Athena is a nurse and nourisher, although until now it was not known of what (nourisher of the deed!).

Metis: either√ma:me + di, or √di as in Dais:Tis, or, as MG 374 maintains, √med, augmented from √me; B 635 (entry *metis*, "wisdom, intelligence, moderation, measure, [factual] knowledge") does not give a root, but only the Indo-European word *meti* and the Sanskrit *mati-h*, both with the same meaning as *metis* and related to *metiesthai*, "to ponder, think," and to French *méditer*, as well as to *medomai*, "to devise, think out, rule" (see for *medomai* also MG 361, which adduces √me); and finally, to this group, according to B, *metron*, "measure," which according to MG 371 f. has the root *me*; see also our remarks in the text, p. 75.

Me'et: Egyptian goddess of law and justice (and hence, of measure). She is probably akin to Metis and Dike (see below);

Hades: according to Drexler (in Roscher, note 12 on p. 182 above, I, 2, column 1778 f.) and the generally accepted viewpoint today—although neither B nor Pauly-Wissowa (article by Latte, note 12, p. 182 above, part-volume 14, column 1541 f.) furnish an etymology—the name *Haides* or *hades* is composed of the alpha privativum (or alpha negativum) and the stem *id*, which forms the verb *idein*, "to see," whose root derives from a *D*-root. Hades, therefore, is only a negation of the *D*- and diurnal principle! It is merely a shadowy dark indeed, near twilight, and has nothing in common with the primordial darkness expressed by √kel. It represents merely what is invisible and hidden from sight, not darkness as such; it comprises the shadowy aspect of light and the dark aspect of the mythical intermediate realm between magic darkness and mental illumination.

Dike: the Greek goddess of law and jurisprudence: W 175, WH 348 f. (entry *dico*, "I say, speak") √deik or deig. W assumes the same root also for Old High German *zihan*, "to accuse, charge"; *zeigan* and New High German *zeigen*, "to show"; Old High German *zeihhan*, "sign"; English "teach"; Greek *deik-nymi*, "to show"; and *deigma*, "proof, example"; see also MG 129√deik, dik. The *K*-principle in Dike follows the *D*-principle, which divides and determines it; Dike is a judge in a much more encompassing sense: she is the judge of the mythical world, directing it toward the mental;

Dionysos: √unknown. Roscher (note 12, p. 182 above), I, column 1029, notes the earliest Aeolian form of the name; Kern, in Pauly-Wissowa (note 12, p. 182 above), part-volume 9 (1903), column 1029, conjectures a derivation from *Dios nysos* = god-son, since *nysos* was the Thracian word for "son"; other conjectures can be found in Preller-Robert (note *107*, p. 111 above), I, p. 664, note 1, and Rohde, *Psyche* (note *3*, p. 274 above), II, 2, p. 38, note 1. The *D*-element (see note *122*, p. 113 above) emphasizes its consciousness-illuminating effect in the "Lenaea" rites (see text, p. 80).

Dioscuri (dioskoroi, Ionian: dioskouri): sons of Zeus, named Castor and Pollux (Polydeukes), twin sons of Leda, brothers of Helen and Clytemnestra; Castor was renowned as a horseman (i.e., the conqueror of the animal originally dedicated to Pluto-Hades!), Pollux was famed as a boxer (!). The name Dioscuri doubtless contains the root da:di = ker, that is, the diurnal as well as nocturnal realm: according to mythical tradition, they lived alternately one day in Olympus, one day in the underworld! (See MG 151). In the names of the sons (*Söhne*) there is an expression of conciliation (*versöhnlich*) which in the names of the sisters, particularly in Clytemnestra's, is irreconcilable (*unversöhnlich*), for when Clytemnestra is slain by her son Orestes, this means in elemental-etymological terms that the aggressive *R*-element and the divisive dental elements (*S* and *T*) with their dental character destroy the kĕl-principle, the initial principle of the name Clytemnestra. Her name, however, also includes the -*taim* (derived from temno?), as well as the *S*-, *T*-, and *R*-elements in the reverse order of that in the son's name (Orestes). Her name, in other words, also contains the elements that destroy the kĕl-principle, which are evident in the Dioscuri, the brothers of the sister-pair Clytemnestra-Helen. The name Clytemnestra reflects what Bachofen expressed in the quotation cited earlier (text, p. 150) that the maternal principle, with its mythical emphasis and its proximity to the kĕl-principle, had itself become deficient: giving birth had been supplanted by murder—by the murder which is suggested in the second and fourth syllables of the name Clytemnestra, who killed her spouse and was killed by her son.

Titan: $\sqrt{}$di:da?

dexiteros, dexios (Greek) = whatever is to the right, straight, dexterous, adroit: B 177$\sqrt{}$de(i)k, dek, dik; MG 131$\sqrt{}$ek;

dexter (Latin) = right: EM 254, WH 346 f., 330 (entry *decet*): $\sqrt{}$dek;

dirigere (Latin) = to direct, steer: WH 353 from Indo-European *dis* + *rego* (from $\sqrt{}$reg).

In conclusion we would also observe, in connection with

tempus (Latin) = time;
tempo (Italian) = time;
tiempo (Spanish) = time; and
temps (French) = time,

that among etymologists there has not been any agreement until now as to the root for these words. Neither Ernst Gamillscheg, in his *Französisches etymologisches Wörterbuch* (Heidelberg: Winter, 1928), p. 838, nor W. Meyer-Lübke, in his *Romanisches etymologisches Wörterbuch* (Heidelberg: Winter, ³1930), p. 714, no. 8634, goes so far as to designate a root. One thing is certain: all of these words can be traced to *temenos, tempos* (or its plural, *tempea*), which, according to H. Usener (*Götternamen*, note 17, p. 183 above, p. 191 f.), like Latin *tempus* and *templum*, mean nothing other than an intersection or crossing, namely that of the east-west parallel with the meridian. But even the conception of the meridian vertically intersecting the so-called eternal or infinite line measured by the sun from east to west during the course of the day fixes time in the intersection of the lines, just as it fixes the infinite line. A simple spatial explanation like that of Usener does not comprehend the characteristic aspects of *temenos*, that is to say, it provides only a haptic explanation appropriate to the nineteenth century, and not for pre-Christian time.

Various roots are conjectured for the Greek verb *temno*, "to cut, cut apart, di-or bisect," which is the basis for all of the words cited above: M 746 f. $\sqrt{}$tem? $\sqrt{}$tma?; E 620 f. conjectures merely an augmented root form t-emp; MG 564 f. $\sqrt{}$tem, tma; B 954 assumes a stem *tem*; Weinstock, in Pauly-Wissowa (note 12, p. 182 above), part-volume 9 (1934), column 481, entry *templum*, mentions only the two conjectures *tem* and *temp*. As for our own discussion, we maintain that *temno* derives from √di + √ma. (Observed with respect to the roots, this central concept is a *metis* in which the *D*-element predominates, and thus assists the rational time element to its breakthrough, just as it comes to the fore in the instance of Metis' daughter, Athena. The *ma:me* principle is still predominantly a measuring principle, while the *di*-principle is already one of severing and rationality.) To illustrate the fact that our manner of considering the content of the consonantal root elements from an elemental-etymological standpoint can on principle provide certain clarifications, we would cite another minor example. Much speculation has surrounded the explication of the Greek suffix *-ta*. This suffix frequently occurs, and is particularly used to form the owner and master of the particular object to which it is attached, as in *naus*, "ship," and *nautes*, "shipman, navigator." These *ta*-forms are thus not just fortuitous; the principle of dividing, aiming, and particularly, directing inherent in the dental element makes of the mere ship in this example the directed ship, and thus the one who directs it, the shipman or mariner.

Index of Names

Index of Subjects

Minor: tonality, 460; triad, 508 *n* 55
Minos, King, 76
Minus: mutation, 38; realm/domain, 280; -side of nature, 424; values, 280
Miracle(s), 132
Miraculous healing, 163
Mirror, 34–35 *n* 62, 67, 70, 97, 217, 232; -roots, 127, 172–173, 243 *n* 77, 557; world, 468
Mirroring, linguistic, 217, 243 *n* 77
Misinterpretation, of parapsychological phenomena, 164
Mneia, 318
Mneme, 318
Mnemetic theory, 395
Mnemosyne, 318, 328
Mobiles, 482, 483 fig. 61
Modalities of consciousness, 204, 403
Model(s), 353, 376, 387, 430; of the atom, 376; of the scale, Einstein's, 353; space-time, 353; -thinking, 430
Moderation, 93, 94, 95, 129, 130
Modernism, 280, 510 *n* 58
Modern times, 434
Modes, church (music), 459
Moebius strip, 256
Moirai, 207
Molecular biology, 536
Moment, the, xxvii, 24, 86, 294
Monarch (sole ruler), 92
Monarchy, 468, 509
Monism, 447
Monochord, 84
Monos ("monarch"), 92
Monotheism, 76, 92, 441 *n* 71; of Mosaic law, 76, 92; primordial (Ur-), 441 *n* 71, 517 *n* 170
Monotheization, 198
Monsters, 538
Montage, 534 *n* 4
Montezuma, 5
Mont Ventoux, 12, 15, 343, 515 *n* 145
Moon, 12, 77, 87, 166, 167, 170, 210–212, 213, 219, 221, 232, 233, 240 *n* 50, 241 *n* 57, 245 *n* 102, 551 entry "Kore/Kora"; astral-mythical, 12; god (Men), 240–241 *n* 50; symbol (sickle), 168; symbolism of, 212, 232; *see also* lunar aspect of Kronos, 551; lunar character of the soul, 210, 232; lunar goddess, 246 *n* 109, 550 entry "Helen(a)"; lunar periodicity, 166, 232; lunar theology, 241 *n* 55
Morality, 419, 426
Morgarten, 8 *n* 6
Morphologists, 429
Morphology of cultures, 432
Mosaic law, 114 *n* 142
Mosaics, 52
Moscia, 514 *n* 138
Moses, 75, 79, 114 *n* 142
Moth, 240 *n* 45
Mother(s), 75, 76, 151, 157 *n* 11, 163, 242 *n* 71;

of all things (peace), 151; of Athena (Metis), 75; domain of the, 393, 394; great, 76, 151, 163; *see also* maternal: attachment, 161 *n* 48; principle, 339, 560–561 entry "Dioscuri"; spirit, 234; world, 150, 198; matriarchal: principle, 76; religions, 10; matriarchy, 79, 149, 150, 160 *n* 43 & 45, 262, 266 *n* 35, 339; matricide, 150, 161 *n* 48, 255, 315, 339, 425
Motion, 201, 228, 253, 308, 533; circular, 228, 253; directed, 167; *see also* movement
Motoricity, 285, 301, 308, 310, 531, 533
Motorization, 306, 537; *see also* mechanization, 280, 301, 311, 531
Mouth, 57, 58, 64, 65, 109 *n* 66, 73, 144, 145, 165; *see also* oral cavity, 172
Mouthlessness, 55, 56 fig. 9–11, 57, 57 fig. 12–14, 58 fig. 15–16, 59 fig. 17–18, 64, 108 *n* 61 & 63, 109 *n* 66 & 77
Movement (directed motion), 166–167, 201, 218, 362, 534 *n* 4; circular, 172, 228, 253; clockwise, 173; inner (psychic), 196; of the soul, 166, 197, 201; of temporicity, 167; toward the left, 64, 174; toward the right, 64; of the world, 166
muitsix, 195
Multi-family homes, 467, 469 fig. 49
Multiplicity, 143, 496; of dimensions, 496
Multivalence, 492
Mummy, 207, 235 fig. 43
Mundificatio, 110 *n* 88
Mu-principle, 177
Murals (of Pompeii), 11, 31–32 *n* 27, 80, 93, 169 fig. 23
Muralistic painting, 512 *n* 111
Muse(s), 17, 64, 184 *n* 30, 192, 208, 214, 218, 240 *n* 43, 246 *n* 108, 317, 320, 325–328, 330 *n* 16, 331 *n* 37, 64 fig. 20, 65 fig. 21
Muse, to (leisure, contemplation), 126, 330 *n* 16; *see also* leisure, 427, 531
Mushroom frenzy (intoxication), 108 *n* 61
Music, 101, 121, 125, 202, 254, 443 *n* 80, 454–464, 466, 505 *n* 1–12, 506–511, 537, 538, 539 *n* 6; atonal, 455, 458, 459; classical, 101, 459; electronic, 455, 537; instrumental, 458; meant to be read, 510 *n* 60; "open," 460; polytonal, 455; primordial, 456, 457; "silenced", 121; spherical, 510 *n* 67; twelve-tone, 456, 459, 462, 510 *n* 58
Muss-Musse, 110 *n* 80, 126, 127; *see also* "must"
"Must" (compunction), 317, 320, 330 *n* 16
"Mustard-Seed Garden, Textbook on the," 202
Mutation(s), xxvii, 1, 29, 36–43, 76, 96, 103 *n* 9, 116, 130, 134, 139, 140, 142, 151, 167, 181, 192, 198, 201, 204, 236, 249, 259, 268, 271, 272, 273, 280, 289, 292, 293 *n* 7, 347, 381; anxiety as sign of, 133 f.; biological, 39, 381; breathing character of, 121; concept of, 37 ff.; of consciousness, 1, 29,

Born in Posen in 1905, Jean Gebser came from an old Franconian family domiciled in Thuringia since 1236. A nephew of German chancellor von Bethmann-Hollweg, he was a descendant on his mother's side of Luther's friend Melanchthon. He was educated in Breslau, Königsberg, Rossleben, and at the University of Berlin.

In 1929 Gebser emigrated to Italy and subsequently lived in Spain where he was attached to the Ministry of Education of the Spanish Republic. From 1937-1939 he lived in Paris in the circle which included Picasso, André Malraux, Paul Eluard, and Louis Aragon. In 1939 he made his permanent home in Switzerland where he became a citizen in 1951. For many years Gebser was Lecturer at the Institute of Applied Psychology in Zürich and was later appointed honorary Professor of Comparative Studies of Civilization at the University of Salzburg, Austria.

For his many publications, including books on Rilke, his friend Federico García Lorca, recent developments in the sciences, East-West relations, evolution, and twentieth century civilization and its antecedents, Gebser received several prizes, including a share of the German Schiller prize, the literary award of the Esslingen Artist's Guild, the Koggen prize of the City of Minden, and the literary award of the City of Berne. He died in Berne on May 14, 1973.

Noel Barstad is Professor Emeritus of Modern Languages at Ohio University and was until 1990 Vice-president of the International Jean Gebser Society (Schaffhausen, Switzerland), of which he is a founding member and a member of the Board of Directors.

Algis Mickunas is Professor of Philosophy at Ohio University.

SYNOPTIC TABLE

Structure	1. Space and Time Relationship		
	a) Dimensioning	b) Perspectivity	c) Emphasis
Archaic:	Zero-dimensional	None	Prespatial Pretemporal
Magic:	One-dimensional	Pre-perspectival	Spaceless Timeless
Mythical:	Two-dimensional	Unperspectival	Spaceless Natural temporicity
Mental:	Three-dimensional	Perspectival	Spatial Abstractly temporal
Integral:	Four-dimensional	Aperspectival	Space-free Time-free

Structure	2. Sign	3. Essence	4. Properties	5. Potentiality
Archaic:	None	Identity (Integrality)	Integral	Integrality
Magic:	Point	Unity (Oneness)	Non-directional unitary Interwovenness or fusion	Unity by Unification and Hearing/Hearkening
Mythical:	Circle ○	Polarity (Ambivalence)	Circular and polar Complementarity	Unification by Complementarity and Correspondence
Mental:	Triangle △	Duality (Opposition)	Directed dual oppositionality	Unification by Synthesis and Reconciliation
Integral:	Sphere ●	Diaphaneity (Transparency)	Presentiating, diaphanous "rendering whole"	Integrality by Integration and Presentation

Cross-sections 1–7: see Part I, Chapter 4, section1   Cross-section 8: see p. 141 ff.
Cross-sections 9–11b and 12–14 see Part I, Chapter 4, section 4
Cross-sections 11c–11g and 15–17 see Part I, Chapter 8, section 1
For some of the ascriptions or attributions not given in the text of Part I, see Part 2, Chapter 10, section 1

Structure	6. Emphasis		7. Consciousness-	
	a) Objective (external) (Aspect of World)	b) Subjective (internal) (Energy or Initiator)	a) Degree	b) Relation
Archaic:	Unconscious Spirit	None or Latency	Deep sleep	Universe-related: Breathing-spell
Magic:	Nature	Emotion	Sleep	Outer-related (Nature): Exhaling
Mythical:	Soul/Psyche	Imagination	Dream	Inner-related (Psyche): Inhaling
Mental:	Space - World	Abstraction	Wakefulness	Outer-related (Spatial world): Exhaling
Integral:	(Conscious Spirit)	(Concretion)	(Transparency)	(Inward-related: Inhaling? or Breathing-Spell?)

Structure	8. Forms of Manifestation		9. Basic attitude and agency of energy	10. Organ emphasis
	a) efficient	b) deficient		
Archaic:	None	Presentiment, foreboding	Origin: Wisdom	—
Magic:	Spell-casting	Witchcraft	Vital: Instinct Drive Emotion	Viscera — Ear
Mythical:	Primal myth (envisioned myth)	Mythology (spoken myth)	Psychic: Imagination Sensibility Disposition	Heart — Mouth
Mental:	*Menos* (directive, discursive thought)	Ratio (divisive, immoderate hair-splitting)	Cerebral: Reflection Abstraction Will/Volition	Brain — Eye
Integral:	Diaphainon (open, spiritual "verition")	Void (atomizing dissolution)	(Concretion) Integral: (Rendering diaphanous) ("Verition")	(Vertex)

Structure	11. Forms of realization and thought		
	a) Basis	b) Mode	c) Process
Archaic:	—	Originary	Presentiment
Magic:	Empathy and Identification Hearing	Pre-rational, pre-causal analogical	Associative, analogizing, sympathetic interweaving
Mythical:	Imagination and Utterance Contemplation and Voicing	Irrational: non-causal, polar	internalized recollection, contemplation — externalized utterance, expression
Mental:	Conceptualization and Reflection Seeing and Measuring	Rational: causal, directed	Projective speculation: oceanic, paradoxical, then perspectival thinking
Integral:	(Concretion and Integration "Verition" and Transparency)	(Arational: acausal, integral)	integrating, rendering diaphanous

Structure	11. Forms of realization and thought			
	d) Expression	e) Formulation	f) Limits	g) Valence
Archaic:	Presentiment	World-origin	—	—
Magic:	Vital experience	World-knowledge, the "recognized" world	conditioned	univalent
Mythical:	Undergone experience	World image or *Weltanschauung:* the contemplated and interpreted world	temporally bound	ambivalent
Mental:	Representation Conception, Ideation	World-conception: the thought and conceptualized world	limited	trivalent
Integral:	Verition	World-Verition: the world perceived and imparted in truth	open, free	multivalent

Structure	12. Forms of Expression		13. Forms of Assertion or Articulation
Archaic:	—		—
Magic:	Magic:	Graven images Idol Ritual	Petition (Prayer): being heard
Mythical:	Mythologeme:	Gods Symbol Mysteries	Wishes (Ideals: Fulfillment "wish (pipe-) dreams")
Mental:	Philosopheme:	God Dogma (Allegory, Creed) Method	Volition: attainment
Integral:	(Eteologeme:)	(Divinity) *(Synairesis)* (Diaphany)	(Verition: Present)

Structure	14. Relationships		
	a) temporal	b) social	c) general
Archaic:	—	—	universal or ["cosmic"]
Magic:	undifferentiated	Tribal world [clan/kith and kin] natural	egoless — terrestrial
Mythical:	predominantly past-oriented [recollection, muse]	Parental world [Ancestor-worship] predominantly matriarchal	egoless "we"-oriented psychic
Mental:	predominantly future-oriented [purpose and goal]	World of the first-born son, individuality [child-adulation] predominantly patriarchal	egocentric — materialistic
Integral:	(presentiating)	Mankind neither matriarchy nor patriarchy but integrum	ego-free amaterial apsychic

Structure	15. Localization of the soul	16. Forms of bond or tie	17. Motto
Archaic:	(Universe)	—	(All)
Magic:	Semen and blood	Proligio (*prolegere*) emotive and point-like	*Pars pro toto*
Mythical:	Diaphragm and heart	Relegio (*relegere*) observing, internalizing (recollecting) and externalizing (expressing)	Soul is identical to life (and death)
Mental:	Spinal cord and brain	Religion (*religare*): believing, knowing and deducing	Thinking is Being
Integral:	Cerebral cortex, humoral	Praeligio (*praeligare*): presentiating, concretizing, integrating	Origin: Present Perceiving and Imparting Truth